# THE FACTS ON FILE
## ENCYCLOPEDIA OF

# WORLD
# MYTHOLOGY
# AND LEGEND

## SECOND EDITION

# THE FACTS ON FILE
# ENCYCLOPEDIA OF

# WORLD
# MYTHOLOGY
# AND LEGEND

## SECOND EDITION

ANTHONY S. MERCATANTE
REVISED BY JAMES R. DOW

VOLUME II
M–Z

Facts On File, Inc.

MID-CONTINENT PUBLIC LIBRARY

3 0000 12580346 4

*Dedicated to all my family*
*—J...*

**THE FACTS ON FILE ENCYCLOPEDIA OF WORLD MYTHOLOGY AND LEGEND, SECOND EDITION**

Facts On File, Inc.
132 West 31st Street
New York NY 10001


**LIBRARY OF CONGRESS CATALOGING-IN-PUBLICATION DATA**

Mercatante, Anthony S.
    The Facts On File encyclopedia of world mythology and legend / Anthony S. Mercatante; revised
by James R. Dow—2nd ed.
    p. cm.
    Includes bibliographical references and index.
    ISBN 0-8160-4708-1 (set: alk. paper) ISBN 0-8160-5780-X (volume I) ISBN 0-8160-5781-8 (volume II)
    1. Mythology—Dictionaries. 2. Folklore—Dictionaries. I. Dow, James R. II. Title.

BL303.M45 2003
291.1'3'03—dc21                                          2003040262

Facts On File books are available at special discounts when purchased in bulk quantities for businesses, associations, institutions, or sales promotions. Please call our Special Sales Department in New York at (212) 967-8800 or (800) 322-8755.

You can find Facts On File on the World Wide Web at http://www.factsonfile.com

Text design by Erika K. Arroyo
Cover design by Cathy Rincon

Printed in the United States of America

VB Logidec 10 9 8 7 6 5 4 3 2

This book is printed on acid-free paper.

# CONTENTS

# M

**Maanhaltija**    In Finno-Ugric mythology, the earth spirit who watches over the fruits of the land.

**1942**

**Maat** (Maa, Maet, Maht, Maut) (truth, justice, righteousness)    In Egyptian mythology, goddess of truth, daughter of the sun god Ra; her name is represented by an ostrich feather, an emblem she shared with the air god Shu. Her presence is indicated in "The Weighing of the Heart" in *The Book of the Dead*, in which the feather of truth is usually found over the balance scales and also appears as the weight against which the heart is weighed. Egyptian judges in the Plotemaic and Roman periods were often portrayed wearing an amulet of Maat around a cord on their necks as emblems of their office. One ancient Egyptian text describes the goddess: "Great is Maat, the mighty and unalterable." Maat was sometimes thought of as a kind of good angel who lived with an individual and accompanied that person into the afterlife. "Joining Maat" became a euphemism for dying.

See also: *BOOK OF THE DEAD, THE*; RA, SHU

**1943**

**Mab** (Welsh, a baby)    In European folklore, queen of the fairies. Shakespeare's *Romeo and Juliet* describes her as the "fairies' midwife," that is, she delivers men's brains to dreams. Specific reference to Mab is made when Romeo says: "I dreamed a dream tonight," and Mercatio replies, "Oh, then I see Queen Mab hath been with you." Berlioz's dramatic symphony *Romeo and Juliet* has a brilliant scherzo depicting Queen Mab.

**1944**

**1945**

***Mabinogion, The***    Welsh collection of medieval legends and tales translated into English by Lady Charlotte Guest in 1838. It is believed the tales were first written in Welsh in the 14th century, though some may date from the 11th century. Most of the tales deal with Celtic myths and legends.

**1946**

**Mabon** (young god)    In Celtic mythology, a Welsh sun god and hero, son of Ruien and Modron, brother of Owain, noted for his hunting, his hound, and his swift horse. Mabon alone is able to seize a razor from behind the ear of a boar. In later Arthurian legend Mabon is a mortal released from prison by King Arthur, who needed his help in the chase of the boar Twrch Trwyth.

See also: ARTHUR, KING

**1947**

**Machaon** (lancet)   In Greek mythology, son of the healing god Asclepius; brother of Acesis, Aegle, Hygieia, Iaso, Janiscus, Panacea, and Podalirius; married Anticleia; father of Alexanor, Gorgasus, and Nichomachus. Machaon was one of the suitors of Helen, and after her abduction he sailed for Troy with Podalirius and 30 ships. He was a doctor who tended the Greeks during the Trojan War. Some accounts say he was hidden in the wooden horse, but others say he was killed before the war began. He was later worshiped as a god. Machaon appears in Homer's *Iliad* (book 2) and Vergil's *Aeneid* (book 2).

See also: *AENEID, THE;* ASCLEPIUS; HELEN OF TROY; *ILIAD, THE*

**1948**

**Machira, Lake**   In the folklore of the Carib Indians of the Orinoco region of South America, magic lake of the dead. It was believed that most of the souls of the dead were swallowed by great serpents in Lake Machira. The dead were then carried by the serpents to "a land of pleasure in which they entertain themselves with dancing and feasting," according to Fray Ruiz, a 17th-century Christian author who wrote about Indian beliefs in *Conversión en Piritú de Indios Cumuanagotos y Palenques.*

**1949**

**Maconaura and Anuanaitu**   In the mythology of the Carib Indian tribes of the Orinoco region of South America, a primeval husband and wife.

After Adaheli, a creator god, had made man and woman, a handsome Indian was born, Maconaura, who lived with his mother. He was a fisherman, and one day he found that his basket net had been broken and his fish stolen. He set out to discover the thief and found that a cayman, a form of South American crocodile, had stolen the fish. Maconaura shot an arrow between the eyes of the cayman, and it disappeared beneath the waters. Then Maconaura heard a noise and found a beautiful Indian girl, Anuanaitu, who was crying. He took her to his home, for she was very young, and they lived with his mother. When she was old enough, he married her. After some time, however, Anuanaitu killed Maconaura and his mother because the cayman, which Maconaura had killed, was her brother.

**1950**

**Macunaima**   In Brazilian folklore, hero who appears in the novel *Macunaima*, "the story of a hero without a backbone," by Brazilian novelist Mario de Andrade (1893–1945). Macunaima is described as "jet black," a child of midnight, who would not talk until he was six. When he finally did speak, he said: "Oh, I'm too lazy."

**1951**

**Madderakka**   In Finno-Ugric mythology, goddess of birth worshiped by the Lapps, with three goddess daughters, Sarakka, Juksakka, and Uksakka. Madderakka was responsible for making women and cattle fertile and for creating the body of the child in its mother's womb. Her daughter Sarakka helped women in childbirth and also reindeer at the birth of their calves. She was invoked by Lapp women during menstruation. Juksakka, the second daughter, was believed to change the girl child in the womb into a boy child and was also invoked to make boys into good hunters. Uksakka, the last daughter, lived underground, protecting people in their comings and goings. At childbirth she received the new child and watched over its first steps so that it would not injure itself.

**1952**

**Mademoiselle Charlotte**   In Haitian voodoo, a loa (deified spirit of the dead) who manifests all the traits of a white European when she mounts or takes possession of a person during voodoo ritual. Thus, when she mounts a black Haitian girl, the girl will then speak eloquent European French. The goddess loves to be shown all the respect due her office and will work only for someone she takes a liking to. Another loa of European background in Haitian voodoo is Dinclinsin, who is believed to have come to Haiti with Mademoiselle Charlotte. Dinclinsin, however, is greatly feared because of his extreme severity.

See also: LOA

**1953**

**Madira**   In Hindu mythology, goddess of wine and wife of Varuna, god of the ocean. Madira is also called Varuni.

See also: VARUNA

**1954**

**Maev** (Maeve, Medb, Meadhbh) (she who intoxicates)   The most vibrant female personality in all of Celtic mythology. She is queen of Connaught, an evil war goddess in the cycle of myths around the hero Cuchulain, who is killed by her sorcery. She is often depicted with a bird and a squirrel on her shoulders wearing a red cloak and carrying a spear that is flaming. She appears in numerous tales and legends as a licentious queen. Her appearance deprived soldiers of their strength; she was therefore the goddess who drained men of sexual powers. In later English folklore, Maev became Queen Mab, queen of the fairies, later replaced by Titania.

See also: CUCHULAIN; MAB

**1955**

**Magen David** (shield of David)   Modern symbol of Judaism, the hexagram formed by two equilateral triangles that have the same center and are placed in opposite directions. The Magen David is not found in the Old Testament nor mentioned in the Talmud. It is believed to have first been referred to by the 12th-century writer Judah Hadassi. Sometimes it is called the Star of David, but this is a misnomer.

**1956**

**Magi**   In the Bible, N.T., wise men who visited the Christ Child and offered gifts. The account of the visit is found in Matthew (2:1–12), which tells that when Jesus was born a star appeared in the east. The Magi (or Wise Men in some Bible translations) started from their own country to follow the star. It guided them to Judea. They went to King Herod and asked him where the royal infant was to be found. Herod did not know but asked the Magi to make inquiries and report Jesus' whereabouts to him. The Wise Men left, and the star reappeared. They followed it, and it guided them to a shed in Bethlehem where Mary and Joseph had taken temporary lodgings. The Wise Men entered and made their offerings. Warned by an angel not to return to King Herod, they left for their own lands.

In Cologne Cathedral in Germany visitors were shown three heads, which they were told were the heads of the three Wise Men. The names given to them are Caspar (The White One), Melchior (The King of Light), and Balthazar (The Lord of Treasures). The New Testament account does not name the Wise Men nor does it say how many there were. The three gifts signify kingly office (the gold); Godhead (the frankincense); and the coming death of Christ (the myrrh).

Other names are given the three Wise Men: Apellius, Amerus, and Damascus; Magalath, Galgalath, and Sarasin; or Alor, Sator, and Peratoras. Some legendary accounts say they were Shem, Ham, and Japeth of the Old Testament, who had fallen asleep and awakened when Christ was born.

In modern-day Germany and Austria children still dress up as the Three Kings and go from house to house and sing for the occupants. When they leave they mark the entrance with C M B. The chalk, sometimes salt, has been blessed by the church.

**1957**

**Magna Mater** (great mother)   In Roman mythology, epithet for Cybele and Rhea, both mother goddesses. In Rome the worship of the Magna Mater was introduced in 204 B.C.E. at the command of a Sibylline oracle, to pray for deliverance from Hannibal in Italy. An embassy was sent to fetch her holy stone from Pessinus, which was conveyed into the city by the most virtuous woman in Rome. A festival was then instituted in honor of Magna Mater. Held 4 to 9 April, it was called Megalesia (Greek, great mother's rites).

See also: GREAT GODDESS

**Magnes** (magnet)   In Greek mythology, a man whose shoe nails became magnetized while he was walking over a mine; thus, our word *magnet*. Magnes was the son of Aeolus and Enarete; father of Dictys and Polydectes by a naiad and father of Eioneas, Hymenaeus, and Pierus. Some accounts say Magnes was a slave of Medea, who transformed him into a magnet.

See also: AEOLUS; MEDEA

**Magpie**   A bird of the crow family with a long tail and black and white plumage, often considered a bird of ill omen in European folklore. In Christian symbolism the magpie represents the devil or vanity. But the bird does possess some good qualities, as in one English rhyme from Lancashire:

One for sorrow two for mirth
Three for a wedding four for a death
Five's a christening six a dearth
Seven's heaven eight is hell
And nine's the devil his ane sel.

Some variants change the fourth line to "four for a birth."

In Oriental folklore, such as Chinese, the magpie is a sign of good luck. A chattering magpie signifies the arrival of guests or some good news. In Nordic mythology the magpie is believed to be a soulbird, one that carries the souls of the dead.

**Mah**   In Persian mythology, the moon goddess, whose light makes the plants grow.

*Mahabharata, The*   (great war of the Bharatas) Hindu epic poem, longest in the world, consisting of 110,000 couplets. It is divided into 18 *parvans* (sections or books). The original authorship or editing of the work is ascribed to the sage Vyasa, though the entire work was written over subsequent centuries, displaying numerous additions. Dates for the compilation of the epic range from 400 B.C.E. to 200 C.E.

The frame tale—the war between two branches of the same family—takes up about one-fourth of the poem; the rest deals with such diverse subjects as mythology, folktales, and cosmology. It also contains philosophical digressions such as the Bhagavad-Gita, perhaps the most famous section of the entire work, inserted as episodes and subepisodes.

The following summary gives the main incidents and details connected with the epic proper, that is, the tale of the great war.

There was once a king named Santanu, a descendant of Bharata, who had a son Bhishma. In his old age King Santanu wished to marry again, but the hereditary rights of his son Bhishma were an obstacle to the king in obtaining a favorable match. Bhishma, in order to assist his father in his quest to marry, gave up his rights to the throne. The king then married Satyavati, who bore him two sons. The eldest, Chitrangada, succeeded to the throne but was killed. He was followed by his brother, Vichitra-virya, who died without any offspring but left two wives, Ambika and Ambalika, daughters of King Kasi. Satyavati then called on Vyasa, the half brother of her husband, to fulfill the law and father children in the name of Vichitra-virya. Vyasa had lived the life of a hermit in the forests, and his severe fasts had completely wasted his body, so he was quite ugly. The two widows were so frightened by his appearance that the elder one closed her eyes when making love; she gave birth to a blind son, Dhrita-rashtra. The younger widow turned so pale that her son was called Pandu (the pale).

Satyavati wanted a child without any physical blemish. So instead of sleeping with Vyasa herself she substituted her slave girl, who bore a son, Vidura. The three children, Dhrita-rashtra, Pandu, and Vidura, were brought up by their uncle, Bhishma, who acted as regent. When they came of age the throne was not given to Dhrita-rashtra because he was blind but went instead to Pandu.

Pandu had two wives, Kunti (Pritha) and Madri, but he did not have intercourse with either. Some believe he suffered from leprosy (his name meaning "pale"). Pandu left for the Himalaya Mountains. His two wives, however, had five children, all fathered by different gods. Pandu acknowledged them as his before he died, and they were called the Pandavas. Kunti was the mother of the three oldest sons, Madri the mother of the two younger ones.

Yudhi-shthira (firm in fight) was the son of Yama, god of the dead; Bhima (the terrible) was the son of Vayu, the wind god; Arjuna (white; bright; silvery) was the son of Indra, the storm god. Nakula and Saha-deva, the sons of Madri, were followed by Surya, the sun god.

The other branch of the family, that of Dhrita-rashtra, had 100 sons and 1 daughter, Duh-sala. From their ancestor, Kuru, they were known as the Kauravas.

Thus the two major branches of the family, and the two contending forces in the epic, are the Pandavas and the Kauravas. The Pandava sons were brought up in the court of King Dhrita-rashtra, their uncle, but because he showed them favor over his own sons (he nominated Yudhi-shthira to be his heir apparent), a feud broke out between the two branches. To stop the fight the Pandavas were sent into exile. However, one cousin, Duryodhana, plotted to destroy the Pandavas completely. He had their house set afire. All five sons were thought to be dead, though they escaped into the forest.

While the Pandavas were living in the forest, they heard that King Draupada had proclaimed a *swayamvara*, a tournament in which the daughter of the king would choose her husband from the contenders. The Kauravas also heard of the contest and went to seek the hand of Draupadi, daughter of the king. Being in exile, the Pandavas disguised themselves as Brahmans (priests). At the contest the Pandavas won every feat. After they had thrown off their disguises, the winner of the bride was seen to be Arjuna. The brothers took Draupadi home and told their mother, Kunti, they had made a great acquisition. Kunti, not knowing they meant Draupadi, told them to share it among themselves. A mother's command could not be evaded, and Draupadi became the common wife of all five brothers. Each husband belonged to her for a specific time, during which the others were not to interfere.

Because they had revealed themselves at the *swayamvara* King Dhrita-rashtra called the Pandu brothers back to court and divided his kingdom. Prince Yudhi-shthira was chosen king of the territory given the Pandavas. After having conquered many other countries, King Yudhi-shthira decided he wanted to perform a great horse sacrifice, to set up his claim as universal ruler and king of kings. This move excited the jealousy of the Kauravas, who plotted to destroy the vain king. They persuaded King Yudhi-shthira to gamble with Sakuni, their uncle, who was a cheat. At the end of the gamble Yudhi-shthira lost his entire kingdom, as well as his family. King Dhrita-rashtra forced the Kauravas to restore both to Yudhi-shthira, but he again gambled them away. This time he and his brothers were forced into exile in the forest for 12 years. In the 13th year they joined, in disguise, the service of the king of Virata.

The Pandavas now determined to recover their lost kingdom. The king of Virata became their ally, and preparations were made for war. Krishna (an incarnation of the god Vishnu) and his brother Balarama, relatives of both the Pandavas and Kauravas, took the side of the Pandavas. Krishna acted as charioteer for his friend Arjuna. It was in this role that Krishna spoke the great Bhagavad-Gita, the most famous philosophical part of the epic, while the rival armies were drawn up for battle at Kurukshetra, a plain north of Delhi.

Many battles follow in the epic, the end result being that the Pandavas are the victors. But that is not the end of the epic, for it goes on with the lives of the survivors. Filled with remorse for all of the slaughter he caused, King Yudhi-shthira abdicated his throne, leaving with his brothers for the Himalayas to reach the heaven of Indra, the storm god, located on Mount Meru. The journey was not easy because sins and moral defects proved fatal to the pilgrims. The first to die was Draupadi because "too great was her love for Arjuna." Next was Saha-deva, who "esteemed none equal to himself." Then Nakula: "ever was the thought in his heart, 'There is none equal in beauty to me.'" The great hero Arjuna was next. He said, "In one day I could destroy all my enemies." He died because he boasted and did not fulfill his boast. When Bhima fell, he asked the reason for his death and was told, "When thou last looked on thy foe, thou hast cursed him with thy breath; therefore thou fallest today." Yudhishthira went on alone with his faithful dog until he reached the gate of heaven. He was invited by Indra to enter, but he refused unless his brothers and Draupadi could also enter. He was told they were already there, but when he entered he saw all of the Kauravas there instead. He left heaven and was sent to hell, where he heard the voices of his family. He then resolved to stay with them. He was told, however, that this was merely a test, an illusion, for he and his brothers and friends were in Indra's heaven.

See also: ARJUNA; BALARAMA; BHARATA; BHIMA; BHISHMA; BRAHMAN; DRAUPADI; FRAME TALE; INDRA; KRISHNA; MERU; SURYA; VAYU

1962
**Mahagir** (Magaye)    In Burmese mythology, a *nat*, or supernatural being, in whose honor a coconut is hung on a porch of every Burmese home. Mahagir is portrayed standing on a platform, holding a sword in one hand and a leaf fan in the other. The platform is held up by three demons who are sitting on a kneeling elephant.

See also: NATS

1963
**Maharajikas**    In Hindu mythology, lesser or inferior gods, whose numbers range from 220 to 236.

1964
**Maharishi** (great sage)    In Hinduism, a term applied to holy men or sages, the term derived from the Prajapatis, the progenitors of the human race in Hindu mythology, who are often called Maharishis.

1965
**Mahasthamaprapta** (he that has obtained great strength)    In Buddhism, an attendant of Amitabha Buddha displaying the *mudra* of worship. In Chinese Buddhism he is called Ta-shih-chih; in Japanese Buddhism, Daiseishi.

See also: AMITABHA; MUDRA

1966
**Mahavira** (great hero)    Believed to have lived in the fifth or sixth century B.C.E., contemporary of the Buddha. Mahavira's original name was Vardhamana. His legendary life is found in the *Kalpa Sutra*, a sacred book in Jainism that contains the lives of the Tirthamkara. According to that account, on the night in which Mahavira "took the form of an embryo in the womb" of his mother, Devananda, the wife of a Brahmin, was "on her couch, taking fits of sleep, in a state between sleeping and waking, and having seen the 14 illustrious, beautiful, lucky, blest, suspicious, fortunate great dreams, she woke up. To wit: an elephant, a bull, a lion, the anointing of the goddess Sri, a garland, the moon, the sun, a flag, a

vase, a lotus lake, the ocean, a celestial abode, a heap of jewels, and a flame. . . ."

All of these symbols were taken as signs that an important son would be born, one well versed in the learning of the Hindu sages. While this was happening, however, Shakra, the chief of the gods decided to take the embryo from Devananda's womb and place it in the womb of Trisala, a member of the warrior caste. When Mahavira was born, "the gods and goddesses came down from heaven to show their joy."

The boy lived a normal life and later married Yashoda, by whom he had a daughter, Riyadarshana, but then decided to leave his worldly life. He gave away his wealth and became an ascetic. When this happened "the gods came down from heaven . . . and did him homage." He continued as an ascetic for 12 years, and then "he sat down near an ancient temple under the sala [teak] tree and remained motionless for two and a half days, fasting and plunged in the deepest meditation. When he arose on the third day enlightenment was complete." After 30 years of preaching he entered Nirvana, and the gods accompanied him. In Oriental art Mahavira is often portrayed enthroned, with a mirror, a vase, a water vessel, a *srivastsa* (said to represent a curl from the god Krishna's breast), and a swastika.

Other Tirthamkara resemble Buddhas but are distinguished from them by being naked, with eyes wide open, lacking a head bump (*usnisa*), and usually having a diamond-shaped mark in the middle of the chest, representing the *jiva* (the indestructible personal life force, or soul).

See also: NIRVANA; TIRTHAMKARA; USHNISHA

1967

**Mahayana** (great way of liberation)    A form of Buddhism that is believed to have appeared sometime between the first century B.C.E. and the first century C.E. It holds that the true teaching of Buddhism is of wider appeal, with a great deal of emphasis on the virtue of compassion, in contrast to what it calls the Hinayana school of Buddhism, which it claims places greater emphasis on wisdom. Mahayana Buddhism has produced many myths and legends in comparison to those produced by Hinayana Buddhism. The other major form of Buddhism, Hinayana (small vehicle or vehicle to be abandoned) is a derogatory name for a series of preliminary teachings and practices preserved in fossilized form within Mahayana Buddhism. Hinayana is similar to but by no means identical with the living lineage of Theravada. Mahayana is more complex than Theravada, but recent research has illuminated the supposed difference between them as being that Mahayana stands more for "wisdom" and Theravada more for "compassion." Some Mahayana teachers take Hinayana to mean the inner motivation to liberate oneself and not help others, whether or not one is outwardly a follower of Mahayana.

1968

**Maheo**    In North American Indian mythology (Cheyenne), creator god, the All-Spirit, who created all life by his power.

1969

**Mahrach**    In Australian mythology, an evil spirit closely connected with death, often called the black ghost. He appears before the death of a person.

1970

**Maia**    In Greek and Roman mythology, mother of Hermes by Zeus; one of the Pleiades; daughter of Pleione and Atlas. Maia is also one of the names of the Great Mother goddess Cybele. The Romans identified Maia with an ancient Italian goddess of spring, Maia Maiestas, and with Fauna, Bona Dea, and Ops. She was said to be the wife of Vulcan, to whom the priests of the god sacrificed on 1 May. The Latin word *maia* gives the name to the month of May in the Roman calendar and may derive from a word for sow (female pig). The Greek word *maia* is probably another form of *maias* (midwife) and was used

*Maia (Cybele)*

as a term of affection for old women (good mother) and nurses (foster-mother), as well as female doctors.

See also: ATLAS; BONA DEA; GREAT GODDESS; HERMES; OPS; PLEIADES; VULCAN

1971
**Maiden of Pohjola**   In the Finnish epic poem *The Kalevala*, elder daughter of Louhi, the evil mistress of Pohjola, the Northland.

Louhi promised her daughter, the Maiden of Pohjola, to Vainamoinen, the culture hero, if he would forge the magic sampo for her. The hero consented, but he commissioned Ilmarinen to forge the sampo for him. When Vainamoinen

left Louhi, he was told not to look to the sky or else some evil would befall him. Of course, as he set out, he looked to the heavens and saw the Maiden of Pohjola, beautifully dressed, spinning. Moved by her beauty, he called to her:

Come into my sledge, O maiden,
In the sledge beside me seat thee.

The maiden, however, was not so easily moved by the old man. When he told her she should be married, she replied that wives "are like dogs enchained in kennel." Vainamoinen insisted that women are actually queens when married. The maiden replied she would no longer listen to his wooing unless he completed some tasks she would assign him. The hero accomplished all except the last, fashioning a ship out of her broken spindle. In the attempt Vainamoinen accidentally cut his knee. He was healed only when he sang the magic words of the origin of iron.

Vainamoinen's bad luck with the maiden did not stop Ilmarinen from forging the magic sampo, which entitled him to the beautiful girl. At first she did not want to marry Ilmarinen, but eventually she agreed. Frequently in the epic she is called Ilmarinen's Lady. She was later murdered by Kullervo, a disgruntled servant.

Sibelius used the wooing of the Maiden of Pohjola by Vainamoinen as the basis for his symphonic poem *Pohjola's Daughter*.

See also: ILMARINEN; *KALEVALA, THE*; KULLERVO; LOUHI; SAMPO; VAINAMOINEN

1972
**Maiden without Hands**   In German folklore, one of the tales in the Grimm Brothers collection. In their version a poor miller is promised riches by an old man (the devil) if he will give the old man what is standing behind his mill. The miller accepts, assuming that only an apple tree is there. He returns home to find that it was his daughter who had been standing behind the mill at that moment. When the old man comes to

claim his prize, the girl has bathed and has drawn a magical chalk circle around herself, which the devil cannot cross. The devil is thus frustrated and demands that the miller cut off the hands of his daughter, which the miller does reluctantly. The girl wanders off into the woods and meets a king who has silver hands made for her. They marry, and the king is then also deceived by the devil when a message announcing the birth of the king's child is changed to read that the queen bore a monster and that the queen and her child are to be put to death. When the queen flees with her child, the king goes in search of his family. He is aided by an angel, and the family is reunited. The story of the Maiden without Hands is tale type 706.

See also: GRIMM BROTHERS; TALE TYPE

1973

**Maidere**   In Siberian mythology, a savior hero in Tartar myth derived from the Buddhist Maitreya, the living or coming Buddha. Maidere will fight Erlik, the devil, at the end of the world. Ulgen, a creator god, will send down Maidere to teach the love of God and convert mankind. Erlik, however, will then kill Maidere out of envy, but the hero's blood will cover the whole earth and burst into flames that will rise to the heavens. Ulgen will then call the dead to rise, and Erlik and his evil companions will be destroyed.

See also: ERLIK; MAITREYA; ULGEN

1974

**Maid Marion** (rebellion, wished for child?)   In British legend, the mistress of Robin Hood. She appears in the late Robin Hood ballads, disguised as a page boy who lived among Robin's men until she was discovered, and she was married to Robin with Christian rites.

See also: ROBIN HOOD

1975

**Mailkun**   In Australian mythology, an evil spirit, wife of Koen. She captures adults in her net and spears children to death. She is also called Tipakalleum.

1976

**Maît Carrefour**   In Haitian voodoo, a loa (deified spirit of the dead) who is master of the demons of the night and is invoked for protection against them. No one whispers or smiles in the presence of Maît Carrefour. He is also called Kalfu.

See also: LOA

1977

**Maît Gran Bois**   In Haitian voodoo, the loa (deified spirit of the dead) who rules over forests, woods, and plant life.

See also: GRAND BOIS D'ILET; LOA

1978

**Maitreya** (he whose name is kindness)   In Buddhism, name of the Buddha of the Future or the Buddha Who Is to Come. Now he lives in the Tushita heaven. When he comes the world will be renewed. The Buddhists have a legend that tells how Ananda, a disciple of the Buddha, asked his master what would happen after Buddha's death.

"Who shall teach us when thou art gone?" asked Ananda. The Buddha replied: "I am not the first Buddha who came upon earth, nor shall I be the last. I came to teach you the truth, and I have founded on earth the kingdom of truth. Gautama Siddhartha will die, but Buddha will live, for Buddha is the truth, and the truth cannot die. He who believes in truth and lives it is my disciple, and I shall teach him. The truth will be propagated and the kingdom of truth will increase for about five hundred years. Then for a while the clouds of error will darken the light, and in due time another Buddha will arise, and he will reveal to you the selfsame eternal truth which I have taught you." Ananda asked, "How shall we know him?" The Buddha replied: "The

Buddha that will come after me will be known as Maitreya."

Often the inscription "Come Maitreya, come" is found carved on rocks in Buddhist Mongolia and Tibet. In Pali the name is rendered Metteyya; in Tibet, Maitreya is called Byams-pa; in China, Mi-lo-fo or Pu-tai Ho-shang; and in Japan, Miroku Bosatsu. Pu-tai was an eccentric monk who was later thought to have been Maitreya. He was also approximated to the god of luck. A fat, jolly figure, he is worshiped for happiness and riches; known as Hotei O-sho in Japan.

See also: ANANDA; BUDDHA, THE; MIROKU BOSATSU

1979
**Maît Source**   In Haitian voodoo, a loa (deified spirit of the dead) who is chosen by a group to watch over streams, lakes, and rivers. Often a cup of water is placed on his altar.

See also: LOA

1980
**Majestas** (greatness, dignity)   In Roman mythology, goddess of reverence, majesty, and honor; daughter of Honor and Reverentia.

1981
**Makara**   In Hindu mythology, a fantastic animal with the head and forelegs of an antelope and the body and tail of a fish. Makara is the mount of the ocean god Varuna, and his figure is shown on the banner of Kama, god of love. He represents the sign of Capricorn in the Hindu zodiac. Makara is also called Jala-rupa (water foam) and Asita-danshtra (black teeth).

See also: CAPRICORN; KAMA; VARUNA

1982
**Makonaima** (Makanaima, Mackonaima, Makunaima, Makaniama) (one who works in the night?)   In the mythology of the Indian tribes of the Orinoco and Guiana regions of South America, a creator god.

"In the beginning," according to the account by W. H. Brett in his book *The Indian Tribes of Guiana*, Makonaima created birds and beasts. They "were all endowed with the gift of speech. Sigu, the son of Makonaima, was placed to rule over them. All lived in harmony together and submitted to his gentle dominion." This ideal paradise did not last. When Sigu uprooted a great tree planted by Makonaima, he found the stump was filled with water, and a great flood ensued. To save the animals, Sigu took some of them to a cave, which he sealed; the others he took to the top of a tree. He dropped large seeds from time to time to test if the waters were receding, until finally the sound of a splash was no longer heard. When the animals came down, however, they had changed somewhat: the arauta howls from his discomfort in the trees, and the trumpeter bird's legs had been chewed by ants, so they are now bony and thin.

Eventually the earth was again populated, but Sigu was persecuted by two evil brothers, who beat him. Each time he was killed he rose again, but finally he ascended a high hill and disappeared into the sky.

In another creation myth about Makonaima, told by Boddam-Whetham in *Roraima and British Guiana*, no mention is made of Sigu. After having created heaven and earth, Makonaima sat down beside a silk-cotton tree by a river, cutting off pieces of its bark. When he cast the bark into the river, fish and birds arose from it. When he cast it on the ground, people and animals arose.

In another myth Makonaima made a "large mould, and out of this fresh, clean clay the white man stepped. After it got a little dirty the Indian was formed, and Spirit [Makonaima] being called away on business for a long period the mould became black and unclean, and out of it walked the Negro."

See also: RORAIMA, MOUNT

1983

**Malec** (Malik)   In Islamic mythology, principal angel in charge of Djahannam (hell). Malec rules the Zabaniya, who are the guardians of Djahannam according to some accounts; in others, angels who carry the souls of the dead to hell. In the Koran (sura 43) sinners call upon Malec to intercede for them with Allah. Malec, however, remains silent and will not answer the sinners until a thousand years after the Day of Judgment. And when he does answer, he will offer no hope, saying that sinners must remain in Djahannam for eternity.

See also: ALLAH; KORAN, THE

1984

**Malingee**   In Australian mythology, the spirit of the night, who during his travels in the dark seeks to find his way home. Malingee's knees knock together as he walks. Both people and beasts fear him, for he kills tribesmen with his stone ax at the slightest provocation. Other animals, such as the eagle hawk, may be killed with the stone knives attached to his elbows. His face is said to be an awful sight, with burning eyes that make him appear to be a devil.

1985

**Mama Allpa**   In Peruvian Indian mythology, earth goddess invoked for a good harvest; depicted with numerous breasts as a symbol of her fertility.

1986

**Mamandabari**   In Australian mythology, two culture heroes, either two brothers or father and son. They emerged out of the ground in the north and traveled south, either underground or by flying, teaching men various rituals and customs.

1987

**Mama Quilla**   In Inca mythology, moon goddess, sister and wife of Inti, the sun, and protector of married women. Many temples were dedicated to her worship, the most famous being the Coricancha at Cuzco, capital of the Inca empire. Cuzco was founded by the first Inca king, Manco Capac, according to some accounts the son of Inti and Mama Quilla.

See also: INTI; MANCO CAPAC

1988

**Mammon** (riches)   In the Bible, N.T., personification of wealth, money, property, and profit. In Matthew 6:24 and Luke 16:13 Jesus says, "You cannot serve God and mammon." Christian folklore turned the word into the name of a demon of avarice, equating Mammon with Lucifer and Satan. John Milton in *Paradise Lost* says Mammon was "the last erected spirit that fell" from heaven. He was, according to Milton, "always downward bent," admiring the gold that paved heaven's floor. Money is sometimes called the "mammon of unrighteousness." Mammon is the ambassador of hell to England in De Plancy's *Dictionnaire Infernal*, written in the 19th century.

See also: LUCIFER; SATAN

1989

**Manabozho** (Manibozho, Manibozoho, Michabo, Nanabozho, Nanabush)   In North American Indian mythology (Algonquian), trickster, transformer, culture hero, creator of the earth.

Many 19th-century scholars confused Manabozho with the historical figure Hiawatha and the mythical figure Gluskap. Today, most scholars agree that all three are different entities. There are many variant myths relating to Manabozho among the Algonquians. In one, told by the Potawatomi, he was the oldest of four children. The fourth, Flint, killed their mother at his birth. Both Manabozho and the second son had human form, but the third became a white hare and magician. When Manabozho grew up he killed his brother Flint, but the gods became angry and killed the second brother as punishment. Manabozho went on a warpath against them. To stop his wrath the gods initiated him in the Midewiwin, the sacred medicine society. The second brother was brought back to life to preside over the souls of the dead, and Manabozho then initiated the Indians in the Midewiwin.

See also: GLUSKAP AND MALSUM; HIAWATHA; TRICKSTER

**1990**

**Managarm** (moon's dog)  In Norse mythology, an evil giant in the form of a wolf, offspring of a giantess. According to the *Prose Edda*, Managarm "will be filled with the life-blood of men who draw near their end, and will swallow up the moon, and stain the heavens and the earth with blood. Then shall the sun grow dim, and the winds howl tumultuously to and fro," at the end of the world, Ragnarok.

See also: GARM; RAGNAROK

**1991**

**Mananaan** (he of the Isle of Man)  In Celtic mythology, son of the sea god Lir, a Tuatha de Danann, husband of Fand and Uchtdelbh, father of Mongan and Niamh. Mananaan had a ship, *Wave Sweeper*, which was self-propelled, as well as a horse, Splendid Mane, with which he traveled over the sea. Mananaan was patron god of Irish seamen, protector of the Isle of Man and the Isle of Aran, where his home, Emhain of the Apple Trees, was located. In Welsh mythology he is known as Manawyddan and possessed a magic chariot as well as a cloak of invisibility. In *Ulysses* James Joyce calls the "whitemaned seahorses, champing, bright-windbridled, the steeds of Mananaan."

See also: AVALON; FLIDAIS; LIR; TUATHA DE DANANN

**1992**

**Manasseh** (making to forget)  In the Bible, O.T., name of the 14th king of Judah; son of Hezekiah (2 Kings 21:1–18), said to have been an evil king. "The Prayer of Manasseh" is not found in the Old Testament but in the Old Testament Apocrypha and is used in some services of *The Book of Common Prayer* (1979 American Version) during times of penitence. Manasseh is also the name of Joseph's first son (Gen. 41:51).

See also: JOSEPH

**1993**

**Manco Capac and Mama Oello Huaco** (Manko Kapak and Coya Mama)  In Inca mythology, first king and queen; they were brother and sister, and children of the sun.

Manco Capac is the culture hero of the Incas. Before he arrived, according to the *Comentarios reales de los Incas* (1609), written by the half-Inca Garcilaso de la Vega, people lived like wild beasts, with "neither order nor religion, neither villages nor houses, neither fields nor clothing." The sun god, pitying the sad plight of mankind, sent his son Manco Capac and his daughter Mama Oello Huaco to earth near Lake Titicaca. He gave them a golden rod that was slightly shorter than a man's arm and about two fingers in thickness.

"Plunge the rod into the earth," the sun god told the two. "The spot where the rod disappears, there you must establish and hold your court."

After some journeying they came to Huanacauri, where the rod sank deep into the earth. Then the couple separated, each taking the good news of the sun god's love to the people. They "taught their subjects everything that had to do with human living."

Some 30 or 40 years after the descent of Manco Capac and Mama Oello Huaco, Manco Capac left his kingdom to his son Sinchi Roca, who became the next Inca king.

Garcilaso's account is but one of many about the first Inca king and the origin of the Incas. In an account by Ramos Gavilan in *Historia del celebre Santuario de Nuestra Señora de Copacabana* (1621), Manco Capac is said to have been merely a human being who dressed in golden robes and fooled the people into believing in his divine origin. This account is prejudiced because the Spanish author wished to destroy the sources of Inca respect for their past.

Another account, given by José de Acosta in *Historia natural y moral de las Indias* (1590), which is earlier than either of of the other two, says that Manco Capac was the founder and chief of the Incas, who came out of "a certain cave by a window, by whom men first began to multiply; and for this reason they call them *Paccari-tambo* [inn of origin]."

1994

**Mandala** (circle) In Hindu and Buddhist ritual, a mystical diagram, usually circular in outline. Its purpose is to gather vital spiritual forces together. The mandala is a sacred mountain or house that presents reality ordered in such a way as to liberate those who meditate on or enter into it, according to Buddhist belief. When drawn in two dimensions, the mandala appears as a circle contained in a square. It is painted on cloth or paper or drawn on the ground with colored rice or pebbles. It may also be engraved on stone or metal. Some mandalas present a detailed representation of the universe, including the Buddhas and Bodhisattvas, gods and spirits, mountains and oceans, and the Zodiac, as well as great teachers. The mandalas have descended from ancient traditions of magic. Carl Jung, the Swiss psychologist, discusses the mandala frequently in his works. He sees it as a symbolic representation of the "nuclear atom" of the human psyche, whose essence we do not know. Jung confused quartermites with mandalas: all mandalas are quartermites; some quartermites are mandalas.

See also: BODHISATTVA; MUDRA

1995

**Mandrake** A narcotic plant of the nightshade family; in world mythology and folklore, believed to be an aphrodisiac. It appears in Genesis (30:14–24) in the conflict between Rachel and Leah, the wives of Jacob. Leah gets the mandrake root from Rachel's youngest son in order to become pregnant. In English the mandrake is often called love apple. The Arabs call the mandrake the "apples of the djinn," or devil's apples, because they consider the rousing of sexual desire evil. In Machiavelli's play *La Mandragola* the plot hinges on the aphrodisiac qualities of the mandrake. Shakespeare's *Henry VI, Part II* (3:2) alludes to some of the folk beliefs about the root, such as that when it is torn from the ground it will utter groans, and the person who pulls it will either go mad, die, or both. Sometimes a cord was fixed to the root and placed around a dog's neck. When the dog drew the root out, it died. Juliet, in *Romeo and Juliet* (act 4, sc.3), before drinking the sleeping potion, lists her fears and apprehensions:

And shrieks like mandrakes' torn out of the earth, That living mortals, hearing them, run mad.

During the Middle Ages, Christians associated the mandrake with the devil. Witches were said to fashion figures of people out of the plant root as a charm to do harm. Ludwig Tieck includes an episode with a mandrake root in his novel *Der Runenberg* (1804). Thomas Newton in his *Herball to the Bible* said: "It is supposed to be a creature having life engendered under the earth, of the seed of some dead person put to death for murder."

See also: JACOB; LEAH

1996

**Manes** (good or kindly spirits) In Roman mythology, good spirits believed to preside over the burying places and monuments of the dead. Their mother was believed to be the goddess Mania, mother of Lares and Manes, father of Cottys by Callirrhoë. Sacrifices of food were offered to the Manes, and the blood of black sheep, pigs, and oxen were poured over graves during their festival, the Feralia, held between 18 and 21 February, during which time the temples were closed. Vergil's *Aeneid* (book 3) cites the Manes.

Often *Dis Manibus sacrum* was inscribed on tombstones with the name of the dead person.

See also: *AENEID, THE;* CALLIRRHOË; LARES; MANES

Wheel of the Law. A lion supports his throne, or he is shown riding on a lion.

See also: BODHISATTVA; BUDDHA, THE; DHARMA; MAHAYANA; MUDRA

1997

**Mani**   In the mythology of the Indians of Brazil, a culture hero who taught his people various arts. When he was about to die, he predicted that a year after his death the people would find a great treasure, the manioc plant (*manihot esculenta*). One year after Mani's death the plant was found. This myth forms the basis for José Viera Couto de Magalhaes's *O Selvagem,* in which a variant of the story is told.

1998

**Manitou**   In North American Indian mythology, a word used in various Algonquian languages for spirit or divine being. This spirit inhabits all living things, wind, thunder, animals, plants, rocks, as well as the sun and the moon. The manitou often appears in dreams and gives special power or protection. In Germany there is a "Manitou and Indian" club that celebrates the writings of Karl May (1842–1912) every year in Radebeul. May was a writer of adventure books still read by young German boys, and the name manitou appears often in his books.

1999

**Manjushri** (wisdom)   In Mahayana Buddhism, the personification of the Transcendent Wisdom of the Buddha. In Chinese Buddhist legend he was a Bodhisattva who was told by the Buddha that it was his duty to turn the Wheel of the Dharma and convert the Chinese. He chose a five-peaked mountain in Shan-shi province; one peak was made of diamonds, the next of sapphires, then emeralds, rubies, and lapis lazuli. On each grew a flower of a special color, and a pagoda was on the summit of each peak. Manjushri's symbols are the sword of wisdom, a book, and the blue lotus; his *mudra* is turning the

2000

**Manman Brigitte**   In Haitian voodoo, a loa (deified spirit of the dead) invoked by people who are constantly embroiled in disputes. Manman Brigitte does not have her own altar in the Oum'phor (voodoo temple) but is invoked in her favorite tree, the weeping willow or the elm. She is asked to bring disaster on one's enemies, who are assumed to be enemies of the goddess as well. Her principal site of worship was located in the main cemetery of Port-au-Prince, Haiti, but her sacred elm was cut down by government and Catholic authorities because many people were seen praying to Manman Brigitte by placing lighted candles at the foot of her tree. Also known as Mademoiselle Brigitte.

See also: LOA

2001

**Manta** (Huecu)   In the folklore of the Araucanian Indians of Chile, a cuttlefish that lives in deep lakes. When it cries, it causes the water to boil. If any person enters the water, the Manta rises to the surface, drags him down, and eats him. Sometimes it has intercourse with other animals and produces monsters. To kill it, one must throw it branches of the quisco, a bush covered with spines that grows in Chile. A similar monster cuttlefish, called Trelquehuecuve, whose tentacles end in hooves, will squeeze to death anything that comes within its reach.

2002

**Manticore** (man-eater)   Fantastic animal with a lion's body, human head, and scorpion tail. In medieval Christian belief the manticore was a symbol of the devil. Sometimes the animal appears in artworks showing the Hebrew prophet Jeremiah.

*Manticore*

The Great Flood came, and Vaivaswata fastened the cable of the ship to the fish's large magic horn. He passed over the northern mountain and later tied the ship to a tree when the waters receded. Vaivaswata saw that all men and women had been destroyed. Desiring to have children, he prayed and made sacrifice. A woman was produced who came to Vaivaswata, saying she was his daughter. With her he lived "worshiping and toiling in arduous religious rites, desirous of offspring. With her he begat the offspring which is the offspring of Manu."

See also: BRAHMA; NOAH

2003

**Manu** (man)   In Hindu mythology, a word for the 14 progenitors of the human race, each of whom hold sway for 4,320,000 years. The names of the 14 are Swayam-bhuya (self-created), an epithet of Brahma; Swarochisha; Auttami; Tamasa; Raivata (brilliant); Chakshusha (perceptible by the eye); Vaivaswata or Satya-vrata; Savarna; Daksha (dextrous); Brahma-savarna; Savarna or Rudra-savarna; Rauchya; and Bhautya. Vaivaswata, the seventh Manu, is connected with one version of the myth of the Great Flood in Hindu mythology.

One morning, while Vaivaswata was washing his hands, he caught a fish.

"Take care of me and I will preserve you," the fish told Vaivaswata.

"From what will you preserve me?" Vaivaswata asked.

"A flood will carry away all living beings; I will save you from that," the fish replied.

The fish then told Vaivaswata to keep him alive in an earthen vessel and to put him in a larger container as he grew, eventually placing him in the ocean. The fish grew rapidly and was moved from the smaller container to larger ones and then to the ocean. The fish then told Vaivaswata to construct a ship, or ark, in which Vaivaswata was to go abroad. Vaivaswata did as he was told.

2004

**Maori**   In African mythology (Makoni of Zimbabwe), sky and creator god; creator of Mwuetsi, the first man, and Massassi, the first woman. Maori gave Mwuetsi (Mwuetse) a horn filled with magic oil and settled him at the bottom of a primeval lake. But Mwuetsi wanted to live on the earth and complained to Maori, who finally consented to his wish. When Mwuetsi was placed on earth he saw it had no plant life; all was waste and desolate. "See," said Maori when Mwuetsi began to cry, "I told you. Now you are set on a path that will only lead to death. But I will give you a companion." So Maori created Massassi, the first woman and gave her the gift of fire-making. When Maori touched the oil in the horn to his finger and then touched Massassi, she became pregnant and gave birth to plant life on earth.

In time Massassi had to die. At her death Mwuetsi was so distraught that Maori created another woman, Morongo, the evening star, to replace her. She too was touched with the oil, but she said he must have intercourse with her. Then she became pregnant and bore sheep, goats, cattle, chickens, and children. Maori then told Mwuetsi that he was going to die and should no longer have sexual intercourse with Morongo. But the couple continued to sleep together, producing lions, leopards, scorpions, and snakes. One day Mwuetsi tried to force Morongo to have sexual intercourse with him, but a snake, favored by Morongo, bit Mwuetsi. As he weakened from the snake bite, the earth, as well as people and animals, began to die. When Mwuetsi's children learned that only by returning him to the lake could they be saved, they murdered him and placed him back in the lake.

See also: ABUK AND GARANG; ADAM AND EVE; ASK AND EMBLA

**2005**
**Mara**   In Buddhist mythology, the Evil One who attempted to destroy the Buddha but never succeeded. He appears in numerous Buddhist myths and legends. He corresponds to Satan in the Christian world. Mara assaulted the contemplative Buddha beneath the Bodhi Tree. The enticements of Mara's daughters, who were skilled in the arts of desire and voluptuousness, did not affect the Buddha. Also unheeded were the threats of hideous devils. When Mara threw his ultimate weapon, a fiery discus, it turned into a canopy of flowers.

Originally Mara was a Hindu demon, Namuchi, often called Vritra, who constantly fought against the storm god Indra. He was a mischievous spirit who prevented rain and produced drought; his name means "not letting go the waters." In many Hindu myths Indra forces Namuchi to send down fertilizing rains and restore the earth.

Mara is also called Papiyan (more wicked; very wicked) and Varshavarti (he who fulfills desires). In this last version his true nature is revealed, fulfilling the desire for existence, the desire for pleasure, and the desire for power. Mara therefore appears in Buddhist mythology as the arch-tempter of the Buddha. *Mara* is also used as a common noun denoting any hindrance to enlightenment. In Zen, hallucinations are called Makyou (Mara pictures).

See also: BODHI TREE; INDRA; NAMUCHI; SATAN

**2006**
**Marasta**   In Haitian voodoo, a loa (deified spirit of the dead) who represents twins, who are considered sacred.

See also: LOA

*Marduk*

**2007**
**Marduk** (bull calf of the sun)   In Near Eastern mythology (Babylonian), hero-god who defeated the monster of chaos, Tiamat, and was proclaimed king of the gods. Marduk's myth is told in the Babylonian creation epic poem *Enumu Elish* ("When on high . . ."). Recited at Zag-Muk, the New Year celebration, the poem was composed between 1200 and 1000 B.C.E.

"When on high . . ." is the opening of the poem, when the sky was not yet named and "the earth below was nameless." Only Apsu, the abyss, and Tiamat, or chaos, existed. From their mingled waters came forth Mummu, the "tumult of the waves," and the monstrous serpents Lakhmu and Lakhamu. These two in turn gave birth to Anshar and Kishar, two primeval gods. Anshar and Kishar then gave birth to the gods Anu (lofty); Ea, god of sweet waters, earth, and wisdom; Marduk, the hero god; the Igigi, a group of gods who took up their post in the heavens; and the Anunnaki, another group of gods who took their position in the underworld.

Shortly, this new creation angered the peace of Apsu, and he complained to his wife. "During the day I have no rest and I cannot sleep at night," he said to Tiamat.

The married couple then argued about what to do. Their son Ea overheard the argument in which Apsu planned to destroy his offspring. Using magic incantations, Ea seized Apsu and Mummu. Tiamat, angered at this move, gathered a host of gods and gave birth to a group of monsters to fight Ea. Among the monsters were some "with sharp teeth, merciless in slaughter," terrible dragons, storm monsters, savage dogs, scorpion men, fish men, and rams. At the head of her army she appointed Kingu, another monster.

Ea then went to his father, Anshar, to tell of Tiamat's plans to destroy them all. Anshar sent Anu with a message to Tiamat:

Go and step before Tiamat.
May her liver be pacified, her heart softened.

Anu obeyed his father, but as soon as he saw how ugly Tiamat's face was, he took flight. Failing with Anu, Anshar then sent his son Ea, but he was no more courageous. Finally, Anshar decided to send his son Marduk against Tiamat:

Marduk heard the word of his father.
His heart rejoiced and to his father he spoke.

Marduk told his father he was ready to have a contest with Tiamat and would come out the victor. He addressed the assembled gods:

When I shall have become your avenger,
Binding Tiamat and saving your life,
Then come in a body,
In Ubshu-kenna [chamber of fate or destiny],
    let yourselves down joyfully,
My authority instead of yours will assume
    control,
Unchangeable shall be whatever I do,
Irrevocable and irresistible, be the command
    of my lips.

The gods, in no position to offer resistance, accepted Marduk's claim to full authority. Marduk then took his weapon, the thunderbolt, mounted his chariot drawn by fiery steeds, and went forth to the enemy camp:

The lord comes nearer with his eye fixed on
    Tiamat,
Piercing with his glance Kingu her consort.

Kingu, unable to endure the "majestic halo" of Marduk, was killed. Then all of the host of Tiamat left the battlefield except for Tiamat.

"Stand up," cried Marduk. "I and thou, come let us fight."

When Tiamat heard these words of challenge, she "acted as possessed, her senses left her," and she shrieked "wild and loud." All of her rage, however, had no effect on Marduk. The poem describes her undoing:

The lord spread out his net in order to
    enclose her.
The destructive wind, which was behind him,
    he sent forth into her face.
As Tiamat opened her mouth full wide,
Marduk drove in the destructive wind, so that
    she could not close her lips.
The strong winds inflated her stomach.
Her heart lost its reason, she opened her
    mouth still wider, gasping for breath.
He seized the spear and plunged it into her
    stomach,
He pierced her entrails, he tore through her
    heart,

He seized hold of her and put an end to her
life.

He threw down her carcass and stepped upon
her. (Jastrow translation)

Finished, he then cut her "like one does a
flattened fish into two halves." From one half he
created a covering for the heavens, from the
other, the earth. From the blood of the monster
Kingu he created the first man.

In the Old Testament Marduk is often called
Bel. Jeremiah (50:2) uses both names when he
writes: "Declare ye among the nations, and publish, and set up a standard; publish, and conceal
not: say, Babylon is taken, Bel is confounded,
Merodach [Marduk] is broken in pieces." In art
he is often depicted as a composite of a snake and
a dragon holding a *marrn*, a hoe shaped instrument.

See also: ANU; APSU; EA; NABUR; ZAG-MUK

*St. Margaret*

2008
**Margaret, St.** (pearl)   In Christian legend, a
female saint who went in the disguise of a man
for most of her life. Feast, 8 October.

St. Margaret's life is told in *The Golden Legend*,
written in the 13th century by Jacobus de Voragi-
ine. She came of a noble family who married her
off to a noble youth. On the wedding night, however, she "abstained from the society of her husband, garbed herself in the habit of a man," and
fled the house. She reached a monastery and
passed herself off as Brother Pelagius. She continued in the disguise for years, eventually being
made the overseer of the nuns. When one of the
nuns became pregnant, Margaret, as Brother
Pelagius, was charged, convicted, and locked in a
cave, where she was fed bread and water. Years
passed. When she was about to die, she wrote a
letter to the monastery telling them the true
story of her life. In a variant legend, Margaret
was swallowed by a dragon, but he dislodged her
when she made the sign of a cross, and later she
was beheaded at Antioch in Pisidia.

See also: DRAGON; *GOLDEN LEGEND, THE*

2009
**Margawse, Queen**   In Arthurian legend, half
sister of King Arthur, wife of King Lot, and
mother of Gwain, Gareth, Gaheris, and
Agravaine. Malory's *Morte d'Arthur* makes her
the mother of Mordred by King Arthur. Margawse was killed by her son Gaheris when he discovered her with her lover, Sir Lamorok. Later
Gwain killed Lamorok. Tennyson's *Idylls of the
King* uses the name Bellicent for Margawse.

See also: ARTHUR; GARETH; GWAIN; LOT, KING

2010
**Marindi**   In Australian mythology, a dog
whose blood turned the rocks red. One day
Marindi was passing by the dry bed of a water
course when he heard a voice saying "Come out
and fight." It was Adno-artina, the gecko lizard,
who offered the challenge. Marindi agreed to the
fight, but the lizard, seeing Marindi's huge teeth,
decided the battle should be put off until the evening, when he would be able to see better. The
lizard tied a string around the root of his tail to
prevent courage from leaving his body. As they

fought, Adno-artina seized Marindi by the throat. The dog's blood poured out and dyed all of the rocks in the creek red. To this day red ochre, used extensively for decorative purposes, is obtained from the spot where the battle took place.

See also: ADNO-ARTINA

2011

**Marishiten**   In Japanese Buddhist mythology, goddess of light. She is portrayed in a martial aspect, mounted on a boar, elephant, tiger, dragon, or snake. Marishiten has three faces; two are gentle, and the left one is fierce. She carries in her eight arms the sun, moon, spear, a bow and arrow, a sword, and a war fan. Warriors worship Marishiten because she has the power to make herself invisible. Sometimes she is called the queen of heaven.

2012

**Marjatta** (Mariatta) (berry)   In the Finnish epic poem *The Kalevala* (rune 50), virgin mother of a child who becomes king of Karelia and replaces the culture hero Vainamoinen.

Marjatta, who lived in the Northland, was a virgin, "always pure and holy." One day she asked a cuckoo how long she would remain unmarried and was answered by a berry, who told her to "come and pluck" him. The girl did as she was told and became pregnant. Her family, thinking her a whore, threw her out of the house, and the poor girl sought shelter. She found a stable in a clearing and prayed to the horse in the stable to blow his warm breath on her so that she would not freeze to death. When the horse breathed on her, the whole stable was filled with steam, and she gave birth to a boy. While she was sleeping, however, the child disappeared and was found only with the aid of the sun, who told her the boy was in the swampland or a fen. The boy grew up to be "most beauteous" but had no name. He was called Floweret by his mother and Sluggard by strangers. Marjatta wanted to have the boy baptized, but an old man would not do

the ceremony without the father present. Vainamoinen came to investigate the matter and decided the child should be put to death, but the child upbraided Vainamoinen. The boy was then christened and made the king of Karelia, and the angry Vainamoinen left the land.

The 50th rune, which is the last section of the epic, displays a good deal of Christian influence, particularly in the the story of the virgin and her son, and is probably a poetical explanation of the ending of the pagan gods, symbolized by Vainamoinen, and the coming of Christianity. For instance, the Jalo Synty, or Suuri Mies (great birth), referred to in this rune is a title for Jesus Christ, used by the Greek Orthodox Karelians, who view Christ's birth as the birth par excellence.

See also: *KALEVALA, THE*; VAINAMOINEN

*St. Mark*

2013

**Mark, St.** (from Mars, the Roman god of war) First century. In the Bible, N.T., Evangelist, author of the Gospel that bears his name. Patron saint of Venice and of glaziers and notaries. Invoked by captives. Feast, 25 April.

Mark has been identified as the young man who ran away when Jesus was arrested in the garden (Mark 14:51–52) and is believed to be the same "John surnamed Mark" in the Acts of the Apostles (12:12).

According to early Christian legend, Mark preached in Egypt and founded a church at Alexandria, being the first bishop of the city. The pagan population, however, was angry at his miracles and accused him of being a magician. At the feast of the god Serapis the saint was seized, bound, and dragged along the streets until he was dead. At the moment the saint died the police who had arrested him were killed by a bolt of lightning. The Christians at Alexandria buried the mangled remains. Mark's tomb then became a great shrine. About 815 some Venetian merchants trading in Alexandria stole his relics and brought them to Venice, where they were placed in the church dedicated to the saint, San Marco. There is a painting by Tintoretto of the finding of the saint's body.

The saint has proved popular in Christian art. When he is represented as one of the four Evangelists, either singly or grouped with the others, he is usually accompanied by a lion, winged or unwinged. Scenes from his legendary life are quite common in Venetian art. There is a painting by Gentile Bellini, based on one of the legends, of Mark preaching at Alexandria.

One day St. Mark saw a poor cobbler, Anianus, who had wounded his hand severely with his awl. The saint healed the wound, and Anianus was immediately converted to Christianity. Later, after Mark's death, Anianus became the next bishop of Alexandria.

One of the most popular legends, painted by Giorgione and Paris Bordone, tells how the saint saved Venice from a flood in 1340 by appearing with St. George and St. Nicholas and making the sign of the cross to let the storm demons flee.

Another episode from the saint's life tells how a Christian slave prayed at the shrine of St. Mark even though he was forbidden to do so by his master. As a punishment the man was to be tortured, but St. Mark descended from heaven and the instruments of torture were broken or blunted. There is a painting of this scene by Tin-

toretto, and a poem, *The Legend of St. Mark*, by John Greenleaf Whittier.

In English north country villages, people sit in the church on 24 April from eleven at night until one in the morning for three years in a row. In the third year it is said that they can see the ghosts of those who will die that year come into the church.

See also: GEORGE, ST.; LION; NICHOLAS, ST.

2014

**Marko, the Gravedigger**   In Russian folklore, a monk who restored the dead to life. Marko was a gravedigger for the Holy Crypt Monastery during the Middle Ages. One day he dug a grave that was not very wide. When the body was brought to the grave, the monks "began to grumble at Marko, for it was neither possible to adjust the dead man's robes nor to anoint him with holy oil." Marko told the monks that he had not felt well when he dug the grave, but they continued to complain until Marko addressed the dead man: "Brother, your grave is so narrow we cannot even anoint you with holy oil. Take the oil and anoint yourself." The dead man rose up slightly, anointed himself with the holy oil, and then lay down and "once more died." Marko performed other such miracles, and when he died was buried in a grave he had dug for himself.

2015

**Mars**   In Roman mythology, god of war, originally an ancient Italian god who watched over agriculture; identified by the Romans with the Greek war god Ares. Mars was the son of Jupiter and father of Romulus (Quirinus) by Rhea Silvia. March, the first month of the old Roman year, was dedicated to Mars as the fertilizing god of spring. Mars was invoked, along with the goddess Dea Dia, to bless the fields during a festival in May. As god of war Mars was called Gradivus (the strider) because of his rapid march in battle. His symbols were the wolf, woodpecker, and lance. When war broke out, the cry was *Mars vigila!* (Mars awake!). Numerous sacrifices were

*Mars*

offered to Mars and warlike exercises, Equirria, were held in his honor on 27 February, 14 March, and 15 October. On the last day a horse was sacrificed on his altar in the Campus Martius (field of Mars), a plain lying to the north of Rome, outside the Pomerium, between the Tiber, the Quirinal, and the Capitoline Hills. The blood of the horse was collected and preserved in the temple of Vesta and used at the Palilia for the purposes of purification. Mar's cult had a special priest, the *flamen martialis*, and a group of Salci (dancers). During Mars's feast in March the Salci sang, danced, and beat their shields with staves. Augustus honored Mars as Mars Vitor (avenger of Caesar) in a temple erected in 2 B.C.E.

Mars was the patron god of pagan Florence, later replaced by St. John the Baptist, whose church is believed to stand on the spot where Mars's temple originally stood. Dante's *Divine Comedy* (Inferno 13; Paradise 16) cites the legend that the statue of Mars, hidden in the Arno tower, had to be restored before Florence could be rebuilt. Western paintings depicting Mars usually portray his love affair with Venus. Botticelli, Piero di Cosimo, Tintoretto, Veronese, Poussin, and David have all treated the subject.

See also: ARES; JUPITER; VENUS; VESTA; WOLF; WOODPECKER

2016

**Marsyas** (battler?)    In Greek mythology, a Phrygian flute player, son of Olympus; sometimes called Silenus; follower of the Great Mother goddess Cybele. Marsyas, who took up the flute after it had been discarded by its creator, Athena, challenged Apollo to a contest between his flute and Apollo's lyre. Marsyas lost, and Apollo bound him to a tree and flayed him until he died. All of the spirits and deities of the woods lamented Marsyas's death, and their tears became the river Meander. King Midas, who had taken Marsyas's side in the contest, had his ears turned into those of an ass as punishment. The figure of Marsyas bound to a tree influenced many portrayals of the Crucifixion. In Plato's *Symposium* the great philosopher Socrates is called a Marsyas and a Silenus. Plato's *Republic* mentions the flute as an instrument that evokes the darker Dionysian, unruly passions, as opposed to Apollo's lyre, which represents harmony. Dante's invocation to Apollo in *The Divine Comedy* (Paradise, canto 1) uses the same imagery. Ovid's *Metamorphoses* (book 6) and Matthew Arnold's *Empedocles on Etna* deal with the myth. Raphael, Perugino, Tintoretto, Titian, and Rubens are among the artists who have treated the subject.

See also: APOLLO; ATHENA; GREAT GODDESS; MIDAS; OVID

2017

**Martha, St.** (lady)    First century. In Christian legend, patron of cooks and housewives. Sister of Mary of Bethany and of Lazarus, whom Christ raised from the dead. Feast, 29 July.

Tertullian and other early Church Fathers identify Mary of Bethany with Mary Magdalene, though this is not accepted by most biblical scholars today. In Christian art, however, Tertullian's interpretation has made its impact. In *Il Perfetto Legendario* the two sisters are contrasted. "Martha was a chaste and prudent Virgin, and the other publicly contemned for her evil life; notwithstanding which, Martha did not despise her, nor reject her as a sister, but wept for her shame, and admonished her gently and with persuasive words; and reminded her of her noble birth, to which she was a disgrace, and that Lazarus, their brother, being a soldier, would certainly get into trouble on her account. So she prevailed, and conducted her sister to the presence of Christ."

In a Provençal legend Mary Magdalene went to preach in Marseilles, while Martha went to preach in Aix and the surrounding countryside. There was a fearful dragon, called the Tarasque, which St. Martha overcame by sprinkling it with holy water and binding it with her girdle or, in other accounts, her garter. Rubens painted the scene of *Christ in the House of Martha and Mary*, which portrays a simple Martha with an apron, while Mary is richly dressed, listening to Christ's words. She is depicted in art holding a bunch of keys and a ladle or pot of water.

See also: LAZARUS; MARY MAGDALENE

*St. Martin*

2018

**Martin of Tours, St.** (from Mars, Roman god of war; Latin variation, Sanctus Martinus; Italian, San Martino)     Fourth century. In Christian legend, patron saint of armorers, beggars, calvary, coopers, domestic animals, girdlers, glovers, horses and horsemen, millers, innkeepers, tailors, wine merchants, and wool weavers. Invoked against drunkenness, storms, and ulcers. Feast, 11 November.

Martin was born in the Roman province of Pannonia (modern-day Hungary) during the reign of Constantine. His parents were pagan. He was a tribune in the army and was sent into Gaul on a campaign. The *Dialogues* of Sulpicius Severus gives the well-known legend of St. Martin and the beggar. When he was 18, he was stationed at Amiens during a very severe winter. One bitterly cold day a beggar, naked and shaking, came near his station. Martin, like all the other soldiers, was in armor, but over his steel he had a large military cloak. As none of his companions took notice of the beggar, Martin cut his cloak into two with his sword and gave half of it to the beggar. At night Christ appeared to Martin in a vision. He was dressed in the parted cloak and asked Martin if he recognized the garment, adding, "What is done to the poor in My name is done unto Me." Martin then resolved to be baptized. After leaving the army Martin retired to a religious life and was made bishop of Tours in 371.

Many other miracles are recorded of him: he raised a widow's son to life, restored a slave of the proconsul from the possession of the devil, held converse with angels, and quenched fire by prayer. He is usually pictured on horseback, dividing his cloak with a beggar. There is a well-known painting of this incident by El Greco in which the saint is portrayed in 16th-century Spanish costume with a ruff. The cathedral in Mainz, Germany, is named after St. Martin, and a large statue on the roof depicts the scene with the beggar.

2019

**Marunogere**   In Melanesian mythology, Kiwai Papuan god and culture hero. He created the first pig and coconut tree, built the first house, and instituted sacred ceremonies. Two dogs are his companions.

2020

**Maruts** (flashing)   In Hindu mythology, wind gods who form part of the entourage of Indra, the storm god, or of Rudra (another name for Shiva). Their number varies in different texts, the seven major ones being Vayuvega (wind speed), Vayubala (wind force), Vayuha (wind destroyer), Vayumandala (wind circle), Vayujvala (wind flame), Vayuretas (wind seed), and Vayucakra (wind disk). Maruts are also called Rudras.

See also: INDRA; RUDRAS; SHIVA

2021

**Marwe**   In an African folktale told by the Chaga of Tanzania, Marwe and her brother were instructed to keep the jungle monkeys from eating the family's beans. After keeping a long watch they grew thirsty and went off to a distant pool to find water. Marwe threw herself into the pool when she learned that in her absence the monkeys had eaten all of the beans. She preferred to die rather than face the anger of her parents. When she reached the bottom of the pool, she met an old woman who permitted Marwe to live with her.

In time Marwe became homesick and was given the opportunity to return to her parents. First, however, she was asked to choose between hot and cold. Marwe, not knowing what the choice involved, chose cold. She was startled to find her arms and legs covered with expensive bangles. When Marwe appeared by the side of the pool, all of the young men wanted to marry her. She chose Sawoye, whose skin had many blemishes. Soon, however, his skin cleared, and he became a very handsome mate. Marwe and Sawoye prospered, but jealous neighbors killed him. Marwe, however, was able to bring him

back to life and hid him in their home. As the neighbors advanced on the home in an effort to take her riches from Marwe, Sawoye suddenly appeared and killed them.

*St. Mary Magdalene*

2022

**Mary Magdalene, St.** (rebellion? wished-for child?)   First century. In the Bible, N.T., penitent woman. Western art, following Christian legend, makes no distinction between Mary, the sister of Martha and Lazarus, Mary Magdalene, and the "woman which was a sinner," though they appear to have been historically three distinct persons. Feast, 22 July.

In the New Testament Mary Magdalene was a follower of Christ and "ministered" to him. She had been possessed by seven devils, which Christ drove from her. Her courage is illustrated by the fact that she was at the foot of the cross with Mary, the mother of Jesus and John, whereas the other disciples fled. Mary was also the first one to see the risen Christ, according to the account in John's Gospel (20:11–17). This episode is called in Latin the *Noli me tangere* (touch me not). It is frequently found in medieval and later Christian art. The New Testament tells us nothing of the later life of the saint, though medieval Christian legend has supplied much. According to legend, Mary Magdalene and her brother Lazarus and sister Martha, accompanied by Maximin and

Marcella (later sainted), set out in a ship without sail or oar and came to Marseilles. Here they converted the people, with Lazarus becoming the first bishop of Marseilles.

Despite Mary Magdalene's reformation, the sinful aspect of her life has appealed to both poets and artists, who often portray her as a penitent. Richard Crashaw, the 17th-century English poet, in his *Carmen Deo Nostro*, has a poem, *St. Mary Magdalene or the Weeper*, in which numerous lines are expended on the profusion of tears the saint shed over her sinful life. In paintings St. Mary Magdalene is usually portrayed as a beautiful woman with long fair hair. She has near her a box of ointment, referring to the spices to anoint the dead Jesus. Sometimes, however, she is portrayed as a wasted woman. When she is shown in the desert, praying or reading, the emblems of penance, such as a skull or bones, are nearby. Titian, the great painter of the Italian Renaissance, painted her in this manner.

See also: LAZARUS; MARTHA, ST.

*St. Mary of Egypt*

2023
**Mary of Egypt, St.** (rebellion? wished-for child?)   Fourth century. In Christian legend, prostitute who became a saint. Feast, 2 April.

St. Jerome wrote that in Alexandria there was a woman "whose name was Mary, and who in the infamy of her life far exceeded Mary Magdalene." After having passed 17 years in "every species of vice," one day she spotted a ship that was ready to sail to Jerusalem "to celebrate the feast of the true cross." She was "seized with a sudden desire to accompany them" but had no money, so she paid her way with "every means in her power." When they arrived at Jerusalem, all of the worshipers entered the church except for Mary, whose "attempts to pass the threshold were in vain," for a supernatural power drove "her back in shame, in terror, in despair." Convinced that she should mend her ways, she prayed and renounced her wicked life. She bought three loaves of bread and "wandered forth into the solitude" until she had reached the desert. She lived in the Syrian desert as a female hermit. She was finally discovered by St. Zosimus after 47 years. He was asked to bring the Holy Communion to the saint at the end of the year. When he returned, he was not able to pass over the Jordan, but Mary, "supernaturally assisted," passed over the water and received the Holy Communion. St. Zosimus was to return the next year to give her Communion, but when he arrived he found she had died. He buried her body with the assistance of a lion who helped him dig the grave.

St. Mary of Egypt, though sometimes confused with St. Mary Magdalene, is frequently shown in art as a wasted woman, stripped of her clothes, her long hair covering her body, with three loaves of bread. She is thus portrayed in Quentin Massys's painting *St. Mary of Egypt*, as well as in a painting by Emil Nolde.

See also: JEROME, ST.; MARY MAGDALENE

2024
**Masewi and Oyoyewi** (Masewa and Uyuyewa) In North American Indian mythology (Acoma), twin war spirits who were sent by their mother to place the sun in the sky in its correct position and to assign clans to the people. They were credited with killing monsters and releasing the rains.

2025
**Masnavi, The** (Mathnawi, Mathnwi-i-Ma'nawi, Mesnevi) (couplets)   Persian mystical poem in 27,000 couplets, divided into six books, written in the 13th century by Rumi, a Sufi mystic. It

embodies fables, folklore, legends from the Koran, and religious and moral teaching.

*The Masnavi* is considered Rumi's major work, being one of the most important documents of the Sufis, a mystic order related to Islam that employs the language of the senses to express longing for reunion with God. Rumi's text is an attempt to explain the doctrines of Sufism in popular form. Though the Persian poet Omar Khayyam is better known among Westerners because of the 19th-century translation by Edward Fitzgerald, Fitzgerald's teacher, the Reverend Edward B. Cowell, hated the doubting Omar Khayyam but loved *The Masnavi* as one of the most brilliant religious poems in the world.

See also: KORAN, THE

2026

**Mason wasp**   One of the most common of African insects, the mason wasp builds its mud nest on almost any type of object. It often creates a nest near a fireplace and for that reason is commonly credited in mythology with having brought fire to earth. According to the Ila people of Zambia, the mason wasp volunteered to go to heaven, along with three birds, to ask God for fire so that all of the birds and insects of the world could keep warm during winter. Each of the three birds died en route to heaven, leaving only the mason wasp to petition God for fire. God pitied him and decided to grant his wish. He made him chief of all birds and insects and told him to build his nests near fireplaces.

2027

**Mass**   In Christianity, common name for the central act of worship, also called the Holy Eucharist, the Liturgy, the Lord's Supper, and Holy Communion. Based on Jewish and pagan rituals, the Mass uses bread, which is basic to the human diet, and wine, which is associated with vitality and fellowship, for communion with Christ, the risen Lord. The earliest account of the ritual is found in St. Paul's first letter to the Corinthians (I Cor. 11:2–26, New Jerusalem Bible):

For the tradition I received from the Lord and also handed on to you is that on the night he was betrayed, the Lord Jesus took some bread, and after he had given thanks, he broke it, and he said, "This is my body, which is for you; do this in remembrance of me." And in the same way, with the cup after supper, saying, "This cup is the new covenant in my blood. Whenever you drink it, do this as a memorial of me."

For centuries Christians have debated the meaning of the words, sometimes killing one another over their disagreements. Some Christians, such as Roman Catholics, believe that the bread and wine literally become the body and blood of Christ, calling it transsubstantiation; Anglicans believe in the real presence, though they do not define it; Lutherans believe in consubstantiation—the bread and wine exist along with the body and blood of Christ; and still other Christians hold that the rite is merely symbolic and that the bread and wine remain bread and wine. The ancient mystery cults that existed at the time of the birth of Christianity also had communion meals in which bread and wine were part of the ritual. Worship of Orpheus, Osiris, Mithra, Attis, and Dionysus each had a ritual meal as part of the cult.

The Latin Mass, which was fixed by the Council of Trent in the 16th century, broke down as follows: the Ordinary, with unchanging text, and the Proper, with a changing text, depending on whether the Mass was for a special feast day or a saint's day or was a Requiem Mass for the dead. Settings of the musical section of the Mass usually were

Kyrie (Lord, have mercy)
Gloria (Glory to God in the highest)
Credo (The Nicene Creed, beginning "I
   believe in One God")
Sanctus and Benedictus (Holy, Holy, Holy)
Agnus Dei (Lamb of God)

The Mass text has been set by many composers, among them Guillaume de Machaut, Dufay, Ockeghem, Obrecht, Josquin Des Prés, Byrd, Tallis, Palestrina, J. S. Bach, Haydn, Mozart, Beethoven, Cherubini, Schubert, Liszt, Bruckner, Franck, Gounod, Verdi, Villa-Lobos, Poulenc, Stravinsky, and Vaughan Williams. A setting of the Russian liturgy was composed by Tchaikovsky.

See also: MITHRAS; DIONYSUS; ORPHEUS; OSIRIS; PAUL, ST.

2028
**Masterson, Bat**   1855–1921. In American history and folklore, William Barclay Masterson was a sheriff noted for his fine suits, pearl-gray bowler, diamond stickpin, and notched gun. In 1875, Bat killed his first man at Sweetwater, Texas. The incident occurred over a woman named Molly Brennan. Bat and Molly were both wounded by the gunfire of her jealous ex-lover, Melvin A. King, before Bat killed him. After Bat recuperated, he returned to Dodge City, where he worked as a deputy marshal under Wyatt Earp. Once a man pestered Bat to sell him his gun as a souvenir. Not wishing to part with his gun, Bat went out and purchased a Colt .45 to sell to the gentleman. To make the gun even more interesting he put 22 notches on it. When the collector called for his souvenir, Bat handed him the notched gun. Stunned, the man asked him if he had killed 22 men. According to legend, Bat replied: "I didn't tell him yes, and I didn't tell him no, and I didn't exactly lie to him. I simply said I hadn't counted either Mexicans or Indians, and he went away tickled to death." Bat Masterson appeared as the subject of a television series.

2029
**Mater Matuta.** (Mother Dawn)   In Roman mythology, goddess of sea travel, originally an early Italian goddess of birth, dawn (often identified with Aurora), harbors, and the sea, and as such identified with the Greek Leucothea. Her festival, Matralia (festival of mothers), was celebrated on 11 June.

2030
**Mati-Syra-Zemlya** (moist Mother Earth)   In Russian mythology, earth goddess. The worship of Mati-Syra-Zemlya continued in Russia up to the eve of World War I, when peasants invoked her protection against the spread of cholera.

At midnight the old women of the village would gather, summoning one another without the knowledge of the men. Nine virgins would be chosen to go with the old women to the village outskirts. There they would all undress down to their shifts. The virgins would let down their hair, and the widows would cover their heads with white shawls. A widow would then be hitched to a plow, which was driven by another widow. The nine virgins would take up scythes, and the other women took up such objects as the skulls of animals. They would all march around the village, howling and screaming as they plowed a furrow to allow the spirits of Mati-Syra-Zemlya to emerge and destroy all evil spirits, such as the cholera. If a man happened to see this ceremony, he would be seized and killed.

Some Russian peasants would listen to Mati-Syra-Zemlya by digging the earth with a stick or their fingers. If the digging sounded like a well-stocked sleigh moving over the snow, it meant crops would be good. If it sounded like an empty sleigh, the crops would be bad. In the spring bread was buried for her to eat, and beer or wine for her to drink.

Igor Stravinsky's ballet *Le Sacre du printemps* (*The Rite of Spring*), deals with the worship of Mother Earth in pagan Russia. The ballet's subtitle is *Pictures of Pagan Russia*. The work was first performed by Diaghilev's Ballets Russes in Paris with choreography by Vaslav Nijinsky, who Stravinsky thought completely misunderstood the ballet. The sets and costumes were by Nicholas Roerich, who was also responsible, with Stravinsky, for the scenario of the ballet. At the ballet's first performance there was a near riot between those who accepted the modern effects of the score and those who violently protested, saying the work violated all known principles of music. Today *Le Sacre du printemps* is recognized as one of the greatest innovations in 20th-century music.

See also: MIKULA

**Matowelia** In North American Indian mythology (Mojave), culture hero who led the Mojave Indians from the White Mountain to their home along the Colorado River. At death the spirits of the Indians would return to the White Mountains. If they were not ritually burned, they would become screech owls.

2031

**Matronalia** In Roman cult, festivals in honor of Mars and Juno, celebrated by married women in commemoration of the rape of the Sabines and of the peace that later ensued. Flowers were offered in the temple of Juno, who was also called Matrona because she presided over marriage and childbirth.

See also: JUNO; MARS

2032

*Ma Tsu P'o*

2033

**Ma Tsu P'o** In Chinese Taoist mythology, Queen of Heaven and Holy Mother, invoked by sailors to grant good weather and safe sailing. Jesuit missionaries compared Ma Tsu P'o to the Virgin Mary.

See also: VIRGIN MARY

2034

**Matthew, St.** (gift of Yahweh) First century. In the Bible, N.T., Evangelist and Apostle. Author of the Gospel bearing his name. Patron of bankers and tax collectors. Feast, 21 September.

Little is known of his life. The gospels give only the account of his calling by Jesus (Mark 2:14). It is a widely accepted theory that Levi and Matthew are the same person. Jesus is believed to have given Levi the name Matthew. There are two different traditions of the death of St. Matthew. According to Greek legend, he died during the reign of Domitian, but according to Western legend, he was martyred in Ethiopia by either a sword or a spear. In art, aside from his symbol as an angel with a book in his role as Evangelist, he is often portrayed at the moment he answered Christ's call, as in Caravaggio's painting.

2035

**Mátyás** 1440–1490. In Hungarian legend, a king noted for his just rule. He became popular among the peasants during his lifetime for his humane measures in alleviating the hard life of the serfs. Shortly after his death Mátyás became the subject of numerous legends in the manner of King Arthur or King Solomon. Up to the beginning of the 20th century Hungarian peasants believed that King Mátyás would reappear again and their lives would then be better. The belief is similar to the English belief that King Arthur will return in a dark time and restore justice, and the German belief about Barbarossa. A well-known Hungarian proverb is "King Mátyás is dead; justice has passed with him."

See also: ARTHUR; BARBAROSSA; SOLOMON

2036

**Maui** (Mowee)   In Polynesian mythology, great trickster and culture hero who snared the sun and brought fire to mankind but died while attempting to give man immortality.

Maui's father was Tama, the sky, and his mother was Taranga, who gave birth to him prematurely. When he was born, she wrapped him in a tuft of her hair and cast him into the surf, but a jellyfish surrounded the body of the young child, protecting him from any harm. Tama saw the object floating in the ocean and came down to investigate. When he removed the jellyfish he found the baby and took him to his home in the sky, placing the boy on the roof of his house so that he would be warmed by the fire inside. After a short time Maui became restless and decided to go to earth to see his mother and brothers. He entered the assembly hall while his family was attending a dance. Sitting behind his brothers, he waited for his mother, Taranga, to come and count her sons. When she reached Maui, she said he was not one of her children. But when the lad told her his story, she was convinced and said, "You are indeed my last born son." She brought him home and let him sleep in her bed, which annoyed his brothers.

When Maui's father, Tama, saw his son, he was pleased and decided to perform a naming ceremony, which would make Maui sacred and would cleanse all impurities. After the ceremony it was discovered that some prayers had been omitted and that the gods would punish Maui because of the omission.

Maui is credited with setting the length of the day. Annoyed with the shortness of the day, Maui persuaded his brothers that they should capture the sun in a net and force him to slow down.

His brothers at first objected to his plan but later agreed. They made a noose, and Maui took his magic jawbone that he had procured from his grandmother Muri-ranga-whenuam. The brothers then traveled all night to the desert where the sun rises and hid themselves. Maui made a large circle with a length of rope.

Maui said to his brothers, "Keep yourselves hidden, and do not show yourselves to the sun; if you do, you will frighten him. Wait patiently until his head and forelegs are well into the snare, then I will shout. You haul away as hard as you can on both ends of the rope, and I will rush out and beat him until he is nearly dead. And, my brothers, do not let him move you to pity with his shrieks and screams."

When the sun was caught, Maui beat him until he began to move at a slower pace, thus setting the length of the day.

Maui also captured fire for humankind. He went to the underworld and asked Mahu'ike for some fire with which to cook. She (in some accounts a male) gave him one of her fingernails, which contained fire. He later returned to her and said the fire had gone out, and he needed another fingernail, which she gave him. This went on until the goddess was left with only one toenail, and she then realized what Maui was up to. She threw her last toenail to the ground, and it immediately burst into flame. Maui then transformed himself into an eagle in order to escape, but his wings were singed. Mahu'ike saved some of the flames by throwing them into the treetops. To this day men make fire by rubbing two sticks together.

Maui next tried to obtain immortality. He set off with some birds to find Hina-nui-te-po (great goddess of the night), the goddess who ruled the dead. When he arrived in the underworld, he found her asleep.

"My little friends," he said to the birds, "when you see me enter the body of this old chieftainess, be careful not to laugh. If you do, she will awaken and kill me. But when you see me coming out of her mouth, you can laugh, and I will live and Hine-nui-te-po will die."

Maui took off his clothes and entered the goddess through her vagina. When the birds saw his feet sticking out of the goddess's vagina, they almost burst into laughter. One wagtail could not contain himself and let out a laugh, which awoke Hine-nui-te-po, who crushed Maui inside herself. So Maui failed to achieve immortality for humankind.

To this day the Maori recite this proverb: "Men make heirs, but death carries them off."

This account of Maui is based on Sir George Grey's *Polynesian Mythology*. Maui is also known as Amorshashiki, Ma-tshikt-shiki, Mosigsig, and Motikitik.

See also: SUN SNARER; TRICKSTER

2037

**Maundy Thursday**   In Christian ritual, the Thursday of Holy Week before Good Friday, sometimes called Holy Thursday, Shere, or Chare. The main rite during the day is the washing of the feet of the poor by a priest, based on the command in John's Gospel (13:34), in which Jesus said, "A new commandment I give unto you, love one another as I have loved you." With these words Jesus washed the feet of his disciples. During the Middle Ages it was the custom for a bishop or priest to wash the feet of 12 beggars or a group of pilgrims. St. Oswald, archbishop of York (972–992) instructed his clergy to feed 12 poor men and wash their feet every day. English kings also would follow the sacred rite. St. Thomas More tells how King Henry VIII washed the feet of the poor and gave them food and money. Queen Elizabeth I also washed the feet of a pauper, but she first had them washed in herb-scented water by her servants before she performed the rite. The rite of washing the feet is still observed in the Roman and Anglican churches, and by some Anabaptists, but was discontinued by Luther, who denounced it. In 1718, 12 Lutherans were forced to do public penance for having a duke wash their feet. (The name Maundy is believed to derive from the Latin translation of Jesus' command, *Mandatum novum de vobis*.)

See also: OSWALD, ST.; THOMAS, ST.

2038

**Maurice and the Theban Legion, St.** (Moorish, dark-skinned)   Died 286. In Christian legend, Roman captain of the Theban Legion. Patron of armies, armorers, infantry, hatters, and knife grinders. Invoked against demonic possession, enemies of religion, and gout. Venerated at St. Maurice-en-Valois, St. Moritz, and Zofingen. One of the patron saints of Austria. Feast, 22 September.

Among the legions that made up the Roman army at the time of Diocletian and Maximin was one called the Theban Legion because it originated in Thebald. All of the 6,666 soldiers were Christians, and their leader was Maurice, or Mauritius. About the year 286 Maximin summoned the legion from the East to reinforce the army about to march into Gaul. After the passage through the Alps, some of the army was sent on to the Rhine while the rest remained on the banks of Lake Geneva, where Emperor Maximin ordered sacrifices to pagan gods, accompanied by games and ceremonies. Maurice and the Christian soldiers retired some three leagues away and made camp at Aganum, now Saint-Maurice. In the account of *The Golden Legend*, when Maximin heard of this,

. . . he sent knights to them, and commanded that they should come hastily unto the sacrifices of the gods. . . . and they answered that they might not so do because they held the faith of Jesu Christ. And then the emperor . . . said: "The injury celestial is meddled with my despite, and the religion Roman is despised with me. Now shall each contumacious knight feel not only for me, but to avenge my gods." Then Caesar commanded his knights that they should go and constrain them to do sacrifice to the gods, or else they should slay always the tenth man. Then the holy saints stretched tofore that other to come to the death. And after, S. Maurice arose up and said to his fellows among other things: "Enjoy ye with us, and I thank you, for we be all ready for to die for the faith of Jesu Christ." . . . And when the emperor heard that, he commanded to behead yet the tenth man of them. (Caxton translation)

Some of the Theban Legion were trampled down by the cavalry, some hung on trees and shot with arrows, some killed by the sword. Maurice and some of his officers knelt down and were beheaded.

St. Maurice is usually shown in complete armor; he bears in one hand a standard, in the other a palm. Southern European art often shows him dressed as a Roman soldier, as in El Greco's painting of the saint. German art shows him as a Moorish knight, as in Hans Baldung Grien's painting.

**Mauvais**    In Haitian voodoo, an evil man or woman who uses the evil eye against a person, often causing death.

**Mawu Lisa**    In African mythology (Fon of Benin), bisexual god—part male, part female—who became the source of all other gods. Each pair of their children (for all were born as sets of twins) was given an area to rule. Lisa, the male twin, is associated with the sun; Mawu, his female counterpart, is the moon. The first pair was given the earth to rule, and the other six were assigned the sea, weather, hunt, human life span, and similar things to control. Mawu, as the moon, is more inclined to softness, whereas Lisa is forceful and unrelenting. Mawu is the older of the two and is regarded as the embodiment of wisdom; Lisa is the personification of physical strength. Da, the son of the divine pair, assists in ordering the cosmos. At times Mawu is referred to as the Supreme Being without any reference being made to Lisa. Some accounts say Nana Buluka, an androgynous deity, existed before Mawu Lisa and created the god.

See also: AVONAWILONA; DA; YIN AND YANG

**Maya**    Fifth century B.C.E. In Buddhist legend, mother of the Buddha. She led a pure life, entitling her to be the mother of the coming Buddha. Maya had a dream in which the future Buddha appeared to her as a white elephant and entered her right side. The dream is frequently portrayed in Buddhist art.

See also: BUDDHA, THE

**Maya** (the maker)    In Hindu mythology, the architect of the demons. In the epic poem *The Mahabharata* he built a palace for the Pandavas. *Maya* is also the word used to mean the created world as experienced independently by its creator and often is mistakenly translated as "illusion."

See also: *MAHABHARATA, THE*

**Mayauel**    In Aztec mythology, goddess of pulque, the intoxicating drink made from the fermented sap of the agave, and hallucinogens. She is not to be confused with Mayahuel, the wife of Ehecatl. Mayauel was the wife of a farmer. One day she chased a mouse away from the maguey (agave) plantation. She found that the mouse had eaten the heart from one of the plants and had drunk its juice. As a result the mouse swayed unsteadily and was in fact drunk. Mayauel and her husband put some of the juice from the plant in a gourd and left it while they went to work in the fields. When they returned, they took a drink. They soon swayed unsteadily and became drunk. The gods, not wanting to miss out on such a discovery, took the spirit of Mayauel and made her into a goddess. In some accounts the pulque god is called Ometochtli (two rabbits). He was killed by Texcatlipoca, the Aztec creator-trickster god.

See also: EHECATL

2044

**Mazeppa, Ivan** 1644–1709. In Slavic history and legend, Cossack hero and leader. Born of a noble family, Mazeppa became a page at the court of the Polish king. He had an affair with the young wife of a nobleman and as a punishment was tied naked to a wild horse, which was then turned loose. Mazeppa was saved by Cossacks and in time became a hetman, or leader, and prince of the Ukraine under Peter the Great of Russia. Later, however, Mazeppa betrayed Russia to Charles XII of Sweden, when the king invaded the Ukraine. He appears in Lord Byron's poem *Mazeppa*, Pushkin's poem *Poltava*, and Tchaikovsky's opera *Mazeppa*. Victor Hugo's poem *Mazepla* tells of the hero's ride while tied to the wild horse; Liszt's tone poem *Mazeppa* and Delacroix 's painting deal with the same subject.

2045

**Médard of Noyon, St.** Died 545. In Christian legend, patron saint of brewers, peasants, and prisoners. Invoked on behalf of idiots and lunatics; also for fruitfulness, both in childbearing and the fields, for rains and vineyards, and against bad weather and toothache. Feast, 8 June.

Once a sudden shower fell, wetting everyone in the town except St. Médard, who remained perfectly dry, for an eagle had spread its wings over him. Ever after he was called *maître de la pluie* (master of the rain), and it was believed that if it rained on Médard's feast day, it would rain for 40 days thereafter. Médard founded the Rose Festival at Salency in which the most virtuous girl in the parish received a crown of roses and a purse of money. De Maupassant's tale "Le Rosier de Madame Husson," which Benjamin Britten used as the basis for his opera *Albert Herring*, describes the festival.

2046

**Medea** (cunning) In Greek mythology, great sorceress and enchantress, daughter of Aëetes, king of Colchis, and Eidyia; sister of Absyrtus and half-sister of Chalciope; wife of the hero Jason. To assist Jason in his quest for the Golden Fleece, the goddess Aphrodite caused Medea to fall in love with the handsome hero. Medea aided Jason through her skill in magic and witchcraft. She was a priestess of Hecate, goddess of night and witchcraft, according to some accounts. Medea so loved Jason that she killed her brother Absyrtus when he pursued her as the couple fled. When Medea and Jason arrived at Iolcos, Medea rejuvenated Jason's father Aeson by boiling him with a mixture of magical herbs in a vat. Then, in an evil plan, she encouraged the daughters of Aeson's brother Pelias to do the same for their father. The girls eagerly did as told, and the old man was boiled to death. Again the couple fled, this time to Corinth. Here Jason grew tired of Medea and decided to marry Glauce (or Creusa), the king's daughter. Medea destroyed the girl with a poisoned robe and diadem, which caught fire when Glauce put them on. When Glauce's father attempted to save his daughter, he too was destroyed. Not yet satisfied, Medea further punished Jason for his betrayal of her by killing their two sons, Mermerus and Pheres. Leaving Jason desolate, Medea then fled to Athens in a chariot drawn by two dragons. She married Aegeus, king of the city, but later became jealous of his son Theseus and had to flee again. Eventually, she returned to Colchis, where she was believed to be immortal.

Medea appears in Euripides' *Medea* and the modern English version by the American poet Robinson Jeffers; Seneca's *Medea*; Ovid's *Heroides* (12) and *Metamorphoses* (book 7); Apollonius Rhodius's short epic poem *Argonautica* (Voyage of the Argo); Gower's *Confessio amantis*; Chaucer's *Legend of Good Women*; Corneille's *Médée*; Cherubini's opera *Medea*; Jean Anouilh's *Médée*; Pasolini's film *Medea*, with Maria Callas, who also sang the role in Cherubini's opera; Delacroix's painting *Medea*, which portrays her about to kill her children; and Samuel Barber's *Medea's Meditation and Dance of Vengeance* in the ballet

"Cave of the Heart" with choreography by Martha Graham.

See also: AEGEUS; APHRODITE; GOLDEN FLEECE; HECATE; JASON; MERMERUS AND PHERES; OVID

**2047**

**Mehen**   In Egyptian mythology, a great serpent. Mehen surrounds the sun god in his boat to protect him from the monster serpent Apophis. The sun god is portrayed as a ram-headed deity in his role of crossing the heavens at night. He usually wears a solar disk. Around the sun god in this form is a cabin, and Mehen is often portrayed coiling around the cabin as a sign of protection.

See also: APOPHIS; SNAKE

*Melchizedek*

**2048**

**Melchizedek** (king of righteousness)   In the Bible, O.T., king and high priest of Salem. Abraham met Melchizedek when Abraham was returning from rescuing Lot. Melchizedek blessed Abraham and gave him food and wine (Gen. 14:18). In medieval Christian symbolism, based on the Epistle to the Hebrews (5:6) in the New Testament, Melchizedek is seen as a prefiguration of Christ because his offering of food and wine seemed to echo the Christian Eucharist.

See also: ABRAHAM

**2049**

**Meleager** (guinea fowl)   In Greek mythology, a hero, an Argonaut son of Ares or Oeneus and Althaea; brother or half brother of Deianeiras, Gorge, and Toxeus; husband of Cleopatra, daughter of Idas; father of Polydora. He was one of the members of the Calydonian boar hunt. In Homer's *Iliad* (book 9) Meleager is cited as a hero who long defended his city and was killed during the Calydonian boar hunt. In Ovid's *Metamorphoses* (book 8) Meleager's life is snuffed out by his mother. She had been told by the Fates at his birth that as long as a firebrand then in the fireplace did not burn down, Meleager would live. Althaea removed the log and stored it in a chest. When she discovered that Meleager had killed her brothers after the Calydonian boar hunt, she took out the log and cast it into the flames, causing his death. The best-known treatment of the myth in English literature is Swinburne's poetic drama *Atalanta in Calydon*.

See also: AREA; ARGONAUTS; CALYDONIAN BOAR HUNT; *ILIAD, THE*; MELEAGER; OVID

**2050**

**Melisenda**   In medieval Spanish legends, daughter of Charlemagne and the wife of Gayferos. She was captured by the Moors and held prisoner for seven years. Eventually, she was freed by her husband. Cervantes's *Don Quixote* (part 2) has the tale acted out by puppets before the Don. This section of the novel was used by Manuel de Falla for his opera *El retablo de maese Pedro*.

See also: CHARLEMAGNE

**2051**

**Melusina**   In European folklore, a being that is half woman, half fish-serpent, who lived some of the time in a well. Melusina was a full woman during most of the week, but on Saturday she had to return to her snake-fish form. In one medieval French tale she married Raymond, nephew of the count of Poitier, on the condition that she be free on Saturday nights. One day her husband caught Melusina in her snake-fish transformation and she fled. She left two children and is regarded as an ancestor of three noble French families. Occasionally Melusina is depicted in British heraldry as a mermaid with two tails. Mendelssohn's overture *The Fair Melusina* is based on her tale.

See also: UNDINE

2052

**Menelaus** (might of the people)   In Greek mythology, king of Sparta; son of Atreus and Aerope; younger brother of Agamemnon, Anixibia, and Pleisthenes; husband of Helen. He returned to Sparta with Helen after the Trojan War. His return voyage is described in Homer's *Odyssey* (book 4), and Theocritus's *Idyll 18* is a marriage song for Menelaus and Helen. Menelaus and Helen were worshiped as demigods at Therapne near Sparta. He appears in Homer's *Iliad* and *Odyssey*, Euripides' *Helen*, and Vergil's *Aeneid*.

See also: *AENEID, THE*; AEROPE; AGAMEMNON; ATREUS; HELEN OF TROY; *ILIAD, THE*; *ODYSSEY, THE*

2053

**Menorah** (candelabrum)   In Judaism, a seven- or eight-branched candlestick. The seven-branched candlestick was used in the Temple and is described in Exodus (37:17–23): "And he [Bezaleel] made the candlestick of pure gold: of beaten work made he the candlestick . . . three branches of the candlestick out of the one side thereof, and three branches of the candlestick out of the other side. . . . And he made his seven lamps, and his snuffers, and his snuffdishes, of pure gold."

The arch of Titus in Rome portrays the menorah of the Second Temple being taken away after the Romans had captured the city. The base consists of squares. Recent research, however, indicates that the menorah of the Second Temple had three legs, not a square base.

The eight-branched menorah is used for the feast of Hanukkah; it has a ninth socket for the

candle that lights the other branches. The Kabbalah calls the menorah the Tree of Life. According to one Jewish tradition, the Temple menorah was never extinguished until the destruction of the Temple.

See also: HANUKKAH

*Menthu*

2054

**Menthu** (Mentu, Mont)   In Egyptian mythology, a sun god associated with war, often combined with the god Ra and known as Menthu-Ra. The ancient Greeks equated the Egyptian god with their god Apollo.

See also: APOLLO; RA

2055

**Mephistopheles** (he who loves not the light) In Jewish and Christian folklore, either a minion of the devil or the devil himself.

Mephistopheles' most prominent role in folklore is found in the various treatments of the Faust legend, which originated in the late Middle Ages and were a popular topic in chapbooks. *The Historie of the Damnable Life, and Deserved Death of Doctor John Faustus*, translated from the German by P. F. in 1592, describes an early ap-

*Mephistopheles*

pearance of Mephistopheles to Faust, or Faustus. "Suddenly there appeared his Spirit Mephostophiles [sic], in likeness of a fiery man, from whom issued most horrible fiery flames. . . . the Spirit began to blare as in a singing manner. This pretty sport pleased Doctor Faustus well."

Mephistopheles assumes various animal forms to entertain the doctor and then takes on the "apparel" of a friar and offers a document to Faust to sign away his soul. "Faustus being resolute in his damnation, wrote a copy thereof, and gave the Devil the one, and kept in store the other." In this account Mephistopheles is himself the devil. In Marlowe's play *The Tragical History of Doctor Faustus*, Mephistopheles is the leading demonic character, though Lucifer and Beelzebub also appear. When Faustus asks Mephistopheles how he is "out of hell," the demon replies:

Why, this is hell, nor am I out of it:
Thinkest thou that I, who saw the face of God,
And tasted th' eternal joys of heaven,
Am not tormented with ten thousand hells,
In being depriv'd of everlasting bliss?

In Goethe's working of the Faust legend in his mammoth drama *Faust*, Mephistopheles makes a wager with God, much as Satan does in the book of Job in the Old Testament, about how faithful Faust is to God. Mephistopheles says:

What will you wager? Him you yet shall lose,
If you will give me your permission
To lead him gently on the path I choose.

The Lord answers:

As long as on earth he shall survive,
So long you'll meet no prohibition
Man errs as long as he doth strive. (George
   M. Priest translation)

In Goethe's play Faust is saved; in Marlowe's work he is lost.

Mephistopheles is the main character in Arrigo Boïto's opera *Mefistofele*, based on Goethe's work and on Ferruccio Busoni's *Doktor Faust*, another opera based on Goethe. In Franz Liszt's *Faust Symphony* the last movement depicts the character of Mephistopheles in grotesque variations because according to the philosopher Hegel, he "represents the negative principle." Thomas Mann also treated the theme in his novel *Dr. Faustus*. Perhaps the best graphic representation of Mephistopheles is in the series of lithographs by Eugene Delacroix published in 1828 to illustrate Goethe's *Faust*, though a series done by Harry Clarke in a Beardsleyesque style capture better some of the grotesque qualities of the demon.

See also: FAUST; JOB; LUCIFER

2056

**Mera** (glistening)   In Greek mythology, a faithful dog who was transformed into the Lesser Dog Star, Canis (or Sirius). Mera showed Erigone, Icarius's daughter, where her murdered father had been thrown. Immediately after the discovery, Erigone hanged herself, and the Mera dog pined away. The myth is found in Ovid's

*Metamorphoses* (book 7). The name Mera is also borne by a priest of Aphrodite.

See also: APHRODITE; ERIGONE; OVID

**Mercurius, St.** (Mercury [Roman god])   Died 250. In Christian legend, warrior saint who murdered Julian the Apostate. Venerated in the Eastern Orthodox Church. Feast, 25 November.

According to legend, Julian sold his soul to the devil when he renounced Christianity. On the night he was to go to battle against the Persians, St. Basil the Great had a vision of the Virgin Mary seated on a throne and around her a great multitude of angels. She commanded one of them, saying, "Go forthwith, and awaken Mercurius [who had been killed by Julian for being a Christian], who sleepeth in the sepulchre, that he may slay Julian the Apostate, that proud blasphemer against me and my son!"

When St. Basil awoke, he went to the tomb of Mercurius and saw that the body was missing. He returned the next day and found the body back in place, dressed in full armor, with the lance stained with blood. One medieval account says: "For on the day of battle, when the wicked emperor was at the head of his army, an unknown warrior, bareheaded, and of a pale and ghastly countenance, was seen mounted on a white charger, which he spurred forward, and, brandishing his lance, he pierced Julian through the body and then vanished suddenly as he had appeared."

Julian was then taken to his tent. Taking a handful of the blood that flowed from his wound, he flung it into the air, saying, "Thou hast conquered, Galilean! Thou has conquered!" The devils then came and took his body to hell.

This fanciful Christian version of history has no basis in fact. Julian was killed by a javelin flung by an unknown hand.

See also: BASIL, ST.; MERCURY

*Mercury (Laurence Housman)*

**Mercury** (merchant)   In Roman mythology, ancient Italian god of merchants and traders; son of Jupiter and Maia; the Romans equated Mercury with the Greek god Hermes. Mercury was protector of the wheat trade, especially in Sicily. He was honored in Rome by a temple near the Circus Maximus. Here, a merchants' guild, known as Mercuriales, established by the state presided over Mercury's worship. At the yearly festival of the temple and guild on 15 May the merchants sacrificed to Mercury and his mother, Maia. At the Porta Capena they sprinkled themselves and their merchandise with holy water. Mercury is cited or appears in Vergil's *Aeneid* (book 4); Ovid's *Fasti* (5); Chaucer's Knight's Tale, part of *The Canterbury Tales*; Shakespeare's *Troilus and Cressida* (2.2.45), *Hamlet* (3.4.58),

*King Henry IV, Part I* (4.1.106), *Anthony and Cleopatra* (4.15.36); and Milton's *Paradise Lost* (4.717–5.285) and *Comus* (637). The element mercury, also called quicksilver, was named after the god known for his swiftness. His attributes are the winged hat, winged shoes, and caduceus.

See also: CADUCEUS; CHAUCER; HERMES; JUPITER; MAIA

*Merlin (A. Beardsley)*

2059

**Merlin** (Merddin, Myrddin) (sparrow hawk) In Arthurian legend, the great enchanter, or magician. Some scholars believe that a person named Merlin lived in the fifth century and served under the British chiefs Aurelius Ambrosius and King Arthur. Legend says he lost his mind after the battle of Solway Firth, broke his sword, and retired into the forest, where he was later found dead beside a riverbank. This thread of Merlin's story was greatly amplified during the Middle Ages.

According to various medieval sources, King Constans, who drove the Jute Hengist from England, was the father of three sons, Constantine, Aurelius Ambrosius, and Uther Pendragon. The dying Constans left the throne to his eldest

son, Constantine, who chose Vortigern as his prime minister. Shortly after Constantine's accession, Hengist again invaded England. Constantine was deserted by Vortigern and was treacherously killed. In reward for his defection Vortigern was offered the crown, which he accepted. But Constans's other two sons (who, according to a variant account, were called Uther and Pendragon) were still alive and sought vengeance.

To defend himself against any army that might attempt to deprive him of his throne, Vortigern built a great fortress on Salisbury Plain. But although the masons worked diligently by day, building high, thick walls, they always found them overturned the next morning. Astrologers were consulted, and they said the walls would not stand until the ground had been watered with the blood of a child who could claim no human father.

Five years prior to this prediction, the demons, seeing that so many souls escaped hell owing to a Divine Child (Jesus Christ), had decided to have the devil father a child by a human virgin. A beautiful girl was chosen for the purpose. As she daily went to confession to a priest named Blaise, he soon discovered the evil plot of the demons and resolved to frustrate it.

On Blaise's advice the girl, instead of being immediately put to death for intercourse with the devil, was locked up in a tower, where she gave birth to a son. As soon as he heard the child's cries, Blaise ran in and baptized him, giving him the name Merlin. The Christian rite annulled the evil purpose of the demons, but nevertheless the child was gifted with strange and marvelous powers. When he was five years old, he defended his mother from charges of witchcraft and proved her innocent.

His fame grew, and he came to the court of Vortigern. When asked why the walls of Salisbury would not stand, Merlin replied that two dragons—one red and one white—fought underground each night. A search was made, the dragons were discovered, and a battle was fought between the two. The white dragon won and then disappeared. Work on the walls then continued. Vortigern, however, was very uneasy because Merlin foresaw the coming conflict with Constans's sons and Vortigern's ultimate defeat. Merlin's prediction was soon fulfilled. Uther and his brother Pendragon landed in Britain with an army, and Vortigern was burned to death in his castle.

Shortly after the victory a war arose between the Britons, under Uther and Pendragon, and the Saxons, under Hengist. Merlin, who aided Uther and Pendragon, said they would be victorious, but only one would survive. Pendragon was killed, and Uther added his brother's name to his own, becoming Uther Pendragon. His first care was to bury his brother, and he asked Merlin to erect a suitable monument to Pendragon's memory. Merlin conveyed great stones from Ireland to England in the course of a single night and then set them up at Stonehenge.

*Merlin and Viviane (Nimuë) (A. Beardsley)*

Merlin then went to Carduel (Carlisle) and through magic constructed a beautiful castle and established a round table for Uther Pendragon. Merlin also aided Uther Pendragon in a deception that enabled him to sleep with Igraine in the guise of her husband. From their union King Arthur was born.

When Arthur was made king, Merlin became his adviser. As Merlin could assume any shape he pleased, Arthur often used him as a messenger. Once he went to Rome in the guise of a stag to bear Arthur's challenge to Julius Caesar (not the conqueror of Gaul but the mythical father of Oberon) to single combat.

Merlin was said to have made many magic objects, among which was a cup that would reveal whether the drinker had led a pure life. It always overflowed when touched by "polluted lips." He was also the artificer of King Arthur's armor and of a magic mirror in which one could see whatever one wished. But Merlin had a fatal weakness: women. Viviane, the Lady of the Lake, sometimes called Nimuë, beguiled him and learned all of his magic secrets. Then she went with him to the magic forest of Broceliande in Brittany. Wishing to rid herself of her aged lover, she cast a magic spell over him, enclosing him in a hawthorn tree, where he would dwell forever. There are, however, other legends accounting for Merlin's end. According to one, Merlin, having grown old, once sat down at the Siege Perilous (the seat at the Round Table commemorating Judas's betrayal), forgetting that only a sinless man could sit upon it. He was immediately swallowed up by the earth. Another version says Viviane imprisoned Merlin in an underground palace, where she alone could visit him. There he dwells, unchanged by time, and daily increases his store of knowledge.

He appears in all retellings of the Arthurian legends. Tennyson's "Merlin and Vivien," part of *Idylls of the King*, and E. A. Robinson's *Merlin* include him. Ernest Chausson's symphonic poem *Viviane* deals with Merlin's seduction and end as does Burne-Jones's painting *The Beguiling* of Merlin, in which Viviane is casting her magic spell over the old magician.

See also: ARTHUR; BARBAROSSA; HENGIST; IGRAINE; LADY OF THE LAKE; OBERON; ROUND TABLE; SHAPESHIFTER; STONEHENGE; UTHER PENDRAGON; VIVIANE; VORTIGERN

*Mermaid and merman*

**2060**
**Mermaid**    In European folklore, fantastic beings, half fish, half woman, with gold or green hair. Mermaids can be spotted on moonlit evenings, looking in a mirror as they comb their hair. Often they lure sailors to their death and are credited with knowing the future. In 16th-century English the word *mermaid* was often used for a courtesan, as in Shakespeare's *Comedy of Errors* (3.2, etc.). Hollywood's *Mr. Peabody and the Mermaid* tells of a very respectable businessman who falls in love with one of the beautiful creatures. In the 1984 movie *Splash*, Daryl Hannah plays the role of a modern-day mermaid.

See also: DUGONG; SIRENS

**2061**
**Mermerus and Pheres** (care-laden and bearer) In Greek mythology, children of Medea and Jason. When Jason betrayed Medea, she killed the children to punish him.

See also: JASON; MEDEA

**2062**
**Merseburg Charms**    In German literary folklore, two charms in alliterative verse recorded from oral sources around 800 C.E. The first is to be used for freeing prisoners from their bonds, while the second is for curing an injury. Several Germanic gods are named in the second charm.

Phol and Wodan went to the forest.
Where Balder's horse sprained its foot.
Then Sinthgunt charmed it, and Sunna her sister;
Then Friia sang charms, and Volla her sister;
Then Wodan sang charms, as he well could:
be it bone-sprain, be it blood-sprain, be it limb-sprain
bone to bone, blood to blood,
limb to limb, be they thus glued together.

See also: CHARM; HILDEBRANDSLIED

**2063**
**Meru**    In Hindu mythology, a fantastic golden mountain, the *axis mundi*, situated in the navel of the earth; on it is Swarga, Indra's heaven. It contains the cities of the gods and the homes of celestial spirits.

See also: INDRA

**2064**
**Mesede**    In Melanesian mythology, the great marksman, whose bow ignites when it is drawn. Once Mesede rescued Abere's son from a crocodile, but he took Abere's daughters as a prize. Mesede's wife was angry at this and had the girls killed. The head of the youngest was cast into the sea, where it turned into a log. When it was washed ashore, flies hollowed it out. Morave, another hero, covered one end with skin, creating the Dibiri drum that is symbolic of a human body and is used in various rituals.

See also: ABERE

2065

**Metatron** (Metratton, Mittron, Metaraon, Merraton) (one who occupies the throne next to the divine throne?)   In Jewish folklore, angel who led the children of Israel through the wilderness after the Exodus from Egypt. In the biblical account (Exod. 12:5), however, the Israelites are guided by Yahweh, the Hebrew god himself. In some Jewish legends Metatron is said to have been the patriarch Enoch, transformed into an angel after his death. Genesis (5:24) records that Enoch did not die but was taken bodily to heaven by God. Metatron is sometimes called Lad (tender age).

　　See also: ENOCH; YAHWEH

2066

**Methuselah** (man of the dart)   In the Bible, O.T., son of Enoch and grandfather of Noah; he lived 969 years (Gen. 5:27). In Gershwin's opera *Porgy and Bess* he is cited for his old age in one of the songs. Methuselah is a common epithet for a very old man.

　　See also: ENOCH; NOAH

2067

**Metis** (counsel)   In Greek mythology, a Titaness, daughter of Oceanus and Tethys; first wife of Zeus, according to Hesiod's *Theogony* (886 ff). When Zeus was told by Heaven and Earth that his wife was to bear a child who would overthrow him, he swallowed Metis through trickery. Athena was born fully armed from Zeus's head, which was split open by Hephaestus's ax, or by Prometheus. In Greek religion Metis was a personification of counsel, prudence, and insight.

　　See also: ATHENA; HEPHAESTUS; HESIOD; PROMETHEUS; ZEUS

2068

**Metsanneitsyt** (forest virgin)   In Finnish mythology, a spirit who lures men to make love to her. She is beautiful in front, but her back is hollow, like a tree stump or trough.

2069

**Metztli** (Metzli)   In Aztec mythology, moon goddess. In order to make a light for the daytime Metztli sacrificed herself and Nanahuatl the Leper in a fire. When she disappeared into the flames, the sun was created. The male form of the moon was called Tecciztecatl. He was portrayed as an old man with a large seashell on his back.

2070

**Mezuzah** (doorpost)   In Judaism, small parchment talisman that contains the Jewish *Shema* or creed (Deut. 6:4): "Hear, O Israel: The Lord our God is one Lord." The command to the Jewish people to attach mezuzahs to their doorposts is found in Deuteronomy (6:8–9). It was commanded: "And thou shalt bind them for a sign upon thine hand, and they shall be as frontlets between thine eyes. And thou shalt write them upon the posts of thy house, and on thy gates." The parchment is placed so that the word *Shaddai* (Almighty) is visible through an opening. It is placed at head height beside the door because it is a Jewish custom to kiss the mezuzah on entering or leaving a house.

2071

**Mice in Council, or Belling the Cat, The** Aesopic fable, probably originally from India, found in numerous European collections.

For many years the mice had been living in constant dread of their enemy, the cat. It was decided to call a meeting to determine the best means of handling the situation. Many plans were discussed and rejected.

At last a young mouse got up. "I propose," said he, looking very important, "that a bell be hung around the cat's neck. Then whenever the cat approaches, we always shall have notice of her presence and so be able to escape."

The young mouse sat down to tremendous applause. The suggestion was put to a motion and passed almost unanimously. But just then an old mouse, who had sat silent all the while, rose to his feet and said: "My friends, it takes a young mouse to think of a plan so ingenious and yet so simple. With a bell about the cat's neck to warn us we shall all be safe. I have but one brief question to put to the supporters of the plan—which of you is going to bell the cat?"

Moral: *It is one thing to propose, another to execute.*

The fable is told in the Prologue to *Piers Plowman* by Langland, where the cat is the symbol of John of Gaunt. Archibald Douglas, fifth earl of Angus (d. 1514), was called Archibald Bell-the-Cat because he killed some of the minions of James III who had been created earls. When the Scottish nobles held a council in the church of Lauder for the purpose of putting down the favorites of the king, Lord Gray asked, "Who will bell the cat?" "That will I," said Douglas, who then, in the king's presence, proceeded to kill the young men.

See also: AESOPIC FABLES

2072

**Michael** (who is like unto God)    In Jewish, Christian, and Islamic mythology, archangel leader of the Jews and prince of the Church Militant, guardian of redeemed souls against the devil. Feast: 29 September in the Western church, called Michaelmas Day.

In the Old Testament Book of Daniel (12:1) the archangel Michael is "the Great Prince which standeth for the children of thy people." Thus, Michael is considered the guardian of the Hebrew people. In the New Testament (Rev. 12:7–9) Michael fights the devil. "And there was war in heaven: Michael and his angels fought against the dragon; and the dragon fought his angels, and prevailed not; neither was their place any more in heaven. And the great dragon was cast out, that old serpent, called the Devil, and Satan, which deceiveth the whole world: he was cast out into the earth, and his angels were cast out with him."

In the Epistle of Jude (chap. 9) the myth that Michael fought the devil for the body of Moses is

*Michael*

alluded to: "Yet Michael the archangel, when contending with the devil he disputed about the body of Moses, durst not bring against him a railing accusation, but said, the Lord rebuke thee." The myth is found in later Jewish and Christian writings. The Koran (sura 2) says that "who so is an enemy to God or his angels . . . or to Mikail (Michael) shall have God as his enemy: for verily God is an enemy of Infidels."

Michael owes his popularity in Western Christianity to three legendary apparitions. In the first, which occurred during the fifth century C.E., Michael descended to Mount Galgano in Italy and ordered a church to be erected and sanctified there in his honor. When the people entered the cavern at the foot of the mountain, they found three altars already erected, one of them covered with a rich altar cloth of crimson and gold. A stream of limpid water springing from the rock healed all diseases. The church was built, and it attracted many pilgrims. Michael is commemorated there on 8 May.

The second apparition of Michael was in the sixth century, when he healed a pestilence at Rome. St. Gregory the Great dedicated the tomb of Hadrian to the saint and called it Castel Sant' Angelo. The third apparition was to Aubert, bishop of Avranches (706) in the Gulf of Avranches in Normandy. St. Michael appeared to the bishop and ordered that a church be erected in his honor. The legend is in many ways similar to that of Mount Galgano.

Both Dante and Milton mention Michael in their works, as does Longfellow in his poetic drama *The Golden Legend* (not to be confused with the medieval book of saints' lives) and Yeats in his poem "The Rose of Peace," in which Michael is called "leader of God's host." John Travolta plays Michael in a 1996 film comedy. He is a grubby angel who has one more good deed to perform before he returns to heaven. Michael is often portrayed in medieval armor, standing over the devil, whom he has defeated. In the final judgment he holds a pair of scales with which he weighs the souls of the risen dead.

See also: KORAN, THE; MOSES; SATAN

2073
**Mictlantecuhtli** (Mictlanteculi) (lord of death) In Aztec mythology, death god, lord of the land of the dead, who with his wife, Mictlantecihuatl,

*Mictlantecuhtli*

cared for the dead who came to their kingdom, Mictlan (Mictlancalco), the place of the dead. Mictlantecuhtli was portrayed as an open-mouthed monster ready to devour the souls of the dead. Sometimes he was portrayed as an owl, with skull and bones. He was associated with the north, and his color was red. Mictlantecuhtli is regarded in some texts as an aspect of the god Tezcatlipoca (mirror that smokes), the Aztec creator-trickster god. Mictlantecuhtli was also known as Tzontemoc (he of the falling hair), perhaps indicative of his role as death god.

See also: TRICKSTER

2074
**Midas** (seed?) In Greek mythology, king of Phrygia; son of the goddess Cybele and a satyr. Midas helped Silenus, a follower of Dionysus (Bacchus), to find his way back to his god, and Dionysus rewarded Midas by granting him any wish. He wished that whatever he touched would turn to gold. Eventually he had to ask that the gift be revoked, because even his food turned to gold and he was unable to eat. To rid himself of his gift Midas had to wash in the Pactolus River, whose sands then became gold. Because he favored Marsyas in his contest with Apollo, Midas was punished by having his ears turned into those of an ass. Ovid's *Metamorphoses* (book 11), John Lyly's *Midas*, Shakespeare's *Merchant of Venice* (3.2.101), Pope's *Dunciad* (3.324), Swift's *Fable of Midas*, Shelley's "Hymn of Pan," and W. S. Landor's *Silenus* all deal with Midas or cite him. Poussin's *Midas and Bacchus* portrays Midas with Silenus.

See also: APOLLO; DIONYSUS; OVID; SATYRS

2075
**Midgard** (middle world [yard]) In Norse mythology, the world of people, midway between the home of the gods, Asgard, and the home of the frost giants, Jotunheim. Midgard was formed from the giant Ymir's body. His blood or sweat became the oceans; his bones, the

mountains; his teeth, the cliffs; and his hair, the trees and other plant life. Ymir's skull formed the vaulted heavens, held up by four dwarfs—Nordi, Sudi, Austri, and Westri. Midgard appears in the *Poetic Edda*, the *Prose Edda*, and Matthew Arnold's narrative poem *Balder Dead*. Midgard is also called Mana-heim.

See also: ASGARD; JOTUNHEIM; *POETIC EDDA*; *PROSE EDDA*; YMIR

2076

**Midgard Serpent** (middle world serpent)   In Norse mythology, a venomous monster, fathered by the fire-trickster god, Loki. Odin cast the Midgard Serpent into the sea, where its movements caused storms. The serpent's body encircled the whole earth, and it bit its own tail. The god Thor took on the monster in battle. The *Prose Edda* tells how Thor "launched his mallet at him, and there are some who say that it struck off the monster's head at the bottom of the sea, but one may assert with more certainty that he still lives and lies in the ocean." Another name for the Midgard Serpent is Jormungand (wolf-serpent).

See also: ANGURBODA; HYMIR; LOKI; MIDGARD; ODIN; THOR

2077

**Midrash** (to examine)   In Judaism, genre of rabbinic literature, consisting of verse by verse interpretation of the Hebrew Scriptures, using homily (sometimes parables and folktales) and exegesis. The tradition began when the Temple at Jerusalem was destroyed.

2078

**Mihr**   In Armenian mythology, the fire god, derived in part from the Persian god Mithras. His worship was added to that of Vahagn, who was a sun, lightning, and fire god native to Armenia.

See also: MITHRAS; VAHAGN

2079

**Mike Fink**   (1770–1823). In American folklore, a legendary keelboat man, the strongest ever. Mike Fink spent most of his time on the Ohio and Mississippi Rivers, but he was actually born near Fort Pitt (Pittsburgh). His nicknames were "Snag" on the Mississippi and "Snapping Turtle" on the Ohio. The stories that sprang up around him were a rich part of a growing form of humorous American folklore. Fink was called the king of the keelboaters, one of those men who guided rafts, flatboats, and keelboats down the rivers. He was particularly famous for his brawls, boasts, jokes, and deadly marksmanship. Even his gun had a nickname, "Bang-All," and he was well known for shooting, winning many local competitions. As entertainment, he and his friends often shot cups of whiskey from the tops of each other's heads. Once he shot the tails from eight baby pigs on shore, some 40 or 50 yards away. Davy Crockett described the river man as "half horse and half alligator," a tribute to his hardiness and strength. Fink introduced himself in taverns by saying, "Whoo-oop! I'm the original iron-jawed, brass-mounted, copper-bellied corpse-maker from the wilds of Arkansas! Look at me! I'm the man they call Sudden Death and General Desolation! Sired by a hurricane, dam'd by an earthquake, half-brother to the cholera, nearly related to the smallpox on the mother's side! Cast your eye on me, gentlemen! And lay low and hold your breath, for I'm 'bout to turn myself loose!" He was proud of the red feather he wore in his cap, signifying his victory over every strong man up and down the river. Fink died at the hands of one of his companions in 1822 while scouting, trapping, and rafting in the Rocky Mountains as a result of an argument over a *chère amie*, as Mike called his many romantic interests.

The story of Mike Fink first appeared in print in 1821 and was soon spread orally. Fink is often linked with Davy Crockett in printed almanacs. He has become a representative of the 19th-century folk hero described by Richard Dorson as "Ring-tailed Roarers, bullies, brawlers, and daredevils."

See also: CROCKETT, DAVY; JOE MAGARAC; PAUL BUNYAN; PECOS BILL

2080

**Mikula Selyaninovich**   In Russian folklore, hero, with superhuman strength, who possibly owes his origin to Volos. He appears in the *bylini*, the epic songs, as well as in folktales, and is depicted as representative of tremendous masculine beauty. His eyes are like falcons' his hair is in tight ringlets, and his brows are as black as sable. Mikula is a *bogatyr*, an epic hero, whose little wooden plow was so heavy that a whole troop of men could not lift it, though Mikula could with one hand. Part of Mikula's power came from Mati-Syra-Zemlya (moist Mother Earth), since he was her lover.

See also: *BYLINA*; MATI-SYRA-ZEMLYA; VOLOS

2081

**Milarepa** (Mila the cotton clad)   1038–1122. Tibetan Buddhist poet and saint, author of numerous songs. In his early life he was a black magician but later converted. He is portrayed with his right hand to his ear, listening to the many hymns he composed, or listening to the "sound" of emptiness, which his songs embody.

2082

**Milkmaid and Her Pail, The**   Aesopic fable, probably derived from the Indian collection *The Panchatantra*.

A milkmaid was on her way to market, carrying a pail of milk on the top of her head. As she walked along the road in the early morning she began to turn over in her mind what she would do with the money she would receive for the milk. "I shall buy some hens from a neighbor," said she to herself, "and they will lay eggs every day which I shall sell to the pastor's wife. And with the egg money I'll buy myself a new frock and ribbon. Green they shall be, for green

becomes my complexion best. And in this lovely green gown I will go to the fair. All the young men will strive to have me for a partner. I shall pretend that I do not see them. When they become too insistent I shall disdainfully toss my head—like this."

As the milkmaid spoke she tossed her head back, and down came the pail of milk, spilling all over the ground. And so all of her imaginary happiness vanished, and nothing was left but an empty pail and the promise of a scolding when she returned home.

Moral: *Do not count your chickens before they are hatched.*

La Fontaine's version of the fable is perhaps the best known. The Frenchman derived the work from Bonaventure des Periers's *Contes et Nouvelles*, which in turn derived it from other sources.

See also: AESOPIC FABLES; LA FONTAINE, JEAN DE; *PANCHATANTRA*

2083

**Milomaki**   In Brazilian Indian folklore, culture hero, from whose ashes grew the paxiuba palm. Long ago a little boy was sent from the great waterhouse, the home of the sun, to earth. He sang so beautifully that the people came to hear him. When he was finished, they returned home and ate their fish, after which they fell down dead. Their relatives then seized Milomaki, blaming him for the deaths, and burned him. As he went to his death, Milomaki sang even as the flames flickered around his body. When his body was ready to burst from the heat, he sang: "Now bursts my body! Now I am dead!" Though his body was destroyed, his soul went to heaven. The same day a long green blade sprang from his ashes. It grew into the first paxiuba palm.

2084

**Mimir** (memory)   In Norse mythology, a giant noted for his wisdom; uncle of Odin. Mimir was at one time the keeper of a magic caldron, Odhrerir, or a magic well at the roots of the world tree, Yggdrasill. Mimir drank from the caldron or well and knew all things—past, present, and future. He once allowed Odin to drink, but the god had to give one of his eyes as the price. Thus, Odin is often portrayed as one-eyed, the socket being covered by his broad-brimmed hat or a lock of hair. In other accounts Odin, after having tasted the well, never smiled again. Mimir lived among the gods even though he was of the giants' race. He was sent as a hostage to the Vanir, another group of gods, who beheaded him. Odin got back Mimir's head, breathed life into it, and consulted it on very important matters. The myth is told in the *Prose Edda*.

See also: ODHRERIR; ODIN; *PROSE EDDA*

**2086**

**Minawara and Multultu**    In Australian mythology, kangaroo men of the Nambutji tribe in central Australia. Created after a great flood, they instituted sacred rites for the men of the tribe.

**2087**

**Mindi**    In Australian mythology, the great evil snake who sends diseases such as smallpox, which is called Mindi's dust.

**2085**

**Min**    In Egyptian mythology, god of fertility, rain, and crops. Min was honored in harvest festivals, during which the first-cut sheaf of the harvest was offered to him by the king. According to some texts, he was also worshiped as a god of roads and travelers and was evoked by caravan leaders before setting out through the desert.

Min is portrayed as a man with an erect phallus holding a whip in his right hand. On his head he wears a crown surmounted by two tall plumes, with a streamer descending from its back. During the festival of Min, the queen of Egypt assumed the role of the "mother of Min" so that the royal *ka* (vital force) could be passed on to the next king. In narratives, this ritual becomes the rape of Isis by her son Min-Horus. In later times the Egyptians identified Min with Amun-Ra, and the Greeks with Pan. He was also closely associated with Horus, who was in some texts addressed as Min-Horus. A classical writer suggested that Min was promoted to the role of a fertility god after he made love to all of the women in Egypt while the men were away fighting wars.

See also: AMUN; HORUS; PAN

*Minerva*

2088

**Minerva**   In Roman mythology, ancient Italian goddess of wisdom and the arts and sciences; the Romans equated Minerva with the Greek goddess Athena. Minerva had a temple on the Capitoline Hill, her chief seat of worship, along with Jupiter and Juno. Her main festival in Rome, the Quinquatria or Quinquatrus (fifth day), began on 18 or 19 March and lasted five days. Sacrifices and oblations were made on the first day, but no blood was shed. On the second, third, and fourth days, gladiators performed, and on the fifth day there was a solemn procession through the streets of the city. During the festival scholars were on holiday and prayed to the goddess for wisdom. Most of the Greek myths attached to Athena were adopted by the Romans for Minerva. Minerva appears in Mantegna's painting *Triumph of Wisdom over Vice*, where she is seen routing the sex goddess Venus. Minerva also appears in Perugino's painting *Combat of Love and Chastity*, in which she aids Diana, goddess of virgins. In English poetry she appears in Lord Byron's "The Curse of Minerva," in which he attacks Lord Elgin for removing the famous marbles from the Parthenon to the British Museum. The goddess also appears in Poe's poem "The Raven," in which a bird of ill omen perches on a bust of Pallas, another name for Minerva.

See also: ATHENA; JUNO; JUPITER; VENUS

2089

**Minos**   In Greek mythology, one of the judges of the dead, once a king of Crete, son of Zeus and Europa; brother of Rhadamanthys and Sarpedon; married to Pasiphae; father of Acacallis, Androgeus, Ariadne, Catreus, Deucalion, Euryale, Giaucus, Lycastus, Phaedra, and Xenodice. In some accounts Minos is a wise king, in others a tyrant who was killed by Daedalaus, whom Minos had imprisoned. He was made a judge of the dead along with Rhadamanthys and Aeacus or Sarpedon. Dante's *Divine Comedy* (Inferno) makes Minos the king of hell. Rodin's statue of *The Thinker*, part of his *Gates of Hell*, has been identified by some art scholars as Minos. Sir Arthur Evans, a British archaeologist, in about 1900 gave the name "Minoan" to prehistoric Cretan civilization. The name Minos may have been a hereditary title rather than an actual name, and is likely not Greek in origin.

See also: AEACUS; ANDROGEUS; ARIADNE; DAEDALAUS; DEUCALION; PASIPHAE; PHAEDRA; RHADAMANTHYS; SARPEDON

2090

**Minotaur** (Minos bull)   In Greek mythology, a monster, half man and half bull, born of Pasiphaë, a wife of King Minos II, and the Cretan (or Marathonian) bull. The Minotaur, also called Asterius, was kept in the labyrinth built by Daedalus and was fed young boys and girls, one of each once a year. The monster was killed by the hero Theseus. In Dante's *Divine Comedy*, the Minotaur, called *l'infamia di Creti* (the infamy of Crete), guards the Seventh Circle of Hell. The Minotaur appears in L. Cottrell's *The Bull of Minos*, Mary Renault's novel *The King Must Die* (1958), and André Gide's *Thésée* and is pictured in Picasso's 15 plates in his Vollard Suite (1930–1937).

See also: DAEDALUS; PASIPHAË; THESEUS

2091

**Minuchihr**   A hero king appearing in the Persian epic poem *Shah Namah* by Firdusi. Minuchihr killed his two evil uncles, Silim and Tur, who were responsible for the death of his father, Irij. When the great hero Faridun, his grandfather, died, Minuchihr came to the throne and was deeply loved by the people. He reigned for 120 years. One day his astrologers told him that his death was close at hand. "The time approaches when thou must die," they told the beloved king. "Before you are placed in the damp earth, prepare for a successor." Minuchihr called his son Nauder to his side and instructed him. He then closed his eyes and died.

See also: *SHAH NAMAH*

*Miriam*

**Miriam** (rebellion)   In the Bible, O.T., sister of Moses and Aaron, who watched over the infant Moses when he was in the ark of bulrushes in the river Nile (Exod. 2:1–10). After the Exodus from Egypt she was known as a prophetess and assisted Moses and Aaron, but she complained, as did Aaron, when Moses married a Cushite (Ethiopian) woman (Num. 12:1–16). For this rebellion she was stricken with leprosy. She died and was buried in the Wilderness of Wandering.

See also: AARON; MOSES

**Miroku Bosatsu**   In Japanese Buddhist mythology, the name given to Maitreya (friendly; benevolent). According to Buddhist legend, before the Buddha was born as a human he lived in the Tushita heaven. Before leaving, he commissioned Maitreya as his successor. Some Buddhist traditions say Maitreya has already appeared in the form of a fat, jolly, eccentric monk, Hotei (Pu-tai), the so-called Laughing Buddha.

See also: MAITREYA

**Mister Dooley**   In American literary folklore, Irish American who runs a small saloon on Archey Road in Chicago, created by Peter Finley Dunne (1867–1936) in newspapers and later col-
lected into books. Martin Dooley usually comments on political situations. One of his most famous remarks was "Whether th' Constitution follows th' flag or not, th' Supreme Court follows th' illiction return." A collection, *Mr. Dooley at His Best*, edited by Elmer Ellis, has an introduction by Dunne. Mr. Dooley's remarks were read by Henry Adams and Henry James, who took delight in them.

**Mistletoe**   A parasitic plant found growing in various deciduous trees; in European mythologies, a sacred plant and symbol of fertility and immortality. The Druids called mistletoe "all healer" when found on an oak. In Norse mythology the mistletoe was sacred to Baldur, and in Roman mythology, the magical Golden Bough plucked by the hero Aeneas has been identified as the mistletoe. The early Italians collected mistletoe on the first day after the full moon; a common European practice until recently was to gather mistletoe on Midsummer's Eve or Day. They were also said to use it as part of a human sacrifice. Probably for this reason mistletoe is excluded from Christian church decorations.

See also: AENEAS; BALDUR; DRUIDS; OAK

**Mithras** (Mithra)   In Persian mythology, god of life, heat, fertility, a mediator between the gods and men, and chief aide to the good god, Ahura Mazda, in his war against the evil spirit, Ahriman.

In pre-Zoroastrian times Mithras and Ahura were probably twin sky gods, called *payu-thworeshtara*, the "two creator-preservers" of the cosmos. Between 1400 B.C.E. and 400 C.E. Persians, Indians, Romans, and Greeks all worshiped the god Mithras, who originally may have been the sun god, Mitra, mentioned in the Indian Rig-Veda. During Roman times the worship of Mithras was converted into a mystery religion. The god was worshiped by the soldiers and imperial officials of Rome.

Rudyard Kipling's poem "A Song to Mithras" captures the mood of the Roman belief in the god's powers:

> Mithras, God of the Morning, our trumpets waken the Wall!
> Now as the names are answered, and the guards are marched away,
> Mithras, also a soldier, give us strength for the day!
> Mithras, God of the Midnight, here where the great Bull dies,
> Look on Thy Children in darkness. Oh, take our sacrifice!
> Many roads Thou hast fashioned—all of them lead to Light!
> Mithras, also a soldier, teach us to die aright!

Part of Kipling's poem refers to the repeated reliefs or statues that portray Mithras slaying a bull. The scene portrays a young man wearing a Phrygian cap slaying a massive bull while a dog licks the blood, a serpent crawls nearby, and a scorpion seems to be removing the bull's testicles. On either side of the scene is a young man, one with a torch uplifted, the other with the torch facing downward.

What exactly this scene symbolizes has puzzled scholars and thinkers. Carl Jung, picking up the similarity between the mysteries of Mithras and of Christianity, sees the slaying of the bull as "essentially a self-sacrifice, since the bull is a world bull which was originally identical with Mithras himself. . . . The representations of the sacrificial act, the tauroctony [bull slaying], recall the crucifixion between two thieves, one of whom is raised up to paradise while the other goes down to hell."

Jung, however, was not the first to recognize the similarities. Tertullian, the early Church writer, seeing that the pagan cult contained baptism and the use of bread, water, and wine consecrated by priests, called fathers, wrote that the similarities of the Mithraic cult to Christianity were inspired by the devil, who wished to mock the Christian sacraments in order to lead the faithful to hell. The French author Ernest Renan, in the skeptical 19th-century tradition, wrote: "If Christianity had been arrested in its growth . . . the world would have been Mithraist."

The religion of Mithras was suppressed by Emperor Constantine when he established Christianity as the state religion in the Roman Empire. Present-day Zoroastrians, however, still worship Mithras as a god.

See also: AHRIMAN; AHURA MAZDA; RIG-VEDA; ZARATHUSTRA

---

2097

**Mitokht**   In Persian mythology, demon of falsehood; son of the evil spirit, Ahriman.

See also: AHRIMAN

---

2098

**Mixcoatl** (Yemaxtli, Yoamaxtli) (cloud serpent) In Aztec mythology, god of hunting, lord of the chase, often identified with the god Tezcatlipoca, the Aztec creator-trickster god worshiped by warriors and magicians. He was also said to be the father of Quetzalcoatl. The Spanish cleric Fray Diego Durán, in his *Book of the Gods and Rites* (c. 1576), says that Mixcoatl was the "inventor of the ways and manners of hunting." The god was portrayed as a man with long hair and black eyes. He wore a crown of plumes on his head, and his nose was pierced with a berry pit. In one hand he held a basket containing food, in the other a bow and arrow. His body was covered with white stripes from the top to the bottom. Human sacrifices were made to him. Mixcoatl was also known as Iztac Mixcoatl (the white cloud serpent). He was a progenitor, father of seven sons who were the founders of the seven cities speaking the Nahuatl language. His first wife was Ilamatechtli, a form of Coatlicue, and his second wife was Chimalmatl (green shield).

See also: COATLICUE; QUETZALCOATL; TRICKSTER

**Mnevis bull**    In Egyptian mythology, Greek name for the Egyptian sacred bull Wer-mer, who was worshiped at Heliopolis. Mnevis was said to be an incarnation of the sun. He was portrayed as a bull with a disk and the uraeus between his horns. Some artworks portray him as a bull-headed man.

See also: APIS; BUCHIS; URAEUS

**Moccus** (Mocco)    In Celtic mythology, a swine god worshiped in Britain and on the Continent. He may have been the guardian of boar hunters. Ancient Roman writers equated Moccus with their god Mercury.

See also: MERCURY

**Mokoi** (evil spirit)    In Australian mythology, a mischievous trickster that wanders about, playing tricks and bringing harm to the living. His evil spirit is invoked by sorcerers among the Murngin of northern Australia.

**Mokos** (Mokosh) (moist)    In Slavic mythology, a goddess who appears in many folktales as Mokusa. She ensured that men's semen was rich in sperm and protected women and sheep during labor and birth. During Lent in Novgorod she wanders about at night disguised as a woman, visiting houses, worrying wool spinners, and guarding and fleecing sheep herself. At night strands of fleece are laid beside stoves to appease her anger.

**Mole**    Burrowing mammal with a pointed nose, small eyes, and tiny teeth. In Egyptian mythology the mole was a symbol of blindness because it was believed the animal neither heard nor saw. In medieval Christianity the mole was seen as symbolic of the earth and avariciousness.

In medieval folk belief, if a man ate the heart of a mole when it had just been removed from the dead animal, he could foretell the future.

**Molimons**    In African mythology (Upotos of the Congo), the souls of the dead, who begged the sky god Libanza not to let the sky fall.

See also: LIBANZA

**Molly Pitcher**    1754–1832. In American history and folklore of the Revolution, the popular name of Mary L. Hays McCauley, who earned her nickname "Molly Pitcher" by bringing pitcher after pitcher of cool spring water to exhausted and thirsty soldiers. She took her husband's place at a cannon after he was killed in battle. Legend says a cannon ball shot through her legs, taking off her petticoat. Whittier's poem "Molly Pitcher" deals with the legend. It is believed, however, that a Margaret Corbin (1751–1800) was the woman who performed the heroic act. For her heroic role, it is said that General Washington himself issued her a warrant as a noncommissioned officer. Thereafter, she was widely hailed as "Sergeant Molly." A flagstaff and cannon stand at her gravesite at Carlisle, Pennsylvania. A sculpture on the battle monument commemorates her deed.

See also: GEORGE WASHINGTON

**Moly**    In Greek mythology, plant with a black root and white flower that saved Odysseus from Circe's enchantments on her island, Aeaea, where he was detained for a year. The plant was given to Odysseus by Hermes. Moly is cited in Homer's *Odyssey* (book 10), Spenser's *Faerie Queene*, Milton's *Comus*, Arnold's *The Strayed Reveller*, and D. G. Rosetti's *The Wine of Circe*.

See also: HERMES; ODYSSEUS; ODYSSEY, THE;

2107

**Momotaro** (peach boy)   In Japanese folktales, a hero who emerged from a peach and defeated the demon Akandoji.

One day the wife of a poor woodcutter went to the river to wash some clothes. As she was about to return she saw a large object floating in the water. She pulled it close to land and saw that it was a large peach, larger than any she had ever seen. She took it home, washed it, and handed it to her husband to open. As the man cut it, a boy emerged from the kernel; they adopted him as a present from the gods to comfort them in their old age. They called the boy Momotaro (the elder son of the peach). He grew up big and strong, surpassing other boys his age. One day Momotaro decided to leave his foster parents and go to Onigashima (Okinawa), the Island of Devils, to seek his fortune. The foster parents gave him some dumplings to take with him. He soon met a dog that asked him for a dumpling and promised to accompany him. Then a monkey and a pheasant came with similar requests. With the three companions he reached the Devil's Fortress. They made their way in and had a terrible battle with the demons, but the animals helped Momotaro. Finally, they reached the inner part of the fortress, where the chief devil, Akandoji, was waiting for them with an iron war club. He was thrown down by Momotaro, who bound him with ropes and made him disclose the secret of his treasures. Then Momotaro helped himself to Akandoji's treasures and left with his three companions for home, where he became a rich and honored member of the community.

The story is Tale Type 130, "The Animals in Night Quarters," best known in the Western world as the "Bremen Town Musicians."

See also: TALE TYPE

2108

**Momus** (reproach, disgrace)   In Greek mythology, a son of Nox (or Nyx, night). Momus was god of criticism, ridicule, or fault-finding, according to Hesiod's *Theogony* (214). He was thrown out of heaven by the gods when he criticized Zeus for placing a bull's horns on its head rather than on its shoulders, which were stronger, and for ridiculing the feet or shoes of Aphrodite, though he did not complain about her naked body. Momus is now used as a term for someone who makes fun or carps at things, though George Meredith's poem "Ode to the Comic Spirit" uses the god as a symbol of healthy criticism. In Greek art Momus is often portrayed raising a mask from his face and holding a small figure in his hand.

See also: APHRODITE; HESIOD; NOX; ZEUS

2109

**Monan** (ancient one)   In the mythology of the Tupi Indians of Brazil, creator god. Though creator, Monan also twice destroyed the earth, once with fire and once by flood. He was followed by Maire-Monan, the transformer, who changed people and animals into other forms and punished them for their sins.

2110

**Monica, St.** (alone?, to advise?)   332–387. In Christian legend, patron of married women and mother of St. Augustine. Feast, 4 May.

Her story is found in her son's autobiography, *The Confessions*. Although she was a Christian, her son Augustine was not brought up in the faith. She prayed continually for his conversion. One day she had a dream. Augustine writes, "She saw herself standing on a certain wooden rule, and a bright youth advancing towards her, joyous and smiling on her, whilst she was grieving and bowed down with sorrow. But he having inquired of her the cause of her sorrow and daily weeping . . . and she answering that it was my perdition she was lamenting, he bade her rest contented, and told her to behold and see where she was, there was I also." Eventually the prayers of Monica were answered, and her son was converted. She died at Ostia on the way back to Africa with Augustine after they had been to Italy. In Christian art she is often portrayed with her son, wearing either a black or a gray habit of a nun.

See also: AUGUSTINE, ST.

**2111**

**Montezuma II** (Monteczoma, Motechuzoma, Moctezuma, Montecuzomatzin) (sad or angry lord)   1466–1520. In Aztec history and legend, last ruler, who ascended the throne when he was 23 and engaged in a campaign to extend his empire. He was noted for his martial prowess, having taken part in nine battles and being a member of the Quachichin, the highest military order of his nation. According to W. H. Prescott in *The History of the Conquest of Mexico* (1843), Montezuma II's court was lavish with pomp and "forms of courtly etiquette unknown to his ruder predecessors. He was, in short, most attentive to all that concerned the exterior and pomp of royalty." He "received the Spaniards as being predicted by his oracles. The anxious dread, with which he had evaded their proffered visit, was founded on the same feeling which led him blindly to resign himself to them on their approach." Roger Sessions composed the opera *Montezuma*, with a libretto by Giuseppe Borgese.

**2112**

**Moo-roo-bul**   In Australian mythology, an evil water spirit who drags his victims to the bottom of a river.

**2113**

**Mora** (tormenting spirit)   In Slavic folkore, a person possessing two souls. A *mora* could assume any shape, animal or vegetable, though frequently it could be identified by its bushy black eyebrows growing together above the nose. Kikimora of Russian folktales is sometimes said to be a *mora*.

See also: KIKIMORA

*Morgan le Fay (Howard Pyle)*

**2114**

**Morgan le Fay** (bright, great fairy)   In Arthurian legend, a witch, the sister or half sister of King Arthur, who continually plots his downfall. In Malory's *Morte d'Arthur* she steals the sword Excalibur and gives it to her lover so that he can kill Arthur. Though the rest of Arthur's enemies are defeated at the end of the work, Morgan le Fay is not. She appears in Ariosto's *Orlando Furioso* and Boiardo's *Orlando Innamorato*. She is also called Fata Morgana, which is the name Longfellow uses in his poem about her.

See also: ARTHUR; EXCALIBUR

**2115**

**Morgante** (sea dweller?)   In the Charlemagne cycle of legends, a ferocious giant converted by Orlando to Christianity. He appears in *Il Morgante Maggiore*, a comic epic poem by Luigi Pulci published in 1483. Morgante aids Orlando (Roland) and other paladins of Charlemagne in their various adventures but then dies from the bite of a crab. Byron translated the first canto of the poem into English in 1822.

See also: CHARLEMAGNE; PALADINS, THE TWELVE

**2116**

**Morkul-kua-luan** In Australian mythology, the spirit of the long grass, portrayed with a beaklike nose and half-closed eyelids that protect him as he glides through the fields of wild grain containing prickling grass seeds.

**2117**

**Morpheus** (fashioner) In Greek mythology, god of dreams; one of the sons of Hypnos (Somnus), who was god of sleep. His brother Icelus created dreams in animals, and his brother Phantastus created dreams in inanimate objects. Ovid's *Metamorphoses* (book 11) describes the Cave of Sleep. Chaucer's *Book of the Duchess* (137) calls Morpheus "the god of sleep." The word *morphine* is derived from the god's name.

See also: CAUCER; HYPNOS

**2118**

**Morrigu, The** In Celtic mythology, a major war goddess, the great queen associated with other war goddesses such as Badhbh and Nemhain, or Macha. It is believed all of those goddesses are merely different manifestations of the Morrigu. She was portrayed as a woman with red eyebrows, wearing a blood-stained garment, fully armed, and drawn in a chariot by red horses. Her bellicosity is often combined with an alluring sexuality. In Arthurian legends she appears as Morgan le Fay, sister of King Arthur. She appears in William Butler Yeats's play *The Death of Cuchulain* as "a woman with a crow's head," referring to her role as a death goddess.

See also: ARTHUR, KING; CUCHULAIN; MORGAN LE FAY

*Moses*

**2119**

**Moses** (a son) In the Bible, O.T., leader of the Israelite departure from Egyptian bondage. Moses was a prophet and lawgiver whose legend is told in the first books of the Hebrew Bible; Exodus, Leviticus, Numbers, and Deuteronomy. It was once believed that Moses was the author of these works, but scholars now agree that he was not.

Moses was born in Egypt to Hebrew parents, Amram, a Levite, and Jochebed. When Pharaoh ordered that all newborn Hebrew male children be put to death, Moses' mother hid him in a basket among the reeds by a stream. Pharaoh's daughter, coming to bathe, found the babe and raised him as her own, giving him the name Moses, which is Egyptian. Moses' wet-nurse was his own mother, though the Egyptians were not aware of this (Exod. 2:1–10).

As a young man Moses saw an Egyptian strike a Hebrew. In anger, he killed the Egyptian, fled the royal court, and lived with Midian shepherds. He served the shepherd-priest Jethro for many years and married Jethro's daughter Zipporah, by whom he had a son, Gershom (Exod. 2:11–22).

While tending sheep on a mountainside in the Sinai Peninsula, Moses heard the voice of Yahweh, the Hebrew cult god, commanding him to lead the children of Israel out of Egypt. He knew it was Yahweh because God appeared "unto him in a flame of fire out of the midst of a bush: and he looked, and, behold, the bush burned with fire, and the bush was not consumed" (Exod. 3:2).

Moses appeared before Pharaoh with his brother Aaron, asking that the people be freed. Pharaoh refused until Yahweh produced a series of plagues, the last one bringing about the death of the male firstborn among the Egyptians. To appease Yahweh, Pharaoh then let the Israelites go.

After the Israelites left, Pharaoh changed his mind, and the Egyptian army pursued them. When they overtook the Israelites on the shores of the Red Sea, "Moses stretched out his hand over the sea; and the Lord caused the sea to go back by a strong east wind all that night, and made the sea dry land, and the waters were divided" (Exod. 14:21).

The Israelites crossed safely, but the Egyptians were all drowned as the waters closed over them. Moses and his people then wandered 40 years in the desert. In lean times Moses sustained the people with manna, a wild sweet edible, and with quail. Once he brought water from a rock by striking it with his rod (Exod. 17:6).

After three months of wandering Moses went up on a high peak of Mount Sinai and received from Yahweh, who was originally a storm and thunder god, the Ten Commandments (Exod. 20:1–17). When Moses came down from the mountain he found that his brother Aaron had made a golden calf to be worshiped by the people. Moses was so angry that he broke the tablets and destroyed the golden calf.

Moses died at Mount Pisgah, and leadership passed to Joshua. Moses was not allowed to enter the Promised Land because he had earlier defied Yahweh by striking the rock to obtain water before commanded to do so by Yahweh.

In art Moses is often portrayed with two blunt lumps resembling horns because of a mistranslation in the Vulgate Bible by St. Jerome, in which he mistook the Hebrew word for "rays" as the word for "horns," which it closely resembles (Vulgate Exod. 34:29). The horns can be seen on Michelangelo's statue of Moses in San Pietro in Vincoli, Rome.

Various legends about Moses not included in the Bible are found in other Jewish writings. One tells of Moses as a child sitting on Pharaoh's lap. The child threw a crown, decorated with an Egyptian god, to the ground. The wise men of the court said this indicated that Moses would overthrow the throne and suggested that the child be killed. To test the child, two platters were put before him; one was heaped with hot coals and the other with cherries. Moses reached for the coals, then, screaming, put his burned hand into his mouth, a sign that he should be allowed to live. His burned mouth caused him speech difficulties throughout his life. The biblical narrative relates that Moses was slow of speech and Aaron often spoke for him. Numerous paintings exist of Moses, among them *The Finding of Moses* by Sebastian Bourdon and *Moses Before the Burning Bush* by Dierk Bouts. In music, Rossini's *Moses in Egitto* (Moses in Egypt) and Arnold Schoenberg's *Moses und Aron* deal with the Hebrew hero. In Islamic legend Moses is called Musa.

See also: JEROME, ST.; JOSHUA; PHARAOH; YAHWEH

*Manna*

**Mot** (death, sterility)   In Near Eastern mythology (Phoenician), god of death produced from the primeval egg, a child of air and chaos. Mot was the father of the sun, moon, and stars.

**Motif**   A motif is the smallest meaningful component of a story. In the folktale Cinderella, for example, the pumpkin that turns into a carriage is motif D451.3.3. "Transformation: pumpkin to carriage." This motif is then related to Tale Type 510 "Cinderella and Cap o' Rushes." In the same tale type, under the section II. Magic Help, the other motifs for this tale are also listed, such as "magic wand furnishes clothes," "transformation of mouse to horse," and "helpful bird."

See also: TALE TYPE

**Mountain in Labor, The**   Aesopic fable found in various European collections.

One day the people of a certain country heard a mighty rumbling in the nearby mountain. Smoke was pouring from the summit. The earth was trembling, and great rocks came hurtling down into the valley. The mountain seemed to be in labor, and all of the people rushed to a vantage point where they could see what terrible thing was about to happen.

They waited and waited, while the sky grew dark and the rumblings and thunderings increased. Finally, as the people watched, there was one earthquake more violent than all of the others. Suddenly, a huge fissure appeared in the side of the mountain. The people threw themselves down on their knees. Some of them fainted. The rest waited with bated breath to see what would happen next. The thundering stopped. A deep silence fell. And out of the gap in the side of the mountain popped a mouse!

Moral: *Magnificent promises often end in paltry performances.*

The fable is referred to both by Lucian in his *True History* and by Horace in his *Art of Poetry*.

When Horace is giving instructions on how to write, he says: "Begin not as did the cyclic writer of old: 'Of Prima's fate and farfame war I'll sing.' What will this braggart produce worthy of so bombastic a boast? Mountains are in labor; to the birth comes a most absurd mouse."

See also: AESOPIC FABLES

**Moyna**   In African mythology (Dogon of the Republic of Mali), hero who discovered the principle of the bull-roarer, a flat object made of wood or metal that creates a peculiar sound when whirled at the end of a rope. Many people are frightened by its sound, and it is often used in African secret societies. According to Dogon mythology, Moyna discovered the bull-roarer by tying a piece of metal to a string and whirling it about. At a masked dance, which women were not allowed to view but often did, Moyna began to whirl the bull-roarer. All of the women ran away in fright. Moyna explained to them later that the sound they heard was the voice of the Great Mask and that women and children must remain indoors when it sounded or they would be destroyed by it. Moyna passed the secret of the bull-roarer on to his sons, telling them to use it at the death of an important person because its irregular sounds are like the voices of the spirits of the dead.

**Mrarts**   In Australian mythology, evil spirits of the dead, often found around burial grounds.

**Mrs. O'Leary's Cow**   In American history and folklore, the cow of Mrs. Patrick (Kate) O'Leary; it supposedly started the Great Chicago Fire in 1871 when it kicked over a lighted lantern while it was being milked. According to the legend, Kate told different people the morning after the blaze began that she was in the barn when one of her cows, Daisy, kicked over a lantern. A few curiosity-seekers claimed to find the broken pieces of such a lantern while snooping behind her cottage, whose survival was one of the great ironies of the disaster. The fire killed several hundred people and destroyed nearly $200 million worth of property.

2126

**Mudgegong**   In Australian mythology, an evil spirit created by Baiame. Mudgegong destroyed all of Baiame's children, who were turned into wild animals.

See also: BAIAME

2127

**Mudra**   In Oriental art, ritual gesture of the hands, fingers, and arms, signifying powers and special actions. Mudras are closely associated with mantras. As the mantras contain the secrets of sounds and images, the mudras contain the secrets of touch. Each deity has its own mudra, which is to be imitated by the worshippers. Among the most common forms are the following:

*Abhaya mudra*, symbol of protection or reassurance. The right arm is raised and slightly bent. The palm is open and held outward, the fingers extended and directed upward; the hand is level with the shoulders.

*Anjali mudra*, symbol of offering or salutation. Both arms may be raised fully upward above the head, the palms turned up and fingers extended. The joined palms can be held downwards, straight in front, in front of the face, or over the head, depending on the degree of honor being offered.

*Bhumisparsa mudra*, symbol of witness, the Buddha's earth- touching gesture. The right arm is pendant over the right knee. The hand has all fingers stretched downward, touching the earth, with the palm inward.

*Dharmachakra mudra*, symbol of the preaching of the Wheel of the Dharma in Buddhism. The hands are held against the chest, the left hand covering the right hand.

*Dhyana mudra*, symbol of meditation. Hands lie in lap, one on the other, palms upward and fingers extended. Figure seated with legs crossed.

*Vara mudra*, symbol of giving or bestowing. The arm is pendant, the hand palm outward with fingers fully extended.

*Vitarka mudra*, symbol of discussion. The hand is held up, palm outward, with the index finger or ring finger touching the thumb.

*Vyakhyana mudra*, symbol of exposition. The right arm is raised and slightly bent, with the thumb and forefinger touching.

2128

**Muhammad** (praised one)   The Apostle of Allah; the Seal of the Prophets (570–632).

Muhammad was born in the Year of the Elephants into an impoverished family of the Koreish (Quraish) tribe. After the death of his mother and father, Abdallah and Amina, he was affectionately cared for by his grandfather, Abd Al Muttalib. When the grandfather died, the boy was left to the guardianship of his son, Muhammad's uncle Abu Talib. Muhammad tended sheep and goats, an occupation that to the present day is considered by the Bedouin as degrading to the male. At the age of 24, Muhammad was employed by a rich widow named Khadijah (also Hadigah, Hadija) to drive the caravans of camels with which she carried on an extensive trade. He did so well that she offered him her hand in marriage, although she was 40 years old and he barely 25. Long after her death his love for Khadijah remained fresh in his heart, and he never let an opportunity pass to extol her virtues. He would often kill a sheep and distribute its flesh to the poor in honor of her memory.

While married to Khadijah, Muhammad would spend time on Mount Hirâ, a wild and lonely mountain near Mecca. An angel, identified as Gabriel, appeared to him and said: "Recite!"

"I am no reader!" Muhammad replied, whereupon the angel shook him violently and again told him to read. This was repeated three times. Then the angel uttered the fives lines of sura 96 of the Koran:

Read! in the name of thy Lord, who did
    create—
Who did create man from congealed blood.
Read! for thy Lord is the most generous,
Who has taught the use of the pen,—
Has taught man what he did not know.

Terribly frightened, Muhammad hastened home to his wife. Not certain of his calling, he had thoughts of suicide. On a few occasions he climbed the steep slopes of Mount Hirâ with the intention of killing himself. At last a glorious angel appeared, and Muhammad in terror ran to his wife, Khadijah, and cried: *"Daththiruni"* (Wrap me up). He lay down entirely wrapped in his cloak. The angel spoke to him: "O thou covered! Rise up and warn! and thy Lord magnify! and thy garments purify; and abomination shun! and grant not favors to gain increase; and for thy Lord await!" (sura 74). After this the revelations came in rapid succession, and Muhammad no longer doubted the urgency of his inspiration.

At first his only convert was his wife, who was afterward called Umm el Mu'minin, "the mother of believers." Next were his daughters, then his cousin Ali, Abu Talib's youngest son, whom Muhammad had adopted. Then came Zaid (Zayo), his freedman and favorite companion, and then Abu-Bakr, who because of his reputation was called El Ziddiq, "the true."

Muhammad's other converts were among the women and slaves at first, and then some influential men of the community became believers. The majority of the citizens of Mecca threw insults and even injured the prophet when he attempted to deliver his message. In time Muhammad made his migration from Mecca to Yathrib, later Medina. This historic act, called the Hegira or Hijra (departure), is the starting point of the Islamic era. The date of the arrival at Medina is not precisely known, set on 16 June in some accounts and 30 September in others. The year usually assigned is 622 C.E. Once Muhammad was established at Medina, he proceeded to set out the rites and ceremonies of Islam, and he built a mosque to serve as a place of prayer and hall of general assembly. He appointed Bilal, his Abyssinian slave, as crier to call the faithful to prayer five times a day.

Soon afterward he turned his attention to his native Mecca. Feeling sufficiently strong to take the offensive, he began to preach the Holy War to convert the infidel. After some petty raids on the enemies' caravans, a fierce encounter took place between the Muslims and the Meccans. During the first part of the battle the Muslims, by Muhammad's order, stood firm at their posts while he encouraged them by promising the immediate reward of paradise to those who should fall martyred in the cause. A strong winter windstorm suddenly arose in the faces of the enemy. Muhammad called the storm the work of the archangel Gabriel, whose thousands of angels were now fighting for Islam. Muhammad took a handful of dirt and threw it toward the Meccans. "May their faces be covered with shame!" he cried. "Muslims, to the attack!" The Meccans were completely routed. Of the captives six were executed by Muhammad's order; others embraced Islam. Mecca was conquered in 630, and the citizens eventually became devoted followers of the Prophet.

In March 632, Muhammad made his last pilgrimage to Mecca, the "farewell pilgrimage." Standing on Mount Arafat he addressed the people, more than 40,000, telling them to stand firm in the faith he had taught them, and he called Allah to witness that he had delivered His message and fulfilled his mission. In June he fell sick and died that month in the arms of Ayesha, his wife and the daughter of Abu-Bakr. Legend has it that Muhammad's coffin is suspended in midair at Medina.

Numerous legends have arisen around Muhammad that are part of the folklore of the Islamic cultures. It is said in one Swahili legend that Allah created the seeds of the prophets out of a handful of his light. There were 25 sparks. The first was given to Adam, and the last was placed in the loins of Abdullah, the father of Muhammad. His mother, Amina, was visited by an angel at night and told that Allah had filled her womb with the light of paradise. The angel said to her: "You will become the mother of the lord of all the Arabs, of the last prophet God will send to earth before Judgment. When he is born, call him Muhammad, the praised one, for that is his earthly name." As soon as Muhammad was born, "he made all the movements of the ritual prayer." An angel came and carried him to the four corners of the earth, to show him his future kingdoms and acquaint him with all of the peoples and spirits of the world.

When Muhammad was a boy of 12, he was examined by a hermit who found "between the boy's shoulder blades" the seal of prophecy in the form of a star, with the words: "There is no god but Allah and Muhammad is his Prophet."

The most famous legend associated with Muhammad concerns his Ascension or Assumption into heaven. Muhammad said he saw himself transported to heaven and brought face to face with God. He reported: "I saw there an angel, the most gigantic of all created beings. It had 70,000 heads, each had 70,000 faces, each face had 70,000 mouths, each mouth had 70,000 tongues, and each tongue spoke 70,000 languages; all were employed in singing God's praise." This must be understood as a mode of emphasis. The Ascension is referred to in the Koran (sura 17): "Celebrated be the praises of Him who took His servant a journey by night from the Sacred Mosque to the Remote Mosque, the precinct of which we have blessed, to show him our signs!" This passage and a few others in the Koran form the basis of a fantastic legendary voyage through the heavens. In the *Ascension of Muhammad*, the journey is described in elaborate detail, as it is in *The Life of Muhammad* by Ibn Ishaq, which survives in parts of the biography compiled by Ibn Hisham.

In the biography Muhammad tells how the angel Gabriel kicked him to awaken him and

then placed him on Burak, the fabulous animal that transported Muhammad to Jerusalem, where "he found Abraham and Moses and other prophets." Muhammad then describes the prophets. Moses was a "tall, dark, lively man with curled hair and a long nose"; Jesus was "neither tall nor short, with flowing hair, and a countenance shining as if he had just come out of a bath"; and Abraham looked just like Muhammad.

Several miracles are traditionally ascribed to Muhammad. One of the best known concerns the moon. Habid the Wise asked Muhammad to prove his mission by cleaving the moon in two. Muhammad raised his hands toward the heavens and commanded the moon to do Habid's bidding. Accordingly, it descended to the top of the Kaaba, made seven circuits, and, coming to the Prophet, entered his right sleeve and came out of his left. It then entered the collar of his robe, descended to the skirt, and clove itself into two plaits, one of which appeared in the east of the sky and the other in the west. The two parts ultimately reunited.

To Western readers, the best-known legend concerns Mount Safa. Muhammad was again asked for proof of his mission. He commanded Mount Safa to come to him, but it did not move. He said: "Allah is merciful. Had it obeyed my words, it would have fallen on us to our destruction. I will therefore go to the mountain, and thank Allah that He has had mercy on a stiff-necked generation."

Muhammad is the spelling of the Prophet's name preferred by Muslim scholars writing in English, although there are many variants: Mohammad, Mohammed, Mahomet.

See also: ABRAHAM; ALI; ALLAH; AYESHA; BORAK; GABRIEL; KHADIJA; MOSES

2129
**Mujaji II**  In African mythology (Lovedu, a Bantu tribe of the Transvaal), the name of the rain queen, who is believed to live forever. Mujaji II was the daughter of an incestuous union of a

daughter and father, Mugede. Her mother's name was also Mujaji, and both ruled for a time over the people. The two were often confused with one another. Mujaji I lived in seclusion and was called "white-faced" and "radiant as the sun." She is not simply the rainmaker; she is also the changer of seasons, and she guarantees their cycles. The tale of the two influenced H. Rider Haggard's novel *She*, which tells of a land ruled by an ageless queen and of the magic fire that enabled her to live thousands of years. The novel was filmed in 1935 and again in 1965.

2130
**Mukasa**   In African mythology (Buganda of Uganda), a demigod. As a child, Mukasa would not eat the food his parents prepared for him. He left home to live by himself, under a tree on an island named Bukasa. He was called Mukasa, which means a man from the island of Bukasa. A man discovered him there and took the child with him to his garden. At the man's home Mukasa would not eat anything until an ox was killed. He then asked for its heart, liver, and blood. From that time on the people of the village came to regard Mukasa as a god. (Asking for these special things to eat was an indication to them of his divinity.) Mukasa married and lived very well among these people, but one day he disappeared. In time mediums claimed to be able to receive messages from Mukasa. The female mediums would smoke tobacco in a hut in front of Mukasa's cone-shaped house. Once having served as mediums, the women had to live the rest of their lives removed from men.

See also: KIBUKA

2131
**Mu Kung** (Duke Good)   In Chinese mythology, the spirit of wood, who made himself clothes of hawthorn leaves. He is one of the Wu Lao, spirits of the five natural forces.

See also: WU LAO

2132
**Mulberry**   A tree used in silkworm culture. In Greek mythology, it was a symbol of tragic love. Originally white, it became blood red from the blood of the lovers Pyramus and Thisbe. The Romans dedicated the mulberry to Minerva, their counterpart of the Greek Athena. In Hebrew mythology and legend, King David consults a mulberry tree to learn when to attack the Philistines. God tells him: "And let it be, when thou hearest the sound of a gong in the tops of the mulberry trees, that then thou shalt bestir thyself; for then shall Yahweh go out before thee, to smite the host of the Philistines" (2 Sam. 5:24). David does as Yahweh commanded and defeats the Philistines. "Balsam" is substituted for "mulberry" in the Revised Standard Version of the text. In China the mulberry is sacred to the goddess San Ku Fu Jén. But in Chinese folklore, the mulberry is never planted in front of a house, as it might bring sorrow or disaster. If a Chinese woman carries a mulberry staff, this indicates that she is in mourning for a child.

See also: ATHENA; DAVID; MINERVA; PYRAMUS AND THISBE; YAHWEH

2133
**Mullion**   In Australian mythology, an eagle hawk who built his nest on the top of an enormous tree that reached almost to the sky. From this location he would swoop down, catch solitary victims, and bring them back to his eaglets for food. In an effort to bring an end to this practice, two headmen decided to climb the great tree. Their plan was to set fire to the nest at the top. First Koomba tried, but he could not reach the top. Then Murriwunda climbed up. He came back down exhausted, saying that he too had been unable to reach the top. Actually, he had instructed the fire not to burn until after he and the other headmen had left the site of Mullion's tree. When they were a safe distance away, a blaze broke out that lit the evening sky. It completely burned the tree, even its roots. Today it is

said that hollows can be traced in the ground where the roots once grew.

**Mullo** (mule)    In Celtic mythology, a tutelary god of mule drivers, worshiped by the Continental Celts. Ancient Roman writers equated Mullo with their god Mars, because he was as a healing god, especially for diseases of the eyes.

See also: MARS

**Mulungu**    In African mythology (Nyamwezi of Tanzania), supreme being equated by African Christians, who make up more than 40 percent of the population, with God. Most Christian translations of the Bible in various African languages have adopted Mulungu for the word *god*. Humans were originally intended to live forever, and Mulungu sent a chameleon to give them the news. It lingered on the way, however, and stammered when delivering the message. Thus, Mulungu sent a bird that told the people they would die and disappear like the roots of a tree.

See also: OLORUN; UNKULUNKULU; WELE

**Mummy** (bituminized thing)    The body of a human being or animal that has been intentionally preserved. The dogs and jackals that lived at the edge of the desert were carrion eaters and often dug up corpses that were buried in shallow graves. To avert this, the Egyptians tried to placate Anubis, "the dog who swallows millions." Anubis plays a role in the Osiris myth as the god who invented mummification in order to preserve the body of Osiris. The Egyptians evolved the ritual and practices of mummification over the course of several centuries, and the methods used varied widely throughout the course of time. In general, the soft tissues of the body were removed through the nose and via an incision in the flank of the torso. Those internal organs deemed worthy of preservation were entrusted

to the care of the canopic jars. The body was then treated with natron, a drying agent, and in the better examples was bathed in unguents and ointments and anointed with oils as it was wrapped in strips of linen. Throughout the wrapping process various amulets were used to ensure certain protections and prerogatives of the deceased in his journey to the underworld were wrapped within those bandages. It is thought that the embalming process in its most elaborate form took up to 70 days. One description of the process is found in Herodotus's *History* (book 2). Mummies, or parts of mummies, were used as medicine for centuries in Christian Europe. In Scotland, for example, in 1612 a mummy cost eight shillings a pound. When genuine Egyptian mummies were not available, the bodies of criminals were used instead. The 17th-century English author Sir Thomas Browne wrote that "Mummy is become merchandise." Interest in mummies increased with the discovery of Tutankhamen's tomb in 1922. Various Hollywood films deal with them, the most famous starring Boris Karloff in 1932, titled *The Mummy*.

See also: ANUBIS; OSIRIS

**Mu-monto**    In Siberian mythology, hero in a Buriat myth who visited the land of the dead. Once Mu-monto went to the land of the dead to demand the return of a horse he had sacrificed at his father's funeral. To reach the land of the dead, Mu-monto went due north and found a rock, which he lifted. He said, "Come here." Suddenly a black fox appeared from under the rock and led him the rest of the way. When he arrived in the land of the dead, he saw all types of punishments meted out to those who had led evil lives. Thieves were bound, liars had their lips sewn up, and adulterous wives were tied to thorn bushes. Mu-monto also saw the reward for the good. There was a poor woman who now lived a life of luxury and an evil rich woman who lived in rags. (The myth does not tell if Mu-monto recovered his horse.)

**Mungan-Ngana**  2138

In Australian mythology, culture hero who taught the people crafts and gave them names. His son was Tundun, who taught men initiation ceremonies. However, the ceremonies were then revealed to women, and as a result Mungan-Ngana sent fire between heaven and earth, killing all life except for Tundun and his wife, who were turned into porpoises and later founded the Kurnai tribe.

**Munkar and Nakir**  2139

In Islamic mythology, two angels who command the dead to sit upright in their tombs when they are to be examined on the Day of Judgment.

Both the faithful and sinners are questioned on the role of Muhammad. If the correct answer is given (that he is the Prophet, or Apostle, of Allah), the body will receive air from paradise. If no answer or an incorrect one is given, the sinner is beaten, then feels pressure from the earth, and is finally gnawed or stung by dragonlike beasts until the Day of Resurrection, when faithful and sinners alike will have to answer to Allah.

In the *Fikh Akbar*, a collection of laws for Islam written through the centuries, it is stated that "the interrogation of the dead in the tomb by Munkar and Nakir is a reality and the reunion of the body with the spirit in the tomb is a reality." It goes on to say that the pressure and punishment felt by the body are also "a reality."

According to other Islamic traditions, however, the angel Ruman will deliver the dead person over to punishment. At the sound of his voice the tomb will contract, almost crushing the body within it, until the first Friday of Rajab, the seventh month of the Muslim calendar. If a man is lucky enough to die on Friday (a sacred day of the week) he is not questioned.

See also: ALLAH; MUHAMMAD

**Mura** (Muru)  2140

In Hindu mythology, a demon slain by Krishna (an incarnation of the god Vishnu). Krishna not only killed Mura but "burnt his seven thousand sons like moths with the flame of the edge of his discus."

See also: KRISHNA

**Murile**  2141

In African mythology (Chaga of Tanzania), culture hero who brought fire. One day a young boy named Murile was being scolded by his mother for his misbehavior. He took his father's stool and commanded it to go into the air. First it went up into a tree and then into the sky. Murile then set out to find the home of the moon-chief, asking people he met for directions. After he had worked for some of these people for a period of time, they told him the way. When he arrived at the moon-chief's village, he saw people eating uncooked food. The moon-chief explained that they knew nothing of fire and so obviously could not cook their food. Murile was promised animals as gifts if he would show them how to make fire. He did so, and in time prospered greatly among these people. By and by, however, he wished to return to his own home and sent a mockingbird back to his people as a messenger. His family did not believe the bird, thinking that their son, who had been gone so long, must be dead. So Murile set off on the journey home with all of his herds, but gradually he grew very tired. A bull promised to carry him if Murile agreed never to eat his flesh. Murile agreed and directed his parents to spare the bull. His father, however, disregarded Murile's command and killed the bull. Not realizing it, Murile ate some food prepared by his mother with fat that had come from the animal. As he sank into the ground, he called out to his mother, saying that she had disobeyed him.

**Muses** (song, inspiration)  2142

In Greek and Roman mythology, the nine daughters of Zeus and

*Erato*

*Euterpe*

Mnemosyne (memory), according to Hesiod's *Theogony*. They were called Camenae by the Romans. They were born at the foot of Mount Olympus in Pieria. Mount Helicon in Boeotia was sacred to them. The nine Muses are Calliope, Muse of epic poetry, mother of Orpheus by Apollo; Clio, Muse of history, whose attribute is a laurel and scroll; Erato, Muse of lyric poetry, love poetry, and marriage songs, whose attribute is a lyre (Erato was invoked by lovers in April); Euterpe, Muse of music and lyric poetry, whose attribute is a flute; Melpomene, Muse of tragedy, whose attribute is the tragic mask and *cothurnus* (buskin); Polyhymnia (Polymnia), Muse of sacred song, oratory, lyric, singing, and rhetoric, whose attribute is a veil; Terpsichore, Muse of dancing, whose attribute is a crown of laurel and a musical instrument in her hand; Thalia, Muse of comedy, whose attribute was the comic mask and the "sock," a shoe worn by comic actors; and Urania, Muse of astronomy, whose attribute is a glove and a pair of compasses. Urania was the mother of Linus by Apollo and of Hymenaeus by Dionysus. In Renaissance poetry she is often said to be the Muse of poetry.

*Clio*

See also: CALLIOPE; ERATO; HESIOD; TERPSICHORE; URANIA; ZEUS

2143

**Mushroom**   An edible fungus. In ancient Egypt, the pharaohs forbade any commoner to touch mushrooms because they were sacred. The Hebrews had a general taboo against fungus eating. The Romans, however, loved mushrooms, though the philosopher-poet Seneca called them "voluptuous poison." Certain types of fungi grow in the form of fairy rings, small circles within which fairies are believed to dance at night. Shakespeare's *The Tempest* (5:1) has Prospero invoke the fairies:

> You demi-puppets, that
> By moonshine do the gree-sour ringlets
>   make,
> Whereof the ewe not bites.

2144

**Muspellheim** (home of destruction)   In Norse mythology, the realm of fire, the heat from which helped in the creation of the world. Surt guards Muspellheim with a flaming sword. He will destroy the gods and the world by fire at Ragnarok, the end of the world.

See also: RAGNAROK; SURT

2145

**Mustard Seed, The**   Buddhist parable about the reality of death, found in various collections. Krisha Gautami, a young orphan girl, had only one child. One day the child died, and Krisha was heartbroken. She carried the dead child to all of her neighbors, asking them for medicine to restore the child to life. Finally, she met a man who said to her, "I cannot give you medicine for your dead child, but I know a physician who can." The man sent Krisha to the Buddha. When she arrived she asked, "Lord and Master, give me the medicine that will restore my son to life." The Buddha replied, "I want a handful of mustard seeds taken from a house where no one has lost a child, husband, parent, or friend." Krisha went from house to house. "Here is mustard seed. Take it," they would say. But when she asked,

"Did a son or daughter, a father or mother, die in your family?" They answered her, "Yes, the living are few, but the dead are many." She then realized that death is common to all humankind. She buried her son and returned to the Buddha, taking comfort in his teaching.

See also: BUDDHA, THE

*Mut*

2146

**Mut** (Mout) (mother)   In Egyptian mythology, a great mother-goddess, believed to possess both male and female reproductive organs. She has been linked to a myth in which Ra and his daughter take on the shape of cats to slay the Apophis serpent. When she quarreled with her father, she too assumed the shape of a cat and roamed the Libyan desert. When she was persuaded to come back to Egypt her return was cause for great celebration among the gods, people, and even animals. Mut's temple at Thebes had a horseshoe-shaped Sacred Lake. Her sanctuary there was in use for 2,000 years. Mut is usually portrayed in Egyptian art as a woman wearing on her head the united crowns of Upper and Lower Egypt and holding in her hands the papyrus scepter and the ankh, sign of life. Sometimes she is portrayed standing upright, with her large winged arms stretched out full length. At her feet is the feather of Maat, or Truth, and on her head is the vulture headdress. Sometimes, however, this versatile deity is portrayed with the head of a man or a vulture and with a phallus and lion claws. The Greeks identified Mut with Hera, the wife of Zeus.

See also: ANKH; APOPHIS; GREAT GODDESS; HERA; MAAT; RA

2147

**Muta** (silence)  In Roman mythology, goddess of silence and quiet. Ovid's *Fasti* (book 2) cites the goddess.

See also: OVID

2148

**Mwambu and Sela**  In African mythology (Luyia of Kenya), the first man and woman. Wele, the creator god, made the sun shine for them and gave them water from heaven to drink. This water eventually made all of the lakes and rivers of the earth. Mwambu and Sela were told which kinds of meat to eat and which to refrain from eating, which types of food were permitted and which were not. Wele gave them young calves, male and female, so that they might prosper. Mwambu and Sela lived in a house on stilts and were always careful to pull the ladder up because there were monsters prowling about. They remained in the house, but their children descended and peopled the earth.

See also: ABUK AND GARANG; ADAM AND EVE; ASK AND EMBLA; WELE

2149

**Myo-o** (kings of wisdom)  In Japanese Buddhist mythology, the five fierce or terrible manifestations of the Buddha; their fierce ap-

pearance destroys ignorance, the major hindrance to enlightenment. They are Dai-itoku-Myo-o, Fudo-Myo-o, Gonzanze, Kongo-yasha-Myo-o, and Aizen-Myo-o. The most important is Aizen-Myo-o, who is equated in Japanese folklore with the god of love. He is portrayed with a ferocious face, having three eyes, one of which is in the middle of his forehead, placed vertically between his eyebrows. On his head is a lion headdress. He usually has six arms and carries a metal bell, a quiver and bow, a wheel, a thunderbolt, a man's head or hook, and a lotus flower. Various Buddhist texts explain some of the symbolism of his iconography. If his body is painted red, it symbolizes his compassion, which issues from every pore of his body like drops of blood. His three eyes allow him to behold heaven, earth, and hell. He wears a lion's headdress because he is like a lion. The bell awakens enlightenment; the thunderbolt symbolizes a pure heart or is a means to strike down the wicked. The bow and arrow drive away forgetfulness, and the lotus calms the agitation of guilt.

See also: BUDDHA, THE

2150

**Myrmidons** (ants)  In Greek mythology, ants who were turned into soldiers to accompany Achilles during the Trojan War. King Aeacus of Aegina, a son of Zeus, prayed to his father to replenish the population of his kingdom, which had been destroyed by a plague sent by Hera to punish one of the women her husband, Zeus, had loved. A variant account says there were no people to begin with. Zeus answered the prayer of Aeacus by transforming ants into warriors, who later joined Achilles in the Trojan War. Today the term Myrmidons is used for warriors "who execute an order, especially a military command, with ruthless indifference to its baseness or inhumanity" (Bergen Evans). Homer's *Iliad* (book 2) and Ovid's *Metamorphoses* (book 7) tell of the Myrmidons.

See also: ACHILLES; AEACUS; HERA; ILIAD, THE; OVID; ZEUS

2151

**Myrrh** (Smyrna)    A tree resin used for incense, associated in Greek mythology with a tale recounted by Ovid in his *Metamorphoses* (book 10) about a princess, Myrrha, in love with her father, Cinyras, king of Cyprus. In remorse for her incestuous feelings she attempted suicide but was rescued by her nurse, who then promised to help her. She told the king that a very beautiful girl longed to sleep with him and arranged an assignation. Drunk with wine, the king did not recognize Myrrha when she came to him, but after several encounters he discovered that his mistress was his own daughter. Horrified to discover his incest, he tried to kill her, but she fled to the land of Sabaea, where she bore a son, Adonis, and afterward she turned into a tree, the myrtle. Her tears became the fragrant resin of the tree. Adonis was worshiped with burning of myrrh at his festival.

See also: *METAMORPHOSES, THE*

2152

**Myrtle**    An evergreen shrub; in European mythology and folklore, often associated with birth and resurrection. Greek colonists carried myrtle boughs to their new countries to symbolize the end of one life and the beginning of another. The myrtle was associated with Aphrodite, Greek goddess of sex, love, and fecundity, as well as with her Roman counterpart, Venus. Among Romans the myrtle was a symbol of marriage, a rite over which both Venus and Juno presided. Its blossoms were worn by brides, and bridegrooms wore myrtle sprigs. Yet the Romans also saw an evil side to the myrtle: it was identified with unlawful and incestuous love and was not allowed to be displayed at some public functions. The ancient Jews believed that eating myrtle leaves gave one the power to detect witches. In the Old Testament the myrtle is a token of the goodness of Yahweh, for he promised to plant a myrtle in the wilderness for the children of Israel (Isa. 41:19).

See also: APHRODITE; JUNO; VENUS; YAHWEH

2153

**Mystère**    In Haitian voodoo, the sun, one of the main symbols in voodoo worship; also a loa (deified spirit of the dead).

See also: LOA

# N

**Na Atibu**   In Micronesian mythology, a creator god of the Gilbert Islands. Earth and people were formed from Na Atibu's body. From his spine the sacred tree Kai-n-tiku-abu (tree of many branches) sprang, with people as its fruit. But one day a man named Koura-abi got angry when some excrement fell on him from the tree. He attacked the tree, breaking its branches and scattering the people throughout the world.

2154

**Nabu** (announcer)   In Near Eastern mythology (Babylonian), god of wisdom, speech, and writing; son of Marduk. Nabu appears in the Old Testament (Is. 46.1) as Nebo, where he is ridiculed, along with the god Bel, for his helplessness.

See also: BEL; MARDUK; ZAG-MUK

2155

**Naenia** (dirge)   In Roman mythology, goddess who presided over funerals. Her temple was outside the city gate in Rome.

2156

**Naga** (Naia, Naja, Naje) (snake)   In Hindu and Buddhist mythology, fantastic beings with the head of a man or woman and the body of a snake,

2157

ruled over by Shesha, the serpent king. The Nagas guard various treasures, especially pearls. Sometimes Nagas' upper bodies are human and their lower bodies serpentine. They are said to inhabit Nagaloka, Niraya, or Patala. Often the Buddha is shown surrounded by Nagas in complete serpentine form.

See also: PATALA; SHESHA

**Naglfar** (conveyance made of nails)   In Norse mythology, the ship of the giants, made of dead men's nails. Naglfar will carry the giants to their final battle, Ragnarok, against the gods. It was an ancient Nordic custom to cut short the nails of deceased persons to delay the coming of Ragnarok. Thus, the size of Naglfar depends on how many people are buried with long fingernails that were not cut. At Ragnarok, the end of the world, Naglfar will bring the Jotunn giants to fight the Aesir gods. Naglfar appears in the *Prose Edda*. Naglfari is the name of a giant who was the first husband of Nott.

See also: AESIR; JOTUNN; RAGNAROK

2158

**Nain Rouge** (red dwarf)   In American folklore, a ghost of a red-faced creature who is believed to be responsible for the burning of Detroit in 1805. To avoid its evil spell some citizens paint

2159

the sign of the cross on their homes. Tales of a Red Dwarf date back over 200 years. Witnesses of this goblin-like creature describe it as no more than two-and-half feet tall, covered in dark red to black skin or fur with blazing red eyes. Cadillac, the founder of Detroit (1701), is rumored to have encountered and even attacked the Red Dwarf. Within days Cadillac lost both his fame and fortune. On 30 July 1763, the day before the battle of Bloody Run, the creature was seen dancing along the banks of the Detroit River. Several citizens of Metro Detroit supposedly spotted the Red Dwarf the day before the 1967 riots. On 1 March 1976, two employees of Detroit Edison saw a small "child" climbing a utility pole. Fearing the child might fall, the two men called out to him, and much to their surprise, the child leaped from the top of the 20-foot pole and scurried away. The next day Detroit was buried in one of the worst snowstorms in its history.

2160

**Nairyo-sangha**   In Persian mythology, messenger of the good god, Ahura Mazda, who lives in the navel of kings and is a companion of the god Mithras. Nairyo-sangha is worshiped along with Sraosha, one of the seven Amesha Spentas, who will help judge the world.

See also: AHURA MAZDA; MITHRAS

2161

**Najara**   In Australian mythology, a spirit who lures young boys away from their tribes and makes them forget their language. Najara was a tribesman of the Djauan country. One day he went off to spear an emu. He sat down at the base of a palm tree and saw some dingoes—wild dogs—come along smelling the ground. They killed Najara and ripped his body to pieces. The moon god, Deert, found Najara's body and buried it. At the end of three days Najara returned to life and rose from his grave. Deert asked him how he was able to accomplish this. Najara answered that the moon god did not need his "clev-

erness." Najara knew that Deert too had the secret of returning from the dead.

Najara went off into the desert. When he came upon a boy from his tribe, he whistled to him. The boy came over, and the two camped together for several months. When they were at last sighted by other members of the tribe, the boy fled. Eventually he was caught and brought back to the tribal camp. Najara, on the other hand, showed no fear. He suddenly disappeared and was never seen again. It was a long time before the boy would eat the food of his tribe or speak their language. To this day it is believed that when the spirit of Najara whistles in the grass, boys will be lured away and forget their tribe's language.

See also: DEERT; GIDJA

2162

**Nakaa**   In Micronesian mythology, the guardian of a primordial tree. According to a Gilbert Island myth, it was Nakaa who watched over a tree given to women at the beginning of time. Men, who were made to lie apart from women, were innocent and were forbidden to touch the tree. The men were given a fish trap that supplied them with plentiful fish. They were also given a tree of their own, which bore a single nut. Each time the nut was picked, another would grow in its place. One day when Nakaa was away, the men disobeyed him and touched the women's tree. When Nakaa returned, he found some of the men's hairs on it and knew they had been there. He grew very angry and permitted death to enter the world.

Nakaa sat down by the entrance to the spirit world and wove a net, which he used to capture the spirits of the wrongdoers as they attempted to seek rest for their souls. The spirits of the good people were free to enter the realm of the afterlife, but the spirits of the violators could not. Depending on which tribe is telling the myth, the souls of the blessed go either to an island, somewhere underground, or to a place in the sky.

**Nakk**  In Finno-Ugric mythology, evil water spirit living in the deepest spot in the water. Nakk could appear in many different shapes, both human and animal, though the Estonians usually imagined him as a gray old man who swallowed everything in the water that came his way. Sometimes he seated himself on the shore to watch people or bewitched them with his songs, which forced men and animals to dance until they fell into the sea and were drowned. The female counterpart of Nakk was Nakineiu (Nakk's maid), a beautiful girl who sat on the surface of the water, on a stone on the shore, or in the shadow of a tree growing near the river, combing her long golden-yellow hair. Sometimes she appeared naked with a half human and half fish body. Like her male counterpart, she too sang.

See also: LORELEI

**Nalul**  In Australian mythology, a man of unknown origin who one day came out of the desert to a lovely green place of fig trees, palms, and flowers. He heard the sound of laughing girls and ever so gradually crept up to them. Unseen by them, he parted the reeds and saw a beautiful girl with long hair. Nalul caught her by the hair, but she fought him. Finally, he threw sand into her eyes and while she was blinded, he tied her to a tree. In time he brought her some honey to eat, but she seemed not to know what it was and apparently did not understand his language. Only after he rubbed the sweat of his body across her mouth, ears, and eyes could she understand him. He then heated some bark and placed it by the girl's ears so she could hear the sound of water. When he had finished, Nalul called her Nyal-Warrai-Warrai, the girl from the water. Now she freely went with him and no longer had to be tied. When they passed the country where her sisters lived, they called to her. Although she did not want to, she felt compelled to go back to the water whence she had come. She was never seen by Nalul again. It is said that she went to be with her father, the rainbow snake.

**Nama**  In Siberian mythology, hero of the flood myth as told by the Altaics. Nama was commanded by the creator god Ulgen to construct an ark. Because Nama was partly blind, he asked the assistance of his three sons, Sozun-uul, Sar-uul, and Balyka. When the ark was finished Nama, his wife, his sons, some other people, and animals were placed aboard. When the flood came, all were saved. After many years, when Nama had grown old and was near death, his wife asked him to kill all of the people and animals he had originally saved so he could be lord of the dead in the next world. However, his son Sozun-uul convinced his father that this was wrong, so instead the old man killed his wife by cutting her in two. When Nama died, he took his son Sozun-uul to heaven with him, where he was later transformed into a constellation of five stars.

In later mythology Nama became lord of the dead and is called Jaik-Khan (the flood prince). He is invoked as an intermediary between God and man, living in the Third Heaven, that of the Kudai, seven spirits who watch over men's destinies. When Nama sends the life force to each child born into the world, he is called Jujutshi.

See also: ULGEN

**Namuchi** (not releasing the heavenly waters) In Hindu mythology, a demon slain by Indra, the storm god. When Indra conquered the demons, Namuchi alone resisted so strongly that he overpowered Indra, making him a prisoner. Namuchi offered to let Indra go if Indra promised not to kill him by day or night, wet or dry. Indra promised and was released. Later, however, the god cut off Namuchi's head at twilight, between day and night, and with water foam, which was neither wet nor dry. In the Hindu epic poem *The Mahabharata*, the severed head of Namuchi follows Indra, crying out: "O wicked slayer of thy friend." The same myth is recounted with Narasinha, an incarnation of Vishnu, as the slayer.

See also: INDRA; *MAHABHARATA, THE*; VISHNU

2167

**Nana**   In African mythology (Yoruba of southwest Nigeria and Fon of Benin), earth goddess; married to Obaluwaye, the earth god; mother of Omolu, another earth god. Nana, Obaluwaye, and Omolu also appear in African cults of Brazil and Cuba.

2168

**Nanda**   In Buddhist legend, a woman who gave rice pudding or, in other versions of the legend, very rich cream (the cream of the cream of the milk from 100 cows) to the Buddha after he had given up mortifications, finding them useless to Enlightenment.

See also: BUDDHA, THE

2169

**Nandin** (the happy one)   In Hindu mythology, the bull-vehicle of Shiva, who watches the *lingam* outside the temple. He has one leg crooked, ready to stand up and go as needed. Nandin is also called Viraka (little hero).

See also: LINGAM; SHIVA

2170

**Nane** (Hanea)   In Armenian mythology, goddess, daughter of the supreme god, Aramazd. She may have been derived from the Sumerian goddess Nana, though in Hellenistic times Nane was often identified with the Greek goddess Athena as a wise and warlike goddess.

See also: ARAMAZD; ATHENA

2171

**Nanimulap**   In Micronesian mythology, god of fertility in the Caroline Islands. His sacred animal is the turtle, which may be eaten only by chiefs.

2172

**Nanna** (mother of the brave)   In Norse mythology, the wife of Baldur and mother of Forseti. After Baldur's death Nanna died of anguish at his funeral fire and was burned along with him. She accompanied him to Hel and sent back cloth for Frigga and a ring for Fulla, just as Baldur had returned the ring Draupnir to Odin. Nanna appears in the *Prose Edda* and in Matthew Arnold's narrative poem *Balder Dead*.

See also: BALDUR; FRIGGA; ODIN

2173

**Naomi Wise**   American ballad of the 19th century that tells how Naomi was murdered by her lover. The ballad is believed by some to be based on the murder of Naomi Wise by Jonathan Lewis in Randolph County, North Carolina, in 1808. When Lewis had a chance to win a local heiress, he decided to rid himself of Naomi Wise, whom he had gotten pregnant. The ballad describes the murder in full detail:

> The wretch then did choke her, as we
>     understand,
> And threw her in the river below the
>     milldam;
> Be it murder or treason, O! what a great
>     crime,
> To drown poor Naomi and leave her behind.

2174

**Napi** (old man, creator)   In North American Indian mythology (Blackfoot), creator god, culture hero, and trickster. Napi created the first people out of clay. He then appeared to his creatures near a river. A woman asked him if people were to live forever. He replied that he had not thought of that question. "We must decide what shall happen. I will toss a piece of wood into the river. If it floats, when people die they will return to life in four days. But if the wood sinks, death will be forever." The wood was cast into the river, and it floated. Then the first woman picked up a stone and said, "If it floats, we will live forever; but if it sinks, we will die." The stone was cast into the river and immediately sank. "You have chosen," replied the god. Some accounts say that Napi left after the creation and went to live in the mountains, promising to return one day.

See also: TRICKSTER

*Narcissus*

2175

**Narcissus** (benumbing, narcotic)   In Greek mythology, son of Cephisus and Lirope. Narcissus scorned the love of Echo, a nymph (or according to another account, a male lover). As punishment, the gods made Narcissus fall in love with his own reflection in a pool. Because he received no answer from his image, the youth killed himself and was transformed into a flower. In another variation Narcissus had a twin sister who died. When he looked into the pool, he thought he saw her image, not his own. Narcissus has been cited in English literature by many poets, among them, Spenser in *The Faerie Queene* (3.6.45) ("Foolish Narcisse, the likes the watry shore"), Christopher Marlowe in *Hero and Leander* (1.74–6), Keats in *I Stood Tip-toe upon a Little Hill* (163), and Shelley in *The Sensitive Plant* (1.18–20). Narcissus was painted by Caravaggio, Tintoretto, Claude, Poussin, and Turner.

See also: ECHO; NYMPHS

2176

**Nareau** (Naareau, Narleau, Na-areau, Areopenap) (spider lord)   In Micronesian mythology, two creator gods, Ancient Spider and Young Spider. According to some accounts, Ancient Spider is a preexistent being, living in either darkness, a void, endless space, or the sea. Other accounts say he was born when Te Bo Ma (darkness) and Te Maki (the cleaving together) had sexual intercourse, producing Void, Night, Daylight, Thunder, Lightning, Ancient Spider, and Younger Spider.

In the account of the Gilbert Islands, Ancient Spider made heaven and earth from a shell. He commanded the sand and water to have sexual intercourse. Their children included Nakika, the octopus; Riiki, the eel; and a son whose name was also Nareau, or Young Spider. Young Nareau's task was to transform fools and mutes into normal human beings. He loosened their tongues and limbs and opened their eyes and ears. Then he commanded them to lift the sky, but they could not. So he called on Riiki and Nakika to assist him. While Young Spider chanted, Riiki raised the sky and the earth sank. Young Spider pulled the sides of the sky down to meet the edge of the horizon, leaving the fools and deaf mutes in the middle of the sea. Four women were placed in position to support the heavens. Exhausted with his labors, Riiki died and became the Milky Way. Ancient Spider became the sun and moon, his brains became the stars, trees, and rocks, and humans sprang from the remainder of his body.

See also: SPIDER

**2177**

**Narguns**   In Australian mythology, evil beings, half human and half animal, made of stone. They cannot be killed.

**2178**

**Nari** (Narvi)   In Norse mythology, son of the fire-trickster god, Loki, and his wife, Siguna. Nari appears in the *Prose Edda*.

See also: LOKI; SIGUNA

**2179**

**Nasnas**   In Persian-Islamic folklore, a demon who appears in the shape of a feeble old man. Nasnas usually sits on the bank of a river, and when a traveler approaches, Nasnas asks for help in crossing. If the traveler consents, Nasnas mounts his shoulders. When they reach midstream, he wraps his legs around his victim and drowns him.

**2180**

**Nasu** (Nas, Nasus, Nasrust, Druj Nasa)   In Persian mythology, corpse demon, the personification of corruption, decomposition, contagion, and impurity. Nasu often appears in the form of a fly that hovers above rotting bodies. He is driven away by the glance of a dog in the rite called *sag-did* (dog-sight). In some texts Nasu is regarded as a demoness.

**2181**

**Natigay** (Natigai)   In Siberian mythology, the earth god worshiped by the Tartars to protect children, cattle, and grain. Marco Polo, in his *Travels* (book 1), has a description of the images of Natigay he encountered on his journeys. They were "covered with felt or cloth," and one was placed in each dwelling. At mealtimes the images of Natigay and of his wife and children were "fed" by having grease from the meal rubbed on their mouths. Natigay is probably a corruption of Otukhan, a pagan Turkish god adopted by the Tartars.

**2182**

**Nation, Carry**   1846–1911. In American history and folklore, fanatic temperance leader who hatcheted her way to fame. Later she was best known as Mother Nation. She believed that God had given her a divine mission to destroy saloons and the drinking of hard liquor. She lectured extensively on her divine call and told her story in a book, *The Use and the Need of the Life of Carry A. Nation*. She is the focus of Douglas Moore's opera *Carry Nation*, as well as in limericks and tales.

**2183**

**Natos**   In North American Indian mythology (Blackfoot), the sun, whose wife is Kokomikeis, the moon. All of their children were destroyed by pelicans except Apisuahts, the morning star.

**2184**

**Nats**   In Burmese mythology, generic name for supernatural beings, both good and evil, who inhabit air, land, and sea. In some accounts they are believed to be the spirits of the dead who have to be placated by offerings. The most famous group appears in the work *Maha Gita Medani*, a handbook in verse that contains short biographical sketches. Verses from the book are recited at festivals by a *nat-kadaw*, or female medium, who is believed to be under the possession of a *nat*. The most famous *nat* is Thagya Min, whose yearly descent to earth marks the beginning of the Burmese new year. In Burmese art Thagya Min is portrayed standing on a lotus, which in turn rests on three elephants.

**2185**

**Natty Bumppo**   In American literary folklore, hero of James Fenimore Cooper's *Leather-Stocking Tales*, a series of novels deriving its name from Natty Bumppo's long deerskin leggings. Natty is Cooper's vehicle for the expression of the author's personal views about the mores of 18th and early 19th century America. Throughout *The Leather-Stocking Tales*, Natty agrees with

Cooper's concept of a class-structured society. He dislikes the French, Iroquois, and Catholics, and reveals a disdain for miscegenation. Natty Bumppo is called Bumppo or Deerslayer in *The Deerslayer*, Hawkeye in *The Last of the Mohicans*, Pathfinder in *The Pathfinder*, Natty Bumppo or Leatherstocking in *The Pioneers*, and the trapper in *The Prairie*. Natty Bumppo, whose character is based in part on Daniel Boone, is the ideal outdoorsman: kind, strong, honest, and resourceful. He appears in two Hollywood movies called *The Last of the Mohicans*, starring Randolph Scott (1936) and Daniel-Day Lewis (1992).

2186

**Naumann, Hans**   1886–1951. German folklorist who in the 1920s introduced two concepts into the study of folk traditions. His concepts of "primitive communal goods" and "sunken cultural goods" were intended to explain the survival of primitive traditions that had sunk down from higher strata of society to the common peasant folk. Folktales were thus the remnants of ancient myths and heroic legends. Folksongs had likewise sunk down from earlier variants to the peasantry, and their folk costumes were seen as the remnants of more formal attire in the past.

Naumann was severely criticized by his contemporaries and by the Nazi regime for not appropriately valuing the German peasantry. Such statements as the following brought on the criticism:

One should shy away from using comparisons with the animal kingdom, but still it offers the closest parallels. . . . When the peasants of a Lithuanian village go to the market in the next town, perhaps to Lida, they move along their streets like ants, each one following the next. And just like them they are indistinguishable for strangers. In addition to a common shaped beard and a similar hair cut they also have common facial characteristics and a similar body shape. . . . The clothing is the same, their demeanor is

the same, the small sleds or the wagons that the Lithuanian peasants are sitting on, are all the same. In front of them they all have the same small horses with the same harnesses, and behind them they all seem to have the same woman sitting on a bundle of hay, her head covered, her upper body in a short sheep skin and her lower body in a brightly colored skirt made from homespun coarse linen: in brief, the concept of a primitive communal culture appears to be convincingly displayed among the Lithuanian peasants. . . . At the market place they stand around in bunches, they all make the same movements, they are all spirited by the same viewpoints and thoughts. When one laughs they all laugh along; when one curses they all do the same thing. . . . And just as they all arrived at the market place following one another, they all disappear at the same time, following one another, they go waddling home like geese all walking there the same way, completely without any individualism and conduct their completely uniform life.

2187

**Nausicaa** (burner of ships)   In Greek mythology, daughter of Alcinous, king of Phaeacia, and Arete. In Homer's *Odyssey* (book 6) Nausicaa befriended Odysseus, bringing him to the home of her father before the hero was sent on his way back to his wife. In later tradition Nausicaa married Telemachus, the son of Odysseus, and was the mother of Perseptolis or Poliporthus. Samuel Butler, the English novelist who translated both *The Iliad* and *The Odyssey* into English prose, also wrote a book in which he argued that Nausicaa, not Homer, or at any rate a woman, was the real author of *The Odyssey*.

See also: ALCINOUS; ODYSSEUS; *ODYSSEY, THE*; TELEMACHUS

2188

**Ndauthina**   In Melanesian mythology, Fijian trickster god of fire and of fishermen. He protects fishermen but causes trouble for others.

See also: TRICKSTER

2189

**Ndengei**   In Melanesian mythology, Fijian creator god in serpent form whose movements cause earthquakes. Offerings of pigs and first fruits are made to the god. Ndengei's son, Rokomautu, who is sometimes called a creator god, gave fire to humankind.

2190

**Nebuchadnezzar** (Nebuchadrezzar) (Nebo protects the crown)   In the Bible, O.T., king of Assyria who reigned from 604 to 561 B.C.E. He rebuilt Babylon, restored the temple of the god Bel, and may be responsible for the Hanging Gardens. He appears in many legends. He supposedly went mad at the height of his achievements, as described in Daniel (4:33) when he "did eat grass as oxen. . . . his hairs were grown like eagles' feathers, and his nails like birds' claws." William Blake painted the ruler in this state, and a 15th-century Umbrian panel from a cassone (marriage trunk) portrays scenes from the life of Nebuchadnezzar.

See also: BEL; SEVEN WONDERS OF THE AN-CIENT WORLD

2191

**Nectar**   In Greek mythology, the magical drink of the gods that conferred immortality. It was given to the gods in golden cups by Hebe or Ganymede. Ambrosia was the food of the gods.

See also: AMBROSIA; GANYMEDE; HEBE

2192

**Nefer**   In ancient Egyptian cult, an amulet of the windpipe and stomach, often made of a semiprecious stone. It is the sign for the concept of "good" and is the plural for "beauty."

2193

**Nefertiti** (the beautiful one has come)   fl. 1372–1350 B.C.E. Egyptian queen, wife of Akhenaten, who worked with her husband in establishing the worship of Aten. The famous head of Nefertiti in the Egyptian Museum of Berlin is but one of many fine portraits of the ruler.

See also: AKHENATEN; ATEN

*Neith*

2194

**Neith** (Neit, Net, Nit) (the terrifying one)   In Egyptian mythology, goddess of the city of Saïs, which served as Egypt's capital during the Twenty-Sixth Dynasty. When Saïs became the major city, Neith's importance increased considerably. A great festival, called the Feast of Lamps, was held in her honor. During the festival, according to Herodotus's *History* (book 2), devotees burned a multitude of lights in her honor all night in the open air. Neith became associated with creation myths, similar to those surrounding Hathor. As a goddess of weaving and the domestic arts, Neith was said to have woven the world with her shuttle. She was sometimes called the first birthgiver, the mother who bore the sun before anything else existed and thus could be considered the oldest of beings. On her temple wall was inscribed: "I am all that has been, that is, and that will be." In Egyptian art Neith was usually depicted as a woman wearing the crown of Lower Egypt, holding a scepter in one hand and the ankh, sign of life, in the other. The Greeks identified Neith with their goddess Athene.

See also: ANKH; ATHENE; HATHOR

**Nei Tituaabine** In Micronesian mythology, Gilbert Island tree goddess. She was once a mortal who fell in love with a chief, Auriaria, but died when she bore no offspring. From her body sprouted various trees and fruits.

*Nekhebet*

2196
**Nekhebet** (Nechbet) In Egyptian mythology, the vulture goddess of Upper Egypt, a patron of childbirth. She was called "the father of fathers, the mother of mothers" in some texts. Often she was portrayed as a vulture, though she also appeared in Egyptian art as a woman wearing the vulture headdress surmounted by the white crown of Upper Egypt. The Greeks identified her with their goddess Eileithyia.

See also: VULTURE

2197
**Nemesis** (due enactment, retribution) In Greek mythology, goddess of vengeance or personification of the righteous anger of the gods; daughter of Erebus and Nox; sister of Cer, Aether, Dreams, Hemera, Hypnos, Momus, Thanatos, and Charon. She was seduced by Zeus, and some accounts say she was the mother of Helen. Nemesis punishes *hubris* (presumption or pride), as when she pursued Agamemnon for his pride in victory. Dürer made a woodcut of the goddess. Byron's dramatic poem *Manfred* has Nemesis as a servant of Arimanes, the devil.

See also: AGAMEMNON; HELEN OF TROY; NOX; ZEUS

2198
**Nemterequeteba** In the mythology of the Chibcha Indians of Colombia, a culture hero, often identified with the chief of the gods, Bochica. He was similar to Tonopa, of whom he may be one version. He was pursued by Huitaca, but he changed her into an owl or a moon. Nemterequeteba organized a cult, appointed a high priest, and taught chastity, sobriety, social order, and the arts of spinning, weaving, and textile painting. When his task was finished, he disappeared. In Chibcha art he is portrayed as an old man with long hair and a beard down to his girdle. Nemterequeteba is also called Chimizapagua, the messenger of Chiminigagua (the creator god) and Sugumonxe or Sugunsua, the person who disappears.

See also: BOCHICA

2199
**Nephthys** In Egyptian mythology, Greek form of Nebthet; sister of Osiris, Set and Isis; often associated with darkness, decay, and death. In early Egyptian mythology Nephthys was usually regarded as the female counterpart of the evil god Set, with whom she had remained barren, and was thus called an "imitation woman with no vagina." She then went to her other brother, Osiris, whose wife was Isis, and tricked him into copulating with her. She conceived Anubis, the jackal-headed god. Later, however, she became the faithful friend of Isis and helped her sister collect the scattered limbs of Osiris, who had been dismembered by Set, and reassemble his body. She and Isis were both present when Anubis mummified the body. In the Pyra-

*Nephthys*

with the Greek Poseidon; possibly called Nethunus by the Etruscans; called Poseidon by the Greeks; husband of Salacia. Generally, in English literature Neptune is seen as a personification of the ocean. Shakespeare's *Macbeth* says: "Will all great Neptune's ocean wash this blood / Clean from my hand" (2.2.60–61). Neptune also was seen as the god who watched over England, and he is cited in Shakespeare's *Cymbeline* (3.2.19–20) as such. He also is cited or appears in Milton's *Comus* and his epic *Paradise Lost*, Ben Jonson's *Neptune's Triumph*, and the opening masque in Beaumont and Fletcher's *The Maid's Tragedy*. The most famous image of the god is probably that by Bernini in the Trevi Fountain in Rome. The artist also did a *Neptune and Triton*. Neptune's attributes are the trident, a weapon favored by Mediterranean fishermen, and the

mid Texts she is considered the friend of the dead, and the same role is attributed to her in *The Book of the Dead*.

Although Nephthys was a goddess of death, she was also the female counterpart of the ithyphallic god Min, who symbolized virility, reproduction, and regeneration. Nephthys was also skilled in magic and "words of power," and as a healing deity she was, with Isis and Osiris, one of the great deities of Mendes in the delta region. She often appeared with Isis on the walls of coffins, with winged arms outstretched in a gesture of protection. Among her many titles were "mistress of the gods," "great goddess, lady of life," "sister of the god," and "lady of heaven, mistress of two lands."

Egyptian art portrays Nephthys as a woman wearing on her head a pair of horns and a disk surmounted by the hieroglyph of her name.

See also: ANUBIS; *BOOK OF THE DEAD, THE*; ISIS; MIN; OSIRIS; PYRAMID TEXTS; SET

2200

**Neptune**   In Roman religion, the early Italian god of freshwater pools who became identified

*Neptune riding on a dolphin into Venice harbor (Jacopo de Barberi)*

whip, reminding his worshiper that he was also a god of horses. Neptune's festival date was 23 July.

See also: POSEIDON

*Thetis ordering the Nereids into the sea (John Flaxman)*

**Nereids** (the wet ones)   In Greek mythology, sea nymphs or mermaids, the 50 or 100 daughters of Nereus, a sea god, and Doris. Among them were Actae, Agave, Amatheia, Amphinome, Amphithoe, Amphirite, Apseudes, Callianassa, Callianeira, Clymene, Creusa, Cymodoce, Cymothoe, Dexamene, Doris, Doto, Dynamene, Erato, Eudora, Galatea, Glauce, Halie, Iaera, Ianassa, Ianeira, Limnoreia, Maera, Melite, Nemertes, Nesaera, Oreithyia, Panope, Pasithea, Pherusa, Proto, Psamanthe, Speio, Thalia, Thetis, and Thoe. The Nereids were attendants on Poseidon. The most famous are Amphirite, wife of Poseidon, and Thetis, mother of Achilles. Images of Nereids were often carved on Roman sarcophagi indicating the passage of the soul to the other world.

See also: ACHILLES; AMPHIRITE; DORIS; MERMAID; NYMPHS; POSEIDON; THETIS

2202

**Nergal** (lord of the great city)   In Near Eastern mythology (Babylonian-Assyrian), war god, lord of the underworld, husband of Ereshkigal, goddess of the underworld. When he trespasses against a taboo of the underworld, sexual intercourse, he is doomed to stay forever. In some accounts he is said to be the son of Bel. He was addressed as "the hero of the gods, who marches in front of them" to battle, and among his names (when identified with the planet Mars) are those of Allamu and Almu. Assyrian kings regarded Nergal as the patron god of hunting. Nergal was portrayed wearing a crown and was waited on by 14 attendants. His sacred city of the dead was Cutha.

See also: BEL; ERESHKIGAL

2203

**Nero, Claudius Caesar**   Ruled 54–68 C.E. In Roman history and legend, emperor who "fiddled while Rome burned" and then blamed the Christians for the fire. The fiddling is legend and has no historical basis. Nero's mother, Agrippina, was suspected of killing the emperor Claudius, her uncle, so that Nero would succeed instead of Britannicus, Claudius's own son. Nero later had his mother killed. He was tutored by Seneca, the author and philosopher. Poppaea Sabina, his mistress from 58 C.E. and then his wife from 62 until her death in 65, was believed responsible for the death of Nero's mother and his divorce from Octavia for sterility. When Nero's armies revolted on the Rhine, the emperor killed himself, but for some time rumors circulated that he had not really died. His dying words were "what an artist dies in me." After the fire in Rome he built the *domus aurea* (golden house) in a park overlooking an artificial lake. In front stood a massive statue of the emperor as the sun god. Monteverdi's opera *Poppaea* deals with Nero and his mistress and wife. Nero's life is given in Suetonius's *Lives of the Twelve Caesars*.

2204

**Nerthus** (Nertha, Hertha) (earth)   In Germanic mythology, mother earth, fertility goddess of tribes. The Roman writer Tacitus in his

*Germania* (40) calls her Terra Mater. Processions in Nerthus's honor, in which she was worshiped as goddess of fertility, peace, and plenty, were elaborate. During the spring, cows pulled a statue of Nerthus on a cart to a holy meadow on an island in the sea. The festival lasted several days. When it was over, the cart and the statue were part of a cultic cleansing process. Slaves dedicated to the goddess were drowned in her honor. The origin of the name is unclear, but it is probably related to Erda (earth).

See also: ERDA; FREY; NJORD

2205

**Nessus** (young bird or animal)   In Greek mythology, a centaur, son of Ixion and a cloud, who attempted to rape Deianira, wife of Heracles. Nessus was killed by Heracles with an arrow poisoned with the blood of the Lernean Hydra. Some of the blood spilled on Nessus's shirt, which later was given to Heracles by Deianira in the belief that it would reclaim Heracles' love for her. In fact, the shirt caused Heracles' death. The expression "shirt of Nessus" is used to indicate a fatal gift.

Ovid's *Metamorphoses* (book 4) tells the tale, and it is alluded to in Shakespeare's *All's Well That Ends Well* (4.3.283) and *Anthony and Cleopatra* (4.12.93). In *The Divine Comedy* (Inferno, cantos 12, 13) Vergil points out Nessus to Dante. Later Nessus is deputed by Chiron to escort Vergil and Dante and to show them the ford across the river Phlegethon.

See also: CENTAUR; DEIANIRA; HERACLES; HYDRA; IXION; OVID

2206

**Nestor** (newly speaking)   In Greek mythology, a wise man, son of Neleus and Chloris, noted for his eloquence during the Trojan War. Homer's *Iliad* (book 1) identifies Nestor as king of Pylos. His wife was Eurydice, according to Homer, but other sources name Anaxibia. He had two daughters and seven sons. According to late accounts, Nestor lived to be 300 years old, having

been blessed by Apollo, who added the years to compensate for the god's murder of the sons of Niobe and Amphion, Nestor's uncles. Nestor also appears in Homer's *Odyssey* (book 3), where he entertains Telemachus, the son of Odysseus. Nestor's tale is told in Ovid's *Metamorphoses* (book 12). He appears in Shakespeare's *Troilus and Cressida*.

See also: APOLLO; *ILIAD, THE*; NIOBE; ODYSSEUS; *ODYSSEY, THE*; TELEMACHUS

2207

**Net-net**   In Australian mythology, small, hairy, mischievous people who have claws instead of fingernails and toenails.

2208

**Neulam-kurrk**   In Australian mythology, an evil female spirit who kidnaps children and eats them.

2209

**Ngalalbal**   In Australian mythology, wife of the gigantic old god Baiame and mother of the creator god Daramulum.

See also: BAIAME

2210

**Ngallenyook**   In Australian mythology, an evil spirit who sends sickness. Medicine men cannot destroy Ngallenyook.

2211

**Ngarangs**   In Australian mythology, evil beings who resemble men, with long, flowing hair and beards. They live at the roots of old gum trees, coming out at night to capture victims, whom they eat.

2212

**Ngunung-ngunnut**   In Australian mythology, the bat who created the first woman to remedy the imbalance in nature in which only men existed, according to the Wotjobaluk.

See also: ABUK AND GARANG; ADAM AND EVE; ASK AND EMBLA; KHADAU AND MAMALDI

**2213**

**Ngunza**   In African mythology (Mbundu of Angola), a hero who captured Death. Ngunza was one of two brothers. While he was on a trip away from home, he dreamed that his brother had died. When he returned, his mother explained that Death had taken his brother. So Ngunza set a large trap to capture Death. When Death was caught, he begged to be set free, arguing that he was not responsible for killing people. Death said that it was invariably the fault of some human being, often the person himself. Death and Ngunza set off together to visit the land of the dead so that Ngunza could see this for himself. Ngunza found his brother living well, better than he had lived when he was on earth. Ngunza returned home and was given the seeds of all of the significant plants that grow in Angola. In time Death came looking for him. Ngunza resented the persistent way in which he was pursued by Death. Finally, however, Death threw an ax at Ngunza, who quickly died and turned into a spirit.

**2214**

**Nhangs**   In Armenian mythology, evil spirits, often in the form of mermaids, who lured people to their death. One Armenian commentary on the Bible calls Salome, the girl who danced for the head of St. John the Baptist, more bloodthirsty than "the Nhangs of the sea," referring to the belief that Nhangs, vampirelike, sometimes sucked the blood from their victims.

See also: MERMAID; SALOME

**2215**

*Nibelungenlied* (lay of the Nibelungs)   Thirteenth-century epic poem of 2,327 stanzas by an

*Siegfried and Kriemhild*

unknown Austrian. The work is divided into 39 adventures or chapters.

*First Adventure.* Three Burgundian princes, or Nibelungs, live at Worms on the Rhine. Their sister Kriemhild has a vision in which she sees two eagles pursue a falcon and tear it to pieces when it seeks refuge on her breast. Knowing her mother is skilled at interpreting dreams, Kriemhild asks her what the dream means. She is told that her future husband will be attacked.

*Second Adventure.* At Xantan on the Rhine, King Siegmund and his wife hold a tournament for the coming of age of their only son, Siegfried, who distinguishes himself greatly at the feast. His mother lavishes great gifts upon him.

*Third Adventure.* Siegfried hears of Kriemhild's beauty and goes to woo her, taking with him only 11 men. He arrives at Worms. Hagen, a cousin of King Gunther, Kriemhild's brother, tells the king that Siegfried once killed a dragon and now is the owner of the Nibelungen hoard (the dwarfs' gold). The hoard had belonged to two brothers, who asked Siegfried to divide it between them. He undertook the task in exchange for a sword, Balmung, which lay on top of the heap of gold. But no sooner had he made the division than the brothers killed one another, leaving Siegfried with the treasure.

On hearing that Siegfried has come to challenge Gunther to a duel, the Burgundians are very upset. They persuade Siegfried to disarm and stay as a guest for a year. Kriemhild watches Siegfried from a window and falls in love with him.

*Fourth Adventure.* Siegfried aids Gunther by defeating the kings of Saxony and Denmark. He defeats the enemy with only 1,000 men against their 4,000. When the messenger comes to announce Siegfried's victory, Kriemhild flushes with pleasure.

*Fifth Adventure.* A tournament is held at Worms in honor of the victory. Siegfried and Kriemhild meet face to face and fall in love. Siegfried then asks Gunther for Kriemhild's hand.

*Sixth Adventure.* Gunther bargains with Siegfried, asking that before he claims Kriemhild he should go with Gunther to Isenland and help him win Brunhild. Gunther needs Siegfried's help in wooing because Brunhild has vowed to marry only a man who can throw a spear and a stone farther than she can and surpass her in jumping. Siegfried, failing to dissuade Gunther, decides to accompany him on his quest and suggests that Hagen and another knight join them. Kriemhild provides them with handmade garments, and they reach Isenland 12 days later. As their ship nears the land, Siegfried asks his companions to tell everyone that he is Gunther's vassal, and he behaves as if that were his true station.

*Seventh Adventure.* Brunhild sees the ship arriving and believes Siegfried, who had come to her realm once before, has come to woo her. Siegfried guides Gunther and his men through a ring of fire to reach Brunhild's castle. When she realizes that it is Gunther who wishes to win her, she warns him that if he fails to hurl the spear and stone farther than she, he and his men must die. When Gunther sees Brunhild's spear, which

took 12 men to lift, he loses heart. Siegfried whispers in his ear not to fear but to go through the motions. Siegfried, concealed by his Tarnkappe, a cloak of invisibility, will accomplish the tasks. Siegfried does so, and Gunther wins Brunhild, though she is upset by the outcome.

*Eighth Adventure.* Brunhild summons to her castle a large number of warriors in the hope of not having to marry Gunther. Siegfried sails off to the land of the Nibelungs, forces them to recognize him as their lord, and brings 1,000 back with him to Isenland. When Brunhild sees his force she does not resist.

*Ninth Adventure.* The bride, escorted by all of the men, sails across the sea and up the Rhine. As they near Burgundy, Gunther decides to send word of their arrival. He persuades Siegfried to act as his messenger, assuring him that he will earn Kriemhild's gratitude.

*Tenth Adventure.* Siegfried marries Kriemhild, and the two couples sit side by side at an evening meal. When Gunther goes to their bedroom with Brunhild, she picks him up, hangs him on a peg, and leaves him there all night, taking him down in the morning. The next day all notice that Siegfried is radiant but Gunther is not at all happy. Gunther then tells Siegfried what happened. Siegfried says he will help by putting on his magic cloud cloak in the evening and teaching Brunhild how to treat her husband. That night Siegfried, unseen, follows Gunther and Brunhild into their room. When the lights are put out, he wrestles with Brunhild until she acknowledges herself beaten. She believes she is yielding to Gunther, but it is Siegfried who snatches her girdle and ring, before leaving Gunther alone with her. Once Brunhild has submitted to a man, she loses all of her miraculous power. Siegfried returns to Kriemhild, tells her all that happened, and gives her the girdle and ring.

*Eleventh Adventure.* Siegfried returns to Xantan with Kriemhild, and his parents relinquish the throne to them. They have a son.

*Twelfth Adventure.* Ten years pass, and Brunhild asks Gunther why Siegfried and Kriemhild have not visited them. Gunther invites the couple to visit.

*Thirteenth Adventure.* Siegfried and Kriemhild arrive with Siegmund, Siegfried's father. A feast is held, at which Brunhild curtly informs Kriemhild that Siegfried can scarcely be as great as Kriemhild pretends, since he is one of Gunther's vassals.

*Fourteenth Adventure.* Kriemhild denies this. Brunhild insists and declares she will prove her point at church when the two attend mass. Both women, angry, arrive simultaneously at mass escorted by imposing trains. Seeing Kriemhild make a motion to enter first, Brunhild bids her pause. The two get into a verbal duel. In the heat of the argument Kriemhild insinuates that Brunhild granted Siegfried sexual favors. She then shows her the girdle and ring. The men enter; Siegfried denies taking advantage of Brunhild. Brunhild refuses to listen, and Gunther refuses to avenge her. She finally persuades Hagen, her kinsman, to take up her quarrel. Believing Brunhild had been wronged by Siegfried, Hagen urges Gunther to kill Siegfried.

*Fifteenth Adventure.* Hagen devises a plan to kill Siegfried. He discovers that Siegfried is invulnerable, having bathed in the blood of the dragon Fafnir, except for one spot between his shoulders, where a linden leaf, sticking fast, prevented the blood from touching. Hagen tells Kriemhild to embroider a cross on her husband's garment over the spot to protect Siegfried. They then go off hunting in the Odenwald.

*Sixteenth Adventure.* The three, Gunther, Hagen, and Siegfried, race to a neighboring spring to drink. When Siegfried stoops over the spring to drink, Hagen runs a spear through the mark of the cross. Mortally wounded, Siegfried turns, grasps his shield, and hurls it at Hagen with such force that he dashes it to pieces. As he dies, he asks Gunther to take care of Kriemhild.

*Seventeenth Adventure.* The funeral train arrives at Worms. Hagen tells the bearers to lay Siegfried's body at Kriemhild's door. Kriemhild comes out in the morning to attend mass and falls over the body. Realizing it is her husband, she faints. The Nibelung knights arrive to carry the body to the minster, where Kriemhild insists that all those who took part in the hunt shall file past the body. It was believed that a dead man's wounds would bleed whenever his murderer drew near. Siegfried's wounds drop blood at Hagen's touch. Kriemhild publicly denounces him as the murderer, but he says he did his duty.

*Eighteenth Adventure.* Siegmund, the father of Siegfried, asks that Kriemhild come home to Xantan with him. Throughout it all, Brunhild shows no pity.

*Nineteenth Adventure.* Three years pass before Hagen suggests to Gunther that Kriemhild send for the Nibelung hoard, which was given her in marriage. Kriemhild consents, and the treasure arrives. It is so large that Hagen fears it will cause Kriemhild to become too independent, so he has it buried and tells no one its location but his masters.

*Twentieth Adventure.* Kriemhild is wooed by Rudiger for Etzel, king of Hungary. She accepts when Rudiger tells her Etzel will aid her in avenging Siegfried's death. Then, escorted by her faithful Ekkewart and carrying off with her the small portion of the Nibelungen treasure that still remains to her, she starts off for Hungary.

*Twenty-first Adventure.* Kriemhild proceeds on her way and is met on all sides by ovations of her future subjects.

*Twenty-second Adventure.* Kriemhild meets Etzel and other heroes, such as Dietrich of Bern. Under his escort they proceed to Vienna for the marriage festivities, which last 17 days.

*Twenty-third Adventure.* Seven years pass. Kriemhild has a son by Etzel, but she still grieves for Siegfried. One day she suggests that King Etzel invite her kinsmen to Hungary. When he consents, she gives special instructions to make sure that Hagen accompanies her brothers.

*Twenty-fourth Adventure.* Hagen is invited and comes fully armed, with an escort of 1,000 men.

*Twenty-fifth Adventure.* The Burgundians leave Brunhild and her son in the care of a steward and set out. As they are now the possessors of the Nibelung hoard, the poem terms them Nibelungs in the remainder of the work. Under the guidance of Hagen, who alone knows the way, the party reaches the banks of the Danube. They find no vessels to ferry them across, so Hagen asks them to wait until he can provide means of transportation.

Walking down to the river, he surprises three swan maidens bathing. He captures their garments and forces them to tell the future. Although one promises him sexual pleasures, her companions, having recovered their garments, warn Hagen that none of his party but a priest will return safely to Burgundy. They inform him that he can secure a boat by telling the ferryman on the opposite bank that his (Hagen's) name is Amalung. Hagen induces the ferryman to cross the river and springs into his boat before the man, discovering the trick, attacks him with his oar. Forced to defend himself, Hagen kills the man. He then proceeds to convey relays of the Burgundian army across the river. Casting off for the last crossing, Hagen notices the priest on board and, wishing to prove the swan maidens wrong, casts the cleric overboard. When the priest swims back to shore, Hagen realizes that none of the rest will return.

*Twenty-sixth Adventure.* The Burgundians continue their journey, and though warned by Ekkewart, they go on to visit Bishop Pilgrin and Rudiger.

*Twenty-seventh Adventure.* At Hagen's suggestion a marriage is arranged between Giseler, the youngest Burgundian prince, and Rudiger's daughter. Rudiger then guides the Burgundians to Etzel's court, where Kriemhild rejoices.

*Twenty-eighth Adventure.* Kriemhild meets the guests and asks Hagen for her gold. He says it will stay at the bottom of the Rhine until the Last Judgment. Hagen's men spend the next three days armed, fearing what is to come.

*Twenty-ninth Adventure.* Kriemhild asks her men to kill Hagen. She points him out and accuses him, but they are fearful of him and flee. Hagen then joins Etzel, who is portrayed as an old, inoffensive man.

*Thirtieth Adventure.* A night attack is made on Hagen, but again he frightens the Hungarians by his menacing glance.

*Thirty-first Adventure.* A tournament is held, at which the Huns and Burgundians argue. To calm them, Etzel invites the Burgundians to a banquet. They arrive fully armed.

*Thirty-second Adventure.* While the banquet is on, the Huns attack the Burgundians, who are outside.

*Thirty-third Adventure.* Hagen, hearing what has happened outside the banquet hall, takes out his sword and cuts off the head of Etzel and Kriemhild's child, which bounces into Kriemhild's lap. The king and queen are saved by Dietrich of Bern.

*Thirty-fourth Adventure.* The Burgundians pause after the slaughter but are again attacked by the Huns. Kriemhild cries that she will reward with gold anyone who will bring her Hagen's head.

*Thirty-fifth Adventure.* Attempts are made to kill Hagen, but all fail.

*Thirty-sixth Adventure.* Kriemhild orders the hall where the Burgundians are holding out to be set afire. It is built of stone, and they quench the fire with the blood of the dead and even drink the blood.

*Thirty-seventh Adventure.* Rudiger, in obedience to Kriemhild, enters the hall. Gernot, one of Kriemhild's brothers, and Rudiger slay each other.

*Thirty-eighth Adventure.* More battle ensues, and of the Burgundians only Hagen and Gunther remain alive.

*Thirty-ninth Adventure.* Dietrich enters the hall and attacks Hagen. He captures him and brings him to Kriemhild.

"Fair and noble Kriemhild," thus Sir Dietrich
   spake,
"Spare this captive warrior who full amends
   will make
For all his past transgressions; him here in
   bonds you see;
Revenge not on the fetter'd th'offences of the
   free."

While Dietrich is securing Gunther, Kriemhild, left alone with Hagen, again demands her treasures. Hagen answers that, having promised never to reveal its hiding place as long as his lords live, he cannot reveal the secret to her. Kriemhild, who now is insane, orders the death of her brother Gunther. She carries his head to Hagen as proof that there is no reason to keep the secret. Hagen still will not tell her, so she cuts off his head with Siegfried's sword. Neither Etzel nor the hero Hildebrand is quick enough to stop Kriemhild when her fierceness overpowers them. Hildebrand then kills Kriemhild.

This epic was very popular with German Romantic poets and dramatists. In 1810 Friedrich Heinrich Karl La Motte-Fouqué wrote a Nibelungen trilogy titled *The Hero of the North*. It consisted of *Sigurd the Dragon Slayer*, *Sigurd's Revenge*, and *Aslauga*. Ernst Raupach wrote a five-act drama with a prologue called *The Nibelungen Hoard*, and Emanuel Geibel's drama *Brunhild* dealt with the love of Brunhild and Siegfried. Christian Friedrich Hebbel's trilogy *The Nibelungen* was followed by *Sigfrid and Chriemhilde* by Wegener and later by *Sigfrid Sage*, the first part of Wilhelm Jordan's epic poem entitled *Die Nibelunge*; the second part, *Hildebrant's Homecoming*, appeared in 1874. Richard Wagner's great *Der Ring des Nibelungen*, although using many of the names from the *Nibelungenlied*, actually follows the plot of the *Volsunga Saga*.

See also: BALMUNG; BRYNHILD; DIETRICH OF BERN; ETZEL; NIBELUNGS; *RING DES NIBELUNGEN, DER*; TARNKAPPE; *VOLSUNGA SAGA*

2216

**Nibelungs**   In Norse mythology, the dwarfs or elves who possessed a hoard of gold and lived in the land of mist (Nebel). In the Norse *Volsunga Saga* Nibelung is the son of Hogni and grandson of Giuki. In later Norse myth the name Nibelungs is used for the followers of Sigurd (Siegfried), since he possessed the gold ring crafted by

the dwarfs. It is also used in the Germanic epic *Nibelungenlied* for the Burgundians under King Gunther. In *Der Ring des Nibelungen* Richard Wagner uses *Nibelungs* for the gnomes, dwarfs, or elves, such as Alberich and Mime. They are portrayed in Arthur Rackham's illustrations for Wagner's Ring Cycle.

See also: *NIBELUNGENLIED*; *RING DES NIBELUNGEN, DER*; SIEGFRIED; SIGURD

*St. Nicholas (Dürer)*

2217

**Nicholas, St.** (victory people, prevailing among the people)    Died 350. In Christian legend, bishop of Myra; as Santa Claus, patron saint of children, patron of bankers, captives, pawnbrokers, Russia, Aberdeen, Greek fishermen, and sailors. Feast, 6 December.

According to legend, Nicholas was born of Christian parents in their old age. As soon as he was born he arose in his bath and joined his hands, praising God that he had been brought into the world. From that day on he would only nurse at his mother's breast on Wednesdays and Fridays. When he was still young, his parents died and left all of their wealth to Nicholas. The saint devised means to get rid of the money. *The Golden Legend*, a collection of saints' lives written in the 13th century by Jacobus de Voragine, tells how the saint gave gold to save three girls who would have to become whores if they did not have doweries.

After this episode, the see of the bishop of Myra was vacant, and the Church assembled to choose a successor. One bishop had a dream that the first man who should come through the church doors should be consecrated bishop. Nicholas walked through the doors and was therefore chosen.

St. Nicholas's role as patron of sailors is related to the legend that when a ship on the way to the Holy Land was about to be destroyed, the sailors called on St. Nicholas, who appeared to them and stilled the storm. He was said to have been at the Council of Nicea (325), where he struck Arius on the jaw.

At the Reformation his feast day was abolished in many Protestant countries, but when the Dutch Protestants came to establish the colony of New Amsterdam they still celebrated the old "visit of St. Nicholas" the night before 6 December. When the English took over New Amsterdam and renamed it New York, the custom stayed, and the visitor was called Sinter Klaas. Since he appeared as a bishop and many English Protestants disliked the idea of a bishop, St. Nicholas was stripped of his ecclesiastical robes and turned into a figure that combined the old saint with that of the Germanic god Thor. The feast day was then moved to Christmas. The final development of the legend was the poem *A Visit from St. Nicholas* by Clement Clarke Moore, which became the standard version of the legend.

St. Nicholas was removed from the calendar of saints of the Roman Catholic Church in 1969.

See also: *GOLDEN LEGEND, THE*; THOR

2218
**Nicodemus** (conqueror of the people)    First century. In the Bible, N.T., a Pharisee and member of the Sanhedrin, or Jewish governing body, who followed Jesus but in secret. Nicodemus assisted at the burial of Jesus and brought a mixture of myrrh and aloes to anoint Jesus' body (John 19:39). In paintings of the Eastern Church he is often shown in portrayals of the descent from the cross and the entombment of Christ. In some paintings he is shown bending down, extracting one or more nails from Jesus' feet and placing them in a basket, the so-called Basket of Nicodemus.

2219
**Nidaba**    In Near Eastern mythology (Sumerian), grain goddess who brought the arts of civilization to humankind.

2220
**Nidhogg** (Nithogg, Niohoggr) (hateful)    In Norse mythology, the dragon in Nifelheim at the foot of the cosmic tree, Yggdrasill; he gnaws at its roots. The squirrel Ratatosk "runs up and down the ash," according to the *Prose Edda*, "and seeks to cause strife between the eagle and Nidhogg." In some accounts Nidhogg is described as a flying dragon that eats corpses.

See also: NIFELHEIM; *PROSE EDDA*; RATATOSK; YGGDRASILL

2221
**Nidra** (sleep)    In Hindu mythology, a personification of sleep, sometimes said to be a female form of the god Brahma. Other accounts say Nidra was produced at the Churning of the Ocean, when the gods and demons sought the Amrita, or water of life.

See also: AMRITA; BRAHMA; CHURNING OF THE OCEAN

2222
**Nifelheim** (world of fog)    In Norse mythology, the ancient underworld, the land of dark, cold, and mist; distinguished from Hel, the land of the dead. Odin cast Hel into Nifelheim, where

she had her domain. In the midst of Nifelheim was Hvergelmir (bubbling caldron), the fountain from which and to which all waters found their way. From Hvergelmir flowed the river Elivagar (rivers whipped by passing showers). Nifelheim was located at the foot of the world tree, Yggdrasill, and was the home of Nidhogg the dragon and of the Fenrir wolf. Nifelheim appears in the *Prose Edda*.

See also: ELIVAGAR; FENRIR; HEL; NIDHOGG; YGGDRASILL; *PROSE EDDA*

**2223**

**Nightingale**    A small migratory thrush noted for its song, which is a warning to all other male nightingales to stay out of the singer's territory, as well as being an invitation to the females to join the male. In Greek mythology Philomila was transformed into a nightingale. The nightingale is often associated with death, as in Keats's "Ode to a Nightingale." Hans Christian Andersen's tale "The Nightingale" has the bird bargain with death to save the Chinese emperor's life. Stravinsky's opera *The Nightingale* is based on Andersen's tale.

See also: PHILOMILA

**2224**

*Nihongi* (*Nihonshoki*) (Chronicles of Japan) Japanese Shinto book completed in 720. It is longer than the earlier *Kojiki*, the original authoritative work on Japanese Shinto, but contains many of the same myths, often giving variant accounts. Many of the gods appear under different names or are rendered in Chinese characters. The *Nihongi* traces myth, legend, and history up to 697.

See also: *KOJIKI*

**2225**

**Nijuhachi Bushu**    General term in Japanese mythology for the 28 gods who symbolize the constellations. The group is generally made up of the following: Basosennin, Daibenzaiten,

Naraen, Misshakukongo, Daibonten, Teishakuten, Makeshura, Tohoten, Konshikikujaku, Zochoten, Bishamon-ten, Mawaraten, Mansenshao, Shimmoten, Gobujo, Nadaryu-o, Karura-o, Kinnara-o, Magora-o, Ashira-o, Konda-o, Kendatsuba, Shakara-o, Kompira-o, Mansen-o, Sanshi-taisho, Hibakara-o.

**2226**

**Nike** (victory)    In Greek mythology, winged goddess of victory called Victoria by the Romans. In Hesiod's *Theogony* (383) Nike is said to be the daughter of the Titan Pallas and Styx and sister of Zelos (eager rivalry), Kratos (strength), and Bia (force). There are numerous references to Nike in Greek literature because she was closely associated with Athena. Sometimes Athena was worshiped as Athena Nike. Whereas Athena was the goddess of wisdom, Nike was the embodiment of victory in athletic and musical contests, as well as in battle. In one ancient Greek work, the Bacchylides *Fragment XI*, her role is clearly stated: "Nike, dispenser of sweet gifts, standing beside Zeus on Olympus, bright with gold, allots to mortals and the immortals the prize of valor." The most famous statue of the goddess is the Nike of Samothrace, now in the Louvre. Roman art often portrayed the goddess as the symbol of victory over death, and these statues may have influenced early Christian art.

See also: ATHENA; HESIOD; PALLAS; STYX; TITANS; VICTORIA; ZEUS

**2227**

**Nikitch, Dobrynya**    In Russian history and folklore a brave and fierce warrior, second only to Ilya Muromets. He was also a good singer and skillful chess player. He defeats the dragon Zmei Gorynytch, but he unwisely spares the creature from death. The dragon then abducts Princess Zabava, and Dobrynya sets out to rescue her and kill the dragon. His quest takes him down into the underworld before he finds and kills Zmei and his female companion. One *bylina* called

"Dobrynya and Aloisha" is clearly based on the Odysseus and Penelope story. When Dobrynya departs to slay the dragon, he tells his wife of only one day that he will be gone for seven years. He asks her to wait for him. When her husband does not return after more than the seven years, his wife is forced to make plans to marry Aloisha Popovich. On the wedding day Dobrynya returns, but in disguise, and reveals himself at the wedding by dropping his ring, into the wedding cup. His wife recognizes the ring, and the wedding is halted. Other *bylyni* tell of his fights with the dragon Gornynych and of his search for a bride for Prince Vladimir. According to legend, he is finally beaten by a giant female warrior, but in history he was killed fighting the Tatars at the battle of Kalka in 1224.

See also: ALIOSHA POPOVICH; BYLYNA; DRAGON; ILYA MUROMETS

2228
**Nikkal**  In Near Eastern mythology (Canaanite), goddess of the fruits of the earth; daughter of Hiribi, god of summer; and wife of Yarikh, the moon god. Her marriage to Yarikh is celebrated in an ancient poem in which the Kathirat, wise goddesses, act to settle the marriage affair, and Hiribi acts as an intermediary for the bridal payment.

2229
**Nine Worlds**  In Norse mythology, the worlds that made up the cosmos, watched over by Odin. They are Asgard, the home of the Aesir gods; Vanaheim, the home of the Vanir gods; Midgard, the home of humankind; Alfheim, the home of the light dwarfs or elves; Jotunheim, the home of giants; Svartalfaheim, the home of the dark elves; Nifelheim, the land of dark, cold, and mist; the ninth is unknown, though some accounts say it is Nithavellir, the land of the dwarfs.

See also: ALFHEIM; ASGARD; JOTUNHEIM; MIDGARD; NIFELHEIM

2230
**Nine Worthies, The**  In medieval European folk belief, a series of nine ideal types of people, taken from the Bible, the Greek and Roman world, and the Middle Ages. The nine worthies represent a numerical configuration drawing on the mystery of the number three and its square. They are usually listed as three Jews, Joshua, David, Judas Maccabaeus, all from the Bible; three pagans, Hector, Alexander the Great, and Julius Caesar from the Greek and Roman world; and three Christians, King Arthur, Charlemagne, and Godfrey of Bouillon from the Middle Ages.

The most extensive literary treatment in English literature is found in *Morte Arthure* (c. 1360). They are portrayed on a panel piece at the Chateau Coucy in France, in the Hansa Saal in the cathedral in Cologne, in the Schöner Brunnen in Nürnberg in Germany, and in tapestries in the Cloisters Museum in New York City.

See also: ARTHUR

2231
**Ninib** (Nerig, Nineb, Nin-ip, Nirig)  In Near Eastern mythology (Babylonian), god of the summer sun who opposes Marduk, the hero god and god of the spring sun and vegetation.

See also: MARDUK

2232
**Ninurta** (Ningirsu, Nimurta, Nimurash)  In Near Eastern mythology (Sumero-Akkadian), war god and patron of hunting, son of Enlil or Bel and Innini. He was called "the arrow, the mighty hero." Some scholars believe that Nimrod in the Old Testament (Gen. 10:9) is a variant for Ninurta. Ninurta's symbol was an eagle with outstretched wings.

See also: BEL

2233
**Ni-o** (kings of compassion)  In Japanese Buddhist mythology, fierce warrior gods at the gates of temples, whose duty is to prevent evil spirits

from entering. They stem from Hindu mythology, being representations of the gods Indra and Brahma.

See also: BRAHMA; INDRA

*Niobe*

**Niobe** (snowy)    In Greek mythology, daughter of Tantalus and Dione; wife of Amphion; mother of 10 sons and 10 daughters (some accounts say six or seven). Niobe taunted Leto, mother of Apollo and Artemis, for having only two children. As punishment all of Niobe's children except Chloris, wife of Neleus and mother of Nestor, were killed by Apollo and Artemis. The Olympians buried the children, and Niobe was transformed into stone, still dripping tears on Mount Sipylus in Lydia. Niobe's myth appears in Homer's *Iliad* (book 24), Hesiod's *Theogony*, and Ovid's *Metamorphoses* (book 6). In Dante's *Divine Comedy* (Purgatory, canto 12) Niobe figures among the examples of defeated Pride, one of the Seven Deadly Sins in Christianity. Shakespeare's *Hamlet* has the hero say of his mother, "Like Niobe, all tears," referring to Gertrude's tears over her dead husband. Byron's *Childe Harold's Pilgrimage* calls Rome "the Niobe of Nations." Ancient Greek and Roman statues often portray Niobe's vain attempt to save her children from the deities' wrath. David, the French classical artist, painted the death of the children.

See also: APOLLO; ARTEMIS; HESIOD; *ILIAD, THE*; NESTOR; OVID

2235

**Nirvana** (gone out [as a flame], extinction [of passion], cooled, rolled up or away, blowing away or extinguishing)    In Buddhism, the state of enlightenment and liberation, often confused by some Western writers with a sort of Christianlike heaven. D. T. Suzuki writes in his study *Outlines of Mahayana Buddhism* that Nirvana "is the annihilation of the notion of ego-substance and of all desire that arises from this erroneous conception. But this represents the negative side of the doctrine, and its positive side consists in universal love or sympathy (*karuna*) for all beings. These two aspects of Nirvana (i.e., negatively, the destruction of evil passions, and positively, the practice of sympathy) are complementary to each other; and when we have one we have the other."

In Jain mythology Nirvana is the place of liberated souls at "the ceiling of the universe where they live in unconscious, eternal bliss." Nirvana is described negatively as the destruction of the passions and positively as the attainment of selfless bliss. Death after Nirvana is called parinirvana (final Nirvana) and is not followed by rebirth. In Pali it is called Nibbana. The chief characteristic of existence is suffering, and therefore Nirvana is the cessation of suffering. By practicing self-discipline an individual can put an end to passion and craving. When these are extinguished, no more karma is generated and there is no further rebirth. When rebirth stops, an individual has realized Nirvana.

2236

**Nithavellir** (the dark fields)  In Norse mythology, the home of the dwarfs, according to some accounts. Some scholars believe the term should be Nitafjoll (the dark crags).

See also: ALFHEIM; NINE WORLDS

2237

**Nitten**  In Japanese Buddhist mythology, sun goddess, derived from the Hindu god Surya. She is portrayed holding a lotus, on the calyx of which reposes a sphere, symbol of the sun. She is one of the Jiu No O, 12 Japanese Buddhist gods and goddesses adopted from Hindu mythology.

See also: JIU NO O; SURYA

2238

**Nivata-Kavachas**  In Hindu mythology, sea giants "clothed in impenetrable armor" who lived in the depths of the sea. According to the epic poem *The Mahabharata*, there were some 30 million of them.

See also: MAHABHARATA, THE

2239

**Nixie** (Nix, Nixe)  In Germanic folklore, a watery being who is often unfriendly to humans, causing them to drown. They are capable of assuming various forms, and they sometimes marry humans. They are usually depicted as marine creatures, half woman and half fish, and are allied to the Sirens of classical antiquity. In some parts of Germany it is considered bad luck to save a drowning person because the person has been fated as an offering to the nixies, who must have at least one human sacrifice per year.

See also: MELUSINA; MERMAID; SIRENS

2240

**Njinyi** (he who is everywhere)  In African mythology (Bamum of Cameroon), creator god who allowed death to take human life. Njinyi created humans healthy and strong but discovered that in time they died. So he went to Death and asked him if he were responsible for killing people. Death said people really wanted to die, and he would prove it to Njinyi. They went to a roadside, and Njinyi hid behind a tree while Death sat underneath it. Soon an old slave passed by, mumbling to himself, "I wish I had never been born. It's better to be dead." No sooner had the words left his mouth than he fell down dead. Next came an old woman, complaining of her sad lot and wishing she were dead. As soon as she uttered the words, she fell down dead. "Look," said Death to Njinyi, "people want to die. They call me." So Njinyi left, sad that humankind choose death instead of life.

2241

**Njord** (Niord, Njordhr) (humid)  In Norse mythology, one of the Vanir; god of winds, sea, fire, and wealth; husband of his sister Nerthus; father of Frey and Freyja. When Njord went to Asgard, he married Skadi, but she preferred living in her father's home Thrymheim, and Njord loved to reside at his home, Noatun (ships' heaven). According to the *Prose Edda*, "They at last agreed that they should pass together nine nights in Thrymheim, and then three in Noatun." The *Prose Edda* says that Njord "is so wealthy that he can give possessions and treasures to those who call on him for them." The kenning for a sponge is "Njord's glove."

See also: FREY; FREYJA; IDUNA; KENNING; SKADI

2242

**No** (Noh)  Stylized Japanese drama, using masks, that had its beginnings in the 14th century.

Many No plays are Buddhist on Shinto texts, which contain numerous myths and legends, though some are based on secular works, such as the *Tales of the Heike Clan*. One of the most famous No plays is *Aoi-no-ue* by Zeami Motokiyo, written in the 14th century, about a "revengeful ghost." In it Lady Aoi is freed from a sinister incubus, while the ghost of Princess Rokujo, her dead rival in love for Prince Genji, is delivered from the evil spirit haunting her and allowed to enter into the Buddhist paradise. Another play by Zeami Motokiyo, *Takasago*, tells of two pine trees inhabited by gods.

*Sotoba Kimachi* (Komachi and the Gravestone) by Kan'nami Kiyotsugo (1333–1384) tells of an old woman who sits on a *stupa*, a sacred symbol of Buddha. She is accused by a Buddhist priest of sacrilege but tells him all things are sacred, both she and the old *stupa*. Suddenly she goes insane, seeing her old lover, but recovers in time to know she will die and enter the Buddhist paradise.

2243
**Noah** (rest)    In the Bible, O.T. (Gen. 6–9), the son of Lamech; a tenth-generation descendant of Adam, who saved himself and his family during the Great Flood. God entrusted Noah with the construction of an ark or houseboat. Noah took his family and various animals aboard as God sent the floods to destroy all life. When the waters finally began to subside, the ark rested on Mount Ararat, and Noah sent a raven and a dove to determine the degree the waters had receded. The dove returned with a bit of an olive branch, which showed that the waters had abated. God directed Noah to disembark with everything in the ark. Noah erected an altar and made sacrifice, and God blessed him and his sons. Noah was also the first to make wine and is often portrayed as drunken. Various scenes from his life popular with artists are the building of the ark, the Flood, the sacrifice of Noah, and the drunkenness of Noah. Benjamin Britten's cantata *Noyes Fludde* is based on a medieval English play. In Islam Noah is called Nuh, and his story is told in the Koran (sura 2).

Sailors refer to a white band of clouds shaped something like the hull of a ship as "Noah's Ark."

If the clouds go from east to west, sailors expect dry weather; if they go from north to south, sailors expect wet weather.

See also: ADAM AND EVE; LAMECH; RAVEN

2244
**No-no-Kami**    In Japanese mythology, god of the fields and plant life in general.

*Norns*

2245
**Norns** (pronouncers)    In Norse mythology, the fates, women who determine the fate of each person. Three—Urd (past), Verdandi (present), and Skuld (future)—live near a fountain under the massive ash Yggdrasill, the world tree. "These maidens fix the lifetime of all men," according to the *Prose Edda*. "But there are, indeed, many other Norns, for, when a man is born, there is a Norn to determine his fate. Some are known to be of heavenly origin, but others belong to the races of elves and dwarfs." They appear in the *Poetic Edda*, the *Prose Edda*, and Richard Wagner's *Götterdämmerung*, the last music drama of *Der Ring des Nibelungen*. They also appear in Thomas Gray's poem *The Fatal Sisters: An Ode*. In Germanic folklore they appear as fairy godmothers or three spinners.

See also: *POETIC EDDA*; *PROSE EDDA*; *RING DES NIBELUNGEN, DER*; SKULD; URD; VERDANDI; YGGDRASILL

2246
**Nostradamus, Michel**    (1503–1566). A French astrologer who published an annual

*Almanack.* He is still known today for his prophecies published in 1555 in *Centuries*. In 1781 his work was banned by the pope, but it is still often cited when disaster strikes. In 2001, when the World Trade Center was destroyed, frequent references to prophesies by Nostradamus appeared through electronic media, such as:

In the City of God there will be a great thunder,
Two brothers torn apart by Chaos,
while the fortress endures, the great leader will succumb,
The third big war will begin when the big city is burning. — Nostradamus 1654

The quatrain is not to be found in his published works but is a hoax. Nostradamus's vague and ambiguous language is so obscure that many people continue to find meaning in his prophecies.

2247
**Nott** (night)   In Norse mythology, a giantess whose first husband was Naglfar and second husband was Annar, a dwarf. She became the mother of Jord (the earth) and Dagr (day) by her second husband. Nott's horse was Hrimfaxi (frost-maned). Dagr and Nott had a carriage that went around the earth once a day.

See also: DAGR; JORD; NAGLFAR; SKINFAXI

2248
**Nox** (night)   Nyx in Greek, the Latin Nox in Greek and Roman mythology was daughter of Chaos and Darkness; wife of her brother Erebus (the covered pot, often identified with Hades) whose children were the three Fates, Thanatos, Sleep, Dreams, Care, Momus, the Hesperides, Nemesis, Discord, Fraud, Eris, and others. Nox is mentioned in Vergil's *Aeneid* (book 6), which deals with Aeneas's visit to the underworld. Nox is also mentioned in Hesiod's *Theogony*.

See also: *AENEID, THE;* HADES; HESIOD; HESPERIDES; NEMESIS; THANATOS

2249
**Nudd** (silver hand)   In Celtic mythology, a sea god and king of the Tuatha de Danann (people of the goddess Danu). Nudd lost one hand in battle, thus losing his throne because a maimed king could not rule. His hand was replaced by a silver artificial one, thereby regaining his throne for him and earning him the title Argetlam (the silver handed). Some scholars believe that Ludd, the British sea god, is an equivalent of Nudd, who also lost one hand, had it replaced by a silver artificial one, and was called Llawereint (silver handed). Ludd's temple in London was located near St. Paul's Cathedral, and Ludgate Hill is named after the god. Sometimes Ludd was known as Nudd in Britain.

See also: LUDD; TUATHA DE DANANN

2250
**Nuga** ( Nugu, Nugi)   In Melanesian mythology, the crocodile father of the Kiwaians. Nuga was originally carved from wood by a man named Ipila. While carving a wooden human figure, Ipila put some sago milk on its face, and the figure came to life. The first sound it made was that of a crocodile. Nuga asked Ipila to make three other men for him so that he would not be lonely. The men he made wanted more than sago for food, so they began killing animals. Soon they became half crocodile, and no one wanted anything to do with the crocodile men. They tried to reproduce, but only male children were born to them. From these poor beings descended those who claim the crocodile as ancestor. Ipila was displeased with his creations and forced Nuga to hold the earth on his shoulders forever.

See also: CROCODILE

2251
**Nules-murt**   In Finno-Ugric folklore, a forest spirit appearing in human form with one eye. Nules-murt can lengthen and shorten his body at will, though he usually prefers to be as tall as a tree. He lives in the forest with his vast treasures

of gold, silver, and cattle. Offerings are made to him by the people. Other spirits of the forest are Pales-murt (half man), who has half the body of a man; Yskal-pydo-murt (cow-footed man), an evil spirit; Surali, a hairy spirit; Cheremiss Kozla-ia, another forest spirit; and Ovda, an evil forest spirit who lives in the chasm in the rocks and ruins of old buildings. Nules-murt is also called Unt-Tongk and Mis-khun.

**2252**

**Numbakulla**    In Australian mythology, self-created sky gods who created humans from amorphous creatures.

**2253**

**Nummo** (Nommo)    In African mythology (Dogon of the Republic of Mali), twins, one male and one female, produced when Amma, or God, united with the Earth.

Amma, male, was lonely and came close to the female Earth for intercourse. The union was at first blocked by a red termite hill, which had to be removed. The resultant act was therefore imperfect, and a jackal was born instead of twins, which would have been the proper outcome. Amma and Earth united again, this time creating a cosmic egg with twin placenta, one male and one female, called Nummo; they were green, hairy, waterlike creatures. Their top halves were human and their bottom halves snakelike. They had forked tongues and red eyes. The Nummo went to Amma, their father, for instructions. He told them they were the essence of water. From heaven they saw that Earth was in need of help, so they came with heavenly plants, the fibers of which were used later by man to make clothing. Earth developed the basis of a language, but she was raped by her son, the jackal, who was jealous of his mother's possession of language. Amma then wanted to create things without the help of Earth, but the Nummo spirits drew male and female outlines on the ground to be sure that twin births would continue. As a result, all human beings have two souls at birth and are bisex-

ual. At circumcision the female spirit is removed from the male, and at excision the male spirit is removed from the female.

In heaven the Nummo spirits served as blacksmiths. Once an ancestor stole some of the sun from their smithy, and as he was escaping, the Nummo threw a thunderbolt at him. The ancestor slid down a rainbow to earth so fast that he broke both his arms and his legs. Since then men have joints at both elbows and knees. This first ancestor was a blacksmith, but with time others learned to develop other occupations.

See also: DA; MAWU LISA

**2254**

**Nunyunuwi** (dressed in stone)    In North American Indian mythology (Cherokee), cannibal monster whose body was covered with a skin of solid stone. Nunyunuwi loved to kill and eat hunters, but he could not bear the sight of menstruating women. In one myth, he came upon seven such women, and when he saw the last one, "blood poured from his mouth, and he fell down on the trail." The medicine men then drove seven sourwood stakes through his body and placed logs underneath him, which they ignited. As the fire burned, Nunyunuwi spoke "and told them the medicine for all kinds of sickness." When the fire had burned down, some red paint and a magic stone was left. The medicine man took the stone for himself, but the red paint he used to paint the faces and chests of the people. The red paint granted its wearer hunting success, skill, or a long life.

**2255**

**Nure Onna** (wet woman)    In Japanese folklore, a female ghost having long hair and a flickering tongue to taste the wind. For many Japanese she is the personification of all evil.

**2256**

**Nut** (Nout) (water)    In Egyptian mythology, goddess who personified the sky. Nut was the

*Nut*

wife of Geb, the earth god. Nut was also Geb's twin sister and copulated with him against the wishes of Ra. In revenge Ra had the couple separated by Shu, who held up the sky, and said that Nut could not bear any children during any month of the year. Thoth, the god of wisdom as well as scribe of the gods, took pity on Nut and constructed five epagomenal (new) days not part of the curse. Thoth played a board game with the moon and won sufficient light to create these five extra days. On these days Nut gave birth to Osiris, Horus, Set, Isis, and Nephthys, according to some texts. The sycamore was sacred to Nut. Each morning the sun god Ra passed between the goddess's two turquoise-colored sycamores at Heliopolis when he began his journey across the sky.

In Egyptian art Nut was usually portrayed as a woman bearing a vase of water on her head. She sometimes wears a headdress of horns and the disk of the goddess Hathor and holds a papyrus scepter in one hand and the ankh, symbol of life, in the other.

See also: GEB; HORUS; ISIS; NEPHTHYS; OSIRIS; RA; SET; SHU

2257
**Nut** Fruit of numerous trees; in European mythologies and folklores, often a symbol of fertility because of its resemblance to testicles. At weddings in ancient Rome the bridegroom would scatter nuts as he led his bride to the temple. This signified that the husband was giving up his childhood habits and sports. Catullus's *Carmen Nuptialis* says: "Give nuts to the slaves, boy; / your time is past. / You have played with nuts long enough." The nut's connection with childhood is symbolized in Jewish custom in a game children traditionally play at Passover in which nuts are the stakes. In Russian folklore, peasants would carry nuts in their purses as a charm to make money. In English folklore, the discovery of a double nut indicated that good fortune was on the way. To make sure of the good luck the finder had to eat one nut and throw the other over his or her shoulder.

See also: HAZEL; PASSOVER

2258
**Nyame** (shining one) In African mythology (Ashanti of Ghana), creator god, often symbolized by the moon or as Nyankopon, the sun. Lightning, Nyame's thunderbolts, are called God's axes. Stone axes are placed in sacred forked posts standing by doorways, and pots with special offerings are also made for the god. Nyame is the god to whom people confidently turn in times of stress and hardship. He creates in mankind an appetite for life and makes it worth living.

*A nymph*

**Nymphs** (young unmarried women)   In Greek mythology, lesser female spirits of nature, often cited as daughters of Zeus. Among the various nymphs were the oreads (mountain), dryads and hamadryads (tree nymphs), naiads (spirits of fountains and rivers), oceanides (spirits of the great stream Oceanus), and Nereids (50 daughters of Nereus who watched the Mediterranean). Though nymphs lived long, they were not immortal and often would fall in love with mortals. Among some of the most important nymphs were Echo, Arethusa, Oenone, Dryope, Calypso, Thetis, Amphitrite, and Panope. Nymphs are cited in Spenser's *Epithalamion* (37–39), Pope's *Rape of the Lock* (2.19–20), T. S. Eliot's *Waste Land* (178–183), Milton's "Lycidas" (50–51, 98–102) and his masque *Comus*, in which he invents a nymph he calls Sabrina.

See also: AMPHITRITE; ARETHUSA; CALYPSO; DRYADS; ECHO; NEREIDS; OCEANUS; OENONO; THETIS; ZEUS

**Nzambi**   In African mythology (Bakongo of Angola), bisexual creator god, identified with the sky and Mother Earth. Nyambe, Njambi, and Nzame are names by which the deity is known among other African tribes. The Bakongo people say: "He is made by no other, no one is beyond him." He shows kindness to even the most destitute members of society.

*Oak (Arthur Rackham)*

oracles after listening to the rustling of the oak leaves. In both Greek and Roman mythology, the first food of humankind was the acorn, seed of the oak. North American Indians, who ate acorns, believed the oak was a gift from Wy-ot, the firstborn of the sky and earth. In Germany, when St. Boniface wanted to convert the populace, one of his first acts was to destroy an oak tree sacred to the Druids. The oak was thought to be the home of demons, dragons, and dwarfs. In some northern areas the punishment for injuring an oak was to have one's navel cut out and nailed to the wound in the tree, then to have one's intestines wound around the tree. The expression "knock on wood" is based on the belief that gods dwelled in the trees and could be called upon by knocking on the trunk. In England Royal Oak Day, 29 May, commemorates the restoration of King Charles II; it is named for the oak that sheltered him in its thick branches when he was fleeing Cromwell's troops.

See also: BONIFACE, ST.; DRUIDS; JOVE; JUPITER; ZEUS

2261

**Oak**   A hardwood tree, sacred to the Greek sky god Zeus and his Roman counterpart, Jupiter or Jove. The oracle of Zeus at Dodona was located in an oak grove, where the priestess pronounced

2262

**Oakley, Annie**   1860–1926. In American history and folklore, stage name of Phoebe Anna Oakley Mozee, a markswoman and member of Buffalo Bill's Original Wild West Show. While the Wild West show was performing in Europe in 1890 and 1891, Crown Prince Wilhelm visited several times and watched Annie shoot the ashes off cigarettes. Intrigued, Wilhelm asked Annie to shoot his cigarette. Annie put the cigarette in Wilhelm's hand and not his mouth. Later it was said that if Annie had shot Wilhelm and not his cigarette, she could have prevented World War I. On 29 October 1901, two trains collided near Linwood, North Carolina. Five stock cars of horses and other animals belonging to Buffalo Bill's Wild West show were killed or mortally wounded. It was reported that Annie was so traumatized by the accident that her hair turned white within 17 hours. Another story says that Annie liked to visit an Arkansas Hot Springs resort. On one such visit in December 1901 or early January 1902, she was left alone by her attendant. After about 45 minutes, she fainted in her hot bath. Her hair turned white and her skin was speckled with brown spots.

Irving Berlin's *Annie Get Your Gun* starred Ethel Merman as Annie. The Hollywood film *Annie Oakley* starred Barbara Stanwyck. Annie Oakleys are free passes to a theatrical performance, so called because they usually have holes punched into them.

See also: BUFFALO BILL

**Obatala** (king of the white cloth)    In African mythology (Yoruba of southwestern Nigeria), second son of Olorun, the sky god, who helped create land on the water. He is Olorun's representative on earth and the one who shapes human beings. He is said to have founded the first Yoruba city, Ifé.

See also: OLORUN

**Oberon** (elf king)    In medieval European folklore, king of the elves or dwarfs, believed by some scholars to be derived from Alberich in Norse mythology. At his birth the fairies bestowed gifts on him: one gave him insight into men's thoughts, and another gave him the power to transport himself to any place instantaneously. Oberon appears in the medieval French romance *Huon of Bordeaux*, in which he is said to be the son of Julius Caesar and Morgan le Fay, the sister of King Arthur. Shakespeare uses him in *Midsummer Night's Dream*, Christoph Martin Wieland in his *Oberon* (1780), and he is the subject of Karl Maria von Weber's opera *Oberon*.

See also: ARTHUR

**Obumo**    In African mythology (Ibibios of southern Nigeria), the thunder god, usually regarded as the principal deity and the creator of all things. His home is in the sky. Being too far away to trouble about the petty affairs of men, he leaves these in the hands of lesser powers, reserving to himself the ordering of the great events of the years, such as the succession of the seasons. At the beginning of the rainy season Obumo descends in the form of a fish hawk to woo his terrestrial wife, Eka Abassi.

See also: EKA ABASSI; OBATALA

**Oceanus**    In Greek mythology, an early sea god, eldest son of Uranus and Gaea; married to his Titan sister Tethys; father by Tethys of the 3,000 sea nymphs, Oceanides, and other sea gods. Originally portayed as a great river encircling the disk of the earth and flowing back into itself, as portayed encircling the outer rim of the shield of Achilles in the *Iliad* (book 18). Later, the name of the great outer sea (as opposed to the inner sea, the Mediterranean). Among his children are Doris, Eidyia, Electra, Callirrhoë, Perseis, Proteus, Pleione, Styx, Inachus, Melia, Meliboea, Arethusa, and Fortuna. Oceanus appears in Aeschylus's *Prometheus Bound*, and his 3,000 sea-nymph daughters inspired Jean Sibelius's tone poem *Oceanides* (1914).

See also: ARETHUSA; CALLIRRHOË; DORIS; ELECTRA; FORTUNA; GAEA; HOMER; *ILIAD, THE*; STYX; TITANS; URANUS

**2267**

**Odhrerir** (Odherir, Odhroerir, Odrorir) (heart stirrer)  In Norse mythology, a magic kettle containing a magic potion, the mead of poets. It was prepared by the dwarfs Fjalar and Galar from honey mingled with the blood of Kvasir, the wisest of men, who had been created from the spittle of the Aesir and Vanir gods. (The treaty of peace between the two groups had been sealed by each side spitting into a vessel.) The drink conferred wisdom and knowledge of runes and magic charms, as well as poetic facility. Odin, the chief Aesir god, was aware of its power and transformed himself into a snake to capture the mead. It was under the control of the giant Suttung, whose daughter Gunlod guarded it. In his snake form Odin bored his way through a rock to where Gunlod sat on her golden stool. She let the snake drink as it lay in her arms for three days. Having drained the caldron dry, Odin flew away in the form of an eagle. When he arrived in Asgard, he spit the drink into a vessel. Odhrerir was also known as Eldhrimir.

See also: AESIR-VANIR WAR; BAUGI; KVASIR; SUTTUNG

**2268**

**Odin** (Othin) (leader of the possessed, frenzy) In Norse mythology, one-eyed chief of the Aesir gods; god of wisdom and war; son of Bor and the giantess Bestla; brother of Vili and Ve (or Hoenir and Lodur); married to Frigga; father of Thor (Tyr) and Baldur. Odin was called Voden, Woden, Wotan, Wuotan, or Votan in Germanic and Anglo-Saxon mythologies. The *Prose Edda* describes Odin as the god who "governs all things."

Odin was the wisest of the gods, and all the other deities came to him for advice. He drew his wisdom from the well of the giant Mimir. Odin gave up one of his eyes to Mimir as a pawn to gain wisdom and was sometimes portrayed as a one-eyed old man. Occasionally, however, he appears as a heroic man with a spear and shield. In Valhalla and Vingolf Odin gave elaborate banquets, but he only drank wine, which was all he needed to sustain himself. The meat served to the god was given to his wolves, Freki and Geri (the greedy one). Odin had two ravens called Hugin (thought) and Munin (mind) that perched on his shoulders. Every day they flew forth throughout the universe and brought news home to the god. Odin was often called God of Ravens. From his throne Hlithskjalf in Valaskkalf, the god could see everything pass before him. His horse was Sleipnir, an eight-footed animal; his spear was called Gungnir and could hit anything aimed at; and on his arm he wore a precious ring, Draupner, from which dropped eight other rings every nine nights.

It is believed that part of Odin's worship consisted of human sacrifices. It was believed that the god once hung on a gallows, wounded with the thrust of a spear, and thus gained wisdom. Some of his worshipers were hung on gallows in the same manner. Odin was called God of Hanged Men or Lord of the Gallows because of this. He would tell one of his ravens to fly to the hanged man, or he would go himself to talk to the man. An 11th-century account by Adam of Bremen tells of a sacrificial grove near a temple at Uppsala where human bodies hung from the branches of the sacred trees.

*Odin (W. G. Collingwood)*

Among the many kennings for the god are Ygg (the awful), Gagnrad (he who determines victories), Herjan (god of battles), Veratyr (lord of men), Har (the high one), Jafnhar (even as high), Thridi (third), Bileyg (one with evasive eyes), Baleyg (one with flaming eyes), Bolverk (the worker of misfortune, applied to Odin's role in granting or not granting victory to his followers), Sigfather (the father of battle or of victory), Gaut (the creator), and Tveggi (the twofold). Odin appears as Wotan in Wagner's *Der Ring des Nibelungen* and is portrayed in Arthur Rackham's illustrations for Richard Wagner's Ring Cycle.

See also: AESIR; AUDHUMLA; BALDUR; HLITHSK-JOLF; KENNING; MIMIR; *RING DES NIBELUNGEN, DER*; VALHALLA

*Odysseus offering the Cyclops wine*

2269

**Odysseus** (sufferer)   In Greek mythology, a hero, king of Ithaca, son of Laertes or Sisyphus and Anticleia; married to Penelope; father of Telemachus. Noted for his cleverness and strength, he appears in Homer's *Iliad* and *Odyssey*. The Latin name form Ulysses (or Ulixes) was used by the Romans, evidently from a dialect where *od-* was pronounced *ol*.

Odysseus began to demonstrate his heroic strength at an early age. Once when his grandparents came to visit him, Odysseus saved them from a wild boar attack. He killed the boar, but not before he had been wounded on the knee, which left a permanent scar. He received his mighty bow from Heracles' friend Iphitus, whose father, Eurytus, had given it to him. Only Odysseus with his massive strength could string the bow. When he reached manhood, his father, Laertes, gave up the throne, and Odysseus became king. He tried to win Helen's hand, failed, and later married Penelope, who bore him a son, Telemachus. While Telemachus was still a baby, the Trojan War broke out, and Odysseus, not wishing to honor his vow to fight, pretended to be insane. He yoked a horse and cow together and pretended to plow when the officials came to call him to the war. To test if he were really mad, the officials placed the infant Telemachus in the way of the plow, and Odysseus immediately stopped plowing, so he was judged sane and recruited. His mission was to convince Achilles to join the war. During the Trojan War Odysseus mediated the quarreling between Agamemnon and Achilles, rescued the body of Achilles, and was awarded his armor. When the Trojan prophet Helenus was captured and asked what the Greeks must do to win the war, he named three things: enlist Neoptolemus, the son of Achilles, to fight; capture the bow and arrows of Heracles; and capture the Palladium, the sacred statue of Athena that protected Troy. Odysseus succeeded in all three tasks. Finally, prompted by Athena, he proposed the trick of the wooden horse, which destroyed Troy.

After Troy fell, the Greeks set out for home. Odysseus, who had offended the sea god Poseidon, was not allowed to return home for 10 years. His adventures from that point form the basis of Homer's *Odyssey*. A later myth, not recorded in Homer, tells how Odysseus grew tired of simple home life and set out again, seeking adventure, and how he later died at sea. Dante's *Divine Comedy* (Inferno, canto 26), using the Latin name form, places Ulysses among the Fraudulent Counselors because of the wooden horse. Dante has Ulysses tell how he and a few companions set out beyond the Pillars of Heracles to gain experience of the world and see human goodness and evil, telling his men: "You were not made to live like beasts, but to follow virtue and knowledge." The crew reached the Mount of Purgatory, where a storm destroyed the ship, and Ulysses died. In medieval literature Odysseus is generally seen as a dishonest rogue. He appears as such in the *Tale of Troy*, a medieval reworking of the Greek legends, and in Gower's *Confession amantis* he appears as a magician who was taught his skills by Calypso and Circe, two enchantresses. Tennyson's "Ulysses" is a poem treating the Dante myth. The major modern work dealing with the character is James Joyce's novel *Ulysses*, in which Leopold Bloom is a modern-day Ulysses. Nikos Kazantzakis's epic *The Odyssey: A Sequel* takes up where Homer's *Odyssey* leaves off. Other works that treat Odysseus are Shakespeare's *Troilus and Cressida*, Monteverdi's opera *Il ritorno d'Ulisse* (The Return of Ulysses), Giraudoux's *Tiger at the Gates*, and Gide's *Philoctète*.

See also: ACHILLES; ATHENA; HERACLES; *ILIAD, THE*; *ODYSSEY, THE*; PENELOPE; SISYPHUS; TELEMACHUS

2270

**Oedipus** (swollen foot)   In Greek mythology, son of Jocasta and King Laius of Thebes; he unknowingly killed his father and married his mother. An oracle had informed Laius and Jocasta that their son would bring about the death of Laius, his father. When Oedipus was born, Laius had the boy exposed to die on the slopes of Mount Cithaeron, his ankles pierced by a long pin. The baby was rescued by a shepherd, who took him to King Polybus of Corinth, who brought the boy up as his own son. Hearing rumors that Polybus was not his natural father, Oedipus went to Delphi to ask the oracle of Apollo his true parentage. The oracle informed him that he would cause the death of his father and marry his mother but did not reveal that Laius and Jocasta were his natural parents.

Oedipus then left Corinth and became a wanderer. One day on a narrow road in the mountains, Oedipus met Laius, who was himself returning from the oracle at Delphi. Oedipus blocked the narrow road, not letting Laius or his servants pass. A confrontation ensued, and one of Laius's servants killed one of Oedipus's horses. In a rage the young man killed not only the servant but King Laius as well. Thus, the first part of the oracle was fulfilled, although Oedipus was completely unaware of the fact. He then arrived in Thebes, where he discovered that the city was being ravaged by the Sphinx, a winged monster with the body of a lion and the head and breasts of a woman. The Sphinx would ask travelers a riddle, then cast them from a high rock when they did not answer correctly. The Sphinx asked Oedipus the riddle: "What animal in the morning goes on four feet, at noon on two, and in the evening on three?" Oedipus replied that it was man who went on all fours when a child, on two feet as a man, and on three (two feet plus a staff) as an old man. The Sphinx was so infuriated at being outwitted that she threw herself off the rock and was killed. The people of Thebes, unaware that Oedipus was the killer of Laius, offered him the throne and Jocasta, Laius's widow, as a reward for saving Thebes from the Sphinx. Oedipus and Jocasta had two daughters, Antigone and Ismene, and two sons, Eteocles and Po-

*Oedipus and the Sphinx*

lynices. When a famine struck the land, the blind prophet Tiresias was called to determine what must be done. Tiresias said that the murderer of Laius must be found and punished. Oedipus agreed, and in a short time it was discovered that it was he who was responsible for Laius's death and that Laius had been Oedipus's father. Jocasta was horrified at the discovery and committed suicide. In despair Oedipus blinded himself and was led into exile by Antigone, his daughter. He reached Colonus in Attica after years of wandering and was given the protection of Theseus of Athens. Oedipus's sons then fought to regain his throne in an expedition known as the Seven against Thebes. Both sons knew from an oracle that whoever had Oedipus's blessing would be victorious. His son Polynices went to Attica to ask Oedipus's blessing but was cursed instead. Eteocles sent Creon to bring Oedipus back for his side, but Theseus prevented his going, and Oedipus cursed Eteocles as well. The sons then killed each other. Oedipus died (or disappeared) in a grove sacred to the Eumenides at Colonus, not far from Athens. Oedipus's body was not allowed to be buried at Thebes and Colonus and finally found a resting place at Eteonos at a shrine named Oedipodion, sacred to Demeter.

Sophocles' *King Oedipus*, also known as *Oedipus Rex* or *Oedipus Tyrannus*, as well as his *Oedipus at Colonus*, deal with the major myth. The *King Oedipus* play served as the basis for Cocteau's Latin version, *Oedipus-Rex*, with music by Stravinsky. It was also the basis for Cocteau's play *The Infernal Machine*. The Sophocles play was translated into English by W. B. Yeats. Other treatments are by Gide in his *Oedipe* and *Théséa* and by Pasolini in his film *Oedipus Rex*. Ingres painted *Oedipus and the Sphinx*. Homer's version in the *Odyssey* tells us that Oedipus, the son of Laius, accidentally killed his father and later married his mother. When the truth came out, Jocasta hanged herself, but Oedipus continued to reign. Homer's *Iliad* adds that Oedipus was buried with full honors after he was killed in battle. Statius's epic poem the *Thebais*, in

12 books, part of which was translated by Alexander Pope, tells the story of Oedipus's curse on his sons and the fight between Polynices and Eteocles. Freud coined the term *Oedipus complex* to refer to men with unresolved sexual conflicts concerning their relationship with their mothers.

See also: ANTIGONE; APOLLO; DELPHI; ETEOCLES AND POLYNICES; JOCASTA; TIRESIAS

*Oenone warning Paris*

2271

**Oenone** (queen of wine)    In Greek mythology, a nymph of Phrygian Mount Ida, daughter of Cebren, a river god; mother of Corythus and Daphnis; a wife of Paris. Oenone knew Paris would leave her for Helen and bring destruction on Troy. When Paris was fatally wounded, Oenone, unable to forgive him, refused him help. One of Ovid's *Heroides* (5) tells her tale, as do Tennyson's *Oenone* and *The Death of Oenone* and William Morris's poetic tale *The Earthly Paradise*.

See also: DAPHNIS; HELEN OF TROY; NYMPHS; OVID; PARIS; TROY

2272

**Ogier the Dane** (wealth-spear)    In the Charlemagne cycle of legends, one of the paladins who lives in Avalon. As Holger Danske he is still a traditional hero in Denmark.

Charlemagne made war against the king of Denmark and took his son Ogier as hostage. The young Danish prince was favored by the fairies from the time of his birth. Six of them appeared to him. Five promised him every earthly joy, and the sixth, Morgan le Fay, foretold that he would never die but would dwell with her in Avalon, the land where King Arthur also lives forever. While in prison Ogier fell in love with and secretly married the governor's daughter, Bellissande. When Charlemagne was about to depart for war, he freed Ogier to aid him because Ogier was known for his heroic nature. Ogier returned to France after the war and learned that Bellissande had borne him a son and that his father had died. He was now the rightful king of Denmark.

Charlemagne gave him permission to return home, where he ruled for some years, and then he returned to France. His son, now grown up, had a dispute with Prince Charlot over a game of chess. The dispute became so bitter that the prince used the chessboard as a weapon and killed Ogier's son. Outraged at the murder of his son and unable to achieve any satisfaction from Charlemagne, Ogier insulted the emperor and fled to Didier (Desiderius), king of Lombardy, with whom Charlemagne was at war.

Charlemagne attacked Didier, but Ogier escaped from the besieged castle. Shortly after, however, when asleep near a fountain, Ogier was taken by Turpin, the archbishop and friend of Charlemagne. Ogier was led before the emperor and refused all offers of reconciliation. He insisted that Charlot be killed for the death of his son. Then an angel from heaven appeared, telling Ogier not to demand the death of Charlot. Ogier consented and was fully reinstated.

He attacked a Saracen giant, defeated him, and earned the hand of Clarice, princess of England. He was then made king of England but soon grew weary of ruling and journeyed to the East, where he besieged Acre, Babylon, and Jerusalem. On his way back to France, his ship was attracted by a magic lodestone, and all his companions perished. Ogier alone escaped to land. He then came to an adamantine castle, invisible by day but radiant at night, where he was welcomed by Papillon, a magic horse. The next day, while wandering across a flowery meadow, Ogier met Morgan le Fay, who gave him a magic ring. Although Ogier was now 100 years old, as soon as he put on the ring, he became a young man again. Then, putting on the crown of oblivion, he forgot his home and joined King Arthur, Oberon, Tristram, and Lancelot in Avalon, where he spent 200 years.

At the end of that time his crown accidentally dropped off, and Ogier remembered the past. He returned to France riding Papillon. He reached the court during the reign of one of the Capetian kings. Ogier was amazed at the changes in court life. One day he had his magic ring playfully taken from his finger and placed on that of the countess of Senlis. When she realized that it made her young again, she wanted the ring for herself. She sent 30 knights to take it from Ogier, who defeated them all. The king having died, Ogier next married the widowed queen. But Morgan le Fay, jealous of his love for the queen, spirited Ogier away in the midst of the marriage ceremony and bore him to the Isle of Avalon, from which, like King Arthur, he will return only when his country needs him. Longfellow, in one of his *Tales of a Wayside Inn*, tells the legend of Ogier and Didier (Desiderius). William Morris also relates the tale in his *Earthly Paradise*.

See also: ARTHUR; AVELON; BARBAROSSA; CHARLEMAGNE; LANCELOT OF THE LAKE; MORGAN LE FAY; OBERON; TRISTAM

2273

**Ogma** (Ogham)   In Celtic mythology, orator, warrior of the Tuatha de Danann, Irish god of literature, eloquence, fertility, healing, poetry, prophecy, and war; husband of Etain; father of Cairbe, MacCecht, MacCool, MacGreiné, and Tuirenn. He is also the fabled inventor of the Ogham alphabet, the earliest form of writing in Irish. The Latin alphabet is adapted to a series of twenty "letters" of straight lines and notches carved into wood or stone. Ancient Roman writers identified Ogma with both Hercules and Mercury. On the Continent he was worshiped under the name Ogmios.

See also: HERCULES; MERCURY; TUATHA DE DANANN

**2274**

**Ogoun**    In Haitian voodoo, god of war and fire, who is known as a healer and shows concern for the welfare of children. As a god of fire, Ogoun's sacred color is red, and rum is poured out as an offering to him, then set afire. Ogoun is sometimes depicted in the likeness of St. George. The association stems from the fact that the warrior-god is associated with the slayer of a monster dragon-serpent.

See also: GEORGE, ST.

**2275**

**Ogun Onire** (Ogun) (owner of the town of Ire) In African mythology (Yoruba of southwestern Nigeria), god of iron and war; married to Yemoja, the female spirit of the Ogun River; patron of blacksmiths and hunters.

Ogun Onire once descended to earth by a spider's web with his iron ax in hand. He wanted to go hunting. Olorun, the sky god, asked him if he could borrow his iron ax because Olorun had only a bronze one that would not cut down trees. Ogun Onire consented after he was offered the gift of a crown. At first he was pleased, but then decided he just wanted to go hunting and live away from the other gods. Because of his love of hunting, the other gods avoided him. Human sacrifices were offered to Ogun Onire in past centuries, and blacksmiths in Yoruba sacrifice dogs to him every two weeks. Once a year the people hold a three-day feast in Ogun Onire's honor at which they dance and eat dogs.

See also: GU

**2276**

**O-Ikazuchi**    In Japanese mythology, one of the Ikazuchi, the eight gods of thunder.

See also: IKAZUCHI

**2277**

**O Kiku**    In Japanese legend, the spirit of a girl who was thrown into a well.

O Kiku was the maid of a great man, Aoyama. He was given 10 precious plates, which he entrusted to O Kiku's keeping. He constantly told O Kiku that he loved her, but she refused all of his offers. In anger Aoyama hid one of the plates and then asked O Kiku to produce the whole set. A hundred times she counted the pieces, but each time only nine came up. Aoyama then suggested that if she became his mistress he would overlook the loss. O Kiku refused and was killed by Aoyama, who threw her body into an old well. Since then her ghost has visited the place of the murder, counting one, two, three . . . up to nine.

In a variant of the legend, O Kiku is said to have actually broken a plate. She was imprisoned by Aoyama but escaped, eventually drowning herself. O Kiku is portrayed in Hokusai's *Manga* (Ten Thousand Sketches).

**2278**

**Okonorote**    In the mythology of the Warau Indians of the Guianas, a young hunter who discovered a hole in the sky and descended to the earth. In the beginning the Warau had lived in the sky. One day Okonorote, a young hunter, shot an arrow and missed his target. Searching for the arrow, he found it had fallen through a hole in the sky. Okonorote looked down and saw the earth below, covered with forests and pampas. Using a cotton rope, he climbed down to look around. When he came back up, he told the Warau what he had seen and persuaded them to go down also. One fat woman could not get through the hole and was stuck, which prevented the Warau from returning to the sky after they had descended to earth.

See also: STAR HUSBAND

### 2279

**Olaf, St.** (forefather)   c. 995–1030. In Christian legend, King Olaf II Haraldson of Norway. Feast, 29 July.

As a young man Olaf fought in England for King Ethelred against the Danes. He became a Christian, tried forcibly to convert the Norwegians to the new faith, and was murdered. Soon after his death numerous miracles were reported. Snorri Sturluson's *Heimskringla* contains a long section on the life and death of St. Olaf. He writes that the king's body was found complete, with no decay. A bishop then trimmed the beard and hair of the dead king, saying the hair was sacred. This was doubted by some, so the bishop set the hair on fire, but "it was not consumed." When a spring arose at the site of Olaf's murder, it became a cult site and "infirmities were cured by its waters."

Henry W. Longfellow, in his *Tales of a Wayside Inn*, has *The Saga of King Olaf*, which captures some of the vigor and style of the old Nordic poems. Tooley, a street in London, is believed to be a corruption of St. Olaf's name. Formerly it was a colony of Scandinavians in the Southwark district.

### 2280

**Old Man and Death, The**   Aesopic fable found in various collections throughout the world.

An old laborer, bent double with age and toil, was gathering sticks in a forest. At last he grew so tired and hopeless that he threw down the bundle of sticks. "I cannot bear this life any longer," he cried out. "Ah, I wish death would only come and take me!"

As he spoke, death, a grisly skeleton, appeared and said to him: "I heard you call me."

"Please, sir," replied the woodcutter, "would you kindly help me to lift this faggot of sticks onto my shoulder?"

*Moral: We would often be sorry if our wishes were gratified.*

This fable forms part of the collections of Lôqman, La Fontaine, and L'Estrange. There is a similar fable from India, called *The Messengers of Death*.

See also: AESOPIC FABLES; LA FONTAINE, JEAN DE

### 2281

**Olelbis** (he who sits in the sky)   In North American Indian mythology (Wintun), creator god. Before Olelbis created humankind, he sent two buzzards, called Hus, to the earth to build a stone ladder from it to the sky. Halfway up the ladder they were to place a pool to drink from and a place to rest. At the top were to be two springs, one to drink from and the other for ritual bathing. "When a man or woman grows old," Olelbis said, "let him or her climb to Olelpanti (heaven), bathe and drink, and their youth will be restored." So the two buzzards left and began to build the ladder. Coyote, called Sedit in this myth, said to the two: "I am wise. Let us reason about this matter. Suppose an old woman and an old man go up, go alone, one after the other, and come back alone, young. They will be alone as before, and will grow old a second time, and go up again and come back young, but they will be alone, just the same as the first time. They will have nothing on earth to rejoice about. They will never have any friends, any children. They will never have any pleasure in the world. They will never have anything to do but to go up this road old and come back down young again. Joy at birth and grief for the dead is better, for these mean love." The two buzzards agreed, but one said to Coyote, "You too shall die and lie in the ground." Realizing what he had done to himself, Coyote tried to fly to heaven with wings made of sunflowers, but he fell back to earth and was dashed to pieces. "It is his own fault," Olelbis said. "He was killed by his own words. From now on all people will fall and die."

See also: COYOTE

2282
**Olifat** (Olofat)    In Micronesian mythology, trickster and culture hero, son of a mortal woman and the sky god Luk (Lukelong).

Olifat was born from his mother's head when she pulled a twist of coconut leaf rib that was tied around a lock of her hair. He was no sooner born than he began to run about. Luk told his wife that the boy was never to drink from a coconut with a hole bored at its top. But one day Olifat did just that. As he tipped back his head to get the last drop of juice, he saw his father in the sky. Immediately, he decided to visit his father's home. Riding on a column of smoke that rose from a fire of coconut shells, he arrived to see that workmen were building a Farmal, or house, for the spirits of the dead. Though his father recognized him, he did not let the workmen know who the boy was. The workmen decided to sacrifice Olifat to ensure the foundations of the house. They had planned to put him in a hole and then jam the house post on top of him. But Olifat knew their plans. While the hole was being dug, he made a hollow to one side of it at the bottom. When the men threw him in, he climbed into the side hole as the post was pushed down. With the help of some termites, Olifat made his way to the top of the pole and shouted, almost frightening the men to death. After that he went on various adventures, many of which concerned seducing relatives' wives. Once he turned himself into a mosquito so that he could be swallowed by his brother's wife in her drinking water in order to father a son with her. In a more beneficent role Olifat sent a bird down to earth with fire in its beak. The fire was placed in different trees so that men might learn to obtain fire from rubbing sticks together.

2283
**Oliver** (olive tree)    In the Charlemagne cycle of legends, Charlemagne's favorite paladin and close friend of Roland (Orlando). He appears in the *Chanson de Roland*, which describes his death, as well as in Pulci's *Il Morgante Maggiore*,

Boiardo's *Orlando Innamorato*, and Ariosto's *Orlando Furioso*.

See also: CHARLEMAGNE; MORGANTE; PALADINS, THE TWELVE; ROLAND

2284
**Olokun** (owner of the sea)    In African mythology (Yoruba of southwestern Nigeria), sea goddess or god. Beliefs vary as to the sex of Olokun, indicating that perhaps at first Olokun was a bisexual deity. In one myth Olokun is a male god in conflict with Olorun, the sky god. Once Olokun asked Olorun to appear dressed in his finest clothing. Olokun agreed to do the same so that the people would be able to decide which of the two gods was the greatest. But Olorun sent the chameleon, dressed in clothing exactly like Olokun's. Olokun then put on ever more splendid robes to outdo this display, but each time he changed his robes to surpass the raiment of the chameleon, the chameleon was able to match him. This frustrated Olokun, who came to accept the fact that Olorun's power was greater than his own if his messenger, the chameleon, could outdo him. From that day on Olokun has taken second place to Olorun. In African art Olokun is portrayed with a royal coral dress and mudfish legs. Both of his hands hold lizards.

See also: OLORUN; MULUNGU; UNKULUNKULU; WELE

2285
**Olorun** (owner of the sky)    In African mythology (Yoruba of southwestern Nigeria), sky god, the head of the Yoruba pantheon, who is not interested in man's affairs but lives in the heavens. He delegated his creative power to Obatala or Oshala, who fashioned human children in the mother's womb. Obatala is wedded to Odudua. Obatala and Odudua had Aganju, lord of the soil, and Yemaja, the goddess of water. The two in turn got married and had Orungan, the god of the upper air. But the lustful Orungan raped his mother, Yemaja, and from the incestuous union a whole brood of gods was

born at a single birth, including Orun, the sun god; Oahu, the moon god; Shango, the storm god; Dada, god of vegetation; Orisha Oko, god of agriculture; Oshossi, god of hunting; Ogun, god of iron; and Shankpana, god of smallpox.

Olorun is also known as Oba-Orun (king of the sky), Ododumare (owner of endless space), Eleda (creator), Oluwa (lord), and Orisha-Oke (sky god).

See also: ESHU; OBATALA; OLOKUN; OSHOSSI; SHANGO

2286
**Olrik, Axel**  1864–1917. Danish folklorist who attempted to describe what he called the "epic laws of folk poetry" in 1909. He presented folk narrative as structured according to formulas for opening and closing and for repetition (particularly of the number 3). He also emphasized that there were usually no more than two individuals per scene, who often represented the good and the bad, or the large and the small, and he pointed out the importance of the initial and final positions in a tale. His assumption was that scholars "can determine the characteristics of particular peoples, their special types of composition and cultural themes." His work helped lay the basis for further structuralist studies of folk narrative.

See also: PROPP, VLADIMIR

2287
**Olympian Gods**  In Greek mythology, the 12 (sometimes 13) major gods (with Roman names in parentheses): Zeus (Jupiter), Hera (Juno), Poseidon (Neptune), Demeter (Ceres), Apollo (Apollo), Artemis (Diana), Hephaestus (Vulcan), Pallas Athena (Minerva), Ares (Mars), Aphrodite (Venus), Hermes (Mercury), Hestia (Vesta), and Pluto or Hades (Orcus or Dis). The Romans called the Olympian gods *di majorum gentium*. They lived on Mount Olympus, the highest

mountain, 2,980 meters, in Greece, on the border of Macedonia in northern Greece.

See also: APHRODITE; APOLLO; ARES; ARTEMIS; ATHENA; DEMETER; HEPHAESTUS; HERA; HERMES; HESTIA; PLUTO; POSEIDON; ZEUS

*Zeus (Jupiter)*

2288
**Om**  In Hinduism, a sacred sound used in prayer and meditation. It is a single syllable formed by the combination of other syllables, and it is so sacred that when it is uttered, no one should hear it. The monosyllables represent the Hindu triad, *a* being Vishnu, *u* being Shiva, and *m* being Brahma. It signifies creation, maintenance, and destruction of a cosmic cycle. One Hindu text, *The Mandukya Upanishad*, says: "Om. This syllable is all. Its interpretation is that which has been, that which is, and that which is to be. All is Om, and only Om, and whatever is beyond trinal time is Om, and only Om." According to one myth, only Agni, the fire god,

possessed immortality; the other gods did not. Fearing that death would destroy them all, the gods took refuge in the sound of Om, which was given the epithet "slayer of death."

See also: AGNI; BRAHMA; SHIVA; VISHNU

2289

**Omacatl** (two reeds)    In Aztec mythology, god of joy, festivity, and happiness; worshiped by the rich, who held banquets in his honor. He represented a late aspect of Tezcatlipoca, after that deity had absorbed several lesser-known deities. According to Fray Bernardino de Sahagún in *Historia general de las cosas de Nueva España* (1570–1582), the god would sometimes appear at festivals for him. If for any reason he was not satisfied, he would say: "Wicked men, for what reason hast thou omitted to honor me with respect? I will henceforth abandon thee, and thou wilt pay dearly for the injury thou hast put upon me." Then many of the guests would become ill, suffering dizziness and headache. Omacatl is regarded in some texts as an aspect of Tezcatlipoca, the Aztec creator-trickster god.

See also: TEZCATLIPOCA; TRICKSTER

2290

**Ometecuhtli** (Ometecutli) (the dual lord, lord of duality)    In Aztec mythology, supreme being, who was outside of space and time and was the source of all life. He was the husband of Omechihuath, who gave birth to an obsidian knife, which she threw down to earth. From it 1,600 heroes were born, the first inhabitants of the earth. C. A. Burland in *The Gods of Mexico* (1967) writes that the Mexicans "were quite sure that in everything there was a unity of opposing factors, of male and female, of light and dark, of movement and stillness, of order and disorder. This opposition and duality was an essential of everything, and they felt that it was through this principle that life came into being. Hence, this god was a revelation of something very deep but so unknowable that he was the only god with no material temple."

2291

**Omphale** (navel)    In Greek mythology, a Lydian queen, daughter of Iardanus and married to Tinolus, who bought Heracles as a slave and kept him three years in her service. Omphale became his mistress and mother of several of his children, Agelaos, Alceus, and Lamus. During Heracles' stay he dressed as a woman. Saint-Saëns tone poem *Omphale's Spinning Wheel* (1871) is, according to the composer, about "feminine seduction, the victorious struggle of weakness against strength."

See also: HERACLES

2292

**Oni**    In Japanese folklore, word for ogres or devils. Usually an oni is of giant size and has claws, a square head with two horns, sharp teeth, and sometimes three evil eyes surmounted by big eyebrows. Three toes and three fingers are also common among oni. They can fly, but seldom do. Occasionally they wear trousers made of tiger's skin. Sometimes, however, they take on another form, such as that of a begging monk or a woman. In some Japanese tales an oni is converted to Buddhism and becomes a monk, first having his horns sawed off. Often in Japanese art priests are shown sawing off the horns of oni, who then become temple guardians who beat gongs and perform other menial ceremonies. Oni occasionally march at night in groups of 100 in imitation of religious ceremonies. When they are thus aligned they are called Hiakku no Yako. At the beginning of the year, a ceremony called *oni-yarai* is held, during which beans are cast around a house to rid it of any oni that might be lingering in corners.

2293

**Onion**    A pungent edible bulb, related to the leek. Plutarch writes in *Isis and Osiris* that Egyptian priests "kept themselves clear of the onion, because it is the only plant that thrives in the waning of the moon. It is suitable neither for fasting nor festival, because in the one case it causes thirst, and in the other tears for those who partake of it." In Poland a folk custom says that childbearing is eased if the expectant mother sits over a pail of boiling onions. On the other hand, a 12th-century Egyptian-Jewish physician, Ibn al-Jamil, recommended rubbing onion juice on the penis as a contraceptive.

**Onyankopon** (the great one)    In African mythology (Ashanti of Ghana), sky god who became disgusted with humankind and returned to his sky home.

When Onyankopon lived on the earth, there was a very old woman who pounded her yams so hard with her pestle that she knocked against Onyankopon. "Why do you always do that?" he asked the old woman. "If you continue, I will leave for my home in the sky." Taking no heed of Onyankopon, the old woman continued, and Onyankopon kept his word and left for his home in the sky. Then the old woman told her children to use mortars piled one on top of another to reach Onyankopon's home in the sky. They piled one on the other and almost reached the top, but they needed one more mortar. The old woman told them to remove the one from the bottom of the pile. When they did, all of the mortars crashed to the ground, killing the children and many onlookers. After this incident the Great One remained at a distance from humans.

Onyankopon is also called Otumfoo (the powerful one), Ananse Kokroko (the great wise spider), and Otomankoma (the eternal one).

See also: ANANSI; DENG

**Opochtli** (the left-handed)    In Aztec mythology, god of fishing and bird snaring, who invented the fishing rod and harpoon. Opochtli was portrayed as a naked man painted black, his head decked with plumes from wild birds and a coronet in the shape of a rose. He was portrayed surrounded by green paper and wore white sandals. In his left hand he held a red shield, and a

white flower of four petals was placed crosswise on it. In his right hand he held a cup.

**Ops** (abundance)    In Roman mythology, goddess of fertility; wife of Saturn; she was either the same as Rhea-Cybele or a separate deity. As goddess of plenty, human growth, and birth, Ops was invoked by touching the earth. Her major festivals were the Opalia (19 December), the Opiconsivia (25 August), and the Volcanalia (23 August).

See also: SATURN

**Oral-Formulaic Theory**    Also known as the Parry-Lord theory, named after its founders Milman Parry and Albert Lord. This theory of oral tradition is based on patterned phrases, or formulas, which are used in narratives as the basis for their composition. Both Parry and his student Lord applied the theory to living traditions, specifically to the *guslari* (bards who play a stringed instrument called a *gusle*) of the former Yugoslavia.

Through field trips from 1933 to 1935 and by Lord alone from 1950 to 1951, they were able to record and study living south Slavic oral traditional epics. Parry was interested in the systematic recurrence of particular phrases, like "swift-footed Achilles," and reasoned that longer epics might not be simply shorter works loosely joined by a performer, but represent "an expression regularly used, under the same metrical conditions, to express an essential idea." Albert Lord then took the theory to its conclusion in the first line of *The Singer of Tales* (1960) when he said: "This book is about Homer." The performance by *guslari* served as a model for understanding not only the lengthy national epics like those attributed to Homer, but also for Anglo-Saxon, Old French, and Byzantine Greek epics. In this way the oral-formulaic theory was able to clarify some typical actions, such as preparing for battle, but it was also able to identify story patterns common in stories across cultures.

One of the conclusions drawn from this field work and theory is that they offered documentation for the oral origins of these texts. What is missing in this theory are the extralinguistic aspects of oral tradition and the restricting of originality and expressivity by individual verbal artists.

*Orange*

Oduduwa, the father of Oranyan, was the brother of God and helped create the earth when God grew tired of his work. Because of this Oduduwa felt that he should become owner of the land. The Yoruba regard him as their founder and say that Oduduwa was their first king. Oranyan, his son, was a great hunter who, as he grew older, spent most of his time in a grove. He came out only to help his people when they were attacked by enemies. One day during a celebration a drunken man called out that the village was being attacked. The aging Oranyan came out on horseback and randomly began killing his own people. The people cried out to him to stop. Oranyan did, promising never to fight again, and he thrust his staff into the ground. Then, according to some accounts, both he and his wife were turned to stone. Pieces of his staff have been carefully placed together at the sacred city of Ifé, forming what is called the staff of Oranyan. The 20-foot staff has many nails driven into it, though its exact symbolism is not known.

2298
**Orange**    A citrus fruit whose blossom was a traditional decoration for brides. The orange indicates the hope for fruitfulness, while the white blossoms are symbolic of innocence. Sometimes it is identified in European folklore as the fruit eaten by Adam and Eve; the exact fruit is not named in the Genesis text. It also was associated with the Virgin Mary as a symbol of purity, chastity, and generosity. Both Italian and English witches traditionally used the orange to represent the victim's heart. The name of the victim was written on a paper and pinned to the fruit, which was then placed in a chimney to rot until the victim died.

See also: ADAM AND EVE; VIRGIN MARY

2299
**Oranyan**    In African mythology (Yoruba of southwestern Nigeria), hero king, son of Oduduwa.

2300
**Orcus** (boar)    In Roman mythology, one of the names of the god of the underworld, identified by the Romans with the Greek god Hades, who had a temple in Rome. Orcus also was often used as a name for the underworld. In Vergil's *Aeneid* (book 6) the hero Aeneas passes through the Gate of Orcus, where Harpies, Gorgons, and other monsters dwell. Orcus was the god who brought death rather than a king of the dead. He had a store chamber in which he gathered his harvest, for Orcus was often pictured as a reaper cutting the ripened grain. In some accounts Orcus is believed to be a form of Dis Pater, a Roman god of the dead to whom sacrifices of black animals were made.

See also: AENEAS; *AENEID, THE*; GORGONS; HADES; HARPIES

2301
**Order of the Garter, The Most Noble**    In British history and tradition, the highest order of

knighthood. The tradition began with King Edward III around 1348 and was revived in 1805. According to legend, Joan, countess of Salisbury, dropped her garter accidentally during a court ball. The king picked it up but diverted the eyes of the guests away from the countess by placing the blue band around his own knee while saying: "*Honi soit qui mal y pense*" (Shame on him who thinks evil of it). The order is limited to the sovereign and the members of the royal family and 25 knights. Foreign royalty may also be admitted. The only females in the order are the sovereign's queen and the eldest daughter if she is the heir apparent to the throne. Garters were common on the hat or the knee, and brides traditionally wore several on their legs, which were then distributed following the wedding. Some of this tradition still survives in the wearing of a blue garter for a wedding and the tossing of it to the attendants after the ceremony.

*Orestes and Electra at the tomb of Agamemnon*

2302

**Orehu**  In the mythology of the Arawak Indians of the Guianas, a water spirit, somewhat resembling a mermaid. One day an Arawak was walking beside the water when he saw an *orehu* arise from the stream, bearing a branch in her hand. She told him to plant the branch, which he did. Its fruit was the calabash, until then unknown among the Arawaks. The *orehu* appeared a second time with small white pebbles. She told the Indian to enclose them in the gourd so as to make a magic rattle, which was then used by the Semecihi, the medicine men of the Arawaks, to ward off the Yauhau, demon spirits.

2303

**Orestes** (mountaineer)  In Greek mythology, son of Agamemnon and Clytemnestra, brother of Electra, Iphigenia, and Chrysosthemis. Orestes killed his mother and her lover, Aegisthus, in revenge for the murder of Agamemnon. When Agamemnon returned from the Trojan War, his wife and her lover, Aegisthus, killed him and seized his throne. Orestes, Agamem-

non's son, was taken by his sister Electra to the court of Strophius, the king of Phocis, then Electra returned to her mother. After seven years the oracle of Apollo at Delphi ordered Orestes to avenge his father's murder. Orestes and his male lover, Pylades, son of King Strophius, went to Argos, where, with Electra, they planned the killing of Clytemnestra and Aegisthus. Orestes and Pylades went to the palace disguised as messengers, ostensibly to announce the death of Orestes. Eager to hear the news, Aegisthus was caught off guard and was the first killed. The two then turned to Clytemnestra, who protested that a son would not kill his mother. Orestes almost relented, until Pylades reminded him of the oracle, and they then killed Clytemnestra. Guilt for his deed followed Orestes in the form of the Erinyes (Furies). Eventually, Athena calmed the Erinyes, changing them into the Eumenides (kindly ones), and forgave Orestes. Aeschylus's trilogy, the *Oresteia*, made up of *Agamemnon*, *The Choephoroe*, and *The Eumenides*, with the myth. Sophocles' *Electra* and Euripides' *Andromache*, *Iphigenia in Tauris*, and *Orestes*, also deal with the Orestes myth but make the Furies imagined fantasies of Orestes' guilt-ridden mind. Others who deal with or cite the myth are Homer, Herodotus, Ovid, Pausanias, and Vergil among the ancient authors and Alfieri, Goethe, Giraudoux, O'Neill, and Sartre in modern times. Strauss's *Electra*, with a libretto by Hofmannsthal, and Darius Milhaud's *Choephoroe* treat the subject musically.

See also: AEGISTHUS; AGAMEMNON; APOLLO; DELPHI; ELECTRA; IPHIGENIA; TROY

2304

**Orion** (man of the mountains)  In Greek mythology, handsome hunter-hero, son of Poseidon, Zeus, or Hermes and Euryale; husband of Side (pomegranate), who was cast into the underworld for boasting she was more beautiful than the goddess Hera. Orion then fell in love with Merope, daughter of King Oenopion of the island of Chios. While wooing Merope, Orion cleared the island of wild beasts. King Oenopion, however, tried various schemes to prevent the marriage. One day Orion got drunk and raped Merope and was blinded by Oenopion as a punishment. Learning that he could regain his sight from the rays of the rising sun, Orion persuaded an attendant to the smith god Hephaestus to guide him to the island of Lemnos, where the sun restored his sight. In another myth he was a follower of Artemis and was accidentally slain by the goddess or was killed when he attempted to rape her. In another variant Orion was in the service of Artemis when he was seen by Eos, dawn goddess, who fell in love with him and carried him away. Artemis killed him out of jealousy according to some accounts by having a scorpion bite him. Both the scorpion and Orion were then made into a heavenly constellation. Vergil's *Aeneid* (book 1) and Ovid's *Metamorphoses* (book 12) tell of Orion. Spenser's *The Faerie Queene* (1.3.31) tells the myth of his death; Milton's Latin poem "Ad Patrem" deals with Orion; Keat's *Endymion* (2.198) has the line "blind Orion hungry for the dawn"; and Longfellow's "Occultation of Orion" also

uses the myth. Nicholas Poussin's painting *Blind Orion Seeking the Rising Sun* is one of his greatest works.

See also: *AENEID, THE*; ARTEMIS; HEPHAESTUS; HERMES; HERA; OVID; POMEGRANATE; POSEIDON; ZEUS

2305

**Orisha**  In African mythology (Yoruba of southwestern Nigeria), the gods, demigods, or deified ancestors. There are hundreds of orishas, ranging from the original sky god Olorun to local protective deities.

See also: OLORUN

2306

**Oro**  In Polynesian mythology, Tahitian war god, son of Hina-tu-a-uta (Hina of the land) and Ta'aroa, the creator god. Celebrations in Oro's honor, involving singing and dancing, were arranged by hereditary priests. Oro had three daughters, To'i-mata (ax with eyes), 'Ai-tupuai (eater of summit), and Mahu-fatu-rau (frog of many owners). Hoa-tapu (sworn friend) was his only son. Sometimes Oro was called Oro-i-teamoe (Oro of the laid down spear), making him a god of peacetime.

2307

**Orokeet**  In Australian mythology, a name given to both a male and a female evil spirit.

2308

**Orpheus** (sea perch)  In Greek mythology, poet and musician son of Apollo and Calliope (or Oeagrus and Cleio) who could enchant gods, people, animals, trees, and rocks with the sound of his magic lyre, given him by Apollo; married to the Dryad (or nymph) Eurydice. Orpheus sailed with the crew of the Argonauts in their quest for the Golden Fleece. He helped them through the magic of his music when he played his lyre as they passed through the Clashing Rocks and the region of the Sirens. On his return from the adventure he married Eurydice, but according to Vergil's account in *Georgics* (4), she died when the beekeeper Aristaeus tried to rape her. As Eurydice ran from her attacker, she stepped on a poisonous snake, which bit and killed her. Distraught by his wife's death, Orpheus went to the underworld to bring her back. Orpheus's music so charmed Pluto and Persephone, king and queen of the dead, that either one or both agreed that he could take Eurydice back to the upper world. Orpheus was told, however, that he must not look at Eurydice until they reached the upper world. Orpheus could not resist the temptation to look at Eurydice and lost her. This version of the myth is told by Vergil, Ovid, and Seneca, but in a variant Orpheus was told he could have Eurydice for only one day; then Hermes, as guide for the dead, would come to bring her back to the underworld. After losing Eurydice, Orpheus wandered about Thrace. He died on Mount Rhodope, either killed by the Maenads, followers of Dionysus, because he failed to honor their god or torn to pieces by women jealous of his love for Eurydice. The pieces of his torn body were gathered up by the Muses. His head, still singing, and his lyre floated on the river Hebrus to the island of Lesbos, where they were dedicated to Apollo. Orphism, discussed by Plato and Vergil, is a mystical religion that taught death and resurrection and that one could become purified only when the soul was separated from the body.

Ovid's *Metamorphoses* (book 10) formed the basis for Politian's *Orfeo*, the first Italian drama on a classical subject; Monteverdi's opera *Orfeo*; Gluck's *Orfeo ed Euridice*, in which Eurydice is restored to Orpheus; Stravinsky's ballet *Orpheus*; Jean Anouilh's play *Eurydice*; Marcel Camus' film *Black Orpheus*; two plays by Cocteau plus some art work; and Rilke's *Sonnets to Orpheus*. Orpheus is cited in numerous English poems and plays, among them Spenser's *Amoretti* (44); Shakespeare's *The Merchant of Venice* (5.1.79–82) and *Henry VIII* (3.1.3–8); Milton's "Il Penseroso" (107–8), "L'Allegro" (149–50), "Lycidas," (58–63) and *Paradise Lost* (book 7.26–27, 32–39);

William Morris's *Life and Death of Jason*; and Robert Browning's *Eurydice to Orpheus*. Moreau, Redon, and Lord Leighton used Orpheus as a subject for paintings.

See also: ARGONAUTS; ARISTAEUS; APOLLO; CALLIOPE; DIONYSUS; DRYADS; EURYDICE; GOLDEN FLEECE; HERMES; MUSES; NYMPHS; OVID; PERSEPHONE; PLUTO

2309

**Orunmila** (the sky knows who will prosper)    In African mythology (Yoruba of southwestern Nigeria), god of divination; eldest son of Olorun, the sky god. By the reading of palm nuts or cowries he perceives the meanings and intentions of Olorun. As god of divination Orunmila is called Ifa, a word that means divining. As Ifa, the god came to improve the health of his people and assist in supernatural matters. Ifa visited many villages but finally made his home in the sacred city of Ilé-Ifé. Ifa could speak all of the languages known to humankind. Because of his gifts he is seen as an intermediary between his father, Olorun, and the people.

See also: ESHU; ILÉ-IFÉ; OLORUN

2310

**Osa**    In African mythology (Edo of Benin), sky god, supreme being who lives in heaven. Osa created the world, while his evil counterpart, Osanoha (Osa of the bush), made a house in which diseases live. When men and women on their way from heaven to earth came near the house, rain fell and drove them to it for shelter; thus sickness came to the earth. And because the wicked Osanoha created animals, man became their enemy and hunted them. In a variant myth Osa and Osanoha agreed to reckon up and compare their riches. Osa had more children than Osanoha, and the two have been enemies ever since.

Osa's emblem is a long pole with a white cloth attached. In some villages Osa is represented by a pot; in others, by a tree with a white cloth tied to it.

**2311**

**Osawa**   In African mythology (Ekoi of Nigeria), sky god who sent two messages to man, one of life and one of death. Osawa sent a frog with the message that death ends all things. Then he sent a duck with a message that said that the dead will come back to life. The frog arrived with his message, but the duck stopped on the way and never delivered his message.

See also: MULUNGU; OLOKUN; UNKULUNKULU; WELE

**2312**

**Oshossi**   In African mythology (Yoruba of southwestern Nigeria), god of the forest and hunt, whose worship is found today in Cuba and Brazil. His followers dance to him carrying a small bow, his symbol.

**2313**

**Oshun**   In African mythology (Yoruba of southwestern Nigeria), goddess of the Oshun river and and fresh water; wife of Shango, the thunder god. Her worshipers wear amber beads, and her cult is found in Africa, Cuba, and Trinidad.

See also: SHANGO

**2314**

**Oshunmare**   In African mythology (Yoruba of Nigeria), the rainbow serpent, whose worship is found in parts of Brazil.

See also: SHANGO

**2315**

**Osiris** (mighty one?)   In Egyptian mythology, Greek form of the Egyptian Asar, Ausar, or Ser; god of death and resurrection; the brother-husband of Isis; father of Horus; brother of Set and Nephthys. There are a few texts that depict Osiris as a terrifying figure who sends out demon messengers to drag the living into the realm of the dead. However, the main source for the connected narrative of the myth of Osiris is Plu-

*Osiris*

tarch's work *Isis and Osiris*, which deals with Egyptian beliefs. In some cases Plutarch was mistaken about Egyptian beliefs, though his narrative has left its mark on Greek and Roman sources.

When Osiris was born, a voice was heard to say that the lord of creation was born. In the course of time Osiris became the king of Egypt and devoted himself to civilizing his subjects and teaching them the craft of husbandry. He established a code of laws and taught men to worship the gods. Having made Egypt peaceful and flourishing, he set out to teach other nations of the world. During his absence his sister-wife, Isis, ruled the state. When Osiris returned, his evil brother Set (identified by Plutarch with Typhon) plotted with 72 others, including Aso, the queen of Ethiopia, to slay Osiris. The conspirators built a chest to the measurements of Osiris's body. The box was brought into Osiris's banqueting hall while he was eating, and by a ruse he was induced to lie down in the chest, whereupon Set and his cohort closed the box and took it immediately to the mouth of the Nile, where they set it afloat.

These events happened on the 17th day of the month of Hathor, when Osiris was in the 28th year of his reign. This day was subsequently marked on the calendar as triply unlucky because it was the day Isis and Nephthys began their great lamentation for Osiris.

When the report of the treachery reached Isis, she cut off a lock of her hair, a sign of mourning, and set out to find her husband's body. In the course of her wanderings she discovered that Osiris had slept with their sister Nephthys and that the offspring of the union was the jackal-headed god Anubis, whom Isis found and brought up to guard her. Actually, Osiris had not lusted after Nephthys, who was in love with him, but had been unwittingly tricked by his sister into sleeping with her.

Isis learned that the chest had been carried by the waves to the coast of Byblos and there lodged in the branches of a bush, which quickly shot up into a large and beautiful tree, enclosing the chest on every side so that it could not be seen. The king of Byblos was attracted by the tree's unusual size and had it cut down to make a pillar for one of the rooms of his palace. Isis learned of this and went to Byblos, where she was taken to the palace to become nurse to one of the queen's sons. The goddess would transform herself into a swallow at every opportunity and hover around the pillar, bemoaning her sad fate. Each night she placed the queen's son in a special fire to consume his mortal parts, until the queen finally discovered her son in the flames and cried out. Isis revealed her story and begged for the pillar that supported the room. The queen took pity and ordered that the pillar be cut open and the chest containing Osiris's body be removed. When Isis saw the body of her dead husband, she cried out with such a fierceness that one of the queen's children died of fright.

Isis set sail for Egypt, where she again embraced the corpse and wept bitterly. She hid Osiris's body in a secluded spot. The evil Set stumbled on the chest when he was out hunting one night, realized what it contained, and proceeded to cut Osiris's body into 14 pieces, which he dispersed all over Egypt.

When Isis heard of this, she took a boat made of papyrus, a plant abhorred by the crocodile, and sailed about collecting the fragments of Osi-

*Osiris-Seker*

ris's body. Wherever she found a part of her husband, she built a tomb. It is said that that is why there are so many tombs of the god scattered throughout Egypt. Isis collected all of the pieces of her husband but one, the penis, which had been devoured by the lepidotus, the phagrus, and the oxyrhynchus, fish that the Egyptians thereafter especially avoided. Isis then constructed a phallus to take the place of her husband's penis, and a festival was held in its honor.

After some time Osiris's spirit returned from the dead and appeared to his son Horus, encouraging Horus to avenge his father's death. Horus and Set engaged in a great battle that lasted for three days. Horus was the victor, but Isis, taking pity on her brother, let him go free. Then Horus, enraged, cut off his mother's head, which the god Thoth replaced with a cow's head. (The goddess sometimes appears cow-headed.) Set appeared before the gods and accused Horus of being a bastard, but Thoth defended Horus. Thereupon two more battles ensued between the two combatant gods, and Horus again proved victorious.

This is the general outline of the Osirian myth as written by Plutarch. Osiris was the man-god (he was first human and later deified) who had conquered death, and so, the Egyptians believed, would his followers. In every funeral inscription from the Pyramid Texts to the Roman period, rituals performed for Osiris were also done for the deceased, the deceased being identified with Osiris.

Osiris absorbed the characteristics of so many gods that he became both the god of the dead and the god of the living. Originally, he was the personification of the flooding of the Nile. He also may have represented the sun after it had set, and as such symbolized the motionless dead. Some later texts identify him with the moon. The Egyptians said that Osiris was the father of the gods who had given birth to him, as he was the father of the past, the present, and the future (immortality).

In Egyptian art Osiris is usually portrayed as a mummy with a beard wearing the white crown of Lower Egypt on his head and the *menat*, an amulet, around his neck. Sometimes he appears as the Tet pillar, symbol of strength and stability in life and renewed power after death, and is called Osiris Tet. Other composite forms of Osiris frequently appear:

*Osiris-Seker*—the god as a hawk-headed mummy, sometimes standing upright, sometimes sitting. When seated, he holds in his hands the whip, scepter, and crook. This composite god signifies that Osiris became overlord of Duat, the underworld, and absorbed the death god Seker into himself.

*Osiris-Neper*—combination in which Osiris was coupled with one of the oldest grain gods of Egypt, Nepra.

*Osiris Aah* (Osiris as the moon god)—the appearing with a crescent moon and full moon on his head. In his hands he holds the signs of life, stability, serenity, power, and dominion.

*Osiris-Sah* or *Osiris-Orion*—as such his female counterpart was Isis-Sept, or Isis-Sothis.

*Osiris-Horus*—Osiris coupled with his son; together they become a form of the rising sun.

*Osiris-Ra*—composite god in which Osiris represented the day and night suns.

*Osiris-Neb-Heu* (Osiris, lord of eternity)—the god in the form of a mummy with the head of the benu, or phoenix.

*Osiris-Seb*—Osiris fused with the ancient creation god, who produced the world from the Cosmic Egg.

*Asar-Hep* or *Serapis*—Osiris coupled with the old bull god Apis. Osiris is also called Unnefer (he who is continually happy), referring to his role in defeating death.

See also: ANUBIS; APIS; BENU; HATHOR; HORUS; ISIS; NEPHTHYS; RA; SEKER; SET; THOTH

2316

**Ossian** (Oisin) (little dear)    Third century C.E.? Legendary Celtic poet whose "works" were published by James Macpherson as *Fragments of Ancient Poetry Collected in the Highlands of Scotland, and Translated from the Gaelic or Erse Language*; *Fingal, an Ancient Epic Poem in Six Books*; and *Temora* (1760-1763). The books claimed to be translations of ancient poems, but Dr. Johnson remarked that he considered the poems "to be as gross an imposition as ever the world was troubled with." In fact, the poems were mainly the work of Macpherson's vivid imagination and not of the poet as claimed, though they were based on the character Oisin, as found in Scottish ballad tradition. Nevertheless, Europe was taken by storm with the poems. German Romantics placed Ossian on a level with Homer. In Goethe's novel *Werther* the hero and Charlotte weep over the poems. The French artist Ingres painted *Ossian's Dream*, and James Joyce cites the bard in *Ulysses*.

2317

**Oswald, St.** (god power)    c. 605–642. In Christian legend, king of Northumbria. Feast, 5 August.

Oswald defeated the Welsh king Caedwalla near Hexham in 634 and was made king of Northumbria. He was baptized at Iona and with the aid of St. Aidan tried to convert his people to Christianity.

One medieval legend records his charity. At a dinner he was told that there were some beggars outside his door. He had before him a silver plate filled with meat. Oswald told his servant to give the food and the plate to the beggars. St. Aidan, who was present, held the king's right hand, saying, "May this hand never wither."

When Oswald was killed in battle at Masefield fighting against pagans and their Welsh Christian allies, his right hand, which had been amputated, remained whole and "free from decay." His head was taken to a church at Lindisfarne and buried between the arms of St. Cuthbert. His right hand was carried to Bamborough Castle.

"May God have mercy on their souls, as Oswald said when he fell," was a common proverb for many years in England.

See also: CUTHBERT, ST.

2318

**Otoroshi**   In Japanese folklore, a fantastic animal that protects temples and shrines from impious people. If an impious person enters the grounds, the otoroshi will pounce on the person and tear him or her to shreds.

2319

**Otshirvani**   In Siberian mythology, a creator god who defeated the evil giant snake Losy. In a Mongolian myth Losy lived in the water and spent his time spitting out venom over the earth, trying to kill men and animals. God decided to have the monster killed and asked Otshirvani to battle him. Otshirvani took on the beast but was losing the battle until he fled to Sumer, the world mountain, where he was changed into the Garide Bird. As this fantastic bird, he seized Losy by his head and dragged him three times around Mount Sumer, finally smashing the monster's head against a rock. Losy, however, was so large that his body wrapped around the mountain three times, and his tail was still in the ocean. Ot-

shirvani appears in some Siberian myths with the creator god Chagan-Shukuty.

See also: CHAGAN-SHUKUTY; GARIDE BIRD; LOSY

2320

**Otter**   An aquatic, fur-bearing mammal having webbed feet and a long, slightly flattened tail. In medieval Christian belief the otter symbolized Christ because it was believed that the otter killed the crocodile (the devil) by entering its mouth and devouring its bowels before reappearing. This was seen as symbolic of Christ's descent into hell (the devil's mouth) to free Adam and Eve and all of the Old Testament saints and holy men and women. But in contrast the medieval symbolists also saw the animal as the devil because it insinuated itself into a person's heart in order to bring about its destruction. In the Norse *Volsunga Saga*, Otter, son of a human father, is killed by the trickster god Loki, and to appease Otter's father the gods agree to pay him enough gold to cover Otter's body inside and out. Fafnir, a brother of Otter, kills his father to obtain the gold. Fafnir then turns himself into a dragon to guard the gold and is in the end killed by the hero Sigurd.

See also: ADAM AND EVE; CROCODILE; FAFNIR; LOKI; SIGURD

2321

**Oum'phor** (Hounfor, Hunfor)   In Haitian voodoo, temple resembling Moses' design for the Ark of the Covenant and the Tabernacle (Exod. 25–27). The Oum'phor consists of a large area, usually covered, with a center post called *poteau-mitan*, which recalls the staff of Moses in the Bible. All important voodoo rituals are conducted around the *poteau-mitan*, the top of which is believed to be the center of the sky, and the bottom the center of hell. The *poteau-mitan* is usually square and set in a circular pedestal made of masonry. Around the pedestal are triangular niches. The pedestal itself is a form of altar on which are placed various ritualistic implements.

These include the jars called *pot-de-tête*, containing spirits of the people who worship at the Oum'phor, and *govis*, jars that receive the voodoo loas (deified spirits of the dead) when they are called down by the *houn'gan* and *mam'bo*, the priest and priestess of the cult. The loa is identified by the behavior of the individual who is "mounted." The large area is the Oum'phor proper, a square house resembling the Holy of Holies of the Bible.

According to voodoo legend, Moses was taught voodoo by Jethro, called Ra-Gu-El Pethro in voodoo belief. Zipporah, the daughter of Jethro, was Moses' wife and bore the prophet two mulatto sons, which so upset Aaron and Miriam, the brother and sister of Moses, that Moses eventually divorced Zipporah. The voodoo loas were so angry at this that they caused Miriam to turn white with leprosy. The voodoo version of the biblical account is, of course, at variance with the explanations offered in the Hebrew narrative (Num. 12:1–15).

See also: AARON; ARK OF THE COVENANT; LOA; MIRIAM; MOSES

**Ouroboros**   2322   In world folk belief, a serpent or dragon devouring its own tail; often a symbol of eternity.

*Ouroboros*

2323

**Ovid**   43 B.C.E.–18 C.E. Publius Ovidius Naso, Roman poet best known for his great poem *The Metamorphoses* in 15 books that tells Greek and Roman myths from the creation of the world to the deification of Julius Caesar. In 8 C.E. Ovid, who had held minor official posts, was exiled by the emperor Augustus to Tomi (Costanza), a town on the Danube near the Black Sea. The exact cause of the exile is not known, though some scholars believe it is related to a scandal concerning Augustus's granddaughter Julia, who was also exiled. While in exile, Ovid continued to write his *Tristia* (Elegies) and *Epistulae ex Ponto* (Letters from Exile). Earlier he had written *Ars amatoria* (The Art of Love), which Augustus did not like because of its frankness about sexual matters; *Remedia amoris* (Remedy for Love), a series of short love poems; *Amores* (Loves); and the *Heroides*, verse letters from women of myth and history. Aside from these, he left the *Fasti*, a calendar of the Roman year, but it was incomplete, covering only the first six months of the calendar. Ovid's fame, however, rests on his masterpiece, *The Metamorphoses*, which inspired many poets and writers, among them Dante, Chaucer, Wordsworth, Pope, Dryden, Goethe, Marlowe, Spenser, and Shakespeare. In *The Divine Comedy* Dante places Ovid with Homer as one of the greatest poets. In art *The Metamorphoses* influenced most major European artists, especially Rubens, Poussin, and Picasso. Delacroix's *Ovid among the Scythians* portrays the poet in exile.

2324

**Owl**   A nocturnal bird of prey with large eyes and a broad head. The Egyptian hieroglyph for owl symbolized death, night, cold, and passivity and was also used to indicate the sun below the horizon when it crossed the sea of darkness in its daily journey. In Aztec mythology Techolotl, god of the underworld, was symbolized by a night owl. In North American Indian mythology (Pimas) the owl was a symbol of the souls of the dead. If an owl happened to be hooting at the

*Owl*

time of death, it was certain that the owl was waiting for the soul of the dying person. Owl feathers were always given to a dying person to help him or her in the next world. If a family had no owl feathers, they would obtain them from a medicine man, who traditionally kept a stock of them. In Greek and Roman mythology the owl was sacred to the goddess of wisdom, Athena, and her Roman counterpart, Minerva. The city of Athens had so many owls that the proverb "taking owls to Athens" was an ancient equivalent of "coals to Newcastle." On the other hand, the Romans ritually purified Rome if an owl accidentally strayed into the capital city, considering it an ill omen. In medieval Christian folklore the owl was seen as a demonic bird.

One British folktale tells how Jesus changed a girl into an owl for being stingy. One day Jesus, in disguise, went into a baker's shop and begged for some bread. The mistress of the shop immediately put some dough in the oven. "That is too much," cried the woman's daughter. The girl went to the oven and reduced the amount to half.

Not satisfied with that, she went back to the oven and reduced the dough again. But the dough began to rise and rise in the oven, pushing open the doors and falling across the floor. "Heugh, heugh, heugh," cried the girl, owl-like, and at that moment Jesus turned her into an owl. Shakespeare was familiar with the legend, since he has Ophelia say in *Hamlet* (4:5): "They say the owl was a baker's daughter."

To Shakespeare and many of his contemporaries the owl was a demonic bird. It was the "vile owl" in the poet's *Troilus and Cressida* (2.1) and the "obscure bird" in *Macbeth* (2.3). The poet inherited the medieval bias that identified the bird with Jews, who "lived in darkness." In Jewish folklore Lilith, the first wife of Adam before Eve, flew about as a night owl, making off with children. Although the Old Testament does not contain the Lilith myth, the prophet Isaiah (34:11–15) chooses the owl as one of the demonic birds that will haunt the land of Edom. There are numerous motifs associated with the owl in the *Motif Index of Folk Literature*.

See also: ATHENA; BIG OWL; MINERVA

2325

**Ozymandias**   Greek name for the Egyptian Rameses; used by the Greek historian Diodorus Siculus when he translated an inscription at the foot of a gigantic statue of Rameses II. It ran: "My name is Ozymandias, king of kings: if any would know how great I am and where I lie, let him surpass me in any of my works." The English poet Shelley, who hated all despots, used the quotation with a twist in his poem *Ozymandias*. Shelley's poem concludes:

"My name is Ozymandias, King of Kings:
Look on my works, ye Mighty, and despair!"
Nothing beside remains. Round the decay
Of that colossal wreck, boundless and bare
The lone and level sands stretch far away.

# P

**Pabid**    In the mythology of the Tupi Indians of Brazil, spirit of the dead. When a person died, it was believed that the eyes left the body, which changed into a *pabid*; then the *pabid* would pass over two great crocodiles and two giant snakes into the land of the dead, beyond the river Mani-Mani. Once there the *pabid* would be greeted by two fat worms, which would bore a hole in the belly, removing all of the intestines. When they had finished their meal, they would present the *pabid* to Patobkia, the head magician, who would sprinkle pepper juice into the eye sockets, restoring the lost sight. In the land of the dead a male *pabid* had to have intercourse with Vaugh'en, the ancient giantess. Female spirits had to have intercourse with Mpokalero. After this one sexual experience, no further sexual acts took place—men had merely to place leaves on the backs of women, who then bore children. When *pabids* wished to sleep, they would lean against the poles in their huts, cover their eyes, and sleep standing up. While the *pabid* lived in the land of the dead, the heart of the dead person would sprout after three days a *ki-agpga-pod*, a little man who grew bigger and bigger until it burst the heart. A magician then called up the spirit, which assumed a visible form and was sent up into the air.

**Pachacamac** (earthquaker, he who sustains or gives life to the universe)    In the mythology of the ancient coastal people of Peru, supreme god, often identified with the god Virachocha, supreme god and creator of the Incas.

Pachacamac created man and woman but failed to provide them with food. When the first man died of starvation, the sun aided the woman by giving her a son. This child taught her how to live on wild fruits. His action angered Pachacamac, who killed the young man. From his buried body, however, maize and other cultivated plants arose. The sun then gave the woman another son, Wichama. Angered again, Pachacamac killed the woman. In revenge Wichama pursued Pachacamac, driving him into the sea. Wichama then burned up the lands and turned men into stone.

In another myth Pachacamac is the son of the moon and sun. In this version, Con, who may have been an earlier supreme god, filled the land with men and women he had created, giving them all of the necessities of life. When some of the people annoyed the god, he turned the fertile land into barren wastes. He left the people only the rivers so that they might support themselves by irrigation and hard work. Pachacamac came and drove out Con, changing his men into monkeys. He then created the men and women whose descendants exist today.

The chief center of the worship of Pachacamac was a temple built on a small hill in the fertile coastal valley of the same name south of present-day Lima, Peru. His cult included priests and sacrifices, and he was consulted as an oracle.

See also: CUN; VIRACHOCHA

**2328**

**Pachamama** (mother earth) In Inca mythology, earth goddess to whom coca was offered to ensure good crops. She is still worshiped in some parts of Bolivia, Ecuador, Peru, and northwestern Argentina. Her festivals take place at the beginning and end of the various agricultural cycles. Among Christian Indians her cult has been absorbed into that of the Virgin Mary.

**2329**

**Padmasambhava** (lotus-born) Eighth century C.E. Indian Buddhist worshiped in Tibet as founder of Buddhism in that country. He is said to have been born from a lotus in the north Indian pilgrimage town of Ujjain (Tibetan: Odiyan), where the elbow of the dismembered goddess fell to earth. At the request of King Thi-Sron Detsan, Padmasambhava came to Tibet to subdue and pacify the native demons. He remained for 50 years, teaching the doctrine of Tantra-Yogacara. He destroyed all of the evil gods of the country and converted those remaining to Buddhism. After 50 years Padmasambhava miraculously disappeared. Legend says he entered the body of a demon king, Me-wal, where he reigned.

He is often called Guru Rinpoche (precious master) and is portrayed in art seated on a lotus with his legs locked, his right hand holding the *vajra*, the thunderbolt, and the left hand lying in his lap holding a bowl made from a human skull. A trident with three heads—peaceful, sorrowful, and a skull symbolizing the Hinayana, Mahayana, and Vajrayana—is supported against his left side by his elbow. His garments are usually red. He has eight forms: Guru Pädma

Jungnä (born of a lotus), for the happiness of the three worlds, the central figure in the plate; Guru Pädma-sambhava (savior by the religious doctrine); Guru Pädma Gyélpo (the king of the three collections of scriptures); Guru Dorje Dolö (the Dorje, or diamond comforter of all); Guru Ñima Od-zer (the enlightening sun of darkness); Guru S'akya Sen-ge (the second Sakya—the lion), who does the work of eight sages; Guru Seng-ge da dok (the propagator of religion in the six worlds, with the roaring lion's voice); and Guru Lo-ten Ch'og-Se (the conveyer of knowledge to all worlds).

See also: MAHAYANA

**2330**

**Pa-Hsien** (eight immortals) In Chinese Taoist mythology, eight beings who as mortals followed the Tao (the way) and achieved the status of enlightened spirits. They are Chung-li Ch'üan, Chang Kuo-lao, Lu Tung-pin, Ts'ao Kuo-chu, Li T'ien-kuai, Han hsiang Tzu, Lan Ts'ai-ho, and Ho Hsien-ku.

See also: CHANG KUO-LAO; CHUNG-LI CH'ÜAN; HAN HSIANG TZU; HO HSIEN-KU; LAN TS'AI-HO; LI T'IEN-KUAI; LU TUNG-PIN

**2331**

**Pahuanuiapitasitera'i** (the great one that opens the sky) In Polynesian mythology, Tahitian sea spirit, feared by sailors along with other sea spirits, such as Arematapopoto (short wave), Aremataroroa (long wave), and Puatutahi (coral rock standing alone).

**2332**

**Pairikas** In Persian mythology, evil beings who act as enchantresses, aiding the evil spirit, Ahriman. One of the group, the demoness Pairika, symbolizes idolatry. She is put to flight by the proper prayers and rites.

See also: AHRIMAN

2333

**Paiva and Kuu**    In the Finnish epic poem *The Kalevala*, the sun and moon.

Both Paiva and Kuu attempted to woo the beautiful Kyllikki, the "flower of the islands," to become the wife of their respective sons. Kyllikki refused the offer of Paiva. She did not want to live at Paivala, the sun's abode, because it was too hot. She also refused Kuu's offer because she did not want to live in Kuutola, the moon's abode. Eventually, Kyllikki was abducted by the hero Lemminkainen, but he later left her for being unfaithful.

Sibelius composed *Terve Kuu*, for chorus, on rune 49 of *The Kalevala*, in which Vainamoinen calls on Kuu, the moon, in a mystic invocation.

The sun spirit is called Paivatar or Paivan Tytar (sun's daughter); Kuutar is the moon spirit or daughter in the poem.

See also: *KALEVALA, THE*; LEMMINKAINEN

2334

**Pajana**    In Siberian mythology, a creator god of the Black Tartars. Pajana formed creatures from the earth, but seeing that they lacked life, he went to the Kudai (seven spirits who watch over men's destinies) to obtain from them life-giving spirits to instill in his new creatures. Pajana left a naked dog to guard them while he was away. Erlik, the devil, came and said he would cover the dog with golden hair if the dog would give him the soulless bodies. The dog agreed, and Erlik then spat on the bodies. When Pajana returned and saw what had happened, he turned the bodies inside out; that is why man's insides are filled with the devil's dirt.

See also: ERLIK; ULGEN

2335

**Pajanvaki** (smithy folk)    In Finno-Ugric folklore, spirits who preside over metals.

2336

**Paladins, The Twelve** (officer of the place) In the Charlemagne cycle of legends, 12 knights devoted to Charlemagne's service. The number 12 is derived from the 12 Apostles surrounding Jesus. The usual 12 are Roland (Orlando), nephew of Charlemagne; Rinaldo (Renault), of Montalban, Roland's cousin; Namo (Nami), duke of Bavaria; Salomon (Solomon), king of Brittany; Astolpho of England; Archbishop Turpin; Florismart; Malagigi (Maugis), the magician; Ganelon (Gan), the traitor; Ogier the Dane; Fierambras (Ferumbras), the Saracen; and Oliver. Other names given in various legends are Ivon, Ivory, Otton, Berengier, Anseis, Gerin, Gerier, Engelier, Samson, and Gerard.

See also: APOSTLE; ASTOLPHO; CHARLEMAGNE; FIERAMBRAS; GANELON; OLIVER; RINALDO; ROLAND

2337

**Palden Lhamo**    In Tibetan Buddhism, a goddess, portrayed with eye teeth four inches long, with three eyes, sitting on a chestnut colored mule. Her clothes consist of a girdle made of the skin of a recently flayed man. Her mule, with girth and cropper made of living snakes, tramples underfoot the mangled remains of a human body. The goddess drinks human blood out of a skull.

2338

**Pales**    In Roman mythology, one of the Numina; a goddess of herds and shepherds, invoked for fertility, worshiped at Rome. Pales' festival, Palilia, was celebrated on 21 April, the date Romulus laid the foundations of the city of Rome. Vergil's *Georgics* (3) and Ovid's *Fasti* (book 4) mention the goddess.

See also: OVID; ROMULUS AND REMUS

**2339**

**Pali** An ancient Indian literary language that was used for writing down the canon of Theravada Buddhism.

See also: AGAMA; ANURUDDHA; ARHAT; BHIKKHU; BODHISATTVA; DHARMA; JATAKA; MAHAYANA; MAITREYA; NIRVANA; PRATYEKA-BUDDHA; SUTRA; TRI-RATNA; WESAK

**2340**

**Palinurus** (making water again) In Roman mythology, the helmsman of Aeneas who guided the ship through a storm past Scylla and Charybdis after the defeated Trojans left Carthage. Tempted by the god of sleep, Palinurus closed his eyes and fell overboard. He was found by local tribesmen, who killed him. In Vergil's *Aeneid* (books 3, 5, 6) Palinurus describes his fate when the Trojan hero Aeneas visits the underworld. Because his body had been left on the seashore without proper burial rites, Palinurus was unable to cross the Styx, the river of death. The Sibyl who accompanied Aeneas on his underworld journey then promised Palinurus that, even though denied burial, a shrine (Capo Palinuro in Lucania) would be erected in his honor.

See also: AENEAS; *AENEID, THE*; SIBYLS; STYX

**2341**

**Palis** (foot licker) In Persian-Islamic mythology, a demon who attacks those who fall asleep in the desert. Palis kills his victim by licking the soles of the feet until he has sucked out all of the blood. Once two camel drivers found a way to ward off attacks from Palis. They lay down foot-to-foot on the ground and covered themselves with their clothes. The demon arrived and began to go around the sleepers trying to find their feet but found nothing but their two heads. In despair the demon gave up, crying out: "I have traveled a thousand valleys and thirty-three but never met a man with two heads."

**2342**

**Palladium** (shield of Pallas) In Greek and Roman mythology, a token of Athena that was believed to protect the city of Troy. When it was stolen by the clever Odysseus and Diomedes, it signified that Troy would fall to the enemy. It was believed by the Trojans that the statue or image was sent down from heaven by Zeus to Dardanus, Troy's founder, to ensure Troy's protection. In a variant myth, the Trojan Aeneas rescued the Palladium from Troy and eventually brought the image to Rome. On several occasions it helped save the city. Homer's *Iliad* (book 10), Vergil's *Aeneid* (book 2), and Ovid's *Metamorphoses* (book 13) all tell of the sacred image. The London Palladium derives its name from the mistaken idea that the Palladium was a circus. In English usage the word is figuratively applied to anything on which the safety of a country or people is believed to depend.

See also: DARDANUS; DIOMEDES; *ILIAD, THE*; ODYSSEUS; OVID; TROY

**2343**

**Pallas** (maiden, shield, youth) In Greek and Roman mythology, an epithet often given to Athena. Botticelli's *Pallas and the Centaur* and Edgar Allan Poe's poem "The Raven" both use the title for Athena. Some scholars believe the name Pallas derives from one of the Titans who Athena flayed and whose skin she then used as a covering. Pallas is also a common name for humans in Greek and Roman mythology. One of the best known is a son of Evander who fought with Aeneas in Italy, killing many of the Rutuli. That Pallas was killed by Turnus, king of the Rutulians, according to Vergil's *Aeneid* (books 8–10). Others include a giant son of Uranus and Gaea; a brother of Aegeus, king of Athens and uncle of Theseus, who tried to usurp his brother's kingdom; and a Titan who was the son of Crius and Eurybea, married to Styx and father of Nike, goddess of victory.

See also: AENEAS; *AENEID, THE*; ATHENA; CENTAUR; EVANDER; GAEA; THESEUS; TITANS

2344

**Pallian** In Australian mythology, brother of Pundjel, a creator god.

See also: PUNDJEL

2345

**Pallor and Pavor** (paleness and fear) In Roman mythology, companions of the war god Mars. On Roman coins Pallor is portrayed as a boy with dishevelled hair and Pavor as man with bristling hair and an expression of horror.

See also: MARS

2346

**Palm** A tropical evergreen tree; in Near Eastern mythology, associated with the Tree of Life. In the Old Testament the palm is sometimes a symbol of the ruler of Israel (Isa. 19:15 RSV). In the New Testament the blessed are clothed in white and have "palms in their hands" (Rev. 7:9) as tokens of their martyrdom. St. Christopher's staff was said to be from a palm tree. In the Christian rite of Ash Wednesday the ashes are made from the palms used the previous year on Palm Sunday. In Sicily the palms blessed on Palm Sunday are not only used to remember Christ's triumphant entry into Jerusalem but are hung in homes to induce rain and plentiful harvests.

See also: ASH WEDNESDAY; CHRISTOPHER, ST.

2347

**Pan** (pasture) In Greek mythology, an Arcadian god of flocks, fertility, shepherds, forests, and wild life; son of Hermes and Dryope or Penelope, or of Zeus and Hybris; called Faunus by the Romans. Pan was often portrayed with an erect phallus, though later Greek and Roman art portrayed him as a horned man with a beard and the lower part of a goat (which Christianity later identified with Satan). Pan invented the seven-reed flute, calling it Syrinx, after the nymph Syrinx, who, when he tried to rape her, was transformed into a reed, which Pan used for his

*Pan*

first flute pipe. The English word *panic* derives from the fear inspired by Pan, though in some accounts, Panic is the son of Ares, the war god, and the brother of Eris (discord), Phobos (alarm), Metus (fear), Demios (dread), and Pallor (terror). One of the Homeric Hymns (attributed to Homer but not by him) deals with Pan, as does the poet Pindar. Other literary works about Pan are Shelley's "Hymn of Pan" and E. M. Forster's "Story of Panic." Elizabeth Browning's poem *The Dead Pan* (1844) deals with the myth that when Christ died on the cross, the cry "Great Pan is dead" swept across the world, telling all that the pagan gods were no more. One of the most famous paintings of the god, Luca Signorelli's *The Realm of Pan*, was destroyed in World War II.

See also: ARCADIA; ARES; FAUNUS; HERMES; HOMER; NYMPHS; PENELOPE; ZEUS

2348

**Panacea** (heal-all) In Roman mythology, goddess of health, daughter of Aesculapius and sister of Hygeia, Machaon, and Podalirius. The word *panacea* comes from the name of the goddess.

See also: HYGEIA; MACHAON

**2349**

**Panathenaea** (all-Athenian festival)   In ancient Greek ritual, the summer festival in honor of Athena's birthday. As part of the rite the people presented a peplum to the goddess in a long procession along the Sacred Way to the Parthenon. This scene is depicted on one of the temple friezes of the Elgin Marbles.

See also: ATHENA; ELGIN MARBLES

**2350**

**Panchajana**   In Hindu mythology, a demon who lived in the sea in the form of a conch shell. Panchajana seized the son of Sandipani, but Krishna rescued the boy and killed the demon. Krishna then used the conch shell for a horn. Later the conch shell became one of the symbols of Krishna and Vishnu.

See also: KRISHNA; VISHNU

**2351**

*Panchatantra, The* (five books)   Hindu collection of fables and tales within a narrative framework; some were composed about 200 B.C.E., although the standard text dates from 1199 C.E.

There once lived a king called Immortal Power who had three sons, Rich Power, Fierce Power, and Endless Power. All three sons "were supreme blockheads," and the king therefore called his wise men to see what could be done to educate his sons and prepare them for their duties. He chose a wise Brahman (priest), Vishnusharman, who promised to render the king's sons wise and intelligent in six months, or else, he told the king, "His Majesty is at liberty to show me His Majestic bare bottom."

Vishnusharman took the three princes home and assigned them to learn "by heart five books" of fables that he had composed, as follows:

*The Loss of Friends*, telling of the broken friendship between a lion, Rusty, and a bull, Lively. There are more than 30 tales in this section, told by two jackals, Victor and Cheek.

*The Winning of Friends*, which has as its framing story the tale of the friendship of the crow,

the mouse, the turtle, and the deer, who are called, respectively, Swift, Gold, Slow, and Spot.

*Crows and Owls*, telling of the war between the crows and owls.

*Loss of Gains*, containing some 12 tales, one of which is the well-known *The Ass in the Tiger Skin*, which is found in many Aesopic collections as *The Ass in the Lion's Skin*.

*Ill-Considered Action*, containing 11 tales relating to that subject.

In the various tales in *The Panchatantra* the actors are animals that conform to most folkloric motifs associated with animals: the lion is strong but dull-witted; the jackal, crafty; the heron, stupid; the cat, a hypocrite; and so on.

In his translation of *The Panchatantra* Arthur W. Ryder writes that it "contains the most widely known stories in the world. If it were further declared that the *Panchatantra* is the best collection of stories in the world, the assertion could hardly be disproved, and would probably command the assent of those possessing the knowledge for a judgment."

By the 17th century *The Panchatantra* had been translated into all major European languages. One of its most important influences was on various Aesopic collections of fables. One tale in the collection influenced Hans Christian Andersen, whose *The Princess and the Pea* was inspired by one of the Indian fables.

See also: AESOPIC FABLES; *ASS IN THE LION'S SKIN, THE*; BRAHMAN; FRAME TALE; MOTIF

**2352**

**Pancras, St.**   Fourth century? In Christian legend, martyr, patron saint of children. Invoked against cramp, false witness, headache, and perjury. Feast, 12 May.

Pancras was martyred at 14 after he told Emperor Diocletian that if the ruler's servants behaved as the Roman gods did he would "haste to put them to death." The emperor did not like the quick wit of the boy and had him beheaded. According to St. Gregory of Tours, whenever a "perjurer nears the tomb of St. Pancras, either he falls dead on the flagstones, or else, a demon seizes him and sets him writhing in a fit." Formerly, French kings confirmed treaties in the name of St. Pancras, feeling that either party swearing falsely would drop dead immediately. One legend recorded in *The Golden Legend*, written in the 13th century by Jacobus de Voragine, tells how two men were on trial and "the judge knew which of them was the culprit," but he let them swear their innocence before the altar of St. Peter. When they both remained unharmed he said, "Old Saint Peter is too merciful! Let us consult the young Saint Pancras." They did, and the liar "fell dead in a moment."

See also: *GOLDEN LEGEND, THE*; GREGORY OF TOURS; NICHOLAS, ST; PETER, ST.

2353

**Pandarus** (he who flays all)  In Greek and Roman mythology, the go-between of the lovers Troilus and Cressida. Pandarus was killed by Diomedes during the Trojan War. Pandarus appears in Homer's *Iliad* (book 2), Vergil's *Aeneid* (book 5), Boccaccio's *Filostrato*, Chaucer's *Troilus and Criseyde*, and Shakespeare's *Troilus and Cressida*. The word *pander*, meaning procurer, comes from Pandarus.

See also: *AENEID, THE*; CHAUCER; DIOMEDES; *ILIAD, THE*

2354

**Pandora** (all gifts)  In Greek mythology, the first woman. After Prometheus had created man, Pandora was made of clay by Hephaestus at Zeus's command, in order to punish men. Pandora was given a jar (or box) that contained all of the evils of the world and was told not to open it. She did open it and let loose all evils. All that remained in the box was Elpis (Hope). The expression "Pandora's box" comes from the myth, which is cited by Apollodorus *Bibliotheca* (Library) and Hyginus's *Fables*. It inspired Milton's lines in *Paradise Lost* (book 4.714) that described the fatal beauty of Eve. Pandora also is the subject of Spenser's "Sonnet XXIV," Dante Gabriel

Rossetti's poem "Pandora," and Longfellow's *Masque of Pandora*.

See also: APOLLODORUS; HEPHAESTUS; PROMETHEUS; ZEUS

2355

**P'ang Chu, P'ang Ch'ê, and P'ang Chiao**  In Chinese mythology, three goddesses of the corpse, portrayed as Buddhist nuns, one dressed in green, one in white, and one in red. The three live in the body. When they leave the body they tell the gods of the sins committed by the dead.

2356

**Panis** (misers)  In Hindu mythology, a race of demons who stole cows and hid them in caverns. In the sacred collection of hymns, the Rig-Veda, they are called "the senseless, false, evil-speaking unbelieving, unpraising, unworshiping Panis." Some scholars believe them to be the native inhabitants of India, who were enemies of the invading Aryans.

See also: RIG-VEDA

2357

**P'an-ku** (Phan-ku)  In Chinese mythology, primeval being, creator of humankind.

In some texts P'an-ku emerged from the cosmic hen's egg, which was all that existed before heaven and earth were created. The contents of the egg then divided, producing the Yin and Yang. The heavy elements descended, bringing forth the earth, while the lighter elements produced the sky. For 18,000 years P'an-ku grew at the rate of ten feet a day between heaven and earth, filling the space between the two. When he died, his body became the natural elements making up the earth. In a variant myth P'an-ku made the world, plants, and animals while he was alive. Realizing that there were no people, he made figures out of clay. When they were dry, they were to be impregnated with the vital forces of Yin and Yang. Before full life came to them, however, a storm arose, and P'an-ku brought into his house all of the figurines that were out baking in the sun. Some of them were damaged, and that is why some people are born lame or sick.

In Chinese art P'an-ku, though a giant, is portrayed as a dwarf, dressed either in a bearskin or in leaves. Sometimes he holds the symbol for Yin and Yang.

See also: YIN AND YANG

2358

**Parameshthin** (who stands in the highest place) In Hindu mythology, a title often applied to the gods or to distinguished mortals; a name in the Vedas for a son of Prajapati.

See also: PRAJAPATI; VEDAS

2359

**Paran-ja**   In Hindu mythology, the sword of the storm god, Indra.

See also: INDRA

2360

**Pariacaca**   In the mythology of the Huarochiri (Warachiri) Indians of the western side of the coastal cordillera of Peru, a hero-god. The myth of Pariacaca is told by Francisco de Ávila, a Roman Catholic priest of San Damian, a parish in the district of the Huarochiri, in *A Narrative of the Errors, False Gods, and Other Superstitions and Diabolical Rites . . . [of] the Indians* (1608).

There was a great flood, and five eggs were deposited on Mount Condorcoto. From the eggs were born five falcons who turned into men, Pariacaca and his brothers. They went about doing many marvelous things.

Pariacaca decided to try his strength against the rival god, Hulallallo Caruincho, and went in search of him. Pariacaca's strength lay in wind, rain, and flood; Caruincho's, in fire. Passing through a village called Huagaihusa in the guise of a poor man, he was not well received except by one young woman, who brought him chicha to drink. He destroyed the place by rain and flood,

having first warned the woman and her family so that they could escape. He defeated Hulallallo Caruincho and caused him to flee toward the Amazonian forest.

But Caruincho only pretended to enter the forest. He turned himself into a bird and hid on a cliff on Mount Tacilluka. This time the five sons of Pariacaca swept the mountain with thunderbolts and a storm, and Caruincho had to flee again, but he left behind an enormous serpent with two heads that was changed to stone by Pariacaca. Closely pursued, Caruincho took refuge in the jungle. The sons of Pariacaca went to Mount Llamallaku, where they called together all of the peoples and established the cult of Pariacaca. Long afterward when the Inca came to power, they took over this cult.

Pariacaca is believed by some scholars to be a god of the waters or a deified mountain that gives both rain and irrigating streams.

*Hector chiding Paris (John Flaxman)*

2361

**Paris** (wallet)   In Greek mythology, abductor of Helen, second son of King Priam of Troy and Queen Hecuba; brother of Aesacus, Cassandra, Creusa, Deiphobus, Hector, Helenus, Polyxena, and Troilus; married to Oenone; father of Corythus and Daphnis. Before Paris was born, Hecuba dreamed she would deliver a firebrand that would destroy Troy. Priam, therefore, had

Paris, also called Alexander (champion), exposed at birth on Mount Ida. But the child was suckled by a she-bear for five days and then raised by a shepherd, Agelaus, as his own son. While a youth, Paris married the nymph Oenone, whom he later deserted. To settle an argument among the goddesses about who would receive a golden apple and have the honor of being called the fairest, Zeus, who did not wish to make a choice, sent his messenger god Hermes to Paris to ask him to make the choice. The three goddesses, Aphrodite, Artemis, and Hera, appeared before the youth in what has come to be known as the Judgment of Paris. Hera, wife of Zeus, promised Paris royal power, Athena promised victory in war, and Aphrodite promised him the most beautiful woman in the world. Paris chose Aphrodite as the fairest and gave her the golden apple. Of course, he made enemies of the other goddesses by his decision. His prize, the most beautiful woman in the world, was Helen, wife of King Menelaus of Sparta and mother of Hermione. Keeping her word, the goddess Aphrodite led Paris to Sparta, where he was entertained by Menelaus and Helen as a guest. While Menelaus was away, Aphrodite made Helen fall in love with Paris, and the two fled. Eventually this rash act led to the Trojan War when the Greek forces under Agamemnon sought to return Helen to Menelaus.

During the Trojan War, Paris's reputation was that of a coward because he was apt to run away from the fight and go home to have sexual intercourse with Helen. After 10 years of war Paris and Menelaus met one to one on the battlefield. It was believed that the war would end when the duel was over. Paris threw his spear at Menelaus, but Menelaus turned the spear aside with his shield. Then Menelaus cast his spear, which only ripped Paris's tunic. The two men then drew their swords. Menelaus's sword broke during the first exchange, but he was so angry he grabbed Paris by his helmet and dragged him toward the Greek camp by his helmet's chin strap. Aphrodite, fearful that her favorite would die, cut the strap, covered Paris in a cloud, and

took him to Helen's bedroom to make love. Homer's *Iliad* does not tell us of the end of Paris, but later Greek myth says he killed Achilles with a poisoned arrow in the hero's vulnerable heel and was then killed by a poisoned arrow of Philoctetes. Paris asked his men to take him to Oenone, the nymph he had deserted. She refused to save his life, but when he died she killed herself. Paris appears in Homer's *Iliad*; Vergil's *Aeneid* (books 1, 7); Ovid's *Metamorphoses* (book 12) and *Heroides* (16, 17); William Morris's "Death of Paris" in *The Earthly Paradise*; W. S. Landor's *Death of Paris and Oenone*; Tennyson's "Dream of Fair Women," *Oenone*, and *Death of Oenone*; and in David's painting *Paris and Helen*.

See also: *AENEID, THE*; AESACUS; AGAMEMNON; APHRODITE; ARTEMSI; CASSANDRA; DAPHNIS; HECTOR; HELENUS; *ILIAD, THE*; MENELAUS; OENONE; POLYXENA; PRIAM; TROY; ZEUS

*The Judgment of Paris (John Flaxman)*

2362

**Parnassus** (surrounding island)   In Greek history and mythology, mountain of Phoas near Delphi, northwest of Athens, consecrated to Apollo, the Muses, and Dionysus. Its slopes contained the famous oracle of Apollo. The boat of Deucalion came to rest on the mountain's slopes after the flood. The theme of Apollo and the Muses was painted by Raphael, Mantegna, Poussin, and Domenichino, all using images from Ovid's *Metamorphoses*. The name of the culture center in Paris, Montparnasse, is derived from

Parnassus. Between 1860 and 1876 a group of young artsts published a periodical, *Le Parnasse contemporain* (The Modern Parnassus), in which they showed their love for Greek and Roman art and cultue.

See also: APOLLO; DELPHI; DEUCALION; DIONYSUS; MUSES

2363

**Parsley**   An herb in ancient Greek and Roman ritual, associated with death and resurrection. The Greeks and Romans often decked their tombs with parsley wreaths. The ancient Greek expression "to be in need of parsley" was a way of saying someone was close to death. According to Greek mythology, the parsley herb sprang up from the blood of the hero Achemorus when he was slain by a great serpent. The Nemean Games were held in Achemorus's honor, with foot, horse, and chariot races, boxing, and wrestling. Wreaths of parsley crowned the winners. In Homer's *Odyssey* Calypso's magic island is covered with parsley, which connects the herb with sexual love. In English folklore, it was believed that babies were found in parsley beds. The magical qualities of parsley are referred to in the refrain to Simon and Garfunkel's song "Scarborough Fair": "parsley, sage, rosemary and thyme."

See also: CALYPSO; ROSEMARY; SAGE

2364

**Parthenope** (maiden face)   In Greek mythology, one of the Sirens, daughter of Achelous and Calliope; sister of Ligeia and Leucosia. She drowned herself after she failed to lure Odysseus to his death. Homer's *Odyssey* (book 12) tells of her fate.

See also: ACHELOUS CALLIOPE; LIGEIA; ODYSSEUS; *ODYSSEY, THE*; SIRENS

2365

**Parthenos** (virgin, unwed)   In Greek cult, title frequently applied to Athena as virgin goddess but also used for other female deities. The Par-

thenon, on the highest part of the Acropolis in Athens, was dedicated to Athena Parthenos. Begun in 447 B.C.E., the temple was dedicated in 438; it was designed by Callicrates and Ictinus and contained what are now called the Elgin Marbles as well as the statue of the goddess Athena by Phidias (c. 490–415 B.C.E.). The temple became a Christian church dedicated to the Virgin Mary; later it was converted into a mosque.

See also: ATHENA; ELGIN MARBLES

2366

**Partridge**   Fowl-like bird with a short beak, short legs, and a short tail. In Greek mythology the partridge, symbolic of fecundity and fertility, is sacred to both Aphrodite and Zeus. In ancient Hebrew folk belief the female partridge was believed to steal the eggs of other birds (Jer. 17:11). An early Christian work, *The Acts of John*, sees the bird as a symbol of the soul, but St. Ambrose, writing later, sees it as the devil. Ambrose's concept is reflected in a 12th-century Latin bestiary that cites the bird for its evil sexual habits: a male partridge coupled with another male.

See also: AMBROSE, ST.; APHRODITE; BEAST EPIC; ZEUS

2367

**Paruksti** (the wonderful)   In North American Indian mythology (Pawnee), storm and thunder personified as all of the life-giving and self-renewing powers of the earth.

2368

**Pasiphaë** (she who shines for all)   In Greek mythology, daughter of the Titan sun god Helios and Perseis (Perse); sister of Aeetes, Circe, and Perses; married to King Minos of Crete; mother of Acacallis, Androgeus, Ariadne, Catreus, Deucalion, Euryale, Glaucus, Lycastus, Phaedra, and Xenodice. She was also mother of the Minotaur by the white bull. Minos had requested from the sea god Poseidon a magnificent bull for sacrifice. The god sent a white bull, but Minos substituted another. In revenge, Poseidon had Pasiphaë fall in love with the bull. Daedalus built a wooden cow for Pasiphaë to hide in while having sexual intercourse with the white bull. Their offspring was the Minotaur, half bull and half man. The monster, which fed on human flesh, was hidden in a labyrinth constructed by Daedalus. Pasiphaë bewitched Minos so that all of his mistresses died after having sexual intercourse with him. Pasiphaë appears in Boccaccio's *Genealogy of the Gods*, in which she is a symbol of the soul, while her husband is human. She also appears in Henri de Montherlant's *Pasiphaé* with illustrations by Henri Matisse in 1944 and Jean Cocteau in 1948.

See also: ARIADNE; DAEDALUS; HELIOS; MINOS; MINOTAUR; PHAEDRA; POSEIDON; TITANS

2369

**Passover** (Pesah)    In Judaism, feast held from the 15th to the 22nd of Nisan (13–20 April) commemorating the Exodus of the Hebrews from bondage in Egypt; it is one of the three seasonal festivals, the others being Shavouth (Pentecost), also called the Feast of Weeks, and Sukkoth, or Feast of Booths. The narrative and ritual of the feast is told in the Book of Exodus (chaps. 12–15). Originally, according to some biblical scholars, at the first full moon in the first month of spring it was the custom for a lamb or goat to be slaughtered at twilight, then eaten at a common meal in the middle of the night along with unleavened bread and bitter herbs. This was to be done in haste. Whatever portion remained uneaten was to be burned before daybreak. As soon as the slaughtering had been done, a bunch of hyssop was dipped into the lamb's or goat's blood and used to sprinkle a few drops on the lintels and doorposts of each house. This ritual was known as *pesah*. It was followed by a Feast of Unleavened Bread, during which no fermented food was allowed to be eaten. It is believed that the Exodus from Egypt coincided with the traditional *pesah* ceremony and was later incorporated into the Hebrew feast. It is now believed by most biblical scholars that not all of the tribes of Israel went down to Egypt nor came out of it at the Exodus.

The main ceremony of Passover is the *Seder* (order of service or formal procedure), in which various foods are eaten and the narrative, called *Haggadah* (recital) of the Exodus is recalled. Some of the foods eaten are *matzah* (unleavened bread), bitter herbs (e.g., horseradish), and *haroseth* (a mixture of chopped apples, raisins, nuts, and cinnamon), recalling the mortar used to build the cities of Pithol and Rameses by the Hebrews for their Egyptian masters. Wine, at least four cups, is also drunk during the ceremony. At the conclusion of the meal an extra cup of wine is filled for Elijah the prophet, who will come, it is believed, on Passover night to herald the final redemption of Israel. The door of the house is flung open to allow the prophet to enter. Some biblical scholars believe that Jesus was celebrating the Passover at the Last Supper, though many others believe it was a simple Jewish meal. In the liturgy (Mass) of the Holy Eucharist in Roman and Anglican churches, the priest says "Christ, our Passover is sacrificed for us," and the people answer with "Therefore let us keep the feast." This is based on Paul's writing in 1 Corinthians (5:7–8).

See also: ELIJAH; SUKKOTH

2370

**Patala**    In Hindu mythology, collective name for the lowest region of the underworld, inhabited by Nagas. It consists of Atala, Sutala, Vitala, Tatala, Mahatala, Rastala, and Patala. In contrast to most underworlds Patala is a place filled with sensual gratification, not punishment.

See also: NAGAS

2371

**Patrick, St.** (noble man)    c. 373–464. In Christian legend, Apostle of Ireland. Feast, 17 March.

Part of the biography of St. Patrick is supplied by the saint himself in *The Confession of Saint Pat-*

*St. Patrick*

*rick*, which is considered authentic by most scholars. In the *Confession* Patrick tells us that his father's name was Calpurnius and that he collected taxes for the Romans. Patrick lived with his family on a farm that was raided by Pictish pirates when he was 16. He was captured and carried off to Ireland, where he was sold as a slave. He eventually escaped and returned to his parents in Britain. Some time later he left to study for the priesthood in Gaul under St. Martin of Tours. He rose to the rank of bishop and was sent to convert the Irish.

The legends surrounding the saint's activities in Ireland are numerous. The most famous legend is that he drove all of the snakes out of Ireland. When St. Patrick ordered the snakes into the sea, one of the older reptiles refused to obey. St. Patrick made a box and invited the serpent to enter, pretending it was a place for the creature to rest. The serpent said the box was too small, but St. Patrick said it was large enough. The serpent kept insisting it was too small, while St. Patrick said it was just right. Eventually the serpent entered the box to prove his point, and Patrick closed the lid and threw the box into the sea.

A tale recorded in *The Golden Legend*, written in the 13th century, tells how Patrick "traced a wide circle with his staff, and a very deep pit opened within it. And it was revealed to Patrick that the pit was the opening to a purgatory, and that those who chose to go down in it could expiate their sins, and would be spared their purgatory after death."

In actuality, St. Patrick's purgatory was a small cave on the island of Lough Derg, a lake near Pettigoe in Donegal. St. Patrick had the walls painted with various scenes of torment to instill fear in those who visited the cave. The cave became a place of pilgrimage for those who wanted to experience the pains of Purgatory and hell in this life, to avoid them in the next. Pilgrims would spend nine days fasting as part of the ritual. Henry of Saltrey tells how Sir Owain visited it. The hero Fortunatus also was supposed to have been to the place. The cave was blocked on St. Patrick's day in 1497 by orders of the pope. Calderón's play *El Purgatorio de San Patricio* deals with the legend. In art St. Patrick is usually depicted banishing the serpents and with a shamrock leaf. When he explained the Trinity to the heathen priests on the hill of Tara, he used the shamrock as his symbol.

See also: FORTUNATUS; *GOLDEN LEGEND, THE*; PIED PIPER OF HAMELIN; SNAKES

**Patroclus** (Patrocles) (glory of the father)    In Greek mythology, friend and cousin of Achilles; son of Menoetius and Periopis or Sthenele. Patroclus was killed by the Trojan hero Hector, who in turn was killed by Achilles in revenge. Twelve Trojan nobles were sacrificed on Patroclus's funeral pyre. In post-Homeric literature, it was taken for granted that Patroclus and Achilles were lovers, though there is no trace of that relationship in the *Iliad*. In later Greek mythology, it was said that his ashes were mixed with those of

*Patroclus's funeral pyre*

Achilles. Both were worshiped on the White Island as semideities. The funeral games of Patroclus form book 23 of Homer's *Iliad*. Patroclus also appears in Ovid's *Metamorphoses* (book 13) and Shakespeare's *Troilus and Cressida*.

See also: ACHILLES; HECTOR; *ILIAD, THE*; OVID

*The conversion of St. Paul*

2373

**Paul, St.** (small, little)   First century. In the Bible, N.T., Apostle to the Gentiles. Patron of tent makers, weavers, saddlers, basket weavers, theologians, and workmen's associations. Invoked in stormy weather on the ocean and as protection against snakebite. Patron of many countries and cities such as London, Rome, Malta, Frankfurt, and Berlin. Feast, 29 June.

Nearly all of the original materials for the life of St. Paul are contained in the Acts of the Apostles and in his Epistles, or letters, in the New Testament. Added to these biblical works is the apocryphal *Acts of St. Paul*, written in the latter half of the second century, which gives legends not contained in the biblical works (though it also covers those with a romantic interpretation) and *The Golden Legend*, written in the 13th century, which incorporates the earlier works.

Paul was born in Tarsus, a city in Cilicia, Asia Minor, about 1 B.C.E. His Jewish name was Saul, and his Latin name, to which as a Roman citizen he was entitled, was Paul. The latter was used exclusively after he became the Apostle to the Gentiles. Of his parents we know nothing, except that his father was of the tribe of Benjamin (Phil. 3:5) and a Pharisee (Acts 23:6). Paul dictated his letters in Greek. He was sent to Jerusalem for his education "at the feet of Gamaliel," one of the most eminent of all Doctors of the Law. As was the custom with rabbis, Paul also learned a trade, tent making. Saul was yet a "young man" (Acts 7:58) when St. Stephen was stoned to death. Among those who disputed with Stephen were some "of them of Cilicia." Paul held the cloaks of those who stoned Stephen while he was witnessing the act of murder. St. Augustine believed that when Paul saw St. Stephen pray for his enemies the seeds of his conversion to Christ were planted. At first, however, Paul wished to pursue this new group of Christians and punish them by reporting them to the Jewish high priest. On a mission to Damascus to arrest some Christians and bring them to Jerusalem for trial, the decisive event in his life occurred. His conversion is told three times in the Acts of the Apostles (9:1–10; 22:5–16; and 26:12–18). According to these accounts Paul saw a great light and heard the words, "Saul, Saul, why persecutest thou Me?" In reply to the question, "Who art thou, Lord?" Paul heard, "I am Jesus, Whom thou persecutest." Paul was then blinded for some time. Soon afterward he received baptism and the imposition of hands from Ananias (Acts 9:17) and then left for Arabia (Gal. 1:17). He then went on three important missionary journeys and returned to Jerusalem. He was met by a hostile mob, who accused him of transgression of the law of Moses. He was beaten by the mob and rescued by Roman soldiers, who put him in protective custody (Acts 21:27–36). After a time he was sent to Rome for trial (he was a Roman citizen).

On the way he was shipwrecked on Malta, where he miraculously escaped being bitten by a poisonous snake. The Acts of the Apostles ends with the statement that St. Paul remained in captivity in Rome for two years. The rest of his life is not told us. Christian legend, however, has supplied the remainder.

According to *The Golden Legend*, "When Paul came to Rome, Nero's reign had not as yet been confirmed." When Nero heard that Paul and the Jews were quarreling about Jewish law and Christian faith, he paid so little attention to Paul that the saint was free and could go "wherever he wished and could preach without obstacles." Paul became well known as a preacher. One day "Nero's cup-bearer" and one of his favorites, named Patroclus, climbed up onto a window ledge so he could hear Paul preach. He fell asleep, fell out of the window, and was killed. Paul thought Nero would grieve for him, so he asked that the body of the young man be brought to him. "When the corpse was lying in front of Paul he awakened him and sent him to the Emperor." Nero, however, was very upset that his old lover returned and had him, along with others who now professed belief in Christ, imprisoned. He also had Paul handcuffed and brought before him. Paul was freed, however, after the Roman mob threatened Nero, but he was brought again before the emperor, who accused Paul of being a magician. "Behead this deceiver. Make an end to this criminal," Nero cried. Paul was beheaded. "When his head was severed from his body . . . there flowed a stream of milk" from his neck. Paul's ghost then appeared to Nero, who became so terrified that "he became mad and no longer knew what to do."

The scene in St. Paul's life that is most usually painted is the Conversion of St. Paul. Among the most famous works are those of Peter Brueghel, painted in 1567, Caravaggio, and Jacopo Tintoretto's fantastic canvas in the National Gallery of Art, Washington, D.C. Rembrandt painted *Paul in Prison* in 1627, and Giotto painted *The Beheading of St. Paul* about 1311. In many paintings and sculptures St. Paul is shown with a sword. If placed downward it symbolizes his death; if placed upward, his preaching. Often he carries a book, the symbol of the Epistles in the New Testament. His physical features were described in the *Acts of Paul* by a man named Titus, who had personally seen the saint. He was "small, bald, had bowlegs but a strong body, with eyebrows meeting and with a slightly bent but graceful nose, and at times he looked like a human being and then again he had the face of an angel." Sholem Asch's novel about St. Paul, entitled *The Apostle*, has a major portion devoted to Paul's Jewish background.

See also: AUGUSTINE, ST.; *GOLDEN LEGEND, THE*; STEPHEN, ST.

2374
**Paul Bunyan**  In American folklore, giant lumberjack of the Great Lakes and the Pacific Northwest. Various places claim Paul Bunyan as their own: Maine, Michigan, Minnesota, Oregon, and the Canadian woods. As a baby Paul grew so fast that his father could not keep making cradles to fit him. At one month Paul was 20 feet tall and still growing. Tired of his parents' arguing, he took his cradle and left home to begin a life of adventure as a lumberjack. Stories deal with the large size of his camps; the size and eating habits of Babe the Blue Ox; and the creation of American geography. Paul dragged a spiked pole behind him to create the Grand Canyon, and a leak in Babe's water trough started the Mississippi River. Among Paul's companions are Hot Biscuit Slim, a cook; Little Merry, who got the food; Johnny Inkslinger, the camp secretary; Shanty Boy, who could sing any song; and Galloping Kid, who gave up being a cowboy to be with Paul.

Folklore scholars question whether Paul Bunyan is true oral folklore. There is a trickle of oral tradition associated with Old Paul, but he enters print in an article written by James McGillivray for the Detroit *News-Tribune* of 24 July 1910, titled "The Round River Drive." He later sums up his acquaintance with Paul with this statement:

"My first knowledge of such a lumber camp character now known as Paul Bunyan came to me when I was scaling logs at the logging camp of Rory Frazer, twenty-two miles east of Grayling on the north branch of the Au Sable river. I was thirteen years of age, but big, like an adult man. . . . The men had a lounging shanty by themselves, removed from Rory's domicile, and hardly an evening went by that some lumberjack did not bring out some new angle on the prowess of a mythical 'Paul Bunyan.' I had never heard the name before, despite the fact that I lived in the renowned lumbermill area of Oscoda-Au Sable, twin towns that led the world in sawmill production back in the eighties."

The early oral tradition is supported in a diary kept by Edward O. Tabor, a teacher who worked as a lumberjack during the summer in Palmer Junction, Oregon. He records a few fragmentary tales about Paul and his blue ox. By 1914 W. B. Laughead produced a small booklet, *Paul Bunyan and His Big Blue Ox*, a pamphlet for the Red River Lumber Company, originally located in Minnesota but relocated to California. Laughead wrote: "It should be stated that the names supporting characters, including the animals, are inventions by the writer of this version." The oral chronicles did not, in his hearing, call any of the characters by name except Paul Bunyan himself.

Both Douglas Malloch's narrative poem "The Round River Drive," which appeared in *The American Lumberman*, and Carl Sandburg's "Who Made Paul Bunyan?" in *The People, Yes* deal with Paul's legend, as did Virginia Tunvey, Father Shepard, James Stevens, Glen Rounds, Dell J. McCormick, and Louis Untermeyer. Robert Frost's poem "Paul's Wife" deals with the hero's wife. During the 1950s Richard M. Dorson coined the term *fakelore* in his writings about Paul Bunyan in an attempt to distinguish between living oral traditions and individuals' spurious, synthetic writings consciously contrived and usually for financial gain.

See also: FAKELORE; JOE MAGARAC; MIKE FINK; PECOS BILL

## 2375

**Pausanias**   Second century C.E. Greek travel author of the *Description of Greece*, which covers topography, legends, myths, rituals, and histories of various places. It is an invaluable source for many myths and lost artworks. The 10 books are (1) Attica and Megara; (2) Argolis, and others; (3) Laconia; (4) Messenia; (5–6) Elis and Olympia; (7) Achaia; (8) Arcadia; (9) Boeotia; and (10) Phocis and Delphi.

## 2376

**Pawang** (wizard)   In the Malay Peninsula, wizard, medicine man, or magician. The office is usually hereditary, or the appointment is practically confined to the members of one family. The *pawang* or *bomor* is the intermediary between man and the supernatural. He attends new projects and important rites, such as those connected with birth, marriage, and death. He also acts as a spirit medium and pronounces oracles while in a trance; he possesses considerable political influence; he occasionally practices austerities; and he observes some degree of chastity. A related term, *pantang*, is used for anything that is forbidden or taboo in the culture.

## 2377

**Pawang Pukat**   In Malayan mythology, a wizard who was turned into a porpoise. Once there was a Pawang Pukat who had bad luck all of the time. He resolved to use magic to change his fortune. One day, having caught nothing, he asked his friends to collect an immense quantity of mangrove leaves in their boat. He carried the leaves out to the fishing ground, scattered them on the surface of the water, together with a few handfuls of parched and saffron-stained rice, and repeated a series of spells over them.

The next time he went fishing, the leaves had been transformed into fish of all shapes and sizes, and an immense haul was the result. The fishing wizard gave directions to have all the proceeds divided among his family and debtors. Then, without warning, he plunged into the sea, reappearing as a porpoise.

**Pax** (peace)    In Roman mythology, goddess of peace; equivalent to the Greek goddess Eirene; also associated with Salus and Concordia by the Romans. Her cult became popular during the reign of Augustus Caesar, and her most famous monument was the Ara Pacis, a large altar dedicated on 30 January, 9 B.C.E., by the Roman Senate to commemorate Augustus's safe return from Gaul and Spain. The feast of Pax was held 3 January.

See also: EIRENE

**Paynal** (Paynalton) (he who hastens)    In an Aztec rite, name given to the man who played the part of the war god Huitzilopochtli. According to Fray Bernardino de Sahagún in *Historia general de las cosas de Nueva España* (1570–1582), this deputy god "had to go personally to summon men so that they might go forthwith to fight the enemy." When Paynal died he was honored by the people.

See also: HUITZILOPOCHTLI

**Peach**    A fruit tree. In China the peach stands for immortality and springtime. The Chinese god of longevity is often portrayed emerging from a peach. In European Christian tradition, the peach is a sign of salvation, often appearing in paintings of the Virgin and Child.

See also: MOMOTARO

**Peacock**    The male peafowl, having long, spotted, iridescent tail feathers that can be spread out like a fan. In world mythology and folklore the peacock is sometimes a symbol of pride and vanity. In *Henry VI, Part I* (3.3) Shakespeare writes:

Let frantic Talbot triumph for a while
And like a peacock sweep along his tail;
We'll pull his plumes and take away his train.

Shakespeare knew the Greek myth of the origin of the peacock's colorful tail feathers. Hera, the wife of Zeus, sent the hundred-eyed giant Argos to watch Io, a mistress of Zeus who had been transformed into a heifer. Zeus, in the guise of a woodpecker, led the god Hermes to slay the giant. Hera, unable to take revenge on either Hermes or Zeus, contented herself with taking the giant's eyes and placing them in the tail of her favorite bird, the peacock, which made the bird quite proud.

In Buddhist mythology the peacock is a symbol of vanity but also a symbol of compassion and watchfulness. In Chinese mythology and folklore the peacock is a symbol of rank, beauty, and dignity and was an emblem of the Ming Dynasty. In Hindu mythology the peacock is the mount of Brahma, Kama, and Skanda and emblem of Sarasvati.

In Christian symbolism the peacock's tail was sometimes used as the All-Seeing Eye of the Church. It also symbolized immortality of the soul since it was believed that the peacock's flesh did not decay. St. Augustine wrote in *The City of God*: "Who except God, the Creator of all things, endowed the flesh of the dead peacock with the power of never decaying." Christian legend says the saint experimented with a dead peacock and found this to be true. In early Christian art two peacocks facing each other was symbolic of the souls of the faithful drinking from the Fountain of Life.

In Islamic folklore the peacock was the original guardian of the Gates of Paradise, but it ate the devil, who then, inside the bird, entered Paradise and worked the fall of Adam and Eve. In Persian mythology two peacocks facing on either side of the Tree of Life symbolize man's dual nature of good and evil.

See also: ADAM AND EVE; AUGUSTINE, ST.; BRAHMA; HERMES; HERA; IO; KAMA; SKANDA; WOODPECKER; ZEUS

2382

**Pecos Bill**    In American folklore, a tough Western hero who was the subject of many adventures. Edward O'Reilly created the figure of Pecos Bill for the *Century* magazine in 1923. After the hero had killed "all the Indians and bad men," as one tale says, he headed West. First, he encountered a 12-foot snake, which he killed, and then a big mountain lion, which he used as his riding mount to replace his wounded horse. When he arrived at a cowboy campsite, he grabbed a handful of beans and crammed them into his mouth, then he grabbed the coffeepot to wash them down.

He said, "Who in the hell is boss around here, anyway?"

"I was," said a big fellow about seven feet tall, "but you are now, stranger."

Other legends tell how he first invented roping. He had a rope that reached from the Rio Grande to the Big Bow, and he would amuse himself by throwing a loop up in the sky and catching buzzards and eagles. He could also rope bears, wolves, and panthers. The first time he saw a train he thought it was some varmint, and he threw his rope around it and brought it to a halt. There are at least two accounts of his death. One tale says he died laughing when he saw a Boston man dressed up in "a mail-order cowboy outfit," and another tale says he "died of solemncholy" when he heard a country lawyer talk about keeping "inviolate the sacred traditions of the old west."

Pecos Bill was depicted on a box of Kellogg's Cocoa Krispies cereal, and Walt Disney featured him in the 1948 film *Melody Times*.

2383

**Pedro the Cruel**    1334–1369. In medieval history and legend, king of Castile and León, who appears in numerous Spanish ballads. Don Pedro was popular with the people but hated by the nobles. Legend credits him with the death of his wife, Queen Blanche, and the murder of her three brothers. When Pedro died in battle, his head was cut off and his remains buried. Later they were disinterred by his daughter, the wife of the English John of Gaunt, and deposited in Seville.

See also: BALLAD

*Pegasus*

2384

**Pegasus** (of the springs)    In Greek mythology, a winged horse who sprang from the blood of the slain Gorgon Medusa when her head was cut off by the hero Perseus. Bellerophon, another Greek hero, captured the winged horse with the aid of a golden bridle given him by Athena when she encountered Pegasus drinking from the Pierian spring. With Pegasus's aid Bellerophon killed the monster Chimera. When Pegasus's hoof touched the earth, the magical spring Hippocrene gushed forth. Bellerophon, becoming overly ambitious, tried to reach Mount Olympus on Pegasus, but Pegasus knew better and threw his rider. Finally, Zeus gave Pegasus a home on Mount Olympus. Homer's *Iliad* (book 6), Ovid's *Metamorphoses* (book 4), Horace's *Odes IV* (11.27), Spenser's *Faerie Queene* (1.9.21), Shakespeare's *King Henry Part I* (4.1.109), Milton's *Paradise Lost* (book 7.4), Pope's *Essay on Criticism* (1.150), and Schiller's *Pegasus im Joche* all deal with the mythical animal.

See also: ATHENA; BELLEROPHONE; CHIMERA; GORGONS; *ILIAD, THE*; OVID; PERSEUS; ZEUS

2385

**Peklo** In Slavic mythology, a name for the underworld, the land of the dead. The name apparently comes from *pech'* (to bake). The word suggests the warmth of paradise, not the heat of hell.

2386

**Peko** (Pekko) In Finno-Ugric mythology, a barley god worshiped by the Estonians. Peko's image, made of wax, was the common property of the community, with each farm having the privilege of hosting the god's image for a year. For Peko's feast (which was held at Whitsuntide) a special beer was brewed, and prayers were offered to the god, calling on "Peko, our god, shepherd our herds," to "look after our horses, protect also our corn from snow, from hail!" The image of the god was then left at the feast, and a wrestling contest took place outside. The person who was first bruised was then chosen the guardian of the god for the next year.

See also: WHITSUNDAY

2387

**Pele** In Polynesian mythology, Hawaiian volcanic goddess who lives in the crater of Kilauea on Hawaii.

In some myths Pele is said to have come to Hawaii from Tahiti, fleeing from her sister, whose husband she had seduced. In another account she is said to have fled from a flood, and a third version says she simply liked to travel. A sister, Hi'iaka, is Pele's constant companion. When Pele settled at Kilauea she fell in love with a young chief, Lohiau, from Kana'i. She told him she would send someone to fetch him in three days. Back at her volcano home, she instructed her sister Hi'iaka to fetch her husband. When Hi'iaka arrived she discovered that Lohiau had died of a broken heart, but she caught his fleeing spirit, placed it back in his body, and brought him to her sister.

However, during this delay Pele had become so jealous of her sister that she caused a lava stream to destroy Hopoe, her sister's close friend. Finally, the two sisters played a game of kilu (similar to quoits) to determine who would have the love of Lohiau. Hi'iaka won, but Pele was not happy and tried to kill the couple. Hi'iaka's magic protected her from Pele's flames, but Lohiau was destroyed, only to be restored once again to life by Hi'iaka's magic.

2388

**Peleus** (muddy) In Greek mythology, king of the Myrmidons and an Argonaut; son of Aeacus, king of Aegina and Endeis; husband of the sea nymph Thetis; father of Achilles. In Catullus's poem 64, *Peleus and Thetis*, it was at Peleus's marriage feast that Eris (discord) threw an apple with the inscription "for the fairest" into the gathering and caused a dispute among the goddesses for possession of the apple. That dispute led to the Judgment of Paris and the Trojan War. Homer's *Iliad* (book 9), Euripides' *Andromache*, Apollodorus's *Bibliotheca* (Library), and Ovid's *Metamorphoses* (book 11) all refer to Peleus or tell his tale.

See also: ACHILLES; AEACUS; APPLE OF DISCORD; MYRMIDONS; THETIS

2389

**Pelican** A large, web-footed, fish-eating bird having a large bill with a distensible pouch. In medieval Christian belief the pelican was a symbol of a pious, self-sacrificing creature identified with Christ. St. Jerome writes that the pelican was known to restore life to its dead young by shedding its own blood after the offspring had been killed by a serpent. The saint then explained that the serpent was the devil; the off-

*Pelican*

the one she had eaten. As a man, Pelops fell in love with Hippodameia. To win her hand, he had to enter a chariot race against her father, Oenomaus. He won by bribing Oenomaus's charioteer, Myrtilus, to remove the axle pin of Oenomaus's chariot just before the race. After his victory Pelops killed Myrtilus, either to avoid paying him or perhaps to silence the only witness to his crime, by casting him in the ocean afterward called Myrtoan, Myrtilus, or Oenomaus. His tale appears in Pindar, Appollonius, Hyginus, and Ovid's *Metamorphoses* (book 6). The preparations for the chariot race appear on the east pediment of the Temple of Zeus at Olympia.

See also: ATLAS; ATREUS; DEMETER; HERMES; NIOBE; OVID; PELOPS; PERSEPHONE; TANTALUS; ZEUS

spring, mankind trapped in sin; and the pelican, Christ, who shed his blood to save mankind. Dante's *The Divine Comedy* calls Christ *nostro pelicano* (our pelican).

See also: JEROME, ST.

2390

**Pelops** (muddy face)   In Greek mythology, a hero, son of Tantalus and Atlas's daughter, Dione; brother of Niobe; father of Atreus and Thyestes. When he was a child, his father killed him, cooked him, and served him at a feast of the gods to test whether a god would recognize human flesh. Only Demeter, mourning the loss of Persephone, ate part of Pelops's shoulder bone. Hermes reconstructed Pelops's body, and Demeter gave him an ivory shoulder to replace

2391

**Penanngga Lan**   In Malayan mythology, a vampire woman, often a woman who has died in childbirth, returning to torment small children with her horrible face and her entrails hanging out.

See also: LA LLORONA; VAMPIRE

2392

**Penates** (of the inner chamber, storehouse)   In Roman mythology, household gods, originally spirits of the dead. Their images were generally made of wax, ivory, silver, or earth, and offerings of wine, incense, fruits, and sometimes lambs, sheep, or goats were made to them. When a family moved from one house to another or from one place to another, it was customary for the head of the family to remove his Penates and establish them in the new house even before he thought of his family's comfort. Vergil's *Aeneid* (book 2) tells how Aeneas, before fleeing burning Troy, placed the Penates and Lares on his father's back and then carried his father on *his* back. Raphael painted the scene of the flight.

See also: AENEAS; *AENEID, THE*; TROY

*Penelope and Telemachus*

**Penelope** (with a web over her face, striped duck)   In Greek mythology, the faithful wife of Odysseus, daughter of Icarius and Periboea or Asterodia. Penelope was mother of Telemachus. When Odysseus sailed for the Trojan War, Penelope was left to manage the household affairs in Ithaca. In a short time she was hounded by local suitors to remarry. She kept them at bay by saying she first had to finish weaving a shroud for her father-in-law, Laertes. Each day she would weave, but at night she would undo the work. Finally, after three years, she was betrayed by one of her maids and forced to finish the piece. Athena, who protected Penelope and her husband, told her to offer herself to the suitor who could string the great bow of Odysseus and shoot through a row of double-headed axes. By this time Odysseus, who had been gone some 20 years, had returned and was disguised as a beggar in the hall. He not only strung the bow but also killed the suitors. The couple were then reunited. In Homer's *Odyssey* (books 16, 17) Penelope is characterized as a model of feminine virtue and chastity, being called "wise" and "prudent." In later, post-Homeric legend, she maintained that characterization, except in Peloponnesus, where it was believed she had committed adultery.

There was a cult to Penelope associated with a duck or other species of bird in eastern Arcadia, supposedly the site of her death. Ovid's *Heroides* (1) and *Ars amatoria* (3.15) deal with her love for Odysseus. Shakespeare's *Coriolanus* (1.3.92), Spenser's "Sonnet XXIII," and W. S. Landor's *Penelope and Pheido* all cite or deal with Penelope. In opera the myth of Penelope has been treated by Cimarosa, Fauré, Galuppi, Piccinni, Jommelli, and Libermann.

See also: ATHENA; HOMER; LAERTES; ODYSSEUS; *ODYSSEY, THE*; OVID; TELEMACHUS; TROY

**Penthesilea** (forcing men to mourn)   In Greek mythology, an Amazon, daughter of Ares and Otrera, who fought for the Trojans during the Trojan War after Achilles had killed Hector. Penthesilea was killed by Achilles' spear. When he saw her great beauty, Achilles fell in love with her and returned her body to King Priam for proper funeral honors. Achilles' display of sentimentality made Thersites ridicule him, and Achilles killed him. The myth is told in Vergil's *Aeneid* (book 1), Ovid's *Metamorphoses* (book 12), and the *Aethiopia*, an anonymous epic poem that continues Homer's *Iliad*, written about 775 B.C.E. Hugo Wolf's symphonic poem *Penthesilea* is based on Heinrich von Kleist's poetic tragedy *Penthesilea*. Penthesilea's death is often portrayed in ancient Greek art. It was one of the subjects painted by Panaenus around Phidias's statue of Zeus.

See also: ACHILLES; AMAZONS; ARES; HECTOR; *ILIAD, THE*; PRIAM; THERSITES; TROY

**Pentheus** (grief)   In Greek mythology, king of Thebes, son of Echion and Agave. Pentheus refused to worship Dionysus and was killed when the god inspired a frenzy in his worshipers, the Bacchae. Believing Pentheus to be a wild boar, they tore him to pieces. The first to attack was Agave (highborn), his mother, followed by Pentheus's two sisters, Ino and Autonoe. Euripides'

*Perceval (Louis Rhead)*

*The Bacchae*, Vergil's *Aeneid* (book 4), and Ovid's *Metamorphoses* (book 3) tell the tale.

See also: *AENEID, THE*; DIONYSUS; OVID

**2396**

**Perahera** In Buddhism, a torchlight procession held every August at Kandy, where the Tooth Relic of the Buddha is carried around the city on the back of an elephant.

See also: BUDDHA, THE

**2397**

**Perceval** (Percival, Percivale, Parsifal, Parzival) (pierce valley) In Arthurian legend, a knight of the Holy Grail. Medieval versions of his legend vary greatly in detail, but all tell of a boy brought up in the forest ignorant of knights and courtly manners. He goes to the court of King Arthur,

eventually becomes a knight of the Round Table, and goes in quest of the Holy Grail. He is allowed to view the Grail because he is pure. Perceval makes his first appearance in medieval legend in Chrétien de Troyes's *Perceval, le conte del Graal*. He then appears in "Peredur, Son of Efrawg," a tale in *The Mabinogion*. His legend is also told in Wolfram von Eschenbach's long poem *Parzival* and Malory's *Morte d'Arthur*. Wagner took most of his material from Wolfram von Eschenbach's telling for his opera *Parsifal*.

See also: ARTHUR; HOLY GRAIL; ROUND TABLE

**2398**

**Perdix** (partridge) In Greek mythology, culture hero, Athenian inventor of the saw, compass, and potter's wheel; son of Perdix, the sister of Daedalus. He was murdered by Daedalus and transformed into a partridge. The story is in Ovid's *Metamorphoses* (book 8).

See also: DAEDALUS; OVID; PERDIX

**2399**

**Persephone** (bringer of destruction) In Greek mythology, goddess of the underworld; a pre-Greek goddess, also called Kore (maiden) and later Proserpina by the Romans; daughter of Demeter and Zeus. Pluto (Hades or Dis), god of the underworld, wished to marry Persephone, but his offer was refused by her parents. One day while Persephone was out gathering flowers, Pluto came in a chariot drawn by four black horses and abducted Persephone, taking her to his underground kingdom. Her mother, Demeter, was wild with madness and withdrew all

*Rape of Persephone*

plant life from the earth. Zeus, fearful that all life would die without Demeter's help, sent Hermes to the underworld to retrieve Persephone, but she had eaten pomegranates (fruit of the underworld) and was compelled to stay in Pluto's kingdom for as many months as the number of fruits she had eaten. When Persephone returned to her mother, the earth's vegetation was restored. Thus, Persephone became a goddess of fertility, of the birth and death of vegetation. Under the name Kore she was worshiped, along with Demeter and Dionysus, at the Eleusinian Mysteries.

Ancient Greek art portrayed Persephone as a beautiful maiden. Her attributes were a horn of plenty, a sheaf of wheat, a cock (the rising sun), a torch, and a pomegranate (rebirth after death). Homer's *Odyssey* (book 11), Hesiod's *Theogony*, the Homeric Hymns (not by Homer), Vergil's *Aeneid* (books 4, 6,), Ovid's *Metamorphoses* (book 5), Shelley's "Song of Proserpine, While Gathering Flowers on the Plain of Enna," Tennyson's "Demeter and Persephone," Swinburne's "Hymn to Proserpine" and "The Garden of Proserpine," George Meredith's "The Appeasement of Demeter," and Stravinsky's *Perséphone* (1934) with libretto by André Gide all have dealt with the myth.

See also: *AENEID, THE*; DEMETER; DIONYSUS; HADES; HERMES; HESIOD; *ODYSSEY, THE*; POMEGRANATE; ZEUS

2400
**Perseus** (destroyer) In Greek mythology, hero, son of Zeus and Danaë. When Perseus was a baby, his grandfather Acrisius was warned by an oracle that Perseus would kill him when he grew up. Fearful, he placed Danaë and Perseus in a wooden box and had them thrown into the sea. They were cast ashore and found by Dictys, a fisherman on the island of Seriphus. Dictys brought up Perseus and took care of Danaë. After some time, when Perseus was a young man, King Polydectes fell in love with Danaë and wanted to marry her. She refused, and Polydectes believed it was because of Perseus, so he

*Perseus carrying the head of Medusa*

sent him on a quest to retrieve the head of Medusa, the snake-haired Gorgon. Polydectes hoped Perseus would die in the quest. But Hermes, messenger of the gods, helped Perseus, and the hero returned with Medusa's head. When the giant Atlas refused Perseus shelter, Perseus showed him the Gorgon's head, and Atlas turned to stone. As he flew home on the winged sandals given him by Hermes, he saw Andromeda chained to a rock by the sea, waiting to be devoured by a sea monster. Perseus slew the monster from the air with one blow and then married Andromeda. At the wedding feast a former suitor of Andromeda appeared and wished to fight the hero. Perseus exposed Medusa's head to him, and the suitor and all of the guests were turned to stone. Returning to his mother with his bride, he found Danaë had hidden herself from Polydectes' sexual advances. Again he exposed Medusa's head at a feast held by Polydectes and turned the king and his guests to stone. Perseus put Dictys on the throne and gave Medusa's head to Athena for her shield, the Aegis. At Argos, while attending funeral games, Perseus accidentally killed his grandfather, Acrisius, fulfilling the oracle. He was killed by Megapenthes.

Cellini's *Perseus* and Antonio Canova's statue *Perseus with the Head of Medusa* are among the best representations of the myth. Perseus's myth is found in Apollordorus's *Bibliotheca* (Library); Ovid's *Metamorphoses* (book 4); William Morris's "Doom of King Acrisius," part of *The Earthly Paradise*; Charles Kinglsey's *Heroes*; Nathaniel Hawthorne's *Wonder Book*; as well as works by Tennyson, Browning, Hopkins, and Auden.

See also: ACRISIUS; ANDROMEDA; APOLLORDORUS; DANAË; GORGONS; HERMES; ZEUS

*Christ giving the Keys to St. Peter*

2401

**Peter, St.** (rock, stone)    First century. In the Bible, N.T., "Prince of the Apostles." Patron of bakers, bridge builders, butchers, carpenters, clockmakers, fishermen, fishmongers, glaziers, masons, net makers, potters, stationers, and shipwrights. Invoked against fever, foot troubles, frenzy, snakebite, wolves, and for a long life. Feast, 29 June.

Peter's original name was Simon (snub-nosed). He was the son of a man named Jonas or John, who was a fisherman. Peter and brother Andrew followed their father's profession. They were partners with John and James, the sons of Zebedee. Both Peter and Andrew were followers of John the Baptist, but when Jesus said, "Follow me, and I will make you fishers of men," Peter immediately joined him. He was always regarded as the first of the Apostles and is so listed in every account given in the New Testament as well as in legendary sources. Peter appears in the most important happenings in the life of Christ. He is present at the raising of Jairus's daughter (Luke 8:41–51), the Transfiguration (Matt. 17:1–2), the Last Supper (Luke 22:8ff.), the Agony in the Garden (Matt. 26:37–40), and the Resurrection (John 24:12). It is Peter who catches the fish with the coin in its mouth needed to pay the tribute when Christ says, "Render unto Caesar the things that are Caesar's and unto God the things that are God's."

The high position of Peter among the Apostles both during Christ's life and later are summed up in the words Christ addresses to him. "Thou art Peter [rock], and upon this rock I will build my church: and the gates of hell shall not prevail against it. And I will give unto thee the keys of the kingdom of heaven: and whatsoever thou shalt bind on earth, shall be bound in heaven: and whatsoever thou shalt loose on earth shall be loosed in heaven."

Yet in his high position (differently interpreted by Catholics and Protestants from the text) Peter is also weak and sometimes blind to Christ's mission. He rejects the idea that Jesus must suffer. Jesus is so angered by this that he tells Peter, "Get thee behind me, Satan; thou art an offence unto me; for thou savorest not the things that be of God, but those that be of men." Toward the close of Christ's ministry Peter's role becomes very prominent. At the Last Supper he asks the reason Jesus is washing his disciples' feet. He also says he would never deny Christ, which he does. He is reminded by the cock crowing.

Peter's story is continued in the Acts of the Apostles in the New Testament. In the first part of the work Peter is clearly the leader of the Apostles. Accompanied by his wife, he travels to various cities bringing the Gospel. We are not told, however, how he died, nor are we told about a journey to Rome, where he and St. Paul, according to legend, were martyred on the same day. Christian legend, however, has supplied what is lacking in the biblical accounts. The most important legend concerns the magician Simon Magus. The miracles of Peter were so superior to any done by Simon Magus that the magician fled to Rome. St. Peter followed him there. Many years passed, and Simon Magus became a favorite of the emperor Nero. According to *The Golden Legend*, written in the 13th century, Simon said he was the Son of God, who, if his head were to be cut off, would rise again on the third day. "Nero ordered the executioner to cut off his head; but Simon, by his magic art, caused the executioner to behead a ram, thinking the while that he was beheading Simon himself." The magician then hid for three days, made his appearance, and the emperor eventually put up a statue to "the holy god Simon." After some time Peter and Simon came into a contest before the emperor. The final feat was Simon's journey to heaven, "since the earth was no longer worthy of him." On the set day he climbed to the top of a high tower and began his flight with a laurel crown on his head. Nero called out to Peter to look at the flight of Simon Magus. But Peter called out, "Angels of Satan, who hold this man up in the air, in the name of my master Jesus Christ, I command you to hold him up no longer." Simon was then dashed to the earth, "his skull was split, and he died."

When Rome was burning the Christians asked Peter to flee for his safety because the Christians were being blamed for the deed. As he went along the Appian Way, he met Christ walking toward Rome. He said, "Lord, whither goest thou?" And Christ replied, "I go to Rome to be crucified anew." "To be crucified anew?" asked Peter. "Yes," said Christ. "Then, Lord, I too return to Rome, to be crucified with thee."

Peter, not being a Roman citizen like St. Paul, was "condemned to die on the cross." He asked that he be crucified with his "head toward the earth" and his feet pointing to heaven, for he said, "I am not worthy to die as my master died."

In Christian art, Peter is usually shown holding the keys of heaven, sometimes a fish or a cock. The number of art works dealing with him is staggering. Among the most noteworthy are those of Giotto, Crivelli, Caravaggio, Raphael, Michelangelo, Masaccio, Giovanni Bellini, Quentin Massys, Hans Holbein, Rubens, Francisco de Zurbarán, Murillo, Fra Bartolommeo, and El Greco. The location of his tomb under the high altar of St. Peter's cathedral in Rome was verified in 1950.

See also: ANDREW, ST.; APOSTLE; *GOLDEN LEGEND, THE*; JOHN THE BAPTIST, ST.; PAUL, ST.; SIMON MAGUS

2402
**Peter Martyr, St.** (St. Peter of Verona) (stone, rock)   1205–1253. In Christian legend, patron saint of inquisitors and midwives. Venerated in Verona, Italy. Feast, 29 April.

Peter was a noted Dominican preacher who hounded heretics and Jews and was finally murdered by a group of hired assassins in the forest on his way from Como to Milan. One of the assassins struck him on the head with an ax and then went in pursuit of Peter's companion. When the assassin returned, he found Peter had written the Apostles Creed with his own blood on the ground, or according to another account, was reciting the creed aloud. In either case, the murderer pierced Peter with a sword.

2403
**Peter Rugg**   In American folklore, a man who cannot die and spends his years in constant wanderings. He does not age but rides around in his buggy on New England roads around Boston. William Austin's tale *Peter Rugg, The Missing Man* narrates the legend.

See also: VANISHING HITCHHIKER

2404
**Petra Loa**   In Haitian voodoo, a group of loa whose rites were introduced from Santo Domingo by a man named Don Pedro. The symbol of the Petra loa is a whip, suggesting some connection to the imposition of slavery.

These loa have red eyes, and they make the initiates writhe and grimace, especially when the initiates fail to make payment to the loa for their services. They are in contrast to the benevolent and dignified Rada loa.

See also: LOA

**2405**

**Petro Simbi**   In Haitian voodoo, a loa (deified spirit of the dead) of rain; patron of magicians. Petro Simbi is both benevolent and aggressive. Symbolized by a glowing iron rod stuck upright in a charcoal fire, his color is red. Sacrifices of goats and pigs are made to him.

See also: LOA; PETRA LOA

**2406**

**Phaedra** (bright one)   In Greek mythology, daughter of Minos and Pasiphae; sister of Acacallis, Androgeus, Ariadne, Catreus, Deucalion, Euryale, Glaucus, Lycastus, and Xenodice; wife of Theseus; mother of Acamas and Demophon; in love with Hippolytus, her stepson. Phaedra married Theseus after the death of Antiope, his previous wife. Being much younger than Theseus, Phaedra fell in love with her stepson Hippolytus, but the youth rejected Phaedra's advances. In retaliation for the rejection Phaedra accused Hippolytus of attempting to rape her and then hanged herself. Theseus banished Hippolytus and prayed for vengeance on him, and Hippolytus was then killed by Poseidon. Phaedra appears in Euripides' *Hippolytus*, Seneca's *Phaedra*, and Ovid's *Heroides* (4). Racine's *Phèdre* was used as the basis for the Jean Cocteau ballet with music of Georges Auric. Others works using Racine's text were Ildebrando Pizetti's opera *Phaedra* (1915) and a modern movie version of the plot, *Phaedra*, (1961) staring Melina Mercouri.

See also: ACAMAS; ANDROGEUS; ANTIOPE; CATREUS; DEMOPHON; DEUCALION; HIPPOLYTUS; MINOS; OVID; POSEIDON; THESEUS

**2407**

**Phaethon** (shining)   In Greek mythology, son of Apollo or Helios, both sun gods, and the nymph Clymene. Phaethon was laughed at by his companions when he said he was the son of Apollo. He went to Apollo and begged to be allowed to drive Apollo's sun chariot across the heavens. Reluctantly consenting, Apollo gave Phaethon his horses and chariot. After a time Phaethon could not control the chariot. It plunged to the earth and parched Libya. Zeus, in response, killed the boy with a thunderbolt. Phaethon fell into the Eridanus or Po River and was transformed into a swan. There his sisters, the Heliades, mourning him, were transformed into willow trees and their tears into drops of amber. Ovid's *Metamorphoses* (books 1, 2) tell the myth in detail. Spenser's "Tears of the Muses" calls Phaethon "Phoebus foolish sonne." In Shakespeare's *Two Gentlemen of Verona* (3.1.154–5) the Duke compares Valentine to Phaethon when he plans to elope with Silvia: "Wilt thou aspire to guide the heavenly car / And with thy daring folly burn the world?" Shakespeare also cites the image of the falling Phaethon in *Richard II* (3.3.178–79). The Heliades appear in Andrew Marvell's poem "The Nymph Complaining for the Death of Her Faun" (99–100). In music Lully's opera *Phaeton* (1683) and Saint-Saëns' tone poem *Phaëton* (1873) deal with the myth. In art Hans Rottenhammer's *Fall of Phaeton* portrays the ride.

See also: APOLLO; HELIADES; HELIOS; OVID; SWAN; ZEUS

**2408**

**Phaon** (shining)   In Greek legend, a boatman of the Mytilene in Lesbos, loved by the poet Sappho. Phaon rejected Sappho's love, and as a result she killed herself by leaping off a cliff on the island of Leucas. Originally Phaon was old and ugly, but he received from Aphrodite a small box containing an ointment that made him young and handsome. Ovid's *Heroides* (15) has a letter from Sappho to Phaon. David's painting of Sappho also pictures Phaon.

See also: APHRODITE; OVID

**Pharaoh** (great house)   In ancient Egypt, title for the kings, who were believed to be incarnations of Horus, the son of Osiris. When a pharaoh died he became Osiris, one with the god of the dead. In the Bible the word *pharaoh* is used as if it were a proper name. We have no evidence as to which pharaoh is referred to in the story of the Exodus from Egypt by the Hebrews.

See also: BIBLE (EXODUS); HORUS; OSIRIS

2409

**Philip, St.** (lover of horses)   First century. In the Bible, N.T., Apostle. Patron of hatters, pastry cooks, Brabant, and Luxemborg. Feast, 1 May.

Born at Bethsaida, Philip was one of the first men called by Jesus early in his ministry at Bethany, beyond the Jordan where John was baptizing (John 1:28). He was present with the faithful disciples when they prayed in the upper room in Jerusalem after Christ's Ascension (Acts 1:12–14).

According to legend, Philip went to preach in Scythia, where he worked for some 20 years. Then, according to the account in *The Golden Legend*, written in the 13th century but based on earlier sources, he was taken by the pagans.

2410

. . . which would constrain him to make sacrifice to an idol which was called Mars, their God, and anon under the idol issued out a right great dragon, which forthwith slew the bishop's [king's] son that appointed the fire for to make the sacrifice, and the two provost also, whose servants held St. Philip in iron bonds; and the dragon corrupted the people with his breath that they were all sick, and St. Philip said: "Believe ye me and break this idol and set in his place the cross of Jesu Christ and after, worship ye it, and they that

be here dead shall revive, and all the sick people shall be made whole." And anon St. Philip commanded the dragon that he should go in to desert without grieving or doing any harm to any person, and anon he departed. (Caxton translation)

The pagan priests were upset by Philip's power, so they bound him on a cross and stoned him to death, "and his body was worshipfully buried there, and his two daughters died long after him and were also buried, that one on the right side, and the other on the left side of the body of their father."

When St. Philip is shown in art, alone or in a series of Apostles, he is generally a man in the prime of life, with a small beard and a benign countenance. His attribute is a cross, sometimes a small one carried in his hand, a high cross in the form of a T, or a tall staff with a Latin cross at top. The cross symbol, according to Jameson in *Sacred and Legendary Art*, may "allude to his martyrdom; or to his conquest over the idols through the power of the cross; or, when placed on the top of the pilgrim's staff, it may allude to his mission among the barbarians as preacher of the cross of salvation."

See also: APOSTLE; DRAGON; *GOLDEN LEGEND, THE*; MARS

**Philoctetes** (love of possessions)   In Greek mythology, an Argonaut, male lover of Heracles, great archer, son of Poeas and Demonassa. Philoctetes joined the expedition against Troy. On the way to the city he and his companions landed on a small island to offer sacrifice to a local goddess. In one account he was bitten by a snake, in another he was scratched by one of his own poisoned arrows. In either case, the wound festered, and his companions left him on the island of Lemnos, where he lived for 10 years. Near the close of the Trojan War the Greeks captured the Trojan prophet Helenus, who informed them that only if the bow and arrows of Heracles were

2411

obtained could they be victorious. The bow and arrows were in the possession of Philoctetes, who had obtained them when he lit Heracles' funeral pyre on Mount Oeta. Odysseus and Neoptolemus (or Diomedes) were sent to Philoctetes to obtain the bow and arrows. Only when Heracles appeared, risen from the dead, did Philoctetes, give up the bow and arrows. Machaon, a son of Asclepius, the god of healing, cured Philoctetes' wound. Philoctetes later founded two cities in Italy. Homer's *Iliad* (book 2), Sophocles' *Philoctetes*, and Ovid's *Metamorphoses* (books 9, 13) all deal with Philoctetes.

See also: ARGONAUTS; ASCLEPIUS; DIOMEDES; HELENUS; HERACLES; ODYSSEUS; TROY

2412

**Philomela** (song lover)    In Greek mythology, sister of Procne; daughter of King Pandion of Athens and Zeuxippe. Procne's husband, Tereus, king of Thrace, raped Philomela and then cut out her tongue so she could not speak. However, the girl wove her sad tale on a tapestry and sent it to her sister Procne. As revenge, the two sisters killed Itylus, the five-year-old son of Tereus, and served the boy to the father at dinner. During the dinner, Philomela threw Itylus's head on the table. The gods then transformed Philomela into a nightingale, Tereus into a hawk (or hoopoe), Procne into a swallow, and Itylus into a pheasant (or sandpiper). Ovid's *Metamorphoses* (book 6) and Chaucer's *Legend of Good Women* narrate the myth. Other works that have dealt with or referred to the myth are Sir Philip Sidney's "The Nightingale"; Edmund Spenser's *Virgils Gnat* (401–3); Shakespeare's *Titus Andronicus*, in which part of the plot is similar to the myth; Milton's "Il Penseroso" (56–62); Matthew Arnold's "Philomela"; Swinburne's "Itylus"; Oscar Wilde's *The Burden of Itylus*; and T. S. Eliot's "Sweeney among the Nightingales" and *The Waste Land*.

See also: CHAUCER; OVID

2413

**Phlegethon** (blazing)    In Greek mythology, one of the five rivers of Hades, the underworld in which those who have committed violence against their families are cast until they are forgiven. Homer's *Odyssey* (book 10) and Ovid's *Metamorphoses* (book 15) mention the river. In Dante's *Divine Comedy* (Inferno) it is one of the three rivers of Hell (the others being Acheron and Styx); sinners who have shed blood are cast forever into this river of boiling blood. In Plato's dialogue *Phaedo*, the river is called Pyriphlegethon (river of fire).

See also: HADES; *ODYSSEY, THE*; OVID

2414

**Phlegyas** (fiery)    In Greek mythology, king of Lapithae and son of Ares and Chryse. Phlegyas burned Apollo's temple at Delphi when he discovered that the god had raped Coronis, Phlegyas's daughter and the mother of Aesculapius. Apollo killed Phlegyas and placed him in the underworld with a massive stone above his head, which constantly threatened to fall on him. Vergil's *Aeneid* (book 6), which narrates Aeneas's visit to the underworld, tells of Phlegyas's fate.

See also: *AENEID, THE*; APOLLO; ARES; DELPHI; PHLEGYAS

2415

**Phocas, St.**    Third century. In Christian legend of the Eastern Church, patron saint of gardeners. Feast, 3 July.

Phocas lived outside the gate of Sinope, in Pontus, where he cultivated a garden and gave the produce to the poor. One night as he was at supper, some strangers came in, and as he kept open house, he invited them to stay. They said they had come to find a certain Phocas, whom they were hired to kill. Phocas said nothing. He gave them a night's lodging, and while they were asleep he went out and dug a grave in his garden among the flowers. In the morning he told his guests that Phocas was found and "insisted on their beheading him at the grave, and they buried him there." In Byzantine art St. Phocas is presented as an aged man holding a spade.

*Phoenix*

**Phoenix**   In world mythology, fantastic bird that is reborn from its own ashes. The standard ancient account of the phoenix is found in Herodotus' *History* in which he says he never saw the creature but was told that it lived for 500 years, and upon its death was reborn from its own ashes, which were lit in the Temple of the Sun in Heliopolis, Egypt. In Christian symbolism the phoenix became a sign of the Resurrection of Christ. St. Clement, a convert of St. Paul, refers to the phoenix in one of his letters to attest to the truth of Christ's Resurrection. A 12th-century Latin bestiary also cites the phoenix as proof of Christ's Resurrection. "If the phoenix has the power to die and rise again, why silly man are you scandalized at the word of God . . . . who offered himself on the Altar of the cross to suffer for us and on the third day rise again?" (T. H. White translation). The phoenix was later adopted as a sign over apothecary shops because of the association of alchemists with this bird.

See also: CLEMENT, ST.; PAUL, ST.

**Phyllis** (leafy)   In Greek mythology, daughter of King Lycurgus (or Phyleus or Sithon, all kings of Thrace); sister of Dryas. She married Demophon, son of the hero Theseus but was loved by his brother Acamas, by whom she had a son, Munitus. Phyllis killed herself and was turned into an almond tree when Demophon did not return to her after a month's absence. One of Ovid's *Heroides* (2) and Chaucer's *Legend of Good Women* tell her tragic tale.

See also: ACAMAS; CHAUCER; DEMOPHON; OVID; THESEUS

**Picus** (woodpecker)   In Roman mythology, son of Saturn; father of Faunus and husband of Canens. Picus also loved Pomona. When the enchantress Circe fell in love with Picus, he rejected her advances, so she turned him into a purple woodpecker. Ovid's *Metamorphoses* (book 14) and Vergil's *Aeneid* (book 7) tell of the transformation.

See also: AENEID, THE; CANENS; FAUNUS; OVID; SATURN

**Pied Piper of Hamelin**   In medieval German legend, a magician who rid Hamelin of a rat plague in 1284. The Pied Piper appeared dressed in multicolored clothes and offered to rid the city of the rats for a fee. The town fathers agreed, and the Pied Piper began playing his pipe. Rats came swarming out of their holes and began to follow the magician to the Weser River, where they were drowned. When he tried to collect his fee, the town fathers refused to pay it, so the Pied Piper began to play his pipe again. This time children came out and followed him to Mount Poppen, where they vanished.

There have been many attempts to relate this loss of children to a historic event, including the Children's Crusade, but the most likely source seems to be that of Bishop Bruno of Olmütz sending emissaries to Lower Saxony in the 13th century to recruit families to colonize his Bohemian diocese. The motif of driving out creatures is repeated in Saint Patrick's driving the snakes out of Ireland. The legend was used by Robert Browning in *The Pied Piper of Hamelin*.

See also: PATRICK, ST.

**Pien ch'eng**   In Chinese mythology, ruler of the sixth hell of Ti Yü, the underworld.

See also: TI YÜ

2420

**Pien Ch'iao**   Sixth century B.C.E. In Chinese legend, a deified innkeeper honored as a god of medicine. Pien Ch'iao was the first man to dissect the human body. He had a transparent abdomen and could not only follow the course of his blood but also watch the action of drugs. He is usually portrayed as a handsome man in fine clothes, whereas his spirit teacher, Ch'ang Sangchün, is shown nude, ugly, and unkempt. In Japanese legend Pien Ch'iao is called Henjaku.

2421

*Pilate washing his hands (Dürer)*

**Pietas** (devotion)   In Roman mythology, goddess of piety, respect, and duty toward the gods, parents, and country. A temple in her honor was erected in Rome on the reputed spot where a woman had fed with her own milk her aged father, who had been imprisoned by the Roman senate and deprived of food. In Roman art Pietas was portrayed as a woman, often with a stork, a symbol of piety. Aeneas, the greatest Roman hero, was often called *pius Aeneas*, "loyal Aeneas," referring to his high religious, social, and patriotic ideals.

See also: AENEAS; STORK

2422

**Pikoi**   In Polynesian mythology, Hawaiian hero called the rat shooter. Once he strung 40 rats by their whiskers with one arrow.

2423

**Pilate, Pontius**   First century. In the Bible, N.T., Roman procurator in Judea, about 26–36, who plays a prominent part in the Passion of Christ. Although Pilate was convinced of Jesus' innocence, according to the Gospel accounts, he still allowed Jesus to be crucified. He "absolved" himself from the act by washing his hands. In Christian art Pontius Pilate is portrayed publicly washing his hands, saying, "I am innocent of the blood of this just person" (Matt. 27:24). Pilate was finally brought to Rome for slaughtering Samaritans and either was executed or killed himself. Ironically, in some calendars of the Eastern Church he is placed among the saints, and his feast day is 25 June, alluding to a Christian legend that he became converted to Christ by his wife, Claudia Procla, who had asked him not to condemn Jesus. The Gospels try to downplay Pilate's responsibility because they did not want the Romans blamed for Jesus' death; instead, they place the blame on the Jews.

2424

**Pilwiz** (Bilwis)    In Germanic folklore, a spirit with a sickle on his big toe. He is a demonic figure who goes into grain fields at night, cuts the stalks, and delivers them to a magician neighbor. He is generally of an evil temper, but offerings to him help to appease his spirit.

**Pine**    A cone-bearing evergreen tree; in Near Eastern mythology, associated with the worship of the Great Mother goddess Cybele and her lover-consort Attis. On 22 March a pine tree was felled and brought into the goddess's sanctuary. Its trunk was swathed like a corpse in woolen blankets and decorated with wreaths of violets, said to have sprung from the blood of Attis when he was castrated by a wild boar and transformed into a pine tree. On 24 March, the Day of Blood, the high priest drew blood from his arms and presented it to the goddess. His offering was followed by those of other men, some of whom castrated themselves on the altar. They then would run through the city carrying their genitals. When a man threw his genitals into a particular house, that house was considered honored and had to furnish him with female attire and ornaments, which he would wear the rest of his life. In Greek mythology, the pine was associated with Dionysus, and in Greek art a wand tipped with a pine cone often is carried by the god or his worshipers. For the Romans the pine cone was a symbol of virginity. In Japan the pine is a symbol of longevity, constancy, and marital faithfulness under the spirits of Jo and Uba. In modern-day Germany and Austria, a pine is placed on a new building when the highest point is reached. This moment is the *Richtfest* (construction feast), and the owner must supply the workers with food and drink. This guarantees that the new inhabitants will also have enough to eat and drink.

See also: ATTIS; DIONYSUS; JO AND UBA

**P'ing-Teng**    In Chinese mythology, ruler of the eighth hell of Ti Yü, the underworld.

See also: TI YÜ

**Piper, The**    Aesopic fable found in various European collections.

There was a piper who was walking by the seaside when he saw some fish. He began to pipe, thinking they would come out of the water onto the land. After some time he realized that his music did not charm them, so he got a net and cast it into the sea. A great draft of fishes was drawn up. They began to leap and dance. The piper said, "Cease your dancing now, as you did not dance when I piped for you."

Moral: *Pay attention and come when you are called.*

The fable was told by Cyrus of Sardis to a group of Ionian and Aeolian Greeks who had come to plead with the conqueror. Cyrus had earlier urged them to revolt against Croesus—whom he had since defeated—but they had refused. "It was in anger, therefore, that he made them this reply," according to Herodotus in his *History of the Persian Wars* (book 1). There is an English proverb, "Fish are not to be caught with a bird call," which may stem from this fable.

See also: AESOPIC FABLES

**Pisachas** (flesh eaters)    In Hindu mythology, demons created by the god Brahma from stray drops of water that fell from the water used to create gods and men. They are vile, the most malignant order of malevolent beings.

See also: BRAHMA

**Pleiades** (sailing ones, flock of doves)    In Greek mythology, seven daughters of Atlas and Pleione: Alcyone (winter storm), Celaeno (darkness), Electra, Maia (fertility), Merope (mortality), Sterope (Asterope), and Taygeta (nymph of the mountain in Lacedaemon). They were born in Arcadia on Mount Cyllene. They were pursued by the giant Orion and transformed into the heavenly constellation Pleiades, or they wept at the suffering of the father, Atlas, and were transformed into stars. One of the Pleiades is invisible. Some accounts say it is Merope, who married a mortal and hides out of shame; other accounts say it is Electra, who hides from grief for the destruction of Troy. Ovid's *Metamorphoses* (book 13) tells the myth. Lord Byron's *Beppo* (14) refers to "the lost Pleiad." The term the *Pleiad* is frequently given to groups of seven illustrious persons, such as the 16th-century French Pleiad that wrote poetry. Their leader was Ronsard.

See also: ALCYONE; ARCADIA; ATLAS; CELAENO; ELECTRA; MAIA; ORION; OVID; TROY

2431

**Pluto** (wealth giver)   In Greek and Roman mythology, Hades, god of the dead and the underworld; also called Ades, Aides, Aidoneus, Pluton, Dis; married to Persephone. No temples or offerings were made to Pluto. Shakespeare's *Henry IV, Part II* (2.4.109) refers to "Pluto's damned lake by this hand, to the infernal deep, / With Erebus and tortures vile also," describing the realm of the underworld.

See also: HADES; PERSEPHONE

2432

**Plutus** (wealth)   In Greek mythology, god of wealth, son of Demeter and the Titan Iasion. Plutus was originally connected with agricultural prosperity but later became the god of riches. He was believed to be blind because wealth was given indiscriminately to good and bad alike. In Thebes and Athens the god was portrayed as a child on the arm of Tyche and of Eirene, goddess of peace. Hesiod's *Theogony* cites the god, as do Aristophanes' comedy *Plutus*, in which his sight is restored so that he can give wealth to the deserving, and Dante's *Divine Comedy* (Hell),

where he appears as Pluto, the Italian form of Plutus (not to be confused with Pluto, the god of the underworld).

See also: DEMETER; EIRENE; HESIOD; TITANS

2433

**Pocahontas** (playful one)   c. 1595–1617. In American history and folklore, popular name of Matoaka, daughter of the Indian chief Powhatan. In legend as recorded in Captain John Smith's *Generall Historie*, she saved the life of John Smith when Powhatan was about "to beate out his brains." Pocahontas intervened, placing Smith's "head in her armes, and laid her owne upon his to save him from death" (book III, chapter 2). Pocahontas later became a Christian, married John Rolfe in 1614, went to England, and died there.

Pocahontas is mentioned in Ben Jonson's *Staple of News* and Thomas Fuller's *Worthies of England*, as well as various novels, poems, and plays, among them John Davis's *The Indian Princess, or La Belle Sauvage*, John Esten Cooke's *My Lady Pokahontas*, Vachel Lindsay's poem "Pocahontas, Our Mother," and Hart Crane's poem "The Bridge." Though most historians have rejected Smith's account, Bradford Smith (*Captain John Smith, His Life and Legend*) believes there may be some truth in the tale. The Disney movie *Pocahontas* (1995) is accurate in some respects. It captures the spirit of the woman Pocahontas and her people, and the spirit of the early days of Jamestown. Pocahontas's life ended on a high note, with a triumphal tour of England as a visiting princess. This part of her life is covered in Disney's *Pocahontas II: Journey to a New World* (1998). When she started home, disease took her life, and she was buried in the church at Gravesend, England (17 March 1617) at age 21 or 22.

2434

*Poetic Edda*   Collection of poems on Norse mythological and legendary themes, believed to date from the eighth or ninth century C.E., sometimes called the *Elder Edda* or *Saemund's Edda*.

*Poetic Edda (W. G. Collingwood)*

The title *Saemund's Edda* was given by Icelandic scholars in the 17th century in the erroneous belief that the poems were written or collected by Saemund the Learned. Actually, the poems were first written down from oral tradition in the 12th or 13th century. The oldest part of the *Poetic Edda* deals with myths of the Norse gods in the form of dialogues between Odin and another—either a giant, human being, or another deity. The most important poem of the group is the *Voluspa* (the Wise Woman's Prophecy), which deals with a visit by Odin to the oracle and gives an account of the origins of the world, its present state, Ragnarok (the end of the world), and the new world that will emerge after Ragnarok. The other poems are *Hovamol* (the Lay of the High One), *Vafthruthnismol* (the Lay of Vafthruthnir, "the Mighty in Riddles"), *Grimnismol* (the Lay of Grimmer), *Skirnismol* (the Lay of Skirnir), *Harbarthsljoth* (the Lay of

Harbarth, "Gray-Beard," that is, Odin), *Hymiskvitha* (the Lay of Hymir), *Lokasenna* (Loki's mocking), *Thrymskvitha* (the Lay of Thrym), *Alvissmol* (the Lay of Alvis, "All-Knowing"), *Baldrs Draumar* (Baldur's Dream), *Rigsthula* (the Lay of Rig), *Hyndluljoth* (the Lay of Hyndla, "She-Dog"), and *Svipdagsmol* (the Lay of Svipdog, "Swift-Day").

Aside from poems dealing with Norse gods, other poems or lays deal with heroes of the Northlands, such as *Helgakvioa Hjorvarossonar* (the Lay of Helgi the Son of Hjorvaror), which tells of the wooing of Svava by King Helgi. Some of the poems of the *Poetic Edda* were translated into English by William Morris in the 19th century. Earlier, the English poet Thomas Gray used the *Vegtamskvioa* (the Lay of the Wayfarer), which is a supplement to the *Voluspa*, in writing his poem "The Descent of Odin, an Ode."

See also: *PROSE EDDA;* RAGNAROK

**Poinsettia**    2435    The legend of the poinsettia concerns Pepita, a poor Mexican girl who had no gift to present the Christ Child at Christmas Eve services. Walking to the chapel with her cousin Pedro, Pepita's heart was filled with sadness. "I am sure, Pepita, that even the most humble gift, if given in love, will be acceptable in his eyes," said Pedro. Pepita then knelt by the roadside and gathered a handful of weeds, making a small bouquet of them. She became even sadder looking at the bunch of weeds. She fought back tears as she entered the small village chapel. When she approached the alter, she remembered Pedro's words. Her spirit lifted as she placed the bouquet at the foot of the nativity scene. Suddenly the bunch of weeds burst into bright red flowers, and everyone who saw them was sure it was a miracle. Ever since, those bright red flowers have been known as *Flores de Noche Buena*, flowers of the holy night, and they bloom every year during Christmas.

Poinsettias are not poisonous. The rumor that they are has continued to circulate because of one unfounded story in 1919. An army officer's two year old child allegedly died after eating a poinsettia leaf. The story was never proven and was most likely hearsay, but it has taken on a life of it's own. According to the American Medical Association's *Handbook of Poisonous and Injurious Plants*, other than occasional cases of vomiting, ingestion of the poinsettia plant has been found to produce no ill effect.

2436

**Polednice** (the noonday witch)  In Slavic folklore, a noonday witch. She appears in Karel Jaromir Erben's literary folk ballad *Kytice* (The Garland). It tells of a mother who threatens her unruly child with a visit from Polednice if the child does not behave. At noonday a "little shriveled spectral woman leaning on a crooked stick" arrives and kills the child. This gruesome ballad was used by Dvořák in his symphonic poem *Polednice*. The Czech title is sometimes translated *The Midday Witch*.

*Polevik (I. Bilibin)*

2437

**Polevik** (polevoy, polevoi) (field spirit)  In Slavic folklore, spirit of the field, whose nature is variable. Sometimes he is mischievous, causing people to lose their way, or even worse, he sometimes strangles them, particularly if they are drunk. If a worker fell asleep in a field at noontime or before sunset, the *polevik* would ride over him with his horse or send some disease. To earn the *polevik's* good will, two eggs must be placed in a ditch with an elderly cock that can no longer crow. The performer of this rite must complete it before being seen by anyone, or it will have no power. When the *polevik* appears, he is often dressed in full white. He often has a black body, and each eye is a different color. In northern Russia the *poludnitsa*, a female field spirit, will sometimes lure children away. She is a tall creature and wears white.

See also: COCK

2438

**Polong**  In Malayan mythology, a demon about as big as the first joint of a little finger. It will fly through the air wherever it is told to go, but it is always preceded by its pet or plaything, the *pelesit*, which is a species of house cricket.

To create a *polong*, the blood of a murdered man is placed in a bottle with a wide bottom and a long, narrow neck. Prayers are recited over the bottle for 7 or 14 days (depending on which account of the ritual is followed) until a sound like the chirping of young birds is heard from the bottle. The creator then cuts one finger and inserts it into the bottle so that the *polong* can suck the blood. If the creator is a man, he is called its father, if a woman, its mother. Every day the parent feeds the *polong* with his or her blood to keep the demon under its control so that the *polong* will afflict whomever it is directed to. Sometimes the *polong* is rented out for a fee by its creator.

A person attacked by a *polong* cries out and loses consciousness, tears off clothing, bites and strikes, and is blind and deaf to everything. To effect a cure, formulas are chanted by a medicine man over the head of the afflicted, his or her thumb is pinched, and medicines are applied. When the remedy is successful, the sick person cries out: "Let me go, I want to go home." The medicine man then replies, "I will not let you go if you do not make known who it is that has sent you here, and why you have come, and who are your father and mother."

Sometimes the *polong* will not answer or confess, but at other times it will give all of the particulars, though it is also capable of lying and accusing the wrong persons of the evil deed. If it tells the truth, the sick person will recover; if not, the victim shrieks and yells in anger and dies in a day or two. After the death, blood pours forth bubbling from the mouth, and the whole body is blue with bruises.

**Polycrates**   Sixth century B.C.E. In Greek history and legend, tyrant of Samos; son of Aeacus; known for his wealth and as a patron of the arts. According to a legend recorded in Herodotus's *History* (book 3), Polycrates was told he could avoid an evil fate if he would throw away his most precious possession. He therefore cast his favorite ring into the sea, only to have it returned to him in the belly of a fish. The ring was said to have been kept in the temple of Concord in Rome. Polycrates was crucified by Oroetes, a Persian governor who was envious of his good fortune.

**Polydamna** (much controlling)   In Greek mythology, wife of Thonis, king of Egypt. She entertained Helen of Troy, giving her a magic drug to help banish melancholy and care. The myth is a late one that says Helen never went to Troy, only her shadow; the true Helen was in Egypt. This version forms the basis for Richard Strauss's opera *Die Aegyptische Helena* (1928) with a libretto by Hugo von Hofmannsthal.

See also: HELEN OF TROY

**Polyphemus** (famous or talkative)   In Greek mythology, the one-eyed Cyclops from Sicily in the *Odyssey* (book 9), blinded by Odysseus; son of Poseidon and Thoosa. Polyphemus had earlier killed Acis, whom Galatea loved. Vergil's *Aeneid* (book 3), Ovid's *Metamorphoses* (book 13), Euri-

pides' *The Cyclops*, where he appears as a comic character, and Turner's painting *Ulysses Deriding Polyphemus* all deal with Polyphemus. Handel's *Acis and Galatea* also features the Cyclops.

See also: AENEID, THE; ODYSSEUS; *ODYSSEY, THE*; POSEIDON

**Polyxena** (many strangers)   In Greek mythology, a daughter of King Priam of Troy and Hecuba; sister of Aesaus, Cassandra, Creusa, Deiphobus, Hector, Helenus, Paris, and Troilus; she was loved by Achilles. Polyxena does not appear in Homer, but later Greek mythology says she was sacrificed to the ghost of Achilles by his son Neoptolemus as the Greeks were leaving Troy. A variant account says she killed herself. Euripides' tragedy *Hecabe* deals with her tale, as does W. S. Landor's *The Espousal of Polyxena*.

See also: ACHILLES; CASSANDRA; HECTOR; PARIS; PRIAM

**Pomegranate**   Semitropical fruit-bearing tree, often cited in both Jewish and Christian folklore as the fruit eaten by Adam and Eve, though the account in Genesis does not say which fruit was eaten. In Greek mythology, the pomegranate is associated with Persephone and the underworld. In Mesopotamia the pomegranate was believed to increase sexual potency. According to one myth, the god Attis was conceived when his mother, Nana, a virgin, put a pomegranate on her bosom. Variants of the myth cite the almond. In European folklore, a dream about pomegranates means love is on the way.

See also: ADAM AND EVE; ALMOND; ATTIS; PERSEPHONE

**Pomona** (tree fruits)   In Roman mythology, goddess of fruit trees. She married Vertumnus, who, disguised as an old woman, successfully prevailed on her to break her vow of celibacy.

*Pomona*

Her other suitors were Pan, Picus, Priapus, and Silonus. Ovid's *Metamorphoses* (book 14) tells how Vertumnus fell in love with Pomona.

See also: OVID; PAN; PICUS; PRIAPUS; VERTUMNUS

**2445**

**Pope Elhanan**   In medieval Jewish legend, a Jew who became pope. In some accounts Elhanan left the papacy and, according to one medieval legend, "became a Jew greatly respected in the eyes of all the people." Elhanan's legend is placed by some scholars in the 13th century. Anacletus II, who was pope from 1130 to 1138, was of Jewish descent and was called Judaeopontifex (the Jewish pope); he may have inspired the legend.

**2446**

**Pope Joan** (Yahweh has been gracious)   In medieval legend, a woman who disguised herself as a man and was elected pope as John VIII. Joan was English by birth. She disguised herself as a man when she went to Athens to study. She then went on to Rome, where, according to Bartolomeo Plantina in his *Lives of the Popes*, "she met with few that could equal, much less go beyond her, even in the knowledge of Holy Scriptures; and by her learned and ingenious readings and disputations, she acquired so great a respect and authority that upon the death of Leo ... by common consent she was chosen pope in his place." As she was going to the Lateran Church for a service, labor pains came upon her, and she died after having been pope for a little more than two years. The legend inspired Emmanuel Royidis's novel *Pope Joan*, translated into English by Lawrence Durrell. A popular card game played without the eight of diamonds is called the Pope Joan.

**2447**

**Popol Vuh** (book of the community?)   Sacred book of the ancient Quiché Maya Indians of Guatemala.

The *Popol Vuh* was first written down in the Quiché language, but in Latin characters, sometime in the middle of the 16th century by an unknown Mayan convert to Christianity. The now-lost manuscript was copied at the end of the 17th century by Father Francisco Ximénez, a parish priest of the village of Santo Tomás Chichicastenango in the highlands of Guatemala. The work was rediscovered by the Austrian scholar Carl Scherzer in 1857.

The *Popol Vuh* is divided into four parts. The first deals with the creation of the world. The second and third books are concerned with the heroes of the Indians, such as Hunahpú and Xbalanqué. The last section gives myths of cult origins, accounts of tribal wars, and records of historic rulers. Tales from the *Popol Vuh* were used by Charles Finger in his *Tales from Silver Lands*.

See also: HUNAHPÚ AND XBALANQUÉ

**2448**

**Poro**   In African cult (Mende of Sierra Leone), a group of secret societies. They serve a variety of functions, including the initiation of youths into manhood during puberty rituals and the perpetuation of old customs. The society is arranged in a hierarchy controlled by the elders of the community. Women may join but rarely become leaders. The members meet at a secret location that they refer to as a "sacred bush," located near the spot where the founder of their group is buried. The masked spirit of the society is the Gbeni, which may be viewed only by fellow members. A society similar to this one, used for the initiation of girls, is the Sande.

**Po' Sandy**   2449   In American folklore, a runaway slave who was transformed into a tree in order to escape capture. The African-American novelist Charles W. Chesnutt narrates the tale in his *Po' Sandy* (1888).

See also: MOTIF

*Poseidon rising from the sea (John Flaxman)*

**Poseidon** (lord light, shining lord)   2450   In Greek mythology, one of the 12 Olympian gods, god of the sea, earthquakes, and horses; son of Cronus and Rhea; brother of Zeus, Demeter, Hades, Hera, and Hestia; identified by the Romans with their god Neptune. Poseidon ruled the Mediterranean and the Black Seas; rivers not navigated by the Greeks were ruled by Oceanus and Pontus, the latter also a Titan god as old as Oceanus. Poseidon and his wife, Amphitrite, a daughter of Nereus, lived in a palace of gold at the bottom of the sea. When the god appeared in his golden chariot, drawn by horses with brass hooves and golden manes, the waters grew calm, though he could raise sudden storms or cause shipwrecks. Black bulls were sacrificed to him. Poseidon and Athena had a contest to determine who would rule Athens. It was agreed that the deity who could create the most useful gift for humankind should rule Athens. Poseidon, striking a stone with his trident, produced the horse. Athena, however, invented the olive tree, and the city was awarded to her patronage because the olive branch was a symbol of peace and the horse a symbol of war. Poseidon also lost in his attempt to win Argos from Hera and Corinth from the sun god Helios.

During the Trojan War Poseidon sided with the Greeks. Before the war Poseidon and Apollo had to build the walls of Troy as a punishment for offending Zeus. When the walls were completed, Laomedon, the ruler, refused to pay the gods. In revenge Poseidon sent a monster to kill the Trojans. To appease the angry god, Laomedon offered his daughter Hesione as a sacrifice, but Heracles saved the girl. Never forgetting the wrong done him, Poseidon aided the Greeks in the Trojan War until Troy was burned to the ground. Like his brother Zeus, Poseidon loved to have numerous mistresses, among them Gaea, Demeter, Aphrodite, the Gorgon Medusa, and many nymphs. Among his numerous offspring were Amyous, Antaeus, Arion, Pegasus, Polyphemus, and Triton.

Poseidon appears or is cited in Homer's *Iliad* and *Odyssey*; Hesiod's *Theogony*; Vergil's *Aeneid*; Ovid's *Metamorphoses*; Spenser's *Faerie Queene*; Shakespeare's *Coriolanus* (3.1.256), *The Tempest* (5.1.35), and *Cymbeline* (3.1.20); and Pope's *Rape of the Lock* (5.50), as well as works by Milton, Jonson, Beaumont, Fletcher, and W. B. Yeats, among others. Most of these cite him under his Latin name form, Neptune.

In ancient Greek and Roman art Poseidon is portrayed as a strong older man with thick, curly hair and beard holding a trident (three-pronged fork) and with a dolphin nearby, often with his wife, Amphitrite, and sometimes with Triton, one of his many sons. His contest with Athena for Athens is featured on the west pediment of

*Poseidon riding on a Hippocampus*

the Parthenon. One of his most famous temples is on the promontory of Sunium in Attica, dating from the fifth century B.C.E.

See also: APOLLO; ATHENA; DEMETER; HADES; HERA; HESTIA; NEPTUNE; TITANS; ZEUS

**2451**

**Potato**    An edible tuber of the nightshade family, at one time condemned by 18th-century Scots because it was not mentioned in the Bible and therefore was considered unholy. It was once believed to be poisonous, and in Elizabethan England it was believed to restore sexual potency. In Shakespeare's *Troilus and Cressida* (5:2) Diomedes says to Cressida, "How the devil luxury, with his fat rump and potato-finger, tickles these together! Fry, lechery, fry!" In this context potato-finger means penis.

See also: TROILUS AND CRESSIDA

**2452**

**Pothos**    In Greek mythology, personification of longing and desire; companion of Aphrodite.

See also: APHRODITE

**2453**

**Potkoorok**    In Australian mythology, mischievous spirits who play tricks on fishermen.

**2454**

**Potok-Mikhailo-Ivanovich** (Mikhail Potyk) In Russian folklore, a *bogatyr*, or epic hero, with superhuman strength, who appears in the *bylini*, the epic songs, as well as in many folktales. When Potok-Mikhailo-Ivanovich married, he and his wife made a pact. When one died, the other would follow into the tomb. When his wife died, he attached a rope to the church bell in case he changed his mind. He then went to her grave with his horse and sat there all night. At midnight many serpents appeared, one of which turned into a dragon, all aflame. Potok-Mikhailo-Ivanovich killed the monster with his sharp saber and cut off its head. He then took the head and anointed the body of his wife with its blood, and she immediately was restored to life. Mikhail rang the bell, and they were released from the tomb. The two were allowed by the priest "to live as formerly." When Potok-Mikhailo-Ivanovich died, his wife "was buried alive with him in the dank earth."

See also: *BYLINA*

**2455**

**Potoyan**    In Australian mythology, a tribal name for the evil spirit. He can be driven away by fire because he is afraid of it.

**2456**

**Pourquois Story** (why story)    A narrative that has both fable and myth elements and is told to explain the nature of existence or of certain phenomena. An example is "How People Sang the Mountains Up." This Apache story tells how animals, humans, and even the gods sang to the mountains to make them grow up to the heavens, to the sun and the moon, the source of earthly strength. Another Native American story describes abnormal weather as the result of a beaver's despair and weeping when his proposal of marriage was rejected. Common to many of the stories is a fault or an evil that must be removed, and in this way the pourquois story is like a fable that illustrates human defects and shortcomings, with a concluding moral often found in the title itself. This genre of stories has also often been taken up by modern authors, such as Joel Chandler Harris in his Uncle Remus tales (1905), and to some degree even by Rudyard Kipling in his *Just-So Stories* (1902).

See also: AESOPIC FABLES; UNCLE REMUS

**2457**

**Pradyumna**   In Hindu mythology, a son of Krishna (an incarnation of the god Vishnu). Pradyumna, when he was six days old, was stolen by the demon Sambara and thrown into the ocean, where he was swallowed by a fish. When the fish was later caught, Pradyumna was released. He was brought up by Maya-devi (Maya-vati), a mistress of the demon Sambara. Later, when Pradyumna grew up, he challenged Sambara and killed him. Pradyumna himself was killed in the presence of his father, Krishna, during a drunken brawl. In a variant myth Pradyumna is said to be a form of the god of love, Kama, while in the epic poem *The Mahabharata* Pradyumna is said to be the son of the god Brahma.

See also: BRAHMA; KAMA; KRISHNA; *MAHAB-HARATA, THE*

**2458**

**Prajapati** (lord of creatures)   In Hindu mythology, an epithet of the god Brahma or an epithet applied to sages who were the progenitors of the human race. Their number varies from seven to 21 in different accounts. In the Hindu epic poem *The Mahabharata*, for example, there are 21 Prajapatis, whereas in the Vedas the term is also applied to Indra, the storm god, and to the 10 mind-born sons of Brahma. The term, therefore, is fluid in its uses. The major Prajapatis are Angiras, Atri (an eater), Atharvan, Bhrigu, Daksha, Kasshhyapa, Kratu, Marichi, Narada (bringing to man?), Pulaha, Pulastya, Pracetas, Vasishtha (most wealthy), Viswamitra (friend of all), Viraj (ruling afar), and Virana (heroic).

See also: BRAHMA; *MAHABHARATA, THE*; VEDAS

**2459**

**Prakriti**   In Buddhist legend, a woman of low caste who fell in love with Ananda, a disciple of the Buddha. She followed Ananda and met the Buddha, who converted her to his doctrine.

See also: ANANDA

**2460**

**Prana** (breath of life)   In Hinduism, a name for the supreme spirit. The sacred Atharva-Veda calls for "Reverence to Prana, to whom all this universe is subject, who has become lord of the all, on whom the all is supported."

**2461**

**Pratyeka-Buddha** (isolated enlightened one)   In Buddhism, a Buddha who obtains enlightenment without a teacher and cannot proclaim his enlightenment. Sometimes the term Silent Buddha is used. In Pali it is called Pacceka-Buddha. There are two other paths to salvation. Some attain Nirvana through Arhatship, and some, the Supreme Buddhas, attain perfect enlightenment and teach the Dharma to others.

See also: ARHAT; DHARMA

**2462**

**Prayer Wheel** (precious Dharma wheel)   In Tibetan Buddhism, a wheel containing either passages from sacred writings or a series of mantras, such as the *Om Mani Padme Hum*, an untranslatable formula representing the entire Buddhist teaching, learned in childhood and repeated constantly up to one's death. Prayer wheels can be small enough to be held in one's hand or taller than a man's head. They are like barrels turned by hand or water or wind, and they can be made from any material, including wood, ivory, copper, and silver. A prayer wheel is a means of disseminating the spiritual power of a mantra, which is a sound or sequence of sounds that sacramentally effect what it signifies. Thus, the mantra *Om-Ah-Hum* signifies the entry of Buddha-nature into the manifest work and effects the manifestation when it is recited or otherwise disseminated. The power of the mantra is made available whenever a prayer wheel is rotated, but its fullest effect is felt by those who through faith open themselves to its power.

See also: MANTRA; OM

*Iris advising Priam to obtain Hector's body (John Flaxman)*

2463

**Prester John** (John the Prester)   In medieval legend, a Christian king and priest who ruled over a country in Asia or Africa. In the 12th century letters purportedly written by Prester John circulated in Europe. He describes his country, writing that "our land streams with honey, and is overflowing with milk." Prester John also appears in medieval Jewish legend. Joshua Lorki, a Jewish physician to Pope Benedict XIII, wrote that some people "live in a place under the yoke of a strange people . . . governed by a Christian chief, Preste-Cuan [Prester John]." Benjamin of Tudela, another Jew, traveled in the East between 1159 and 1173 and wrote that Prester John was a Jewish king who ruled with great splendor over a realm inhabited by the Jews. According to the later account of Sir John Mandeville in his *Travels*, Prester John was a lineal descendant of Ogier the Dane, who reached the North of India with 15 of his barons. Marco Polo, in his *Travels*, says Genghis Khan "fought against Prester John and, after a desperate fight, overcame and slew him."

See also: OGIER THE DANE

2464

**Preta** (ghosts)   In Hindu mythology, a ghost or evil spirit animating a dead body and haunting cemeteries.

2465

**Priam** (ransomed back or chief)   In Greek mythology, king of Troy; son of Laomedon and Strymo (or Placid); husband of Hecuba; father of 50 sons and 50 daughters, among whom were Hector, Paris, Troilus, Cassandra, and Creusa.

When Heracles took the city of Troy, Priam was one of the prisoners. His sister Hesione freed him by ransom, and he changed his original name, Podarces, to Priam (ransomed back). (His name is probably derived from a word indicating chief or first; the story of his name change represents a back-formed folk etymology.) Heracles later placed him on the throne of Troy. Priam had earlier married Arisba but divorced her to marry Hecuba. He then wished to recover his sister Hesione, whom Heracles had carried to Greece and married to his friend Telamon. To carry out his plan, Priam manned a fleet and gave his son Paris command of it. But Paris returned with Helen, wife of Menelaus, as a prize for choosing Aphrodite to receive the Golden Apple in the incident of the Judgment of Paris, and thus the seeds of the Trojan War were sown. In Homer's *Iliad* Priam is portrayed as an old man. When his son Hector is killed by Achilles, Priam goes to the Greek hero and begs the body of his dead son. According to post-Homeric accounts, Priam was killed at the altar of Zeus by Neopotolemus.

Among ancient authors Priam appears in Homer's *Iliad*, Vergil's *Aeneid* (book 2), and Ovid's *Metamorphoses* (books 12, 13). In English literature references to Priam are found in the works of Chaucer, Spenser, Shakespeare, Milton, Dryden, Pope, Byron, Wordsworth, Tennyson, Keats, William Morris, D. G. Rossetti, Robert Bridges, and John Masefield. Priam appears in a series of wall frescoes in Pompeii. Berlioz's *The Trojans* and Tippet's *King Priam* are operas that feature the tragic king.

See also: ACHILLES; APHRODITE; CASSANDRA; HECTOR; HELEN OF TROY; HESIONE; *ILIAD, THE* MENELAUS; PARIS; PRIAM; TROY

**Priapus**   2466   In Greek and Roman mythology, god of gardens and vegetation, associated—because of his portrayal with an erection—with good luck and lewd behaivior; son of Dionysus and Aphrodite. Priapus also was called Lutinus and Mutinus by the Romans. Originally a god from the Hellespont region, his cult spread to Greece, Alexandria, and Italy. Donkeys, symbols of lust, were sacrificed to him. Horace, Tibullus, and Martial wrote of him, and he appears in Petronius's novel *Satyricon*, in which the hero Encolpius's inability to have an erection is a punishment of Priapus. Priapus was portrayed with an erection, and statues of him were placed in gardens. He is mentioned in Chaucer's *Parliament of Fowls*, Shelley's *Witch of Atlas*, Swinburne's *Dolores*, D. H. Lawrence's "Hymn to Priapus," and T. S. Eliot's "Mr. Apollinax." Poussin's *Dance in Honor of Priapus* portrays the god as a *Herm*, a square pillar supporting a bust of Hermes and having erect male genitals. Herms often stood at the crossroads in Greek cities as a protection. A sculpture series was designed by Poussin for the gardens at Versailles in which Pan, Faunus, Heracles, Flora, Pomona, and Venus are portrayed.

See also: APHRODITE; CHAUCEER; DIONYSUS

**Primary Chronicle**   2467   In Russian history and legend, an 11th-century chronicle that provides an important source for stories, particularly those in the spirit of *dvoeverie* (double faith), a continuation of pagan traditions after the adoption of Christianity. It is also sometimes called the *Tale of Bygone Years*.

See also: TALE OF BYGONE YEARS

**Priya-vrata**   2468   In Hindu mythology, a son of the god Brahma. Priya-vrata was unhappy about the fact that only half the earth at a time was lit by the sun. One day he "followed the sun seven times round the earth in his own flaming car of equal velocity, like another celestial orb, resolved to turn night into day," according to the *Bhagavata Purana*. Before his father, Brahma, stopped him, "the ruts which were formed by the motion of his chariot wheels were the seven oceans. In this way the seven continents of the earth were formed."

In the *Vishnu Puranas* he had 10 sons and two daughters. Three of his sons adopted a religious life, and he divided the seven continents among the others.

See also: BRAHMA; PURANAS; VISHNU

**Procrustes** (stretcher-out)   2469   In Greek mythology, robber, tyrant of Attica; son of Poseidon; also called Damastes or Polypemon. He tied travelers to his iron bed, cutting off their legs to make them fit if they were too long or stretching them if too short. He was killed by the hero Theseus, who forced Procrustes to lie in his own bed. "Procrustean" has come to symbolize tyranny and enforced labor. Apollodorus's *Bibliotheca* (Library) and Ovid's *Metamorphoses* (book 7) and *Heroides* (book 2) all deal with Procrustes.

See also: OVID; POSEIDON; THESEUS

**Prometheus** (forethought)   2470   In Greek mythology, Titan culture hero who gave humankind fire; invented architecture, astronomy, medicine, navigation, metalworking, and writing; son of the Titan Iapetos and either the goddess Themis (later married to Zeus) or Clymene (Asia), an Oceanide; brother of Atlas Epimetheus (afterthought), and Menoetlus, married to Hesione; father of Deucalion by Hesione or Pronoea.

After the gods had defeated the Titans in the battle to rule the universe, the gods negotiated with man about the honor man was to pay to the gods. Since Prometheus, though a Titan, had sided with the gods, he was chosen to decide how sacrificial victims were to be offered. Prometheus cut up an ox and divided it into two parts. He wrapped the choice cuts in the skin of the ox and placed the stomach on top of it to make it look unappetizing. The remainder of the animal, which was made up of bones, Prometheus covered with fat to make it look desirable. Zeus had to make the choice of which portion was to be set aside for the gods. Zeus knew that Prometheus had set up a trick but still chose the heap of bones and fat. Then, as a punishment to mankind, Zeus deprived them of the gift of fire, leaving them in darkness and cold.

That did not stop Prometheus, who, according to Hesiod's *Theogony*, "cheated him, and stole the far seen splendor of untiring fire in a hollow fennelstalk" and gave it to man. Zeus, angered that man now had fire, called on the smith god Hephaestus to make a beautiful woman of clay, whom Zeus called Pandora. Until that time man had lived alone. Zeus called on the goddess Athena, who, according to Hesiod, "girded and arrayed Pandora in silver-white raiment (and) placed around her head lovely garlands fresh-budding with meadow-flowers." Hermes, the messenger of the gods, then carried to Pandora a jar (or box) as her dowry. In the jar was every evil that was to come into the world. Pandora was brought before Epimetheus. Though Prometheus had warned his brother not to accept any gifts from Zeus, Epimetheus was so moved by Pandora's beauty that he married her. Pandora removed the lid from the jar, and out flew all the evils, troubles, and diseases that were unknown to man until that time. Only Hope remained in the jar when Pandora closed it again. The misogynist Hesiod wrote: "Just so to mortal men high-thundering Zeus gave woman as an evil." But Zeus was not satisfied with punishing man; he now turned on Prometheus and had him bound in adamantine chains to a pillar, with an eagle (or vulture) who ate Prometheus's liver

*Epimetheus accepts Pandora from Mercury*

each day. The liver was restored at night only to be eaten again the next day.

In a variant myth recorded in Ovid's *Metamorphoses* (book 1), Prometheus is made the actual creator of humankind: ". . . Prometheus tempere'd into paste, / And, mix't with living streams, the godlike image cast" (John Dryden translation). Goethe used this image in his poem *Prometheus*, which was set to music by Franz Schubert and Hugo Wolf. The combination of defiance of omnipresent authority and godly powers of creation have made Prometheus one of the most popular subjects in Western art, music, and literature. Among the most important works is Aeschylus's *Prometheus Bound*, part of a trilogy. The other two plays in the trilogy, *Prometheus the Firebringer* and *Prometheus Released*, have been lost. Other works include Shelley's *Prometheus Unbound*; Beethoven's *Die Geschöpfe des Prometheus* (The Creatures of Prometheus) (1801); Alexander Scriabin's *Prometheus, Poem of Fire*; Franz Liszt's symphonic poem *Prometheus* (1850), as well as his setting of texts of the German Romantic poet Herder, who wrote a play *Prometheus*; and André Gide's *Le Prométhée mal Enchaîné*, in which the eagle or vulture is kept as a pet by Prometheus. Others who have treated the theme are Lord Byron, Henry Wadsworth Longfellow, Robert Bridges, James Russell Lowell, and Robert Graves. Painters using Prometheus as a subject include Piero di Cosimo, Rubens, Jordaens, and Jacob Epstein. The best-known modern sculpture is in Rockefeller Center in New York City and portrays Prometheus giving the gift of fire to humankind.

See also: ATLAS; DEUCALION; HESIONE; OVID; THEMIS; TITANS; ZEUS

*Prometheus forming man out of clay*

2471

**Propp, Vladimir**   1895–1970. Russian folklorist best known as the author of a 1928 book called *Morfologija skazki* (Morphology of the Folktale), in which he postulated that, "fairy tales possess a quite particular structure which is immediately felt and which determines their category, even though we may not be aware of it." For his analysis Propp chose 100 Russian fairy tales recorded by A. N. Afanasiev. In his study of these tales, Propp noted the recurrence of 31 "functions," a term he used to describe a structural component, "an act of a character, defined from the point of view of its significance for the course of the action." He was thus able to reduce these folktales to two necessary functions: they must have a villain (lack), and the villain must be defeated (lack liquidated). No other functions are absolutely necessary, although many of them are to be found in the tales. Other functions include absentation (one of the members of a family is absent from home), interdiction (an interdiction is addressed by the hero/heroine), violation (the interdiction is violated), and so forth. Propp was also able to verify that no matter how many functions appeared in an individual tale, they always appeared in the same sequence. This

study laid the groundwork for formal or structural studies of folktales. Alan Dundes used the same methodology for analyzing North American Indian tales.

2472

**Prose Edda**   Handbook of Norse mythology for poets, written by Snorri Sturluson (1179–1241 C.E.). The work is sometimes called the *Younger Edda* to distinguish it from the *Poetic Edda*, or *Elder Edda*.

The *Prose Edda* was designed as a handbook for poets who wished to compose in the style of the scalds of the Viking ages. It consists of three parts. The first part, "Gylfaginning" (the deluding of Gylfi), tells the myths of the Norse gods. It is often our major source for the tales. The second part, "Skaldskaparmal" (poetic diction), consists mainly of a catalog of kennings (figurative expressions of various kinds), whose use in ancient Viking poetry is illustrated by numerous examples from old poems. It also contains some mythological and legendary tales. The third part, "Hattatal" (account of meters), is a poem Snorri composed about King Haakon and Earl (later Duke) Skuli Baroarson, between 1221 and 1223. This is made up of some 100 stanzas and is accompanied by a prose commentary on the variations of meter and style exemplified by each verse.

The major interest of the *Prose Edda* today is the first part, which deals with tales of the deities of Norse mythology. The *Prose Edda* had a major influence on Matthew Arnold's narrative poem *Balder Dead*.

See also: KENNING; *POETIC EDDA*; SKALD

2473

**Proteus** (first man)   In Greek mythology, sea god; the old man of the sea; son of Oceanus and Tethys. He had the gift of prophecy and the ability to change his shape until caught and held firmly down. Homer's *Odyssey* (book 4) and Ovid's *Metamorphoses* (book 8) deal with Proteus. In Spenser's *Faerie Queene* (book 1) the great deceiver Archimago can take "As many formes and shapes in seeming wise/ As ever Proteus to himselfe could make." Milton's *Comus* calls Proteus "the Carpathian wizard," referring to Vergil's comment in the *Fourth Georgic* that the sea god lived most of the time in the Carpathian Sea between Crete and Rhodes. Other poets who have used Proteus are Pope in *The Dunciad*, Archibald MacLeish in *Men of My Century Loved Mozart*, Rolfe Humphries in *Proteus, or the Shapes of Conscience*, and Wordsworth in "The World Is Too Much with Us." From his name come the English words *protean* (of changeable shape) and *protein*.

See also: ODYSSEY, THE; OVID

2474

**Pryderi** (Phyderi) (anxiety)   In Celtic mythology, hero who was the son of Pwyll, the god of Arawn, the underworld, and Rhiannon, the "great queen." He appears in the *Mabinogion*. As a child Pryderi was stolen by Teyrnon Twry Bliant, a ruler of part of Wales lying between the Wye and the Usk. He was given the name Gwri (he of the golden hair), but when he was returned to his parents he was named Pryderi. Later in life Pryderi exchanged some valuable swine for illusory horses and hounds offered by Gwydion, the British king and magician. A fight ensued, and Pryderi was killed. His story may have contributed to the conception of Perceval in the Arthurian legends.

See also: ARTHUR, KING; GWYDION; PERCEVAL; *MABINOGION*

2475

**Psyche** (soul)   In Greek and Roman mythology, a girl loved by Eros (Cupid), who was god of love; mother of Voluptas, who was goddess of pleasure. Psyche was a beautiful girl, so admired by many young men that they neglected the worship of Aphrodite, goddess of love. Angry, Aphrodite sent her son Eros to cause Psyche to fall in love with an ugly monster, but instead Eros fell in love with Psyche. He had her sent to

a secret palace and made love to her each night under cover of darkness, telling her she must not look upon him in the light. Curious about her lover, Psyche, carrying a lamp, came into the chamber when Eros was asleep and dropped hot oil on him, causing him to flee. Psyche went in search of him, but Aphrodite thwarted her with a series of mishaps. In the end the two lovers were reunited and married. Apuleius's novel *The Golden Ass*; William Morris's "Cupid and Psyche," part of *The Earthly Paradise*; and Keats's "Ode to Psyche" all deal with the subject. Numerous paintings and sculptures have portrayed Psyche and Eros, including a Hellenistic marble group called *Invention of the Kiss*, Raphael's frescoes for the Loggia di Psyche in the Farnese Palace in Rome, sculptures by Canova and Rodin, and a painting by Edward Burne-Jones called *Psyche in Her Chamber*. César Franck wrote a symphonic poem called *Psyche*.

See also: APHRODITE; EROS;

*Ptah*

2476

**Ptah**   In Egyptian mythology, a creator deity who made the world with his heart and his tongue: the chief god of Memphis; the craft god, protector of artisans; his wife was Sakhmet; his son, Nefertem. His scepter included the *djed* symbol of stability, the *was* symbol of dominion, and the *ankh* symbol of life. He bestowed these qualities on Egyptian kings, who were often crowned in his temple at Memphis. Ptah was identified by the Greeks with their god Hephaestus and by the Romans with their god Vulcan. Ptah filled many roles in Egyptian belief. He was the master craftsman who brought forth everything, according to one myth. He fashioned the gods, made the cities, founded the *nomes* (provinces), installed the gods in their shrines, established offerings for them, and made likenesses of them to their satisfaction. In Egyptian art Ptah was portrayed as a bearded man with a tight-fitting cap and a tight-fitting garment from which his hands extended. In Verdi's *Aida* the priests call upon Ptah in the last scene of the opera.

See also: ANKH; HEPHAESTUS; SAKHMET; VULCAN

2477

**P'u Hsien**    In Chinese Buddhism, a Bodhisattva who becomes patron god of Mount O-mei in Szechuan, portrayed with a greenish face, wearing a yellow robe with a red collar, and riding on an elephant. At one time the elephant was a man who battled and was defeated by P'u Hsien. P'u Hsien is derived from the Sanskrit name A Samantabhadra, the Bodhisattva of the protection of worldly activity or of religious practice.

See also: BODHISATTVA

2478

**Puloman**    In Hindu mythology, a demon killed by Indra, the storm god, when he cursed Indra for raping his daughter Sachi.

See also: INDRA

2479

**Pundjel**    In Australian mythology, a creator god who first created man. He made the first couple, two men, from clay on pieces of bark. The black creature was called Kookinberrook,

the lighter-colored creature, Berrokborn. Pundjel breathed on them and danced them to life. Then Pallian, the brother of Pundjel, discovered two female forms gradually emerging head first from muddy waters. One was Kunewarra; the other was Kuurook. They became the wives of the first two men. The men were given spears; the women, digging sticks. In time children were born, and the earth was inhabited, but Pundjel and Pallian found the children to be evil and cut them into pieces. A great wind then came and scattered the pieces, and they were turned into whole people.

See also: ABUK AND GARANG; ADAM AND EVE; ASK AND EMBLA; BERROKBORN; KHADAU AND MAMALDI; KOOKINBERROOK; PALLIAN

2480

**Puntan**    In Micronesian mythology, preexistent creator god. When Puntan was about to die, he ordered his sister to create from his body a place for humans to live. His breast and back became the earth and sky; his eyes, the sun and moon; and his eyebrows, the rainbow.

See also: YMIR

2481

**Purah** (Puta, Poteh) (fire?)    In Jewish folklore, angel associated with the close of the Sabbath. Purah appears in Isaac Bashevis Singer's short story "Jachid and Jechidah."

2482

**Puranas** (ancient)    Popular Hindu texts, later than the epics, in which the myths of the gods are given. There are 18 commonly accepted Puranas of varying length and content. Usually a Purana is devoted to the praise of one god. The Puranas reflect popular folk beliefs and the various cults that arose in India over the centuries. They are as follows:

*Vishnu Purana*, in which Vishnu is praised as the creator, sustainer, and controller of the world.

*Kurma*

*Narada Purana* (Naradiya), in which the sage Narada describes the duties of man in society.

*Bhagavata Purana* or *Srimad Bhagavatam*, which narrates the life of Krishna (an incarnation of the god Vishnu).

*Garuda Purana*, named after the fantastic bird Garuda, which carries Vishnu; it deals with death rites.

*Padma Purana*, which describes the creation of the world when it was a golden *padma* (lotus) and describes Patala, the lowest part of the underworld.

*Varaha Purana*, a revelation of Vishnu as the boar incarnation, Varaha.

*Matsya Purana*, a revelation of Vishnu as the Matysa (fish) incarnation.

*Kurma Purana*, a revelation of Vishnu as the Kurma (tortoise) incarnation.

*Lingam Purana*, which explains the worship of the *lingam* (phallus) of the god Shiva.

*Vayu Purana*, devoted to the god Shiva.

*Skanda Purana*, devoted to Skanda, god of war and a son of Shiva.

*Agni Purana*, a mixture of various matters told by the fire god, Agni, to the sage Vasishtha.

*Brahma Purana*, devoted to the sun god Surya.

*Brahamanda Purana*, devoted to the *anda* (egg) of the god Brahma.

*Brahma-Vaivasvata Purana*, devoted to the worship of Krishna and his mistress Radha.

*Markandeya Purana*, which tells how birds recite the sacred Vedas as well as the myth of Shakti, as mother goddess, who saved the earth from demons.

*Bhavishya Purana*, a handbook of rites.

*Vamana Purana*, a revelation of Vishnu as the dwarf incarnation, Vamana.

See also: AGNI; BRAHMA; GARUDA; LINGAM; SHIVA; SKANDA; VAYU; VISHNU

2483
**Purusha** (man)   In Hindu mythology, the primeval male, according to some accounts. The title is sometimes applied to the god Brahma, and Purushottama (best of men) is used for the god Vishnu or for any deity regarded as supreme.

See also: BRAHMA; VISHNU

2484
**Pushan** (nourisher)   In Hindu mythology, a sun god, keeper of herds and bringer of prosperity. Pushan protects and multiplies cattle, is a guide on roads and journeys, and is patron god of conjurers, especially those who discover stolen goods. He is also connected with marriage and is invoked to bless the bride. Pushan is toothless because the god Shiva knocked out his teeth. As a result he eats gruel and is known as Karambhad (pap). In Indian art Pushan is often portrayed carrying an ox goad in a chariot drawn by goats.

See also: SHIVA

**Pushpa-danta**    In Hindu mythology, one of
the eight elephants that protects the eight points
of the compass. Pushpa-danta is also an attendant of Shiva, condemned to be reborn as a man
for recounting a private conversation between
Shiva and his wife Parvati.

See also: SHIVA

**Pu-tai Ho-shang** (hemp bag master)    In Chinese Buddhism, an eccentric monk regarded as a
manifestation of Maitreya, the Buddha of the Future, portrayed as a fat man with the upper part
of his body exposed. Called the Laughing Buddha, he is often shown with a bundle of papers
and a pilgrim's staff or a fly-whisk. He is also
shown carrying a hemp bag and surrounded by
children. The hemp bag is said to contain junk
he picked up. He called it "The Bag of Wonderful Things," and the children would crowd
around as he drew mysterious objects out of it
and gave them away. In Japanese mythology he is
called Hotei o-sho.

See also: MAITREYA

**Putana** (stinking)    In Hindu mythology, a demoness who attempted to kill the infant Krishna
(an incarnation of the god Vishnu) by suckling
him to death. Her breasts were filled with poison, but Krishna suckled and dried them up, and
she died. In Hindu folklore Putana is regarded as
a demoness who causes disease in children.

See also: KRISHNA; VISHNU

**Pyan-ras-gsigs**    In Tibetan Buddhism, name
of Avalokiteshvara, the Bodhisattva of Perfect
Compassion, one of the five Dhyani-
Bodhisattvas, who is known as Kuan-Yin in
China and Kwannon in Japan; also an independent entity. In Pure Land Buddhist iconography
he is, together with Mahasthemaprapta, one of

*Four-handed Avalokiteshvara*

the two Bodhisattvas attendant on Amitabha
Buddha. He is recognized by the small figure of
Amitabha in his crown and is often shown holding a lotus, in which the devotee is reborn into
the Pure Land.

See also: AMITABHA; AVALOKITESHVARA; BOD-
HISATTVA; DHYANI-BODHISATTVAS; KUAN-YIN;
KWANNON; MAHASTHEMAPRAPTA

**Pyerun** (Perun, Peruw) (to strike, to thunder)
In Slavic mythology, god of thunder and war. He
had a golden beard and rode a flaming chariot
across the sky, piercing the clouds with his
miraculous bow. The oak was his sacred tree.

The idol of Pyerun was erected under the
open sky in Kiev, Russia, and served by the *kniaz*
(a prince), the military chief of the city. It is believed, therefore, that his cult was in many ways a
warrior cult. When Prince Vladimir of Kiev
(who was later sainted by the Russian church)
was converted to Byzantine orthodoxy in 988, he
ordered the image of Pyerun to be cut down and
thrown into the river. The god's attributes were

transferred to other figures in Russian folklore and mythology.

In White Russian mythology Pyerun lost his chariot but still roamed the sky with his bow. The folk hero Ilya Muromets, though a Christian, possessed some of the attributes of Pyerun, and the prophet Elijah from the Old Testament also was identified with the god because he ascended to heaven in a fiery chariot (2 Kings 2:11). (In the Russian church Elijah is called Iliya the Prophet, and his feast day is 20 July.)

Variants of Pyerun's name among Slavic peoples are Perkunas, the Lithuanian god who created the universe from the warmth of his body; Perkons, the Lettish god of thunder and lightning; Piorun among the Poles; Peranu among the Bohemians, and Peroon among the Serbians.

See also: DAZHBOG; ELIJAH; ILYA MUROMETS; OAK; VLADIMIR, ST.

2490

**Pygmalion** (shaggy fist)   In Greek mythology, a king (or sculptor) of Cyprus, who made a statue of a woman and fell in love with it. Pygmalion prayed to Aphrodite, goddess of love, to help him, and she turned the statue into a living woman called Galatea. Galatea bore Pygmalion's son, Paphus. The story is told in Ovid's *Metamorphoses* (book 10), which in part inspired the final scene of the living statue in Shakespeare's *Winter's Tale*. A one-act opera by Rameau also treats the tale. William Morris's *Earthly Paradise* recounts the myth, and George Bernard Shaw's *Pygmalion* also uses it. Shaw's play was the basis for the musical play *My Fair Lady*. The movie *One Touch of Venus*, with a score by Kurt Weill and starring Ava Gardner, also uses the story, but in the movie it is a statue of Venus that comes alive in a department store.

See also: APHRODITE; OVID; VENUS

2491

**Pyramid Texts**   Ancient Egyptian texts found in the pyramid of King Unas of the Fifth Dynasty, as well as in other pyramids of the Sixth Dynasty. The texts, engraved on the walls, consist of prayers, magic formulas, and various rubrics to help the deceased in his journey to the other world.

See also: *BOOK OF THE DEAD, THE*; COFFIN TEXTS

2492

**Pyramus and Thisbe**   In Greek and Roman mythology, two lovers. Pyramus and Thisbe lived in adjoining houses in Babylon. They were forbidden to see or speak to each other by their feuding families. They managed, however, to whisper through a chink in the wall separating the two properties. One day they agreed to meet at night in a wooded spot outside the city. Thisbe, arriving first, was frightened by a lion and fled, dropping her scarf. Pyramus, reaching the spot later, found the lion's footprints and the torn scarf. Believing Thisbe dead, he killed himself by falling on his sword. Thisbe returned, found Pyramus's body, and killed herself. From their blood the mulberry tree grew blood-red fruit. The tale is told in Ovid's *Metamorphoses* (book 4) and is played out by Bottom the weaver and his friends in Shakespeare's *A Midsummer Night's Dream*. Pyramus and Thisbe are also reminiscent of Shakespeare's *Romeo and Juliet*. The tale is also told by Chaucer in his *Legend of Good Women* and by Gower in *Confession Amantis*. Poussin painted a canvas called *Pyramus and Thisbe*.

See also: MULBERRY; OVID

2493

**Pythia** (she who discovers)   In Greek ritual, priestess of Apollo at Delphi, who delivered oracles called the Pythia. Her name is derived, according to some accounts, from Python (serpent), a giant snake that was produced by Gaea, goddess of earth, and haunted Mount Parnassus. The etymology is supposed to connect Python with *pythein*, "to rot," because the serpent's body rotted on the site, but it is more likely to derive from *pynthanein*, "discover by asking." The monster was slain in the cave at Delphi by Apollo with his first arrow. A sacred rite, called the Pythian Games, was enacted in ancient Greece to commemorate the event. A bronze column in the form of a three-headed snake supporting a gold tripod was placed at the site. The myth is told in the Homeric Hymn to Pythian Apollo (attributed to Homer but not by him) and Ovid's *Metamorphoses* (book 1). Keats's *Hymn to Apollo* and Byron's *Childe Harold* (III, 81) make reference to Pythia.

See also: APOLLO; DELPHI; OVID

# Q

**Qat**   In Melanesian mythology, hero, trickster, and creator god, whose companion is Marawa, a spider.

Qat, according to some accounts, made the first humans by shaping wood into men and women and beguiling them into life. His companion, Marawa, did the same. But when Marawa's figures began to move, he buried them in a pit. Seven days later Marawa dug them up and found only rotting corpses. That is why there is death in the world. In other accounts Marawa is a wood sprite who aids Qat in various adventures. Once he saves him from his evil brothers, called Tangaro, who try to crush him to death. Another myth tells how Qat brought night into the world. His brothers complained because the sun always shone and they could not rest. So Qat went to Oong (night) for help. He then told his brothers how to fall asleep. When the cock crowed, he took a red flint stone and cut Oong, causing the dawn. In other sections of Melanesia, Qat's adventures are credited to Tagaro.

See also: ASK AND EMBLA; SPIDER; TAGARO; TRICKSTER

**Questing Beast**   In Arthurian legend, a monster called Glatisaunt, which had the head of a serpent, the buttocks of a lion, the body of a leopard, and the feet of a deer. It made "the noise of 30 couple of hounds questing [baying]," according to Malory's *Morte d'Arthur*. The Questing Beast was hunted by King Pellinore, who was later killed by Sir Gawaine to avenge the death of Gawaine's father, King Lot.

See also: GWAIN; LOT, KING

**Quetzalcoatl** (feathered serpent, precious serpent, precious twin)   In Toltec mythology, wind god. Another Quetzalcoatl was a culture hero. In his purely mythical form the god Quetzalcoatl was one of four brothers born in the 13th heaven. Of the four, one was called the black and one the red Tezcatlipoca, and the fourth was Huitzilopochtli. Tezcatlipoca (the black and red are combined) was the wisest. He knew all thoughts and could see into the future. At a certain time the four gathered together and consulted concerning creation. The work was left to Quetzalcoatl and Huitzilopochtli. First they made fire, then half a sun, the heavens, the waters, and a great fish called Cipactli; from Cipactli's flesh they made the solid earth.

The first people were Cipactonal, a man, and Oxomuco, a woman. They had a son, but there was no wife for him to marry, so the four gods made one out of the hair taken from the head of their divine mother, Zochiquetzal.

The half sun created by Quetzalcoatl and Huitzilopochtli was a poor light for the world, and the four brothers came together to find a means of adding another half to the sun. Not waiting for their decision, Tezcatlipoca transformed himself into a sun. The other brothers then filled the world with giants, who tore up the trees with their hands. After some time Quetzalcoatl took a stick and "with a blow of it knocked Tezcatlipoca from the sky into the waters." He then made himself the sun. Tezcatlicopa transformed himself into a tiger and emerged from the waves, attacking and devouring the giants; then, passing to the nocturnal heavens, he became the constellation of the Great Bear.

As the sun, Quetzalcoatl made the earth flourish, but Tezcatlipoca was merely biding his time. When the right moment came, Tezcatlipoca appeared in his tiger form and gave Quetzalcoatl such a blow with his paw that it hurled him from the skies. Quetzalcoatl then swept the earth with a violent tornado that destroyed all of the inhabitants except for a few "who were changed into monkeys." Then, when Tezcatlipoca placed Tlaloc, the rain god, as the sun in the heavens, Quetzalcoatl "poured a flood of fire upon the earth, drove Tlaloc from the sky, and placed in his stead, as sun, the goddess Chalchiutlicue, the Emerald Skirted, wife of Tlaloc." When she ruled as sun, the earth was flooded, and all humans were drowned again except for those who were changed into fishes. As a result, "the heavens themselves fell, and the sun and stars were alike quenched."

The two then realized that their struggle had to end, so they united "their efforts and raised again the sky, resting it on two mighty trees, the Tree of the Mirror (*tezcaquahuitl*) and the Beautiful Great Rose Tree (*quetzalveixochitl*) on which the concave heavens have ever since securely rested."

The earth still had no sun to light it, and the four brothers met again. They decided to make a sun, one that would "eat the hearts and drink the blood of victims, and there must be wars upon the earth, that these victims could be obtained for the sacrifice." Quetzalcoatl then built a great fire and took his son, born of his own flesh without any mother, and cast him into the flames, "whence he rose into the sky as the sun which lights the world." Tlaloc then threw *his* son into the flames, creating the moon.

The Quetzalcoatl of that myth is a god. Another Quetzalcoatl is a culture hero, a high priest of the city of Tula. He was the teacher of arts, the wise lawgiver, the virtuous prince, the master builder, and the merciful judge. He lived a life of fasting and prayer.

The hero (not the god) Quetzalcoatl either came as a stranger to the Aztecs from an unknown land or was born in Tula, where he reigned as priest-king. For many years he ruled the city and at last began to build a very great temple. While it was being constructed Tezcatlipoca (who in other myths is a creator-trickster god but here is a demonic force, or sorcerer) came to Quetzalcoatl one day and told him that toward Honduras, in a place called Tlapallan, a house was ready for him. He should leave Tula and go to live and die in the new home.

Quetzalcoatl said that the heavens and the stars had already warned him that after four years he must leave, and he would therefore obey. He left with all of the inhabitants of Tula. Some he left in Cholula and others in Cempoal. At last he reached Tlapallan, and on the day he arrived he fell sick and died.

There is another, better-known account in the *Annals of Cuauhtitlan*. When those opposed to Quetzalcoatl did not succeed in their designs to rid themselves of his presence, they summoned Tezcatlipoca. He said: "We will give him a drink to dull his reason, and we will show him his own face in a mirror, and surely he will be lost."

Then Tezcatlipoca brewed an intoxicating drink, the pulque, and taking a mirror he wrapped it in a rabbit skin and went to Quetzalcoatl's house.

"Go tell your master," he said to the servants, "that I have come to show him his own flesh."

"What is this?" asked Quetzalcoatl when the message was delivered. "What does he call my own flesh? Go and ask him." But Tezcatlipoca said he would speak only with Quetzalcoatl. He was then admitted into the presence of Quetzalcoatl.

"Welcome, youth. You have troubled yourself much. Whence come you? What is this, my flesh, that you would show me?"

"My lord and priest," replied Tezcatlipoca, "I come from the mountainside of Nonoalco. Look now at your flesh; know yourself; see yourself as you are seen by others." And with that he handed him the mirror.

As soon as Quetzalcoatl saw his face in the mirror, he said: "How is it possible my subjects can look on me without affright? Well! might they flee from me. How can a man remain among them filled as I am with foul sores, his face wrinkled and his aspect loathsome? I shall be seen no more: I shall no longer frighten my people."

But Tezcatlipoca said he could conceal the defects on Quetzalcoatl's face. He painted the ruler's cheeks green and dyed his lips red. The forehead he colored yellow, and, taking the feathers of the quetzal bird, he made a beard. Quetzalcoatl looked at himself in the mirror and was pleased with the artifice.

Then Tezcatlipoca took the strong pulque he had brewed and gave some to Quetzalcoatl, who became drunk. He called his attendants and asked that his sister Quetzalpetlatl come to him. She instantly obeyed and, drinking some of the pulque, also became drunk.

It is not clear whether Quetzalcoatl slept with his sister in the myth, but the next morning he said, "I have sinned, the stain on my name can never be erased. I am not fit to rule this people. Let them build for me a habitation deep underground; let them bury my bright treasures in the earth; let them throw the gleaming gold and shining stone into the holy fountain where I take my daily bath."

He then journeyed eastward to a place where the sky, land, and water met. There his attendants built a funeral pyre, and he threw himself into the flames. As his body burned his heart rose to heaven, and after four days he became the planet Venus, the Morning Star.

In a variant of the end of the legend, Quetzalcoatl departed on a raft toward the east, saying he would one day return. When Spanish conquistador Hernán Cortés arrived in the 16th century, the Aztecs believed that their hero had returned to them as he had promised, a belief that helped seal their doom. The conflict between the two cultures is told in W. H. Prescott's *The History of the Conquest of Mexico* and in the novels *The Fair God* by Lew Wallace and *Captain from Castile* by Samuel Shellabarger, which was made into a film.

See also: TEZCATLIPOCA

**Quiracus, St.**    Third century. In Christian legend, bishop of Ostia who was stabbed in the back and beheaded. His dog retrieved and returned his head, and he appears in medieval art holding his head in his hands. Feast, 23 August.

# R

*Ra*

**Ra** (Re, Phra, Pre) (sun, creator, creative power?) In Egyptian mythology, the major sun god, often merged with the god Amun, forming the composite god Amun-Ra. He was the King of the Gods, on earth and later from heaven.

One of the first acts of creation in Egyptian mythology was the appearance of Ra's sun disk above the waters of Nun (chaos). Time was said to have begun with the first rising of Ra. Because the Egyptians believed that the sun was made of fire and could not have risen directly out of the waters of chaos without some means of conveyance, it was assumed that Ra made his journey over the waters in a boat. The morning boat was called Matet (becoming strong) and the evening boat, Semktet (becoming weak). The course of Ra was said to have been mapped out by the goddess Maat, who was the personification of physical and moral law. In the evening after the sun had set in the west, Ra entered Duat, the underworld. With the help of the gods there he successfully passed through that region in a boat and appeared in the sky the next morning. As he passed through Duat he gave air, light, and food to those who were condemned to live there. Two fishes, Abtu and Ant, swam before Ra's boat and acted as pilots.

Each morning just before he left Duat and was about to enter the sky, Ra engaged in a battle with Apophis, a giant serpent and night demon. Apophis's attacks failed because Ra cast a spell on him, making the monster incapable of moving. Then the supporters of the sun god bound Apophis in chains and hacked him to pieces, after which he was destroyed by the flames of Ra—symbolic of the sun destroying the vapors and dampness of the night. In the *Books of the Overthrowing of Apophis* a ritual is prescribed to be recited daily in the temple of Amun-Ra at Thebes. It cataloged in great detail the destruction that was to befall Apophis and his monstrous helpers, Sebau and Nak.

All of the kings of Egypt in the early empire believed themselves to be the sons of Ra. It was said that whenever the divine blood of the kings needed replenishing, the god took the form of the reigning king of Egypt and visited the queen in her chamber, becoming then the true father of the child born to her. When the child was born, it was regarded as the god incarnate. In due time it was presented to the sun god in his temple. This gave the priests of Ra great power in Egypt.

One myth, however, tells how Ra was almost destroyed by the goddess Isis, who sought his true name. The ancients believed that to possess the true name of a god enabled one to have power over him. Many gods had more than one name, one by which the god was generally known and another that might be called his real name, which he kept secret lest it come into the hands of his enemies, who would use it against him. Isis once wished to make Ra reveal to her his greatest and most secret name. "Cannot I by means of the sacred name of God make myself mistress of the earth and become a goddess of like rank and power to Ra in heaven and upon earth?" she asked. Using her magic skill, she made a venomous reptile out of dust mixed with Ra's spittle, and by uttering certain words of power over the reptile she made it sting Ra as he passed through the heavens. The sun god, finding himself on the point of death, was forced to reveal his hidden name. Having achieved her goal, Isis spoke an incantation that drained the poison from Ra's limbs, and the god recovered.

In the Fifth Dynasty, when the cult of the man-god Osiris spread over the delta region from Busiris (the northern center of the cult) and throughout Upper Egypt from Abydos (the southern center), the priests of the sun god fought to maintain Ra's authority. However, before the end of the Sixth Dynasty the cult of Osiris prevailed, and Ra was relegated to an inferior position, with the greatest of his attributes ascribed to Osiris. From the Twelfth Dynasty onward all of the attributes of Ra were absorbed by Amun, who was the dominant god of Upper Egypt. During the 19th and 20th dynasties 75 forms of Ra were known, constituting part of a litany to Ra, which is believed to have been sung

*Eye of Ra*

during services in the temples. The litany was painted on the walls of several tombs, such as those of Seti I and Rameses IV.

Ra was connected at a very early period with the hawk god Horus, who personified the height of heaven, and in Egyptian art Ra is usually portrayed as a hawk-headed man and sometimes simply in the form of a hawk. On his head he wears the disk of the sun encircled by a serpent. When he appears in human form, he holds the ankh, sign of life, in his right hand and a scepter in his left. Mau, the great cat, is sometimes equated with Ra. In this form he cuts off the head of the evil monster serpent Apophis. From the 26th century B.C.E. to the Roman period, all kings and rulers in Egypt referred to themselves as Sons of Ra.

See also: AMUN; ANKH; APOPHIS; DUAT; HORUS; ISIS; MAAT; OSIRIS

2499

**Rabbi Eliezer**    Jewish folktale found in the Talmud. Rabbi Eliezer, who was as much distinguished by the greatness of his mind as by the extraordinary size of his body, once paid a visit to Rabbi Simon. The learned Simon received him most cordially and, filling a cup with wine, handed it to him. Eliezer took it and drank it off in one gulp. Another cup was poured, and it went just as quickly. "Brother Eliezer," said Simon jestingly, "remember what the wise men have said on this subject of drinking?" "I well remember," answered the corpulent Eliezer, "the saying of our instructors—that people ought not to take a cup at one draught, but," he added, "the wise men have not so defined their rule to admit of no exceptions. And in this instance, friend Simon, there are no less than three: the cup is small, the receiver large, and your wine delicious!"

See also: TALMUD

**Rabi'a al-'Adawiya**   714–801. In Islamic legend, saint and mystic; born in a poor home, she was kidnapped and sold into slavery. She gained her freedom, however, and gathered around her a group of followers. Her life was one of extreme asceticism and otherworldliness; she was noted especially for her sayings dealing with mystic love.

She is credited with many miracles, such as feeding a crowd on very little food. One legend tells of a camel that she restored to life after it had died during a pilgrimage. When she was dying she asked that all of her friends leave so that the messengers of Allah would have free access to her. Her friends could then hear her reciting the end of sura 89 of the Koran: "O thou my soul which art at rest, return unto thy Lord, well pleased with thy reward, and well pleasing unto Allah; enter among my servants; and enter my paradise."

She appeared in a vision after her death and told how she answered the angels Munkar and Nakir when they questioned her: "I said, return and tell your Lord, 'Notwithstanding the thousands and thousands and thousands of Thy creatures, Thou hast not forgotten a weak old woman. I, who had only Thee in all the world, have never forgotten Thee, that Thou shouldst ask, Who is thy Lord?'"

The tradition that angels appear to the soul immediately after death to impose a minor judgment before the final major judgment at the end of the world is a late belief.

See also: CAMEL; MUNKAR AND NAKIR

**Rabican**   In the Charlemagne cycle of legends, a horse that fed on air and was unsurpassed for swiftness. He appears in Ariosto's *Orlando Furioso*.

See also: CHARLEMAGNE; ROLAND

**Radish**   A small, potent, edible root. During the Jewish feast of Passover radishes are a part of the traditional meal. In today's celebrations of the rite the radish is symbolic of spring and a sign of "the perpetual renewal of life and ever-sustaining hope of human redemption."

See also: PASSOVER

**Ragnarok** (judgment by the powers)   In Norse mythology, the final battle between the gods and the giants that will bring about the end of the world. The battle will take place at Vigrith (field of battle). The destruction, however, will not be the complete end. The *Prose Edda* gives an account of a new "earth most lovely and verdant, and with pleasant fields where the grain shall grow unsown." Some of the gods will return, such as Baldur and Hodur from Hel, the underworld, and a new couple, Lifthrasir and Lif (life), will repeople the land "and their descendants shall soon spread over the whole earth." The *Poetic Edda* contains a description of the end in the poem *Voluspa*. Wagner's last music drama in the cycle *Der Ring des Nibelungen*, titled *Götterdämmerung*, deals with the destruction of the gods.

See also: BALDUR; GJALLAR-HORN; HEIMDALL; HODUR; LIF; LIFTHRASIR; LOKI; ODIN; *RING DES NIBELUNGEN, DER*; THOR

**Rahu** (the seizer)   In Hindu mythology, a demon who seizes the sun and moon, causing eclipses. It is also the name for eclipses. Rahu has four arms, and his body ends in a dragon's tail. When the gods and demons were fighting for the Amrita, the water of life, at the Churning of the Ocean, Rahu disguised himself and drank some of the Amrita. When the sun and moon saw what he had done, they told the god Vishnu, who then cut off Rahu's head and two of his arms. Rahu, however, had gained immortality by drinking the Amrita, and his body was placed in the heavens. The upper part is represented by a dragon's head, the ascending node, and the lower part, the descending node.

The *Vishnu Purana*, one of the 18 Puranas, tells how "eight black horses draw the dusky chariot of Rahu, and once harnessed are attached to it for ever.... Rahu directs his course from the sun to the moon, and back again from the moon to the sun."

Rahu is also called Abhra-pisacha (the demon of the sky) and Kabandha (the headless).

See also: AMRITA; CHURNING OF THE OCEAN; PURANAS

**2505**

**Raiden** (Raijin, Kaminarisan)  In Japanese mythology, thunder god, portrayed with the features of a demon: horns on his head, a tusk, and a wide mouth. Sometimes he carries a circle of 12 round, flat drums, which he beats with sticks; or he is portrayed caught by Uzume, goddess of mirth, who is shown in her bath. Raiden likes to eat navels. Thus, children are dressed to cover their abdomens.

**2506**

**Rainbow Snake**  In Australian mythology, name of the gigantic snake whose body arches across the sky as the rainbow. Known as Taipan among the Wikmunkan people, he is associated with the gift of blood to humankind, controlling the circulation of the blood as well as the menstrual cycle of women. Looked on as a great healer, Taipan demands that his sexual laws and customs be followed. His anger at the breaking of any of them is expressed by thunder and lightning. Medicine men and rain makers invoke Taipan by using quartz crystal and seashells in their rituals. Called Julunggul among the people of the eastern Arnhem Land, the Rainbow Snake is believed to swallow young boys and later vomit

them up. This is symbolic of their rebirth, or the transition from youth to manhood. Known as Kunmanggur in a myth told by the Murinbata of the northwest of the Northern Territory to W. Stanner, the Rainbow Snake is either bisexual or a woman. Sometimes he is described as a male but is portrayed with female breasts. Other names by which the Rainbow Snake is known in Australia are Galeru, Ungur, Wonungur, Worombi, Wonambi, Wollunqua, Yurlunggur, Langal, Muit, and Yero.

See also: WALWALAG SISTERS

**2507**

**Rais, Gilles de**  1404–1440. In medieval history and legend, marshal of France who fought with St. Joan of Arc against the English invaders. He was accused of sorcery, as was Joan, and was executed for heresy and the rape and murder of children. It is believed by some scholars that the legend of Bluebeard is based on his life.

See also: BLUEBEARD; JOAN OF ARC, ST.

**2508**

**Raji**  In Hindu mythology, a man who usurped the throne of the storm god Indra. When there was a war between the gods and demons, the god Brahma declared that the victory should be given to the side that Raji joined. The demons sought Raji's aid but would not make him king as he requested. However, the gods promised Raji that if he sided with them he would be made king of the gods, and Indra, the king of the gods, would worship him. After the demons were defeated, Raji was made king of the gods as promised. Later, when he returned to his own city, he left Indra as his deputy in heaven. On Raji's death Indra refused to acknowledge the succession of his sons (he had 500 sons) and retained the title for himself.

See also: BRAHMA; INDRA

**2509**

**Rákóczi, Ferenc** 1675–1735. In Hungarian legend, prince who led a revolt against Austrian oppression. According to some tales, he did not die but is resting, waiting for the time to come to Hungary's aid. Rákóczi has given his name to a well-known Hungarian marching tune used by Hector Berlioz in his cantata *The Damnation of Faust* and by Franz Liszt in Hungarian Rhapsody No. 15, written in the 1840s.

See also: ARTHUR; BARBAROSSA; MÁTYÁS; SOLOMON

**2510**

**Rakshasas** (Raksasas) (to be guarded against) In Hindu mythology, a class of demons under the leadership of the demon king Ravana. In the Hindu epic poem *The Ramayana*, when the monkey chief Hanuman enters the Lanka (Sri Lanka), Ravana's capital, he sees "the Rakshasas sleeping in the houses were of every shape and form. Some of them disgusted the eye, while some were beautiful to look upon. Some had long arms and frightful shapes; some were very fat and some were very lean; some were mere dwarfs and some were very tall. Some had only one eye and others only one ear. Some had monstrous bellies, hanging breasts, long protruding teeth, and crooked thighs, while others were exceedingly beautiful to behold and clothed in great splendor. Some had two legs, some three legs, and some four legs. Some had the heads of serpents, some the heads of donkeys, some the heads of horses, and some the heads of elephants."

See also: HANUMAN; *RAMAYANA, THE*; RAVANA

**2511**

**Ram** In Egyptian mythology the ram, a male sheep, was sacred to the god Khnum, who was portrayed as a ram-headed god. A ram was sacrificed to the god Amun-Ra once a year. It was skinned and the skin placed over the image of the god, recalling the time when Amun-Ra was incarnated in the form of a ram. In ancient Hebrew belief the ram was sacrificed instead of Isaac when Isaac's father, Abraham, was commanded by god to sacrifice his son (Gen. 22:13). In later Jewish folklore the ram had been trapped in a thicket since the sixth day of creation, waiting for Abraham's sacrifice. From the bones of that sacrificed ram the foundations of the Holy of Holies of the Temple were built; the ram's veins became the strings for King David's harp, and its skin was made into the prophet Elijah's belt and girdle; its left horn made the shofar used by Moses on Mount Sinai; and its right horn the shofar that the prophet Elijah will blow on Mount Moriah to announce the coming of the Messiah. In Islamic belief Abraham's ram was admitted into heaven. In Hindu mythology the ram is the steed or mount of the fire god Agni.

See also: ABRAHAM; AGNI; AMUN; DAVID; ELIJAH; ISAAC; KHNUM; MOSES; RA; YAHWEH

**2512**

**Ram** In Persian mythology, spirit of the air, or angel, who receives the good soul on its way to the other world after death.

**2513**

**Rama** (charming) In Hindu mythology, a hero, chief character in the epic poem by Valmiki, *The Ramayana*. In some Hindu texts, such as Tulasi Das's vernacular version of the Sanskrit *Ramayana*, titled *Ramacheritamanasa* (the holy lake of the acts of Rama), Rama is regarded as an incarnation of the god Vishnu. As such, Rama, along with his wife Sita, is worshiped in many parts of India. One line in Tulasi Das's epic captures the love of the people for their hero god: "Rama knows the hearts of all; in him dwell meekness, love, and mercy. Comfort your heart with this assurance, and come, take rest." Rama appears in Bhavabhuti's plays *The Acts of Rama* and *Later Acts of Rama*. Gandhi's dying words were "Long live Rama," not "O God!" as recorded in the movie *Gandhi*.

See also: *RAMAYANA, THE*; VISHNU

**Ramadan** (Ramazan)   In Islam, ninth month of the lunar year; the time of an annual fast. It is the only month mentioned in the Koran (sura 2), which says that the Koran "was sent down" from heaven in that month.

During Ramadan the believer is commanded to fast the whole month every day, from the first appearance of daybreak until sunset. He must abstain from eating, drinking, smoking, smelling perfumes, and every unnecessary indulgence or pleasure of a worldly nature, even from knowingly swallowing his spittle. When Ramadan falls in summer (since the year is lunar, each month retrogrades through all of the seasons in the course of about every 33½ years) the fast is very severe. Therefore, persons who are sick or on a journey and soldiers in time of war are not obliged to fast. But if they do not fast during Ramadan, they should fast an equal number of days at another time. Fasting is also dispensed with for nurses and pregnant women.

'Id al-Fitr, commonly called *al-'id al-saghir*, or the lesser festival, is a feast for the breaking of the fast when Ramadan is ended. Alms are dispensed, people give gifts, and there is general celebration. In *Moby-Dick* Melville titled chapter 17 "The Ramadan," which refers to Queequeg's "fasting and humiliation."

See also: KORAN, THE

*Ramayana, The* (the tale of Rama)   Hindu epic poem of 24,000 *Shlokas* (48,000 lines), attributed to the sage Valmiki in the third century C.E.. It is divided into seven *kandas*, books of unequal length.

*Bala-Kanda* (book 1). King Dasa-ratha ruled over Ayodhya, a beautiful city. His one complaint, however, was that he had no children. He therefore performed a great sacrifice in the hope of obtaining offspring. The gods accepted his sacrifice, and Dasa-ratha received the promise of four sons. At the request of the god Brahma, the god Vishnu agreed to become incarnate in the body of Rama, one of the four sons to be born, and the other sons, Bharata and the twins Lakshamana and Satru-ghna, also shared some of Vishnu's godhead.

While King Dasa-ratha was performing the sacrifice, Vishnu appeared to him in full glory from out of the sacrificial fire. Vishnu gave the king a pot of nectar for his wives to drink. Dasa-ratha gave half of the magic drink to Kausalya, who became the mother of Rama; a quarter to his wife Kaikeyi, who became the mother of Bharata; and a fourth to his wife Su-mitra, who became the mother of the twins Lakshmana and Satru-ghna.

The four brothers grew up together at Ayodhya. While they were still young, the sage Viswamitra sought Rama's help in protecting him from demons who had been tormenting him. Though unwilling to have his sons leave his court, Dasa-ratha consented, and Rama and Lakshmana went to the hermitage of Viswamitra. There Rama killed the demoness Taraka. Viswamitra had earlier supplied Rama with magic arms that aided the hero in his conquest of Taraka. After the defeat of the demoness, Viswamitra took Rama and Lakshmana to the court of Janaka, king of Videha. At the court was Sita, daughter of the king, who was offered in marriage to anyone who could bend the bow that had belonged to the god Shiva. Rama not only bent the bow but broke it, winning the hand of Sita. Rama's brothers were also married. Urmila, Sita's sister, became the wife of Lakshmana; Mandavi and Sruta-kriti, cousins of Sita, became the wives of Bharata and Satru-ghna.

*Ayodhya-Kanda* (book 2). When the four couples returned to Ayodhya, the king decided to name Rama, his eldest, heir to the throne. The announcement angered the king's wife Kaikeyi, the mother of Bharata. She reminded the king that he had once promised her any two wishes she asked. The angered king, realizing what she wanted, swore to keep his word. The queen then asked that Rama be banished for 14 years and that her son, Bharata, be appointed viceroy in his place.

Rama, being a dutiful son, left with his wife Sita and his brother Lakshmana for the Dandaka forest. Soon after his departure King Dasa-ratha died, and Bharata was called on to be king. Bharata declined, leaving for the forest to bring back Rama. When the two brothers met there was a long discussion, Rama refusing to return until the 14 years had been completed. It was agreed, however, that Bharata should return and act as regent for Rama. As a sign that Rama was king, Bharata brought back a pair of Rama's shoes, placing them on the throne.

*Aranya-Kanda* (book 3). Rama passed his years of banishment moving from one hermitage to another. At last he arrived at the hermitage of Argastya, a sage, near the Vidhya Mountains. Argastya told Rama to live at Panchavati on the river Godavari. Rama's party went to live at Panchavati, but the area was found to be infested with demons. One of them, Surpa-nakha, a sister of the demon king Ravana, fell in love with Rama. When Rama rejected her advances, the demoness attacked Sita. Lakshmana then cut off Surpa-nakha's ears and nose. Calling on her demon friends, Surpa-nakha tried to avenge the wrong, but all of the demons were destroyed. Surpa-nakha then went to her brother Ravana. He became so excited by the physical description of Sita's beauty that he decided to abduct her. Ravana took his magic cart and kidnapped Sita while Rama was lured away from home by Maricha, a demoness who took the form of a deer.

*Kishkindha-Kanda* (book 4). Rama and Lakshmana went in pursuit of Ravana. On their way they killed Kabandha, a headless monster whose disembodied spirit told Rama to seek the aid of the king of the monkeys, Sugriva. The two brothers went to Sugriva and formed an alliance. They also obtained the aid of the monkey leader Hanuman, son of the wind god Vayu.

*Sundara-Kanda* (book 5). With Hanuman's extraordinary powers of leaping and flying, the monkey armies were transported over Ramasetu (Rama's bridge) and entered Lanka, Ravana's country.

*Yuddha-Kanda* (book 6). After a series of battles, Lanka was conquered and Ravana killed by Rama. Sita, to prove she had been faithful to Rama, then underwent an ordeal of fire. Sita entered the flames in the presence of men and gods. Agni, the fire god, led her and placed her in Rama's arms unhurt after the ordeal. Rama then returned to his kingdom with his brothers.

*Uttara-Kanda* (book 7). Rama, however, could not rest, still having doubts of Sita's faithfulness, especially since the populace doubted that she had remained faithful. In order to please the public Rama sent Sita away to spend the rest of her life at the hermitage of the sage Valmiki (the supposed author of the poem). There Sita had twin sons, Kusa and Lava. When they were about 15 years old, they wandered accidentally into Ayodhya and were recognized by Rama as his children. Rama then called Sita back. She declared in public that she had been faithful to Rama, calling on the earth to verify her words. The ground opened, receiving "the daughter of the furrow." Unable to live without Sita, Rama asked the gods to release him. He was told by Time in the form of an ascetic that he must stay on earth or ascend to the heavens. Lakshmana tried to save his brother from Time, but as a result was sentenced to death and sent bodily to the storm god Indra's heaven. Rama then went to the Sarayu River. Walking into the water, he heard the voice of the god Brahma, and he entered into heaven. In a variant ending to the epic, Rama and Sita live happily together, and she is not swallowed by the earth.

The story of Rama and Sita is acted every autumn in many parts of India during a 10-day celebration. At the end of the festival Ravana and his demon hordes are burned in effigy. A suite for orchestra, *Ramayana*, by the American composer Bertram Shapleigh is based on the epic poem.

See also: AGNI; BHARATA; BRAHMA; JANAKA; LAKSHMANA; RAVANA; SHIVA; VAYU; VISWAMITRA

**2516**

**Ran** (robbery)    In Norse mythology, wife of the sea god Aegir. She caught the dead at sea in her net and took them to her underworld. Human sacrifices were made to Ran by pre-Christian Scandinavian sailors before embarking on a voyage. In northern folklore, when she lost her status as goddess, she became a siren who was often seen reclining on the shores combing her hair. In Sweden the spirit Sjöran is believed to be derived from Ran. The kenning for waves is "Ran's way."

See also: AEGIR; SJORAN

**2517**

**Ranieri, St.**    c. 1100–1161. In Christian legend, patron saint of Pisa, Italy. Called St. Ranieri dell Agua or St. Ranieri of Water. Feast, 17 June.

St. Ranieri's life was written by Canon Benincasa, a personal friend, shortly after the saint's death. Ranieri spent his youth in pleasure, but one day while he was playing on a lyre amid his mistresses, a holy man passed by and looked at him with pity. Struck with sudden feelings of guilt for his past, Ranieri followed the man. Shortly afterward he left for Jerusalem, where he took off his rich garments and wore a *schiavina*, or slave shirt, a tunic of coarse wool with short sleeves. While doing penances in the desert he had a vision of a silver and gold vase set with jewels but filled with pitch, oil, and sulfur. The contents were set on fire, and the vase burned. A ewer full of water was put near Ranieri. He placed his hands in it and put two or three drops of water on the flames, and they were extinguished. According to Jameson in *Sacred and Legendary Art*, "The vase signified his human frame . . . the pitch and sulphur burning within it were the appetites and passions . . . the water was the water of temperance. Thenceforward Ranieri lived wholly on coarse bread and water."

Another legend tells of Ranieri and an innkeeper in Messina who diluted his wine, which was then sold to his customers. St. Ranieri revealed the fraud when he unmasked the devil, seated on one of the wine casks in the shape of a huge cat with batlike wings.

St. Ranieri's life was painted by Simone Memmi and Antonio Veneziano in Pisa in 1356.

**2518**

**Raphael** (God has healed)    In the Bible, archangel in Jewish and Christian mythology, patron of humanity. Feast: 21 September in the Western church.

The most prominent role given to Raphael is in the Book of Tobit in the Old Testament Apocrypha. He acts as a companion and guide to Tobit's son Tobias and helps him rid Sara, the intended wife of Tobias, from her demon-lover Asmodeus, who had slain her seven previous husbands. In Tobit (12:15) Raphael describes himself as "one of the seven holy angels, which present the prayers of the saints, and which go in and out before the glory of the Holy One." According to Rabbi Abba in *The Zohar I*, Raphael is "charged to heal the earth, and through him . . . the earth furnishes an abode for man, whom also he heals of his maladies." Raphael appears in Milton's *Paradise Lost* as the "sociable spirit" or as the "affable archangel." (VII, 40). He is often pictured accompanying Tobias and shown holding a pilgrim's staff and a fish (which was used as the charm to rid Sara of her demon-lover). Tobias, often shown as a mere youth, walks close to the angel with his dog nearby.

See also: ANEAL; ASMODEUS

**2519**

**Rapithwin**    In Persian mythology, god of the noonday heat and the summer. When the good god, Ahura Mazda, performed the sacrifice that created the world, it was at the time of day belonging to Rapithwin. When Rapithwin returns at springtime, it is a foreshadowing of the final victory over evil by good, an event at which he will be present.

See also: AHURA MAZDA

**2520**

**Rasetsu Ten**   In Japanese Buddhist mythology, king of demons, portrayed bearded and with upright hair. He holds a sword in his right hand. and his left hand is raised in a sign of fearlessness. He is one of the Jiu No O, 12 Japanese Buddhist gods and goddesses adopted from Hindu mythology.

See also: JIU NO O; MUDRA

**2521**

**Rashnu** (just judge)   In Persian mythology, angel of justice who weighs the good works and sins in his golden scales when the soul's account is balanced in the third night after death. Rashnu is assisted in his work by the angel Astad. The soul is assisted in crossing the "bridge of separation" by a fair maiden who personifies the soul's good deeds.

See also: CHINVAT

**2522**

**Rat**   In Egyptian mythology, wife of the sun god Ra. She was called "mother of the gods," as Ra was called "father of the gods." However, she was really a late development in the cult of Ra and amounts to little more than Ra's name feminized. The sun god was said to have sired the first divine couple without recourse to a female. Rat was portrayed in Egyptian art as a woman wearing on her head a disk with horns and the uraeus. Sometimes there were two feathers on the disk.

See also: RA; URAEUS

**2523**

**Rat and Mouse**   A rat is a long-tailed rodent resembling a mouse but much larger. The two rodents are often confused in world mythology and folklore. In Greek mythology the mouse was sacred to Apollo in his role as sender of plague. Apollo was appealed to as "O Smintheus" (O mouse) when he was invoked in his role as plague sender. Many ancient peoples realized that there

was a connection between mice and plague, though the scientific explanation was unknown to them. The mouse or rat, therefore, often became a symbol of death.

The pagan Germans worshiped a goddess called Nehalennia or Hludana, whose symbol was a rat and whose function was to accompany the souls of the dead. St. Gertrude, a 12th-century saint, was also credited with helping the souls of the dead and was nearly always portrayed with a rat as her companion. One German medieval tale tells how Bishop Hatto was destroyed by mice and rats after he had his flock burned to death in a barn where they had gathered after he had promised them grain.

In America Walt Disney's cartoon character Mickey Mouse, who first appeared in *Steamboat Willie*, has since sung his way to fortune, minus his demonic character and genitals.

See also: APOLLO; PIED PIPER OF HAMELIN

**2524**

**Ratatosk** (swift-tusked)   In Norse mythology, the squirrel that runs up and down the cosmic or world tree, Yggdrasill, carrying abusive language from the dragon Nidhogg at the bottom of the tree to the eagle at the top, and vice versa. Ratatosk appears in the *Poetic Edda* and the *Prose Edda*.

See also: NIDHOGG; *POETIC EDDA*; *PROSE EDDA*; YGGDRASILL

**2525**

**Rati** (love play)   In Hindu mythology, goddess of love, wife of Rama, the god of love. Rati is also called Kama-priya (beloved of Kama); Raga-lata (vine of love); Mayavati (deceiver); Kelikila (wanton); and Subhangi (fair-limbed).

See also: KAMA

**2526**

**Ratnapani** (jewel in hand)　　In Mahayana Buddhism, one of the five Dhyani-Bodhisattvas, whose symbol is a magic jewel.

See also: DHYANI-BODHISATTVAS; MAHAYANA

**2527**

**Ratu-mai-mbulu**　　In Melanesian mythology, Fijian serpent god of the dead, who lives in a cave. A beneficent being, he causes trees and crops to grow. One month of the year is dedicated to him. During that month no singing or dancing is allowed so as not to disturb the god.

**2528**

**Rausch, Bruder** (Brother Rush)　　In Germanic folklore, a house spirit who made people drunk. He appears in English folklore as Friar Rush, and his tale is told in a prose *History of Friar Rush.*

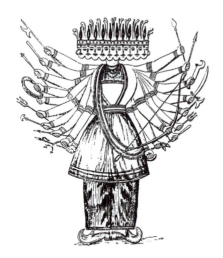

*Ravana*

**2529**

**Ravana** (screaming)　　In Hindu mythology, the demon king of Lanka (Sri Lanka), leader of the Rakshasas, demons and evil spirits. Ravana overthrew his brother Kubera (later made god of wealth) and set himself up as king of Lanka. Ravana was made invulnerable against gods and demons by the god Brahma or Shiva because of his penance and devotion to the god. The only way Ravana could meet death was through a woman, though in actuality he was killed by the hero Rama for having abducted Rama's wife, Sita. In a sense, then, Ravana was killed through a woman. In the Hindu epic poem *The Ramayana*, Ravana is described as having "ten heads, twenty arms, and copper-colored eyes, and bright teeth like the moon. His form was as a thick cloud or a mountain, or the god of death with open mouth. He had all the marks of royalty, but his body bore the impress of wounds inflicted by all the divine arms in his warfare with the gods. It was scarred by the thunderbolt of Indra, by the tusks of Indra's elephant Airavata, and by the discus of Vishnu. His strength was so great that he could agitate the seas and split the tops of mountains. He was a breaker of all laws and a ravisher of other men's wives. . . . Tall as a mountain peak, he stopped with his arms the sun and the moon in their course, and prevented their rising."

Ravana's deeds cried to heaven. Vishnu came to earth in the form of Rama to destroy the demon king. Rama cut off one of Ravana's heads with his sharp arrow, "but no sooner did the head fall on the ground than another sprang up in its place." Rama then took an arrow that had been given to him by the god Brahma. He shot it at Ravana's chest, and it came out of the demon's back, went into the ocean, and then returned clean to Rama's quiver. "Ravana fell to the ground and died, and the gods sounded the celestial music in the heavens, and assembled in the sky and praised Rama."

One sect in south India, however, assigns the victory to Ravana and celebrates the demons' victory over Rama.

Ravana was not alone in his evil works. He was helped by the Naikasheyas, carnivorous imps descended from Nikasha, mother of Ravana. Sometimes his demon aides are called Pistasanas or Nikashatmajas.

See also: BRAHMA; INDRA; KUBERA; RAKSHASAS; RAMA; *RAMAYANA, THE*; SHIVA; VISHNU

**2530**

**Raven**   A large black bird of the crow family having a loud, harsh call. In Greek mythology, the raven was once believed to have been white but was transformed into a black bird by Apollo for informing the god of the infidelity of Coronis, a beautiful maiden loved by the god. The bird was associated with Apollo as god of prophecy.

In Norse mythology two ravens, Hugin and Munin, brought news to Odin of each day's happenings. As a result Odin was sometimes called God of Ravens. The ominous character of the raven is cited in Shakespeare's *Julius Caesar* (5.1); Cassius tells how the ravens "Flay o'er our heads and downward look on us / As we were sickly prey," reflecting the belief that the bird would "smell death" and was therefore a dreaded visitor. But in a Roman legend the raven is a symbol of good. It alighted on the helmet of Valerius, a soldier, when he was about to fight a Gallic warrior. Valerius took this as a good sign and prayed to the gods to aid him in battle. They did, sending the raven to pluck out the eyes of the Gallic warrior. In Christian art the raven symbolizes God's providence, an allusion to the ravens that fed Elijah. In Arthurian legend King Arthur still lives in the guise of a raven, and therefore the birds are never killed. In Eskimo mythology the Great Raven is the creator of animals and women. Poe's *The Raven* is the best-known poem on the raven. There are numerous motifs associated with the raven in the *Motif Index of Folk Literature*.

See also: APOLLO; ARTHUR; DJOKHRANE; HUGIN AND MUNIN; ODIN

**2531**

**Raymond Nonnato, St.** (counsel-protection) 1204–1448. In Christian legend, patron saint of children, domestic animals, innocent persons falsely accused, and nurses. Invoked during childbirth and fever. Venerated in Spain. Feast, 31 August.

St. Raymond was a member of the Order of Mercy, or Mercedarians, who worked to free captive Christians from the Moors. *Les Petits Bollandistes* (vol. 10), a collection of saints' lives, gives the legend of St. Raymond speaking when his lips were locked.

Raymond went to Algiers to redeem Christian captives but was captured by the Moors and imprisoned. Though a captive he still preached the Gospel, which upset the ruling pasha Setim, who ordered him to be whipped, naked, at every street corner. Then a red-hot iron padlock was fastened through his lips. The key was kept by the jailer, and the lock was opened only when he was given food. Yet one day when the jailer came in, he found Raymond reciting one of the Psalms. The jailer, convinced he was a sorcerer, kicked him and left without feeding him.

Eventually, Raymond made it back to Christian lands and was made a cardinal and general of the Order of Mercy. Both Pope Gregory IX and King James of Aragon attended his funeral.

St. Raymond is shown as a Mercedarian with a white badge on his breast and a chain and padlock on his lips. Sometimes he is shown surrounded by Moors and captives.

**2532**

**Raymond of Pennaforte, St.** (counsel-protection)   13th century. In Christian legend, patron saint of canon lawyers, venerated in Spain and Majorca. Feast, 23 January.

Raymond was born of a noble Spanish family. He joined the Dominican Order and through his preaching was partly responsible for the expulsion of the Moors from Spain. His miracles, which are numerous, fill some 16 pages of *Les Petits Bollandistes*, a collection of saints' lives. One legend, included in Leandre Alberti's *Life of St. Raymund*, tells how St. Raymond sailed some 160 miles on his cloak.

King James was living in adultery with a lady of the court. St. Raymond reprimanded him, but the king ignored him. St. Raymond then said he could no longer live in a court where sin was tolerated. The king strictly forbade any shipper, under pain of death, to convey St. Raymond across the water. St. Raymond spread his cloak on the water, jumped on it, held up on his staff a corner of the cloak to make a sail, and sailed all the way to Barcelona. On reaching shore he drew his cloak up and threw it across his shoulders—and it was dry. When the king heard of the miracle, he abandoned his mistress and became an ideal king. The same legend of using a cloak as a sail is also told of St. Bernardino in the 15th century, St. Isidore's wife, and Elijah, who in 2 Kings (2:8) took his mantle and, wrapping it together, "smote the waters, and they were divided hither and thither, so that they two went over Jordan as dry land."

St. Raymond is shown in the Dominican habit kneeling on his magic mantle.

2533

**Raziel** (secret of God)   In Jewish folklore, angel entrusted with guarding or transmitting the "mysteries" or "secrets" of God. Raziel is credited with authorship of *The Book of the Angel Raziel*, a medieval Jewish work popular in eastern Europe, where a copy of the book was believed to keep a house safe from fire. The book says that the "secrets" contained in it were given by the angel Raziel to Adam after he was cast out of the Garden of Eden, then passed on to Noah before he entered the ark, and finally came into the possession of King Solomon, who is credited in both Jewish and Islamic folklore with being a great magician.

See also: ADAM AND EVE; NOAH; SOLOMON

2534

**Razin, Stenka**   d. 1671. In Russian legend, a Cossack leader. Numerous tales grew up around his character. One, which influenced the Russian composer Alexander Glazunov, relates to Razin's death. Stenka Razin was on his magnificent boat with a captive Persian princess when she told him a dream she had had. She had seen her own death as well as the destruction of Stenka Razin

and his followers. Fearful of what she said, Stenka Razin killed her, offered her as a sacrifice to the Volga River, and went out to fight the czar's troops, who defeated him. He was executed in 1671. Glazunov's symphonic poem *Stenka Razin*, which uses as a main theme the traditional song of the Volga boatman; Shostakovich's *The Execution of Stepan Razin*, for bass, chorus, and orchestra, based on a poem by Yevgeny Yevtushenko; and a group sculpture *Stepan Razin and His Troops* by Sergei Konenkov, all portray the hero.

2535

**Rebekah** (ensnarer)   In the Bible, O.T., a daughter of Bethuel and the wife of Isaac; mother of Jacob and Esau. The story of her marriage is told in Genesis (chap. 24). When Abraham, Isaac's father, was old, he wanted to be sure that his son was married. He sent his trusted servant Eliezar back to Chaldea, his native land, to choose a wife for Isaac. Near the city of Nahor the servant prayed for Yahweh's guidance. He asked that when he should stop by the public well with his animals, whichever maiden drawing water there who first offered to draw water for him would be his choice for Isaac's wife. The prayer was answered when Rebekah offered the water. A scene frequently painted is Rebekah at the well, such as the painting by Murillo.

See also: ABRAHAM; ESAU; ISAAC; JACOB; YAHWEH

2536

**Regin**   In Norse mythology, youngest son of Hreidmer and brother of Fafnir and Otter. Exiled by his brother Fafnir over possession of the Nibelung gold, Regin became the great teacher of all craft to mankind. He educated Sigurd, made him promise to avenge the wrongs done him by Fafnir, and forged Sigurd's magic sword. Regin appears in the *Volsunga Saga*.

See also: FAFNIR; NIBELUNGS; SIGURD

2537

**Regulus, St.**   Third century. In Christian legend, first bishop of Senlis, France, as well as its patron saint. Feast, 30 March.

One day St. Regulus encountered a man possessed by a devil. "If you cast me out of the man," said the devil, "let me go into the nearby ass." The saint agreed, but the ass made the sign of the cross with its forefoot, and the devil fled. Another legend tells how the saint, when preaching, told some frogs to stop croaking. They complied. One chapel dedicated to the saint contains images of frogs.

2538

*Reliques*   In 1765 Bishop Thomas Percy published his *Reliques of Ancient English Poetry*, a collection of English and Scottish ballads. These old songs were filled with action and pathos as well as energy and rhythm. His collection came shortly after the work of James MacPherson, who had published his *Poems of Ossian* in 1760–1763, likewise filled with strong sentiment. Unfortunately, MacPherson's publication of verse by the third-century Celtic bard, Ossian, was a hoax; he himself wrote the poetic songs. Still, these two publications had an impact on European poets and scholars that would cause such individuals as Johann Gottfried Herder to collect folksongs and ballads and publish them. European Romanticism would take this inspiration even further, sending the likes of the Grimm Brothers in search of old and traditional fairy tale, myths, and legends.

See also: GRIMM BROTHERS; OSSIAN

2539

**Rémy, St.**   430–533. In Christian legend, bishop of Rheims, France; converted and baptized Clovis, the king of the Franks, in 496. Feast, 1 October.

Rémy was made bishop of Rheims when he was 22 because of his brilliance and great learning. After the conversion of Clovis the king

helped him in his great project of bringing Christianity to the Franks.

There are numerous legends connected with his life recorded in Hinomar's *Life of St. Remi*, written in the ninth century. One section tells how St. Rémy stopped a fire from destroying Rheims by making the sign of the cross before it. The fire kept moving back as the saint walked toward it until it reached the city gates "when it rolled itself into a ball" and disappeared in the fields. Another legend tells that when St. Rémy was an old man he had a dream that there would be years of plenty followed by years of dearth. So he stored corn in Celtum against the years of famine. The villagers, supposing he was going to market the corn to their loss, set fire to his granaries. As the fire was raging, the old saint appeared and said, "Be sure of this, that God will not forget to punish those who have done this mischief." Immediately the persons who had set the fire became hunchbacks. Hincmar, who records the legend, says, "I have often seen the peasants of Celtum, some of whom have certainly crooked backs."

The most famous painting of the saint is by the Master of St. Giles and is called *The Baptism of Clovis*.

2540

**Renpet** (Renenutet, Rannut, Remute, Ernuted) (rising goddess?)   In Egyptian mythology, goddess of the year's duration. She was particularly associated with springtime and youth. In Egyptian art she was portrayed as a woman wearing above her head a long palm shoot curved at the end, which was the ideogram of her name.

2541

**Reshpu** (Resheph, Reshef, Reshep, Reshiph-Mical) (fiery bolt?)   In Near Eastern mythology (Syrian), god of lightning and the thunderbolt, the "Great God, Lord of Eternity, Prince of Everlastingness, Lord of Twofold Strength among the Company of the Gods." Reshpu was worshiped at Reshp in Egypt, where he was depicted as a warrior with a shield and spear in his left hand and a club in his right hand.

### 2542

**Revati**   In Hindu mythology, wife of the hero Balarama, brother of Krishna (an incarnation of the god Vishnu). Revati was given to Balarama by the god Brahma, but the hero thought Revati was too tall for him and "shortened her with the end of a ploughshare, and she became his wife." The couple had two sons.

See also: BALARAMA; BRAHMA; KRISHNA; VISHNU

### 2543

**Revenant**   A term used for a deceased person who is believed to reappear after death. The belief is based on conceptions of life and death, particularly life after death. In most cases a revenant returns to complete some unfinished duty or to fetch personal belongings that he or she might need in the afterlife. They can be divided into two groups, the innocent and the guilty. The former would include mothers who died in childbirth or those who were unhappy at the time of burial or in the final place of rest. Among the latter, the guilty, there might be those who are punished and made to return in order to rectify improper behavior during life. One legend tells of a man named Uncle James who was killed in a car accident. When his family came home from the funeral, they all sat in the parlor and grieved for their loss. Because the house had two front doors, as is common in many rural neighborhoods, they became aware of someone walking up the steps of the house and entering the second door, the one always used by the deceased to go into his own bedroom. There was noise around the dresser in the other room, and then the family heard footsteps once again, going out of the house and down the steps. When they went into the bedroom to see what had transpired, they noticed that a comb, brush, and razor were missing. There was no other explanation than that the deceased had returned from the dead to fetch his own personal items.

### 2544

**Revere, Paul**   1735–1818. In American history and folklore, patriot, craftsman, and political cartoonist. A skilled silversmith, Revere also did portraits and produced false teeth. When the conflict between the colonies and Great Britain broke out, Revere issued crude cartoons attacking the British. He is noted in American legend for his famous midnight ride from Boston to Lexington on 18–19 April 1775 to warn the colonists of the Redcoats' approach. Longfellow's literary ballad "The Midnight Ride of Paul Revere," included in his collection *Tales of a Wayside Inn*, tells how Revere waited for a signal in the Old North Church tower before he began his famous ride. Longfellow's ballad, however, is more legend than fact. Paul Revere did not make the whole ride. A young Dr. Prescott carried the news to Concord, and Revere went to Lexington.

### 2545

**Reynard the Fox** (hard counsel)   In medieval folklore, a clever fox who outwits other animals. His tale was a popular subject in chapbooks and begins with all of the animals complaining about Reynard, who has robbed them. Noble, the lion king, decides to send Bruin, the bear, to arrest Reynard. Bruin, however, is outwitted, as is Tybert, the cat. Finally, Grymbart, the badger, brings in Reynard for trial. He is found guilty and sentenced to be hanged. The clever fox, however, convinces Noble, who is judge, that he has hidden treasure. In hope of obtaining the treasure, Noble unties Reynard, who escapes and continues stealing and raping his neighbors. Arrested for the second time on charges of raping the wife of Isengrin, the wolf, Reynard not only kills Isengrin in a duel, but is made second in command by Noble. William Caxton translated a Flemish version of the tale into English in 1481. Goethe's long narrative poem *Reynard the Fox* and Stravinsky's *Renard the Fox*, for soloists and orchestra, also treat the tale.

See also: AESOPIC FABLES; BESTIARY; CHAPBOOK

2546

**Rhadamanthus** (he who divines with a wand) In Greek mythology, son of Zeus and Europa; brother of Minos and Sarpedon; married to Alcmene; father of Erythus and Gortys. He was born on Crete and ruled over the Cyclades and later was made one of the three judges of the underworld along with Minos and Sarpedon (or Aeacus). He is cited in Homer's *Iliad* (book 4), Vergil's *Aeneid* (book 6), and Ovid's *Metamorphoses* (book 9).

See also: *AENEID, THE; ILIAD, THE;* MINOS; SARPENDON; ZEUS

2547

**Rhampsinitus, Treasure of**   Ancient Egyptian literary folktale told by Herodotus in his *History* (book 2). Herodotus claimed that it had been told to him by Egyptian priests. In the tale a rogue tricks everyone—even the pharaoh, who exclaims at the end: "The Egyptians excelled all the rest of the world in wisdom, and this man excelled all other Egyptians."

2548

**Rhesus** (breaker)   In Greek mythology, king of Thrace, ally of Priam; son of Strymon (or Eioneus) and Calliope (or Euterpe); married Arganthoe. His horses protected Troy. Homer's *Iliad* (book 10) tells how Rhesus was killed by Odysseus and Diomedes in a night raid in which his magnificent white horses were taken. Euripides' *Rhesus*, Vergil's *Aeneid* (book 1), and Ovid's *Metamorphoses* (book 13) also tell the tale.

See also: *AENEID, THE;* DIOMEDES; ODYSSEUS; PRIAM

2549

**Rhoecus**   In Greek mythology, a handsome young man who propped up a fallen oak tree, thus saving the life of the nymph or dryad who lived in the tree. As a reward, Rhoecus asked that the nymph love him. She said she would send a messenger to tell him when to meet her. When

the bee messenger arrived, Rhoecus had already forgotten the incident and waved the bee away. In punishment, the nymph blinded Rhoecus. Rhoecus is also the name of a centaur killed by Dionysus at the wedding of Pirithous and Hippodameia, according to Ovid's *Metamorphoses* (book 12), as well as the name of a Titan killed by Dionysus in the war between the gods and the .

See also: DIONYSUS; DRYADS; NYMPHS; OVID; TITANS

2550

**Ribhus** (clever, skilful)   In Hindu mythology, mortals who were raised to divine status after they fashioned the storm god Indra's chariot and horses. They live in the solar atmosphere and are supporters of the sky.

See also: VISHNU

2551

**Rice**   A cereal grain. In some parts of Java, just before rice is to bloom, farmers bring their wives into the rice field and have sexual intercourse to ensure a successful crop. The Kayans of central Borneo precede the sowing of rice by an elaborate dance, in which dancers wear masks with gogglelike eyes, large teeth and ears, and beards made of goat hair, dressing themselves in banana leaves to look like walking plants. With a hook they ceremonially catch the soul of the rice, which otherwise might wander away, causing crop failure. The custom of throwing rice at weddings comes from India. For Hindus rice was a symbol of fecundity. The bride and the bridegroom each throw three handfuls at each other.

2552

**Richard the Lion-Hearted**   1157–1199. In English history and legend, king of England, also called Richard Coeur de Lion, who took part in the Crusades, though he never reached Jerusalem. He became a prisoner of the emperor Henry VI in 1193 but was ransomed by his English subjects. He died while besieging a castle.

His character appealed to Walter Scott, who at the tournament in *Ivanhoe* introduced him disguised as the Black Knight. Scott's *The Talisman* portrays Richard crusading in the Holy Land, both the friend and the enemy of Saladin.

See also: SALADIN

2553

**Rig-Veda** (Rg-Veda) (Veda of praise)   In Hinduism, the most ancient and sacred part of the Vedas (knowledge), consisting of more than 1,000 hymns to the gods and various natural phenomena, composed between 1400 and 1000 B.C.E.

The Rig-Veda is divided into 10 *mandalas* (circles), or books, consisting of hymns by various *rishis* (sages). In some versions the name of the *rishi* who is reputed to be the teller or reciter is prefixed to each hymn because the hymns are believed to have been "breathed out" by the god Brahma. They were transmitted orally from generation to generation until, according to tradition, they were collected by Krishna Dwaipayna (the arranger).

F. Max Müller, the 19th-century German scholar who was the first to produce a critical Sanskrit text of the Vedas with the traditional commentary and who edited the *Sacred Books of the East*, wrote of the Rig-Veda: "What can be more tedious than the Veda, and yet what can be more interesting, if once we know that it is the first word spoken by the Aryan man? . . . The Veda has a two-fold interest: it belongs to the history of the world and to the history of India. . . . As long as man continues to take an interest in the history of his race, and as long as we collect in libraries and museums the relics of a former age, the first place in that long row of books which contains the records of the Aryan branch of mankind, will belong forever to the *Rig-Veda*."

The greatest impact of the Rig-Veda on Western music is contained in *Choral Hymns* by Gustav Holst. Early in his career he had written for baritone an *Invocation to Dawn*, based on his own translation of some of the Rig-Veda. Later Holst set four groups of hymns to various texts he had translated. In the first group, for mixed voices and orchestra, are *Battle Hymn*, *Hymn to the Unknown God*, and *Funeral Hymn*. The second group, for female voices and orchestra, contains *To Varuna*, *To Agni*, and *Funeral Chant*. The third group, for female voices and harp, includes *Hymn to Dawn*, *Hymn to the Waters*, *Hymn to Vena*, and *Hymn to the Travellers*. The last group is *Hymn to Agni*, *Hymn to Soma*, *Hymn to Manas*, and *Hymn to Indra*. The American composer Bertram Shapleigh composed *Vedic Hymn* on a text from the Rig-Veda.

See also: BRAHMA; VEDAS

2554

**Rimmon** (Ramman, Rammanu) (the thunderer)   In Near Eastern mythology (Babylonian-Assyrian), the storm god, often called Adad or Hadad.

In the biblical book 2 Kings (5:1–18), Naaman, the commander of the Syrian army, worshiped Rimmon, but when he was cured of his leprosy by the prophet Elisha, he said he would worship the Hebrew god, Yahweh, instead. In the Babylonian version of the flood myth, before the Great Flood "the whirlwind of Adad mounted up into the heavens, and all light was turned into darkness." Rimmon was portrayed holding lightning rods in his left hand and an ax in his right. His sacred animal was the bull; his sacred tree, the cypress. His wife was Shala, which may simply mean "woman."

Rimmon was also called Martu (the Amorite) and Kur-Ga (great mountain) in Canaan. He was called Hadad by the Syrians and Teshub by the Hittites.

See also: ELISHA; YAHWEH

2555

**Rinaldo**   In the Charlemagne cycle of legends, son of Aymon, Charlemagne's nephew and one of his 12 paladins. He is also the owner of the horse Bayard. Rinaldo is the rival of his cousin

Orlando for the love of Angelica in Ariosto's *Orlando Furioso*. He also appears in Tasso's *Jerusalem Delivered*. Rinaldo is also called Renault.

See also: AYMON, THE FOUR SONS OF; ANGELICA; BAYARD; CHARLEMAGNE; PALADINS, THE TWELVE; ROLAND

2556

**Rinda** (crust of the earth?)   In Norse mythology, a goddess, a mistress of Odin, and mother of Vali. Odin used various disguises and magic (seid) to sleep with Rinda. Rinda is also Baldur, the avenger.

See also: BALDUR; ODIN

2557

***Ring des Nibelungen, Der*** (The Ring of the Nibelung)   A staged festival-play to be performed over a three-day period and a preliminary evening; words and music by Richard Wagner. First complete performance, Bayreuth, 13–17 August 1876. The work consists of *Das Rheingold*, *Die Walküre*, *Siegfried*, and *Götterdämmerung*.

Wagner wrote the text for his music dramas in reverse order. In 1848 he wrote *Siegfrieds Tod*, which dealt with the death of Siegfried. Realizing that he had to explain more, he wrote *Der Junge Siegfried* (The Young Siegfried). He then felt he needed even more text. *Siegfrieds Tod* became the last work; *Götterdämmerung*, and *Das Rheingold*, the first part, was written last. The texts for all of the dramas were published in 1854. The music, however, was written in the order of presentation.

Wagner used the names found in the *Nibelungenlied*, the medieval German epic, but he used the related plot of the *Volsunga Saga* as the basis for his work. He changed characters and text to suit his artistic purposes, and thus created a "mythology" of his own.

The first drama, *Das Rheingold* (The Rhinegold), had its premiere 22 September 1869 at Munich. Three Rhine maidens guard the precious Rhinegold, which if stolen and forged into a ring will give its owner great powers. But anyone who possesses the gold must renounce love. Alberich, the dwarf, unable to win the Rhine maidens' love, renounces love and carries off the gold to Nebelheim, the land of fog.

As a reward for building Walhalla, Wotan, king of the gods, has promised to give Freia, goddess of youth and love, to the giants Fafner and Fasolt. The other gods refuse to permit this, and Wotan has nothing to offer the giants instead. Loge, the fire god, is called and suggests as a substitute the Rhinegold, of which Alberich is the possessor. The two giants agree.

Wotan and Loge set off to steal it. Wotan and Loge enter Nebelheim. Alberich shows them the treasure, as well as a helmet by which the wearer is able to assume any form (Tarnkappe). Loge persuades Alberich to transform himself into a toad. When Alberich does this, he is overpowered, and Wotan takes the treasure. However, Alberich puts a curse on the ring so that it will bring disaster on all who possess it.

The gold and the fatal ring are given to the giants, who then release Freia to the gods. They joyfully enter their palace over a rainbow bridge,

*Alberich*

but during the last scene the giant Fasolt is killed by Fafner. The curse of Alberich begins to work.

Wotan, knowing of the death of Fasolt, fears that the curse of the ring will fall on the gods. To defend Walhalla against this and the attacks of the Nibelungs, he fathers with Erda, the earth goddess, nine daughters (the Walkyries, chief of whom is Brünnhilde). One of their functions is to ride through the air bearing to Walhalla the bodies of dead heroes, who will be revived and will aid the gods in the coming battle.

To break the curse, it is also necessary to restore the ring to the Rhine maidens, but this task has to be done by a human. Wotan, in the guise of Walse, begets with a woman two Walsung twins, Siegmund and Sieglinde. Wotan hopes Siegmund will be the hero to slay Fafner and return the ring to its rightful owners. To prepare Siegmund for the task, Wotan sets various hardships for him. Sieglinde is made to marry the robber Hunding.

The second music drama is *Die Walküre* (The Valkyries), first performed 26 June 1870 in Munich. Siegmund staggers storm-driven into Hunding's empty hut. Sieglinde enters and finds the stranger—they are unknown to one another, though brother and sister—and they love each other at first sight. Hunding enters, and, enraged at what he finds, he challenges Siegmund to a fight the next day. Sieglinde gives Hunding a sleeping potion, and after a passionate duet the two lovers flee into the night.

Fricka, Wotan's wife, also the protector of the marriage vow, demands that Siegmund, who has sinned by sleeping with his sister, shall die in the coming combat with Hunding. Wotan reluctantly yields and commissions Brünnhilde to bring about Siegmund's defeat. Brünnhilde, however, sympathizes with the lovers and protects Siegmund in the battle. But she is foiled when Wotan enters and allows Hunding to kill Siegmund. Wotan thereupon slays Hunding. Brünnhilde comforts the bereaved Sieglinde, but because of her disobedience Brünnhilde is deprived of her divinity and is put to sleep by Wotan on a fire-encompassed rock. She can be awakened only by a fearless hero, who can then claim her as his bride.

The third music drama, *Siegfried*, had its premiere 16 August 1876. Siegfried is the son of Sieglinde, born after the death of his father, Siegmund. Mime, Alberich's deformed brother, has reared Siegfried in his home in the forest. He hopes that someday Siegfried will slay Fafner, who changed himself into a dragon to guard the treasure. The act ends with Siegfried successfully forging a magic sword.

Siegfried slays Fafner. Mime offers a sleeping potion to Siegfried, who discovers his evil purpose and kills him. Having by chance put his finger, stained with the dragon's blood, to his lips, Siegfried is enabled to understand a bird as it sings. The bird tells of the sleeping Brünnhilde, and Siegfried goes to find her.

On his way Siegfried meets Wotan, who opposes him with his spear, but the spear is shattered by Siegfried's magic sword. Siegfried reaches the fire rock, rushes through the flames, and claims Brünnhilde as his bride.

The fourth and last music drama, *Götterdämmerung* (The Twilight of the Gods), had its premiere 17 August 1876 at Bayreuth. The opera opens in the Hall of the Gibichungs on the Rhine, where Siegfried has arrived, having left Brünnhilde behind. Here he is drugged with a magic love potion by Gutrune, who wants to marry him. The drug causes him to forget his love for Brünnhilde, and he falls in love with Gutrune. Gunther, Gutrune's brother, plots to marry Brünnhilde but knows he lacks the power to overcome her. Siegfried goes with Gunther to capture Brünnhilde. Disguised as Gunther, Siegfried overcomes Brünnhilde and hands her over to the Gibichungs. Siegfried, still under the spell of the drug, becomes Gutrune's lover, and Gunther becomes the lover of Brünnhilde

Hagen stabs Siegfried, who in his last moments recovers his memory. Brünnhilde finds Siegfried dead, and she realizes that he was under a spell. She still loves him. Logs are heaped up for a pyre, and the dead hero is placed on it, but not before Brünnhilde has taken the fatal ring from his finger and cast it into the Rhine. The Rhine maidens appear singing. The sky darkens; the flames rise. Brünnhilde on her horse leaps into the flames. The Rhine rises, and Walhalla is seen to burst into flames.

In 1848 Wagner wrote a "sketch" for the four dramas. His early sketch is important in shedding light on those elements that he kept in the telling of the myth and those he left out of the final version of the dramas. Numerous books have been written to explain Wagner's *Ring*. Among the best known is George Bernard Shaw's *The Perfect Wagnerite: A Commentary of the Niblung's Ring*. Arthur Rackham illustrated the English translation of the *Ring* by Margaret Armour, which was published in 1910.

See also: BRYNHILD; ERDA; FAFNIR; FREY; FRIGGA; NIBELUNGEN; *NIBELUNGENLIED;* TARN-KAPPE; VALHALLA; VALKYRIES; *VOLSUNGA SAGA;* WOTAN

2558
**Ripheus**   In Greek and Roman mythology, a Trojan who joined Aeneas the night Troy was destroyed; he was slain after killing many Greeks. Ripheus is cited for his love of justice and equity in Vergil's *Aeneid* (book 2) and Dante's *Divine Comedy* (Paradise, canto 20). Ripheus is also the name of one of the centaurs killed by Theseus at the marriage of Pirithous and Hippodameia, as told in Ovid's *Metamorphoses* (book 12).

See also: *AENEID, THE;* CENTAURS; OVID; THESEUS

2559
**Rip Van Winkle**   In American literary folklore, creation of Washington Irving in *The Sketch Book*. Rip, who lives with a shrewish wife, one day goes hunting in the Catskills with his dog. There he meets dwarflike beings and drinks some liquor they give him. He falls asleep and awakens 20 years later, an old man, who discovers that his wife has died and the American Revolution has

taken place. He goes to live with his grown daughter and makes new friends.

2560
**Rival Schools of Thought**   Jewish moral tale found in the Talmud. For more than two years two rival schools in the study of the Talmud, that of Shammai and that of Hillel, debated of whether it would have been better if men had not been created. The followers of Shammai said it would have been better if God had not created man, but the school of Hillel said it was good that man had been created. Finally, they concluded their arguments by a compromise: It would have been far better if man had not been created, but since he has been placed on earth, it is his duty to do the best he can to live a righteous life.

See also: TALMUD

2561
**Robert, St.** (fame-bright)   11th century. In Christian legend, abbot, founder of the monastery of Chaise-Dieu in the Auvergne. Feast, 17 April.

As a child, Robert would nurse only at the breasts of good women, not "irreligious ones." When Robert became an abbot, the cook one day informed him that there was not enough food. As Robert was celebrating Mass, an eagle flew into the church and dropped an enormous fish, large enough to feed all the monks. When Robert died his soul ascended to heaven as a globe of fire.

2562
**Robigo** (mildew, rust)   In Roman mythology, goddess invoked to preserve grain from mildew. Her festival, Robigalia, was celebrated on 25 April with offerings of incense and entrails of a sheep and a dog. Ovid's *Fasti* (book 4) describes the feast.

See also: OVID

**Robin** Any of several small birds having reddish breasts. A medieval Christian legend accounts for the red breast. The night of Jesus' birth Mary and Joseph sought shelter in a cave inhabited by a small brown bird. When the angels came to praise the baby Jesus the little brown bird was awakened by the light glowing from the angels and by the heavenly singing. Moved by the beautiful song, the bird joined in and became the first nightingale. Outside the cave another small bird saw shepherds leave their campfire and approach the cave. The bird flew to the fire and fanned it with its wing. The flames soared high into the air and colored the breast of the bird with yellow-red light. The bird became the first robin. In the legend the nightingale is identified as male and the robin as female. Oscar Wilde in *The Nightingale and the Rose* identifies the bird as female. In another Christian legend, when Jesus was on his way to Calvary, a robin plucked a thorn from his crown, and the blood that came from the wound dyed the breast of the bird red.

See also: NIGHTINGALE

**Robin Hood** 12th or 13th century. In medieval British legend, outlaw who stole from the rich to give to the poor. He was believed to be Robert Fitzooth, the outlawed earl of Huntingdon. He had 100 "tall men," all good archers. He took spoils, but according to an account of 1386, "he suffered no women to be oppressed, violated or otherwise molested; poor men's goods he spared, abundantly relieving them with that which by theft he got from abbeys and houses of rich men." Robin Hood's companions in Sherwood Forest and Barnesdale, Yorkshire, were Little John, Friar Tuck, Will Scarlet, Allan-a-Dale, George-a-Greene, and Maid Marion. According to one legend Robin Hood was treacherously slain by a nun at the command of his kinsman the prior of Kirkless, in Nottinghamshire. Another tradition says he died with Little John at the Battle of Evesham. Various operas on the subject of Robin Hood have been written, the most famous being Reginald De Koven's operetta *Robin Hood* (1890). Hollywood made several Robin Hood movies, one of the earliest starring Douglas Fairbanks in 1922.

See also: ALLAN-A-DALE; MAID MARION

**Roch, St.** (Roque) (repose) 14th century. In Christian legend, patron saint of prisoners, the sick in hospitals, and victims of plague. Feast, 6 August.

Roch was the son of the governor of Montpellier, France, who died when the saint was 20 years old. The lad then went to Rome, where a plague was raging, and took care of the sick. He went from city to city in Italy helping the plague-stricken. Then, according to the account in Jameson's *Sacred and Legendary Art*, "One night, being in a hospital, he sank down to the ground, overpowered by fatigue and went to sleep. On waking, he found himself plague-stricken; a fever burned in every limb, and a horrible ulcer had broken out in his left thigh." Fearful that he would disturb the other patients, Roch left for the woods, where he intended to die. However, his dog and an angel took care of him by tending his sore and bringing him bread every day. When he arrived home at Montpellier, he was so changed and wasted by his illness that no one recognized him. He was arrested as a spy, and his uncle, who was the judge, had him locked in prison. After five years the jailor entered his cell one day and was dazzled by a bright light. He found Roch dead and near him a paper with these words: "All those who are stricken by the plague, and who pray through the merits and intercession of Roch, the servant of God, shall be healed." Roch was then buried with honor at Montpellier, but Italian merchants stole his remains (in the Middle Ages it was quite common for saints' bodies or body parts to be removed or stolen from one shrine and placed in another) and brought them to Venice, where they lie in the Church of San Rocco.

St. Roch's attributes are his dog, who daily brought him bread while he was dying of the pestilence, and the physical markings of the plague. He often appears in paintings, as in Parmigianino's work, exposing his groin with its buboes (lymphatic swellings) or pointing to a purpuric spot on his leg. A statue of the saint using this iconography was carried in Constance in 1414 when a plague had broken out, and legend has it that the invocation of St. Roch stilled the plague. A more sedate episode from the saint's life was chosen by Julius Schnoor von Carolsfeld in his *St. Roch Distributing Alms*. The painting, done in sharp outline with clear colors, attempts to capture for the 19th century the religious art of early Italian and German masters.

2566

**Roderick, Don**   Eighth century. In medieval Spanish history and legend, last Visigoth king of Spain, appearing in many Spanish ballads. He was defeated by the Moors in July 711, disappearing on the battlefield. He either was killed, drowned, or escaped. Some legends say he is alive and will return to Spain in its time of need.

See also: BALLAD; BARBAROSSA

2567

**Rodomont**   In the Charlemagne cycle of legends, a Saracen hero who was killed by Ruggiero when he accused Ruggiero of turning traitor by becoming a Christian. Rodomont appears in Ariosto's *Orlando Furioso* and is mentioned by Cervantes in *Don Quixote*: "Who more brave than Rodomont?"

See also: CHARLEMAGNE; ROLAND; RUGGIERO

2568

**Rokola**   In Melanesian mythology, Fijian god of carpenters who taught the people how to navigate.

2569

**Roland** (fame, land)   In the Charlemagne cycle of legends, one of the 12 paladins, called Orlando in Italian legends.

Roland was the count of Mans and knight of Blaives. He was the son of Duke Milo of Aigland and Bertha, the sister of Charlemagne. Medieval legend describes him as eight feet tall, brave, loyal, and somewhat simple-minded.

The most famous work about Roland is the 11th-century French poem *Chanson de Roland* (Song of Roland). When Charlemagne had been in Spain for six years, he sent Ganelon on an embassy to Marsilius, the Saracen king of Saragossa. Out of jealousy Ganelon told Marsilius the route that the Christian army was to take on its way home. Marsilius arrived at Roncesvalles just as Roland was going through the pass with a rearguard of 20,000 men. Roland fought until 100,000 Saracens were slain and only 50 of his own men were left alive. But another Saracen army of some 50,000 now poured in from the mountains. Roland blew his ivory horn, Olivant, which he had won from the giant Jutmundus. The third blast cracked the horn in two, birds fell dead from the sky, and the Saracen army fled, panic-stricken. Charlemagne heard the horn and rushed to the rescue, but it was too late. Roland had died of wounds from the battle.

Roland's sword, Durindana, or Durandal, had once belonged to the Trojan hero Hector. It had on its hilt a thread from the Virgin Mary's cloak, a tooth of St. Peter, one of St. Denis's hairs, and a drop of St. Basil's blood. To prevent Durindana from falling into the hands of the Saracens, Roland hurled it into a poisoned stream.

Roland appears as Orlando in Italian works such as Boiardo's *Orlando Innamorato* (Orlando in Love) and Ariosto's *Orlando Furioso*. Ariosto's poem tells how Orlando goes mad when he is rejected by Angelica, daughter of the king of Cathay. She runs away with a Moor named Medoro. Orlando's wits are then deposited on the moon. Astolpho goes in search of them, using Elijah's chariot. St. John, who lives on the moon, gives Astolpho an urn containing Orlando's wits. On reaching earth again, Astolpho holds the urn to Orlando's nose, and he is cured.

See also: ANGELICA; ASTOLPHO; BASIL, ST.; CHANSON DE GESTE; CHARLEMAGNE; DENIS, ST.; ELIJAH; GANELON; HECTOR; JOHN THE EVANGELIST, ST.; PALADINS, THE TWELVE; PETER, ST.; VIRGIN MARY

2570

**Roma** (strength? river?)    Capital of the Roman Empire, founded, according to Roman mythology, by Romulus on 21 April 753 B.C.E. The city was built on seven hills: Palatium, Cermalus, Velia, Oppius, Cispius, Fagutal, and Sucusa. Roma or Dea Roma, the goddess of the city, was portrayed with a crown, sometimes in the form of Minerva or as an Amazon. On Roman coins she appears with a winged helmet. The emperor Hadrian erected a temple in honor of Roma and Venus as ancestresses of the Roman people. Bizet's symphonic suite *Roma* and Respighi's three tone poems *The Pines of Rome*, *The Fountains of Rome*, and *Roman Festivals* try to capture the city in music.

See also: AMAZONS; DEA ROMA; MINERVA; ROMULUS AND REMUS; VENUS

2571

**Romanus, St.**    Seventh century. In Christian legend, archbishop of Rouen, France; patron saint of merchants. Invoked against drowning, madness, poison, and demonic possession. Feast, 23 October.

Romanus is best known in medieval legend for his destruction of the dragon Gargonille, which was eating the Christians in the area. His only helper in capturing the dragon was a murderer. After making the sign of the cross, Romanus walked into the dragon's den and threw a net over its head. The murderer then dragged the monster through the town to a large bonfire, where it was burned alive. In reward, the murderer was set free. From that day on it was a custom of the chapter of Rouen to pardon a criminal condemned to death. The custom lasted until the

French Revolution. The life of St. Romanus is found on the stained-glass windows of the cathedral of Rouen.

See also: DRAGON

*Romulus and Remus*

2572

**Romulus and Remus** (dweller in Rome? and oar?)    In Roman mythology, twin sons of Mars and Rhea Silvia, who was the daughter of Numitor (Numa), king of Alba Longa. Numitor's brother Amulius deposed Numitor and forced Rhea Silvia to become a vestal virgin. When the twins Romulus and Remus were born, Amulius had Rhea Silvia placed in prison and the twins cast into the Tiber. The boys were discovered and rescued by Faustulus, a shepherd, who found a she-wolf to nurse them. When the boys grew up, they restored their grandfather Numitor to his rightful throne. The two then established a new city on the Palatine Hill, but in an argument about the exact site Romulus killed Remus and later became king. To populate his new city Romulus took fugitives for citizens and helped find them wives by encouraging them to rape the Sabine women. He ruled Rome for about 40 years. Romulus then mysteriously vanished in a whirlwind on the Campus Martius and was later worshiped by the Romans as Quirinus (the lance), a Sabine god, on the Quirinal Hill. His feast, Quirinalia, was celebrated on 13 March, the calends. The tale of Romulus and Remus is told or cited in Plutarch's *Life of Romulus*, Livy's *History of Rome*, Ovid's *Fasti* (book 2) and *Metamorphoses* (book 14), and Vergil's *Aeneid* (book 6). Livy's narrative was used as the basis for Macaulay's *Lays of Ancient Rome*. Machiavelli's *The Prince* singles out Romulus as a hero who helped raise his people out of chaos. The best-known artistic representation of Romulus and Remus is the bronze she-wolf nursing the two babies, which is now in the Capitoline Museum in Rome. The statue of the she-wolf outside the Palazzo Pubblico at Siena, by Giovanni di Turnio (1459), is that city's arms. Rubens also painted the she-wolf and the twins.

See also: *AENEID, THE*; MARS; OVID

2573

**Roraima, Mount** In Brazilian folklore, magic mountain guarded by demons in Roraima, Brazil. One traveler, Boddham-Whetham, in his *Roraima and British Guiana* (1879), tells how he and his party traveled up the mountain. They were met by an "unpleasant-looking Indian," who told them not to go any farther because the demon spirit that possessed the Indian had so ordered it. The mountain, he said, was guarded by an enormous serpentlike creature that could entwine 100 people in its folds. The Indians believed the mountain to be inhabited by white jaguars, white eagles, and didis (half-man, half-monkey creatures). When Boddham-Whetham returned, the Indians rejoiced to see him, "as they had not expected that the mountain-demons would allow us to return," he wrote.

2574

**Rosalia, St.** (rose garden) 12th century. In Christian legend, patron saint of Palermo, Sicily. Invoked against plague. Feast, 4 September.

Rosalia left home at 16 and went to live in a cave, where she wore away the stone with her knees during her devotions. She eventually died there. In time her body was covered with stalactites. When a plague broke out in Palermo in 1624, the people took her body and carried it in procession. The plague then stopped. In gratitude the people constructed a chapel in the cave. The saint is usually portrayed reclining in her cave with a bright light around her. The Virgin Mary crowns her with roses, and she holds a crucifix on her breast. She wears a brown tunic, sometimes ragged, and her hair is loose.

See also: VIRGIN MARY

2575

**Rosamund** Sixth century. In medieval legend, daughter of King Cunimond of the Gepidae. She was forced to marry Alboin, king of the Lombards, after he killed her father. Later he made her drink from the skull of her dead father. In revenge, she had Perideus, the secretary of Helmechis, her lover, murder Alboin. She then married Helmechis and fled to Ravenna, but later planned his death so that she could marry Longines. Helmechis, knowing of the plot, forced Rosamund to drink from a poisoned cup, and she died. Swinburne's play *Rosamund, Queen of the Lombards* deals with the murderess.

2576

**Rose** A thorny shrub with fragrant flowers; in world mythology and folklore, often associated with death and resurrection. The ancient Romans sometimes decked their tombs with roses, and Roman wills frequently specified that roses be planted on the grave. In Switzerland cemeteries still are known as rosegardens. In Christian symbolism the rose is associated with the Virgin Mary, one of whose titles is "The Mystical Rose." It is also associated with St. Dorothy, who

*Rose (Walter Crane)*

carries roses in a basket. For Arabs the rose is a symbol of masculine beauty.

See also: DOROTHY, ST.; VIRGIN MARY

**Rosebush and the Apple Tree, The**   Jewish fable found in the Talmud. A rosebush and an apple tree were having a debate.

"Who can compare with me?" the rosebush asked. "My flowers are beautiful and sweet to smell. True, you are larger, but what pleasure do you give to mankind?"

"Even though you are more beautiful than I," replied the apple, "you are not as good as I am."

"What do you mean?" replied the rosebush. "How are you better than I?"

"You do not give your flowers to man unless you first wound him with your thorns. But I give my fruit to all, even those who throw stones at me."

See also: TALMUD

**Rosemary**   A pungent herb in European folklore, often associated with rejuvenation and love. According to English folklore, it could make one young again and strengthen one's memory. It also was believed that if a girl took rosemary blended with thyme on St. Agnes's Eve (20 Janu-

ary), she would be sent a vision of her lover-to-be. In the language of flowers it means "fidelity in love." The magical qualities of rosemary are referred to in the refrain to Simon and Garfunkel's song "Scarborough Fair": "parsley, sage, rosemary and thyme."

See also: AGNES, ST.; PARSLEY; SAGE

**Rose of Lima, St.** (fame, kind)   1568–1617. In Christian legend, patron of South America and the Philippines. Feast, 30 August.

Born Isabel de Flores y de Oliva, but known as Rose, the saint came of a poor family in Lima, Peru. She was noted for her beauty. Many men asked for her hand in marriage, but she refused. She went so far as to disfigure her face with a compound of pepper and quicklime. When her mother asked her to wear a wreath of roses around her head, they turned into a crown of thorns. St. Rose joined the Dominican Order, where her reputation for ecstasy and mystical transports caused a scandal as well as a church investigation. St. Rose bore it all with patience and spent her time taking care of Indians enslaved by the Spaniards. When Pope Clement X was asked to canonize her in 1671, he refused, saying, "Indian and a saint! That is as likely as roses raining from heaven." Instantly a shower of roses fell on the Vatican until the pope acknowledged his error. The saint was painted by Murillo wearing a thorny crown, holding in her hand the figure of the infant Christ. She was also the subject of a painting by Fernando Botero.

**Rosh Ha-Shanah** (beginning of the year)   In Judaism, feast of the new year, celebrated the first and second days of Tishri (September and October). The feast may originally have been a commemoration of the dead, because it was a common belief of ancient peoples that the dead rejoined the living at the beginning of the year, but as the feast developed, the commemoration of the dead was pushed into the background, and

Rosh Ha-Shanah now begins a time of prayer, penitence, and charity that leads to Yom Kippur, the greatest Jewish feast. One of the main features of the feast is the blowing of the shofar, a ram's horn, recalling the trumpets and thunders heard on Mount Sinai by Moses and the people (Exod. 19:19). It also recalls the belief that Yahweh, the Hebrew god, could dispel the powers of evil (Zech. 9:14–15).

As part of the synagogue service the poem *U-netanneh Tokeph* (let us rehearse the grandeur) is recited, telling of the Day of Judgment when God will judge all people. The poem, according to medieval Jewish legend, was written by Ammon of Mainz (10th century C.E.). He was called by the archbishop of Mainz to renounce his Jewish faith. When he did not respond, the archbishop had him arrested, and his toes and fingers were cut off. Dying, he was brought to the synagogue. As the cantor was about to intone the Sanctification (Holy, holy, holy is the Lord of Hosts), Ammon said, "Pause, that I may sanctify the most holy Name." He began to recite but died when he reached "Yet Thy glories cover us, For Thy name is over us." On Rosh Ha-Shanah Jewish legend says God opens three books. The first book contains the names of pious and virtuous people who will be blessed for the coming 12 months. The second book contains the names of the wicked who are inscribed for death. In the third book, which is the largest, are the names of those who are between, neither very pious nor very evil. These people are given a chance to make a final choice before the record is sealed on Yom Kippur. One ceremony associated with the holiday is called Tashlich (Thou wilt cast), in which it is customary to cast or shake crumbs from one's pocket into the water, symbolizing the casting away of sins. The custom stems from ancient pagan practice in which sops were cast to the spirits of rivers on important days of the year. The Romans, for example, cast straw puppets into the Tiber on the Ides of May. In European folkways offerings used to be cast into the Danube, Rhine, Rhone, Elbe, and Neckar on New Year's Eve.

See also: AMMON OF MAINZ; MOSES; YAHWEH

2581
**Rosie the Riveter** In American folklore of World War II, name given to a fictional woman who symbolized women's contributions to the war effort. In most depictions of Rosie she is shown flexing her muscles. Norman Rockwell's painting *Rosie the Riveter* is modeled on Michelangelo's fresco of the prophet Isaiah in the Sistine Chapel.

2582
**Ross, Betsy** 1752–1836. In American history and folklore, creator of the first Stars and Stripes American flag. Betsy was a widow struggling to run her own upholstery business. Upholsterers in colonial America not only worked on furniture but did all manner of sewing, including making flags. According to an account read before the Historical Society of Pennsylvania on 29 May 1870 by William Canby, Betsy Ross's grandson, the first flag was made in June 1776 at the request of a committee made up of George Washington, Robert Morris, and George Ross, but no evidence exists to support this. In 1781 Francis Hopkinson, who had designed a naval flag, asked Congress to reimburse him for the design of the original Stars and Stripes. Congress declined.

2583
**Round Table** In Arthurian legend, the table made by Merlin at Carduel for Uther Pendragon, the father of King Arthur. Uther Pendragon gave the table to King Leodegraunce of Cameliard, who gave it to King Arthur when Arthur married Guinever, Leodegraunce's daughter. Its circular design eliminated the usual head and foot and therefore assured equality of the knights and prevented jealousy. According to Malory's *Morte d'Arthur*, there were 150 knights

who had "sieges," or seats, at the Round Table. King Leodegraunce brought 100 men to the wedding of King Arthur and Guinever. Merlin filled up 28 of the vacant seats, and King Arthur elected Gwain and Tor. The remaining seats were left to those who might prove worthy of the honor. Always 12 knights, the number of Apostles of Jesus, were associated with the Round Table, though their names vary in different sources. The most frequent names were Lancelot, Tristram, Lamora, Tor, Galahad, Gwain, Gareth, Plaomides, Kay, Mark, Mordred, Accolon, Ballamore, Beleobus, Belvoure, Bersunt, Bors, Ector de Maris, Ywaine, Floll, Gaheris, Galohalt, Grislet, Lionell, Marhaus, Paginet, Pelles, Perceval, Sagris, Superabilis, and Turquine.

See also: ACCOLON; ARTHUR; GALAHAD; GARETH; GUINEVER; GWAIN; LANCELOT OF THE LAKE; MERLIN; PERCEVAL; TRISTRAN AND ISEULT; UTHER PENDRAGON

2584

**Rowan**   A small tree sometimes known as the mountain ash. In medieval Christian belief, the rowan, which had been associated with the pagan Druids, was believed to be potent against witchcraft. In Scotland suspected witches touched with a rowan branch were believed to be then carried away by the devil. Crosses of rowan branches were placed in strategic places, such as over doorways, as protection against evil. In one legend the wood of the True Cross of Christ is rowan, only one of many trees so credited. Another belief was that rowans growing in graveyards kept the dead in their graves until Judgment Day.

See also: CROSS; DRUIDS

2585

**Rubezahl** (turnip remnant)   In Germanic folklore, the turnip-counter spirit. He once abducted a princess who desired turnips. He planted them for her, and she asked him to count the seeds. While Rubezahl was counting, she escaped.

2586

**Rudra** (howler, ruddy one)   In Hindu mythology, a storm god, later identified with Shiva; father of the Rudras or Maruts, wind gods.

In the Rig-Veda, the sacred collection of hymns to the gods, Rudra is portrayed as both beneficent and demonic. He is the god who heals both men and cattle, as in one hymn:

We implore Rudra,
the lord of songs,
the lord of animal sacrifices,
for health, wealth, and his favor.

In his demonic role he is addressed in another hymn:

May the weapon of Rudra avoid us,
may the great anger of the flaring one pass us
    by. . ..
O tawny and manly god, showing thyself,
so as neither to be angry nor to kill,
be mindful of our invocations,
and rich in brave sons,
we shall magnify thee in the congregation.

In some texts Rudra is said to have been born a boy from the forehead of Brahma. In another account he is said to have later divided into male and female, then multiplied, producing the Maruts, or Rudras.

See also: BRAHMA; MARUTS; RUDRAS; RIG-VEDA

2587

**Rue**   An aromatic evergreen, called by Shakespeare the "sour herbs of grace" (*Hamlet* IV.v). It appears in English folklore and literature as a symbol of pity, mercy, and forgiveness, but it also symbolizes grief, repentance, bitterness, and disdain. An early English meaning still current is sorrow or regret. In the Middle Ages witches' brew contained rue because it was a potent force in the working of evil, but it was also an antidote to witchcraft. In Italy rue warded off spells cast by the evil eye. Dipped in holy water, rue branches were used to sprinkle bedrooms to counter demons that were upsetting a couple's sexual relations.

2588
**Ruggiero** (Rogero)   In the Charlemagne cycle of legends, a Saracen hero, also called Roger. He was nursed by a lioness and brought up by Atlantes, a magician, who gave him a dazzling magic shield. He threw it into a well because he thought it unfair to fight with it. Ruggiero deserted the Moorish army for Charlemagne's, becoming a Christian. He married Bradamant, Charlemagne's niece, and later killed Rodomont, another Saracen hero, who at his wedding accused him of being a traitor. Ruggiero appears in Ariosto's *Orlando Furioso* and Tasso's *Jerusalem Delivered*.

See also: ATLANTES; CHARLEMAGNE; RODOMONT

2589
**Ruh** (breath)   In Islamic mythology, angel often identified with Gabriel. Ruh's duty is to bring motion to heavenly spheres, as well as to living beings. With the permission of Allah, Ruh can also stop the heavenly spheres. In the Koran (sura 16) the term *ruh* is used for spirit, as when Allah sends "down angels with the spirit" on "whomsoever He will." In early Arabic poetry, *ruh* meant breath or wind, but in later literature it was used not only for the angel but also for the human spirit and sometimes even to mean the djinn or demons.

See also: DJINN; GABRIEL; KORAN, THE

2590
**Ruhanga** (creator)   In African mythology (Ankore and Banyoro of Uganda), creator god who first allowed humans to return to life after death. All the people had to do was express happiness at the return of the dead. One day a woman refused to put on her best clothes and rejoice when one of the dead returned because her pet dog had died. This so angered Ruhanga that he decided that men and women should die just as the ani-

mals do not return to life. Ruhanga is also known as Kazooba (sun) in his role as sun god; Mukameiguru (he who reigns in the sky) as sky god; and Rugaba (giver) as the giver of life to man, animals, and plants.

2591
**Ruidoso**   In American western folklore, a big maverick steer that brought destruction on all who came in contact with it. At its death it turned into the ghost steer of the Pecos. Its agressive roar, that of a bull ready to charge, can still be heard at night.

See also: WILD HERD

2592
**Rumina** (teat)   In Roman mythology, goddess of suckling infants and animals, consort of Ruminus, her male counterpart. In Rome a sanctuary to both deities stood at the foot of the Palatine Hill in the neighborhood of the Lupercal. In the same place stood the Ruminal fig tree, believed by some scholars to be an early emblem or symbol of Rumina and said to be the one under which Romulus and Remus were suckled by the she-wolf. It is mentioned in Ovid's *Fasti* (book 2).

See also: OVID; ROMULUS AND REMUS

*Rumpelstiltskin*

2593
**Rumpelstiltskin**   Popular European folktale, best known in the Grimms' version. Rumpelstiltskin is a dwarf who promises to help a maiden spin flax into gold if she will give him her first-

born child. In desperation she agrees, but when the child is born, she begs Rumpelstiltskin to let her keep him. He agrees to let her keep the child if she can guess his name within three days. She dispatches all of her servants in an effort to learn his name. One overhears Rumpelstiltskin say his name while reciting a rhyme and dancing in the forest. At the end of three days he returns, and the girl is ready for him and speaks his name. In the Grimms' version she asks: "Is your name Kunz? Is your name Heinz? Can your name be Rumpelstiltskin?" He is so angry that he drives himself into the ground by stamping his foot and tears himself in half trying to extricate himself. In some European versions the dwarf is called Tit-Tot-Tom, Titeliture, Riodin-Riodon, and Dancing Vargaluska.

Rumpelstiltskin is tale type 520, the "The Master Reveals the Riddle." The motif of guessing the name of a supernatural creature which then gives power over him is also widely known in folk tales.

See also: MOTIF; TALE TYPE

---

**Runes**    2594

**Runes**    A Germanic script based on the Latin alphabet from the Gothic *run*, meaning secret or mystery. These inscriptions were made with a sharp instrument on wood, metal weapons, and stone monuments and are symbols with ritualistic, magical, or oracular significance. They occur in all Germanic regions of northern Europe and have a rugged and angular shape. More than 3,000 such inscriptions survive, mostly in Scandinavia. According to Tacitus in his *Germania* (98 C.E.), runes were carved on small pieces of wood and cast as lots by priests in order to foretell the future. During the Nazi period in Germany, Heinrich Himmler's SS (*Schutzstaffel*) used the ancient Germanic rune for writing the SS.

---

**Rusalka** (female water spirit)    2595

**Rusalka** (female water spirit)    In Slavic folklore, female water spirit who lives part of the year in water and part in the forest. A *rusalka* could not live long out of water, but with her comb she was not in danger, for the comb gave her the ability to conjure up water when she needed it.

Two types of *rusalki* are found in Slavic folktales. The northern type is a demonic being, somewhat pale, who entices men with her songs and then drowns them, much like Sirens in Greek mythology or the Lorelei in Germany. The southern variant is an attractive girl, who also entices men but truly loves them. When a man dies in her arms, it is considered a blessing. Among the Bulgarians, the *rusalki* are called *samovily* and are believed to be the spirits of unbaptized dead girls. The Slovaks believe them to be the souls of brides who died after their marriage night. Poles believe them to be beautiful girls punished for leading wicked lives. The Polish variety are good to those who were kind to them in life and punish those where were unkind. The Russian composer Alexander Dargomizhsky composed an opera *Rusalka*, as did the Czech composer Antonin Dvorák. Dvorák's *Rusalka* is based on a story by Alexander Pushkin.

See also: LESHY; LORELEI; SIRENS

*Rustum fighting the White Demon*

---

**Rustum** (Rostastahm, Rustem)    2596

**Rustum** (Rostastahm, Rustem)    In the Persian epic poem *Shah Namah*, by Firdusi, great hero and father of Sohrab.

While yet a child, Rustum displayed great courage and strength. He ate as much as five men could eat in a day and was nursed by 10 women. When Rustum grew up, King Kai-Kaus appointed him captain-general of his army. One day the king decided he wanted to invade Mazinderan, a beautiful and rich city. The idea was planted in the king's mind by a demon who wished the venture to bring about the monarch's destruction. When the king of Mazinderan heard that Kai-Kaus was on his way to invade his kingdom, he called on the White Demon for help. Meanwhile, Kai-Kaus, full of anticipation of victory, was camped on a plain near the city, but hailstorms poured down in the night, destroying most of the army. For seven days the king lamented the loss of his army. Then he heard the voice of the White Demon, which said to him:

O king, thou art the willow-tree, all barren,
With neither fruit, nor flower.
What could induce
The dream of conquering Mazinderan?
(James Atkinson translation).

The White Demon seized the king, but the king managed to send a message asking for help. Rustum started on his journey to free the king. In one day he came to a forest full of wild asses. Hungry, he caught one and cooked it for dinner. While he was asleep a wild lion attacked him, but Rustum was saved by his faithful horse, Ruksh. The next day the two continued on their journey. Coming to a desert, Rustum prayed for some water, which was granted him. After drinking, Rustum addressed his faithful horse:

Beware, my steed, of future strife.
Again, thou must not risk thy life;
Encounter not with lion fell,
Nor demon still more terrible;
But should an enemy appear,
Ring loud the warning in my ear (James Atkinson translation).

After delivering his speech, Rustum lay down to sleep, leaving Ruksh unbridled and at liberty to graze close by. At midnight a monstrous dragon, eight yards long, appeared. Ruksh awoke his master, who attacked the monster. Ruksh helped his master by biting and tearing the monster's scaly hide while Rustum severed its head.

After killing the dragon Rustum resumed his journey, coming to a beautiful green spot where he settled for the night. He found a ready-roasted deer, some bread, and salt. He sat down to eat when suddenly the food disappeared; a flask of wine and a tambourine took its place. Rustum played the instrument, and a beautiful woman appeared. Not knowing she was a demoness, Rustum placed in her hands a cup of wine, calling upon the name of Allah. Suddenly she turned into a Black Demon. Seeing this, Rustum took his sword and cut her in two.

Next the hero encountered Aulad, who ruled part of the land. The two fought, and Aulad lost. Rustum then asked Aulad to give him information as to where King Kai-Kaus was being held prisoner. Rustum promised to make Aulad the next king of Mazinderan if Aulad gave the correct information. Aulad told him where the demons were located, and Rustum went to their hiding place and defeated the demon Arzend. Then the two, Rustum and Aulad, went to the city of Mazinderan. Ruksh, Rustum's horse, neighed so loudly that the sound of it reached the imprisoned king.

Before Rustum could free the king, however, he had to fight the White Demon at Halt-koh (seven mountains). He went to the mountain and found 400 demons. He asked Aulad when to attack and was told that the best time was when the sun was at its hottest because the demons always liked to take a nap during the heat. When the sun was at its height and the demons napping, Rustum dismembered them. A few, however, escaped to tell the White Demon.

Advancing to the White Demon's cave, Rustum looked down and saw that the cave was as dark as hell itself.

"Are you tired of life," the White Demon cried out, "that you invade my kingdom? Tell me your name, since I do not want to destroy a nameless thing."

Rustum then told the White Demon his name, and the battle began. The hero pierced the White Demon's thigh, lopping off a limb. The two fought furiously until at last Rustum grabbed the White Demon, lifted him in the air, and dashed him to the ground. He then tore out the demon's heart, and demons came out of his body as he bled. Rustum then took the heart of the White Demon and restored the sight of King Kai-Kaus, who had earlier been blinded by the demons.

In Persian art Rustum is often portrayed wearing armor and a helmet, with the skin of a leopard as part of his outfit.

See also: ALLAH; *SHAH NAMAH*; SOHRAB

2597
**Ruth** (friendship)    In the Bible, O.T., a Moabite heroine and name of an Old Testament book. She was an ancestress of King David and Jesus. During the days of the Judges, Elimelech and Naomi, with their two sons, went to Moab to escape a famine in their native Bethlehem. The sons, Mahlon and Chilion, married Moabite women, Orpah and Ruth. Then all of the men

died. Naomi, hearing that there was again bread in her native land, decided to return, and her two daughters-in-law wished to go with her. Naomi told them to return to their own families. Orpah agreed, but Ruth said to Naomi, "Intreat me not to leave thee, or to return from following after thee . . . thy people shall be my people, and thy God my God" (Ruth 1:16). In Bethlehem Ruth gleaned in the field of Boaz, a kinsman of Elimelech and "a mighty man of wealth," and she found favor in his eyes. Recognizing her kinship and its customary rights, Boaz protected her by marriage, and from this union King David descended. In Christian art the Tree of Jesse, the father of King David, sometimes portrays Boaz on one of its branches.

See also: DAVID; JESUS; TREE OF JESSE

*Ruth and Boaz (Holbein)*

# S

**Sab-dag** (foundation owner)    In Tibetan folklore, the house-god, devil, or spirit located in a fixed place, who must be appeased or else he will cause harm. To make sure he is in a good mood, once a year the Lamas propitiate him by doing "the water sacrifice for the eight injurers."

**Sachs, Hans**    1494–1576. German cobbler in Nürnberg who wrote numerous shrovetide plays on themes that were common among the German people. One such play tells the story of a wandering student who meets a grieving peasant woman. When he tells her that he is on his way to Paris, she misunderstands him and thinks he is going to Paradise, whereupon she asks him to take along gifts of food and money for her husband who has only recently died. The student quickly sees his advantage and asks for more and more to take along, thus bilking the poor woman of her worldly goods. Hans Sachs's stories deal with knights and priests, peasants and rogues, jealous husbands and greedy merchants, deceitful women and lazy servants. He also wrote numerous fables and jests (*Schwank* in German), about a land of plenty, and even about saints, all of which ended with a moral.

See also: COCKAIGNE, LAND OF

**Sadhyas** (to be attained)    In Hindu mythology, a group of spirits who inhabit the region between the earth and the sun. Their number varies from 12 to 17.

**Sadi**    c. 1184–1263. Assumed name of the Persian poet Sheikh Muslih Addin, whose major works are *The Gulistan* and *The Bustan*, didactic works in prose and verse containing numerous fables.

A descendant of Ali, Muhammad's son-in-law, Sadi studied at Baghdad and, according to some accounts, was made a prisoner by the Christian Crusaders, then ransomed. His major works, *The Gulistan* and *The Bustan*, have been known in the West for centuries, even though his predilection for homosexual liaisons was often masked in translations of his works.

Ralph Waldo Emerson so admired Sadi that he often used Sadi's name as a pseudonym for his poems. One of Emerson's major poems, titled *Saadi*, contains Emerson's summation of the man whom he considered a great poet and moralist.

See also: ALI; ANGRY ACROBAT, THE; *BUSTAN, THE*; DERVISH AND THE KING, THE; *GULISTAN, THE*; MUHAMMAD; SLAVE AND THE MASTER, THE

2602

**Sadko** In Russian folklore, a merchant *bogatyr*, an epic hero. He appears in the *bylini*, the epic songs, as well as in folktales, originally as an ancient water deity. Sadko was a rich merchant who sailed the sea but never paid tribute to the czar of the sea. One day he descended to the watery depths, met the sea czar, and played for him on his *qusli*, a stringed instrument similar to the psaltery. The czar of the sea was so moved that he began to dance, causing a storm that wrecked many ships. When Sadko came to the water's surface again, he sailed on the River Volga for some 12 years. Wishing to return to his city of Novgorod, he cut a slice of bread, put some salt on it, and placed it on the waves of the Volga. The river thanked Sadko for his kindness and told him to see its brother, the lake of Ilmen. In reward for his kindness the lake told Sadko to cast his nets into the waters. They were at once filled with fish, which then were miraculously transformed into silver. Nikolai Rimsky-Korsakov used some of the legends for his opera *Sadko*.

See also: BYLINA

2603

**Saehrimnir** (blackened) In Norse mythology, the magic boar that was partaken of by the heroes (einherjar) in Valhalla. It was killed daily, cooked and eaten, and returned to life the next day, so the ritual could be repeated. Saehrimnir was prepared by Andhrimnir (the sooty-faced), the cook of the gods, who boiled the boar in the magic caldron, Eldhrimir. In the Lay of Grimnir, one of the poems in the *Poetic Edda*, Saehrimnir is said to be "the best of flesh."

See also: EINHERJAR; POETIC EDDA

2604

**Sage** A shrub of the mint family, used as an herb in cooking, also an all-purpose remedy in Greek and Roman folk medicine. It was dedicated to the Greek god Zeus and the Roman Jupiter. In Christian folk medicine, sage was used to freshen the blood, cure nervous stomach, and relieve epilepsy, palsy, fever, and the plague. An English folk rhyme says: "He that would live for aye, / Must eat sage in May." Sage was planted on graves in medieval England. The magical qualities of sage are referred to in the refrain to Simon and Garfunkel's song "Scarborough Fair": "parsley, sage, rosemary and thyme."

See also: JUPITER; PARSLEY; ROSEMARY; ZEUS

2605

**Saints** Holy ones in Christianity, also holy ones in Islamic and Judaic folklore and legend. During the Middle Ages the cult of the saints among Christians was one of the main aspects of religion. Many shrines and relics of the saints were honored and numerous churches built in their honor. The most important saint was the Virgin Mary, whose cult was the most popular, but thousands of other saints were also honored because it was believed that the saints in heaven could plead with God for the people still on earth. St. Thomas Aquinas had written: "A propitious predestination can be helped by the prayers of the saints." From the ninth century on, the legends of the saints abound in medieval thought. Saints were invoked to cure diseases and ills; for example, St. Christopher to protect against bad dreams or St. Thomas à Becket to prevent or cure blindness. St. Agatha was invoked to protect against fire, but St. Florian should be invoked if the fire had already started. Those with toothache called on St. Appolonia because she had all her teeth pulled out at her martyrdom. Saints also were patrons of cities, churches, and countries. St. George protected England, St. Peter protected Flanders, and St. Ursula protected Cologne. Saints were invoked by children, wives, idiots, students; every aspect of medieval life had a patron saint to watch over it. Archers had St. Sebastian, who had been shot at with arrows. Bakers prayed to St. Winifred because he was also a baker. Captives looked to St. Barbara since she had been locked in a tower. The insane, if they could pray, invoked St.

Dymphna. The thousands of saints during the Middle Ages did not receive formal recognition from the Church. Most of the cult grew up under popular support. The first historically attested canonization of a saint took place in 993 when Pope John XV sainted Ulrich of Augsburg. Sometimes a bishop would saint a person in the hope that revenue would come into his diocese from the saint's relics, which would then be encased in an elaborate shrine for the faithful. A reaction against the cult of saints came at the close of the Middle Ages. At the Reformation the practice was attacked by Calvinists and Zwinglians on the grounds that the Bible did not sanction such practice. The Church of England in the Thirty-Nine Articles held: "The Romish Doctrine concerning . . . Images as Relics, and also Invocation of Saints, is a fond thing, vainly invented, and grounded upon no warranty of Scripture, but rather repugnant to the Word of God." (Article 22) The Protestant attack on the saints was countered by the Roman Catholics. The Council of Trent (1563) stated: "The saints, who reign together with Christ, offer up their own prayers to God for men. . . . it is good and useful suppliantly to invoke them, and to have recourse to their prayers, aid, and help for obtaining the benefits of God." The Catholic-Protestant battle of the saints continues into the present. Some Protestant groups have relaxed their attack, and the Roman church has softened its cry for the saints. Secular writers have entered the field. William James, in *The Varieties of Religious Experience*, wrote: "In the life of the saints, technically so called, the spiritual faculties are strong, but what gives the impression of extravagance proves usually on examination to be a relative deficiency of intellect." Mussolini was not so subtle in his attack. In a speech given in 1904 he said, "The history of the saints is mainly the history of insane people." A comic note was struck by Ambrose Bierce in *The Devil's Dictionary*, in which *saint* is defined as "a dead sinner revised and edited."

See also: AGATHA, ST.; APPOLONIA; BARBARA, ST.; BEFANA; CHRISTOPHER, ST.; FLORIAN, ST.;

GEORGE, ST.; SEBASTIAN, ST.; THOMAS AQUINAS, ST.; THOMAS À BECKET, ST.; ULRICH, ST.; URSULA, ST.; VIRGIN MARY;

2606

**Sakatimuna**   In Islamic mythology, enormous serpent killed by the archangel Gabriel. Allah sent Gabriel saying: "Take down for me the iron staff of the 'creed' which dangles at the gate of heaven, and kill the serpent Sakatimuna." Gabriel did as God had commanded, and the serpent was broken apart, the head and forepart shooting up above the heavens and the tail penetrating downward beneath the earth. Some commentators believe this tale is to be taken as an explanation of an eclipse.

See also: ALLAH; GABRIEL; SANG GALA RAJA

2607

**Sakhar**   In Jewish and Islamic legend, a demon who impersonated King Solomon.

King Solomon, having defeated Sidon, slew the king of that city and brought away the king's daughter, Jerada, to be one of his mistresses. The young girl continually cried over the death of her father. To calm her, Solomon ordered the djinn to make an image of the dead king. When it was finished, it was placed in Jerada's chamber, where she and her maids worshiped it every day. Solomon learned from his vizier Asaf that the women were committing idolatry, and he ordered the image destroyed. To atone for his mistake Solomon then went into the desert to ask God for forgiveness. But God wanted more than a plea from Solomon.

It was the king's custom when he washed or "eased himself" to remove his magic ring and hand it to the concubine Amina. One day, when she had the ring in her custody, the demon Sakhar appeared in the shape of Solomon and took the ring. With it Sakhar had complete control of the entire kingdom. Solomon in the meantime had changed in appearance and was not recognized by his subjects. He wandered about for 40 days (the same length of time the image had been worshiped); then Sakhar flew away, casting the magic ring into the sea. The king later recovered it from inside a fish. Solomon eventually captured Sakhar, tied a great stone to his neck, and threw him into the Lake of Tiberias.

See also: DJINN; SOLOMON

**2608**
**Sakhmet** (Sekhmet, Sechmet, Sekhait, Sekhauit, Skhautet, Sekhem) (the powerful one)   In Egyptian mythology, the lion goddess, honored as goddess of war; called Sakhmis by the Greeks. She was the consort of the god Ptah, and together with their son Nefertem they formed the divine triad of gods worshiped at Memphis. Death came into the world when the Eye of Ra was sent down to Sakhmet to punish a rebellious humanity. In Egyptian art Sakhmet is often depicted as a woman with the head of a lioness, which is surmounted by the solar disk encircled by a uraeus. The numerous images of the lioness goddess in hardstone that are often found in museums throughout the world represent Sakhmet and were all originally found in the precinct of the goddess Mut in southern Karnak. It is assumed by scholars that there were two images of Sakhmet for each day of the year to which prayers were addressed to gain her favor.

See also: MUT; PTAH; URAEUS

**2609**
**Sakradhanus**   In Hindu mythology, the bow (rainbow) of the storm god, Indra.

See also: INDRA

**2610**
**Saku-Ikazuchi**   In Japanese mythology, one of the Ikazuchi, the eight gods of thunder.

See also: IKAZUCHI

**2611**
**Salacia** (salt-spring)   In Roman mythology, goddess of spring water; wife of Neptune. She

was identified by the Romans with the Greek Amphitrite.

See also: AMPHITRITE; NEPTUNE

**2612**
**Salamander**   A small amphibian, similar to a lizard, with smooth, moist skin. In world mythology and folklore, the salamander was believed to be poisonous. The antidote for its poison was a drink made by brewing stinging nettle in a tortoise broth. In Greek folklore, according to Pliny, the salamander "seeks the hottest fire to breed in, but quenches it with the extreme frigidity of its body." Christians, echoing this belief, adopted the salamander as a symbol of the Christian struggle against the desires of hot, sinful flesh. Francis I of France, seeking an appropriate symbol for his absolute dictatorial powers, chose a salamander surrounded by flames above the inscription: "I nourish and extinguish." Paracelsus adopted the salamander as the name of the elemental being inhabiting fire.

See also: GNOMES; SYLPHS; UNDINE

**2613**
**Saleh**   In Islamic legend, prophet who preached to the Thamudites. They insisted that Saleh perform a miracle if he wished them to believe in Allah. They suggested that he come to their festival, where they would ask their gods for help and he would ask Allah. They called upon their idols and received no response. Then Jonda Ebn Amru, their leader, pointed to a rock and told Saleh that if he could make a pregnant she-camel come out of the rock he would believe. Saleh called upon Allah, the rock went into labor, and a she-camel appeared and gave birth to a young camel. Seeing this miracle, Jonda believed, although the majority of people did not. Allah then destroyed the unbelievers. The Koran (sura 7) mentions the "she-camel of Allah" but does not give the legend, which was supplied by Islamic commentaries on the sacred text.

See also: ALLAH; KORAN, THE

2614

**Salman al-Parisi**  Seventh century. In Islamic legend, saint, patron of all corporations. A companion of Muhammad, who spoke highly of him, Salman ran away as a boy to follow a Christian monk but eventually was convinced that Muhammad was the prophet sent to restore the faith of Abraham of the Old Testament. Salman is considered one of the founders of Sufism, the mystical sect of Islam. Its name is believed to be derived from the Arabic word *suf*, wool, because of the coarse woolen garments worn by ascetics. Other possible sources of the term are the Arabic word for purity and the Greek word *sophia*, wisdom. The early Sufis dedicated their lives to devotion and seclusion. There are references to them in the *Rubaiyat* of Omar Khayyam, such as the ironic number 87:

> Whereat some one of the loquacious Lot—
> I think a Súfi pipkin—waxing hot—
> "All this of Pot and Potter—Tell me then,
> Who is the Potter, pray, and who the Pot?

See also: ABRAHAM; MUHAMMAD

2615

**Salmon of Knowledge**  In Celtic mythology, a magic fish fed by nuts dropped from the nine hazel trees on the edge of the river Boyne. He is the repository of otherworldly wisdom. According to legend, the bard Finneces had been fishing for the salmon for seven years. A boy named Fionn happened along, and when the fish was being cooked over a fire, Fionn touched it with his finger, burning it, and thrust his finger in his mouth, thus acquiring the otherworldly wisdom that Finneces had sought.

See also: SIEGFRIED

2616

**Salome** (peaceful)  In the Bible, N.T., the wife of Zebedee and the mother of James and John. She witnessed the Crucifixion and was at the tomb on Easter (Mark 15:40). The name is also given to the daughter of Herodias and Herod Philip in Jewish and Christian tradition, though the the girl is not named in the Bible. Her tale is told in Matthew (14:6–8): "But when Herod's birthday was kept, the daughter of Herodias danced before them, and pleased Herod. Whereupon he promised with an oath to give her whatsoever she would ask. And she, being before instructed by her mother, said, 'Give me here John Baptist's head in a charger.'" An executioner then beheaded the prophet. Medieval legend said that Herodias had been in love with John the Baptist and Herod in love with Salome. Hermann Sudermann's tragedy *The Fires of St. John* and Oscar Wilde's *Salome*, illustrated by Aubrey Beardsley, are the best-known versions of the legend. Richard Strauss's opera *Salome* uses the Wilde play in a German translation. Flaubert wrote *Herodias* also using the legend.

See also: EASTER; JOHN THE BAPTIST, ST.

2617

**Saluka-Jataka**  Buddhist folktale, number 286 of the *Jatakas*, or *Birth-Stories of the Former Lives of the Buddha*.

When Brahmadatta ruled as king of Benares, the future Buddha was born as an ox named Big Redcoat. He had a younger brother called Little Redcoat. Both of them worked for a family in a small village. When one of the girls in the family came of age, she was asked for in marriage by a neighboring family for their son. In the girl's family there was a pig, called Celery, who was being fatted to serve as the main meal on the coming wedding day. "Brother," said Little Redcoat one day to Big Redcoat, "we work for this family and help them earn a living. Yet they only give us grass and straw, while they feed Celery, the pig, with rice porridge, and he sleeps comfortably on a platform under the eaves. What can he do for them that we can't?"

"Don't be envious of Celery's porridge," said Big Redcoat. "They want to make him fat for the wedding feast of the young lady of the house. That's why they are feeding him. Wait a few days and you'll see him dragged out, killed, chopped to pieces, and eaten up by the wedding guests."

A few days later, the wedding guests came, and Celery was killed and eaten. Both oxen, seeing what happened, were now quite pleased with their ration.

"In this tale of my former life," said the Buddha, "Ananda, my disciple, was Little Redcoat and I was Big Redcoat."

See also: ANANDA; JATAKA

**2618**

**Samain** (Samhain, Samhuinn, Sauin)  Irish, Scottish Gaelic, and Manx names for the seasonal feast on 1 November. The antiquity of the feast is attested through various sources, the earliest of which is the first century B.C.E. Coligny Calendar, which describes Samain as the period of dark that precedes the light and supports the idea that it was the equivalent of New Year's Day. Julius Caesar also wrote of the Gaulish *Dis Pater*, god of death and winter's cold, who was also worshiped at this time of year. There are also references to human and animal sacrifices as part of the feast. The Christian calendar celebrates All Saints' Day, which was introduced by Pope Boniface IV in the seventh century to replace the pagan festival of the dead. Halloween also continues some of the Samain traditions, such as when the spirits of the dead are suggested by placing burning candles in hollowed out pumpkins.

**2619**

**Samantabhadra**  In Mahayana Buddhism, one of the five Dhyani-Bodhisattvas, representing universal kindness. His symbols are a magic jewel and a scroll; his mount is an elephant. In some Tibetan traditions he is a Buddha, sky blue in color, without clothing or ornaments.

See also: DHYANI-BODHISATTVAS; MAHAYANA

**2620**

**Samaritan, Good**  In the Bible, N.T., a parable told by Jesus (Luke 10:29–37) in answer to: "Who is my neighbor?" It tells of a man left half dead by robbers on the road from Jerusalem to Jericho. A priest and Levite pass him by in turn, but a Samaritan—a group despised by the Jews—took care of him and paid for his lodgings. Jesus ends the parable by saying, "Which of these three, thinkest thou, was neighbor unto him that fell among the theieves? And he said, He that shewed mercy on him. Then said Jesus unto him, Go, do thou likewise" (Luke 20:36–37). The scene has been painted numerous times in Western art. Today anyone who attends to the poor and gives them aid is referred to as a Good Samaritan.

**2621**

**Samba**  In Hindu mythology, a son of Krishna (an incarnation of the god Vishnu) by Jambavati; he scoffed at sacred things. Once he dressed up as a pregnant woman and went to three holy men, asking whether he would give birth to a girl or a boy. They answered, "This is not a woman, but the son of Krishna, and he shall bring forth an iron club which shall destroy the whole race of Yadu . . . and you and all your people shall destroy the race by the club." Samba then gave birth to an iron club, which later formed part of the tip of an arrow that killed Krishna when Jaras (old age) shot at him. In later life Samba became a leper, but the sun god, Surya, cured him through fasting and penance. Later Samba built a temple to worship the sun.

See also: KRISHNA; SURYA; VISHNU

**2622**

**Sambiki Saru**  In Japanese mythology, three apes: Mizaru (not seeing) with hands over his eyes, who sees no evil; Kikazaru (not hearing) covering his ears, who listens to no evil; and Iwarazaru (not speaking) with his hands on his mouth, who speaks no evil. They attend either Saruta Hito no Mikoto, the long-nosed Shinto god whose nasal appendage is said to be some seven cubits long, or the god Koshin. The proverbial saying "Hear no evil, see no evil, speak no evil" came to be associated with monkeys when travelers to China and Japan saw three carved Koshin monkey deities on pedestals alongside the road, with their ears, eyes and mouths covered up.

See also: APE; KOSHIN

2623

**Sam Hart of Woburn**   In American folklore of New England, a horseman who once entered into a race with the devil. The devil appeared to Sam in the form of a country parson riding a black horse and challenged Sam to a race. Both set off at once, but Sam soon realized that the horse and its rider were none other than the devil. He headed for church land, which he knew the devil could not traverse. When he reached the sacred site, the devil's black horse went down on it haunches and threw the devil. Realizing he had lost, the devil said: "You've cheated one whose business is cheating, and I'm a decent enough fellow to own up when I'm beaten. Here's your money. Catch it, for you know I can't cross holy ground, you rascal. And here's my horse. He'll be tractable enough after I've gone home and as safe as your mare. Good luck to you." A whiff of sulfur smoke burst up from the road, and the devil disappeared. But Sam's neighbors never trusted his black horse. One day, they said, it would carry its owner to hell to meet the devil.

2624

**Samiasa** (Azza, Semiaza, Shemhazai, Shamazya, Amezzyarak, Uzza) (the name Azza)   In Jewish folklore, a fallen angel who hangs suspended between heaven and earth, with his nose pierced as punishment for having had sexual intercourse with a mortal woman. Samiasa is responsible for the worship of the sun, moon, and stars because he has the power to move them when men pray to him. The English Romantic poet Lord Byron

has Samiasa as one of the principal characters in his poetic drama *Heaven and Earth*. This drama deals with the biblical myth of the marriage between the Sons of God, or angels, and the daughters of men (Gen. 6:12).

2625

**Sammael** (Satanil, Samil, Seir, Salmail) (poison angel)   In medieval Jewish folklore, principal angel of death, regarded as both beneficent and demonic.

Sammael appears in many Jewish folktales as a dispenser of death, under the control of God. One tells how he was outwitted by two clever foxes. Sammael asks God for permission to kill two of every creature since as yet no one had died in the world. God grants the request with the proviso that nothing be killed before its allotted time. Sammael agreed and then proceeded to break his promise. Coming upon two young foxes, he is about to murder them when they cry out that he has already killed their parents.

"Look into the water," they say to Sammael.

The angel looks down and sees the reflection of the two young foxes. Thinking the reflection to be foxes he already drowned, he allows the young foxes to go free.

Sammael is mentioned in Longfellow's poetic drama *Christus: A Mystery* as "full of eyes," holding a "sword, from which doth fall . . . a drop of gall" into the mouth of the dying, thus causing death. One scene in the drama deals with the young Judas Iscariot, the betrayer of Jesus. Judas is being taught by a rabbi who asks the boy why dogs howl at night. Judas replies that "dogs howl, when the icy breath" of the "Great Sammael, the Angel of Death," is taking flight "through the town."

See also: JUDAS ISCARIOT

2626

**Sampo** (prop of life?)   In the Finnish epic poem *The Kalevala*, magic object forged by the smith Ilmarinen for Louhi, the evil mistress of

Pohjola, the Northland, as part payment for the hand of her daughter, the Maiden of Pohjola.

Louhi set up the magic sampo in a hillside cave, where it took root, producing prosperity for her land. Vainamoinen, the culture hero, determined to steal the sampo from Louhi. He constructed a ship, and the smith Ilmarinen forged a sword for him. Both then set off for Pohjola. On the way the hero Lemminkainen called to them from the shore, asking to accompany them. They took him along, but during the voyage their boat was struck by a giant pike. Vainamoinen killed the pike and made a harp with which he lulled all of the people of Pohjola to sleep. With the help of an ox, the three heroes stole the sampo and started home. However, Louhi awoke and sent fog and wind after the three, causing Vainamoinen's harp to fall overboard. Louhi and her men pursued them in a boat and caught up with them. A battle ensued in which the sampo fell into the lake and was broken to pieces. Only a few pieces floated to the shore. Vainamoinen then planted them for good luck.

In *The Kalevala* the sampo is pictured as a three-sided mill, one side or face grinding out grain, one salt, and one money, all in unlimited amounts. Its *kirjokansai* (lid) is described as being of "many colors." Yet scholars are not at all sure what the sampo actually represents. Some see it as a magic mill, others as a symbol of the North Star, and yet others as a dragon.

See also: ILMARINEN; *KALEVALA, THE*; MAIDEN OF POHJOLA

**2627**

**Sam Slick** In American literary folklore, a Yankee peddler, shrewd, ruthless, and full of wise sayings; created by Thomas Chandler Haliburton (1796–1865). Sam Slick appears in a series of Haliburton's books, the first being *The Clockmaker, or, The Sayings and Doings of Samuel Slick of Slickville*. Some of Slick's sayings are "Time is like a woman and pigs; the more you want it to go, the more it won't" and "Politics

make a man as crooked as a pack does a peddler; not that they are so awful heavy either, but it teaches a man to stoop in the long run." Born in Nova Scotia, Haliburton left for England in 1856 and was elected to the House of Commons.

*Samson and Delilah*

**2628**

**Samson** (sunny or sun-hero) In the Bible, O.T., a hero, one of the Judges, whose tale is told in the Book of Judges (chaps. 13–16). After many childless years Manoah and his wife were told by an angel that she would bear a son, Samson. He later became a leader of the Israelites in their struggle against the Philistines. Brought up as a Nazarene, his hair had never been cut, and he had great strength. On one occasion he caught 300 foxes, tied firebrands to their tails, and set them loose in the Philistine field (Judg. 15:4–6). Three thousand of his compatriots, afraid that the Philistines would punish them for Samson's bravery, tied him up and delivered him to the Philistines. Breaking his bonds, he picked up from a dead carcass the jawbone of an ass and killed 1,000 Philistines (Judg. 15:10–15). After a night in Gaza with a whore he still had enough strength to tear up and carry away the city gates

(Judg. 16:1–3). He then fell in love with Delilah, a Philistine woman, who seduced him into telling her the source of his strength—his hair. While he slept, she had his hair cut off, and his strength was gone. The Philistines then bound him and put out his eyes. During a feast in the temple of Dagon, the Philistine god, the blind and now weakened Samson was paraded before the guests. Feeling his way, he found the pillars supporting the building and pulled down the temple, killing himself and thousands of Philistines (Judg. 16:4–31).

Rembrandt's dramatic *Blinding of Samson*, Milton's dramatic poem *Samson Agonistes*, Saint-Saëns's opera *Samson et Delilah*, and Handel's oratorio *Samson* all deal with the legend, as does a Hollywood film, *Samson and Delilah*, directed by Cecil B. DeMille.

See also: DELILAH

*Samuel anoints Saul as king*

2629
**Samuel** (name of God)   11th century B.C.E. In the Bible, O.T., Prophet, son of Elkanah and Hannah. His legend is told in 1 and 2 Samuel. At his birth he was consecrated to temple service by his mother, Hannah. When still a child, he heard the voice of Yahweh, the Hebrew god, in the night. He continued the work of Moses by reuniting the people. After a long life as priest and leader, he yielded to the people's demand for a king and anointed Saul as Israel's first king. He also anointed David after Saul had been rejected by Yahweh. He appears in Barent Fabritius's painting *Consecration of Young Samuel by the Priest Eli*. In Islamic legend his name is Shamwil and sometimes Ishmawil. He is referred in the Koran (sura 2).

See also: DAVID; MOSES; SAUL; YAHWEH

2630
**Sanaka** (the ancient)   In Hindu mythology, one of the four mind-born sons of Brahma.

See also: BRAHMA

2631
**Sananda** (joyous)   In Hindu mythology, one of the four mind-born sons of Brahma.

See also: BRAHMA

2632
**Sanatana** (eternal)   In Hindu mythology, one of the four mind-born sons of Brahma.

See also: BRAHMA

2633
**Sanatkumara** (eternally a youth)   In Hindu mythology, one of the four mind-born sons of Brahma.

See also: BRAHMA

2634
**Sancus**   In ancient Italian mythology, god of oaths, marriage, treaties, and hospitality identified by the Romans with Apollo or Jupiter. He was also called Semo Sancus or Semo Sancus Dius Fidius.

See also: APOLLO; JUPITER

2635
**Sandalphon** (Sandolphon, Sandolfon) (co-brother)   In Jewish folklore, angel who stands on earth with his head reaching to the door of heaven. The American poet Henry Wadsworth Longfellow, in his poem *Sandalphon*, based on his reading of *The Traditions of the Jews* by J. P. Stehelin, writes of how Sandalphon "gathers the

prayers" of the faithful, turns them into flower "garlands of purple and red," and presents them to God. In the poem Sandalphon is described as "the Angel of Glory" and "the Angel of Prayer."

2636
**Sand Man**   In European folklore, the man who puts children to sleep by sprinkling sand or dust in their eyes and saying "The sandman has arrived."

2637
**Sang Gala Raja** (black king of the djinn)   In Islamic mythology, the mightiest djinn in Malay belief, a combination of the Hindu god Shiva in his destructive role and an Islamic djinn; One account says Sang Gala Raja was formed from drops of blood that shot up to heaven when Habil and Kabil (analogous to the biblical Abel and Cain) bit their thumbs. Another account says Sang Gala Raja was formed from parts of Sakatimuna, the monster serpent, when he was slain by the archangel Gabriel. Sang Gala Raja is believed to live in the heart of the jungle with his wife, Sang Gadin, and his seven children.

See also: CAIN AND ABEL; DJINN; GABRIEL; SAKATIMUNA; SHIVA

2638
**Sangha** (assembly)   In Buddhism, term used for the community of Buddha's disciples. It is divided into four classes: monks, nuns, laymen, laywomen. Monks and nuns are of two sorts: novices, those who have taken *pabbajja* (going forth), and the fully professed, those who have *upasampada* (completion). Sometimes the term is used exclusively to refer to the monks and sometimes it is used to distinguish Buddhists according to a scheme of spiritual achievement without regard to their ecclesiastical status.

2639
**San Hsien Shan** (the three mountains of the immortals)   In Chinese mythology, the three isles

of the blessed, which are P'eng-lai, Fang-chang, and Ying-chou, said to be located in the Eastern Sea. Once an expedition was sent to procure from them the plant of immortality. The expedition failed. The isles are sometimes called Fu-t (blessed land), being part of the Happy Land.

2640
**Sanjna** (conscience)   In Hindu mythology, the wife of Surya, the sun god. Sanjna is also called Dyu-mayi (the brilliant) and Maha-virya (the very powerful).

See also: SURYA

2641
**Sansenjin**   In Japanese mythology, the three gods of war, portrayed as a man with three heads and six arms riding on a boar.

2642
**Santaramet**   In Armenian mythology, goddess of the underworld, or a term for the underworld. Santaramet is derived from the Persian guardian of the earth, Armaiti, one of the seven Amesha Spentas.

See also: AMESHA SPENTAS

2643
**Santes of Monte Fabri, St.**   14th century. In Christian legend, Franciscan lay brother. Feast, 6 September. Medieval legend tells how the saint saw the walls of a church open up. One day, being prevented by his duties from attending mass, St. Santes fell on his knees when he heard the bell announce the elevation of the Host during mass. Immediately the four walls of the church opened so that he might see the altar and the Host, which was radiant with light. When the mass was over, the walls of the church closed.

2644
**San-yu**   In Chinese folklore, three friends—plum, pine, and bamboo—all symbols of lon-

gevity, winter, and the traits associated with a gentleman. The three are also symbols of the three religions of China: Taoism, Confucianism, and Buddhism.

2645
**Sarah** (princess)  In the Bible, O.T., the wife and half sister of Abraham, married to him before they left Ur. Her legend is told in Genesis (chaps. 12–23). Sarah was childless for many years until Yahweh, the Hebrew god, gave her Isaac in her old age. After his birth Sarah became jealous of Abraham's concubine Hagar and drove her and her son Ishmael into the desert.

See also: ABRAHAM; ISAAC; ISHMAEL; YAHWEH

2646
**Sarka** (warrior maiden?)  14th century C.E. In Czech legend, a warrior maiden who, with her followers, killed a troop of male warriors. Sarka swore vengeance on all men when she discovered that her lover, Ctirad, had been unfaithful to her. When Ctirad was heard approaching the forest with a group of his men, the maidens tied one of their group to a tree, and she then feigned crying. Seeing her, Ctirad fell in love with her and freed her. Using a potion, she made his men drunk, and they fell into a deep sleep. She blew the hunting horn, and the other maidens, hidden nearby, rushed out to kill the men. This legend inspired Bedrich Smetana's *Sarka*, part of his cycle of six symphonic poems included in *Má Vlast* (My Country); an opera by Zdenko Fibich, *Sarka*; and one of the earliest operas by Leos Janacek, *Sarka*.

See also: BLÁNIK

2647
**Sarpanitum** (silvery bright one)  In Near Eastern mythology (Babylonian-Assyrian), goddess who presided over the sweet waters, earth, and wisdom. She was the wife of the hero god Marduk and daughter of the god Ea. Often she was merged with Erua, who also was regarded as the

wife of Marduk. The goddess Eria is believed to be identical with Erua.

See also: EA; MARDUK

2648
**Sarpedon** (rejoicing in a wooden ark)  In Greek mythology, hero, son of Zeus and Laodamia or Europa; grandson of Bellerophon. Sarpedon was the commander of the Lycian contingent of King Priam's allies during the Trojan War. At the storming of the Greek camp he and Glaucus, his cousin, were the first upon the enemy walls. Sarpedon, however, was killed by Patroclus. A battle then arose over the possession of Sarpedon's body. Apollo, commanded by Zeus, rescued the disfigured corpse from the Greeks. After washing and anointing it with ambrosia, Apollo had Sleep and Death carry the body through the air to Lycia for burial. He was worshiped as a demigod in Lycia. Sarpedon appears in Homer's *Iliad* (books 2, 12, 16).

See also: AMBROSIA; APOLLO; BELLEROPHON; *ILIAD, THE*; PATROCLUS; PRIMA; ZEUS

2649
**Satan** (adversary)  In the Bible, O.T., part of the heavenly court of God (Job 1:6–7), and in the N.T. (Rev. 12:7–9), the devil.

The concept of Satan as the devil is not found in the Old Testament, since his role is merely as the "adversary" to Job. The Bible makes it clear that Satan is part of God's scheme. God grants Satan the power to be Job's adversary. His power, however, is only over the physical aspects of Job, not the spiritual. But as Judaism developed and came into contact with the dualism of the Persians, in which the conflict between the good god, Ahura-Mazda, and Ahriman, the spirit of evil, was emphasized, Satan took on the characteristics of the evil god of the Persians. By the time of the New Testament Satan was generally regarded as an evil demon or the ruler of demons (Matt. 12:24–30). He not only controls the body but also has power over spiritual nature. Since early Christians could not account for God creating something inherently evil, they concluded that Satan was a fallen angel, "prince of the world" (John 12:31) and even "god of this world" (2 Cor. 4:4). In *Paradise Lost* Milton, following late Jewish sources, makes Satan the monarch of hell, who rules all of the fallen angels. His chief lords, all derived from Near Eastern mythology, are Beelzebub, Chemos, Thammuz, Dagon, Rimmon, and Belial. Satan's character, as portrayed by Milton, is one of daring and ambition and has inspired some critics to say that Satan is the hero of *Paradise Lost*.

In one medieval tale, however, Satan is less proud or heroic. A man named Theophilus gives to Satan a sealed parchment in which he promises to renounce God, the Virgin Mary, and all of the Church in exchange for gold. Satan accepts the offer, and Theophilus becomes rich. Then, realizing what a terrible bargain he has made with Satan, Theophilus runs to a statue of the Virgin and begs her to intercede for him. The Virgin steps down from the pedestal and places the baby Jesus on the floor. She then asks Jesus to help the man, but the child remains mute. Finally, Jesus says, "Why, Mother dear, do you beg so much for this stinking body of a man?" The Virgin insists, however, and Satan is called up from hell to restore the sealed parchment. The Virgin then gives the letter to Theophilus and returns to her pedestal. William Blake's portrayal of Satan in his illustrations for Milton's *Paradise Lost* and the biblical Book of Job are well known. In music, Ralph Vaughn Williams's ballet *Job*, inspired by Blake's illustrations, portrays Satan.

See also: BEELZEBUB; BELIAL; JOB; MEPHISTOPHELES; VIRGIN MARY

2650

**Sati** (Suttee) (the good woman)    In Hindu mythology, a form of the great goddess, Devi. *Sati* is also the word used to refer to a widow who, in a practice now outlawed, throws herself on her husband's funeral pyre.

See also: DEVI

2651

**Saturn** (Saturnus) (the seed-sower)    In Roman mythology, ancient Italian god of harvest and seedtime; husband of Rhea; father of Jupiter; identified by the Romans with the Greek Cronus. Saturn's reign was regarded as the Golden Age. His temple, consecrated in 497 B.C.E., was at the foot of the Capitoline Hill in Rome, and under it was the Roman treasury. Throughout the year, except for his festival, his statue had woolen ribbons wound around its feet. People offered sacrifices to Saturn, especially during the Saturnalia (December 17–23), which was a festival of great mirth and which eventually was replaced by Christmas. During the festival, people exchanged presents, in particular wax tapers and dolls. They played many games, one of the most popular being a game for nuts, symbol of fruitfulness. In English literature, Chaucer, Shakespeare, Spenser, and Keats all write about Saturn. Gustav Holst's symphonic suite *The Planets* also pictures Saturn.

See also: GOLDEN AGE

2652

**Satyrs**    In Greek mythology, creatures of the hills and woods, half-men, half-animal; followers of Dionysus and Pan. Noted for their love of wine, women, and nymphs, they were called by the moralistic Hesiod "good for nothing." In Roman art they appear with goat legs and horns, and were later identified by the Christians with the devil because of their noted sexual appetites. Satyrs appear in Euripides' *Cyclops*, Ovid's *Fasti* (book 3), and Spenser's *Faerie Queene* (I.vi.18). In art Rubens painted a *Nymphs and Satyrs*, while satyrs appear in Botticelli's *Venus and Mars* and Michelangelo's statue *Bacchus*.

See also: DIONYSUS; HESIOD; NYMPHS; OVID; PAN

2653

**Saul** (desired)    11th century B.C.E. In the Bible, O.T., the first king of Israel, anointed by Samuel when the people demanded a king. His legend is

*Saul*

told in 1 Samuel (9–31). Saul was the son of Kish, a Benjamite. He was chosen by Samuel because "from his shoulders and upward he was higher than any of the people." He proved himself in battle against the invading Ammonites and Philistines, but he fell out with Samuel, usurping Samuel's priestly functions and acting as priest-king. Samuel then secretly anointed David to be Saul's successor. Saul became melancholy because Yahweh, the Hebrew god, sent him an evil spirit to torment him. Saul turned against David when he heard people saying that "Saul hath slain his thousands, and David his ten thousands." Open hostilities broke out between David and Saul during the war with the Philistines. Jonathan, Saul's son, sided with David in the dispute. The night before the last battle, Saul consulted the Witch of Endor, calling up the spirit of the dead Samuel, who told him he would die the next day in battle. The Philistines beheaded him and his sons, nailing their bodies to the walls of the temple of Ashtaroth.

William Blake's *The Witch of Endor Summoning the Shade of Samuel for Saul*, Handel's oratorio *Saul*, and Robert Browning's dramatic monologue *Saul* all deal with the legend. Rembrandt's *Saul* portrays Saul grasping a javelin while the young David plays a harp to assuage Saul's melancholy. Saul was also the name of St. Paul before his conversion to Christianity. In Islam Saul is called Talut.

See also: DAVID; JONATHAN; PAUL, ST.; SAMUEL; WITCH OF ENDOR; YAHWEH

**Savitri** (descended from the sun)   In Hindu mythology, a name given to a heroine who brought back her husband from the dead; also a name for the sun and for the daughter and wife of Brahma, as well as an alternate name for Gayatri, the sacred verse used daily by devout Brahmans.

The legend of Savitri is told in the epic poem *The Mahabharata*. It was popularized among English-speaking peoples in the last century by Edwin Arnold's verse translation of the episode *Savitri, or Love and Death*. Savitri was the daughter of King Aswa-pati and was in love with Satyavan, whom she wanted to marry. She was told by a holy man, however, that when she married her husband would die within the year. Nevertheless, she married Satyavan. One day when Satyavan went out to cut wood, she followed him and saw him fall. Standing nearby was Yama, the god of death. Yama told Savitri he had come to take her husband to the land of the dead. Savitri pleaded with Yama, and the god relented, restoring Satyavan to Savitri. The tale was used as the basis for a chamber opera, *Savitri*, by Gustav Holst.

See also: BRAHMA; *MAHABHARATA, THE*; YAMA

**Scaevola, Gaius Mucius**   In Roman history and legend, head of the Mucius family in Rome. Livy's *History of Rome* tells of how he went to the camp of Lars Porsenna, an Etruscan chieftain, and, after failing to kill him, laid his right hand on a burning altar to show his strength and fortitude; this was supposedly the origin of his cognomen *Scaevola*, left-handed. The scene was painted by Tiepolo and Mantegna.

See also: LIVY

**Schildburg**   In Germanic folklore, a city whose residents acquired a reputation for being fools. One tale tells how they built a house without windows and tried to carry the sunlight in.

Their legend is told in a 16th-century work, *The History of the Schildburgers*. The stories are related to a real city in Germany named Schilda or Schildau. In modern Germany someone who behaves foolishly is still called a *Schildbürger*.

2657

**Scipio Africanus Major, Publius Cornelius** 236–184 B.C.E. In Roman history and legend, hero of the Second Punic War against Hannibal, whom he defeated at the battle of Zama in 202 B.C.E. Livy's *History of Rome* (book 26) tells the legend of Scipio being offered a beautiful captive woman as a slave and refusing her, restoring her to the young man she had been pledged to marry. This legend has often been painted under the title *Continence of Scipio*. Giulio Romano did a series of tapestries with that title. Poussin's and Mantegna's paintings of the subject are called *Triumph of Scipio*. Scipio Africanus also appears in Cicero's *Republic* (book 6) in the famous *Somnium Scipionis* (Scipio's Dream) episode. In the dream the hero appears to his grandson and explains the nature of the universe, including Pythagoras's theories of the transmigration of souls and of immortality. The dream influenced *Consolation of Philosophy* by Boethius, who in turn influenced the medieval author of the *Roman de la Rose*; Chaucer's *Parliament of Fowls*; Shakespeare's *Troilus and Cressida* and one of Lorenzo's speeches in *The Merchant of Venice*, beginning "There's not the smallest orb which thou behold'st / But in his motion like an angel sings"; and Milton's *Hymn on the Morning of Christ's Nativity*.

See also: LIVY

2658

**Scorpion**    An arachnid with a long, narrow tail that ends in a venomous sting. Scorpio is the eighth sign of the Zodiac. In Egyptian mythology, the scorpion was an attribute of the evil god Set but was also a protector of the dead. Seven scorpions accompanied Isis on her search for her dead husband, Osiris. In one Egyptian myth Set, in the form of a scorpion, attempts to kill Horus, the son of Isis and Osiris, but the gods restore Horus to life. In European folklore the scorpion is a symbol of evil and treachery. Jesus (Luke 10:19) gives his disciples authority and power over scorpions, which symbolized all that opposed God's rule and kingdom. Medieval symbolism chose the creature, therefore, as a sign of both Judas, the archbetrayer of Jesus, and the Jews, whom medieval Christians persecuted.

See also: HORUS; ISIS; JUDAS; OSISRIS; SET; ZODICA

2659

**Scylla and Charybdis** (she who rends and sucker down)    In Greek mythology, sea monsters. Scylla, according to most accounts, was a daughter of Phorcys and Ceto, and Charybdis a daughter of Poseidon and Gaea. Originally Scylla was a beautiful nymph loved by Glaucus, a man who was transformed into a god. Scylla, however, rejected his love and went to Circe for a magic drug to get rid of Glaucus's romantic attachment. Instead Circe fell in love with Glaucus, who rejected her. So Circe poisoned the water in which Scylla bathed, and the nymph was transformed into a sea monster that devoured ships and men. Opposite Scylla, who was located in the Strait of Messina, between Sicily and Italy, was Charybdis. She also once had another form, that of a woman, but she had a tremendous appetite. Zeus transformed her into a monster who swallowed as much water as she could hold, then spewed it out. Sailors passing between the two monsters had to avoid being eaten by the six ravenous dogs' heads of Scylla or drowning in the whirlpool of Charybdis. The expression "between Scylla and Charybdis" has come to mean that in avoiding one evil, we fall upon an even greater one. Homer's *Odyssey* (book 11), Vergil's *Aeneid* (book 3), Ovid's *Metamorphoses* (book 13), and Spenser's *Faerie Queene* (2.12.9) cite Scylla and Charybdis.

See also: *AENEID, THE*; GAEA; GLAUCUS; *ODYSSEY, THE*; POSEIDON; ZEUS

## Sebald, St. (Seward, Siward, Sigward) Eighth

**2660**

**Sebald, St.** (Seward, Siward, Sigward)  Eighth century. In Christian legend, patron of Nuremberg, Germany. Invoked against cold weather. Feast, 19 August.

Sebald was the son of a Danish king. He left England with St. Boniface to convert the Germans. He traveled through the north of Germany, preaching as a missionary, and settled at last in Nuremberg. Living in a cell not far from the city, he would go there daily to teach the poor, and he was in the habit of stopping on his way at a hut owned by a cartwright. One day when it was very cold he found the family nearly frozen to death in the hut because they had no fuel. Sebald told them to bring him the icicles that hung from the roof, and he used them as fuel for the fire as if they were pieces of wood. Another day Sebald wanted a fish to eat (it was a meatless day), and he sent the same cartwright to buy one in the city. The lord of Nuremberg had an edict that no one was to buy fish until his castle storehouse was supplied. As punishment for having broken the edict, the cartwright was blinded by the soldiers of the lord. St. Sebald restored his sight. His church, the Sebaldskirche in Nuremberg, was begun in 1508 and finished in 1523; it contains a statue of the saint by Peter Vischer that shows St. Sebald as an elderly pilgrim warming his feet at a fire made of icicles. Usually, as in the woodcuts of Albrecht Dürer, he is shown holding the Sebaldskirche, his church, with two towers.

See also: BONIFACE, ST.

**2661**

**Sebastian, Don**  1554–1578. In Portuguese history and legend, king killed in the battle of Alcazar who, according to legend, was not killed but was spirited away to safety and will return to help Portugal in time of need. After his death various pretenders to the throne appeared. John Dryden's tragedy *Don Sebastian, King of Portugal* takes up the legend.

See also: BARBAROSSA

**2662**

**Sebastian, St.** (man from Sebastia, a city in Asia Minor)  Third century. In Christian legend, patron of armorers, bookbinders, burial societies, arrowsmiths, corn chandlers, gardeners, ironmongers, lead founders, needle makers, potters, racquet makers, and stonemasons. Invoked against cattle pest, epilepsy, enemies of religion, plague, and by the dying. Feast, 20 January.

The legend of St. Sebastian dates from the first centuries of Christianity. He was descended from a noble family and, as commander of a company of the Praetorian Guards, was very close to the emperor Diocletian. When it was discovered that Sebastian was a Christian, the emperor asked him to renounce his faith, but Sebastian refused. Then, as *The Golden Legend*, written in the 13th century, tells the tale:

Diocletian was much angry and wroth, and commanded him to be led to the field and there to be bounden to a stake for to be shot at. And the archers shot at him till he was full of arrows as an urchin is full of pricks, and thus left him there for dead. The night after came a Christian woman [St. Irene] for to take his body and to bury it, but she found him alive and brought him to her house, and took charge of him till he was all whole.

With his health restored Sebastian "stood upon a step where the emperor should pass by" and told him to renounce his gods, but Diocletian had him arrested again, "brought into prison into his palace," and stoned to death. St. Sebastian's association with arrows and pestilence betrays him as being a Christian variation of the Greek god Apollo, who was also invoked against plague, which he sent by arrows, as shown in Homer's *Iliad*. In art St. Sebastian is always portrayed as a young man, which gave artists an opportunity to display the naked form without the Church banning the picture as obscene. St. Sebastian is a favorite subject, therefore, with Italian Renaissance painters such as Botticelli, Lotto, Caravaggio, and Mantegna.

Perhaps one of the most moving works, however, is by the French artist Georges de la Tour, showing St. Irene tending the wounded body with two female attendants.

See also: APOLLO; *GOLDEN LEGEND, THE*; *ILLIAD*

*Sebek*

2663
**Sebek** (Sebeq, Suchos, Sobek, Sebak)   In Egyptian mythology, the crocodile god, called Suchos by the Greeks. In Egyptian art Sebek is portrayed as a crocodile-headed man, wearing either a solar disk encircled by a uraeus or a pair of ram's horns surmounted by a disk and a pair of plumes. Frequently, however, the god appears simply as a crocodile. Sometimes Sebek is combined with the sun god Ra to form the composite god Sebek-Ra.

See also: CROCODILE; RA; URAEUS

2664
**Sedna**   In Eskimo mythology, great goddess, queen of Adlivun (those beneath us), the land of the dead under the sea; she is also called Avilayoq, Nuliajuk, Nerrivik, and Arnarquagssaq.

In one myth Sedna was once a beautiful girl who was wooed by many suitors, but she rejected all of them. Once a fulmar (an arctic bird of the petrel family) flew over the ice and sang to her: "Come to me, come into the land of the birds, where there is never hunger, where my tent is made of the most beautiful skins. You shall rest on soft bearskins. My fellows, the fulmars, shall bring you all your heart desires; their feathers shall clothe you; your lamp shall always be filled with oil, your pot with meat."

Sedna listened to the fulmar and decided to become his wife. She discovered, however, that he had lied to her and did not possess all of the things he claimed. In a year her father came to visit her, and she told him she wanted to go home. Angry that his daughter had been mistreated, he killed the fulmar and took Sedna away in his boat. The fulmars, companions of the murdered bird, followed the fleeing couple. A storm arose, threatening to kill both of them. Sedna's father decided to offer Sedna to the birds as a sacrifice. He flung her overboard, but she clung to the boat, The cruel father then cut off the first joints of her fingers. Falling into the sea, the finger joints were transformed into whales, the nails turning into whalebones. The second finger joints fell on the sharp knife and swam away as seals. When the father cut off the stumps of her fingers they became ground seals.

In the meantime the storm subsided, and the fulmars believed Sedna had been drowned. The father then allowed her to come back into the boat. But Sedna now hated her father. One night she called her dogs and had them gnaw off his feet and hands while he slept. When he awoke he cursed himself, Sedna, and the dogs. Suddenly, the earth opened and swallowed the hut, father, Sedna, and the dogs. Ever since, Sedna has reigned as queen of Adlivun, the land of the dead in the sea and has been hostile to humans.

In a variant myth Sedna refused all suitors except a dog or a bird. Her enraged parents cast Sedna, fingerless, into the sea, where she now reigns as queen of the dead. Another variant says

Sedna was a girl who ate so much that her parents were in despair. Once she even started to eat their arms and legs. They awoke and threw her into the sea, first cutting off her fingers.

As goddess of sea creatures, Sedna is invoked for success in hunting. When taboos are broken, the shaman is called and goes into a trance, during which it is believed that his spirit flies to Sedna's land, where he attempts to appease the goddess's anger.

When the Danish explorer Knud Rasmussen asked one Eskimo about the goddess he was told: "We do not believe, we only fear. And most of all we fear Nuliajuk [Sedna]. . . . Nuliajuk is the name we give to the Mother of Beasts. All the game we have comes from her; from her comes all the caribou, all the foxes, the birds and fishes."

See also: GREAT GODDESS; MAIDEN WITHOUT HANDS

**2665**
**Seid** In Norse mythology a form of magic or divination, frequently associated with Odin, but also as practiced by women. The *Prose Edda* gives a description of seid as practiced by Odin:

Odin knew that art called seid, which the greatest power accompanied, and he carried it out himself. Through it he could determine the fates of men and things yet to happen, and also arrange death or bad luck or ill health for people, and take the mind or strength of people and give it to others.

Gullveig and Freyja practiced seid, and it may have been Freyja who brought seid to the Aesir, perhaps causing the Aesir-Vanir War. In one saga, famine has overcome a certain region, and a woman practicing seid is asked to forecast its duration. She climbs on a platform, sings songs, and makes contacts with the spirits. She predicts a quick end to the famine and a prosperous future for those suffering.

See also: AESIR-VANIR WAR; FREYJA; *PROSE EDDA*

**2666**
**Seker** (Sacharis, Seger, Sokar, Solare, Sokaris) In Egyptian mythology, death god of the necropolis of Memphis. Originally, Seker may have been a vegetation god. Later he was combined with Osiris, the god of the dead. The two were also combined with the craft god Ptah to form the god Ptah-Seker-Osiris. Ptah provided new bodies in which the souls of the righteous were to live, thus symbolizing the addition of creative power (Ptah) to death (Seker and Osiris). Egyptian art usually portrayed Seker as a hawk-headed mummy.

See also: OSIRIS; PTAH

**2667**
**Sekhet-Aaru** (field of the reeds) In Egyptian mythology, a paradise, the name originally given to the island of the delta where the blessed souls of the dead lived and saw the sun god Ra each day. The land was filled with wheat as high as five cubits and barley as high as seven.

See also: RA

**2668**
**Selene** (moon) In Greek mythology, ancient moon goddess; daughter of the Titan Hyperion and Theia; sister of Helios and Eos. Selene was a beautiful woman with long wings and a golden diadem that shed a mild light. She rode in a chariot drawn by two white horses. In later Greek and Roman mythology Selene was identified with Artemis, Luna, Hecate, and Persephone. Selene was also known by her epithet, Phoebe (bright moon). She appears riding in her chariot on the east pediment of the Parthenon.

See also: ARTEMIS; HECATE; HELIOS; HYPERION; LUNA; PERSEPHONE; TITANS

**2669**
**Semargl** (family, barley) In Slavic mythology, god of the family and of barley; worshiped among the Russians. He appears in *The Lay of Igor's Army*, and some scholars believe him to

have been invented by the author of that work. There is some disagreement as to whether Semargl is one god or two (known as Sem and Rgl).

See also: *LAY OF IGOR'S ARMY, THE*

**2670**

**Semele**   In Greek mythology, daughter of Cadmus, king of Thebes, and Harmonia, mother of Dionysus by Zeus. Zeus fell in love with Semele and often visited her. Hera, ever jealous of her husband's escapades, took the form of Semele's nurse, Beroe, and convinced the girl to ask Zeus to show himself to her in all his godlike splendor. Zeus agreed to Semele's wish and appeared amid thunder and lightning. Semele was consumed by flames. Before she died she gave birth to a six month's child, Dionysus, whom Zeus saved from the flames and hid in his thigh until it was time for the child to be born. When Dionysus was born he raised his dead mother and placed her in the heavens under the name Thyone. Semele is believed to be a form of Selene or Zemelo, a Phrygian earth goddess. She is cited in Homer's *Iliad* (book 14), Euripides' *The Bacchae*, and Ovid's *Metamorphoses* (book 3) and appears in Handel's secular oratorio *Semele* (1744). *Jupiter and Semele* was painted by Tintoretto.

See also: DIONYSUS; HERA; *ILIAD, THE;* OVID

**2671**

**Semiramis**   In Near Eastern mythology, queen of Assyria; daughter of the goddess Derceto. Semiramis is known chiefly as the murderer of her second husband, King Ninus of Assyria, as well as the builder of many great cities. As a murderess she appears in Rossini's opera *Semiramide* (1823). She was famous for her beauty and wealth.

**2672**

**Semones** (sowers)   In Roman mythology, a name for lesser gods and goddesses, such as Pan, Janus and Priapus, as well as deified heroes.

See also: JANUS; PAN; PRIAPUS

**2673**

**Seng-don-ma**   In Tibetan Buddhism, a woman, often portrayed with the face of a lion, who stamps out human ignorance.

**2674**

**Sennacherib**   (Sin, the mood god, has compensated me for [the loss of my] brothers) 704–681 B.C.E. In Near Eastern history and legend, king of Assyria who captured and destroyed Babylon. He conquered Jerusalem during the days of Hezekiah, but at night, according to the Old Testament (2 Kings 19:35), "the angel of the Lord went out, and smote in the camp the Assyrians an hundred four-score and five thousand." Lord Byron's poem *The Destruction of Sennacherib* was set for chorus and orchestra by Modest Mussorgsky.

**2675**

**Sennadius, Dream of**   In Christian legend, a dream recorded by St. Augustine in one of his epistles to prove that man has two natures.

Sennadius was a physician who did not believe in the duality of man's nature and consequently in a future life. One night an angel appeared to him in a dream and asked him to follow. The angel took Sennadius to the confines of a city, where he was "ravished with celestial music" that the angel told him came from the voices of perfect spirits. Sennadius thought no more about the dream when he awoke. Sometime afterward the angel appeared to him again, recalled to him the memory of the former visit, and then asked him if the vision had occurred while Sennadius was awake or during sleep. Sennadius replied, "During sleep."

"Just so," said the angel. "What you saw and heard was not by your bodily senses then, for your eyes and ears were closed in sleep."

"True," said the physician.

"Then," continued the angel, "with what eyes did you see, and with what ears did your hear?"

Sennadius could not answer. The angel said, "It must be evident, if you see when your bodily eyes are shut and hear when your bodily ears are closed in sleep, that you must have other eyes and ears beside those of your material body. When, therefore, your body sleeps, that other something may be awake. When your body dies, that other something may live on."

See also: AUGUSTINE, ST.

**Seraphim** (Seraph, singular) (burning, glowing) 2676

In the Bible, O.T.,the highest of the nine choirs of angels, stemming from demonic spirits in Babylonian mythology. When the prophet Isaiah (Isa. 6:2–3) describes the throne of Yahweh, the Hebrew god, he says that above it "stood the seraphims: each one had six wings; with twain he covered his face, and with twain he covered his feet, and with twain he did fly. And one cried unto another and said, Holy, holy, holy is the Lord of hosts: the whole earth is full of his glory." Isaiah's seraphim, from the root "to burn," are believed to come from the "fiery serpents" mentioned in Numbers (21:6). From early Christian times, however, the seraphim were made into a category of angels and are mentioned in the Preface to the Roman Mass as well as in the great hymn Te Deum, composed by Niceta of Remesiana, where they repeat the phrase from Isaiah.

See also: CHERUBIM; ISIAH; YAHWEH

**Serapion the Sinonite, St.** (ardent?)    Fourth 2677

century. In Christian legend, a saint known for his generosity not only in giving away his goods to the poor but in selling himself several times for the benefit of the poor. Feast, 2 March.

The first time, according to Alban Butler's account in his *Lives of the Saints*, he sold himself to a comedian for 20 pieces of silver. The comedian was a pagan, but Serapion converted him to Christianity and also persuaded him to leave the stage (considered an evil profession by the early Church). The comedian freed Serapion and offered him 20 pieces of silver, which the saint

refused. Next he sold himself to relieve a poor widow. After having stayed with his master for the allotted time he was again given his liberty as well as a cloak, a tunic, an undergarment, and a copy of the Gospels. He had "scarce gone from the door, when he gave his cloak to one poor man, and his tunic to another." A stranger came up and asked him why he was out in the cold without a cloak. Had he been robbed? Who caused his condition? "This book," replied Serapion, showing the stranger the Gospels. The rest of his life was devoted to selling himself to help the poor. Serapion "at length died in Egypt, in a desert, at the age of sixty years."

**Serapis**    In Egyptian mythology, Greek name 2678

for the composite god made up of the god Osiris, called Ser in Egyptian, and the sacred bull of Memphis, Apis. The date of the introduction of the cult of Serapis is disputed by scholars. Some believe it was the artificial creation of either Ptolemy I or Ptolemy II, who used the cult of Serapis in an attempt to blend the existing Egyptian concepts with those of the Greeks who settled in Egypt after the conquest by Alexander the Great. It was an attempt to give both segments of the population a common religious heritage. Serapis was worshiped by Greeks, Romans, and Egyptians at a common shrine. In the Roman Empire his worship, along with that of Isis, rivaled all other Mediterranean cults. In art Serapis was portrayed as a bull-headed man wearing a solar disk and the uraeus between his horns and holding symbols associated with Osiris.

See also: ALEXANDER THE GREAT; APIS; ISIS; OSIRIS; URAEUS

**Serpent and the File, The**    Aesopic fable 2679

found in various collections throughout the world.

In the course of its wanderings a serpent came into an armorer's shop. As he glided over the floor, he felt his skin pricked by a file lying there.

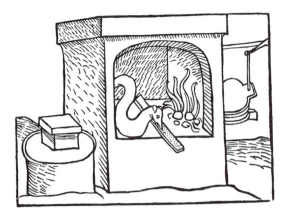

*The Serpent and the File*

In a rage he turned on it and tried to dart his fangs into it. However, he could do no harm to the heavy iron and gave up his anger.

Moral: *It's useless to attack the insensible.*

The fable is told in the Arabic fables of Lôqman. In his version, however, the snake's part is taken by a cat. R. L. Stevenson quotes the fable in his novel *The Master of Ballantrae*.

See also: AESOPIC FABLES

2680

**Serqet** (Selket, Selqet, Selquet)   In Egyptian mythology, scorpion goddess. Serqet protected the body of the dead. She was often seen on the walls of tombs with winged arms outstretched in a protective gesture. She was believed to have special province over the entrails of the deceased. Serqet was a companion of the goddess Isis in her wanderings, and it was said that those who worshiped Isis were never stung by a scorpion. Egyptian art portrays Serqet as a woman with a scorpion on her head or as a scorpion with the head of a woman.

See also: ISIS; SCORPION

2681

**Set** (Seth, Sethi, Sit, Sut, Sutekh)   In Egyptian mythology, the evil god; brother of Osiris, Isis, and Nephthys; called Typhon by the Greeks. He murdered his brother, Osiris, who was avenged by Horus, the son of Osiris. Seth frequently serves as a catalyst, his thoughtless actions leading to favorable outcomes, such as Osiris becoming the ruler of the underworld. He was associated with the dangerous aspects of the desert, sandstorms, and flash floods.

The worship of Set was one of the oldest cults of Egypt. Originally, he was a beneficent god of Upper Egypt, whose realm was the abode of the blessed dead, where he performed friendly offices for the deceased. When the followers of Horus (the elder), the supreme god of Lower Egypt, conquered the followers of Set, Set's place in the Egyptian pantheon of gods fell into disrepute, and eventually the priests of Horus declared Set a god of the unclean, an enemy of all other gods, and ordered all of his images destroyed.

Set was the archenemy of the sun god, and almost all allusions and legends pertaining to him reflect the battles he waged against the sun. In the earliest and simplest form of the myth, Set represented the cosmic opposition of darkness and light. In a later form of the myth, Set is the antagonist of the sun god Ra and seeks, in the form of the monstrous serpent Apophis, to prevent him from appearing in the east daily. The result was always the same. Apophis would be annihilated by the burning heat of Ra, and Set, who

*Set*

could renew himself daily, would collect his noxious cohort and ready himself for the next night's battle against the sunrise.

In the most famous and complex version of the myth, Set is the murderer and dismemberer of his brother, Osiris, who was sometimes called his twin brother. He pursued and persecuted Osiris's widow, Isis, who was also his own sister. He also persecuted Isis and Osiris's child Horus. Later Horus was called on to avenge his father's death, and in a series of battles he defeated Set and would have destroyed him if it had not been for the interference of Isis, who took pity on her brother and spared him.

The Egyptians viewed the battle between Set and Horus as the ultimate victory of good over evil. Yet according to some interpretations, in the sphere of the eternal, where there is no duality, Set and Horus are one; that is, death and life, darkness and light are one. In Egyptian religion this has been referred to as "the secret of the two partners," reflecting the hidden understanding of the two combatant gods. Set, representing strife, is perennially subdued but never destroyed by Horus, representing peace. In the end there is reconciliation. The pharaoh who was sometimes known as the Two Lords was identified with both of these gods as an inseparable pair.

As the great antagonist of light, Set was frequently symbolized by the black boar, whose emblem was the primeval knife, the instrument of dismemberment and death. His female counterpart was his sister Nephthys, who was herself a goddess of darkness and decay.

In Egyptian art Set is usually portrayed as a man with the head of a fantastic beast with pointed muzzle and high, square ears. This unidentifiable beast has been commonly called the Typhonian animal, Typhon being the god with whom the Greeks identified Set. Sometimes Set is portrayed with horns, which made him the ideal image for the devil in Egyptian Christianity. Other animals associated with Set were the antelope, the crocodile, and the ass.

Set was sometimes said to have a mane of red hair, and Plutarch writes in *Isis and Osiris* that an ass was thrown down a precipice because the animal bore a resemblance to Set in its redness. Persons who had red complexions were often treated ignominiously.

See also: ANTELOPE; APOPHIS; ASS; CROCODILE; HORUS; ISIS; MUMMY; NEPHTHYS; OSIRIS; TWO BROTHERS, TALE OF; TYPHON

**Seven Kings of Rome**  2682  In Roman history and legend, they are Romulus, Numa Pompilius, Tullus Hostilius, Ancus Martius, Tarquinius Priscus, Servius Tullius, and Tarquinius Superbus.

**Seven Sages of Greece**  2683  In Greek history and legend, seven men noted for their wisdom. They are Thales of Miletus (seventh century B.C.E.), who believed the material basis for the world was water and was noted for his absentmindedness, as when he fell down a well while not paying attention; Solon of Athens (c. 640–c. 560 B.C.E.), a lawmaker noted for his remark to Croesus, whom he met in Lydia, that no man could be said to have lived a happy life until he was dead; Bias of Priene; Chilo Sparta, who brought back the bones of Orestes; Cleobulus of Rhodes; Periander of Corinth (c. 625–585 B.C.E.), patron of the arts who dedicated the Chest of Cypselus at Olympia, which was decorated with gold and ivory reliefs of scenes from Greek mythology, his court being the setting of Plutarch's *Symposium of the Seven Sages*; and Pittacus of Mytilene (c. 650–570 B.C.E.), a moderate democratic reformer.

See also: ORESTES

**Seven Sleepers of Ephesus, The**  2684  Legend in both Christian and Islamic folklore. In Islamic folklore the seven are called *Ashab al-Kahf* (the people of the cave). They are seven youths who fled to a cave to escape the Decian persecution

(250) for being Christian. They fell asleep, awoke some 200 years later, and died.

St. Gregory of Tours, writing in *De Gloria Martyrum* in the sixth century, gives one Christian version of the legend. According to his account, seven noble youths in the household of the emperor Decian fled the court when the emperor began to persecute Christians. They entered a cave and fell asleep. Some 230 years later the cave was opened, and the youths awoke; they died soon afterward. Their bodies were buried in a large coffin in St. Victor's Church in Marseilles. Their names were Constantine, Dionysius, John, Maximian, Malchus, Martinian, and Serapion.

The Islamic account is found in the Koran (Sura 18) and differs from the Christian account. In it a dog, Katmir, not directly named in the sacred text, "lay . . . with paws outstretched" outside the entry to the cave. (Katmir is one of the 10 animals admitted to Paradise in Islamic belief.) After 309 years the sleepers awoke and sent one of their number into the town to buy bread. As to what happened later the Koran is silent, though various other Islamic accounts fill in the gaps in the tale.

Goethe's poem *The Seven Sleepers of Ephesus* combines both Christian and Islamic accounts, ending with the eight of them (Goethe counts the dog):

Thenceforth from the world were sundered.
The most blessed Angel Gabriel
By the will of God Almighty,
Walling up the cave for ever, Led them unto
    Paradise.

The Koranic account of the legend was used by Taufig al-Hakim in his play *Ashab al-Kahf*. The legend seems to have arisen from taking the expression "fell asleep in the Lord" literally, and not, as was meant, having died. Though many Christian writers through the ages have dismissed the legend, the Feast of the Seven Sleepers is celebrated on 27 July.

The number seven is associated with other medieval "sleepers." Every seven years Barbarossa turns over and Ogier the Dane thunders with his mace on the floor, and Tannhäuser spent seven years beneath the earth in magical enthrallment.

See also: KORAN, THE

2685
**Seven Wonders of the World**    In the ancient Greco-Roman world they were the Pyramids of Egypt, the Hanging Gardens of Babylon, the Tomb of Mausolus, the Temple of Diana of Ephesus (Artemision), the Colossus of Rhodes, the Statue of Zeus by Phidias, and the Tower of Pharos at Alexandria. During the Christian Middle Ages another seven were added. They were the Coliseum (amphitheater) of Rome, the Catacombs of Alexandria, the Great Wall of China, Stonehenge, the Leaning Tower of Pisa, the Porcelain Tower of Nankin, and the Mosque of St. Sophia at Constantinople (now museum of Hagia Sophia at Istanbul).

See also: COLOSSUS OF RHODES; DIANA; ZEUS

2686
**Shahapet**    In Armenian mythology, serpent spirit that appeared as both a man and a serpent. Generally, the Shahapet, who often inhabited vine stocks and olive trees, was a beneficent spirit unless angered. Agathangelos, the Christian historian of Armenia in ancient times, calls Christ the Shahapet of the graveyards.

2687
***Shah Namah*** (book of kings)    Persian epic poem by Firdusi, completed in 1010, narrating the mythical and legendary history of Iran from the days of Gayomart, its first king, to the fall of the Sassanian dynasty in 641 C.E. under the impact of Islam. The epic consists of more than 50,000 couplets, divided into 50 chapters.

Firdusi based his poem on various collections of Persian history and lore. Yezdjird, the last Sassanian king, had collected all of the histories and traditions connected with Persia and had them bound into a book known as *Bustan-Namah*. After the Islamic conquest of Persia, additional material was added to the book, bringing it up to the death of Yezdjird. Mahmud of Ghazna (997–1030), the king of Persia, wished the prose chronicle to be turned into a verse epic. From it he selected seven tales, which he distributed among seven poets of the court, so that he might pick which was to complete the massive work.

Dagiqi, a poet, was given the tale of Rustum and Sohrab, two of the main heroes in the work. The king was so pleased with the poet's treatment of the tale that Dagiqi was commissioned to complete the work. In the meantime Dagiqi had introduced another poet, Abu'l-Qasim Mansur, to the court, and he so captivated the king that the king changed the poet's name to Firdusi (paradise). The legend relates that the king said, "You have made my court as resplendent as *firdusi*."

Dagiqi died in 980, and the task of completing the epic was given to Firdusi. He was promised 1,000 gold pieces for every 1,000 couplets of the work. Firdusi refused payment until the work was completed. When it was completed, the king's prime minister, Hasan Meymendi, a conceited favorite of the king who hated the poet, had silver substituted for the gold. According to legend, Firdusi gave away one-third of the silver payment to the slave who brought it.

"The sultan shall know," he said, "that I did not bestow the labor of 30 years on a work to be rewarded by silver."

In his anger the poet wrote an insulting poem against the king and then, thinking it best to move, fled his city. He finally died in Tus.

Again according to legend, when the king ultimately discovered what his prime minister had done, changing the gold payment for a silver one, he had the gold sent, but it was too late; the poet had died. The money was finally used by the family to build a stone embankment in the city of Firdusi, a dream he had held all his life.

Among the heroes treated in the epic are Bahram Gur, the hero king and the "great hunter"; Jemshid, a culture hero and proud king; Faridun, the hero who defeats the evil king Zahhak; Gayomart, the first king and primeval man; Husheng, a king, culture hero, and discoverer of fire; Kavah, a blacksmith who refused to sacrifice his children to the evil Zahhak; Minuchihr, a hero king who came to the throne on the death of the great hero Faridun; Mirtas, the good king who was the father of Zahhak, the evil king; Rustum, the great hero of the poem, father of Sohrab, whom he accidentally killed in battle; Tahumers, a king who was a slayer of demons; and Zal.

See also: BAHRAM GUR; *BUSTAN, THE*; GAYOMART; HUSHENG; JEMSHID; KAVAH; MINUCHIHR; SOHRAB; THAUMERS; ZAHHAK; ZAL

**2688**
**Shaitans** (sayatin)    In Islamic mythology, evil spirits more dangerous than the djinn. Allah created Al-Shaitan, perhaps another name for Iblis, the devil, who then produced eggs from which other demons were hatched. In a variant myth Allah not only created Al-Shaitan but a wife for him, who then produced three eggs as their offspring. The children are all ugly, having hoofed feet. Shaitans are even more ugly in their eating habits. They like excrement and other dirt and waste and prefer the shade to sunlight. It is believed that every person has a personal shaitan, or demon, just as he has a personal guardian angel. Sometimes the shaitan is considered the muse of poetic inspiration.

See also: ALLAH; DJINN; IBLIS; MALEC

**2689**
**Shakuntala** (Sakuntala, Sakoontala) (bird protected)    In Hindu mythology, a heroine in love with King Dushyanta.

Shakuntala was born in a forest and lived there on the food supplied to her by birds until she was found by the sage Kanwa. The sage brought her up in his hermitage as his daughter.

One day she was seen by King Dushyanta, who immediately fell in love with her. He wooed her, and she accepted him, not in a marriage but in a simple declaration of mutual love. On leaving her to return to his city, he gave her a ring as a pledge of their love.

When later the sage Dur-vasas came to visit Kanwa, Shakuntala was so absorbed in thoughts about King Dushyanta that she paid little attention to the guest. Dur-vasas became so angry that he cursed Shakuntala, saying she would be forgotten by Dushyanta. Relenting later from the harshness of his curse, Dur-vasas said the curse would be removed as soon as King Dushyanta saw the ring he had give Shakuntala as a token of love. Pregnant, Shakuntala, set off to see King Dushyanta. Before leaving she bathed and lost the ring. When she reached the palace, Dushyanta did not recognize her, fulfilling the curse. She was taken back to the forest, where a son, Bharata, was born. Later the ring was found in a fish by a fisherman and brought to the king. He recognized it and then accepted Shakuntala and his son.

Shakuntala forms the basis for the best-known play by the Indian playwright Kalidasa, titled after the heroine. The work was made known to the English-speaking world through a translation by Sir William Jones in 1789. The German poet Goethe wrote of the drama:

> Wouldst thou the young year's blossoms and
>     the fruits of its decline,
> And all by which the soul is charmed,
>     enraptured, fasted, fed?
> Wouldst thou the earth and heaven itself in
>     one sole name combine?
> I name thee, O Shakuntala, and all at once is
>     said. (Eastwich translation)

See also: BHARATA

2690
**Shamash**    In Near Eastern mythology (Babylonian-Assyrian), sun god, (originally female) god of justice and healing, his consort was the goddess Aa, and his attendants were Kittu (truth) and Mesharu (righteousness). He appears in the epic poem *Gilgamesh* as a friend of the hero. He is portrayed in the relief atop the stele of Hammurabi in the Louvre in Paris as the divine source and justification for the laws that were codified under Hammurabi and given to his subjects to obey. Among his epithets were Babbar (shiner) and Ma-banda-anna (sky ship).

See also: AA; GILGAMESH

2691
**Shamba**    In African legend, the 93rd chief of the Bakongo of Congo. It is not at all clear what the rulers before him were like, but he is said to have been a very wise, peaceful, and innovative man. From childhood he had a great desire to travel. He felt that travel was the best teacher, and over the years he visited many countries. From each place he learned about new things, including embroidery, tobacco, weaving, and a game called Mankala. He forbade the use of lethal weapons, rarely killed anyone, and under all conditions spared the lives of women and children. As a judge he showed great wisdom in both criminal and civil cases. Shamba once rebuked a person for offering hearsay evidence at court, saying that only those who have actually seen something with their own eyes have the right to speak.

2692
**Shango**    In African mythology (Yoruba of southwestern Nigeria), thunder god; husband of Oya, goddess of the Niger River, and Oshun, goddess of the Oshun River. Among his servants were the wind, Afefe, and the rainbow, Oshun Mare.

Shango was once a mortal; he served as fourth king of his people. A powerful ruler, he was feared because of his ability to breathe fire from his mouth. But two of his political aides challenged his authority. Shango tried to have the two men fight with each other, thus diverting their anger from him. He succeeded in having one kill the other, but the victor then turned on Shango, trying to kill him. Shango was forced to flee, along with his wife and faithful followers. They wandered about until they arrived at Koso, where he built a palace. A lightning storm came and destroyed the palace, killing all his wives and children. Shango despaired and hanged himself from a tree. Shango's enemies made fun of his remaining followers, but they continued to honor their dead ruler, praying that fire would consume Shango's enemies. Then their prayers seemed to be answered, for numerous fires began to spread and destroy many houses. Fear gripped Shango's enemies, who now believed he had not died but had disappeared into the woods and later ascended to the sky. A temple was erected in Shango's honor at Koso. Today the ram is sacred to the Yoruba for its bellow, which is said to be the noise of Shango's thunder. Shango is also known as Jakuta (stone thrower) and Oba Koso (the king does not hang), in reference to his death and rebirth.

See also: ESHU; OSHUN

**Shang-Ti** (the emperor above)   In Chinese mythology, a sky god, also worshiped as T'ien (sky or heavenly god). When the Jesuits came to China in the 17th century, they created the term T'ien Chu (heavenly or sky lord) to designate the Christian God.

2693

**Shan T'ao**   283–205 B.C.E. In Chinese legend, one of the seven Chu-lin Ch'i-Hsien (Seven Immortals). He is the patron of rising talent, portrayed as an old man with a staff. In Japanese legend he is called Santo.

See also: CHU-LIN CH'I-HSIEN

2694

**Shape-shifter**   The transformation of the body, from human to animal or from animal to human. This is a common motif in most narra-

2695

tive genres, fables, legends, myths, and epics. In some cases the transformation is an example of metempsychosis, "soul travel," but in most cases the transformation is more literal. By the late Middle Ages, shape-shifting was looked upon as devilish sorcery, but it had not always been that way, as one can see in tale type 301 "The Three Stolen Princesses," in which the hero is of supernatural origin, "the son of a bear." This human/animal relationship has been and still is evident in some names, particularly in the Germanic world. The names Bern, Bernd, Bjarki, Bera, and Björn all are related to the bear, or at least suggest ursine origins. Other examples are Arthur (whose name may have its origin from the Celtic word *airth*, "bear"), or the Old English Beowulf (whose name might be a kenning for Wolf of the Bees). In modern Germany the name Wolfgang is quite common, as are some older names like Arnulf, which like Beowulf may suggest canine affinities. Many of the figures in old Norse sagas have names like *berserkir* (berserks) or *ulfhednar* (wolf-cloak). Animals that indicate or suggest travel were also common, such as birds and marine animals. The werewolf is perhaps the most obvious shape-shifter still known in modern society.

See also: BEOWULF; BERSERK; WEREWOLF

**Shatarupa** (the hundred-formed)   In Hindu mythology, daughter and wife of the god Brahma, goddess of wisdom and science, mother of the sacred Vedas. In Indian art Shatarupa is often portrayed seated on a lotus playing a type of banjo, or with four arms holding a book of palm leaves representing learning; with a string of pearls called Sivamala (Shiva's garland), which serves as a rosary; and with a rose, which she presents to her husband, Brahma. Shatarupa is also known as Savitri (descended from the sun); Sarasvati (flowing), referring to her earlier role as river goddess; Vach (speech), as goddess of speech; Brahami, as wife of Brahma; and Gayatri

2696

(song), the sacred verse recited daily by Brahmans.

See also: BRAHMA; VEDAS

**2697**

***Shayast la-Shavast*** (the proper and improper) A ritual text in Zoroastrian belief, written in Pahlavi, a southwestern dialect of Middle Persian; it deals with sin and impurity and gives details on ceremonies. It often quotes from the sacred book, the *Avesta*, as does the *Denkard*, of which large sections summarize the contents of the *Avesta*.

See also: *AVESTA*; ZARATHUSTRA

**2698**

**Shen** (divine, spirit, god) In Chinese mythology, a shen refers to a divinity, spirit, god, or deified mortal. The Japanese word *Kami* is written with the Chinese character *shen*.

See also: KAMI

**2699**

**Shen Nung** (divine farmer) In Chinese mythology, a culture hero, the ox-headed divine farmer, second of the Five Sovereigns. He taught men the art of agriculture as well as the use of healing drugs, being honored as the god of medicine. Shen Nung is also the god of burning wind. During his reign the people were saved by the intervention of Ch'ih Sung-tzu (red-pine sow), the lord of rain.

See also: SHEN

**2700**

**Sheol** (pit) In the Bible, O.T., the place of the dead, under the earth, translated as hell in the King James Version of the Bible. The Revised Standard Version often uses Sheol or Hades. It is not a place of punishment. All of the dead, good and bad, reside there as shadows.

See also: HADES

**2701**

**Shesha** (remainder) In Hindu mythology, a serpent king of the Nagas. Shesha serves as the couch of Vishnu when the god sleeps during the intervals of creation. At the end of each age Shesha vomits fire, which destroys all creation. He is the son of Kadru, who mothered a thousand powerful many-headed serpents, and brother of Manasa-devi, who has special power in counteracting poison. Shesha is also called Mahoraga (great serpent) or Ananta (endless) as a symbol of eternity. He is sometimes identified with the serpent king Vasuki.

See also: NAGAS; VISHNU

**2702**

**Shichi Fukujin** In Japanese Shinto mythology, the seven gods of good luck and fortune. They are Ebisu, the god of daily food; Daikoku, god of wealth; Bishamon, war god and god of riches; Benten, goddess of love, beauty, music and other arts; Hotei, the so-called "Laughing Buddha"; Jorojin, the god of longevity and wisdom; and Fuku-roku-ju, the god of fortune. All of these gods are borrowed from Chinese mythology.

See also: BENTEN; EBISU; DAIKOKU; HOTEI

**2703**

**Shitenno** In Japanese Buddhist mythology, four heavenly guarding kings who live on the slopes of the cosmic mountain, Sumeru, guarding the four corners of the earth. They are Jigoku, Zocho, Komoku, and Bishamon. The Shitenno are Hindu deities believed to have been converted to Buddhism by the Buddha. According to one Buddhist text, *Golden Light Sutra*, they will protect the territories of Buddhist kings; thus, temples were built for them by the Japanese emperors.

See also: BISHAMON; BUDDHA, THE; JIGOKU

*Shiva*

2704

**Shiva** (Seeva, Siva) (auspicious)   In Hinduism, sometimes regarded as the supreme god and sometimes the third god of the Hindu triad made up of Brahma, the creator; Vishnu, the preserver; and Shiva, the destroyer. Shiva is often identified with the earlier god Rudra mentioned in the Rig-Veda.

Shiva is the god of cosmic destruction. In Hindu mythology, however, the term *destroyer* is understood as meaning that Shiva causes beings to assume new forms of existence. He is, therefore, a re-creator, who is perpetually restoring that which has been destroyed. In this role he is worshiped by his symbol, the *lingam* (phallus) or by the *lingam* and the *yoni* (womb) of his wife Devi, who in some texts is regarded as his *shakti*, or female energy.

In Indian art Shiva is often portrayed as a handsome man with five faces and four arms. He is often seated in yogic posture and has a third eye in the middle of his forehead, contained in or surmounted by a crescent moon. In his role as god of the ascetics his matted locks are often gathered up in a coil that bears the symbol of the Ganges, which he caught as the goddess of the river fell from heaven to earth. He wears a *munda-mala*, necklace of skulls, and serpents twine about his neck in a collar called a *naga-kundala*. Shiva's neck is blue from drinking the deadly poison that would have destroyed the world. In one hand he holds the *trishula* (trident), called Pinaka. He is frequently naked but may wear the skin of a tiger, a deer, or an elephant. The god is often accompanied by his sacred bull, Nandin, chief of Shiva's personal attendants, who carries a staff of office. Nandin is also the guardian of all four quarters of the earth. He is portrayed milky white and is often seen at entrances to temples dedicated to Shiva. Other accessories of Shiva are a bow, Ajagava; a drum, Khatwanga, in the shape of an hour glass; and a club with a skull at the end and a cord for binding offenders.

The German poet Goethe, in his poem "The God and the Bayadere," writes of one of Shiva's appearances on earth:

> Mahadeva (Shiva), Lord of earth,
> For the sixth time comes below
> As a man of mortal birth,—
> Like him, feeling joy and woe.
> Hither loves he to repair,
> And his power behind to leave;
> If to punish or to spare,
> Men as man he'd fain perceive. . . .

Shiva sees and falls in love with a *bayadere* (dancing girl) and she with him. One night she falls asleep,

> And she finds the much-loved guest
> On her bosom, lying dead. . . .

When they bury the body of Shiva, the *bayadere* jumps onto the funeral pyre:

> But the youth divine outsprings
> From the flame with heavenly grace,
> And on high his flight he wings,
> While his arms his love embrace. . . .
>     (Bowring translation)

*Shiva and Parvati*

Among the many titles by which Shiva is invoked are Aghora (horrible); Bhagavat (blessed); Ardhanari (half man), a form in which Shiva is shown as half male and half female, typifying the male and female energies in the universe; Chandra-sekhara (moon-crested); Ganga dhara (controller of the Ganges); Girisa (mountain lord); Hara (seizer); Isana (ruler); Jala-murti (whose form is water); Jata-dhara (wearing matted hair); Kala (time); Kalanjara (wearing a garland of skulls); Mahesha (great lord); Mrityunjaya (vanquisher of death); Pashu-pati (lord of animals); Sthanu (the firm); Tryambaka (three-eyed); Ugra (fierce); Virupaksha (of misformed eyes); and Viswanatha (lord of all). Maha-kala (great time), the form in which Shiva is portrayed on the cave at Elephanta, shows him with eight arms. In one hand he holds a human figure; in another, a sword or sacrificial ax; in the third, a basin of blood; in the fourth, the sacrificial bell. With two other hands he is drawing behind him the veil that extinguishes sin. The other two arms of the sculpture found at Elephanta have been destroyed.

Vira-bhadra (gracious to heroes) is considered in some texts to be a son of Shiva, in others, an emanation of Shiva. In one text, *Vayu Purana*, he is described as having "a thousand heads, a thousand eyes, a thousand feet, wielding a thousand clubs, a thousand shafts; holding the shell, the discus, the mace, and bearing the blazing bow and battle ax; fierce and terrible, shining with dreadful splendor, and decorated with the crescent moon; clothed in a tiger's skin, dripping with blood, having a capacious stomach and a vast mouth armed with formidable tusks."

See also: BRAHMA; DEVI; LINGAM; NANDIN; RIG-VEDA; RUDRA; VISHNU; YOM

*Shou Hsing*

2705

**Shou Hsing** (longevity star)   In Chinese legend, the deified sage Tung Fang So, worshiped as the god of longevity.

One day Emperor Wu Ti saw a green sparrow and asked Tung Fang So whether it was an omen. Tung Fang So replied that it showed that Hsi Wang Mu, the goddess of peaches, was coming to visit the emperor with seven peaches from the magic peach tree that grew in her sacred garden. Each magic fruit, *p'an-t'ao*, conferred on the person who ate it 3,000 years of life. As the sage had predicted, the goddess Hsi Wang Mu appeared to the emperor. As the goddess was eating one of the peaches with the emperor she noticed that Tung Fang So was peeping at her through a window. "This man stole and ate three of my peaches," she said to the emperor, "and now he is to live for thousands of years."

Shou Hsing is portrayed as an old man carrying one, two, or three preaches, accompanied by a deer or issuing from a peach. In Japanese legend, Shou Hsing is called Tobosaku.

See also: HSI WANG MU; PEACH

**Shri** (prosperity, luck)   In Hindu mythology, goddess of prosperity and luck, often identified with Lakshmi, another goddess of good fortune. Shri is also associated with fertility. One of her epithets is Karisin (abounding in dung), referring to her role with food and soil.

See also: LAKSHMI

2706

*Shu*

2707

**Shu** (he who holds up?)   In Egyptian mythology, god of the air. He and his twin sister, Tefnut, constituted the first couple of the Ennead of Heliopolis, which was a system of gods worshiped in Egypt.

According to one myth, the sun god conceived Shu and Tefnut without benefit of a partner. He masturbated and then swallowed his own semen, sneezing out Shu and spitting out Tefnut. Others say that Shu was the first son of the sun god Ra and the sky goddess Hathor. At the request of Ra, Shu was said to have separated the sky (Nut) from the earth (Geb) and maintained the division with his upraised arms. As a result, light and space were created as well as heaven above and earth below. Shu is often compared to Atlas in Greek mythology, who supported the heavens with his head and hands. In Egyptian art Shu was almost always portrayed in human form wearing a feather or feathers on his head and holding a scepter in his hand. Sometimes he was pictured with his arms upraised and the four pillars of heaven near his head.

See also: ATLAS; ENNEAD; GEB; HATHOR; NUT; RA

2708

**Shuddhodana**   Fifth century B.C.E. In Buddhist legend, father of Gautama, the Buddha. He was the chieftain of the North Indian Shakya tribe. In some accounts he is said to have been a king. Told by soothsayers that his son would be either a universal monarch or a Buddha, an Enlightened One, he tried to prevent him from becoming a Buddha but failed.

See also: BUDDHA, THE

2709

**Shui Ching-tzu** (son of water essence, water spirit)   In Chinese mythology, the spirit of water, who made himself clothes of ebony bark. He is one of the Wu Lao, the five spirits of natural forces.

See also: WU LAO

**Shvod** In Armenian folklore, guardian house spirit, who is often cited as an ogre and used to frighten children.

2710

**Sibu** In the mythology of the Indians of the Isthmus of Panama, the supreme god. Sibu entrusted a basket containing the seeds of all life to Sura, a lesser god, but demonic powers were continually after the basket. The evil god Jaburu stole it and ate the seeds. When Sura returned, Jaburu killed him. From Sura's grave a cacao tree and a calabash tree rose. Sibu forced Jaburu to drink a mixture made from the cacao tree served in a drinking vessel made of the calabash. Jaburu liked the chocolate taste and drank until his stomach began to swell. When it blew up, Sibu picked up the seeds that came out of Jaburu's body. "Let Sura wake up again!" Sibu declared. He again gave Sura the basket containing the seeds of all life. In another creation myth Sibu and Jaburu threw cacao pods at one another. Sibu used green pods, and Jaburu used ripe pods. At the third throw the pod broke in Jaburu's hand, and humankind was born.

2711

**Sibyls** In Greek and Roman cult, name given to women endowed with prophetic gifts under the god Apollo. Their number varied from one to 10 to 12, and various sites were chosen for their abode. The most famous Sibyl was that of Cumae in Campania, Italy. This Sibyl led Aeneas in the underworld after he broke off the Golden Bough. According to some accounts the Cumaean Sibyl was once the mistress of Apollo. She tells Aeneas that she has lived seven generations already because Apollo granted her wish that she have as many years as their were grains in a handful of dust. The Sibyl, however, forgot to ask the god for perpetual youth and thus aged and shrank. In Petronius's novel *Satyricon* the Sibyl has shrunk to a tiny being, all shriveled up, who is kept in a cage and asks only to die. In another

2712

myth associated with the Sibyl, she offered King Tarquinius Priscus nine books of sibylline oracles. The king, however, refused to buy them at the price she set, so she burned three and again offered the remaining six. Again, he refused, and she burned three more, still asking the full price. Realizing that all of the books would be destroyed, Tarquinius agreed to buy the remaining three for the price of the original nine. The sacred books were kept under the charge of Roman priests and could only be consulted by order of the Senate. In 83 B.C.E. they were destroyed by fire, and another set was produced. Eventually the Christians and Jews began producing sets of sibylline books, and 14 such books appeared that are still extant. During the Middle Ages the Sibyls along with the Hebrew Prophets were said to have predicted the coming of Christ. In the *Dies Irae*, the great medieval hymn for the dead, the Sibyl is cited along with King David. Michelangelo painted five Sibyls on the ceiling of the Sistine Chapel, and Raphael, Mantegna, Rembrandt, and Turner also painted Sibyls. The Sibyl's most famous role is in Vergil's *Aeneid* (book 6).

See also: AENEAS; APOLLO; GOLDEN BOUGH

2713

**Sick Lion, The** Aesopic fable found in various European collections.

The lion allowed word to get around that he was on his deathbed and wished all of the animals of his kingdom to come to his cave to hear his last will and testament. The fox did not wish to be the first to enter the cave. So he lingered near the entrance while the goat and the sheep and the calf went in to receive the last wishes of the king of beasts.

After a time, the lion seemed to make a remarkable recovery and came to the mouth of the cave. Seeing the fox a safe distance away, he bellowed: "Why do you not come in to pay your respects to me, Friend Fox?"

"Please pardon me, Your Majesty," replied the fox, "but I did not wish to crowd you. I noticed the tracks of many of your subjects going into your cave, but so far I have seen none coming out. Until some of them come out and there is more room in the cave, I think I'll stay out here in the open air."

Moral: *Don't believe all you hear.*

The fable is alluded to by Horace in his *Satires* (book 1). In a variation of the fable, *The Ailing Lion and His Visitors*, included in Juan Ruiz's *El Libro de Buen Amor* (The Book of Good Love), the lion is actually sick. When he is visited by the other animals they offer themselves for his supper. The lion chooses a bull for dinner, and the wolf is chosen to do the honors of carving. Thinking to get the better of the lion, the wolf gives him the entrails, saying they will be better for his health. However, the lion raises his paw and tears away the skin and an ear from the wolf's head. The fox is then ordered to do the honors of serving. Fearful and clever at the same time, she gives the whole trunk of the bull to the lion and the entrails to the rest of the party.

"Who taught you, dear madam, to carve so well, so judiciously, so properly?" asked the lion.

"I studied the wolf's head and learned from it," the fox replied.

See also: AESOPIC FABLES

**2714**

**Sido**   In Melanesian mythology, trickster of New Guinea. Sido fell in love with a beautiful woman named Sagaru, only to lose her to a more powerful magician. Battling the magician to try to win her back cost Sido his life. But his spirit was not allowed to enter Adiri, the land of the dead. So he went about seducing women and children. After wandering for some time he entered Adiri and planted a garden to feed the dead. Transforming himself into a pig, he cut out his backbone to form the roof of a house for the dead. The Kiwaians on New Guinea commemorate this event by fastening parts of a pig to the framework of their homes. Sido is also known as Hido and Iko.

See also: ADIRI; TRICKSTER

**2715**

**Siegfried** (victory peace)   In the *Nibelungenlied*, a hero; called Sigurd in the *Volsunga Saga*, an earlier version of the legend.

See also: SIGURD; *NIBELUNGENLIED*; *VOLSUNGA SAGA*

**2716**

**Sif** (kinship)   In Norse mythology, grain goddess, the second wife of Thor and mother of Ull, Thor's stepson. The fire-trickster god, Loki, stole Sif's hair and was forced to replace it with golden hair made by the dwarfs.

**2717**

**Siggeir**   In Norse mythology, king of the Goths and husband of Signy. He took over the Volsung kingdom, slaying Volsung and setting wild beasts to devour Volsung's 10 sons; only Sigmund survived. He was finally killed by being burned alive in a palace set on fire by Sigmund and Sinfiotli. Siggeir appears in the *Volsunga Saga*.

See also: SIGMUND; SIGNY

**2718**

**Sigi**   In Norse mythology, a son of Odin; a murderer and an outlaw. Before he was killed he became the father of Rerir, who was the father of Volsung. A kenning for Thor is the "husband of Sif."

**2719**

**Sigmund** (victory shield)   In Norse mythology, son of Volsung and Ljod. Sigmund was father (by his sister Signy) of Sinfiotli, co-avenger of Volsung's death, and father (by Hjordis) of the great hero Sigurd. Sigmund was killed by the will of the gods for having had sexual intercourse with his sister. He appears in the *Volsunga Saga* and Richard Wagner's *Der Ring des Nibelungen*. Sigmund is portrayed by Arthur Rackham in his illustrations for Wagner's Ring Cycle.

See also: *RING DES NIBELUNGEN, DER*; SIGURD

**Signy**   In Norse mythology, daughter of Volsung and Ljod; sister of Sigmund, and mother by him of Sinfiotli. Signy was forced to become the wife of King Siggeir. She contrived to save one of her brothers, Sigmund, from death by wild beasts. She then deceived him, disguised as a gypsy, and bore him Sinfiotli, who became Sigmund's companion in avenging Volsung's death. She died when Siggeir's palace was set on fire. She appears in the *Volsunga Saga* and as Sieglinde in Richard Wagner's *Der Ring des Nibelungen*.

See also: *RING DES NIBELUNGEN, DER*; SIGGEIR; SIGMUND

**2721**

**Siguna** (Sigyn) (victory giver)   In Norse mythology, the wife of Loki, the fire-trickster god. She tended him when he was finally bound under the earth.

See also: LOKI

*Sigurd (Willy Pogany)*

**2722**

**Sigurd**   In Norse mythology, a hero; in Germanic mythology called Siegfried. Sigurd was the son of Sigmund and Hjordis; husband of Gudrun; and father of Sigmund, Swanhild, and Awlaug (by Brynhild). He appears in the *Volsunga Saga*, in William Morris's *Sigurd the Volsung and the Fall of the Niblungs*, a four-book epic in anapestic couplets, and Richard Wagner's *Der Ring des Nibelungen* as Siegfried. He is portrayed

in Arthur Rackham's illustrations for Wagner's Ring Cycle.

See also: BRYNHILD; GUDRUN; *RING DES NIBELUNGEN, DER*; SIEGFRIED; SIGMUND

**2723**

**Sileni** (moon men)   In Greek mythology, creatures of the hills and woods, often confused with satyrs, having horse's ears, flattened noses, horse's tails or legs, or both. The most famous of the group was Silenus, teacher of Dionysus, who was made drunk by King Midas. The Greeks compared Socrates with Silenus not only because he was a teacher, but because he was also ugly, as was Silenus. Vergil's *Sixth Ecologue*, Ovid's *Metamorphoses* (book 11), Pope's *Dunciad* (III,324), Swift's "The Fable of Midas," Shelley's "Hymn of Pan," and W. S. Landor's *Silenus* also cite or tell of Silenus. Silenus appears in paintings of Titian, Piero di Cosimo, Rubens, and Géricault.

See also: DIONYSUS; SATYRS

**2724**

**Silvanus** (of the woods, forest)   In Roman mythology, god of agriculture, watching over hunters, shepherds, and boundaries; patron god of houses and flocks. Under the Roman Empire Silvanus was credited with protecting parks and gardens. In Roman art he was portrayed as a strong woodsman. Vergil's *Aeneid* (book 8) describes a grove near Caere dedicated to Silvanus that served as the boundary between Latium and Ethruria.

See also: *AENEID, THE*

**2725**

**Simeon Stylites, St.** (hearing)   390–459. In Christian legend, first pillar saint. Patron of shepherds. Feast, 5 January in the Roman Church and 1 September in the Eastern Orthodox Church.

St. Simeon wanted to mortify his body, so according to a fifth-century account in Theodoret's *Ecclesiastical History*, he "elevated himself on a pillar . . . of forty cubits in height, and there stood he for 37 years with a chain around his neck, a spectacle to men and to angels." The account goes on to tell that St. Simeon sometimes made as many as 1,244 "inclinations of the body in one day." He also "stood one whole year on one foot." He died on his pillar. Tennyson's poem *St. Simeon Stylites* deals with the mad saint.

**2726**

**Simon Magus** (Simon the magician)   First century. In the Bible, N.T., a magician rebuked by St. Peter because he attempted to buy the power of the Holy Spirit (Acts 8:9–13). The word *simony*, the buying of ecclesiastical power, derives from his name. Christian tradition not included in the New Testament says that Simon was a constant foe of Peter, even following him to Rome. One account says Simon requested that he be buried alive, certain he would rise up on the third day. Another account says he tried to fly from a tower and was killed when he fell.

See also: PETER, ST.

*Simurugh*

**2727**

**Simurgh** (Saena, Semuru, Senmury, Simorg, Simurg) (thirty)   In Persian mythology, a gigantic bird whose wings were as large as clouds. The Simurgh sat on the magical tree, Gaokerena, which produced the seeds of all plant life. When he moved, a thousand branches and twigs of the tree fell in all directions. They were then gathered by another bird, the Camrosh, which took them to the rain god, Tishtrya, who fertilized them. The Persian mystic poet Farid Al-Din Attar (fl. c. 1180–1220) used the Simurgh as a symbol of the godhead in his poem *Nantiq-al-Tayr* (The Conference of the Birds). The work is an elaborate allegory in which 30 birds (Persian, *si murgh*) set out in search of the Simurgh, only to realize in the end that they are the Simurgh.

See also: TISHTRYA

**2728**

**Sin** (moon)   In Near Eastern mythology (Sumerian), moon god of Ur and son of Enlil, the storm god. Abraham, the Hebrew patriarch in the Old Testament, came from Ur by way of Harran, both cities being devoted to the moon god Sin. Mount Sinai is also believed to have been originally dedicated to Sin.

See also: ABRAHAM; ENLIL

**2729**

**Sinbad the Sailor**   Hero in the tale of "Sinbad the Sailor and Sinbad the Porter" in *The Thousand and One Nights* (nights 536–566), which contains the seven voyages of Sinbad the Sailor. Sinbad was a merchant in Baghdad who acquired great wealth by making seven voyages, which he narrated to Sinbad the Porter, a poor man.

*First Voyage* (nights 538–541): Sinbad, a wealthy youth, squanders all of his money and, attempting to recoup his loss, buys some merchandise and sails away. The ship stops in the Indian Ocean, and he and others of the ship visit what they think is an island but which is actually a large sleeping whale. They light a fire on the whale's back, and the heat wakes the monster, which instantly dives into the ocean. Sinbad is rescued by some merchants and returns home.

*Second Voyage* (nights 543–546): Bored with life on land, Sinbad takes another journey by ship. He falls asleep on an island where the ship has stopped for water, and he is left behind. He discovers the egg of a roc (a fabulous bird) about 50 feet in diameter. When the monstrous roc appears, Sinbad grabs hold of one of its feet and is flown away to the Valley of Diamonds. Here merchants on the cliffs above, unable to reach the valley, throw down meat to the birds in the valley. The diamonds strewn on the valley's bottom stick to the meat, which the birds carry up and deposit in their cliffside nests. The men then come and steal the diamonds. Sinbad attaches himself to a piece of meat and is lifted to an eagle's nest. Later he is rescued by the jewel collectors and returns home to Baghdad a rich man.

*Third Voyage* (nights 546–550): Sinbad's ship is captured by some savage dwarfs and is taken to an island where a giant one-eyed ogre (similar to the Cyclops of Greek mythology) begins eating the crew one by one. Sinbad heats two iron spits and rams them into the monster's eye. The ogre summons two other monsters, and most of the men are killed. But Sinbad and two others escape, only to be lured to an island by a serpent that attempts to swallow Sinbad. He builds a wooden enclosure around himself that makes it impossible for the serpent to reach him. Sinbad is saved by a ship that sails from island to island, and while on it Sinbad sees a fish like a cow, fish like asses, and a bird born from a seashell.

*Fourth Voyage* (nights 550–555): Sinbad is shipwrecked and cast ashore with his companions on an island inhabited by cannibals, who imprison and fatten them for better eating, though Sinbad eats little so as to remain thin. He eventually escapes and reaches a kingdom where bridles and stirrups are unknown. Sinbad makes himself rich by "inventing" them, and the king gives his daughter as wife to Sinbad. When she dies, he is buried alive with her body according to the custom of the land. Sinbad escapes, however, and

returns to Baghdad, rich from rifling the bodies of the dead on his way out of the catacombs.

*Fifth Voyage* (nights 556–559): Sinbad's ship is destroyed by two rocs whose offspring has been eaten by merchants. Seizing a floating piece of wreckage, Sinbad is washed ashore on a beautiful island. He comes upon an old man who appears "weak and infirm" sitting on the bank of a stream. Thinking to help the old man, Sinbad carries him on his back, but the man "clasped his legs nimbly" around Sinbad's neck, making it difficult to walk. Eventually Sinbad makes a liquor to get the old man drunk and then dashes "his head to pieces." After being rescued, Sinbad learns the man was the Old Man of the Sea, and Sinbad is "the first who ever escaped strangling by his malicious tricks."

*Sixth Voyage* (nights 560–562): Sinbad's ship is driven ashore and breaks up on a barren island. Here he finds many precious stones and also an underground river, on which he rides a raft to the city of Serendib, where the king welcomes Sinbad. He is sent home with great wealth plus a present for Caliph Harun al-Rashid.

*Seventh Voyage* (nights 563–566): Caliph Harun al-Rashid sends Sinbad back to Serendib with gifts for the king. On his way, Sinbad is captured by pirates and sold as a slave to a merchant who makes him an elephant hunter. He is so successful that he learns of the burial ground of the elephants, where a huge store of ivory is located. He is rewarded with his freedom and given a stock of ivory, with which he returns home. The romantic adventures of Sinbad appeal to writers of adventure fiction, particularly children's stories, and Hollywood has produced films of many versions of the legends.

See also: *THOUSAND AND ONE NIGHTS, THE*

2730

**Sindri** (cinder)   In Norse mythology, a worker in gold among the dwarfs; Sindri created Odin's arm ring, Draupnir; Frey's golden boar; and Thor's hammer, Mjolnir.

See also: BROK; FREY; THOR

**Sinon** (plunderer)    In Greek mythology, a young Greek soldier, a relative of Odysseus, who pretended to desert to Troy and convinced the Trojans to bring in the wooden horse. When night came, Sinon let the Greeks out of the wooden horse, and Troy was sacked. Vergil's *Aeneid* (book 21) and Dante's *Divine Comedy* (Inferno, canto 30) cite him as an example of treachery. In the latter he is among the falsifiers of words, called *il falso Sinon greco* (the false Greek Sinon).

See also: *AENEID, THE;* ODYSSEUS; TROY

**Sinuhe**    Hero in the ancient Egyptian "Tale of Sinuhe," found in various Egyptian manuscripts. The tale was used by the scribes and students of the 12th and 13th dynasties, who copied it on ostraca (limestone flakes) as part of their studies. The tale is of a man who has to flee Egypt but always wishes to return to his beloved land. Eventually, he is called back. The short tale inspired Mika Waltari's novel *The Egyptian*, which was made into a popular Hollywood film.

**Sirens** (those who bind with a cord, or those who wither)    In Greek mythology, three water nymphs, Ligeia, Leucosia and Parthenope, who with their singing lured seamen to watery graves. They lived on an island between Circe's isle and Scylla, where they sat in a flowery bed surrounded by the rotting bodies of the shipwrecked men. When Odysseus sailed past them, he had the ears of his men stopped up with wax so they could not hear the Sirens' song. He, however, wanted to hear the song so he had his men tie him to the mast. When the Argonauts took the same watery route, they were saved by the song of Orpheus, which defeated the songs of the Sirens. Either Odysseus or Orpheus is responsible for their deaths. The three cast themselves into the sea when they failed to lure Odysseus or Orpheus. They were transformed into sunken rocks. Generally, early Greek art portrayed the Sirens as great birds with the heads of women, or with the upper part of the body like that of a woman, with the legs of a bird, with or without wings. In later Greek art the Sirens were portrayed as beautiful women. They are sometimes associated with the cult of the dead and were believed to guide souls to the underworld. As such they appear on various Greek tombs. Sirens appear in Homer's *Odyssey* (book 12), Apollonius of Rhodes's *The Argonautica*, Dante's *The Divine Comedy*, where they are symbols of sensual pleasure, William Morris's *The Life and Death of Jason*, and E. M. Forster's *Story of the Siren*. Debussy's last section of his *Nocturnes* (1898) for orchestra, "Sirènes," captures the song of the Sirens with a women's wordless chorus.

See also: ARGONAUTS; LIGEIA; NYMPHS; ODYSSEUS; *ODYSSEY, THE;* ORPHEUS; PARTHENOPE

**Sir Patrick Spens**    Late medieval English ballad that tells of a ship sent in wintertime to Norway. On its journey home, Sir Patrick's ship is wrecked, and everyone on board is lost.

See also: BALLAD

**Sisyphus** (shrewd or wise)    In Greek mythology, first king of Corinth, a trickster noted for shrewdness and cleverness; son of Aeolus, king of Thessaly, and Enarete. When Zeus raped the nymph Aegina, daughter of the river god Asopus, Sisyphus promised to tell Asopus what had happened, but only on the condition that Asopus would give Corinth a spring on top of the Acrocorinth, its acropolis. Zeus was so angry at what happened that he sent Thanatos, Death, to kill Sisyphus, only to have Thanatos bound by Sisyphus so that no one could die. Zeus then sent Ares, the war god, to free Thanatos. As soon as Thanatos was free, he killed Sisyphus, but before Sisyphus died he asked his wife, Merope, not to perform the prescribed funeral rites for his burial. This angered both Hades and his wife,

Persephone, deities of the underworld, who sent Sisyphus back to earth to have the burial sacrifices offered. Sisyphus promised to return to the underworld afterwards, but he lived to a very old age before he died again. Zeus, angered, devised a punishment for Sisyphus when he did return to the underworld. He was required to roll a boulder up a hill, but whenever it reached the top, it rolled back down—and had to be rolled up the hill again, over and over. Thus *Sisyphean* came to mean a fruitless, endless task.

Sisyphus appears or is cited in Ovid's *Metamorphoses* (book 4); Spenser's *Faerie Queene* (I.v.35); and Pope's "Ode on St. Cecilia's Day" and supplies the title for Camus' collection of existential essays, *The Myth of Sisyphus* (1942), in which Camus explores the absurdity of life. Titian painted a *Sisyphus*.

See also: AEOLUS; ARES; ASOPUS; HADES; NYMPHS; OVID; PERSEPHONE; THANATOS

2736
**Sivamala** (Shiva's garland)   In Hindu mythology, a rosary that the goddess of wisdom, Shatarupa, gave to Brahma, her husband and father.

See also: BRAHMA

2737
**Sjoran**   In Swedish folklore, a spirit of the sea, derived, according to some scholars, from the Norse goddess Ran, wife of the sea god Aegir.

See also: AEGIR; RAN

2738
**Skadi** (Skade) (damage)   In Norse mythology, a giantess, wife of the sea god Njord and daughter of the giant Thjassi. When her father was slain for stealing Iduna's magic apples, Skadi demanded satisfaction for the deed. She was allowed to choose a husband from among the gods on the condition that she make her choice by seeing only their feet from behind a curtain. She thought she had chosen the handsome god Bal-

dur but instead received Njord. She lived part of the time at her father's home, Thrymheim, and part at her husband's, Noatun. According to the *Prose Edda*, she liked to spend "her time in the chase of savage beasts, and is called the Ondur goddess, or Ondurdis."

See also: IDUNA; NJORD; *PROSE EDDA*

2739
**Skald**   In Norse mythology, the term for a poet. In addition to the anonymous mythological and heroic tales, representative of a continuing oral tradition in the Germanic world, there is a large body of poetry treating the same topics. The god Thor is the most frequent mythological subject of the poetry, and the basic stylistic feature is the kenning, a representational substitution for a noun. Thor is referred to as "son of Jord," or as "husband of Sif." Skaldic poetry is thus ornate oral poetry that requires a knowledge of the ancient myths and indicates their survival after the conversion to Christianity.

See also: JORD; KENNING; SIF; THOR

*Skanda (Karttikeya)*

**Skanda** In Hindu mythology, the six-headed war god, son of Shiva. In some texts Skanda is said to have no mother at all; Shiva cast his semen into fire, and Skanda arose. In other texts Skanda, called Karttikeya (son of the razors), is said to have as his mothers the seven Kritikas (the Pleiades). Sometimes represented as a razor, Skanda is also called Guha (reared in a secret place) and Kumara (the youth). The last epithet is sometimes also applied to Agni, the fire god.

See also: AGNI; PLEIADES; SHIVA

**Skinfaxi** (shining mane) In Norse mythology, horse of Dagr (the day) that drew Dagr and Nott's carriage around the earth once a day. From Skinfaxi's mane, light was shed over the earth and the heavens. Skinfaxi appears in the *Prose Edda*.

See also: DAGR; NOTT; *PROSE EDDA*

**Skipper Ireson's Ride** American literary ballad by John Greenleaf Whittier, written in 1857. It tells how Skipper Floyd Ireson deserted his ship, causing the death of his companions. Whittier said that his ballad "was founded solely on a fragment of rhyme which I heard from one of my early schoolmates, a native of Marblehead." The refrain:

Poor Floyd Ireson, for his hard heart,
Tarred and feathered and carried in a cart
By the women of Marblehead.

In the 1888 edition of his poems Whittier says the poem was "pure fancy." In reality the incident took place in 1808 and Benjamin Ireson, not Floyd, was accused of deserting his men, though in fact the crew was responsible for the wreck. The poem became so well known that Rudyard Kipling incorporated a story about it into his novel *Captains Courageous*. In Samuel Roads's *History of Marblehead* the victim,

contrary to the legend and ballad, was carried in a dory, not a cart, and men, not women, were the principal avengers.

**Skirnir** (he who makes things shine) In Norse mythology, the favorite servant of the god Frey. He acted as a go-between for Frey when he sought Gerda's love.

See also: FREY; GERDA

**Skoll and Hati** (to stick to) In Norse mythology, two wolves that pursue the sun and moon. The *Prose Edda* describes them as finally devouring the sun and moon at Ragnarok, the end of the world.

See also: FENRIR; FREY; GARM; *PROSE EDDA*; RAGNAROK

**Skritek** In Slavic folklore, a household spirit, often in the form of a small boy, who lives behind the oven or in the stable. He protects the family, which in turn leaves portions of their meals for his consumption, especially on Thursdays and Christmas. If for some reason the *skritek* is offended, he causes havoc in the house. His statue, made of wood, portrays him with his arms crossed and wearing a crown. The statue is placed on the table to guard the hearth when the family is away. In Polish folklore the *skritek* appears as a drenched chicken, dragging its wings and tail.

**Skuld** (future) In Norse mythology, one of the three named Norns, the others being Urd and Verdandi. Skuld is portrayed veiled, facing the future with a scroll in her hands.

See also: NORNS; URD; VERDANDI

**2747**

**Slave and the Master, The**   Moral fable by the Persian poet Sadi, in *The Gulistan* (chapter 5, story 2). A gentleman possessed a slave of exquisite beauty, whom he regarded with love and affection. One day he said to a friend, "Would that this slave of mine, with all the beauty and good qualities he possesses, had not a long and uncivil tongue." "Brother," his friend replied, "do not expect service after professing friendship, because when relations between lover and beloved come in, the relations between master and servant are superseded."

See also: *GULISTAN, THE*; SADI

*The Sleeping Beauty (Walter Crane)*

**2748**

**Sleeping Beauty, The**   European folktale, the most popular versions being Perrault's *La Belle au bois dormant* (1697) and the Grimms' *Little Briar Rose* (1812). After many prayers a childless king and queen were rewarded with the birth of a baby girl. The king and queen invited all of the people in the kingdom to her christening, and in addition they invited 12 of the 13 Wise Women (supernatural beings). They omitted asking the 13th because they had only enough gold goblets to serve 12 of them. At the christening each of the Wise Women bestowed a gift on the child. Before the end of the ceremony the uninvited Wise Woman appeared, and in retribution for not being invited, she cursed the baby, saying she would prick her finger on a spindle and die. It happened that one of the 12 Wise Women had not yet bestowed her gift, so she was able to temper the curse with her gift, though not revoke it. For her gift she declared that the princess would not die but would sleep for 100 years when she pricked her finger and could then be awakened by the kiss of a prince.

In an effort to forestall the curse the king ordered all spindles in the kingdom destroyed. However, the 13th Wise Woman disguised herself as an old woman and hid a spinning wheel in a remote tower of the castle, where she sat spinning until the child's 15th birthday. On that day the princess wandered into the remote tower and found the old woman and the spinning wheel. Offering to let her try her hand at spinning, the old woman made sure the girl pricked her finger. The girl began to get sleepy and went to her room to lie down. Sleep then overcame everyone in the castle, and eventually vines grew up over every portal and window, completely covering the structure.

The story of the sleeping princess spread throughout the land, and many princes attempted to scale the fortress to reach her and revive her, but all failed. Then when 100 years had passed, a young prince made an attempt to reach the princess and succeeded. His kiss awakened her, and then the entire castle awoke. The prince and princess then married.

Perrault's version was used by Tchaikovsky for his ballet *The Sleeping Beauty*. Walt Disney's feature-length cartoon *Sleeping Beauty* (1959) deals with the folktale in a sentimental manner.

Sleeping Beauty is tale type 410 and has numerous well-known motifs: fairies preside at child's birth, one fairy sets the course of the child's life, a prick with a spindle causes magical sleep, and disenchantment by a kiss.

See also: MOTIF; TALE TYPE

2749

**Slith** (the dark fields)   In Norse mythology, a river that flowed in the land of the giants. In the *Voluspa*, the first poem in the *Poetic Edda*, which narrates the creation and destruction of the world, the river is said to come from the east "through poisoned vales with swords and daggers," that is, icy cold.

See also: *POETIC EDDA*

2750

**Snake**   A legless reptile. In world mythology and folklore the snake, or serpent, is sometimes a symbol of a beneficent being, sometimes a demonic one. In Jewish and Christian belief the snake is often equated with evil or the devil. In Genesis (3:1) the serpent is described as "more subtile than any beast of the field which the Lord had made." According to Christian tradition, the snake had legs until he caused the downfall of humans by tempting Adam and Eve with the apple. Since then the snake has been condemned to slither on its belly in the dust. The Old Testament does not identify the serpent with the devil, but the New Testament does. According to the Book of Numbers (21:5–9), Moses erected a brass serpent in the desert when the Hebrews were in danger of being wiped out by a snake plague. All of the people who looked upon the brass snake would recover from the poisonous snakebites. The image erected by Moses was similar to the one dedicated to the life-giving god Nin-gis-zida in ancient Sumerian ritual. The brass serpent seems to have been in use for some time, for we are told that it was venerated during the reign of Hezekiah (717–686 B.C.E.) and destroyed by that king because "the children of Israel did burn incense to it: and he called it

Nehusthan" (2 Kings 18:14). Jesus uses the image of the brass serpent when he says: "And as Moses lifted up the serpent in the wilderness, even so must the Son of Man be lifted up: That whosoever believeth in him should not perish, but have eternal life" (John 3:1–15).

In ancient Egyptian mythology the monster-serpent Apophis, enemy of the gods Horus, Amen, Ra, and Osiris, always tried to prevent the sun god Amun-Ra from rising every day. But the clever priests of Amun-Ra devised a magic ceremony to guarantee that the sun would rise. They made a snake out of wax, inscribed it with the name of Apophis, and while reciting spells and incantations cast it into the fire. The magic worked, for every day the sun did rise over the land of Egypt. But the same Egyptians saw the snake as a symbol of resurrection because it shed its skin. One ancient Egyptian text, devised to help the dead achieve resurrection, puts the following lines into the mouth of the deceased:

I am the serpent Sata whose years are many,
I die and I am born again each day. . . .
I renew myself,
and I grow young each day.

The Greeks also used the snake or serpent as a symbol of rebirth and healing. Asklepius, god of medicine, was often shown with the caduceus, a wand with two entwined serpents surmounted by small wings or a winged helmet, both indicating quick movement. In Aztec mythology Quetzalcoatl (green-feathered serpent) was portrayed in serpent form. In Persian mythology the serpent or snake is believed to bring disease and death. Ahirman, the evil spirit, once transformed himself into a serpent, entering human beings and producing lust, greed, falsehood, slander, and revenge. Numerous goddesses in world mythology are also identified with the snake or serpent, such as the Sumerian goddess Inanna, Queen of Heaven, who is often portrayed holding snakes in her hands, symbolic of her control of the phallus. The Minoan Mother Goddess, who was "the master of men," was also pictured with snakes on her person in

Hindu mythology. The serpent is associated with Vishnu, who sleeps on a coiled serpent on the primordial waters. There are numerous motifs associated with snakes in the *Motif Index of Folk Literature*.

See also: AMUN; APOPHIS; ASCLEPIUS; CADUCEUS; HORUS; MOSES; OSIRIS; QUETZALCOATL; RA

2751

**Snegurotchka** (the snow maiden)    In Russian mythology, lovely daughter of King Frost and Fairy Spring. Snegurotchka was brought up in the cold forest because sunlight would destroy her. As long as she knew nothing of love, she was safe from the sun god's fatal caress. But one day she heard the song of a shepherd's son, Lel, and asked her father to let her join humanity. She was so overjoyed at sharing in human emotions that she asked Fairy Spring to give her the power to love. The wish was granted, and she fell in love with Prince Mizgyr, who left his betrothed, Kupava, for Snegurotchka. But when the two declared their love for each other, the sun's rays touched Snegurotchka, and she melted. Mizgyr cursed the gods and drowned himself in a lake. The legend of Snegurotchka was used by Alexander Ostrovsky in his play *Snegurotchka*; Tchaikovsky wrote incidental music for the first performance. Rimsky-Korsakov used Ostrovsky's play as the basis for his opera *Snegurotchka*.

2752

**Sodom and Gomorrah** (burning and submersion)    In the Bible, O.T., two cities of the plain of the River Jordan, destroyed by fire and brimstone by Yahweh, the Hebrew god. The legend, told in Genesis (19:1–29) tells how the patriarch Abraham asked Yahweh to spare Sodom if 10 righteous men could be found (women did not count). But none were found. Yahweh sent three angels to the city, and the angels encountered Lot as they entered through the gates. Lot offered them lodging and brought them to his house. Some men of the city knocked at Lot's

*Sodom and Gomorrah*

door and demanded that Lot send the three strangers outside "that we may know [have sexual intercourse with] them" (Gen. 19:5). Lot refused, offering instead to send out his virgin daughters to be abused sexually. The angels intervened and told Lot to prepare his family to flee the city because it was to be destroyed by God. While Abraham and his family and Lot and his family fled, the city was destroyed. Lot's wife looked back on the destruction and was turned into a pillar of salt (Gen. 19:26). The city was punished, according to some biblical commentators, because of its homosexual practices, but the biblical text makes it clear that the crime was inhospitality to strangers, since Lot was willing to offer his daughters to the men of the city for sexual intercourse rather than have his guests violated. But the incorrect popular interpretation has stuck, and the word *sodomy* is used to refer to homosexual activity. In Marcel Proust's *Remembrance of Things Past*, the novel *Sodome et Gomorrhe*, translated into English as *Cities of the Plain*, deals in part with the narrator discovering that Baron Charlus is a homosexual.

See also: ABRAHAM; YAHWEH

2753

**Sohrab** (Suhrab)    In the Persian epic poem *Shah Namah*, by Firdusi, son of the hero Rustum; he is killed by his father in battle.

The story of Sohrab and Rustum, that of the combat between a father and a son who did not know one another, forms part of the narrative in Firdusi's epic. Rustum, one of the greatest warriors of the Persians, in the course of his wanderings married the daughter of the king of Aderbaijan but soon left his wife in pursuit of more adventure. She bore him a son named Sohrab, but fearing that Rustum would take the boy and turn him into a soldier, she sent a message saying she had given birth to a girl. Sohrab grew to manhood and, longing to find his warrior father, went into the service of the Tartars. A battle then ensued between the Persians and the Tartars, with Sohrab on the side of the Tartars and Rustum on the side of the Persians. When Sohrab first saw Rustum, he had an intuition who his antagonist was and eagerly inquired if he was Rustum. But Rustum, ignorant of Sohrab's intuition, refused to reveal his identity and challenged Sohrab to combat. In their first encounter, after an exchange of spears, Sohrab evaded his opponent's club, but because of the weight of the club Rustum lost his balance and fell. Sohrab, however, refused to take advantage and offered a truce. Rustum, enraged at his downfall, renewed the struggle. Rustum then called out his own name, and Sohrab, bewildered by the fact that the man he thought was his father seemed to be calling for Rustum, ceased to fight and was fatally pierced by his father's spear. Unsure of the identity of his slayer, he declared that Rustum, his father, would avenge his death. Finally, the truth came out: each discovered the identity of the other, but it was too late; Sohrab was dead.

The legend of a battle between father and son is also found in Germanic heroic legendry. The young warrior Hadubrand engaged his father Hildebrand in a duel when the father returned after 30 years and was not recognized by his son.

This pathetic episode from *Shah Namah* inspired an essay by the French writer Sainte-Beuve, which was read by the English poet Matthew Arnold, who in turn used the essay to form the basis for his blank verse narrative poem *Sohrab and Rustum*. Arnold also consulted an account of the episode he found in Sir John Malcolm's *History of Persia*.

The poem was characterized by English poet Coventry Patmore, writing in the *North British Review*, as a "vivid reproduction of Homer's manner and spirit" but not "a new and independent creation." This criticism was echoed by Douglas Bush in *Mythology and the Romantic Tradition in English Poetry*. He writes that the poem is "academic" and has all of "the defects of a poem written to illustrate a theory."

See also: HILDEBRANDSLIED; *RUSTUM, THE*; *SHAH NAMAH*

2754
**Sol** (sun)   In Norse mythology, the sun, believed to be the daughter of Mundilfari. Sol's brother was Mani, the moon. When Odin asked a wise giant where the sun and moon came from, he answered:

> Mundilfari he is called, the father of Mani
> And also of Sol the same;
> Into heaven shall they turn each day,
> So that people can reckon years.

See also: MUNDILFARI

2755
**Solbon** (Sulbundu, Tscholbon)   In Siberian mythology, god of horses, worshiped by the Buriat; he rides through the sky with a lasso in his hand. Solbon has three wives, one of them a former Buriat girl whom he abducted from her wedding feast. She bore him a son; his two other wives are childless. In one myth Solbon left his horses in the care of his groom, Dogedoi, while he traveled in the western sky (Solbon is identified with the planet Venus). Dogedoi, however, left the horses unattended for three days and went out for a walk with Buto, his dog. When he returned, he found that wolves had scattered some of the horses and eaten the others. When Solbon returned, Dogedoi was severely punished. Some horses are dedicated to Solbon by

the Buriat and are thereby removed from any secular service in the community. During the spring the manes and tails of the horses are cut in preparation for a sacrifice to Solbon. Meats, cream porridge, and wines are also prepared for the god. The wine is thrown into the air in Solbon's honor, and the food is burned.

See also: VENUS

2756

**Solomon** (peaceful)   c. 971–931 B.C.E. In the Bible, O.T., third king of Israel, son of King David and Bathsheba, noted for his wisdom, though this is often in conflict in the various accounts in the Bible regarding the king and his extensive wealth. One rabbinical fable says that Solomon wore a ring with a gem that told him all he desired to know.

Two episodes from his life are most often encountered in art and music: the visit of the queen of Sheba (1 Kings 10) and the judgment of Solomon. The rich and beautiful queen of Sheba arrived at Solomon's court in Jerusalem with a great entourage. She had heard reports of the king's greatness and wisdom. Sheba tested Solomon by asking him many difficult questions, which he answered correctly. When she left Jerusalem, the queen gave him many gifts. The second episode deals with the king choosing the genuine mother between two whores, each of whom claimed to be the mother of a certain baby (1 Kings 3:16–28). The women lived in the same house, each had borne a child, and one of the two children died at night. Both women claimed the surviving child as her own. The dispute was brought before Solomon, who called for a sword to divide the living child in two, saying he would give half to each. The real mother cried out, "O my lord, give her the living child, and in no wise slay it." But the other woman said, "Let it be neither mine nor thine, but divide it" (1 Kings 3:26). Solomon then gave the child to the first woman, because a true mother would rather lose her child than see it die.

Aside from the numerous paintings depicting the subjects, Handel wrote an oratorio *Solomon*. In Islam Solomon is called Sulaiman. Solomon is credited in the Bible with the authorship of the Song of Songs, the Proverbs, Ecclesiastes, and the O.T. Apocrypha Wisdom of Solomon. However, no serious biblical scholar accepts his authorship of these works, even though tradition assigns them to him.

See also: DAVID

2757

**Soma**   In Hindu mythology, a plant and its juice that was ritually filtered and sometimes mixed with water, milk, butter, or barley to produce an intoxicating or even hallucinogenic drink. The ceremony in which this is drunk is the Avestan *haoma*, the central rite of Zoroastrian worship. It was the drink of the priest and those participating in a sacrificial ritual. The soma is said to be "mountain borne" or brought from the sky by an eagle, and thus of divine origin. In the Rig-Veda it is said that Indra draws her strength from soma juice. The juice of the Soma is not to be confused with the moon god of the same name.

See also: AMRITA; CHANDRA; CHURNING OF THE OCEAN; CHYAVANA; GANDHARVAS; GARUDA; INDRA; LOKAPALAS; RIG-VEDA; ZARATHUSTRA

2758

**Sovi**   In Slavic folklore, a hero responsible for originating cremation of the dead. The tale is found in a 13th-century Russian work that may have been derived from a Finnish source.

When Sovi's son died, Sovi buried him in the ground. The next day he asked his son if he had rested well. But the son groaned: "Oh! Worms and reptiles have eaten me!" Sovi then gave his son supper and put the body in the hollow of a tree for the night. The next day he asked the same question, and the boy replied: "Countless bees and mosquitoes have stung me. Oh, I have slept badly." So the following day Sovi made a huge funeral pyre and threw the body of his son into it. The next day when he asked the same question the boy replied: "I slept as peacefully as an infant in the cradle."

The custom of cremation was common in earlier times in Slavic countries. In Lithuania, when Great Duke Algirdas (or Oligerd) was burned in 1377, some 18 saddle horses also were included in the funeral pyre. The body was dressed in a robe of rich purple brocade, a mantle studded with pearls and precious stones, and a belt of gold and silver.

2759

**Spes** (expectation)  In Roman mythology, goddess of hope, invoked at births and marriages and for a good harvest. She had several temples in Rome. Portrayed as a young woman, she held a bud, either closed or just about to open, in her right hand.

*Sphinx*

2760

**Sphinx** (throttler)  In Greek mythology, a monster, half-woman, half-beast; daughter of Echidna and Orthus or Typhon. The Sphinx had the head of a woman and the body of a lion. She was sent by Hera or Apollo to punish King Laius of Thebes. She would sit on a rock and ask the following riddle: "What is it which, though it has one voice, becomes four-footed and two-footed and three-footed." If those questioned could not answer the riddle the Sphinx hurled them from

her rock, or else she ate them. When Oedipus passed by the Sphinx he was asked the riddle and replied that the answer was man, for as an infant he is four-footed, creeping on hands and feet; in his prime he is two-footed; and in old age he uses a cane as a third foot. When the Sphinx heard the correct answer, she threw herself over the cliff and died. Pausanias, to rationalize the myth, wrote in his *Description of Greece* that the Sphinx was a woman bandit who waylaid travelers, her headquarters being on Mount Phicium. Carl Jung, giving a psychological account, says that the Sphinx represents the Great Mother goddess who is destroyed by the stronger masculine force represented by Oedipus. In the Egyptian version of the Sphinx, however, it is always a male and often symbolizes royal strength and dignity. The Great Sphinx at Gizeh represents the god Horus trying to catch sight of his father, Ra, the rising sun, as he journeys across the valley. Ingres and Moreau both painted the Sphinx and Oedipus.

See also: APOLLO; ECHIDNA; HERA; HORUS; LAIUS; OEDIPUS; PAUSANIAS; TYPHON

2761

**Spider**  An arachnid that spins webs that trap prey and serve as nests. In Egyptian mythology the spider is an attribute of the goddess Neith as weaver of the world. In Greek mythology it is associated with Athene, Harmonia, the Fates, the Moirai, and Persephone. Athene transformed Arachne into a spider for challenging the goddess to a weaving contest. The spider is also associated with Holda and the norns in Norse mythology and Ishtar and Atagatis in Sumero-Semitic mythology. In Christianity the spider is a symbol of evil or the devil. The Chibcha Indians, a North Andean tribe of Colombia, believe that the dead cross the lake of death on boats made of spiderwebs. They therefore hold the spider in awe and will not kill it. Some South American Indian mythologies believe the spiderweb to be the means of climbing from the "lower world" to the "upper world." In African mythology, Yiyi, a spider man, brings fire from heaven to help humankind. Yiyi's web is used by the handmaidens of the sun to come down to earth to draw water and then reascend to heaven. According to the Nauru Island natives of the South Pacific, the world was created by Areop-Enap (ancient spider).

In Mark Twain's *Huckleberry Finn* (1885) the author says that spiders are portents of bad luck and even death: "Pretty soon a spider went crawling on my shoulder, and I flipped it off and it lit in the candle; and before I could budge it was all shriveled up. I didn't need anybody to tell me that that was an awful bad sign and would fetch me some bad luck. . . . I got up and turned around in my tracks three times and crossed my breast every time; and then I tied a lock of my hair with a thread to keep witches away."

See also: ARACHNE; ATHENA; HARMONIA; ISHTAR; NEITH; NORNS; PERSEPHONE

2762
**Springfield Mountain** American ballad, believed to be the oldest original American ballad still in circulation. It tells of the death by snakebite of Timothy Myrick at Wilberham (then Springfield Mountain), Massachusetts, on 7 August 1761. There are several variants of this ballad. Some were wild exaggerations made up by vaudeville performers, in which Merrick's wife-to-be died as a result of trying to suck the poison out.

> Now Molly had a ruby lip
> With which the pizen she did sip.
> But Molly had a rotten tooth,
> Which the Pizen struck and kill'd 'em both.

2763
**Sreca** (fate) In Serbian folklore, female personification of fate, often portrayed as a beautiful maiden spinning thread. If in a beneficent mood, she protected the family. When in an evil mood, she was called Nesreca and portrayed as an old woman with bloodshot eyes who paid no attention to the welfare of the family. With the proper

spells the evil Nesreca could be dismissed, but Sreca, a person's fate, was his for his entire life.

2764
**Stag** An adult male deer. In Greek mythology the goddess Artemis (Diana in Roman mythology) punished Actaeon for spying on her nudity by turning him into a stag, which was then devoured by mad dogs. When Agamemnon and his fleet were about to set sail for Troy, the Greeks asked their priest how to placate the goddess. Agamemnon was told to sacrifice his daughter Iphigenia. When the sacrifice was about to take place, Artemis (according to one account) substituted a stag for Iphigenia and took the maiden away to Tauris, where she became a priestess of the goddess. In Christian medieval folklore it was believed that when the stag reached the age of 50 years it would search for a snake, kill and eat it, and then make a mad dash to the nearest pool and drink as much water as possible to renew its antlers for another 50 years. If, however, the animal did not get to the water within three days after eating the snake, it would die. For Christians the stag became a symbol of the soul thirsting after God. There are numerous motifs associated with the stag in the *Motif Index of Folk Literature*.

See also: AGAMEMNON; ARTEMIS; DIANA; IPHIGENIA

2765
**Standish, Miles** c. 1584–1656. In American history and folklore, military leader of the Pilgrims. He appears in Longfellow's long narrative poem *The Courtship of Miles Standish*, which is pure legend. Miles was not in love with Priscilla and never sent John Alden to woo the girl in his name. According to Longfellow's poem, Priscilla's reply when Alden asked her to marry Standish was, "Why don't you speak for yourself, John?" In reality Standish was married twice. He believed in religious tolerance, in contrast to his Puritan contemporaries. He also appears in John Lothrop Motley's *Marry-Mount* and Helen Car-

lisle's *We Begin*, both works of fiction. Aside from Longfellow's legend, James Russel Lowell's poem "Interview with Miles Standish" is also legend. Longfellow's poem was made into operas by seven different composers, but none is still performed.

2766

**Stanislaus of Cracow, St.** (camp glory?) 1030–1070. In Christian legend, martyr bishop of Cracow. Invoked by soldiers in battle. Feast, 7 May. Stanislaus was appointed bishop of Cracow in 1072. Because of the oppressive rule of Prince Boleslaus II, the bishop excommunicated him. In revenge Boleslaus murdered the bishop with his own hands at the altar. The body was then hacked to pieces; parts were placed in goblets and flung out of doors to be eaten by carrion birds. However, four eagles watched over the remains of the saint. Then suddenly the bones came together, sinew to sinew, limb to limb, and the whole body was restored.

2767

**Star Husband Tale**   In American Indian mythology, a tale of two young girls who are seeking husbands and in the process open up a hole in the sky. The two girls are sleeping in the open at night and see two stars. They make wishes that they may be married to these stars. In the morning they find themselves in the upper world, each married to a star—one of the stars a young man and the other an old man. The women are usually warned against digging but eventually disobey and make a hole in the sky through which they see their old home below. They are seized with longing to return and secure help in making a long rope. On this they eventually succeed in reaching home.

This tale was used by the American folklorist Stith Thompson to reconstruct an archetype or hypothetical original form of the tale, "from which all other versions were produced by some individual or group changes." By comparing 86 versions Thompson was able to offer statistics in

support of his hypothetical archetype. Two girls (65 percent) sleeping outside (85 percent) make wishes for stars as husbands (90 percent ). All of the other motifs ranged statistically from 55 percent to 90 percent Thompson also used maps to locate the tale, by means of which he suggested that the tale was probably created in the Central Plains area of North America and diffused in all directions from its place of origin.

See also: TALE TYPE

2768

**Star of Bethlehem**   A flowering plant of the lily family. In medieval Christian legend, it was blessed by the Child Jesus as he lay in his manger because it served as his pillow. At Christmastime in Italy the manger is decked with star of Bethlehem. The French call it *la dame d'onze heures*, because it always opens at eleven o'clock.

*St. Stephen*

2769

**Stephen, St.** (crown)   First century. In the Bible, N.T., proto-, or first, Christian martyr, who was stoned to death. Feast, 26 December.

His legend is told in the Acts of the Apostles (6,7). Medieval legend deals with the recovery of the saint's body, which had been missing for some 400 years after his death. Lucian, a priest of Carsagamala in Palestine, was visited in a dream by Gamaliel, the Jewish doctor of the law who had taught St. Paul. Gamaliel revealed to Lucian that after the death of Stephen he had carried away the body and buried it in his own tomb. Gamaliel had also placed near St. Stephen's body those of Nicodemus and other saints. Lucian had the dream of Gamaliel three times. He went to his bishop, told the dream, and a crew went out to dig at the spot indicated in the dream. The crew discovered the remains of St. Stephen as well as those of some other saints. The relics were first placed in Jerusalem, then later taken to Constantinople, and finally to Rome, where they were placed in a tomb with the body of St. Lawrence. One medieval legend relates that when they opened the tomb and lowered St. Stephen's body, St. Lawrence's body moved on its side, giving place of honor on the right to St. Stephen. From the legend, the Romans called St. Lawrence *Il cortese Spagnuolo* (the courteous Spaniard). The phrase "fed with St. Stephen's bread" means to be stoned to death.

See also: LAWRENCE, ST.; NICODEMUS

2770
**Stonehenge**    A prehistoric circle of very large stones on Salisbury Plain in England. The medieval historian Geoffrey of Monmouth in his *History of the Kings of Britain* says that Stonehenge was erected by Merlin to perpetuate the memory of the teacher of Hengist the Jute, who killed King Vortigern and 400 of his attendants while pretending peace. Merlin was asked by Auralius Ambrosius to devise a memento to this cruel event. By magic Merlin transported the Giant's Dance, stones that had been brought by a race of giants to Killaraus in Ireland from Africa. The stones were said to possess magic properties. Legend also associates Stonehenge with the Druids, but recent scholarship has revealed that it is a much older structure.

See also: DRUIDS; HENGIST; MERLIN; VORTIGERN

2771
**Stone of Scone**    In British legend, believed to be the stone on which Jacob rested his head at Bethel, as recorded in the Old Testament. Medieval legend said that it was carried to Egypt, Spain, Ireland, and finally to Scotland, where it

was placed in the monastery of Scone. Scottish kings were crowned on the sacred stone. The English coronation chair, made for King Edward I, was designed to enclose the Stone of Scone, which he seized from the Scots in 1297. The chair, made of oak, was painted with birds, foliage, and animals on a gilt ground. Since 1308 every English sovereign, except Edward V and Edward VIII, has been crowned on it.

See also: JACOB

2772
**Stork**    A large wading bird having long legs and a long neck and bill. In western European folklore the stork is believed to bring babies. Many Germans believed that if a stork flew over a house it meant a child was on the way. This reflects the early belief that children were brought up out of the water or found in rocky caves. In Greek mythology the stork was sacred to the goddess Hera and in Roman mythology, to Juno, Hera's counterpart. In Christian symbolism the stork represents chastity, purity, and piety and is a harbinger of spring. Aristotle wrote that "it is a common story of the stork that the old birds are fed by their grateful progeny." It was believed in the Middle Ages, partly based on Aristotle, that when a stork grew old its children would surround it, provide it with food, and aid it when it flew by supporting it gently on each side with their wings. There are numerous motifs associated with the stork in the *Motif Index of Folk Literature*.

See also: HERA; JUNO

2773
**Stormalong, Old**    In American folklore, an occupational hero among sailors, particularly well known in chanteys, or sailors' work songs. One chantey begins "Old Stormy was a good old man, ay, ay, ay Mister Stormalong," and ends with a formulaic: "O Stormy's dead and gone to rest, of all the sailors he was best." Old Stormy was also well known in tall tales. When his ship was blown off course by a hurricane and crashed

into the Isthmus of Panama, it cut through the ground just as it had parted the waves, creating the Panama Canal. Like other folk heroes, Old Stormalong is strong beyond belief, and his feats resemble those of other American tall tale heroes.

See also: CROCKETT, DAVY; JOE MAGARAC; JOHN HENRY; MIKE FINK; PAUL BUNYAN; PECOS BILL

2774

**Strap Buckner**   In American Western folk-lore, a giant of a man who could drink any of his companions under the table. Aylett C. (Strap) Buckner (1794?–1832) moved to Texas as a young man from Virginia. Red-headed, of Irish and Scottish ancestry, he was supposedly nick-named "Strap" because of his prodigious size and strength. Though legend has it that the Indians (who, impressed by his strength, reportedly nick-named Buckner the "Red Son of Blue Thunder") offered him marriage with the Indian princess Tulipita, Buckner never married. One historian suggested that his lack of heirs allowed the growth of ever-more outlandish legends of his strength and size. He had a red beard and rode a swift gray horse. One day he was challenged at cards by the devil and lost when the demon grew to nearly 200 feet tall and some 80 feet in girth. Strap Buckner's spirit is still seen astride his gray horse riding through the night.

2775

**Strawberry**   A small bush producing sweet berries. In Norse mythology, the strawberry is associated with the love goddess Frigga; in Christian symbolism, it is associated with the Virgin Mary.

See also: FRIGGA; VIRGIN MARY

2776

**Stribog**   In Slavic mythology, god of winds. In the Russian epic *The Lay of Igor's Army*, the winds are called the grandsons of Stribog. Other Slavic wind gods are Varpulis, who caused the noise of a storm; Erisvorsh, god of the "holy tempest": and Vikhor, god of whirlwinds. In areas with harsh winters Stribog came to be considered the Winter King whose gusts chilled the bones of Mother Earth.

See also: *LAY OF IGOR'S ARMY, THE*

2777

**Stupa** (mound)   A mound of earth covered with masonry, containing at its center a relic, usually of the Buddha or Jina, or a portion of scripture. According to Buddhist legend, when the Buddha was about to die, he was asked by a disciple what would happen to his remains after death. The Buddha answered that a *stupa* should be built to contain them. Ashoka, the Buddhist king, built *stupas* at sites associated with the birth, life, and death of the Buddha. In Ceylon *stupa* is called *thupa*. Various architectural structures and terms developed from the term stupa: in Burma, *asgopa*; in China and Japan, *pagoda*; and in Tibet, *chörten*. Some older accounts call a *stupa* a *tope*. A *chaitya* is a hall containing a *stupa* or an image of Buddha. The *stupa* provides a physical focus for worship so that the mind may ascend to contemplation of spiritual realities.

See also: ASOKA; BUDDHA, THE; JINA

2778

**Stymphalian Birds**   In Greek mythology, bronze-beaked, man-eating, fantastic birdlike beings, expelled from Lake Stymphalus in Arcadia as Heracles' sixth labor. The hero frightened the birds with bronze castanets given him by the goddess Athena. Heracles then shot at them; some escaped and flew to the Black Sea, later to threaten the Argonauts. They were believed to be associated with Artemis's cult. Images of them were carved on the metopes of Zeus's temple at Olympia. Pausanias's *Description of Greece* (book 8) tells of the birds. Dürer's *Hercules Killing the Stymphalian Birds* shows the hero drawing his bow to kill them.

See also: ARCADIA; ARGONAUTS; ARTEMIS; ATHENA; HERACLES; ZEUS

**Styx** (hated)   In Greek mythology, one of the five rivers of Hades, the underworld, over which Charon ferried the spirits of the dead. It was named after Styx, the eldest daughter of Oceanus and Tethys and mother of Zelus (zeal), Nike (victory), Kratos (power), and Bia (strength) by the Titan Pallas. In the battle between the gods and the Titans Styx sided with the gods and was rewarded for her service and made ruler of the river named after her. The gods swore by the sacred Styx, and if they violated their oath, they would be punished by nine years of banishment from the council of the gods and would spend one year speechless and breathless. Though its waters were believed to be poisoned, Thetis immersed her son Achilles in its water to make him invulnerable.

The Styx appears or is cited in Homer's *Odyssey* (book 10), Hesiod's *Theogony*, Vergil's *Aeneid* (book 6), Ovid's *Metamorphoses* (book 3), Dante's *Divine Comedy* (Hell, cantos 7, 9, 14), Shakespeare's *Troilus and Cressida* (V.4) and *Titus Andronicus* (1.11), Milton's "L'Allegro" and *Paradise Lost* (Book 2), and Pope's *Dunciad* (2.338). In art Joachim Patinir's *Charon Crossing the Styx* and Delacroix's *Dante and Virgil Crossing the Styx* are best known.

See also: ACHILLES; *AENEID, THE*; CHARON; HADES; HESIOD; NIKE; OCEANUS; *ODYSSEY, THE*; PALLAS; THETIS; TITANS

**Su-bhadra**   In Hindu mythology, sister of Krishna (an incarnation of the god Vishnu) and a wife of the hero Arjuna. According to some accounts Su-bhadra had an incestuous relationship with her brother Krishna. When the cart Jagan-Natha is brought out, images of Su-bhadra and her elder brother Balaram accompany the idol.

See also: ARJUNA; BALARAM; JAGAN-NATHA; KRISHNA; VISHNU

**Sucellos** (the good striker)   In Celtic mythology, a thunder god, portrayed as an elderly, benign fat man, associated with the underworld. He is most often depicted with a long curling beard and a long-shafted hammer, which was a weapon, a cooper's tool, a fencing instrument, and an emblem of power, like a scepter.

**Suiten** (water god)   In Japanese Buddhist mythology, water god derived from the Hindu god Varuna, portrayed as an old man seated on a *makara*, a mythical animal with the body and tail of a fish and an antelope head and legs. In some representations Suiten is shown as a young man holding a sword in his right hand and in his left hand a snake coiled like a question mark, with five snakes issuing from his hair. Suiten is one of the Jiu No O, 12 Japanese Buddhist gods and goddesses adopted from Hindu mythology.

See also: JIU NO O; MAKARA; VARUNA

**Sukkoth** (booths)   In Judaism, Feast of Booths, or Tabernacles, celebrated from the 15th to the 22nd of Tishri (September and October). Originally it was called the Feast of Ingathering, when the summer crops and fruits were gathered. Parts of the feast, according to the Old Testament (Deut. 16:9–12, Exod. 34:22, Lev. 23:15–21, Num. 29:12–40), were reaping of the crops and fruits, special rituals to induce rain, and dwelling in *sukkoth* (booths), actually trellis-roofed cabins made of plaited twigs of carob and oleander and roofed with palm leaves. Leviticus (23:42–43) says: "All the people of Israel shall live in shelters for seven days, so that your descendants may know that the Lord made the people of Israel live in simple shelters when he led them out of Egypt. He is the Lord your God" (Today's English Version). Of course, this is a later interpretation, because when the Israelites wandered through the desert they lived in tents, not booths; wood and green leaves were unavailable to them. Sukkot is a joyous festival and includes a blessing of the sun. Originally, it was based on a pagan magic rite to rekindle the decadent sun at the time of the autumnal equinox and to hail it when it rose at dawn this folk custom is still found in the Islamic Ashura, New Year, where children and unmarried men leap over flames as did the ancient Romans who leaped over fires and ran through the fields with blazing torches. Bonfires in European folklore are part of the ritual, especially at Halloween, which was the eve of the ancient New Year as celebrated in Europe.

2784

**Sukusendal** In Finnish mythology, a nightmare spirit who has sexual intercourse with people while they sleep, appearing as a person of the opposite sex. Sometimes it replaces rightful children with changelings. To protect children, mothers placed a pair of scissors or some iron object in the cradle; this made the spirit unable to do evil. If a person went to the bathhouse late at night, however, he or she might be killed by the Sukusendal.

2785

**Sul** In Celtic mythology, a goddess of the sun and hot springs, whose temple at Bath, England, had perpetual fires burning in her honor. Some ancient Roman writers equated her with their goddess Minerva as well as with the Italian goddess Salus, who presided over health and prosperity.

See also: MINERVA

2786

**Sumangat** In Malayan mythology, the human soul, believed to be a spirit copy of the human form, which leaves the body during sleep and at death.

2787

**Summanus** In Roman mythology, ancient Italian god associated with evening lightning. He had a temple near the Circus Maximus where on 20 June sacrifices were offered to him.

2788

**Sumsumara-Jataka** Buddhist folktale, number 208 of the *Jatakas*, or *Birth-Stories of the Former Lives of the Buddha*.

When Brahmadatta ruled as king of Benares, the future Buddha was born a monkey at the foot of the Himalayas. He grew strong and sturdy, with a big, muscular frame. He lived near a bend in the Ganges River close to the forest.

At the same time a crocodile also lived nearby in the Ganges. The crocodile's wife one day saw the monkey, and impressed by his massive size, thought how nice it would be to eat his big heart. She said to her husband, "I want to eat the heart of that big monkey that lives nearby."

"Good wife," said the crocodile, "I live in the water and he lives on the dry land. How can we catch him?"

"By hook or by crook," she replied, "but catch him we must. If I don't get him, I'll die."

"All right," said the crocodile, consoling his wife. "I have a plan. I will give you his heart to eat."

One day while the monkey was sitting on the bank of the Ganges, after taking a drink of water, the crocodile drew near.

"Sir Monkey," said the crocodile, "why do you live on rotten fruits in this part of the forest? On the other side of the river there is no end of mango trees and all sorts of delicious fruits, some as sweet as honey. Why don't you let me carry you over to the other side of the river."

The monkey trusted the crocodile and climbed onto his back. After the crocodile had swum well into the center of the river, he plunged deep into the water, and the monkey began to flay about in the water.

"Good friend," cried the monkey, "I will drown."

"What, do you think I agreed to carry you across the river out of the goodness of my heart?" the crocodile answered. "Not a bit. My wife wants to eat your heart, and I promised her that I would get it for her."

"Friend," said the monkey, "that's nice of you to tell me. But I don't have my heart with me. Why, if my heart were inside me when I jump among the trees, it would be all broken to pieces."

"Well, then," said the angry crocodile, "where do you keep your heart?"

The monkey pointed to a fruit-laden fig tree in the distance on the shore. "See," he said, "there is my heart, hanging on the fig tree with the fruit."

"If you show me your heart," the crocodile replied, "then I won't kill you."

"Take me to the shore, then" said the monkey, "and I'll point it out to you hanging right in front of your eyes."

The crocodile took the monkey across the river and brought him to the fig tree. The monkey leaped off his back, climbed the fig tree, and sat on one of its branches.

"You stupid crocodile," he cried from the safety of the tree branch, "you thought that I kept my heart in a tree. You are a fool. I have outsmarted you. You may keep the fruit for yourself. You may have a strong body, but you have no common sense." The crocodile, feeling miserably foolish, went back home.

"In this tale of a former life," said the Buddha, "the crocodile was Devadatta, my life-long enemy, the lady Cinca was his wife, and I was the monkey."

See also: DEVADATTA; JATAKA

2789

**Sung-ti wang**   In Chinese mythology, the ruler of the third hell of Ti Yü, the underworld.
See also: TI YÜ

2790

**Supratika**   In Hindu mythology, one of the eight elephants who protect the eight points of the compass. The group is called Diggajas.

2791

**Surt** (black)   In Norse mythology, a fire giant who is to enkindle the universe at Ragnarok, the end of the world, when the gods and giants will be destroyed. When the world ends at Ragnarok

> Surt travels from the south with the enemy of
>     twigs [fire],
> the sun shines from the swords of the
>     carrion-gods,
> Mountains resound, and ogresses roam,
> Humans tread the road to Hel, and the sky is
>     riven.

He rules Muspellsheim. Surt appears in the *Prose Edda*.
See also: MUSPELLHEIM; *PROSE EDDA*; RAGNAROK

*Surya*

2792

**Surya** (to shine?)   In Hindu mythology, the sun god, whose chariot is drawn by the Harits (green), seven mares, or by one seven-headed horse, Etasha. His wife is Sanjna (conscience), who is also called Dyu-mayi (the brilliant) and Maha-virya (the very powerful).

Sanjna was unable to bear the intense love of Surya, so she gave him Chhaya (shade) as his mistress. Surya, not noticing that there had been a substitution, had three children by Chhaya: Sani, the planet Saturn; the Manu Savarna; and a daughter, the Tapati (heating) River. Sanjna then became jealous of Surya's love for these children by his mistress and fled, but Surya went in search of her and brought her back. Their child was Yama, god of the dead. In Indian art Surya is portrayed drawn by the Harits, or by Etasha, surrounded by rays. His charioteer is Vivaswat (the bright one), also another name for the sun, who is credited with being the father of the Aswins, twin gods who precede the dawn. Closely connected with Surya are Suras, lesser gods or spirits who are part of his heavenly court. An earlier Vedic god, Arusha, representing the morning or rising sun, is considered in some texts to be another form of Surya.

Among Surya's many epithets are Dinakara (the maker of day); Bhaskara (the creator of light); Mihira (he who waters the earth), referring to Surya's drawing the moisture up from the seas so that clouds are formed; Grahapati (the lord of the stars); and Karmasakshi (the witness of men's deeds).

See also: ASWINS; SANJNO; YAMA

2793

**Susano** (swift-impetuous male, the impetuous god)   In Japanese Shinto mythology, storm god, brother of the sun goddess Amaterasu. He was born from the nose of the primeval creator god Izanagi. He is said to have planted the forests of Korea from the hairs of his beard. Because of this he is usually associated with forests.

Susano is both good and evil in Japanese mythology, often displaying the traits of a trickster. After he had driven his sister Amaterasu to hide in a cave, thereby plunging the world into darkness, he was exiled by the gods from the Plain of Heaven to earth. In the *Kojiki* (records of ancient matters) his subsequent fate is told. He arrived at the river Hi in Izumo, where he saw some chopsticks floating down the stream. He thought, therefore, that there must be people above. Proceeding upstream in search of them, he discovered an old man and woman with a young girl between them. They were crying. He asked who they were.

"I am an earth spirit," the old man said, "and my name is Foot-Stroking Elder. My wife's name is Hand-Stroking Elder. And this is our daughter whose name is Mistress Head Comb."

Susano then asked, "And what is the cause of the weeping?"

"Once we had eight daughters," the old man said, "but there is an eight-forked serpent that comes each year and eats one. His time has come round again. That is why we weep."

"What is the serpent's form?" Susano asked.

"Its eyes are as red as the winter cherry. It has one body with eight heads and tails. On that body moss grows, and conifers. Its length extends over eight valleys and eight hills, and if one looks at the belly, it is constantly bloody and inflamed."

Then, looking at the girl, Susano asked, "Your daughter, will you give her to me?"

The old man replied, "With reverence. However, I do not know your name."

"I am the elder brother of the goddess Amaterasu, and I descended here from heaven."

"That being so, with reverence, she is yours," the old man replied.

Susano took the girl at once, changed her into a multitudinously close-toothed comb, and placed it in his hair.

"Distill a brew of eightfold refined liquor," he told the old couple. "Also, make a fence round about, and in that fence let there be eight gates; at each gate let there be eight platforms and on each platform a liquor vat; into each of which pour some eightfold liquor and wait."

They did as they were told. The eight-forked serpent came at the appointed time and dipped a head into each vat. Then, as the dragon became drunk, every one of its heads lay down to sleep. Susano drew his sword and cut the monster into pieces.

See also: AMATERASU OMIKAMI; *KOJIKI*

2794

**Sutra** (thread or row)   A short verse or aphorism, a collection of such sayings, or a work giving the essence of teachings. In Hinduism, sutras may explain the Vedas or the teachings of a philosophical school; they also may be concerned with secular matters such as Sanskrit grammar and courtly love. In Buddhism a sutra is a sermon of the Buddha on a topic of general interest. The sutra is the earliest piece of Buddhist literature in China. Most begin with the phrase "Thus was it heard by me." In Pali, *sutta*.

See also: VEDAS

2795

**Suttung** (heavy with broth)   In Norse mythology, a giant who possessed Odhrerir, a magic caldron containing a potion that conferred wisdom and the gift of poetry. The god Odin seduced Gunlod, the daughter of Suttung, and obtained the potion from her. When Odin fled in the form of an eagle, he was pursued by Suttung. He came so close that Odin could not get the mead back into the possession of the Aesir, and therefore he urinated a small portion. This portion makes bad poets.

See also: BAUGI; GUNLOD; KVASIR; ODHRERIR

2796

**Svadilfare** (slippery ice?)   In Norse mythology, a horse belonging to the giants; father of Sleipnir, Odin's horse. Svadilfare worked in the building of a structure for the gods. The animal was lured away from his task for sexual intercourse by the fire-trickster god, Loki, disguised as a mare, and the gods therefore did not pay the giants because the work was not completed on time. The myth is told in the *Prose Edda*.

See also: LOKI; *PROSE EDDA*; SLEIPNIR

2797

**Svantovit** (strong lord?)   In Slavic mythology, war god; in some accounts the father of all gods, particularly Dazhbog, the sun god, and Svarogich, the fire god.

Portrayed as a four-faced man wearing a hat, he held in one hand a bull's horn containing wine. Once a year the high priest would examine the contents of the bull's horn to see if any wine remained. If some did, it was a good omen, meaning the year would be fruitful and happy. If the wine had diminished considerably, poor crops and trouble were to be expected. Each year a captive Christian was chosen by lottery and sacrificed to the god. When the Christian Danish king Valdemar conquered Arkona in 1168, he destroyed Svantovit's temple and dragged the god's image out to humiliate it. Svantovit's followers waited for their god to destroy the Christians, but instead the Christians hacked the idol to pieces and burned it. A black animal was seen to emerge from the god's burning image and flee the Christian warriors, who said it was the devil.

Closely connected with Svantovit were other gods, who may have been variants of him, such as Triglav, portrayed with three heads, his eyes and lips covered by a golden veil; Rugevit, a warrior god who was armed with eight swords, seven hanging from his girdle and the eighth held in his right hand; and Yarovit, portrayed with a golden shield. Radigast, also a war god, held a double-edged ax. On his chest he wore a bull's head, and on his curly head was a swan with outstretched wings. One statue near the river Zbrucz depicts Svantovit as having breasts. This may be a later representation of the deity showing acceptance or tolerance of women within his sanctuary.

See also: DAZHBOG; SVAROGICH

2798

**Svarogich** (Svarazic) (son of Svarog)   In Slavic mythology, god of fire, son of Svarog (heaven), the sky god, and brother of Dazhbog, the sun god. One custom that survived long after paganism was the taboo on cursing while a domestic fire was being lit. It was believed that Svarog had given fire and could also take it away. Svarogich was portrayed wearing a birdlike helmet on his head and the image of a black bison's head on his breast; his left hand held a double-edged sword. Svarogich was called on for his prophetic powers, and human beings were sacrificed to him. After John, bishop of Mecklenburg, was captured in battle in 1066, his head was offered to the god.

See also: DAZHBOG; SVAROG

2799

**Svyatogor** (Sviatogor) (holy mountains) In Russian folklore, a *bogatyr*, or epic hero, with superhuman strength, who appears in the *bylini*, the epic songs, as well as in folklore. Svyatogor once boasted that if he could find the place where all of the earth was concentrated, he could lift it. He found a small bag on a steppe and touched it with his staff, but it did not move. Nor did it move when he touched it with his finger. Without getting off his horse he grabbed the bag in his hand, but again it would not move. He then got off his horse, took the bag with both hands, and lifted it above his knees until he sweated blood, but as he did he sank deep into the earth. The poem ends: "Svyatogor had indeed found the weight of the earth, but God punished him for his pride."

See also: BYLINA; ILYA MUROMETS

2800

**Swallow** A small bird noted for its swift and graceful movement. In Egyptian mythology the swallow was sacred to Isis as the Great Mother. In Greek mythology the bird was sacred to Aphrodite and in Roman mythology, to Venus, her counterpart. It is also associated with the Sumero-Semitic goddess Nina. According to a Scandinavian legend, the bird received its name when it hovered over the cross of Jesus crying "Svala! Svala!" (console! console!). In medieval Christian belief the swallow became a symbol of

the Incarnation and Resurrection of Christ because the bird disappears in winter and reappears in spring. Many paintings of the Nativity depict a swallow nesting under the eaves, and some Christian artworks portraying the Crucifixion have a swallow hovering above the cross offering Jesus consolation, hence the name "bird of consolation" for the swallow. In Jewish folklore the swallow is said to have convinced God through a trick that the best food in the world for the snake would be a frog, not a man. When the snake found out what the swallow did, it leaped up and caught some of its tail. That is why some swallows have forked tails.

See also: APHRODITE; FROG; ISIS; SNAKE; VENUS

2801

**Swamp Fox** In American history and folklore, popular name of Francis Marion (1732–1795) of South Carolina, who fought on the side of the Patriots during the American Revolution. He used the swamps as his base for guerrilla warfare. One legend tells how he entertained a British officer during an exchange of prisoners. When the officer saw the Americans poorly clad and eating bark, he returned to his post and later resigned his commission, feeling he could never again fight against such dedicated men. G. W. Mark's primitive painting *Marion Feasting the British Officer* illustrates the tale. Marion earned his name Swamp Fox, according to one legend, because he used the cry of a swamp fox as a signal, although no such animal exists.

2802

**Swan** A large aquatic bird with a long slender neck and often white plumage. In Greek mythology swans were sacred to the muses, who were associated with the god Apollo. The best-known Greek myth relating to the swan concerns Zeus and Leda. Zeus, in the form of a swan, seduced Leda beside the river Eurotas. Later Leda laid an egg, which produced Helen, Castor, and Polydeuces. Swans were honored in Sparta as symbols of the goddess Aphrodite. In a late Greek myth Helen is united with the hero Achilles on a spirit isle in northern Pontus, where they are served by swans. In medieval legend Lohengrin is called the Knight of the Swan and appears in a boat drawn by a silver swan. The legend was used by Wagner for his opera *Lohengrin*. In Hindu mythology the god Brahma often rides a swan. In Celtic mythology the swan is a solar symbol and beneficent. In many European tales girls are turned into swans. This motif is used in Tchaikovsky's great ballet *Swan Lake*. According to legend, swans sing beautifully before they die, which is reflected in the term "swan song," the last work of a poet or a composer.

See also: APOLLO; BRAHMA; CASTOR AND POLYDEUCES; HELEN OF TROY; LEDA; ZEUS

*Swine*

**2803**

**Swine** The boar, sow, and pig frequently appear in world mythology and folklore; sometimes one is confused with another. A boar is the uncastrated male swine, a pig is a young swine, and a sow is an adult female swine. The boar is often a phallic symbol and associated with Attis, Adonis, Osiris, Set, Vishnu, Ares, Mars, Tammuz, Odin, and Woden, all male deities. It is also sacred to various goddesses in mythology, such as Aphrodite, Demeter, and Freya, as well as the Greek heroine Atalanta. Norse mythology has the gods and heroes of Valhalla continually feasting on Saehrimir, a magic boar who is constantly replenished after he is eaten. Freya, the Norse goddess, had a lover, Ottar, who was a golden boar. In northern cults a boar was sacrificed to the god Frey at the winter solstice. Part of that custom continues today in the form of roast pig at Christmas feasts. In Egyptian mythology the goddess Nut was sometimes portrayed as a sow with her piglets. It was believed that each morning Nut ate the piglets, that is, the stars were eaten by the sky goddess. The Greek goddess Demeter was often portrayed with a sow at her feet or in her arms, and the Tibetan goddess Vajravareh was also identified with the sow. The ancient Hebrews regarded swine as unclean animals, forbidding the eating of pork, although some Jews did keep swine. In medieval Christian belief the pig was a symbol of lust and sensuality. In Buddhist belief the pig is also an unclean animal and symbol of lust. In Chinese folklore the pig is a symbol of the wealth of the forest, and the Japanese use parts of the boar as a talisman against snakes. There are numerous motifs associated with swine in the *Motif Index of Folk Literature*.

See also: APHRODITE; ARES; ATTIS; DEMETER; FREYA; MARS; NUT; ODIN; OSIRIS; VALHALLA; VISHNU; WODEN

**2804**

**Swithen, St.** (Swithin, Swithun, Swithunus) Died 862. In Christian legend, bishop of Winchester, chaplain and counselor to King Egbert of the West Saxons. Feast, 15 July.

The most famous legend connected with the saint says that if it rains on his feast day, it will rain for another 40 days. According to one explanation of the origin of the legend, St. Swithen asked that his body be buried with the poor people, outside the church, so that the "sweet rain of heaven might fall upon his grave." This was done, but 100 years later it was decided to move the saint's body inside the church because a workman said he had a vision of the saint requesting that his body be moved. When they attempted to move the remains, however, it began to rain and continued for some 40 days, which held up the removal. During the reign of William the Conqueror, Walkelin, bishop of Winchester, laid the foundation for a new cathedral church, and on 15 July 1093, the shrine of St. Swithen was removed, or translated, from the old to the new church. The shrine became very famous. Henry VIII, however, destroyed it along with numerous others but found that its gold and jewels were fakes. A new shrine was dedicated in 1962.

Other saints having legends of rain continuing for some time after their feast days are Sts. Gervase and Protase, St. Médard in France, St. Cewydd in Wales, and St. Godelière in Flanders. An old English couplet captures the folk belief:

St. Swithin's day, gif ye do rain, for forty day
   it will remain;
St. Swithin's day, an ye be fair, for forty days
   twill rain nae mair.

2805

**Syaha** (hail)   In Hinduism, the exclamation spoken when an offering is made to the gods. Syaha is also the name of the wife of the fire god, Agni, where offerings are made over fire.

See also: AGNI

# T

**Tagaro** In Melanesian mythology, trickster and culture hero often in conflict with his brother Suce-mutua. One account tells how Tagaro creates edible fruits for humankind while his evil brother Suce-mutua creates useless ones. Variants give the name of the evil brother as Meragubutto. In one tale Tagaro devises a plot to destroy Meragubutto through a clever trick. He tells his brother that he wishes to gain more magic power, but to do so he must be burned alive in his own house. Meragubutto is only too pleased to set a torch to his brother's house and agrees to help. Tagaro goes into his house and enters a deep pit that he had dug earlier. Meragubutto lights the fire and the house goes up in flames. When the fire dies down, Tagaro reappears. Impressed and believing that Tagaro's magic has been increased by the fire, he resolves to do the same. He enters his house, which is then set afire by Tagaro, and is burned to death.

See also: TRICKSTER

**Tag-Mar** In Tibetan Buddhism, the Red-Tiger Devil, portrayed with the head of a tiger and the body of a man. He was part of a mystery play which appears to have been intended to expel the old year and the demons of bad luck.

**Tahumers** (Tahuras, Takhmoruw, Takhmorup, Takhma-Urupa, Tahmuraf, Tatmurath) In Persian mythology, a king, culture hero, and slayer of demons, appearing in the epic poem *Shah Namah* by Firdusi. Tahumers succeeded his father, King Husheng, and continued his father's role as teacher of the arts of civilization: spinning wool, weaving carpets, training wild animals, and hunting. In Firdusi's epic, Tahumers is often called Diw-bund (binder of demons) because of his power over the demonic underworld.

One day the evil spirit, Ahriman, attempted to destroy Tahumers, but the king "bound Ahriman by his magic spells and rode him like a swift steed. He saddled Ahriman and without respite made him carry him on a tour of the world." While the king was away, however, other demons attempted to take control of his kingdom. Tahumers returned "girded with majesty and master of the world. On his shoulder he bore a massive club."

The demon army was poised against Tahumers and his army, but Tahumers "bound up two-thirds of them by magic and struck down the others with his heavy club." The demons were tied together to be executed.

"Do not kill us," they cried out, "and thou shalt learn from us a new art."

Interested in their offer, the king spared them. The demons immediately brought a pen, ink, and a book and taught Tahumers how to read and write. His mind "with learning was illuminated. The world was blest / with quiet and repose. . . ." Tahumers reigned for some 30 years more and was succeeded by his son, the hero Jemshid.

See also: AHRIMAN; HUSHENG; *SHAH NAMAH*

2809
**Taikó-mol** (solitude walker)   In North American Indian mythology (Yuki), creator god who appeared on the foam of the primeval water wearing an eagle headdress. After he had created the earth by using four *lilkae* (stone crooks), he went up into the sky.

He makes humans from sticks. One day a human did something wrong and died. Taikó-mol buried him and resurrected him the next day, but he smelled so bad that the people all got sick. Taikó-mol then decided not to give them the power to resurrect the dead, but he did give them the Dance of the Dead Spirits.

See also: ASK AND EMBLA

2810
**Taillefer**   Died 1066. In medieval history and legend, Norman warrior and minstrel. Before the Battle of Hastings he sang songs in praise of Charlemagne and Roland. His singing encouraged the troops of William the Conqueror. Taillefer struck the first blow in the battle and was the first Norman casualty.

See also: CHARLEMAGNE; ROLAND

2811
**Taiowa**   In North American Indian mythology (Hopi), creative void, force, mindful presence. Taiowa's first creation was Sotuknang, who undertook creation of people with the aid of Kohyangwuti, the spider woman.

2812
**Taishaku Ten**   In Japanese Buddhist mythology, a god, derived from the Hindu god Indra, portrayed with three eyes, holding in his right hand a thunderbolt trident, called Dokko, and in his left hand a cup. Taishaku Ten is one of the Jiu No O, 12 Japanese Buddhist gods and goddesses adopted from Hindu mythology.

See also: INDRA; JIU NO O

2813
**T'ai-shan kun wang**   In Chinese mythology, ruler of the seventh hell of Ti Yü, the underworld.

See also: TI YÜ

2814
**Talassio**   In Roman mythology, god of marriage; equated by the Romans with the Greek god Hymen. He is associated with the myth of the Rape of the Sabine Women. Livy's *History of Rome* (book 1) tells of Talassio.

See also: HYMEN; LIVY

2815
***Tale of Bygone Years, The***   Medieval Russian chronicle compiled by various hands within 150 years of the adoption of Christianity as the state religion, from about 1040 to 1118. The chronicle relates the stories in the spirit of *dvoeverie* (double faith), a continuation of pagan traditions after the adoption of Christianity. One version of the text is traditionally ascribed to Friar Nestor (1056–1114), who edited and contributed to the chronicles. The work comprises a history of Russia from the creation of the world through the eventual overthrow of the old Slavic gods and the coming of Christianity under Prince Vladimir, who was later canonized by the Russian Orthodox Church. Rich in legends, folktales, and myths, *The Tale of Bygone Years* is also a main source for early Russian history. It is sometimes called *The Primary Chronicle*.

See also: *PRIMARY CHRONICLE*; VLADIMIR, ST.

2816

**Tale Type**    A term first used by the Finnish folklorist Antti Aarne and further developed by the American folklorist Stith Thompson. Their joint publication, *The Types of the Folktale*, first published in 1910 and revised in 1928 and again in 1961, established type sets, or recurring patterns, for the plots of individual tales.

The term *type set* as it is used in folklore studies suggests stories that can be configured into a set and are thus identifiable because they share a common plot. Originally Aarne isolated and indexed 540 distinguishable tale types, leaving nearly 2,000 slots open for later additions. When Thompson revised the original work, he increased the number of identifiable tale types and subtypes to 3,228.

If one looks at an example of one tale type, Snow White (identified as Aarne/Thompson, AT 709), one finds five major elements to the tale: I. Snow White and her Stepmother; II. Snow White's Rescue; III. The Poisoning; IV. Help of the Dwarfs; and V. Her Revival. Motifs for each element are then listed and associated with their motif number. Under number I are the following individual motifs: Z65.1. Red as blood, white as snow; L55. Stepdaughter heroine; M312.4. Prophecy: superb beauty for girl; D1311.6.3. Sun answers questions; D1311.2. Mirror answers questions; D1323.1. Magic clairvoyant mirror. Each tale has thus been broken down into its basic elements, and the many variant motifs used to create the story are listed. Studies of individual tales are listed according to their AT number and can be found in the standard folklore bibliographies and electronic databases.

See also: MOTIF

2817

**Taliesin** (radiant brow)    Sixth century. In medieval Welsh legend, bard who appears in the Book of Taliesin (in *The Mabinogion*), in which he is credited with supernatural powers.

See also: *MABINOGION, THE*

2818

**Talmud** (study or learning)    In Judaism, books of civil and religious law written between 500 B.C.E. and 500 C.E.. The books are not contained in but are largely derived from the Pentateuch. There are two collections, the Babylonian and the Jerusalem, or Palestinian, Talmuds. Part of the Talmud contains *Haggadah* (narration) consisting of myths, legends, and fables to explain various beliefs, rites, and parts of Scripture.

See also: BIBLE, THE

2819

**Talonhaltija** (guardian spirit)    In Finno-Ugric mythology, spirit believed to be the ghost of the first person to die in a house, or else the ghost of the first person who kindled a fire in the house. The *talonhaltija* is beneficent, looking after the welfare of the family.

2820

**Talus** (Talos) (brass or sufferer?)    In Greek mythology, a man created from brass by the smith-god Hephaestus. Talus was given to King Minos of Crete to protect the island. Every time a stranger appeared Talus would greet the visitor, becoming red hot and embracing the person to death. When the Argonauts arrived he threw rocks at them. Eventually he was killed by Poeas, an Argonaut. Another person named Talus was a nephew of Daedalus and credited with the invention of the saw and the compass. Daedalus, however, was quite jealous of Talus's gifts and killed him by hurling him down the Acropolis of Athens.

See also: ARGONAUTS; DAEDALUS; HEPHAESTUS; MINOS

2821

**Tamar** (palm tree)    In the Bible, O.T., Absalom's sister, daughter of King David; she was raped by Amnon, another of King David's sons. Amnon was killed by Absalom (2 Sam. 1:32). Robinson Jeffers's *Tamar, and Other Poems* is based on the biblical tale but deals with a modern Tamar who lives on the Monterey coast. She seduces her brother and brings destruction to her whole family.

See also: ABSALON; DAVID

**Tambora**   2822
In Australian mythology, headless female beings who dragged men to their dark caves.

**Tamburlaine the Great** (Timur the Lame)   2823
1333–1405. In medieval history and legend, despot who ruled by terror over various parts of Asia and India. His capital was Samarkand. He appears in Marlowe's first play *Tamburlaine the Great* (1587), an epic play in two parts written in blank verse.

**Tam-Din**   2824
In Tibetan Buddhism, a "wrathful entity," often portrayed with a horse's head; derived from the Hindu god Haya-griva.

See also: HAYA-GRIVA

**Tammuz** (Dumuzi) (rightful son?)   2825
In Near Eastern mythology (Babylonian), god of corn and vegetation; he died each winter and was resurrected each spring; originally a Sumerian deity, Dumuzi.

Tammuz was originally a sun god, the son of Ea and the goddess Siduri and the lover or husband of the great goddess Ishtar. His love affair and death are told in the ancient poem *Ishtar's Descent into the Underworld*, known in various versions throughout the Near East, in which the goddess offers her youthful lover to be killed in place of herself. In Canaan Tammuz was called Adonai (my lord), and a great festival, celebrating his death and resurrection, was observed in various Near Eastern cities. Gebal was the chief seat of the spring festival in Phoenicia. "Gardens of

Adonis" were planted—pots filled with earth and cut herbs (which soon withered away) in which wooden figures of the god had been placed. Wailing women tore their hair and lacerated their breasts during the seven days of the festival. The Hebrew prophet Ezekiel saw women in the north gate of the temple "weeping for Tammuz" (Ezekiel 8:14).

See also: DUMUZI; EA; EZEKIEL; ISHTAR

**Tancred** (thought, advice)   2826
d. 1112 C.E. In medieval legend, Norman hero, son of Otho the Good and Emma, sister of Robert Guiscard. Tancred served under Godfrey de Bouillon in the First Crusade. Tancred appears in Tasso's *Jerusalem Delivered*, Rossini's opera *Tancredi*, Goethe's *Tasso*, and the earlier Monteverdi work *Il combattimento di Tancredi e Clorinda*.

See also: RINALDO

**Tane** (male)   2827
In Polynesian mythology, creator god, lord of the forest, son of Atea and Papa, father and husband of the goddess Hina.

According to some accounts, Tane tried to have sexual intercourse with his mother, but she rejected his advances. He then left home in search of a wife. He had sexual intercourse with various beings, producing such offspring as rocks, streams, trees, and reptiles. Not satisfied with any of his children because they did not have his human shape, he formed a woman out of soft red sand and breathed life into her. He called her Hina and married her. She is regarded as the first woman in Polynesian mythology and is associated with the moon and with fertility, and she guards the entrance to the land of the dead. In some accounts she is married to Tiki, the first man, and founded a royal line. Hina was portrayed with two faces. Tane's sexual organ was also called Tiki. Tiki appears in some legends as the creator of the first woman.

In Hawaiian mythology Tane is called Kane and is known as a major god who possessed a gigantic penis. In many myths his enemy is Kanaloa, the squid god. Kane's home is Kane-huna-moku (hidden land of Kane).

See also: ADAM AND EVE; ATEA AND PAPA; TIKI

2828

**Tangaloa**   In Polynesian mythology, creator god, who is also known as Ta'aroa, Tangaroa, and Kanaloa.

According to one Samoan myth, Tangaloa lived alone in a limitless, formless void in which there was neither light nor motion. One day he cast down a rock, which became Manu's Groves, the main island in the Samoan group. Next he made the remaining islands. Tangaloa's bird, Tuli, flying over the island in search of rest, pointed out to the god that the land lacked shade. Tangaloa gave Tuli a creeping vine for shade. When the vine withered and decomposed, maggots formed, eventually becoming the first man and woman.

According to a Tahitian account, Tangaloa created himself, having no mother or father, and lived in a shell called Rumia (upset). After a time he became bored and slipped out of the shell, only to find a totally dark void, so he found a new shell in which to hide. For thousands of eons he remained in the shell in deep contemplation. Then, using the new shell for the foundation and the old shell for the dome, he formed the sky. Calling himself Te Tumu (the source), he created various gods, whom he decked out with red and yellow feathers. When the feathers fell to the ground, they turned into trees and plants. Tangaloa then commissioned some artisan gods to fashion "a good-looking boy," though some variants say he first created woman.

Another tradition says Tangaloa and the god Akea Wakea had a dispute about which one was the father of a child born to the goddess Papa. To settle the argument, Papa cut the child in half, giving a half to each god. Akea Wakea threw his half into the sky, and it became the sun. Tan-galoa held his half until it decomposed. He then threw it into the sky, and it became the moon.

See also: ATEA AND PAPA

2829

**Tanner of Tamworth, The**   In medieval legend, English hero who mistook Edward IV for a highwayman. After an altercation they changed horses, the king giving his hunter for the Tanner's cob (a short-legged, stocky horse), worth about four shillings. As soon as the tanner mounted the king's horse, it threw him, and the tanner gladly paid a sum of money to get back his old mount. King Edward then blew the hunting horn, and his courtiers gathered round. "I expect I shall be hanged for this," cried Tanner. King Edward, however, gave him the manor of Plumpton Park, with an income of 300 marks a year.

*The return of Tannhäuser to Venusberg*

2830

**Tannhäuser** (dweller in the house of Tann, a name for Venus)   13th century. In medieval German history and legend, a knight who fell in love with the pagan goddess Venus. His tale is told in many ballads.

Tannhäuser was a minnesinger. One day he wandered near Hörselberg in Thuringia and heard the alluring song of Venus. He entered the Venusberg, her home, through a subterranean cave. He stayed with the goddess, "yielding to Venus's witching spells." After a while, however, his sexual appetite was dulled, and he fled the goddess.

Wishing to return to his betrothed, he felt guilty because of his passion for Venus. He decided to go to Rome and ask the pope for forgiveness.

"No," said Pope Urban, "you can no more hope for mercy than this dry staff can be expected to bud again."

Distraught, the knight left. On the third day after the pope had dismissed him, the papal staff bloomed. Realizing his error, the pope sent to find Tannhäuser, but the knight had returned to Venus.

Wagner's opera *Tannhäuser* (1845) is based on the medieval legend. The composer has the hero return from the Venusberg to the court of the landgrave of Thuringia, where Elizabeth, his betrothed, has remained true to Tannhäuser. At a great singing tournament, Tannhäuser's friend Wolfram von Eschenbach sings of spiritual love, and Tannhäuser sings of erotic love. Wolfram then mentions the name of Elizabeth, and Tannhäuser rejects Venus, who appears briefly on the mountain, singing seductively. A funeral procession then approaches. On the bier is Elizabeth. When Tannhäuser sees her, he dies. The next morning, pilgrims arrive from Rome bearing the pope's staff, which has miraculously bloomed. The blooming staff is a common motif in folk literature (F971.1).

See also: MOTIF; VENUS; VENUSBERG

2831
**Tano**   In African mythology (Togoland), the river god.

God had two sons, Tano and Bia. The older, Bia, was more obedient, and God wanted to give him the fertile lands to control. Tano was to receive the barren lands. A goat told Tano of God's plan. So Tano disguised himself as Bia and arrived at God's house before Bia had a chance to get there. God mistakenly gave the fertile lands to Tano and could not later revoke what he had given.

In another myth, a hunter, after trying for many days, failed to catch anything. He finally hit an antelope, which was transformed into the god Tano. Tano quelled the hunter's fears, offering to protect him. As they traveled together, they came upon Death. Death opposed Tano's traveling with the hunter. Tano resented Death's interference in the matter. The two then started singing songs to one another in a contest. Neither one, however, would agree that the other was better. At last they agreed that when a man became ill, the outcome of that illness would depend on which of the two got to him first. If Tano arrived first, the man would live, but if it were Death, the man would die.

2832
**Tantalus** (lurching or most wretched)   In Greek mythology, king of Sipylos in Lydia; son of Zeus; father of Pelops and Niobe; grandfather of Atreus and Thyestes; punished by the gods for the murder of his son. At first the gods loved Tantalus, inviting him to their numerous feasts. This honor went to his head, and he decided to test the gods' knowledge. He killed his son Pelops and served him at a banquet, hoping to prove that the gods could not tell the difference between human and animal flesh. None of the gods ate the food except for Demeter, who absent-mindedly consumed part of the boy's shoulder. Later Pelops was restored to life and his missing shoulder blade replaced by an ivory one, but Tantalus was sent to Tartarus, the lowest section of Hades, the underworld, to be punished. Homer's *Odyssey* (book 11) describes Tantalus as being in water up to his neck but unable

to quench his thirst because as he reaches for the water, it recedes. Also, close by is a fruit-laden tree, but when he tries to eat, the fruits vanish. According to Pindar, Tantalus is suspended in the air, while above his head hangs a massive rock, ready to fall and crush him at any moment. Euripides uses elements from both versions. Some accounts say that Tantalus was punished for revealing a secret of Zeus, or stealing the nectar and ambrosia of the gods, or taking a dog of Zeus. The word *tantalize* comes from the myth.

See also: ATREUS; DEMETER; HADES; NIOBE; *ODYSSEY, THE*; PELOPS; ZEUS

2833

**Tanuki Bozu**    In Japanese folklore, badger disguised as a Buddhist monk. He is believed to bring luck and wealth and is often enshrined in Japanese stores, though he may also take on various forms to waylay, deceive, or annoy travelers.

2834

**T'ao t'ieh** (ravenous)    In Chinese folk art, an ogre mask of an animal having feline characteristics. Some scholars believe it depicts a stylized tiger because the tiger was the guardian of graves in ancient China and fought off evil spirits. Others see it as symbolic of the dualistic concepts of life and death, light and darkness. It also has been interpreted as symbolic of death, which swallows up all things in its gluttonous mouth.

2835

**Tapio** (worker in Tvaps, i.e., hunting)    In Finnish mythology, forest god. His wife, Mei-likki, his son Nyyrikki, and his daughter, the wind spirit Tuulikki, were all spirits of the forest. Tapio's realm was called Tapiola, which is used in the Finnish epic poem *The Kalevala* for the forest in general and is almost synonymous with *Metsola* (woodland). Sometimes Tapio aided the wanderer in the forest, but if he was in a mischievous mood, he would tickle or smother the person to death. His mysterious spirit and nature

inspired Sibelius's last major symphonic composition, *Tapiola*, which was first performed in New York under the conductor Walter Damrosch. Another name for Tapiola is Kuippana (king of the forest), who was a minor tutelary genius.

See also: KALEVALA, THE

2836

**Tara** (she who carries across [to Nirvana])    In Tibetan Buddhism, a female entity, especially one of two deified wives of King Sron Tsan Gampo, known as the White Tara and the Green Tara; sometimes called Dölma (mother).

One wife, Princess Wen-ch'eng, deified as the White Tara, is portrayed as an Indian woman with a white complexion, seated and holding in her left hand a long-stemmed lotus flower. She has seven eyes—the eye of foreknowledge in the forehead, two others on the face, and one in each palm and each sole. She is called the Seven-Eyed White Tara and uses her eyes to see and aid the suffering. She is worshiped by the Mongols.

The second wife, a Nepalese, was deified as the Green Tara and portrayed as a beautiful Indian woman with uncovered head and a green complexion, seated on a lotus, with her left leg pendant and holding in her left hand a long-stemmed lotus flower.

The following injunction is included in her worship: "If we worship this sublime and pure-souled goddess when we retire at night and arise in the morning, then all our fears and worldly anxieties will disappear and our sins will be forgiven. She—the conqueror of myriad hosts—will strengthen us. She will do more than this! She will convey us directly to the end of our transmigration—Buddha and Nirvana."

Green Tara is regarded as being born from a teardrop of Avalokiteshvara, the Bodhisattva of Infinite Compassion. Tara transcends social distinctions and offers a personal relationship to her devotees. Aside from these two Taras, the Tibetans have a list of 21 others.

See also: AVALOKITESHVARA; BODHISATTVA; NIRVANA

**2837**

**Tara** (star)   In Hindu mythology, wife of Brihaspati, raped by the moon god Soma. As a result of the rape a war broke out between the gods and demons. It was ended with the intervention of the god Brahma. Tara was given back to her husband, but she bore a son, Budha (he who knows), whose father was Soma.

See also: BRAHMA; BRIHASPATI; SOMA

**2838**

**Taranis**   In Celtic mythology, a thunder god mentioned by ancient Roman writers and equated with their god Jupiter. Human sacrifices were offered to the god, who originally may have been a goddess of death. Taranis's symbol was a wheel. He became the basis for Lloyd Alexander's Welsh series of juvenile fiction *Taran Wanderer* (1980).

**2839**

**Tarchon**   In Roman mythology, ancestor of the Etruscan Tarquins, leader of the emigrants from Lydia, and founder of Tarquinii and other Etruscan cities. In Vergil's *Aeneid* (book 8) he joined the Trojan hero Aeneas as an ally.

See also: AENEAS; *AENEID, THE*

**2840**

**Tarkshya**   In Hindu mythology, a fantastic animal, sometimes bird or horse, often equated with the fantastic bird Garuda. In some myths Tarkshya is called the father of Garuda.

See also: GARUDA

**2841**

**Tarnkappe** (camouflage cloak)   In Norse mythology, German name for the magic cap or cloak that rendered its wearer invisible or unrecognizable by transformation into another form. Sigurd in the Norse *Volsunga Saga* and Siegfried, his German counterpart in the *Nibelungenlied*, both have such caps. In Richard Wagner's *Der Ring des Nibelungen* it is called *tarnhelm*

and is at first the possession of the dwarf Alberich, but it is stolen from him by Loge (Loki) and Wotan (Odin).

See also: *NIBELUNGENLIED*; *RING DES NIBELUNGEN, DER*; SIEGFRIED; SIGURD

**2842**

**Tarpeia**   In Roman history and legend, a vestal virgin, betrayer of the Romans; daughter of Spurius Tarpeius, Roman commander of the garrison stationed at the Capitol at the time of the Sabine Wars. Meeting Tatius, leader of the Sabines, Tarpeia was either bribed or volunteered to open the gates of the city's citadel if Tatius would give her what his men "wore on their shield-arms," according to Livy's *History of Rome* (book 1). Expecting rich gold bracelets, Tarpeia was not only given the bracelets but had the shields thrown at her, knocking her to the ground. Then other soldiers crushed her to death with their shields. The Tarpeian Rock, from which convicted criminals were flung to their death, is said to be named after Tarpeia. Ovid's *Metamorphoses* (book 14) tells one version of the myth.

See also: OVID

**2843**

**Tarquin**   In Arthurian legend, a "recreant knight" who held some knights of the Round Table prisoner. Sir Lancelot met a lady who asked him to free the knights from Tarquin's power. Coming to a river, Lancelot saw a copper basin suspended from a tree. He struck it so hard that it broke. This brought out Tarquin. A battle ensued in which Lancelot killed Tarquin. Then some "threescore knights and four, all of the Table Round," were freed.

See also: ARTHUR; LANCELOT OF THE LAKE; ROUND TABLE

**2844**

**Tarquinius Priscus**   Reigned 616–579 B.C.E. In Roman history and legend, fifth king of

Rome, who built temples on the Capitol and started the city's drainage system using Etruscan workmen. He is said to have brought the Sibylline Books, collections of prophecy, to Rome.

**2845**

**Tartarus** (far west?)   In Greek mythology, the lowest section of the underworld, where the most evil were punished. Among its inhabitants were the rebellious Titans, Ixion, Sisyphus, Tantalus, and Tityus. The region is described in Homer's *Odyssey* (book 11), Hesiod's *Theogony*, Vergil's *Aeneid* (book 6), Ovid's *Metamorphoses* (book 4), and Dante's *Divine Comedy* (Hell).

See also: *AENEID, THE*; HESIOD; IXION; ODYSSEUS; OVID; SISYPHYS; TANTALUS; TITANS

**2846**

**Tathagata** (thus come, thus gone?)   Title of the Buddha used by himself and his followers. It may mean, "He who has come and gone as former Buddhas," that is, teaching the same truths, following the same paths to the same goal. Another interpretation is "one who has attained full realization of Suchness," that is, one who has realized that things are such-as-they-are, so that he neither comes from anywhere nor does he go anywhere. The implication is that Buddha was not the founder of Buddhism but was made to appear as one of a series (of four or seven) equally perfect Buddhas.

**2847**

**Taui'goad** (wounded knee)   In African mythology (Hottentot), rain god, creator, who "died" on several occasions but continues to return to life. One day Taui'goad had a battle with Gaunab, a great Hottentot chief. Gaunab won each battle, but Taui'goad kept growing stronger until he finally killed his opponent. Just before he died Gaunab hit Taui'goad's knee, and the god has been known as Taui'goad (wounded knee) ever since.

**2848**

**Taurt** (Taueret, Rert, Rertu, Apet, Opet) (the fat one)   In Egyptian mythology, hippopotamus goddess. She was a patron of childbirth and maternity, often identified with the goddess Hathor. The Greeks rendered her name Thoueris. She was both a beneficent deity, as when she protected the dead, or an avenging deity, when she was the female counterpart of the evil god Set. Egyptian art portrays her as a female hippopotamus with distended teats standing upright on her back legs. Taurt's front foot rests on the *sa*, a sign of protection represented by a stylized life preserver, made of papyrus and worn by river travelers.

See also: HATHOR; HIPPOPOTAMUS; SET

**2849**

**Tawiskaron** (flint)   In North American Indian mythology (Mohawk), an evil being who attempts to build a bridge to allow wild animals to travel so that they can prey on humans. These beasts are associated with the famine that winter can bring. He is foiled in his evil design by Sapling, who sends a bluejay with a cricket's hind legs stuck in its mouth to frighten Tawiskaron. When Tawiskaron sees the sight, he believes it is human legs; he flees, and his bridge disappears.

**2850**

**Tchue**   In African mythology (Bushman), cultural founder hero who gave people the gift of fire. He is capable of transforming himself into various animals and forms such as a fly, lizard, elephant, bird, or water hole.

**2851**

**Tcoxoltcwedin**   In North American Indian mythology (Hupa), creator god who sprang from the earth. When he was born, there was a ringing noise like the striking together of metals. Before he was born, smoke was seen, which settled on a mountainside. When pieces of rotten wood fell into his hands, fire was created.

2852

**Tefnut** (Tefenet) (the spitter?)   In Egyptian mythology, goddess of moisture. She and her twin brother, Shu, constituted the first couple of the Ennead, which was a system of gods worshiped in Egypt.

According to one myth, the primeval sun god created Tefnut and Shu. He is said to have masturbated and then swallowed his own semen, sneezing out Shu and spitting out Tefnut. According to another account, they came from the spittle of his mouth. Then, with Shu, Tefnut conceived the sky goddess, Nut, and the earth god, Geb, and they in turn bore the great gods Osiris, Isis, Nephthys, and Set, thus completing the great Ennead of Heliopolis. Together with Shu, Tefnut helped support the sky and each day received the new sun as it rose in the east. Sometimes she represented the power of sunlight.

Tefnut, however, could also be ferocious. Her original home was said to be the Nubian deserts, where she roamed drenched in the blood of her enemies. When Thoth, the god of wisdom, upbraided her for abandoning Egypt and leaving the country desolate, Tefnut wept great tears, but her tears soon turned to wrath, and she changed into a bloodthirsty lioness whose mane smoked with fire and whose face glowed like the sun. Egyptian art portrays Tefnut as a woman with the head of a lioness surmounted by a disk or the uraeus or both.

See also: ENNEAD; GEB; ISIS: NEPHTHYS; NUT; OSIRIS; SET; SHU; THOTH; URAEUS

2853

**Telegonus** (born far away)   In Greek mythology, son of Odysseus and Circe; brother of Ardea and Agrius; half-brother of Latinus. Telegonus does not appear in Homer, but in Ovid and Plutarch, who narrate that Telegonus accidentally killed his father, Odysseus. Telegonus was either shipwrecked or landed in Ithaca in search of his father. When he landed he began to plunder the land. Odysseus and his son Telemachus came out to defend the land, and in the ensuing fight, Telegonus killed Odysseus with a lance given him by his mother, Circe. He then discovered that the man he killed was his father. Odysseus's body was taken then by Telegonus, Penelope, and Telemachus and buried on Aeaea. Athena then commanded Telegonus to wed Penelope. Their son was named Italus, after which Italy is named. Telegonus and Penelope eventually went to the Blessed Isles, where they were said to live forever.

See also: ODYSSEUS; OVID; PENELOPE; TELEMACHUS

2854

**Telemachus** (far-away battle)   In Greek mythology, son of Odysseus and Penelope, who went in search of his father and aided him in the slaughter of Penelope's suitors. His story appears in Homer's *Odyssey*. In post-Homeric myth, he married either Nausicaa, Circe, or Cassiphone, a daughter of Circe, and had a son, Latinus. Some accounts say he murdered Circe and fled to Italy. Telemachus appears in Fénelon's novel *Télémaque* and inspired the portrait of Stephen Dadalus in James Joyce's novel *Ulysses*.

See also: ODYSSEUS; *ODYSSEY, THE*; PENELOPE

2855

**Telephus** (suckles by a doe)   In Greek mythology, king of Mysia, son of Heracles and Auge. Abandoned by his mother, Telephus was raised on Mount Parthenius by a doe or goat and later adopted by King Teuthras. Telephus was wounded by Achilles' lance and could only be healed by the same lance. He promised to lead the Greeks to Troy if Achilles cured him, which he did, but he refused to take part in the battle because his wife, Astyoche, was a sister of Troy's King Priam.

See also: ACHILLES; AUGE; HERACLES; PRIAM; TROY

**2856**

**Telepinus**   In Near Eastern mythology (Hittite), god of agriculture who left the earth in anger, causing it to dry up and all life to cease reproduction. His father, the storm god, cried out: "Telepinus has flown into a rage and taken every good thing with him." The gods sent an eagle to search for Telepinus, but he could not be found, so Hannahanna, the Great Mother goddess, asked the weather god himself to search for his son. When the weather god had no success, Hannahanna sent a bee to find Telepinus. The bee found Telepinus and stung him to wake him up, but that merely made Telepinus angrier. Kamrusepas, the goddess of magic and healing, finally pacified Telepinus with her medicine. The god returned home, and life was restored to the land and people.

See also: GREAT GODDESS

**2857**

**Telesphorus** (he who brings to an end)   In Greek mythology, an attendant of Asclepius, the god of medicine, who gave strength to recovering patients.

See also: ASCLEPIUS

**2858**

**Tem** (Tum, Temu, Atem, Atum, Atmu)   In Egyptian mythology, a primeval, creator god; one of the most ancient deities worshiped in Egypt.

The priests of Anu, or Heliopolis, made Tem the head of their company of gods, identifying him with a form of the sun god. Tem appears in *The Book of the Dead* as the evening or setting sun (Khepera is the morning sun and Ra the noonday sun). In the Theban recension of the book, Tem is identified with Osiris as being one of the gods whose flesh never saw physical corruption. Many of the attributes of Tem were absorbed by Khepera, who was also a creator god. In later times the Egyptians named a female counterpart of Tem, calling her Temt or Temit. According to one myth, Tem was responsible for the primeval

flood, which covered the entire earth and destroyed all of mankind except those in Tem's boat.

Egyptian art portrays Tem as a man, sometimes a king, wearing the crowns of Upper and Lower Egypt. Like many other gods, he carries in his hands the scepter and ankh, emblem of life.

See also: ANKH; *BOOK OF THE DEAD, THE*; KHEPERA; OSIRIS; RA

**2859**

**Tembo**   In African legend, a king of the Buganda of Uganda. Tembo was the father of two children, a son and a daughter. Two rivers were supposed to have sprung from the bodies of these children. Tembo's son eventually married his sister.

**2860**

**Tengri** (Tangara, Tengeri, Tura) (god, heaven) In Siberian mythology, the sky god and a general term for God among the Mongolians. He created humans from fire, wind, and water and then breathed life into them. There are two aspects to the Mongolian sky god, Blue Tengri, who represents the power of the various phenomena of the sky that bring fruitfulness to the earth, and Eternal Tengri, who rules over the fate of mankind. The two terms are often used interchangeably.

**2861**

**Tengu** (long-nose)   In Japanese folklore, trickster spirits whose bodies are half human and half bird, with wings and claws and frequently a large beak or elongated nose. The long-nosed variety are called *kohola tengu*; the beaked version, *karasu tengu* (crow tengu). They are minor deities and may be descendants of Susano. They inhabit trees in mountainous areas. According to legend they are born from eggs, from which they are often seen emerging, and live in colonies with one tengu in charge.

See also: SUSANO

*Tengu*

2862

**Tennin** In Japanese-Chinese Buddhist mythology, beautiful winged maidens, inhabitants of a Buddhist paradise. They soar into the air, usually clasping lotus flowers or playing instruments. In Chinese tradition they wear feather robes of five colors. In Japanese folklore Hagoromo (feathery robe) was a tennin who left her feather robe on earth. One day she came down to the forest of Mio, near Okitsu. She admired the view and then, after hanging her feather robe on a pine tree, started to dance on the sandy beach. A fisherman, Hakurio, happened to pass by and thought her a beautiful woman. His looks, however, frightened Hagoromo, who fled, minus her robe, which is still preserved in a nearby temple. Her tale is the subject of a No play.

See also: NO

2863

**Tenten and Caicai** In the mythology of the Araucanian Indians of Chile, two serpents who fought, causing a flood that covered the earth. The people sought shelter on two mountains, which were raised by Tenten as the evil Caicai raised the water level. The people on one of the mountains were turned into animals, fish, and birds. In a variant of this flood myth, the waters came about by the evil work of the Guecubus demons. This time the people fled to two mountains, called Tenten and Caicai (the names of the serpents in the other myth). The god Guinechen raised the mountains to save the people from the ever-rising waters.

See also: GUECUBUS; GUINECHEN

2864

**Teresa of Avila, St.** (summer, harvest?) 1515–1582. In Christian legend, Spanish mystical writer and founder of the discalced, or barefoot, Carmelites. Patron of lacemakers and second patron saint of Spain by order of King Philip II. Invoked by those in need of grace. Feast, 15 October.

Born of a part-Jewish family, St. Teresa's father was Don Alphonzo Sanchez de Cepeda. Her mother's name was Beatrix. Her father was of a serious nature, but her mother tended to be of a romantic frame of mind. The young girl inherited both aspects in her personality and vacilated between the two. As a young girl of nine she decided she wanted to die a martyr. She set out for the "land of the Moors" but was caught by her family. Eventually her father thought it best to send her to a convent, but she did not like the religious life and would often become ill, sometimes near death.

The writings of St. Jerome, who wrote numerous letters on how women were to behave, caught her imagination. She writes in her great *Life*, or *Autobiography*, that for 20 years she did not find the repose for which she had hoped. But she adds, "At length God took pity on me. I read the *Confessions of St. Augustine*. I saw how he had been tempted, how he had been tried, and how he had at length conquered."

About 1561, against great opposition that lasted the remainder of her life, she set about reforming the Carmelite order, which had fallen into slack ways. The first convent of the new, reformed rule had eight nuns. By the end of her life there were some 30 convents established according to her rule. Toward the end of her life she was frequently ill. She died in her own convent of St. Joseph. In her last moments she repeated a verse from the psalm *Miserere*, "A broken and contrite heart, O Lord, thou wilt not despise."

The most famous representation of the saint is the *Ecstasy of St. Teresa* by Bernini. In her *Life* she tells how an angel plunged into her breast a golden spear, symbolizing Divine Love. When the spear was withdrawn, she was "utterly consumed by the great love of God." As depicted by Bernini in the Cornaro Chapel, Santa Maria della Vittoria in Rome, the greatest baroque sculpture, the saint ecstatically sinks back onto a cloud, her eyes nearly closed, her lips parted in a soft moan, evocative of repose after orgasm. Rubens painted *St. Teresa Delivering Bernadin de Mendoza from Purgatory*, in which a rather full-faced saint is confronted by a half-clad Christ, while sinners at the bottom of the painting are enveloped in flames.

See also: JEROME, ST.; JOSEPH, ST.

2865

**Terminus** (limit)    In Roman mythology, god of boundaries. Stones, which marked boundaries, were under the protection of Terminus. Any person removing a stone could legally be killed. His festival, Terminalia, was 23 February, with sacrifices around the boundary stones. Terminalis was an epithet of Jupiter, and the god Terminus may be another form of Jupiter. Erasmus, the great Renaissance humanist, used a figure of Terminus for his emblem to signify readiness for death.

2866

**Terpsichore** (rejoicing in the dance)    In Greek mythology, one of the nine Muses, the Muse of Dance; daughter of Zeus and Mnemosyne. Some accounts say she was the mother of the Sirens by Achelous. Her symbols were a laurel crown and a lyre.

See also: ACHELOUS; LAUREL; MUSES; SIRENS; ZEUS

2867

**Terra or Tellus Mater** (mother earth)    In Roman mythology, ancient Italian mother goddess invoked during birth, marriage, and earthquakes. Her feast, Fordicidia, was 15 April. Sacrifices to her were made 13 December, when the dead returned to Mother Earth. Her temple in Rome was dedicated in 268 B.C.E.

2868

**Tethys** (disposer or the nourisher?)    In Greek mythology, Titaness; daughter of Uranus and Gaea; wife of her brother, Oceanus; mother of Asia, Callirrhoë, Clymene, Clytia, Doris, Europa, Eidyia, Electra, Inachus, Meliboea, Perseis, Pleione, Proteus, Styx, the rivers and the 3,000 Oceanides. Milton's *Comus* refers to the deity's "grave majestic pace."

See also: CALLIRRHOË; DORIS; ELECTRA; GAEA; OCEANUS; PROTEUS; STYX; URANUS

2869

**Tezcatlipoca** (mirror that smokes)    In Toltec mythology, creator trickster god worshiped by warriors and magicians, opposed to Quetzalcoatl.

Tezcatlipoca formed the thin air and darkness, presiding over darkness and night. Dreams and the phantoms of gloom were sent by this god. His sacred animals were those associated with night, such as the skunk and the coyote. This demonic nature is commented on by Fray Bernardino de Sahagún in his *Historia general de las cosas de Nueva España* (1570–1582). He says that Tezcatlipoca "caused wars, enmities and discords." Sahagún then gives some of the numerous titles applied to the god: Titlacauan (we are slaves); Telpochtli (the youth), because he never aged; Moyocoyatzin (the determined doer), a name Sahagún says was given to the god because he could do what he pleased on earth or in heaven; Monenequi (he who demands prayers); Teyocoyani (creator of men); and Teimatini (disposer of men). Because Tezcatlipoca was a jealous god who brought plagues and famines, he was also called Yaotzin (the arch enemy); Yaotl Necoc (the enemy of both sides); Moquequeloa (the mocker); and Yoalliehecatl (the night wind).

See also: QUETZALCOATL

2870
**Thais, St.**    Fourth century. In Christian legend, penitent, saint, patron of fallen women and courtesans. Feast, 8 October.

*The Golden Legend*, written in the 13th century, tells the story of the saint from various earlier sources, such as the *Lives of the Fathers*. Thais was a courtesan who through her charms "reduced to the direst poverty" the men who paid for her affections. However, she met Abbot Paphnutius, who not only convinced her of her guilt but "shut her up in a little cell" and "sealed the door with lead." When Thais asked what she was to do with her "natural issue of water," the abbot replied to her to leave it in the cell as "thou deservest!" After three years Thais came out, reformed, and died 15 days later.

The edifying life of the reformed whore inspired the novel *Thaïs* by the cynic Anatole France. In it Paphnutius, a young rake turned monk, lives in the desert and dreams of the courtesan Thaïs. He interprets the dream as a call to reform the woman, which he does. The problem, however, is that Paphnutius still has lustful dreams of the girl even though she is now living the saintly life of a hermit. In an attempt to rid himself of his lust he tries all manner of mortifications until he realizes that he really wants her. He tries to persuade her to flee the convent

with him. As she dies (it was too much for her sensitive soul to bear), the abbess sends Paphnutius away when she sees the lust written on his face. Jules Massenet wrote an operatic version of France's novel.

St. Thais is not to be confused with the Athenian courtesan who convinced a drunken Alexander the Great to set fire to the palace of Persian kings at Persepolis.

See also: *GOLDEN LEGEND, THE*

*Thalia*

2871
**Thalia** (abundance, festive)    In Greek mythology, a name of three different beings. One, whose name meant festive, was the Muse of comedy, daughter of Zeus and Mnemosyne (memory), whose symbol was the mask used by

comedians. The second, whose name meant abundance, was one of the Graces, daughter of Zeus and Eurynome, sister of Aglaea (splendor), and Euphrosyne (good cheer), mother of the Palici by Zeus, chthonic twin deities who were worshiped at the Palica, near Mount Etna. (In early times humans were sacrificed to them, and oaths were verified through divine judgement.) The third Thalia was one of the Nereids, a sea nymph. A famous movie house in New York City devoted to old and classic movies is named for Thalia. The first two of these beings often overlap or are confused.

See also: AGLAEA; EUPHROSYNE; NEREIDS; ZEUS

2872

**Thallo** (sprouting)   In Greek mythology, the spring, one of the seasons; daughter of Zeus and Themis; sister of Carpo and Auxo.

See also: THEMIS; ZEUS

2873

**Thamar** (date palm)   In Russian Georgian legend, an evil queen who feasted with lovers then threw them into a river the next day.

Queen Thamar's castle was located near the mighty Terek River. From her window at night came the sound of her "enchanting voice, whose song lured traveler, merchant, warrior or peasant to see her within the castle." When the gates to the castle were opened and the wanderer entered, he would find himself in a luxurious room, where Thamar, "richly bedecked in brocade and jewels, reclined voluptuously on a couch." She would feast with the man, locking him in "passionate embraces," but the next morning "the waters of the Terek River would bear away his corpse." From her window could be heard the whispered "farewell."

Thamar's legend was used by the Russian poet Mikhail Lermontov in his short narrative poem "Thamar," which in turn was used as the story basis for Mili Balakirev's symphonic poem *Thamar*. Balakirev's score was later used for the ballet *Thamar* by Michel Fokine, with scenery and costumes by Léon Bakst.

Lermontov also used the character Thamar in his long narrative poem *The Demon*. It tells of a former angel who rebels against God. He sees the beautiful Thamar and falls in love with her, thinking it will reconcile him to God, "In Paradise again I'd shine, like a new angel in new splendor." Thamar cannot resist the demon and they kiss, but she dies and her soul goes to heaven. The demon, however, is left alone. Anton Rubinstein used the poem for *The Demon*, his most popular opera during his lifetime. Boris Pasternak wrote a poem, *In Memory of The Demon*, in praise of Lermontov's poem.

2874

**Thamyris** (thick-set)   In Greek mythology, a Thracian musician, son of Philammon and Argiope, who challenged the Muses to a contest of musical skill. Thamyris lost and was blinded, his voice destroyed, and his lyre broken as punishment. He was said to be the lover of Hyacinthus. Homer's *Iliad* (book 2) and Milton's *Paradise Lost* (Book 3:35) cite the musician.

See also: HYACINTHUS; *ILIAD, THE*; MUSES

2875

**Thanatos** (death)   In Greek mythology, death, son of Nyx and Erebus; twin brother of Hypnos; brother of Aether, Cer, Dreams, Hemera, Chron, Momus, Moros, and Nemesis; and called Mors by the Romans. William Cullen Bryant's poem *Thanatopsis* deals with the theme of death.

See also: HYPNOS; NEMESIS

2876

**Than ka** (colored picture)   In Buddhism, any icon that is colored. Its function is to open the consciousness of the beholder to the spiritual world. Woodcuts of similar design but without color are used by poorer people.

**Thecla, St.** (god-famed)    First century. In Christian legend, first female Christian martyr. Patron of Este and Milan, Italy. Feast, 23 September.

St. Thecla was one of the most honored female saints in the early Church becuase of a book called *The Acts of Paul and Thecla*, which said she was a follower of St. Paul. According to the legend, her reputation for holiness and the cures she effected aroused the hatred of local physicians in Iconium. They claimed she was a priestess of Diana. "It is by her chastity she does these cures," they cried. "If we could destroy that, her power would be overthrown." So they sent a delegation to rape Thecla. The saint ran from them, praying all the time, and then she "saw a rock opened to as large a degree as that a man might enter . . . and she went into the rock, which instantly so closed, that there was not any crack visible where it had opened." All the mob found was her veil, lost where she entered the rock.

Though she did not die a martyr's death, the Eastern Church so honors her. In the medieval Roman Church, St. Martin of Tours advocated her cult.

See also: MARTIN OF TOURS, ST.; PAUL, ST.; STEPHEN, ST.

2878

**Themis** (justice, right)    In Greek mythology, a Titaness, later a goddess who presided over hospitality, law, order, justice, and prophecy. Themis was the wife of the Titan Iapetus but later married Zeus after Metis was swallowed. She was the mother of the Horae (seasons), the three Moerae (Fates), and Astraea, and some accounts say Themis was also the mother of Prometheus. When Themis was no longer Zeus's wife she became his trusted adviser, representing divine justice. She was the protector of the oppressed and was called Soteira (saving goddess) in her role as protector. Before Apollo's oracle at Delphi, Themis had a shrine in the same location. In Greek art Themis is portrayed as a woman holding a pair of scales and a cornucopia, symbol of the blessing of order that the goddess gives her people.

See also: APOLLO; DELPHI; HORAE; METIS; PROMETHEUS; TITANS; ZEUS

2879

**Thersites** (son of courage)    In Greek mythology, ugly, hated Greek, son of Agrius. He laughed at Achilles for the hero's lamenting the death of Penthesilea, the queen of the Amazons. Achilles, in anger, killed Thersites. He appears in Shakespeare's *Troilus and Cressida* as a mean-spirited commentator on the play's characters.

See also: ACHILLES; AMAZONS; PENTHESILEA

2880

**Theseus** (founder, establisher)    In Greek mythology, hero, son of Aethra and Aegeus or Poseidon; husband of Hippolyte, father of Hippolytus; husband of Ariadne, father of Oenopion and Staphylus; and husband of Phaedra, father of Acamas and Demophon.

There are two accounts of the birth of Theseus. In one, his father is King Aegeus and he was raised by Pittheus, his grandfather. In a variant account, Theseus's father is the sea god Poseidon. According to this variant account, Theseus was challenged by King Minos of Crete to prove that Poseidon was his father. The king cast a ring into the sea, asking that Theseus recover it. Not only did Theseus recover the ring, but he also was given a golden wreath by the sea goddess Amphitrite to prove Poseidon was his father.

Six labors are usually assigned to Theseus, all of them performed on his way from Troezen to Athens. In each he kills some monster or giant. The six monsters are: Periphetes, Sinis, the Crommyonian sow, Sceiron, Cercym, and Procrustes. For these killings, Theseus was purified near Athens, and then he entered the city a hero. Theseus's father, King Aegeus, was now married to Medea, the former mistress of Jason and a witch. When Medea saw the handsome Theseus she realized that her control over Aegeus would be lessened, so she prepared a poisoned cup for Theseus. Her plot to kill him failed, and Medea fled in a winged chariot. At this time the Athenians were paying a yearly tribute of seven young boys and girls to King Minos of Crete, who offered them as sacrifices to the monster Minotaur, dwelling in the labyrinth of Crete. King Minos demanded the tribute as punishment for Aegeus, who sent Androgeus, the son of Minos, against the Marathonian bull, which had killed the boy. Theseus told his father he would slay the Minotaur and return with all the youths. He set sail in a ship with black sails and promised, when he returned, to change the sails to white if he defeated the monster. Aphrodite, goddess of love, was on Theseus's side, and when he arrived in Crete, she made Ariadne, daughter of Minos, fall in love with Theseus. Ariadne aided Theseus by means of a ball of magic thread, which she gave him, telling him to fasten one end of it to the lintel of the labyrinth as he entered and unwind it until he came to the Minotaur. In order to escape, he would simply rewind the thread. Theseus killed the Minotaur, then offered it as a sacrifice to Poseidon. He then fled with Ariadne, coming to the isle of Naxos, where, while she was asleep, he abandoned her. Either she died of grief or was later made the mistress of the god Dionysus.

Returning home to Athens, Theseus forgot to change the black sails to white as he had promised. When Aegeus saw the black sails he believed that Theseus was dead and committed suicide. Theseus was then made king of Athens. He entered into battle with the Amazons, capturing their queen, Antiope, or as some variant accounts say, winning her love. But as in the case of Ariadne, he grew tired of Antiope and was ready to cast her off. Antiope tried to kill Theseus but failed, and she in turn was killed by Heracles. Theseus then married Phaedra, sister of Ariadne. His new wife, however, fell in love with her stepson Hippolytus and tried to seduce him. When she failed, she killed herself, leaving a note for Theseus saying that Hippolytus had tried to rape her. Furious, Theseus prayed to Poseidon

to destroy his son. Theseus's relations with women were failures. Theseus planned with his friend Pirithous, king of the Lapiths, to abduct Persephone, queen of the underworld. They failed, and Hades chained both men to rocks. Heracles, who had come to the underworld to capture Cerberus as one of his labors, freed Theseus but failed to free Pirithous.

Returning to Athens, he found another ruler on the throne, and the people rejected Theseus, who was now old. He went to King Lycomedes on the island of Scyrus, where he owned some land. Lycomedes pretended to be pleased with Theseus's visit but plotted his death. He took Theseus to a cliff overlooking his vast lands and pushed the hero to his death. In later belief, an image of the ghost of Theseus appeared in full armor, rallying the Athenians against the Persians, in the Battle of Marathon (490 B.C.E.).

Theseus appears in works by Apollodorus, Herodotus, Homer, Hyginus, Ovid, Pausanias, Statius, and Vergil and in English literature in Chaucer, Shakespeare, Christina Rossetti, W. H. Auden, and T. S. Eliot. Mary Renault's novels *The King Must Die* (1958) and *The Bull from the Sea* (1962) also feature Theseus.

See also: ACAMAS; AEGEUS; AETHRA; AMPHITRITE; APOLLODORUS; ARIADNE; DEMOPHON; HIPPOLYTE; HIPPOLYTUS; HOMER; MINOS; OVID; PAUSANIAS; PHAEDRA; POSEIDON

2881

**Thespis**    Sixth century B.C.E. In Greek history and legend, an Attic poet who is believed to be the first actor to appear on stage separate from the chorus. He introduced the prologue and set speeches for himself, removing them from the chorus, which previously had narrated the entire drama. The use of masks in Greek tragic drama as a device to develop character is also credited to him.

2882

**Thespius** (divinely sounding)    In Greek mythology, king of Boeotia who gave his 50, 51, or 52

daughters to sleep with Heracles. Accounts vary. Some say Heracles slept with each one, 51 in all, for 51 nights. Another account says he had sexual intercourse with all 51 on the same night. In either case, only one girl refused, and she was forced to remain a virgin for life. Heracles fathered 51 sons, who later colonized the island of Sardinia.

See also: HERACLES

**2883**

**Thetis** (disposer)   In Greek mythology, sea goddess, daughter of Nereus and Doris; sister of the Nereids; wife of Peleus, mother of Achilles. Both Zeus and Poseidon pursued Thetis, but she avoided both. They gave up their quest when they were told that the son Thetis would bear would be greater than his father. To make it safe for both, the two gods forced Thetis to marry Peleus, king of the Myrmidons in Thessaly. She tried to avoid the unwanted union, transforming herself into various shapes, but eventually she was forced to marry him. Their son was Achilles. At their wedding, Eris, the goddess of discord, threw a golden apple inscribed "For the fairest" into the throng, and all the goddesses tried to claim it. Zeus picked Paris to choose the fairest, and his choice of Aphrodite won him Helen, which eventually led to the Trojan War. Thetis, wishing to make her son Achilles invulnerable, dipped him in the waters of the Styx. She held him by his heel, thus leaving one vulnerable part that did not touch the water. Later in the Trojan War it was this heel that Paris shot, killing Achilles. Thetis appears in Homer's *Iliad* and *Odyssey*, Ovid's *Metamorphoses* (book 11), and in Ingres's painting *Jupiter and Thetis*, which portrays the goddess asking Jupiter (Zeus) to aid her son.

See also: ACHILLES; APHRODITE; DORIS; HELEN OF TROY; MYRMIDONS; *ILIAD, THE;* NEREIDS; *ODYSSEY, THE;* OVID; PARIS; PELEUS; POSEIDON; STYX; TITANS; TROY; ZEUS

**2884**

**Thinan-malkia**   In Australian mythology, evil spirits who capture victims with nets that entangle their feet.

**2885**

**Thistle**   A prickly plant, emblem of Scotland. During the reign of Malcolm I (935–958 C.E.) a party of invading Norsemen or Danes, attempting to surprise Scottish forces at Sterling Castle, approached the camp under cover of darkness. One of them accidentally stepped on a thistle and cried out, thus rousing the Scots, who defeated the invaders. With the thistle the motto was adopted: *nemo me impune lacessit* (nobody touches me with impunity). However, there is no record of the thistle as the Scottish symbol until the reign of James VI, better known as James I of England. On some coins issued at his coronation, half of a thistle is combined with half of a rose, apparently joining the two sides of his family, the Scottish Thistle and the Tudor Rose.

**2886**

**Thomas, St.** (twin)   First century. In the Bible, N.T., one of the Twelve Apostles of Jesus. Patron saint of architects, builders, carpenters, masons, geometricians, and theologians, and of Portugal and Parma. Feast, 21 December.

Thomas is named in the Gospels of Matthew, Mark, and Luke, but he is called Didymus (twin) in John's account (11:16). Thomas refused to believe that Christ had risen until he touched Jesus' wounds with his fingers (John 20:24–29), thus the expression "doubting Thomas."

According to *The Golden Legend*, a 13th-century account of the lives of saints, Thomas was deputized to go as a missionary to India. When he refused, Christ appeared and sold him as a slave to an Indian prince who was visiting Jerusalem. Thomas managed to found a church in India, where he met the three Magi, whom he baptized. According to another legend, while in Caesarea, Thomas had a vision in which Christ appeared and told him that Gondolforus, king of the Indies, needed an architect to build him a palace. Thomas went, and Gondolforus gave him money to build the palace; then he left for two years. When the king returned, he found that Thomas had given all the money to the poor and sick. The king, in anger, put Thomas in prison, but a few days later the king's brother died and "there was made for him a rich sepulchre, and the fourth day he that had been dead arose from death to life, and all men were abashed and fled. And he said to his brother: 'This man that thou intendest to slay and burn is the friend of God, and the angels of God serve him, and they brought me in to paradise, and have showed me a palace of gold and silver. . . . And when I marveled of the great beauty thereof, they said to me: "This is the palace that Thomas hath made for thy brother." ' "

After hearing about the dream, the king freed Thomas. According to another legend, the Portuguese found at Meliapore an inscription saying Thomas had been pierced with a lance at the foot of a cross that he had erected in that city, and his body had been moved to Goa in 1523.

The legend of La Madonna della Cintola (Our Lady of the Girdle) says that when the Virgin Mary ascended to heaven, St. Thomas was not present with the other Apostles. Three days later, when he returned, he could not believe their account and wished to see her tomb. The tomb was opened, and the Virgin dropped her girdle from heaven for Thomas.

When St. Thomas is portrayed as an Apostle, he holds a builder's rule or square; when he is shown as a martyr, he holds a lance. Two scenes from his life are most often portrayed: The Incredulity of Thomas, when he puts his finger in the side of Christ, and La Madonna della Cintola.

See also: *GOLDEN LEGEND, THE*; MAGI

2887
**Thomas à Becket, St.** (twin)   1118–1170. In Christian legend, archbishop of Canterbury and

martyr whose shrine at Canterbury was a famous goal of pilgrims during the Middle Ages.

Thomas was born in London of Norman background. In 1154, after filling various posts, he was ordained a deacon and nominated archdeacon of Canterbury. In the following year he was made lord chancellor by his close friend King Henry II. Though Thomas was known for his hot temper and worldliness, his life seemed to change. He opposed the king in his demands on the liberties of the clergy. Thomas described himself as "a proud vain man, a feeder of birds and follower of hounds," who was now "a shepherd of sheep."

The disputes between the king and the archbishop continued for seven years, with Thomas spending some time in exile in France. He returned to England on 1 December 1170. King Henry was reported to have said then, "Of the cowards that eat my bread, is there none that will rid me of this upstart priest." Four Norman knights then bound themselves with an oath to kill Thomas. They went to Canterbury, at first unarmed, but after meeting with Thomas, who defied their demand, they returned with swords. Thomas then ordered the cross of Canterbury to be borne before him as he passed through the cloister into the church. His followers closed the gates behind him, but he commanded them to be reopened, saying, "God's house should never be fortified as a place of defense."

As Thomas ascended the steps of the choir, the four knights with twelve attendants, all armed, burst into the church.

"Where is the traitor?" one asked. All were silent.

"Where is the archbishop?" asked Reginald Fitzurse.

"Here I am," replied Thomas, "the archbishop and no traitor, Reginald; I have granted thee many favors. What is thy object now? If thou seekest my life, let that suffice. I command thee, in the name of God, not to touch my people."

Thomas was then told he must absolve the archbishop of York and the bishop of Salisbury, whom he had excommunicated.

"Till they make satisfaction, I will not absolve them," he firmly replied.

"Then die," said Tracy, one of the four knights.

The first blow, aimed at his head, was broken in its force by Thomas' cross-bearer so that the archbishop was only slightly wounded. Feeling the blood on his face, he bowed his head, saying, "In the name of Christ and for the defense of His Church I am ready to die."

The murderers then attempted to remove him from the church because they did not wish to kill him in a sacred place. But Thomas could not be moved.

"I will not stir," he said. Again they struck him.

He was so beaten by the four knights that his brains were strewn on the pavement before the altar. The monks of the cathedral then bore Thomas's body on a bier and placed it in the choir of the cathedral. The people collected the blood and remains that were left on the pavement. It was not long before stories of miracles in connection with his relics spread. Eventually, a shrine to the saint was erected in the cathedral, and it became one of the most famous pilgrim sites in medieval Europe. Chaucer's Canterbury pilgrims followed routes from London; others took the Pilgrim Way across the North Downs from Winchester. Other pilgrims came from the Continent.

In 1538 King Henry VIII issued a proclamation to the effect that "from henceforth the said Thomas Becket shall not be esteemed, named, reputed, nor called a Saint, but Bishop Becket, and that his images and pictures through the whole realm shall be put down and avoided out of all churches, chapels and all other places: and that henceforth the days used to be as festival in his name shall not be observed, nor the service, office, antiphons, collects and prayers in his name read, but erased and put out of all books."

As a result of Henry's order no trace can now be found of Thomas's body, since it, along with his famous shrine, were destroyed and the gold and jewels given to the Royal Treasury of Henry.

Thomas's legend, however, continued to fascinate the Middle Ages. After his murder friends and enemies vied with one another in praise of the saint. Within a few years of his murder no fewer than nine Latin and one French lives of the saint were in circulation. Three of the Latin lives were the work of men who said they were present at the events.

Aside from providing a framework for Chaucer's *The Canterbury Tales*, the legend has been used by Alfred Tennyson in his play *Becket*, and by T. S. Eliot in his verse drama *Murder in the Cathedral*, which was made into an opera as *Assassinio nella Catterdrale* by Pizzetti. A French play by Jean Anouilh, *Becket*, was made into a film.

See also: CHAUCER

*St. Thomas Aquinas*

2888
**Thomas Aquinas, St.** (twin)   c. 1225–1274. In Christian legend, Doctor Angelicus (angelic doctor) of the Roman Church. Patron of booksellers, Catholic universities, pencil makers, scholars, and students. Invoked for chastity and learning and against storms and lightning. Feast, 7 March.

Though called the Dumb Ox because of his slowness, St. Thomas became one of the greatest thinkers of the Roman Church during the Middle Ages. He produced the *Summa Theologiae*, the culmination of scholastic philosophy, faith, and reason. He was also noted for some hymns, particularly *Adoro Te*, which was translated into English by the baroque poet Richard Crashaw in the 17th century.

Thomas was probably born at Roccasecca, near Aquino in Campania, Italy. He was educated at Monte Cassino and then the University of Naples. While he was an undergraduate, he decided to become a Dominican. The order was not quite 30 years old, and Thomas's family, of noble blood, thought it shocking that he should waste himself becoming a mendicant friar. The family kidnapped him and shut him up in the family castle, but the Dominicans of Naples went in disguise to the castle and, with the help of Thomas's sister, let him down from the castle by lowering a basket. This episode is similar to St. Paul's escape in Acts (9:25). St. Thomas spent the remainder of his life reading and writing. He died in the Cistercian abbey at Fossa Nova.

Numerous legends circulated during the Middle Ages about the saint. One relates that as he knelt before a crucifix it spoke to him, asking him what he most desired. Thomas replied, "Thyself only, O Lord." Another medieval legend tells that at his birth there were three bright stars in the heavens—one for him, one for St. Ambrose of Siena, and one for St. James of Menavia—all born on the same day.

Toward the end of his life St. Thomas was more and more disengaged from everyday matters. His eyes were often fixed on other horizons. His ecstasies were said to be quite frequent and to last for a long time. After each one he is reported to have said, "Oh, who will deliver me from this body of death?"

Though St. Thomas is recognized by the Roman Church as one of its greatest theologians, there was a time when his writings were condemned by various church councils. The Franciscans, a rival order to the Dominicans, for some time forbade their members to read any of the saint's works.

St. Thomas is portrayed in medieval art wearing the Dominican habit, with a book or pen, or a Host (he defended the Roman Catholic doctrine of transubstantiation), and with a sun or human eye on his breast. Often a star is seen overhead, referring to one of his legends.

See also: AMBROSE, ST.; PAUL, ST.

2889
**Thomas More, St.** (twin)    1478–1535. In Christian legend, martyr and lord chancellor of England under Henry VIII. Feast, 6 July.

Born in Milk Street, Cheapside, London, More studied at Oxford and was called to the bar in 1501. He was married twice. His first wife was Jane Colt and his second, Alice Middleton. In 1516 he published his most famous work, *Utopia*, which dealt with an ideal state of living according to natural law and religion. The book countained many satiric attacks on both secular and religious authority. In 1529, after a quick advancement at court, More was made lord chancellor to replace the disgraced Cardinal Wolsey. During his years in office he dealt with the Lutheran controversy, even writing tracts for the king, who gained the title of Defender of the Faith from the pope for his defense of the seven sacraments against Luther's pamphlet. Yet More also dealt rather harshly with "heretics" and was responsible for enforcing some of the harshest penalties for homosexuality in England. When the problem of the king's divorce came to a head, More resigned his office and retired. He was called back to take the oath imposed by the Act of Successions and refused. He was imprisoned in the Tower of London and wrote devotional works, such as the *Dialogue of Comfort against Tribulation*. On 1 July 1535 he was accused of treason for his opposition to the Act of Supremacy and was beheaded on Tower Hill five days later.

His son-in-law William Roper wrote a life of Thomas More and described More's last day when he was led "towards the place of execution, where, going up the scaffold, which was so weak that it was ready to fall, he said to Mr. Lieutenant, 'I pray you, I pray you, Mr. Lieutenant, see me safe up, and for my coming down let me shift for myself.'" He then turned to the executioner "and with a cheerful countenance spoke to him. 'Pluck up thy spirits, man, and be not afraid to do thine office. My neck is very short. Take heed therefore thou strike not awry for saving of thine honor.'"

The famous painting of Thomas More by Hans Holbein, the court painter to Henry VIII, is in the Frick Collection in New York City. The artist also made sketches of the saint and his family. There is a picture of the saint by Antoine Caron in the museum at Blois, in which he is shown as an old man with a long beard, surrounded by what seem to be Roman soldiers, being embraced by his daughter on his way to execution. More forms the subject of a play by Robert Bolt, *A Man for All Seasons*, which has on its opening page a quotation from Samuel Johnson that More "was the person of the greatest virtue these islands ever produced." A 1967 movie was also entitled *A Man for All Seasons*.

*Thor (W. G. Collingwood)*

2890

**Thor** (Thur, Thunar, Thunaer) (thunderer) In Norse mythology, the sky god; son of Odin and Fjorgyn (earth); husband of Sif; associated with thunder and lightning. One of Thor's main epithets is Vingnir (the hurler); he appears in Richard Wagner's *Der Ring des Nibelungen* as Donner. The *Prose Edda* describes Thor as "the strongest of the gods and men." His realm is called Thrudvang; his mansion of 540 rooms, Bilskirnir (lightning). His chariot is drawn by two goats, Tanngniost and Tanngrisnir. Among his possessions are a magic hammer, Mjolnir (thunderbolt), forged by the dwarf Sindri. When Thor threw Mjolnir, the hammer would return to him of its own power. The evil fire-trickster god, Loki, disguised as a fly, tried to interfere with the forging by flying around Sindri. As a result, the hammer had a short handle. A blow from Mjolnir brought instant death, but it could also restore life. Thor used Mjolnir to bless weddings on Thursday (Thor's day). The giant Thrym (noise) once stole Thor's hammer and demanded the goddess Freyja as payment for its return. Thor, disguised as Freyja, had Thrym lay the hammer in his lap and then slew Thrym and all of his giant companions with it. Thor also possessed a magic belt, Megingjardir, which doubled his strength when he wore it.

His worship continued into the Christian Middle Ages. Thor's temples and images, like Odin's, were made of wood, and the majority were destroyed in the 11th century by King Olaf II, who was later sainted by the church. According to some accounts, the saintly king often forced his subjects to reject Thor's worship in favor of Christ's. Olaf was especially angry at the inhabitants of one province who worshiped a primitive image of Thor which they decked with golden ornaments. Every evening they set food before the image, and the next morning it was gone—they believed Thor had eaten it. When the people were called by Olaf in 1030 C.E. to renounce Thor's worship in favor of the one, true god, Christ, they asked for a miracle. They would believe if it were cloudy the next day; it was cloudy, Then they asked that if they were to believe in the Christian god, the following day should be filled with sunshine. Olaf spent the night in prayer, but at dawn the sky was overcast. Nevertheless, determined to win the people for Christ, he assembled them near Thor's image. Suddenly, while they all were listening to him, Olaf pointed to the horizon, where the sun was slowly breaking through the clouds. "Behold our God!" he cried. While the people looked at the sun coming through the clouds, Olaf's guards destroyed Thor's image. Mice and other vermin came out of the wrecked image. Seeing that the food had been eaten by animals, and not by their god, the people accepted the worship of Christ. Thor appears in the *Poetic Edda*, the *Prose Edda*, and Henry W. Longfellow's *The Saga of King Olaf* (part of his *Tales of a Wayside Inn*) in which the "Challenge of Thor" opens:

I am the God Thor,
I am the War God,
I am the Thunderer!
Here in my Northland,
My fastness and fortress,
Reign I forever!

Thor appears as Donner in Arthur Rackham's illustrations for Wagner's Ring Cycle.

See also: FREYA; GEIRROD; HYMIR; MIDGARD SERPENT; ODIN; *POETIC EDDA*; *PROSE EDDA*; *RING DES NIBELUNGEN, DER*; SINDRI

*Thoth*

**Thoth** (Tahuti, Techa, Thout, Dhouti, Zhouti) In Egyptian mythology, ibis-headed moon god, also patron of wisdom, arts, speech; inventory of hieroglyphics and science; he was believed to be the author of *The Book of the Dead*. Thoth was regarded as both the heart and tongue of the great sun god Ra. When Thoth spoke, the wishes of Ra were fulfilled, as when the heavens and the earth were created and when Isis was given the words by which to revive the dead body of her son Horus. In the judgment scene in *The Book of the Dead*, Thoth, after weighing the words of the deceased, gives to the gods the final verdict as to whether a soul is to be blessed or punished.

Thoth was also called Tehuti (the measurer). In this capacity he had the power to grant life for millions of years to the deceased. When the great battle took place between Horus and Set, Thoth acted as the judge, being called Wep-rehewy (judge of the two opponent gods). During the struggle he gave Isis a cow's head in place of her own, which had been severed by Horus in anger when Isis befriended Set.

The Greeks identified Thoth with their god Hermes. They described him as the inventor of astronomy and astrology, the science of numbers and mathematics, geometry, land surveying, medicine, and botany. They said he was the first to organize religion and government, establishing the rules concerning worship of the gods. He was said to have composed hymns, prayers, and liturgical works and to have invented numbers, hieroglyphics, reading, writing, and oratory. In short, he was the author of every branch of knowledge, both human and divine.

In Egyptian art Thoth usually appears in human form with the head of an ibis, although sometimes he appears as the ibis alone. The bird was sacred to him and was associated with the moon, as was Thoth as the measurer of time. Sometimes he is portrayed as a seated baboon wearing the crescent moon on his head. This image reflects the belief that Thoth, as the moon god, took the place of Ra, the sun god, while Ra made his nightly journey through the underworld. When Thoth is portrayed in human form, he holds a scepter and ankh, sign of life, properties common to all of the gods. His headdress, however, varies according to the particular aspect of the god the artist wished to depict. As the reckoner of time and the seasons, Thoth wears on his head the crescent moon. Sometimes he wears the Atef crown and sometimes the united crowns of Upper and Lower Egypt. In *The Book of the Dead* he appears as the "scribe of Maat," or justice, holding the writing reed and palette. His close connection with the god Ra is sometimes indicated by his carrying the *utchat*, which symbolized the strength of the eye of Ra.

See also: ANKH; *BOOK OF THE DEAD, THE*; HERMES; HORUS; ISIS; MAAT; RA; SET; UTCHAT

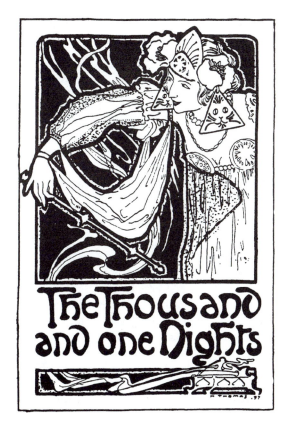

*The Thousand and One Nights (Thomas Henry)*

2892

***Thousand and One Nights, The*** *(The Arabian Nights)*   English translation of the Arabic collection of tales, *Alf Laylah wa-laylah*, which is based on a Persian collection, compiled between 988 and 1011 C.E. The tales are arranged within a narrative framework. The Persian monarch Shahriyar had little trust in women's fidelity, so he adopted the habit of taking a new wife each night and killing her the next morning. However, the clever Shahrazad, or Sheherazade, kept the monarch amused each night by telling a tale that always carried over to the next night so that, as it says at the end of the massive collection, "the Sultan of the Indies could not fail to admire the prodigious store of interesting stories with which the sultana had whiled away the time through one thousand and one nights." He decided not to kill her. The two lived happily together, and "their names were loved and respected throughout the wide territory of the Empire of the Indies."

The collection contains 264 tales of varying length, from short anecdotes of a few lines to novellas of several hundred pages. The tales generally fall into the following categories:

1. Histories or long romances, containing references to actual events. There are few of this type, but they make up the longest tales of the collection.

2. Anecdotes and short stories dealing with historical personages or with incidents of everyday life. These are the most numerous tales in the collection, and they relate for the most part to the period of the Abbaside caliphs El Mensour, El Mutawekkil, El Mutezid, El Mustensir, and Harun al-Rashid. Other tales in this category tell of ancient Persian kings.

3. Romantic tales. There are four types that fit into this category: long romantic and supernatural tales, referring to no particular historical epoch; long purely fictitious tales, laid in some definite historical era and introducing historical personages; novellas of rogues, sharpers, and impostors at the time of the caliphs; and fantastic tales, the most numerous of this section, which

include saints' tales, stories of unfortunate lovers, short purely fictional tales, and tales in a Boccaccio-like mode.

4. Fables and apologues, or short moral tales. The numerous animal fables are derived mainly from Greek, Persian, and Indian sources, though some are even from Chinese and Japanese works.

5. Tales that display wit and learning on the barest thread of narrative. In many of the tales there are poetical compositions, some of high artistic merit and some on the level of doggerel.

The first translation of the tales into a European tongue was done by a French Orientalist, Antoine Galland (1646–1715), who adapted many of the tales to the taste of his age with elaborate fictional detail. This version's influence on European literature was immense. Direct imitation of the collection is found in such works as Beckford's *Vathek* and Marryat's *The Pasha of Many Tales*; the form of the work inspired Robert Louis Stevenson's *New Arabian Nights* and *More Arabian Nights*. Among other writers, Goethe, in his *Westostlicher Diwan;* Platen in *Die Abbassiden;* and Victor Hugo, in *Orientales,* demonstrate the influence of the Arabic work.

In general the English reaction to the work was one of approval. Tennyson's *Recollections of the Arabian Nights* was, according to the poet, based on two tales in Galland's translation. Thomas Carlyle, however, would not allow the book in his house because it was filled with "downright lies." His puritanical attitude is similar to the general one of orthodox Muslims, as reflected by one 10th-century historian, Ali Aboulhusn el Mesoudi, who said the collection was "indeed vulgar."

*The Thousand and One Nights* has influenced other European arts in addition to literature. In music Rimsky-Korsakov's symphonic suite *Scheherezade* attempts, in its four movements, to evoke the mood of the tales. The suite was used by Michel Fokine for a ballet of the same title with fantastical costumes by Léon Bakst. In 1898 Maurice Ravel began an opera to be titled *Shéhézade* but completed only an overture. He did

compose a set of songs to words by Tristan Klingsor, called *Shéhérazade.* One of the most popular operas of the last century, *The Barber of Bagdad* by Peter Cornelius, was based on the collection, and Ernest Reyer's *La Statue,* Issai Obrowen's *A Thousand and One Nights,* and Henri Raboud's *Mârouf* also are based on this source. Other works in the 20th century include British composer Benno Bardi's *Fatme* and Victor de Sabata's *Mille e una notte.*

Filmmakers have been fascinated by the Oriental background of the collection and have produced numerous film epics drawn from the tales. Typical is *Arabian Nights,* starring Maria Montez, Jon Hall, and Sabu.

2893

**Thulur**   In Norse mythology, systematic lists of synonyms found in the *Eddas.* These terms were important because skaldic poetry depended on kennings and heiti for the telling of a story. The kennings, figurative expressions of various kinds, and the heiti, rare poetic names, are of particular importance because they refer to other myths and heroic legends and can only be understood if the listener to these tales also knows the story that is being referred to.

See also: KENNING; *POETIC EDDA; PROSE EDDA*

2894

**Thunderbird**   In North American Indian mythology (North Pacific Coast, in the Plateau, and the Pomo of California), a giant bird, symbol of thunder, who not only causes thunder but brings war and blessings. Lightning is the flashing of his eyes; thunder, the sound of his wings flapping. Like the Aryan thunder-gods (Thor, Zeus, Indra), he is the embodiment of the life force that strikes down man-eating monsters and serpents.

See also: INDRA; THOR; ZEUS

**Thurber, James**  1894–1961. In American literature, an essayist, cartoonist, playwright, and author of collections of fables. His fable characters were both human and animal, bloated husbands and shrewish wives, but also wise and knowing dogs, a mouse, a lion, a wolf, a scorched moth, and perhaps the best known of all, a unicorn. Thurbers's fables appeared in his *Fables for Our Times and Famous Poems Illustrated* (1940) and in *Further Fables for Our Time* (1956). In his story of the "Unicorn in the Garden," Thurber presents a husband who sees a beautiful unicorn wandering around his garden one fine morning. He goes inside several times to tell his wife of his sighting. To each report she shrewishly responds, "The unicorn is a mythical beast, and I am going to have you thrown in the booby-hatch." When the police arrive ready to bind him in restraints and take him off to the mental hospital, they ask him about the sighting of a unicorn in his garden, to which he replies, "The unicorn is a mythical beast." The police then bind his wife and cart her away. The moral: "Don't count your boobies before they hatch." Some of his aphorisms, in which animals often appear, still make interesting points: "The dog has seldom been successful in pulling man up to its level of sagacity, but man has frequently dragged the dog down to his."

**Ti-Albert**  In Haitian voodoo, a loa (deified spirit of the dead) symbolized by a dwarf with one leg. He aids priests and priestesses in driving people insane for wrongdoing. He is offered fruit, eggs, and olive or peanut oil. When he possesses a person, he makes that person a better sex partner.

See also: LOA

**Tiberinus**  In Roman mythology, a king of Italy; son of Janus and Camasena; he drowned in the Albula river, which was renamed Tiber. Some accounts say Tiberinus and the river god Volturnus were combined to form one god, Tiber. In a variant tale Tiberinus, not Helenus as in Vergil, appears to Aeneas, telling him where to found the new city, Rome. His festival was 8 December.

See also: AENEAS; HELENUS; JANUS; VOLTURNUS

**T'ien Hou** (heavenly empress)  In Chinese mythology, a deified mortal worshiped as goddess of the sea. In life she was able to calm a storm by closing her eyes. She also is called Ch'uan Hou (river empress) and portrayed as a princess in elaborate court costume.

**Tiger**  A large animal of the cat family having a tawny coat with narrow black stripes; in Chinese mythology, king of the beasts, taking the place of the lion of Western folklore. In Chinese Buddhist mythology it symbolizes anger, one of the Three Senseless Creatures, the others being the monkey as greed and the deer as lovesickness. In Hindu mythology the tiger is the mount of the goddess Durga, as destroyer, and of Shiva, who sometimes wears a tiger skin. In the West, T. S. Eliot's poem "Gerontion" depicts Christ as a tiger, recalling the terror, strength, and awe the beast conjures up in humankind, as does William Blake's "The Tyger." There are numerous motifs associated with tigers in the *Motif Index of Folk Literature*.

See also: LION; SHIVA

**Tigranes**  In Armenian folklore, a dragon slayer and king. Azadhak, king of Media, had a dream in which a fair-eyed woman gave birth to a dragon slayer who attacked the king and destroyed his idols. When Azadhak awoke, he asked his wise men what the dream signified. They told him that the famous dragon slayer Tigranes was on his way to the kingdom. Wishing to save himself, the king offered to marry Tigranes' sister Tigranuhi, but he told her he planned to kill her brother. The faithful sister so informed her brother. Tigranes came to the king and plunged his triangular spearhead into Azadhak's chest. Azadhak's family was forced to move to Armenia and settle around Massis. They became the children of the dragon, since the first queen of Azadhak was Anush, the mother of dragons. Azadhak is a variation of the Persian demon Azhi Dahaka, who in Persian mythology appears as King Zahhak in the epic poem of Firdusi, *The Shah Namah*.

See also: AZHI DAHAKA; ZAHHAK

2901

**Ti-Jean-Pied-Sec**   In Haitian voodoo, an evil loa (deified spirit of the dead) who makes people commit rape. He is one-legged and eats raw meat.

See also: LOA

2902

**Tiki** (image)   In Polynesian mythology, the first man created by the god Tane from red clay. In a variant myth, Tiki is the name of a creator god who forms a man, Tiki-ahua, who resembles the god's form.

See also: TANE

2903

**Tilaka** (mole)   In Hinduism, the mark on the forehead and/or arms and/or chest made with red, yellow, or white pigment during the morning devotions at the home altar. Sometimes the term *tika* (spot) is used.

2904

**Till Eulenspiegel** (owl glass)   In medieval German legend, a trickster. He was a native of Brunswick, Dietrich (Till) Ulenspegel, who died in 1350 of the plague after a life in which he was noted for often brutal tricks and practical jokes,

played mostly on tradespeople and innkeepers. His adventures were put into book form by Thomas Murner, a Franciscan monk of Strasbourg. The goal seems to have been to contrast city dwellers with unappreciated peasant farmers. Similar figures are found in other countries, such as the Turkish Hodscha Nasreddin. In English he was called Tyll Owlyglass or Tyll Owleglass. Richard Strauss's tone poem *Till Eulenspiegel's Merry Pranks* is a rondo for orchestra. In modern Germany there is an Eulenspiegel Museum in Schöppenstadt.

See also: TRICKSTER

2905

**Tilottama**   In Hindu mythology, a Brahman female who bathed at an improper season and was condemned to be born as Apsaras, a water nymph. She was loved by the god Shiva. He became so enamored of Tilottama's looks that he took on four faces so that he could gaze at her beauty at all times.

See also: SHIVA

2906

**Timon of Athens**   Fifth century B.C.E. In Greek legend, a misanthrope who came to the conclusion that life was a fraud. Timon appears in Plutarch's *Life of Anthony*, which inspired Shakespeare's play *Timon of Athens*.

2907

**Tinirau**   In Polynesian mythology, sea god who had two forms, one divine and the other human. As a human being he was handsome and pleasant, having a liaison with the goddess Hina. In animal form he appeared as a man-of-war bird, hovering above the waters and striking without warning, destroying both men and their boats. Tinirau is also referred to as Sinilau, Kinilau, Timirau, and Tinilau.

See also: KAE; ORO; TANE

**Tintagel** (stronghold of the resplendent mighty god)  In Arthurian legend, a castle on the coast of Cornwall where various episodes from Arthurian legends took place. It was here that Arthur was born and Uther Pendragon died. Its ruins still exist. Arnold Bax's symphonic poem *Tintagel* captures the feeling of the area.

See also: ARTHUR; IGRAINE

**Tipitaka** (three baskets)  Three collections of sacred books in Buddhism, the *Vinaya Pitaka*, the *Sutta Pitaka*, and the *Abhidhamma Pitaka*, converted from the oral to the written tradition sometime in the first century C.E. The first book, the *Vinaya*, contains rules for the monks and nuns; the second, *Sutta*, is a series of sermons on general topics; and the last, *Abhidhamma*, is a collection of material on advanced topics concerning the nature of consciousness. In Sanskrit, Tripitaka.

**Tirawahat**  In North American Indian mythology (Pawnee), the "heaven's circle" of Tirawa, the supreme god, creator of the heavenly bodies. Thunder, lightning, winds, and rain are his messengers.

**Tiresias** (Teiresias) (he who delights in signs)  In Greek mythology, blind prophet; son of Everes and Chariclo; father of Chloris and Manto.

There are variant accounts of why Tiresias became blind. In one version, he saw two snakes mating, killed the female, and immediately was transformed into a woman. After seven years he again saw two snakes mating, but this time he killed the male and was transformed back into a man. When an argument arose between Zeus and Hera as to who had more pleasure during sexual intercourse, man or woman, they consulted Tiresias as the one best able to speak from experience. He answered that women received more pleasure during the sex act. This so angered Hera that she blinded Tiresias as a punishment for telling the truth. Zeus, who could not withdraw the blindness, gifted Tiresias with prophetic powers and a very long life. In a variant account Tiresias was punished for having seen Athena bathe in the fountain of Hippocrene. In another account he was blinded because when he was seven years old he revealed secrets. Tiresias died when he drank from the icy waters of the fountain of Telphusa.

He appears or is cited in Homer, Aeschylus, Apollodorus, Diodorus, Hyginus, Pausanias, Pindar, and Sophocles in ancient literature. In English literature both Tennyson and Swinburne have poems called "Tiresias." He also appears in T. S. Eliot's *The Waste Land*.

See also: APOLLODORUS; ATHENA; HERA; HOMER; ZEUS

**Tirthamkara** (one who makes a ford)  In Jainism, title applied to 23 teachers who have been liberated from continual rebirths, having attained Nirvana. Because they have complete liberation from the world, they are transcendent, omniscient, actionless, and absolutely at peace. This concept, however, is mitigated in Jain practice, in which they are objects of worship.

The 23 Tirthamkara are the following:

Rishabha, who according to one account, "reached the infinite" after "fasting three and a half days without drinking water" and engaged in meditation. He died in the company of "ten thousand monks . . . freed from all pains." His symbol is the bull, and his color is golden.

Ajita (the unconquered). His symbol is the elephant and his color is golden. *Variant spelling*: Ajitanatha.

Sambhava (who opens up possibilities). His symbol is the horse, and his color is golden. *Variant spelling*: Sambhavanatha.

Abhinandana (feeling of voluptuousness). His symbol is the ape, and his color is golden.

Sumati (good sense). His symbol is the heron, and his color is golden.

Padmaprabha (lord of the lotus). His symbol is the lotus, and his color red.

Suparshva (crowned by a five-hooded Naga). His symbol is the swastika, and his color is golden.

Chandrapradha (lord of the moon). His symbol is the moon, and his color is white.

Pushpadanta. His symbol is the dolphin, and his color is white. *Variant spelling*: Subidhi.

Sitala (free from emotion). His symbol is the swastika, and his color is golden.

Shreyamsa (who was born at Sarnath). His symbol is the rhinoceros, and his color is golden.

Vasupujya (universal adoration). His symbol is the buffalo, and his color is red.

Vimalanatha (purity). His symbol is the hog, and his color is golden.

Anantanatha (eternity). His symbol is the falcon, and his color golden.

Dharmanatha (just law; just truth). His symbol is the thunderbolt, and his color is golden.

Shantinatha (lord of peace). His symbol is the antelope, and his color is golden.

Kunthunatha. His symbol is the goat, and his color is golden.

Aranatha (who triumphs over the enemy). His color is golden.

Mallinatha. The only woman on the list. Her symbol is a jar, and her color is blue.

Munisuvrata (observation of monastic laws). His symbol is the tortoise, and his color is black.

Nami. His symbol is the blue lotus, and his color is golden.

Arishtanemi. His symbol is the conch shell, and his color is black.

Parshva. His symbol is two Nagas, and his color is blue.

**2913**

**Tishtrya** (Tistar, Tistrya)  In Persian mythology, rain god, primeval producer of rain, seas,

and lakes, often called the bright and glorious star and identified with Sirius, to whom sacrifices were made to bring purification to the soul. As rain god, Tishtrya was in continual battle against the demons of drought, particularly Apaosha. One day, Tishtrya, in the form of a beautiful white horse, went down to the ocean's depths and met Apaosha, who was in the form of a black horse. The two battled for three days and three nights. Apaosha was gaining the upper hand when Tishtrya called upon the good god, Ahura Mazda, for aid. Ahura Mazda then made sacrifices to Tishtrya to renew his strength. With this newly gained energy Tishtrya defeated the demon Apaosha.

See also: AHURA MAZDA

**2914**

**Titans** (lords, rulers)  In Greek mythology, primeval gigantic beings; children of Uranus and Gaea. Their number varies, though 12 are generally named, coinciding with the 12 Olympian gods who replaced the Titans as rulers. They are Oceanus, Tethys, Hyperion, Thia, Crius, Mnemosyne (Eurybia), Coeus, Phoebe, Cronus, Rhea, Iapetus, and Themis. Added to the list sometimes are Briareus, Cottus, Gyges, Enceladus, Porphyrion, and Rhoetus, though some accounts say they were just giants, not Titans. Also called Titans are Prometheus, Epimetheus, and Atlas. Cronus, their leader, overthrew his father, Uranus, and castrated him. Cronus, in turn, was overthrown by his son Zeus. In the ensuing war Iapetus and all the 12 Titans, except Oceanus, sided with their brother Cronus against Zeus. The war continued for 10 years until Zeus, advised by Gaea, released from Tartarus, the lowest section of the underworld, the Cyclopes and the Hecatonchires, who sided with Zeus and helped him defeat the Titans, who were then cast into Tartarus. Prometheus also sided with Zeus in the battle and was rewarded. The Titans appear in Hesiod's *Theogony*, Hyginus's *Fables*, and Apollodorus's *Biblioteca* (Library). Keats's unfinished epic, *The Fall of Hyperion*, deals with the sun god of the Titans. Mahler's Symphony No. 1 in D is subtitled "Titan."

See also: ATLAS; GAEA; HESIOD; HYPERION; OCEANUS; OLYMPIAN GODS; PROMETHEUS; THEMIS; TITANS; URANUS; ZEUS

2915
**Titha Jumma**   In Burmese mythology, a disciple of the Buddha. Titha Jumma and his brother Zaya Kumma were hatched from eggs left by a dragon woman. They were brought up by two hermit brothers. Titha Jumma died when he was 10 but was reborn when the Buddha appeared in his country, and he became a disciple of the Buddha.

See also: BUDDHA, THE

2916
**Tithonus**   In Greek mythology, handsome young man; son of Laomedon, king of Troy, and Leucippe. Aurora, the dawn, fell in love with the handsome youth and granted him immortality at his request. Tithonus, however, forgot to ask for perpetual youth. As he grew older and older he begged the goddess to kill him. Aurora eventually changed him into a grasshopper. Tennyson's *Tithonus*, a dramatic monologue, deals with his tragic fate.

See also: LAOMEDON; TROY

2917
**Ti Tsang** (Kshitigarbha)   In Chinese Buddhism, a Bodhisattva, god of the underworld and instructor of the regions of darkness, who travels unceasingly throughout the nether world to succor the dead. Ti Tsang is the Chinese form of the Sanskrit Kshitigarbha. As a young man Ti Tsang was a young Brahman who, being converted to the Buddha of that time, took a vow to become a Buddha, but not before he had saved all beings sunk in ignorance and brought them over the river of Samsara to the Happy Land. During his numerous reincarnations he sacrificed himself to fulfill this vow. He is especially

concerned with dead children. Mothers who have lost a child pray to him and place a child's bib around the neck of his image. He is portrayed as a monk. In Japanese he is called Jizo.

See also: BODHISATTVA; BRAHMAN

2918
**Titurel**   In medieval legends associated with the Holy Grail, a knight who was the first guardian of the Grail. He was succeeded by his son Frimutel and later by Amfortas.

See also: AMFORTAS; HOLY GRAIL

2919
**Tiur** (Tir)   In Armenian mythology, scribe of the supreme god, Aramazd; Tiur kept a record of the good and evil deeds of men for future judgment. He also wrote down the decrees that were issued from Aramazd concerning human events. Some scholars believe Tiur was also the of god who conducted the souls to the underworld. The common Armenian expression "May Tiur carry him off!" refers to the god in his possible role as conductor of the dead.

See also: ARAMAZD

2920
**Ti Yü** (the earth prison)   In Chinese mythology, the underworld or hell, made up of 10 sections governed by the Shih-Tien Yen Wang (the Yama kings of the 10 hills). Each king rules over one of the hells. They are Ch'in-kuang wang, Ch'u-kuang wang, Sung-ti wang, Wu-kuan wang, Yen-mo wang, Pien ch'eng, T'ai-shan kun wang, P'ing-Teng, Tu-shi, and Chuan-lun wang.

See also: CH'IN-KUANG WANG; PIEN CH'ENG; P'ING-TENG WU-KUAN WANG; SUNG-TI WANG; T'AI-SHAN KUN WANG; YEN-MO WANG

2921
**Tjinimin the Bat**   In Australian mythology, the trickster bat, son of Kunmanggur, the Rain-

bow Snake. He raped his sisters and eventually killed his father with a spear.

See also: RAINBOW SNAKE

2922

**Tlaloc** (Tecutli, Tlaloque) (path under the earth, wine of earth, long cave?)   In Aztec mythology, god of rain, thunder, and lightning. He controlled mountain springs and weather. Tlaloc lived in a luxurious paradise, Tlalocan, peopled by those who had drowned or had been killed by lightning. One mural from Tepantitla (first to sixth century C.E.) in Teotihuacán portrays the god in his heaven, where there are flowers and butterflies. He is attended by priests, water flows from his hands, and aquatic creatures play at his feet. The souls of those who live in his paradise are portrayed in the lower half of the work and seem to be extremely happy. However, during Tlaloc's feast, called Etzalqualiztli (13 May), children and virgins were sacrificed to him. His offspring by his wife Chalchihuitlicue were the Tlalocs, or clouds.

See also: CHALCHIHUITLICUE

2923

**Tlazolteotl** (Tlaculteutl) (lady of dirt)   In Aztec mythology, sex goddess who produced lust and then forgave the sinner. The ritual freeing people from sins included a number of confessions to the priests of this goddess. The people would then be freed of all sins committed throughout their lives, and they would also be released them from any legal consequences. They were only allowed one such confession in a lifetime. According to Fray Bernardino de Sahagún in *Historia general de las cosas de Nueva España* (1570–1582), the goddess was also known as Ixcuina (two-faced) and had four aspects: the goddesses Tiacapán, Teicu, Tlacotl, and Xocutzin. All four "had the power to produce lust" and "could provoke carnal intercourse and favored illicit love affairs." These four aspects of the goddess are believed by C. A. Burland in *The Gods of*

*Mexico* (1967) to be "the four phases of the moon" and associate the goddess with witchcraft.

*Return of Tobias*

2924

**Tobit** (God is good)   In the Bible, Apocrypha, hero, along with his son Tobias. The tale is included in the Latin Vulgate as part of sacred scripture and was so accepted by the church until the Protestant Reformation. Even Martin Luther, who rejected many books from the standard canon, admired the work, saying he preferred it to Esther, a book that he intensely disliked.

Tobit, a devout and charitable Jew living in exile in Nineveh, was blinded by sparrows "muting warm dung into his eyes." He sent his son Tobias with his faithful dog (in the Bible the dog is always looked on as dirty and unclean, except in this tale) to a distant city to collect a debt. The boy met a companion, a young man who was the angel Raphael in disguise. Tobias, with the help of Raphael, succeeded in collecting the money. Tobias then met a woman, Sarah, who was afflicted with a demon who had killed each of her seven husbands on their wedding nights. With Raphael's aid, Tobias exorcised the demon, married Sarah, returned home with her, and cured his father's blindness. At the end of the tale Raphael reveals himself to them.

Christian art has often portrayed Tobias with the angel and a fish. On Tobias's journey Raphael saved him from being eaten by a great fish. He instructed Tobias to catch the fish, roast it, and eat it but to save the heart, liver, and gall. The first two were used to exorcise the evil spirit haunting Sarah, and the gall was used to cure Tobit's blindness. One of the most famous paintings portraying this legend is *Tobias and the Angel* from the school of Andrea del Verrocchio. Franz Joseph Haydn composed an oratorio *Tobit*.

**2925**

**Toci** (Tozi, Temazcalteci) (our grandmother) In Aztec mythology, goddess and one aspect of Tlalzolteotl. Fray Diego Durán, in his *Book of the Gods and Rites* (c. 1576), calls Toci the "Mother of the Gods and Heart of the Earth." According to C. A. Burland, in *The Gods of Mexico* (1967), Toci was a "life-giving spirit" who "cleansed sins and cared for her little grandchildren." She presided over the sweat bath. Her image was placed above the doorway.

See also: TLALZOLTEOTL

**2926**

**To-Kabinana and To-Karvuvu** In Melanesian mythology, the first two men created by a nameless creator god. One day the creator god drew two male figures on the ground and sprinkled them with his blood, giving them life. To-Kabinana was regarded as the creator of good things, and his brother, To-Karvuvu, was responsible for all of the trouble in the world. Beautiful women were created by To-Kabinana when he dropped two coconuts on the ground. When his brother repeated the act, women with flat noses emerged because the coconuts fell in the wrong position. In another myth To-Kabinana created fish from a wooden image. When his brother repeated the act, he created the shark.

**2927**

**Tomato** A fruit-bearing plant in the nightshade family, introduced in Europe in the 16th century by Spaniards returning from Mexico. In European folklore, the tomato was sometimes identified as the fruit eaten by Adam and Eve in the Garden of Eden, though it is not named in the account in Genesis. The Austrians call the tomato *Paradies Apfel* (paradise apple). In French folklore, the tomato was believed to be poisonous, but in small amounts it was believed to be an aphrodisiac. The French call it *pomme d'amour* (love apple).

See also: ADAM AND EVE

**2928**

**Tom Quick** In American folklore, "Indian Slayer" or "The Avenger of the Delaware." According to one legend, Tom avenged himself on various Indians for the murder of his father by Mushwink, an Indian, whom Tom later met and killed. One legend tells how he tricked the Indians. As he was splitting a log, he found himself surrounded by Indians. They were ready to take him back to camp and torture him, but Tom asked them if they would help him split the log first. The Indians pulled at the log, but instead of driving the wedge in farther, Tom knocked it out and slaughtered the Indians with the ax.

**2929**

**Tonacatecutli** (Tonacateotle) (lord of our existence) In Aztec mythology, consort of Tonacacihuatl, with whom he lived in the ninth, or highest, heaven. They had four sons, who were guardians of the four cardinal points. Tonacatecutli was also known as Tzinteotl (god of the beginning), Tonaca Cihuatl (queen of our existence), Xochiquetzal (beautiful rose), Citallicue (the star-skirted, or the Milky Way), Citaltonac (the star that warms, or the morning), Chicomecoatl (the seven serpents), and Chicomexochit (seven flames).

**2930**

**Tonapa** (Thunupa, Taapac) In Bolivian Indian folklore, culture hero. Tonapa was a blue-eyed man who came from the north with five disciples. He preached against war, drunkenness, and polygamy. Makuri, a cruel tyrant, roused the people against Tonapa's preaching, and they set his house on fire while he was sleeping. He escaped but was later caught by Makuri, who martyred the disciples and left Tonapa for dead.

According to Ramos Gavilan, writing in 1621, Tonapa's body was placed in a boat that "sailed away with such speed that those who had tried so cruelly to kill him were left behind in terror and astonishment for they knew the lake had no current."

Tonapa was identified with St. Bartholomew in some Christian-Indian legends because he carried a cross on his back as he went to see Makuri, and St. Bartholomew was martyred on a cross. Scholars believe Tonapa to be a version of Tupan (Toupan), the thunder god of the Botocudo Indians of Brazil.

See also: BARTHOLOMEW, ST.

2931

**Tonatiuh**   In Aztec mythology, a sun god, fourth in a series of sun gods. Tonatiuh gave strength to warriors, receiving them along with women who died in childbirth, into his paradise, which was identical with Tollan (place of the seed), the Aztec paradise where crops grew in abundance. Offerings of human hearts and blood were made to the god. In some Aztec accounts he was thought of as an eagle who flew near the sun with the souls of the heroic dead.

2932

**Tontuu**   In Finno-Ugric mythology, spirit of a somewhat capricious nature who watches over the welfare of a household, rewarding its members with corn and money.

2933

**Tony Beaver**   In American folklore, comic hero of the West Virginia lumberjacks whose antics often take place in the Cumberland Mountains. In one tale he built a wagon cart that covered ten acres of land to carry watermelons.

When the wagon broke, causing melons to fall into the Eel River, his friends each straddled a seed and rowed away. Tony is credited with inventing peanut brittle: once when a river was overflowing, Tony took some molasses and peanuts, and threw them into the river to stop it up. Tony Beaver's tales are told in Margaret Prescott Montague's *Up Eel River*.

2934

**Too-Roo-Dun**   In Australian mythology, an evil water spirit who seizes his victims and eats them.

2935

**Torongoi and Edji**   In Siberian mythology, the first man and woman. Both Torongoi and Edji were created with fur on their bodies to keep them warm. They were told they could eat fruit from branches that pointed toward the sunrise but were not allowed to eat from branches that pointed to the sunset. To help the couple, God set a dog and a snake to bite the devil if he came. When God returned to heaven, the devil came, crept into the skin of the sleeping serpent, and tempted the woman with the forbidden fruit. She persuaded her husband to eat it too. They both became so frightened afterward that the fur fell off their bodies. When God came down from heaven, Torongoi and Edji hid. God asked them what happened. Torongoi said Edji made him eat the fruit; Edji said the snake made her eat the fruit; the snake said the devil was inside him; and the dog said he had seen nothing.

See also: ABUK AND GARANK; ADAM AND EVE; ASK AND EMBLA; KHADAU AND MAMALDI

2936

**Tortoise and the Birds, The**   Aesopic fable found in various collections throughout the world.

A tortoise became dissatisfied with his lowly life when he beheld so many of his neighbors the birds in the clouds, and he thought that if he could but once get up into the air, he could soar with the best of them. One day he called on an eagle and offered him all of the treasures of the ocean if he would only teach him to fly. The eagle tried to decline the task, assuring him that the thing was not only absurd but impossible, but being further pressed by the entreaties and promises of the tortoise, he at length consented to do the best he could. He took the tortoise up to a great height and loosed his hold on him. "Now, then!" cried the eagle. But before the tortoise could answer a word, he fell on a rock and was dashed to pieces.

Moral: *Don't try to fly if you don't have wings.*

The legend that the Greek dramatist Aeschylus was killed when a tortoise was dropped on his bald head by an eagle is believed to have derived from this fable. The fable appears in the Indian collection the *Kacchapa Jataka*, in which a tortoise, holding a stick in its mouth, is carried by two birds. It falls when it opens its mouth to rebuke the birds that are scoffing at it. Buddha cites it as a lesson to a talkative king.

See also: AESOPIC FABLES; *JATAKA*

2937
**Tou Mu**   In Chinese mythology, goddess of the North Star, who is portrayed on a lotus. She is accompanied by two attendants, Yu Pi and Tao Fu. Sometimes she is seen with the star gods of longevity and affluence.

*The Town Mouse and the Country Mouse*

2938
**Town Mouse and the Country Mouse, The**
Aesopic fable found in various European collections.

A country mouse who had a friend in town invited him, for old acquaintance sake, to pay him a visit in the country. Though plain and rough and somewhat frugal in his nature, the country mouse opened his heart and store in honor of an old friend. There was not a carefully stored-up morsel that he did not produce from his larder—peas and barley, cheese parings and nuts—to please the palate of his city-bred guest.

The town mouse, however, turned up his long nose at the rough country fare. "How is it, my friend," he exclaimed, "that you can endure the boredom of living like a toad in a hole? You can't really prefer these solitary rocks and woods to the excitement of the city. You are wasting your time out here in the wilderness. A mouse, you know, does not live forever; one must make the most of life while it lasts. So come with me and I'll show you life and the town."

In the end the country mouse allowed himself to be persuaded, and the two friends set out together on their journey to town. It was late in the evening when they crept stealthily into the city, and midnight before they reached the great house where the town mouse lived. On the table of the splendid banquet room were the remains of a lavish feast.

It was now the turn of the city mouse to play host. He ran to and fro to supply all of his guest's wants. He pressed dish after dish and dainty after dainty on his friend, as though he were waiting on a king. The country mouse, for his part, pretended to feel quite at home and blessed the good fortune that had wrought such a change in his way of life. But in the midst of his enjoyment, just as he was beginning to feel contempt for his frugal life in the country, the sound of barking and growling could be heard outside the door.

"What is that?" said the country mouse.

"Oh, that is only the master's dogs," replied the town mouse.

"Only!" replied the visitor in dismay. "I can't say that I like music with my dinner."

At that moment the door flew open and a party of revelers, together with two huge dogs, burst into the room. The frightened friends jumped from the table and concealed themselves in a far corner of the room. Finally, when things seemed quiet, the country mouse stole out from his hiding place and, bidding his friend good-bye, whispered in his ear: "This fine way of living may do for those who like it. But give me my barley bread in the security of my country home in preference to your dainty fare partaken with fear and trembling."

Moral: *A crust eaten in peace is better than a banquet partaken in anxiety.*

Horace, in his *Satires* (book 2), tells the fable to point out that wealth brings along with it many problems, though one wonders if his readers were convinced. La Fontaine also tells the tale in his collection of fables, though he substitutes rats for mice.

See also: AESOPIC FABLES; LA FONTAINE, JEAN DE

**Tree and the Reed, The**   Aesopic fable found in various collections throughout the world.

"Well, little one," said a tree to a reed, "why do you not plant your feet deeply in the ground, and raise your head boldly in the air as I do?"

"I am contented with my lot," said the reed. "I may not be so grand as you, but I think I am safer."

"Safe!" sneered the tree. "Who shall pluck me up by the roots or bow my head to the ground?"

That night a hurricane arose and tore the tree from its roots and cast it to the ground, a useless log. The reed, however, bent with the force of the wind during the hurricane and stood upright again when the storm was over.

Moral: *Obscurity often brings safety.*

In the great Indian epic poem *The Mahabharata*, a similar fable is told in which the sea complains that the rivers bring down to it oaks,

but not reeds. Shakespeare, in *Cymbeline* (4:2), seems to refer to the fable in the dirge: "To thee the reed is as the oak," and Wordsworth's poem *The Oak and the Broom* develops the subject in his typical moralistic manner, ending with the oak being "whirled" far away while

The little careless broom was left
To live for many a day.

See also: AESOPIC FABLES; *MAHABHARATA*

**Tree of Jesse**   In Christian lore, tree or root of Jesse, an Old Testament ancestor of Christ. This is frequently seen in medieval art, particularly in stained-glass windows. According to the genealogy in the Gospel of Matthew (1:6), Jesse, father of King David, started the royal line that ended in Christ, the Messiah. Representation of the tree of Jesse in medieval art (usually shown sprouting from the loins of a reclining Jesse) is based on the prophecy of Isaiah (11:1–2): "And there shall come forth a rod out of the stem of Jesse, and a Branch shall grow out of his roots: And the Spirit of the Lord shall rest upon him." Saint Ambrose interprets the passage thus: "The root is the family of the Jews, the stem Mary, the flower of Mary is Christ."

See also: AMBROSE, ST.

**Tree of Life**   In Germanic folklore and mythology, a symbol of life, fertility, blessings, and luck. This symbol is often found in knitting and embroidery works in a dowry, on beds where babies are born, in ironworks produced by a blacksmith, in carvings and painting above a doorway, and on trunks and chests. The tree often appears with six-petaled flowers or stars and sun wheels. Some scholars have sought deeper meanings for the tree, associating it with the tree in the Garden of Eden; the Germanic world tree Yggdrasill, where Odin hung; the Christmas tree; and the tree of fate found in many fairy tales.

See also: CHRISTMAS; *POETIC EDDA*; *PROSE EDDA*; YGGDRASILL

2942
**Tri-loka** (three worlds)    In Hinduism, the three divisions of the universe. An early division was Dyu-loka (bright realm, the sky), Antar-loka (middle realm, the atmosphere), and Bhur-loka (beings realm, the earth). The notion of separate heavens and hells does not occur before the sixth century B.C.E. at the earliest. The three principal gods over the three realms were Surya, Indra, and Agni.

See also: AGNI; INDRA; SURYA

2943
**Trimurti** (having three forms)    In Hinduism, a triad of gods made up of Brahma, Vishnu, and Shiva. The concept, however, is not typical of everyday Hinduism.

See also: BRAHMA; SHIVA; VISHNU

2944
**Tri-ratna** (triple jewel)    In Buddhism, the Buddha, the Dhara, and the Sangha. In Buddhist art the Tri-ratna is sometimes portrayed as three large egg-shaped gems, with the narrow ends directed downward and the central member placed slightly above the other two. The whole composition is surrounded by flames. Called Triratna in Pali, it is an inseparable unit; Buddha manifests Dharma and the Sangha preserves it. Buddhist services commonly begin by taking refuge in the Triratna.

See also: BUDDHA, THE; DHARMA; SANGHA

2945
**Trisiras** (three-headed)    In Hindu mythology, a demon killed by the storm god Indra; he symbolizes heat, cold, and sweating. Trisiras is also used as a name for Kubera, god of wealth.

See also: INDRA; KUBERA

*Tristram and Iseult (A. Beardsley)*

2946
**Tristram and Iseult** (Tristran, Trystan, Ysolde, Ysonde, Yseult, Isold, Isolte, Yseulte, Isot, Izot) (sad, tumult)    In medieval legend, two lovers whose romance became associated with the Arthurian cycle of legends. Tristram's legend is found in nearly all medieval European languages. He was the son of Blanchefleur, sister of King Mark of Cornwall, and Meliadus. The father died in battle at the hands of Morgan when Tristram was born. In another account his mother died in childbirth. Kurvenal (Rohand, Rual), a faithful friend of Blanchefleur, took the child and reared him as his own. Tristram grew up without knowing who his real parents were. He became a knight, a hunter, and a harp player. One day he boarded a Norwegian vessel and eventually landed in Cornwall. He found his way to King Mark's court, and the king informed him of his parents and their fate. After hearing the story of his father's death at the hands of Morgan in battle, he determined to avenge it. He im-

mediately set out, slew Morgan, and recovered his father's lands at Lyonesse, which he entrusted to Kurvenal. When he returned to Cornwall, he found that King Mark had to pay Morold, brother of the king of Ireland, a tribute of 300 pounds of silver and tin and 300 youths to be handed over to slavery. Tristram challenged Morold to combat. Morold, who was a giant and had a poisoned sword, accepted. Morold's sword pierced Tristram's side. Morold told Tristram that if he surrendered he would help him obtain balsam from Iseult (Isolde, Ysolde) to cure him. Tristram would not yield but, in a burst of energy, attacked and slew Morold. He cut through Morold's helmet and pierced the giant's skull, which was so hard that a fragment of his sword remained embedded within the wound.

The people of Cornwall were delighted, and King Mark, who had no son, proclaimed Tristram his heir. Tristram's wound, however, would not heal. He decided to seek Iseult's aid. Knowing that she would not help him if she knew his identity, he arrived in Ireland calling himself Tantris, a minstrel. Iseult, charmed by his music, cured him of his wound. Tristram remained at the Irish court for some time, spending many hours with Iseult. After some months had passed, Tristram returned to Cornwall, where he related to King Mark the story of his cure. He also told of the beauty of the young Iseult, and King Mark expressed a desire to marry her. On the advice of the courtiers, who were jealous of Tristram and hoped he would fail in the mission, the young hero was sent to Ireland to ask for Īseult's hand and to escort her safely to Cornwall.

When Tristram arrived in Dublin, the people were being threatened by a dragon, and he realized that the best way to win Iseult for King Mark would be to kill the dragon. After a fierce battle he slew the monster, cut out the dragon's tongue, and placed it in his pocket. He had gone only a few steps when he fell down exhausted. A few moments later another knight, seeing the dead dragon and the body of a knight nearby, cut off the dragon's head and went back to the palace claiming he had killed the dragon. However,

Iseult and her mother did not believe the knight and went to the scene. They found Tristram with the dragon's tongue in his pocket.

They took him to the palace to nurse him back to health. While the young Iseult sat beside her sleeping patient, she idly drew his sword from its scabbard. Suddenly her eye caught the broken blade, a piece of which had been found in her Uncle Morold's skull. She was about to kill Tristram when her mother stopped her, saying Tristram atoned for the deed by saving them from the dragon. When Tristram had recovered, he challenged the lying knight, won, and then asked for the hand of Iseult for King Mark. Iseult was stunned because she had believed Tristram had come for her hand for himself. But she obeyed her father and prepared to leave. To help save her daughter, her mother brewed a magic love potion, which was put in a golden cup and entrusted to BranGwain, Iseult's attendant. The potion was to be given to Iseult and King Mark on their wedding day. On the journey Tristram entertained Iseult with songs. One day, after singing, he asked for a drink. She went to the cupboard and took the magic potion, not knowing what it was. The two drank from the cup, and the potion aroused in them a passionate love for each other. Still, they resolved to hide their love and continue as planned. Iseult landed in Cornwall and married King Mark. BranGwain, who knew all that had happened, tried to shield her mistress.

In time the love of the two was known, and Meliadus, a knight who hated Tristram, told King Mark. The queen was publicly accused and compelled to prove her innocence by undergoing the ordeal of fire or by taking a public oath that she had shown favor to none but King Mark. On her way to where the ordeal was to take place, Iseult was carried across a stream by Tristram disguised as a beggar and, at his request, kissed him in reward for his service.

When Iseult was called on to take the oath before the judges, she could swear that, with the exception of a beggar, no other man than the king had received her favor. Tristram, however, went mad. When he recovered, he went to the court of King Arthur, but he was again wounded, this time by a poisoned arrow. Again, he could not be cured. Afraid to go again to Iseult for balsam, Tristram went to Brittany, where another Iseult—Iseult of the White Hands—equally skilled in medicine, nursed him back to health. Iseult of the White Hands believed that Tristram loved her as much as she loved him because she heard him sing of Iseult and did not know another existed with the same name. Tristram married Iseult of the White Hands, but he did not love her or show any signs of affection. He could not forget Iseult of Cornwall. When his brother-in-law Ganhardin discovered the truth, he forgave Tristram and asked him to take him to Cornwall, for Ganhardin had fallen in love with a portrait of BranGwain. On their way the two knights aided King Arthur in freeing himself from the Lady of the Lake. They also carried off Iseult of Cornwall to Lancelot's castle of Joyeuse Garde. There Iseult of Cornwall remained with Guinever.

Once again Tristram was wounded. This time Iseult of the White Hands could not cure him, and Iseult of Cornwall was called on. Kurvenal, who went to fetch Iseult of Cornwall, said he would change the black sails of the vessel for white if his mission was successful. Tristram now watched impatiently for the returning sail but died just as it came in sight. When Iseult of Cornwall arrived and saw his body, she too died. Both bodies were carried to Cornwall, where they were buried in separate graves by order of King Mark. But a vine grew from Tristram's grave to Iseult's. It was cut down three times but always grew back.

Tristram's legend has inspired numerous poems, such as *Tristan und Isolde* by Gottfried von Strassburg, *Tristram and Iseult* by Matthew Arnold, *Tristram of Lyonesse* by Swinburne, part of *Idylls of the King* by Tennyson, and *Tristram* by Edwin Arlington Robinson. The most important musical work about Tristram, having a great ef-

*Iseult (A. Beardsley)*

fect on all 19th-century musical development, is Wagner's *Tristan und Isolde*.

See also: ARTHUR

2947

**Triton** (being in the third day)   In Greek mythology, merman, half man, half fish; son of Poseidon and Amphitrite; brother of Albion, Charybdis, Benthesicyme, and Rhode. Triton appears in Vergil's *Aeneid* (book 6), in which he drowns Misenus, a human, for daring to challenge him to a musical contest on conchs. Ovid's *Metamorphoses* (book 2) has him appear in the story of Deucalion, the Flood myth, in which he blows his horn or conch shell to summon the waters to retreat. In European art Triton appears in Bernini's Trevi Fountain and Triton Fountain in the Piazza Barberini in Rome. Wordsworth cites Triton in his "Sonnet" (1807), in which he wishes to "hear old Triton blow his wreathed horn."

See also: *AENEID, THE*; AMPHITRITE; DEUCALION; POSEIDON

2948

**Troilus and Cressida**   In medieval legend, two lovers; he was faithful, but she was not.

The medieval tale developed out of Greco-Roman mythology. Troilus was the son of King Priam of Troy. In Vergil's *Aeneid* (book 1) Troilus is said to have thrown down his arms during a battle and to have fled in his chariot. He was transfixed with a spear thrown by Achilles. In medieval legend he had a love affair with Cressida, an older Trojan woman. Chaucer's long narrative poem *Troilus and Criseyde* is partly based on the *Filostrato* of Boccaccio. Troilus, a prince of the royal house of Troy, scoffs at love and lovers until one day he sees the beautiful Criseyde, a young widow, at the temple of the Palladium. He falls madly in love with her. Pandarus, her uncle and Troilus's friend, coaxes his secret from the timid youth and promises to help him with his niece. Pandarus finds Criseyde sitting with the women, poring over tales of knights and chivalry. Pandarus tells Criseyde that Troilus is madly in love with her. After he leaves, a ballad sung by Antigone sets Criseyde to daydreaming. At this moment, Troilus rides by her window, returning from a battle with the Greeks, amid the shouts of the people. The next day Pandarus returns with a letter, which Criseyde at first refuses to receive but at last consents to answer. Pandarus persuades his niece to go to the palace on a plausible pretext and so contrives to have the lovers meet. He next invites Criseyde to supper at his home, telling her that Troilus is away and cannot be there. Criseyde is induced to spend the night at her uncle's house because of a storm. Pandarus comes to her room with the news of Troilus's unexpected arrival. She consents to see him, and later the two make love.

Criseyde's father is a traitor in the Greek camp. He sends for his daughter in an exchange of prisoners. The lovers are heartbroken at the parting, but Criseyde, with vows that "shake the throned gods," swears to return in 10 days. She soon discovers that no pretext for return will avail because her father, a priest, has foreknowledge that Troy is destined to be destroyed by the Greeks. Diomede, a young Greek, pays court to Criseyde and wins her, though she grieves for Troilus. But there is no need for her to repent; she will make amends by being true to her new lover. When Troilus can no longer continue to believe Criseyde is faithful, he seeks death in battle and is slain by Achilles.

In English the name Criseyde became a byword for faithlessness in love. Shakespeare took up the story in his play *Troilus and Cressida*, with licentiousness as his main theme. Troilus himself is meant to represent constancy, "As true as Troilus." William Walton's opera *Troilus and Cressida* is based on Chaucer's work.

See also: ACHILLES; *AENEID, THE*; *ILIAD, THE*; PRIAM

2949

**Trojanu** (Troiaw)   In Slavic mythology, a spirit of darkness who possessed wax wings. He was believed to be the spirit of the Roman emperor Trajan, who conquered the Dacians in the first century C.E. Often in mythology a feared enemy was worshiped as a demon god in the hope of appeasing his anger. Trojanu is cited in *The Lay of Igor's Army*.

See also: *LAY OF IGOR'S ARMY, THE*

2950

**Troll** (to tread, giant, monster)   In Scandinavian folklore, a dwarf who lives in caves and hills. Originally, trolls were giants. In general they are skillful craftsmen but are not smart.

2951

**Trophonius** (increaser of sales)   In Greek mythology, underworld god; son of Apollo whose oracle at Lebadeia in Boeotia, between Athens and Delphi, was associated with the deities of the underworld. Pausanias's *Description of Greece* (book 9) tells of the elaborate ritual associated with the god. After ritual preparation worshipers were sent down into a hole and swept along by an underground river. When they came out at the end they were in a daze, having heard mysterious voices. A short period of rest was required for them to regain their senses. Trophonius also is the name of a brother of Agamedes, son of Apollo, who built temples at

Delphi. Apollo rewarded them with a peaceful death. Some accounts say both the hero and god are one and the same, the god being a deified mortal.

See also: APOLLO; DELPHI; TROPHONIUS

2952

**Troy**   Ancient Phrygian city, main site of the Trojan War, also called Ilion (Latin, Ilium); believed to be located near present day Hissarlik, in northwest Turkey, some four miles from the Dardanelles. In Greek mythology the city was originally founded by Dardanus, who called it Dardania. He was succeeded by his son Erichthonius, who was succeeded by Tros, who had three sons. One son, Ilus, renamed the city Ilion, and later it was called Troy. In the city was the sacred Palladium, a cult wooden image of the goddess Athena. As long as the city retained the image, no harm could come to it. The image was taken by the Greeks during the Trojan War when they invaded the city and destroyed it. For centuries it was believed that Troy was the invention of Homer in his *Iliad* and never actually existed. Heinrich Schliemann, however, believed in Homer's account and went in search of the city. Between 1870 and 1873 he discovered what he believed, and present-day scholars agree, to be the site of Troy as represented in Homer.

See also: ATHENA; DARDANUS; PALLADIUM; TROY

2953

**Ts'ai Shen**   In Chinese legend, the deified sage Pi Kan, worshiped as the god of wealth. Pi Kan, who is believed to have lived in the 12th century B.C.E., was noted for his profound wisdom. His relative, the emperor Chou, was reproved by the sage for his wickedness. The emperor became so angry that he ordered Pi Kan's heart to be torn out. He had always heard that the heart of a wise man had seven orifices, and he wished to know how wise Pi Kan actually was. Ta'ai Shen is worshiped throughout China, where there are numerous home shrines and

*Ts'ai Shen, god of riches*

temples dedicated to him. In art there are two forms of Ta'ai Shen, a civil form and a military form.

See also: HUN TUN; SHEN

2954

**Tsao Kuo-chiu**   930–999 C.E. In Chinese Taoist mythology, one of the Pa-Hsien, the Eight

*Tsao Kuo-chiu*

Immortals. Of noble birth, he is portrayed in court dress holding a pair of castanets in one hand.

See also: PA-HSIEN

*Tsao Shen*

**2955**

**Tsao Shen**   In Chinese legend, a deified mortal worshiped as the god of the hearth or kitchen. In homes, pictures of Tsao Shen are placed near the stove. He is worshiped with offerings of meat, fruit, and wine in an annual ceremony. After the ceremony is finished, the picture is taken down and burned, together with paper money presented to the god. Then a new picture of the god is placed on the wall for the coming year. Tsao Shen is portrayed in court costume.

See also: SHEN

**2956**

**Ts'ien K'eng**   In Chinese legend, a deified mortal who lived chiefly on mother-of-pearl. He is said to have been the orphan son or grandson of the emperor, being 767 years old at the end of the Yin dynasty in 1123 B.C.E. He is portrayed as

an old man reclining on the waves because he could sleep in the water for a day at a time. He also could lie motionless for a year until covered with dust an inch thick. After living 150 years he looked no more than 20 years old.

**2957**

**Tu** (erect, to stand)   In Polynesian mythology, war god, called Ku in Hawaii, to whom human sacrifices were made. A whole family of gods called Ku existed in Hawaii.

**2958**

**Tuan Mac Carell** (Tuan Mac Cairill)   In Celtic mythology, the sole survivor of the Partholonians, the first people to set foot in Ireland. He was an Irish chief who went through a series of metamorphoses. Tuan Mac Carell's legend is told in the *Book of the Dun Cow*, a manuscript dating from about the 11th century. He tells some Christian monks that he has lived hundreds of years, being a descendant of the first man to set foot in Ireland, Partholan. In his various transformations he was a deer, a boar, an eagle, and a salmon. In his last form he was eaten by Queen Carell and was born again as a man.

**2959**

**Tuatha de Danann** (people, tribe, nation)   In Celtic mythology, the gods and the people or descendants of the goddess Danu, who was a mother goddess and culture heroine. The Tuatha de Danann invaded Ireland from a magic cloud, giving battle to the earlier inhabitants, the Firbolgs, who had arrived years earlier. They pushed the Firbolgs back, taking the best part of the country for themselves. Then the Tuatha de Danann battled and defeated the Fomorians, who had replaced the Firbolgs, but they in turn were defeated by the incoming Milesians, who deified, worshiped, and enshrined the Tuatha de Danann in underground kingdoms.

See also: DANU; FOMORIANS; TUATHA DE DANANN

**Tuisco**   In Germanic mythology, a primeval god who issued from the earth, according to the Roman writer Tacitus in his *Germania*. He traces the origin of the Germans to Tuisco and his son Mannus, who had three sons.

See also: AUDHUMLA

2961

**Tulugal**   In Australian mythology, man's shadow, which is cared for by the creator god Daramulum.

2962

**Tu-lu'kau-guk**   In Eskimo mythology (Unalit peoples at Bering Strait), raven father, creator of everything.

2963

**Tumudurere**   In Melanesian mythology, god of the dead in New Guinea; he rules Hiyoyoa, which lies under the ocean near Maivara on Milne Bay.

2964

**Tunghat**   In Eskimo mythology (Unalit peoples at Bering Strait), supernatural beings whose spirit power is controlled by shamans.

2965

**Tuonetar**   In the epic poem *The Kalevala* (rune 16), daughter of Tuoni (Death).

Once the culture hero Vainamoinen constructed a magic boat but discovered he could not complete the work without the proper magic words. He went in search of them in Tuonela, the land of the dead. When he came to the River of Death, he saw "Death's stumpy daughter," Tuonetar, washing clothes. She asked him how he expected to cross the river without dying. He offered her various lies, which she detected, and finally told her the truth. She then helped ferry him across the River of Death, but he did not

find the magic words. He was informed, however, that the primeval giant Antero Vipunen possessed them. He then went in search of the giant and eventually obtained the magic words.

Tuonetar is also known as Tuonen Tytto (death's maiden) as well as Loviatar (half-blind daughter of Tuoni).

See also: ANTERO VIPUNEN; *KALEVALA, THE*; VAINAMOINEN

2966

**Tuoni** (death)   In Finnish mythology, god of death who rules over Tuonela, the land of the dead, sometimes called Manala or Ulappala (wasteland).

The land of the dead was reached by crossing a black bridge that spanned black water. In the river were *kynsikoski* (rapids) that made the way treacherous. On the black water glided a majestic swan. In his *Four Legends for Orchestra* Sibelius has two movements that deal with Tuonela. "The Swan of Tuonela" evokes, with English horn, the majestic swan, and "Lemminkainen in Tuonela" portrays the death of Lemminkainen at the hands of a herdsman after the hero attempted to kill the swan. Lemminkainen is murdered and his body borne on the icy waters to Tuonela. Tuoni is also called Mana or Kalma (grave).

See also: LEMMINKAINEN; SWAN; TUONETAR

2967

**Turong**   In Australian mythology, mischievous spirits who play tricks on hunters.

2968

**Tursas** (giant)   In the Finnish epic poem *The Kalevala* (rune 2), a water spirit who aided the culture hero Vainamoinen in sowing the earth. At one time Vainamoinen found that although all of the seeds he planted made a rich forest, there was no oak, the "tree of heaven." The reason was that the oak was asleep inside the acorn. The culture hero wondered how he could magically conjure it out of its hiding place. After Vainamoinen consulted five water maidens, the water spirit Tursas arose out of the waves. He burned hay that the water maidens had raked together and planted the acorn in the ashes of the hay. Quickly a tree arose that was so large it blotted out the sun. Terrified at what had happened, Vainamoinen wanted to destroy the oak. He called on his mother, Luonnotar, who sent a pygmy, armed with copper, who transformed himself into a giant and cut down the tree, scattering its trunk to the east, its top to the west, its leaves to the south, and its branches to the north. The chips from the fallen oak were later used to make magic arrows.

See also: *KALEVALA, THE*; VAINAMOINEN

2969

**Turtle and Tortoise**   In world folklore, the turtle and tortoise are often not distinguished from each other. In Chinese mythology the tortoise represents the watery element, the Yin principle, and is called the Black Warrior. In medieval Christian symbolism it represents modesty. In Japanese mythology the tortoise or turtle represents longevity and good luck. In Greek mythology the tortoise was sacred to Aphrodite and Hermes, and in Roman mythology to Venus and Mercury. The well-known fable The Hare and the Tortoise is best known for its moral tag: "Slow and steady wins the race."

See also: APHRODITE; HERMES; MERCURY; VENUS; YIN AND YANG

2970

**Tutankhamen** (the living image of Amen) 1361–1352 B.C.E. Egyptian pharaoh whose tomb was discovered in 1922 by Howard Carter and Lord Carnarvon in the Valley of the Kings in Egypt.

Tutankhamen was the successor of Akhenaten. The young pharaoh was Akhenaton's son-in-law, or possibly his son, brother, or close relation. Originally, the pharaoh was called Tu-

tankhaten (gracious of life is Aten), which indicated that he was a follower of the cult of Aten, the sun disk. He changed his name to Tutankhamen when he came to power because the Theban priests had restored the worship of Amun-Ra, which had been rejected by Akhenaton, who worshiped Aten. The wife of Tutankhamen, following her husband's move, changed her name, Ankhensen-paaten, to Ankhesenamen, indicating her allegiance to the god Amun-Ra. The young pharaoh was probably murdered. He was succeeded by a minister, Ay. Treasures from his tomb have been displayed throughout the world.

See also: AKHENATON; AMUN; ATEN; RA

2971

**Tutugals**   In Australian mythology, spirits who punish children for being evil.

2972

**Tuulikki** (Tellervo) (wind)   In Finnish mythology, the wind spirit, daughter of Tapio, the forest god, and his wife, Meilikki.

2973

**Twashtri** (Tvastr) (architect)   In Hindu mythology, artisan of the gods. Twashtri carries a great iron ax, forging thunderbolts for the storm god, Indra. He is invoked to bestow offspring and forms husband and wife for each other while still in the womb. He also develops the seminal germ in the womb and is the former or shaper of all human and animal life. He corresponds in many aspects with Hephaestus and Vulcan.

See also: HEPHAESTUS; INDRA; VULCAN

2974

**Twe**   In African mythology, a spirit god who inhabits Lake Bosomtive in Ghana. This lake occasionally loses all of its water under the drying rays of the sun. Twe emerged from the lake one day and wished to make love to an old woman. The woman at first refused him, saying that it would be difficult for her to find water and food for a child if she were to become pregnant. Twe assured her that all she had to do was bang on the edge of the lake and fish would come to her. Hearing this, she agreed to their union and bore Twe a son named Twe Adodo. Twe's son was to become the founder of a clan that believes the sprit of Twe, his father, helps them whenever they go fishing.

**Twelve Nights**   2975   In Germanic folklore and mythology, the days before and after Christmas, typically sometime between St. Thomas day (21 December) and Three Kings Day (6 January). Some scholars believe this tradition reached back to a midwinter festival, as with Germanic Yule, or perhaps even further back to an Indo-European festival. These days are considered magical days when many of the usual laws of physics or society do not apply. During this time, the dead or the ghosts of the dead appear, sometimes even well-known figures, such as the White Horseman (*Schimmelreiter*) and Wodan. Some of these festivals feature masked figures. Each of the 12 nights is used to predict the weather during the next 12 months. There are also certain activities that are prohibited, such as washing clothes, baking, fertilizing the fields, and spinning wool, as well as certain foods that are not to be eaten, such as nuts, and taboos about using certain names, such as wolf, fox, rat, and mouse. Other prohibited activities include lending, keeping cattle in the stalls, and covering water, all of which suggest a pre-Christian origin.

See also: MAGI; THOMAS, ST.; WODAN; YULE

**Two Brothers, Tale of**   2976   Egyptian literary folktale, also known as "Anpu and Bata," written about 1225 B.C.E.

Anpu and Bata were brothers. Anpu, the older, was married; Bata, the younger, worked for him in the field, becoming so proficient at his labor that it was said the spirit of God was in him.

Bata was so good at his work, in fact, that even the cattle spoke to him, and he understood them. One day while the two brothers were working in the field, Anpu sent Bata back to the farm to get some grain. Bata did as he was told, but before he could return Anpu's wife tried to seduce him. When he rejected her advances, she told her husband that Bata had tried to rape her. Anpu became enraged and set out to kill his younger brother, but Bata escaped with the help of the sun god Ra. The two brothers later met, and to prove his innocence Bata swore an oath, cut off his penis, and cast it into the water, where it was easten by a catfish. After numerous adventures Bata died and was reborn again as the pharaoh, and Anpu became heir to the throne, thus reversing the order of primogeniture.

The attempted seduction of a virtuous youth by an older woman is found in numerous mythologies. Among the most famous examples are those of Potiphar's wife in Genesis (39:7–20), who attempted to seduce Joseph, and Hippolytus and Phaedra in Greek mythology. According to some scholars, the "Tale of Two Brothers" is based on a myth of two gods, Anubis (Anpu) and Bet (Bata). Anubis was the well-known jackal god of Egypt, and Bet was a pastoral god whose cult image was a mummified ram or bull. There is little agreement as to what the tale actually signifies, although most scholars agree that it served for entertainment rather than for religious or moral purposes.

See also: ANUBIS; HIPPOLYTUS; JOSEPH; OSIRIS; PHAEDRA

**Two Pots, The**   2977   Aesopic fable found in various collections throughout the world.

Two pots, one of brass and one of earthenware, had been left on the bank of a river. When the tide rose they both floated off down the stream. The earthenware pot tried its best to keep aloof from the brass one, which cried out: "Fear nothing, friend, I will not strike you."

"But I may come in contact with you," said the other, "if I come too close; and whether I hit you or you hit me, I shall suffer for it."

Moral: *The strong and the weak cannot keep company.*

An allusion to the fable occurs in the Old Testament Apocrypha, "Have no fellowship with one that is mightier and richer than thyself; for how agree the kettle and earthen pot together?" (Ecclus. 13:2). There is a Talmudic proverb: "If a jug fall on a stone, woe to the jug; if a stone fall on a jug, woe to the jug."

See also: AESOPIC FABLES; *TALMUD*

**2978**

**Two-Toe Tom** In American folklore, a 14-foot alligator, in Alabama marsh country near Montgomery, who ate people and animals. When his pond was dynamited by Pap Haines, the monster escaped by an underground route and later ate Haines's 12-year-old daughter.

**2979**

**Typhon** (hurricane, hot wind, smoke) In Greek mythology, a monster, son of Gaea and Tartarus, with a hundred snake heads that spit out fire. He attacked Zeus, who now was the ruler after he had defeated Cronus, his father. Zeus hurled thunderbolts at Typhon and hurled him down to the underworld. Typhon was said to be buried under Mount Etna, according to some accounts. Before he was imprisoned, however, he fathered with Echidna a host of monsters, including Cerberus, Orthus, the Nemean Lion, the Sphinx, the Chimera, and the Lernean Hydra. Typhon appears in or is cited in Hesiod's *Theogony*, Homer's *Iliad* (book 2), Aeschylus's *Prometheus Bound* and *Seven Against Thebes*, Vergil's *Aeneid*, (book 9), and Ovid's *Metamorphoses* (book 5).

See also: ECHIDNA; GAEA; HESIOD HYDRA; *ILIAD, THE*; TARTUS; ZEUS

**2980**

**Tyr** (god shining) In Norse mythology, one of the Aesir, a war god son of Odin and Frigga. He lost one hand when he placed it in the mouth of the Fenrir wolf. Tyr was the patron of the sword and athletic sports. The *Prose Edda* describes Tyr as "the most daring and intrepid of all the gods. 'Tis he who dispenses valour in war, hence warriors do well to invoke him. . . . He is not regarded as a peacemaker among men." Tuesday was named after the god. In Anglo-Saxon mythology, Tyr is called Tiw, Tiv, or Ziv, or identified with the god Saxnot. During the Roman period Tyr was called Mars Thingsus and associated with an assembly hall where men met to settle disputes. Tyr's name is also given as Tîwaz.

See also: FENRIR; FRIGGA; ODIN; *PROSE EDDA*

**2981**

**Tzitsimine** (the monsters descending from above) In Aztec mythology, spirits of women who died in childbirth and who returned to plague the living. They appeared skull-faced and brought children sickness and injury, as well as contagious diseases. Sometimes a Tzitsimine would appear sitting on a lonely rock, weeping. When a passerby would ask what was wrong, she would display her skull face, frightening the person almost to death.

# U

**Ubshukinna** (Ubshukenna, Upshukkinaku) (chamber of destinies)   In Near Eastern mythology (Babylonian), heavenly council hall of the gods. It was reproduced in the earthly temple complex, where the Zag-Muk, the great New Year celebration, was held. The ceremony honored the hero god Marduk, who on that day told the destiny of men for the coming year from the tablets of fate.

See also: MARDUK; ZAG-MUK

**Uccaihsravas** (neighing loudly, long-eared)   In Hindu mythology, the horse of the storm god, Indra.

See also: INDRA

**Ueuecoyotl** (the old, old coyote)   In Aztec mythology, god associated with sex, useless expenditure on ornament, and unexpected pleasures—all three condemned by the puritanical Aztecs.

**Ugolino, Count**   13th century. In Italian history and legend, a leader of the Guelphs in Pisa. Ugolino was raised to the highest honors, but Archbishop Ruggieri incited the Pisans against his rule. His castle was attacked, two of his grandsons were killed, and the count and his two sons and two surviving grandsons were imprisoned in a tower; its keys were then flung into the Arno River. All food was withheld from the group. On the fourth day, Ugolino's son Gaddo died, and by the sixth day his son Anselm and the two grandchildren died. Last of all the count died. The prison cell has since been called "The Tower of Famine." Dante's *Divine Comedy* (Inferno) portrays Ugolino as devouring the head of Archbishop Ruggieri while frozen in the lake of ice in hell. In *The Canterbury Tales* Chaucer has the monk briefly tell the story of Hugeline of Pise.

See also: CHAUCER

**Uguku and Tskili**   In North American Indian mythology (Cherokee), the hoot owl and the horned owl, who went down to the hollow of a tree where the first fire burned. It burned so fiercely that the smoke nearly blinded Uguku and Tskili, and the wind carried the smoke, making white rings around their eyes.

**Uixtocihuatl**   In Aztec mythology, salt goddess whose festival, Tecuilhuitontli, was held on

2 June. A woman was sacrificed in her honor at the pyramid of the rain god, Tlaloc.

See also: TLALOC

2988

**Ujigami**    In Japanese Shinto mythology, tutelary or special guarding deity of a clan or locality.

2989

**Ukko** (old man)    In Finnish mythology, sky god, often used for God. Ukko replaced the earlier Jumala, a semiabstract term for God, who was sometimes addressed as Kuoja (creator). Ukko is sometimes called Pauanne (thunder), indicating that his role is similar to that of Zeus in Greek and Thor in Norse mythology. He is the most frequently evoked god in the Finnish epic poem *The Kalevala*. He restored fire when Louhi, the evil mistress of Pohjola, the Northland, stole the sun, moon, and fire. Seeing the land plunged into darkness, Ukko struck lightning and sent it down to earth, where it was swallowed by a pike in Lake Alue. Burning inside, the pike swam about madly until it was swallowed by a larger fish, which in turn was caught by the culture hero Vainamoinen, who restored the fire to his people.

Ukko was worshiped in a ceremony called Ukko's Wedding or Ukko's Chest, at which birchbark chests containing sacrifices such as sheep were placed on a holy mountain to be eaten by the god. Ukko ate his share at night, and the people ate the rest the next day. One festival of the god was described by the Christian bishop Agricola in the 16th century. He found that "many shameful things were done" in honor of the great god. The bishop was obviously referring to a sexual orgy that took place after the people had drunk "to excess." Eventually, Ukko's ceremonies were absorbed into Christian ones, and Christ and St. John were evoked instead of Ukko.

Jean Sibelius's *The Origin of Fire* or *Ukko the Firemaker*, based on rune 47 of *The Kalevala*, depicts the re-creation of fire. Scored for baritone,

male chorus, and orchestra, the work is, according to music critic Cecil Gray, of "epic power and grandeur."

See also: JUMALA; *KALEVALA, THE*; LOUHI; RUNE; THOR; VAINAMOINEN; ZEUS

2990

**Ukuhi**    In North American Indian mythology (Cherokee), the black racer snake. Ukuhi went to search for fire, but when he found it, he was scorched black, and ever since he has the habit of darting and doubling back on his tracks as if trying to escape fire.

2991

**Ulfius**    In Arthurian legend, a knight of the Round Table. Ulfius accompanied Uther Pendragon, King Arthur's father, when Uther went to Tintagel. Afterward Ulfius aided King Arthur in his battle against the 11 kings. Ulfius was usually accompanied by Sir Brastias.

See also: ARTHUR; ROUND TABLE; TINTAGEL; UTHER PENDRAGON

2992

**Ulgen** (rich?)    In Siberian mythology, a creator god. Various myths are told of Ulgen's role in creation. According to the Altaics, Ulgen came down from heaven to the waters with the desire to create the earth, though he did not know how to do it. Suddenly Erlik (man) appeared and told him he knew how it could be accomplished. With Ulgen's approval, Erlik dived down to the water's depths and brought up a piece of dirt. He gave part of it to Ulgen and kept part for himself. Ulgen created the earth with his part, and Erlik's piece formed the swamps and bogs of the earth.

A variant tells how Ulgen saw some mud with humanlike features floating on the water. He gave it life and the name Erlik. At first Erlik was Ulgen's friend and brother but later became his enemy and the devil.

In another myth Ulgen created the earth on the waters with three great fish to support it.

One fish was placed in the center and one at each end, and all were tied to the pillars of heaven. If one fish nods, the earth becomes flooded. To prevent this, Mandishire (adopted from Buddhist mythology's Bodhisattva of Miraculous Birth, Manjursi) controlled the ropes so that he could raise and lower the earth. The fish did not like the weight and shook it off, causing an earthquake. The earth fractured, and pieces floated freely until Ulgen anchored them. One of the smallest pieces floating around spoke to Ulgen, saying it did not want to be permanently fixed. Ulgen then took this piece, and instead of an island he created Erlik, the first being.

See also: BODHISATTVA; EARTH DIVER; ERLIK; MANJURSI

---

**Uli-tarra**   In Australian mythology, the first man, who is said to have come from the east. At the beginning of time there was no sea, only the water from a hole that Uli-tarra dug. Uli-tarra was the leader of an aboriginal tribe who left one day to fight a tribe on the other side of the mountain. They painted themselves white and red. On the way to the battle the men came upon two women whom Uli-tarra had once beaten for misbehavior. These two women found two straight sticks and pounded them against the ground, then they departed. The beating of the sticks caused the ocean to form, as well as all other bodies of water, both large and small. As the men returned from their journey they found that the ocean, which had not been there before, blocked their passage. They took the entrails of a deer and blew into them, creating a bridge over the water. One man tried to eat the rope the bridge was made of but was stopped, and the men were able to return to their homes safely.

See also: BIBLE, THE (GENESIS)

---

2994

**Ull** (Ullur, Ullr) (the shaggy one)   In Norse mythology, stepson of Thor and son of Sif, Thor's wife. He lived at Ydalir (yew valley). He is associated with winter and is known as an archer. In the *Prose Edda* it is said: "There is one called Ull, the son of Sif and stepson of Thor. He is such a good archer, and so good on skis that none can compete with him. He is also fair of face and has the ability of a warrior. It is good to call on him in a duel."

See also: *PROSE EDDA*; SIF; THOR

---

2995

**Ulrich, St.** (wolf-powerful)   890–973.   In Christian legend, bishop of Augsburg and patron of weavers. Invoked for a happy birth and a peaceful death; against birth pangs, fever, frenzy, mice, moles, and faintness. Feast, 4 July.

Though of delicate health, Ulrich rose to be the bishop of Augsburg in 923 after the land had been laid waste by the invading Magyars. He was a model bishop according to all accounts of his life. In a biography written by Gerhard, a contemporary of the saint, the legend of Ulrich as the "fish-bishop" is explained. One Thursday Ulrich and his friend Bishop Wolfgang were having a goose for dinner. They talked into the late hours of the night and early morning. Friday arrived (a meatless day), and the messenger of the emperor arrived and saw the two men seated at a table with a goose. Ulrich broke off one of its legs and handed it to the messenger, who put it into his pouch. He hurried away to show the emperor that the two were guilty of eating meat on a Friday. When he arrived at court, he put his hand into the pouch and drew out a fish instead.

Numerous miracles were recorded at the tomb of St. Ulrich, and he was the first saint canonized by Pope John XV in 993—the first solemn canonization by a pope of a saint. Before that local bishops or clergy and laity would proclaim a saint, or legends would grow around a person who would then be venerated as a saint.

In art St. Ulrich is usually portrayed holding a fish. Sometimes he is shown with his copatron of Augsburg, St. Afra.

See also: AFRA, ST.; SAINTS; WOLFGANG, ST.

**2996**

**Ulysses** (sufferer)    Latin name of the Greek hero Odysseus, apparently Latinized to *Ulixes* by way of a dialect where *od-* was pronounced *ol-*. In English translations of Homer's *Iliad* and *Odyssey* as far back as Alexander Pope's, Ulysses is the usual translation of the name. In *The Divine Comedy* Dante places Ulysses and Diomedes among the counselors of evil in the Eighth Circle of Hell. The two are enveloped in a single flame divided at the top. In reply to a request from Vergil (Dante cannot speak Greek, so he cannot question Ulysses), Ulysses relates how, after spending more than a year with Circe, he was impelled to go forth and see "the untravelled world." He set forth with one ship and a few faithful companions and at last came to the narrow strait at the Pillars of Heracles, the limit of the habitable world. He inspired his comrades to go forward with him into the unknown sea and sailed westward for five months, until they sighted a lofty mountain in the dim distance. In the midst of their rejoicing at the sight a storm broke from the distant land, striking their ship, which whirled around three times and then plunged, bow foremost, into the depths of the sea. Medieval tradition said Ulysses was a great liar. Later Shakespeare called him "sly Ulysses" in his poem *The Rape of Lucrece*.

Tennyson's poem "Ulysses" (1842) presents an entirely different aspect of the hero from that provided by Dante. He had read H. F. Cary's translation of Dante, published in 1805. Tennyson's poem was written soon after the death of his close friend Arthur Hallam. The poem ends:

> Though much is taken, much abides; and though
> We are not now that strength which in old days
> Moved earth and heaven; that which we are, we are;
> One equal temper of heroic hearts,
> Made weak by time and fate, but strong in will
> To strive, to seek, to find, and not to yield.

James Joyce's novel *Ulysses* (1922) deals with the events of one day in Dublin in June 1904. Its chapters roughly correspond to the episodes in Homer's *Odyssey*.

See also: ILIAD, THE; ODYSSEUS; ODYSSEY, THE

**2997**

**Uma** (light)    In Hindu mythology, a form of the great goddess, Devi, wife of the god Shiva.

See also: DEVI; SHIVA

**2998**

**Umai-hulhlya-wit**    In North American Indian mythology (Diegueño), giant serpent. He lived in the ocean but was called to a ceremony after Chakopá and Chakomát had created the earth, sun, moon, and stars. The people built a large enclosure of brush for Umai-hulhlya-wit to stay in. He came and coiled himself but could not fit inside. On the third day, when he had coiled as much of his body as possible into the structure, the people set it aflame and burned him. When his body exploded, all knowledge, songs, magic secrets, languages, ceremonies, and customs were scattered over the land.

**2999**

**Unas** (Unus, Unis, Onnos)    In Egyptian mythology, a deified pharaoh of the Fifth Dynasty. Unas was said to have been the son of the god Tem and to have eaten the flesh of gods to become strong. He then journeyed through the heavens and became Orion.

See also: ORION; TEM

**3000**

**Uncle Remus**    In American literary folklore, black house slave, creation of Joel Chandler Harris. Uncle Remus narrates tales of Br'er Rabbit, Br'er Fox, Br'er Wolf, and others, collected in *Uncle Remus: His Songs and Sayings*. His character is based on several blacks who Harris knew, including George Terrell. Uncle Remus appears in Walt Disney's movie *Song of the South* (1947), which combines live actors and cartoon animation.

See also: BR'ER FOX; BR'ER RABBIT; TRICKSTER

**Uncle Sam**   In American folklore, personification of the United States, portrayed as a tall, lean Yankee with long white hair, chin whiskers, striped pants, swallow-tail coat, and star-spangled plug hat. Originally a derogatory nickname used by New England opponents of the federal government's policies during the War of 1812, its exact origin is not fully known. According to some accounts, Uncle Sam is based on Samuel Wilson (1766–1854), known as Uncle Sam, a meat inspector in Troy, New York, who worked for Elbert Anderson. When the initials "E.A.—U.S." were stamped on meat carts, the initials were explained as meaning "Uncle Sam" had inspected the meat. Samuel Wilson died in 1854. His grave is in the Oakwood Cemetery in Troy, New York. Other accounts say Uncle Sam is merely an extension of the initials of the United States.

Thomas Nast, a prominent 19th-century political cartoonist, produced many of the earliest cartoons of Uncle Sam. However, many of Nast's cartoons in fact depict Yankee Doodle or "Brother Jonathan." It is easy to mistake a Brother Jonathan cartoon for one of Uncle Sam, since both figures wear star-spangled suits of red, white, and blue. The first reported book to name the character of Uncle Sam was written by a "Frederick Augustus Fidfaddy" and called *The Adventures of Uncle Sam*. The character of Uncle Sam eventually replaced that of Brother Jonathan, a nickname once used for New Englanders and for Americans in general. The single most famous portrait of Uncle Sam is the "I WANT YOU" army recruiting poster from World War I. The poster was painted by James Montgomery Flagg in 1916–1917.

See also: WASHINGTON, GEORGE

**Undine**   In European folklore, a water sprite who could be mortal if she married a human being. An undine was created without a soul but had the privilege of obtaining one if she married a mortal and bore him a child. She had to suffer all of the pains of being a human. The creature appears in La Motte-Fouqué's *Undine*, Giraudoux's *Ondine*, and Tchaikovsky's *Undine*, an early stage work by the composer, later destroyed, though some parts were used in the ballet *Swan Lake*.

See also: MELUSINA

*Unicorn*

**Unicorn**   In world mythology and folklore, a fantastic animal usually portrayed as a small horselike creature with a single horn protruding from its head. In European mythologies the unicorn is usually viewed as a beneficent being. A medieval description of the fantastic animal is found in *Le Bestiaire Divin de Guillaume Clerc de Normandie*.

The Unicorn has but one horn in the middle of its forehead. It is the only animal that ventures to attack the elephant; and so sharp is the nail of its foot, that with one blow it can rip the belly out of that beast. Hunters can catch the unicorn only by placing a young virgin in his haunts. No sooner does he see the damsel, than he runs towards her, and lies down at her feet, and so suffers himself to be captured by the hunters. The unicorn represents Jesus Christ, who took on Him our nature in the Virgin's womb. . . . Its one horn signifies the Gospel of Truth.

The European belief in unicorns stems in part from ancient pagan Greek sources as well as the Septuagint versions of the Hebrew scripture. When the Hebrew Bible was translated into Greek, the Hebrew word *reem*, which might mean a wild ox, was translated *monokeros* (one-horned). This rendering was followed in later Latin versions of the Bible, which in turn influenced English translations such as the King James Version. The Book of Numbers (23:22) says: "God brought them out of Egypt; he hath as it were the strength of an unicorn." The Revised Standard Version of the Bible in its translation of the verse substitutes "wild ox" for unicorn. One medieval Jewish folktale said the unicorn had perished in Noah's flood because it was too large to enter the ark. Another Jewish folktale argued that God never destroys his own creation; if the unicorn was too large to get into the ark, then God would have let it swim behind the ark.

Along with the unicorn as a beneficent symbol, such as Jesus Christ, the animal was also identified with evil and death. In *The Golden Legend*, a series of saints' lives by Jacobus de Voragine written in the 13th century, the "unicorn is the figure of Death, which continually followeth man and desireth to seize him." Death rides a unicorn in some late medieval Books of Hours. In the *Ancrene Riwle*, a 12th-century book of rules for nuns, the unicorn appears as a symbol of wrath, along with the lion for pride, the serpent for envy, and the bear for sloth. The Church Fathers at the Council of Trent, held in the 16th century, forbade the use of the unicorn as a symbol of Christ. One legend they cited was from Leonardo da Vinci's *Bestiary*, in which the artist made the unicorn a symbol of lust.

The unicorn's horn was thought to have magic curative powers; many late medieval monasteries and cathedrals were believed to possess them, and they appear in inventories of Queen Elizabeth I and other monarchs of the period. Powders purporting to be made from crushed unicorn horns were sold by apothecaries. As late as the French Revolution the unicorn was believed to exist, and a "unicorn's" horn was used to detect poison in food fed to royalty.

In Chinese mythology the unicorn was one of the four animals of good omen, the others being the phoenix, the dragon, and the tortoise. According to one story, when Confucius was born, a unicorn spit out a piece of jade with the inscription announcing the event: "Son of the essence of water, kingdoms shall pass away, but you will be a king, though without a throne." James Thurber, in his *Fables for Our Time* (1940), includes a comical episode called "The Unicorn in the Garden."

See also: CONFUCIUS; *GOLDEN LEGEND, THE*; NOAH; THURBER, JAMES

3004

**Unktomi** (Inktomi)　In North American Indian mythology (Oglala Dakota), spider, the trickster, both culture hero and creator. Variants of his name among the tribes are Iktomé, Ikto, Ictcinike, and Ictinike.

See also: INKTOMI; SPIDER; TRICKSTER

3005

**Unkulunkulu** (chief)　In African mythology (Zulu), a self-originating deity, sky god who instituted marriage. Unkulunkulu sent a chameleon with the message of life and a lizard with the message of death. On the way the chameleon stopped to eat, and the lizard arrived with his death message, which he delivered. To compensate humankind for the loss of immortality, Unkulunkulu instituted marriage so that people's lives were carried on through their children. He also provides doctors to treat diseases and fire for the preparation of food.

See also: OLORUN MULUNGU; WELE

---

3006

**Unquiet Grave**   English ballad, collected in F. J. Child's *English and Scottish Popular Ballads* (1882–1885). In the ballad the dead sweetheart begs the surviving lover to stop mourning over the grave because it disturbs the dead.

---

3007

**Unsinkable Molly Brown**   In American history and folklore, Molly Brown, wife of a Colorado millionaire; she was on the Titanic when it struck an iceberg in 1912. Molly stripped down to her corset and bloomers, had her pistol strapped to her side, and covered a child with her chinchilla coat. She took command of one lifeboat, saying, "Keep rowing, you sons of bitches, or I'll toss you all overboard." When she was asked why she had been saved when so many others died, she replied, "I'm unsinkable." She always went by the name Maggie, not Molly. That nickname was added decades later when her life was dramatized in the Broadway musical comedy *The Unsinkable Molly Brown*, and in a film in 1964 that deals with her life and legend. The script bears only a passing resemblance to her real story.

---

3008

**Untsaiyi** (brass)   In North American Indian mythology (Cherokee), trickster who loved to gamble. Untsaiyi had always won, but once he was fooled by a young boy who beat him at every game. In the end Untsaiyi wagered his life and lost. Untsaiyi's hands and feet were tied by the boy, and a long stake was driven through his chest. He was then placed far out in deep water. But Untsaiyi did not die, and according to the myth, "cannot die until the end of the world." He lies in the water with his face up. Sometimes he struggles to get free. Sometimes the beavers,

his friends, come to gnaw at the ropes to release him, but two crows sitting atop the stake cry out, "ka, ka, ka," and scare the beavers away.

---

3009

**Upanishads** (Sanskrit, from *upa*, "additional," and *ni-sad*, "to sit down at the feet of a teacher")   In Hinduism, a collection of philosophical writings composed over a period of time, the most important being from about 500 B.C.E. The Upanishads are generally in prose, but some are in verse. There are at least 150 of them. They discuss the origin of the universe, the nature of deity, the nature of the soul, and the relationship between mind and matter. The German philosopher Schopenhauer kept a Latin translation of the Upanishads on his table and read it before he went to bed. He wrote of it: "From every sentence, deep, original and sublime thoughts arise, and the whole is pervaded by a high and holy and earnest spirit. . . . They are the products of the highest wisdom. They are destined sooner or later to become the faith of the people."

---

3010

**Upirikutsu** (great star)   In North American Indian mythology (Pawnee), Morning Star, who overcame Evening Star in her realm of darkness. From their union the first human was created. A memorial sacrifice of a captive, often a female, was offered to Morning Star until 1838.

---

3011

**Uraeus**   Ancient Egyptian image of the cobra goddess who guarded the king; commonly found on royal headress.

---

3012

**Urania** (heavenly)   In Greek mythology, one of the nine Muses, the Muse of astronomy and celestial forces; daughter of Zeus and Mnemosyne. Among the ancients Urania was one of the most important of the nine Muses and was considered the arbiter of fate. Some myths say she

*Urania*

was the mother of Linus by Apollo and the mother of Hymenaeus by Dionysus. However, in *Paradise Lost* (book 7.1) Milton calls on Urania as the Muse of poetry. Her symbol is a globe.

See also: APOLLO; DIONYSUS; ZEUS

3013

**Uranus** (heaven, sky)  In Greek mythology, the sky; son and husband of Gaea, the earth; called Coelus by the Romans. Gaea bore him the Titans, the Cyclopes, and the Hecatonchires. He did not allow any of his children to see the light of day but pushed them into Tartarus, a gloomy place in the underworld. Gaea persuaded her Titan sons to attack their father. Led by Cronus, the youngest of the seven, they surprised Uranus as he slept and castrated him with a flint sickle given them by their mother. From the blood dropping upon the earth, Gaea bore the three Erinyes, the Furies, and the Melic nymphs. Some accounts say Aphrodite was born from the sea foam stirred up when Uranus's genitals fell into the sea. Cronus, son of Uranus, became

king. Before he died, Uranus prophesied that Cronus also would be dethroned by a son. Eventually, Zeus dethroned his father, Cronus. Ouranos (overhanging heavens) was another name for Uranus. Hesiod's *Theogony* (133–87, 616–23) tells of Uranus's fate.

See also: APHRODITE; GAEA; HESIOD; NYMPHS; TITANS; ZEUS

3014

**Urban Legend**  In American folklore, the term used to identify contemporary legends, some but not all of which have a modern and urban setting. These tales frequently deal with death, horror, mutilation, sex, foodways, and many other weird happenings or close calls. Stories abound about microwaved animals, roasted babies, creatures in sewers or coke bottles, and devils who frequent dance halls. Most scholars see these stories as commentary on the nature of impersonal industrialized society. A story of a rat found in a basketful of fried chicken suggests anxiety over uncleanliness at fast food emporia and the disappearance of the family meal. A story of placing a baby in the oven to cook is seen as a response to the relaxation of abortion laws and the development of contraceptive pills. Jan Harlold Brunvand has identified more than 500 different legends and has attempted to trace, wherever possible, the source of the tale. The legend of the Blood Libel, for example, has been documented during the Roman Empire.

See also: BLOOD LIBEL LEGEND; VANISHING HITCHHIKER

3015

**Urd** (Urdhr) (the past)  In Norse mythology, one of the three named Norns, the others being Verdandi and Skuld. Urd is the oldest of the Norns and looks to the past.

See also: NORNS; SKULD; VERDANDI

**Uriel** (the light of God)   In Jewish and Christian mythology, one of seven archangels in rabbinical angelology. His name is found on Jewish amulets as a charm to ward off evil.

Unlike the archangels Michael, Gabriel, and Raphael, all of whom are mentioned in the Bible, Uriel appears to be less important since he is not mentioned there, though he is found in the Old Testament Apocrypha Book of Second Esdras (4:1). Uriel also appears in the *Book of Enoch*, a pseudoepigraphic Jewish-Christian work in which he is the watcher over the world and over Tartarus, the lowest part of hell. He serves as the principal guide to Enoch in his various visions.

According to one Christian legend, Uriel, not Christ, appeared to the disciples on the way to Emmaus, though the New Testament text does not support this contention. In Jewish literature Uriel is often called the "one who brings light to Israel." In *Paradise Lost* (book 3:690) Milton, recalling the Jewish belief, calls Uriel the "Regent of the Sun" and "sharpest-sighted spirit" of all in heaven. Dryden, in his poetic play *The State of Innocence*, based on Milton's *Paradise Lost*, pictures Uriel descending from heaven in a chariot drawn by white horses. Less dramatic is Longfellow's Uriel in *The Golden Legend*, in which Uriel is one of the seven angels of the seven planets bearing the star of Bethlehem.

Uriel is rarely portrayed in Christian art. When he is, he is shown holding a book or scroll, symbolic of his role as interpreter of visions and prophecies, as in the cases of Enoch and Esdras. Burne-Jones's painting of Uriel portrays the angel in the traditional pose. Uriel is also known as Nuriel and is sometimes identified with the Flaming Angel.

See also: ENOCH; FLAMING ANGEL; GABRIEL; MICHAEL; RAPHAEL

**Urim and Thummin** (lights and perfection) In the Bible, O.T. (Exod. 28:30), two cult objects used to determine the will of Yahweh, the Hebrew god. Scholars are not quite sure what they were but believe their markings made them resemble dice. They were carried in the breastplate of the high priest. They fell out of use in post-exilic times, perhaps as a result of the development of a higher conception of the deity.

See also: YAHWEH

**Urna** (wool)   In Oriental art, the jewel or small protuberance between the eyes, or circle of hair or eye, seen on gods and Buddhas, representing the third eye for spiritual vision or foreknowledge. The Urna seems to be a circle of hair in the earliest texts. It then becomes an eye and is represented as an eye, a bump, or a jewel. Its symbolism is variously interpreted, but basically it is just a very strong eye that illuminates all universes at once. Eyes are believed to emit light.

**Urre**   In Arthurian legend, one of the knights of the Round Table. When Urre was wounded, King Arthur tried to heal him with his touch but failed. Then Sir Lancelot tried, and Urre was healed.

See also: ARTHUR; LANCELOT OF THE LAKE; ROUND TABLE

**Ursula, St.** (bean)   Fifth century? In Christian legend, virgin martyr. Patron saint of maidens, drapers, and teachers. Invoked for chastity and holy wedlock and against plague. Feast, 21 October.

There are various medieval versions of St. Ursula's life. In one version she is the daughter of Dianotus, a British king, and was sought in marriage by Holofernes, a pagan prince. Dianotus consented to the alliance, but Ursula said she would marry the prince only if he was baptized and she was given three years to travel with her 11 maidens, accompanied by 1,000 companions. The conditions were accepted, and all of the women set sail. They went to Cologne, then to Rome, where they visited the tombs of various saints. When they returned to Cologne, they were all seized by Attila the Hun. All of the women except Ursula were killed.

"Weep not, for though thou hast lost thy companions," said Attila, "I will be thy husband, and thou shalt be the greatest queen in Germany." Ursula screamed back at Attila, causing his anger to flare up, "and bending his bow, which he had in his hand, he, with three arrows, transfixed her pure breast, so that she fell dead, and her spirit ascended into Heaven, with all the glorious sisterhood of martyrs."

Another medieval version makes the legend of St. Ursula a Christian parallel to the rape of the Sabine women in Roman history. This tale is told by Geoffrey of Monmouth in his *History of the Kings of Britain*. Maximian, the British king, having conquered Armonica (now called Brittany), gave it to Conan Meriadoc, his nephew. His country being almost depopulated by war, Conan wished to find wives for himself and his men. He asked for the assistance of Dianotus, brother and successor of Caradoc, king of Cornwall. Dianotus had a daughter named Ursula, whom he promised to Conan as his wife. Dianotus then summoned all of the chief men of his kingdom and also collected 11,000 maidens, whom he shipped to Conan together with his daughter. When on the seas, contrary winds arose, causing the fleet to go off course. It was found in the Rhine by Huns, who attacked the ships and killed all of the women.

See also: ATTILA

3021

**Urvasi**   In Hindu mythology, a nymph loved by the sage Puru-ravas; she bore him several children.

Urvasi agreed to live with Puru-ravas on certain conditions. "I have two rams," she said, "which I love as children. They must be kept near my bedside and never allowed to be carried away. You must take care never to see me when

you are undressed. And clarified butter alone must be my food."

Urvasi came from the storm god Indra's heaven, and its inhabitants were anxious for her return, so they told the Gandharvas, heavenly musicians, to steal the rams. Puru-ravas was undressed when it happened, and so at first he did not pursue the thieves. Urvasi cried, however, impelling him to take his sword and rush after them. The Gandharvas then produced a flash of lightning, which showed Puru-ravas naked, thus breaking the compact. Urvasi disappeared, and Puru-ravas went in search of her. He eventually found her, and she told him she was pregnant and would bring him the child at the end of the year. At the end of the year he met Urvasi, who gave him the son, Ayus. She bore him five or eight more sons.

See also: GANDHARVAS; INDRA

3022

**Ushnisha** (head-band, turban)   In Buddhist art, the protuberance on the top of the head of a Buddha, variously interpreted. In some Buddhist works the form is that of a flame, representing enlightenment. It is one of the major bodily characteristics of a *mahapursusha* (hero)—either of an emperor (*cakravartin*) or Buddha.

3023

**Utchat** (Udjat, Wedjat)   Ancient Egyptian amulet of the eye of the sun god Ra. In the Pyramid Texts the *utchat* is identified with the uraeus cobra, which spat venom and fire against the enemies of the sun god. It appeared on the crown of the pharaoh, the living sun god, who would also defeat his enemies.

According to one myth, the eye of Ra (Tefnut in this version) was separated from her father, Ra, and went to live in the Nubian desert as a bloodthirsty lion. Ra, wanting her back, sent the god Thoth, who persuaded her to return; when she did, she became the goddess Hathor, the great deity who represented the sky. (In Egyptian mythology the gods often change from one form to another.) In a variant of the myth, Tefnut was a cat, a form of the goddess Bast, who became a lion when she was angry. When the eye of Ra was removed from the god (the symbol was also given to other sun gods), it was said that a disturbance occurred in the natural order of the universe, and that when it was returned, the natural order was restored.

The twin *utchats* represent the eye of the sun and the eye of the moon. One myth tells how the powers of evil succeeded in blinding the eye of Ra, the sun god, during an eclipse or prolonged storm. Thoth came to the god and healed his eye. In another myth Thoth healed the eye of the god Horus when it was injured in his battle with the demonic god Set. The restored eye became known as the *utchat*, and its powers as an amulet were thought to be extensive. *The Book of the Dead* contains a spell that will cause Thoth to bring the *utchat* to the deceased during his journey to the kingdom of Osiris.

See also: *BOOK OF THE DEAD, THE*; HATHOR; HORUS; OSIRIS; PYRAMID TEXTS; RA; SET; SHAPE-SHIFTER; TEFNUT; THOTH; URAEUS

*Uther Pendragon (Howard Pyle)*

**3026**

**Uther Pendragon** (chief leader in war)    In Arthurian legend, father of King Arthur by Igraine, wife of the duke of Tintagel. Uther killed the duke and later married Igraine after he had earlier disguised himself as her husband and made love to her. Pendragon is a title conferred on British chiefs in times of great danger. One legend recorded by Geoffrey of Monmouth tells that when the British king Aurelius was poisoned by Ambron, there "appeared a star at Winchester of wonderful magnitude and brightness, darting forth a ray, at the end of which was a globe of fire in form of a dragon, out of whose mouth issued forth two rays, one of which extended from Gaul and the other to Ireland."

See also: ARTHUR; IGRAINE; TINTAGEL

**3024**

**Utgard** (outer place)    In Norse mythology, chief city of Jotunheim, the land of the giants. Its ruler was Skrymir, who was called Utgard-Loki (Magus of Utgard) when he encountered Thor. Utgard appears in the *Poetic Edda* and the *Prose Edda*. In some medieval literature Utgard and Loki are combined to form the name of a devil in Christian folklore. The medieval world view saw the earth as a round, flat disk, with the ocean all the way around it.

See also: ASGARD; JOTUNHEIM; MIDGARD; *POETIC EDDA*; *PROSE EDDA*

**3025**

**Uther Ben** (terrible head)    In Celtic mythology, the head of the father of Arthur, conceived by Eigr by means of an intrigue arranged by Merlin.

See also: ARTHUR, KING; BRAN; BRANWEN

**3027**

**Utnapishtim** (Parnapishtim) (he who saw light? I have found life?)    In Near Eastern mythology, Babylonian hero of the flood myth who was granted immortal life by the gods.

In the epic *Gilgamesh*, Utnapishtim tells his story to the hero of the poem, who came to him seeking immortality.

"I will tell you, Gilgamesh, the marvelous story," said Utnapishtim, "of the decision of the gods. The city of Shurippak was corrupt, so the gods decided to destroy it by bringing a rainstorm upon it. The god Ea, however, warned me, telling me to build a ship, to save myself from the coming deluge."

After the ship, or ark, was completed, Utnapishtim loaded it with gold, silver, and "living creatures of all kinds." He then took his family aboard the ark. When the time came, he entered the ark, closed the door, and entrusted Puzar-Shadurabu, the sailor, with guiding the vessel. When the dawn came, dark clouds arose from the horizon, all of the light was changed to darkness, and a storm began that lasted for seven days. Everything was destroyed; men were turned back to clay, from which they had originally been made. In place of dams constructed by men, marshes were everywhere. Water was over the whole earth.

After "twelve double hours" the waters began to abate, and on the seventh day Utnapishtim sent out a dove, but it found no resting place. Then he sent a swallow, which also returned. Finally he sent a raven, which did not return, indicating that dry land had now appeared. Utnapishtim then left the ship and offered sacrifices to the gods, who had relented—even the great god Bel, who was determined to destroy all life. The god came upon the ship, lifted up Utnapishtim, brought up his wife, and made her kneel by her husband's side. The god then blessed the couple, saying: "Hitherto Utnapishtim was mortal, but now Utnapishtim and his wife shall be gods like us."

Utnapishtim was then placed "at the confluence of the streams," where he and his wife were to live forever.

See also: BEL; GILGAMESH; NOAH

**Utukku**   In Near Eastern mythology, generic name for demons among the Babylonians and Assyrians.

The Babylonians believed that evil spirits resided everywhere, lying in wait to attack people. Each demon was given a name, often describing his or her function. Thus, Lilu (night spirit) and Lilitu, the female form, indicated demonic spirits that worked their evil at nighttime. Eki mmu (seizer) was a shadowy demon that hovered around graves waiting to attack any passersby. Rabisu (the one that lies in wait) and Labartu (the oppressor) were the demons who gave nightmares to the sleeping. Ardat Lili (maid of the night) was a demoness who approached men, aroused their sexual passions, and then did not permit them to have orgasms. Other demons were Akhakhazu (the capturer), Namtar (the demon of plague), Ashakku (the demon of wasting disease), and Namataru, the spirit of fate and son of the great god Bel, who executed instructions given him concerning the destiny of mankind.

To protect themselves against these various demons the Babylonians and Assyrians evolved an elaborate series of incantations to ward off evils. They also pictured the demons as monstrous beings, made of animal heads and bodies resembling human shape. With gaping mouths and armed with weapons, the *utukku* stood ready to attack their next victim. Assyrian kings acknowledged the power of the *utukku* by having statues of them placed at the approaches, entrances, and divisions of their temples and palaces. This was done in the hope of securing their protection instead of their vengeance. The great bulls and lions with human heads often seen on various monuments are part of the same concept. These colossal statues were known as Shedu, another term for demon. Even though the demons assumed animal forms, they could also make themselves invisible.

Because there were so many demonic beings, incantations often would number them, such as the famous text *Seven Are They*:

Seven are they, they are seven,

In the subterranean deep, they are seven,

Perched in the sky, they are seven,

In a section of the subterranean deep they
were reared.

They are neither male nor are they female,

They are destructive whirlwinds,

They have no wife, nor do they beget
offspring.

This ancient text was set to music by the Russian composer Sergei Prokofiev for tenor, chorus, and orchestra as *Seven Are They*. The seven evil spirits are elsewhere compared to various monstrous animals with the power to bewitch even the gods. The eclipse of the moon, for example, was attributed to them. The number seven is not to be taken literally; it means, as in many other mythologies, a miscellaneous group.

3029

**Uwolowu**    In African mythology (Akposso of Togo), sky god. Uwolowu created everything, including the lesser gods. He bestows on men the blessings of offspring and harvest, of rain and sunshine. He also gave man fire. He is almighty and can impart all good things.

Various myths are told of Uwolowu. In one he had two wives. One of them was a frog, and the other was a bird called Itanco. Uwolowu loved his frog wife more than his bird wife; he gave his frog wife all sorts of pretty things but gave nothing to his bird wife. One day he said he would put their love to the test. He gave each of them seven pots and made believe he was dead. His widows were to weep for him and let the tears fall into the seven pots. The frog wife began to weep, but as fast as her tears fell they were licked up by ants. Then the bird wife wept, and her tears filled the seven pots. Uwolowu said, "She whom I did not love has filled seven pots with the tears which she wept for me, and she whom I loved has wept very little." With these words the god lunged out with his foot and kicked his frog wife into the slime, where she has wallowed ever since. But as for his bird wife, Uwolowu set her free to roam forever in the air.

Another myth tells of the origin of death. Once upon a time men sent a dog with a message to Uwolowu to say that when they died they would like to come to life again. Off the dog trotted to deliver the message. But on the way the dog felt hungry and went into a house where a man was boiling magic herbs. The dog sat down and thought to himself, "He is cooking food."

In the meantime a frog had set out to tell Uwolowu that when men died they would rather not come to life again. Nobody had asked the frog to take that message: he had made up the lie. The dog, who still sat hopefully watching the man cook, saw the frog racing by but said to himself, "When I have had a snack, I'll catch up with froggy."

However, the frog came in first and said to Uwolowu, "When men die, they would rather not come to life again."

After the frog delivered his message, the dog entered and said, "When men die, they would like to come to life again."

Uwolowu was puzzled and said to the dog: "I really don't understand these two messages. As I heard the frog's message first, I will heed his and not yours." That is the reason death is in the world.

**Vacub-Caquix** (Uukub Cakix) (seven macaws) In Mayan mythology, an evil giant mentioned in the *Popol Vuh*, the sacred book of the ancient Quiché Maya of Guatemala.

Vacub-Caquix was a being "who was very proud of himself," thinking he was the sun and the moon. He was married to Chimalmat and had two sons: Zipacna, a giant who carried mountains on his back and who ate flesh and crabs, and Cabraca (double giant, or earthquake). Vacub-Caquix and his sons boasted that they had created the earth and were the sun, so the gods decided to destroy them. Two youths, the hero gods Hunahpú and Xbalanqué, were dispatched to kill the giant and his sons.

Vacub-Caquix had a beautiful tropical tree that produced a very aromatic fruit. He ate the fruit of the tree each day, climbing into its branches. One day Hunahpú and Xbalanqué "lay in ambush at the foot of the tree." As soon as Vacub-Caquix appeared they shot with a blowgun and "struck him squarely in the jaw," breaking some of his teeth, and the giant fell from the tree. Hunahpú ran over to the giant to give the coup-de-grâce, but Vacub-Caquix tore off Hunahpú's arm and took it home with him. Hunahpú and Xbalanqué then spoke with Azqui-Nim-Ac (great white wild boar) and his wife, Zaqui-Nim-Tziis (great white coat). These two are the creator man and woman in the *Popol Vuh*.

They appear in different guises throughout the book.

The couple and the two heroes then went to Vacub-Caquix's house. When they arrived they heard the giant "screaming because his tooth pained him." Not realizing that the two youths were the ones who had attacked him and thinking they were the sons or grandsons of the couple, Vacub-Caquix asked if they knew how to cure his toothache. Pretending to help him, the two heroes pulled out all of his teeth, blinded him, and "took all his riches," leaving the giant to die. His wife, Chimalmat, also died soon after, though we are not told how. Later Hunahpú's arm was restored.

The giant's two sons, Zipacna and Cabraca, were undone by Hunahpú and Xbalanqué later on. Zipacna was turned into stone, and Cabraca was fed a bird coated with chalk, which made him weak so that he was easy prey for the two heroes, who threw him to the ground and buried him alive.

See also: ADAM AND EVE; HUNAHPÚ AND XBALANQUÉ; *POPOL VUH*

**Vacuna** In Roman mythology, a Sabine goddess of agriculture, later known as goddess of leisure. She is identified in some ancient accounts with the goddesses Victoria, Venus, Minerva,

Bellona, and Diana. Horace's *Epistles* (1.10.49) cites the goddess.

See also: BELLONA; DIANA; MINERVA; VENUS; VICTORIA

---

3032

**Vagina Dentata** In North American Indian folklore, a vagina with teeth. The motif concerns the matter of pleasure during sexual intercourse, as well as the fear that the penis will be bitten off during sex. Most of the stories are associated with a culture hero or a trickster. Women may have, for example, the teeth of a rattlesnake in their vaginas, with which they kill men during intercourse and then rob them. They may also use this toothed vagina for hunting purposes, capturing animals with it. The culture hero or the trickster often wears down the teeth with a stone penis or some kind of wedge.

See also: CULTURE HERO; TRICKSTER

---

3033

**Vahagn** In Armenian mythology, sun, lightning, and fire god, invoked for courage because he battled dragons. Vahagn was the son of heaven, earth, and the sea. One old poem describes him as having "hair of fire," and a "beard of flame," and says "his eyes were suns." Some scholars believe Vahagn also may have been the patron of game and hunting because his Christian replacement in Armenian folklore, St. Athenogenes, a bishop and martyr of the early fourth century (feast, 16 July), is patron of both. Vahagn survives also in modern folklore as Dsovean (sea-born), who with Dsovinar, an angry female storm spirit, rules over the seas.

---

3034

**Vainamoinen** (Vainanoinen, Wainamoinen) (river's mouth?) In the Finnish epic poem *The Kalevala*, a culture hero, son of Luonnotar, daughter of the air, who brought about creation.

Vainamoinen was the inventor of the harp, "forger of the runes" or poems, and a great magi-cian. In Finnish mythology the heavenly sign Orion is called the scythe of Vainamoinen; the Pleiades, the sword of Vainamoinen. Vainamoinen's home was called Vainola.

The hero's birth forms part of the opening (rune 1) of *The Kalevala*, which tells how the hero "rested in his mother's body" for the space of 30 years as she tossed on the waves. The hero finally reached the shore, where the evil Laplander Joukahainen challenged him to a singing contest and lost, whereupon Vainamoinen plunged him into a swamp. In order to save his life, Joukahainen pledged his sister Aino in marriage to Vainamoinen. However, the girl did not want to marry an old man. Vainamoinen is always portrayed as old in *The Kalevala*, being called "old and steadfast."

Joukahainen again attempted to kill Vainamoinen, but the hero escaped on an eagle, which brought him to Pohjola, the Northland, ruled by the evil mistress Louhi. She promised her daughter to Vainamoinen if he could forge the sampo, which magically made corn, salt, and coins. However, the Maiden of Pohjola, Louhi's daughter, set additional tasks for Vainamoinen, not all of which he could complete, and she eventually married Ilmarinen, who did forge the sampo.

Vainamoinen is portrayed by the Finnish painter Akseli Gallen-Kallela as an old man with a white beard and rather robust or muscular body. Sibelius's tone poem *Pohjola's Daughter* portrays Vainamoinen's wooing of the Maiden of Pohjola. Vainamoinen's departure at the end of the epic when a new king of Karelia is crowned (the king represents Jesus Christ, and Vainamoinen symbolizes the old pagan gods), was used by Longfellow for his description of the departure of Hiawatha in his poem. Sibelius set *The Song of Vaino* for mixed chorus and orchestra, using rune 43, in which Vainamoinen calls on God to protect Finland "from the designs of men" and "the plots of women," while destroying the wicked and laying low the "water wizards."

Vaino is a shortened form of Vainamoinen and is a common name in Finland today.

See also: AINO; HIAWATHA; ILMARINEN; JOUKA-HAINEN; *KALEVALA, THE*; LOUHI; LUONNOTAR; MAIDEN OF POHJOLA; ORION; PLEIADES; SAMPO

3035
**Vairocana** (Intensity Shining)    In Tibetan Buddhism, one of the five Dhyani-Buddhas, the illuminator. In Japanese Shingon Buddhism, he is supreme. He is portrayed in Tibetan art on a blue lotus with the Wheel of Dharma and also mounted on a lion. His *mudra* pose is that of teaching.

In Tibetan Buddhism, Vairocana is subsidiary to the Adi Buddha (Vajradhara or some other Buddha). In Shingon he is the Adi-Buddha and appears at the center of the Two Great Mandalas. In the static mandala his *mudra* is *dhyani-mudra* and in the ninefold dynamic mandala his *mudra* is *vairocana-mudra* (fingers of the right hand enclosing the index finger of the left hand, held upright before the chest). In the Daibutsu of the Todai temple at Nara, he displays *abhaya* and *varada* mudras. In Japanese, he is called Dainichi Butsu.

See also: ADI-BUDDHA; DAIBUTSU; DHARMA; DHYANI-BUDDHAS; MANDALA; MUDRA

3036
**Vajra-Dhara** (Vajra holder)    In Tibetan Buddhism, the name for the Adi-Buddha. He holds a *vajra* in each hand, which he crosses before his chest.

See also: ADI-BUDDHA; VAJRA

3037
**Vajrapani** (wielder of the thunderbolt)    In Tantric Buddhism, a Dhyani-Bodhisattva; god of rain, a form of the Hindu god Indra, and the spiritual son of the second celestial Buddha, Akshobhya. He is often portrayed in a fierce form, black or dark blue, wielding his thunderbolt in his uplifted right hand. In his left hand he holds a

bell, snare, or other implement, according to which title he holds; there are some 15. He is called Chana Dorje in Tibetan Buddhism.

See also: DHYANI-BODHISATTVA; INDRA

3038
**Vajravarahi** (Varahi) (adamantine sow)    In Mahayana Buddhism, goddess of light. According to one myth, a certain Buddhist abbess had an excrescence behind her ear shaped like a sow's head. A Mongol warrior wanted the abbess to show her mark, but when the warrior and his men broke into the monastery, they found only sows and pigs led by a sow bigger than the rest. The warrior was so startled by the sight that he stopped his men from pillaging the place. When they left, the sows and pigs were transformed into monks and nuns, and the large sow into the abbess.

Vajravarahi is usually portrayed riding a chariot drawn by a team of swine. She is shown with three faces, one in the shape of a sow's head, and eight arms. Her hands hold various weapons, including an ax and snare. In Tibetan Buddhism, she is called Marici.

3039
**Vaks-oza**    In Finno-Ugric mythology, mill-ruler spirit appearing as a man or woman. It lived in the mill under the floor or behind the water-wheel. Usually, the *vaks-oza* was friendly to the miller, but if it was not on friendly terms, it had to be appeased by an offering of porridge with a pat of butter on a spoon.

3040
**Valedjád**    In the mythology of the Tupi Indians of Brazil, the first man, an evil magician. At first there was no heaven or earth, only a big block of rock, smooth and beautiful. This rock was a woman. One day it split open amid streams of blood, producing the first man, Valedjád. Valedjád was inherently evil and once even flooded the earth. This caused the Sun to con-

sider how to dispose of him. Later, when the earth was peopled, the magician Arkoanyó hid in a tree and poured liquid wax on Valedjád as he passed by, sealing up his eyes, nostrils, and fingers so he could no longer do evil. To ensure that Valedjád would not free himself, a large bird flew away with him to the cold north country.

**Valentine, St.** (to be strong)    Third century. In Christian legend, patron saint of beekeepers, engaged couples, travelers, and young people. Invoked against epilepsy, fainting, and plague and for a happy marriage. Feast, 14 February.

3041

Valentine was a Roman priest who is believed to have suffered martyrdom during the persecution of Claudius the Goth. The custom of sending valentines on the feast day of the saint is believed to have originated from the popular belief that birds begin to pair on St. Valentine's Day. In his *Midsummer Night's Dream* (IV,1), Shakespeare wrote: "Good morrow, friends! St. Valentine is past; begin these wood-birds but to couple now." Chaucer also makes mention of the fact in his *Parliament of Fowls*. However, 15 February was the festival of Februta Juno (Juno the fructifier), and the medieval church may have substituted St. Valentine for the heathen Roman goddess. An early reference to St. Valentine's Day as a day for lovers is found in the *Paston Letters*, in which Elizabeth Drews wrote to her daughter's prospective bridegroom in February 1477: "And, Cousin, upon Friday is St. Valentine's Day and every bird chooseth him a mate, and if it like you to come on Thursday at night . . ., I trust to God that you shall speak to my husband, and I shall pray that we shall bring the matter to a conclusion."

It was a custom in England to draw lots for lovers on St. Valentine's Day. The person drawn was the drawer's valentine and was given a present, such as a pair of gloves. Chapman, in *Monsieur d'Olive*, written in 1605, refers to the custom when he says, "If I stood affected that way [that is, to marriage] I would choose my wife

as men do valentines—blindfold or draw cuts for them; for so I shall not be deceived in the choosing."

See also: CHAUCER; JUNO

**Valentine and Orson** (to be strong, bean)    In medieval French legend, twin brothers; sons of Bellisant, sister of King Pepin and wife of Alexander, emperor of Constantinople. The twins were born in a forest near Orléans. While Bellisant went in search of Orson, who had been carried off by a bear, Pepin accidentally found Valentine and took the child with him. Valentine later married Clerimond, niece of the Green Knight. Orson was suckled by a bear. When he grew up, he became a wild man and was called the Wild Man of the Forest. His brother Valentine brought him back to civilization.

3042

**Valhalla** (carrion-hall)    In Norse mythology, the home of slain heroes, who are served by the Valkyries. Its outer gate is Valgrind (the death's gate), and it is surrounded by a river, Thund (swollen or roaring). All of the slain heroes (einherjar) are kept at Valhalla waiting for the day when they will join the gods to fight the giants at Ragnarok, the end of the world. The heroes feast on Saehrimnir, a boar whose flesh is restored every night after being slaughtered and cooked. They drink the milk of a goat named Heidrun. The cook is called Andhrimnir and the kettle, Eldhrimnir. While they wait for the last day, the heroes pass the time, according to the *Prose Edda*, by riding out into the fields and fighting "until they cut each other to pieces. This is their pastime, but when mealtime approaches they remount their steeds and return to drink in Valhalla." Valhalla appears in the *Poetic Edda*, the *Prose Edda*, Matthew Arnold's narrative poem *Balder Dead*, and as Walhalla in Wagner's *Der Ring des Nibelungen*.

3043

See also: *POETIC EDDA*; *PROSE EDDA*; RAGNAROK; *RING DES NIBELUNGEN, DER*

**3044**

**Vali** (terrible)    In Norse mythology, son of Odin and the giantess Rinda. He grew to full stature in one day and avenged the death of Baldur by killing blind Hodur.

See also: BALDUR; HODUR; ODIN; RINDA

**3045**

**Valkyries** (Valkyrjr) (choosers of the slain)    In Norse mythology, the fierce daughters of Odin, the chief of the gods. They daily chose those who were to fall in battle, bringing them to Valhalla, the hall of the slain. They often rode horses but could transform themselves into ravens or wolves. Their names vary in different sources. Those listed in the *Poetic Edda* in the poem *Grimismol* are Hrist (shaker), Mist (mist), Skeggjold (ax time), Skogul (raging?), Hild (warrior), Thruth (might), Hlok (shrieking), Herfjotur (host fetter), Gol (screaming), Geironul (spear bearer), Randgrith (shield bearer), and Rathgrith (plan destroyer?).

Richard Wagner's "Ride of the Valkyries," which appears in his music drama *Die Walküre*, part of *Der Ring des Nibelungen*, is one of the most stirring works in 19th-century orchestral repertory. Arthur Rackham portrays the Valkyries in his illustrations for Wagner's the Ring Cycle. In Old English, the word *Waelcyrge* is used for the chooser of the slain.

See also: *POETIC EDDA*; *RING DES NIBELUNGEN, DER*; VALHALLA

**3046**

**Vampire**    In European folklore, a revenant, someone who returns after death to haunt the living. While the body remains buried, it is the spirit that literally attacks the friends and relatives of the deceased. Individuals who might return were generally evildoers during life or those had been the recipients of evil, including murder victims, suicides, and alcoholics.

In order to rid oneself of this evil spirit-creature, it was necessary to exhume the revenant's body and examine it for evidence. There are, in fact, many reports of such exhumations, many of which indicate that the body had not completely decomposed, that there was blood in the mouth, and that hair had continued to grow after death. Vampires reputedly sucked the blood of their victims, but the appearance of blood on the lips of the corpse can be scientifically explained. A decomposing body bloats, and blood is forced out through the skin, including the mouth and lips. The traditional way to "kill" a vampire is with a stake driven through the heart, but there were other ways, such as decapitation with a shovel, excoriation, and cremation. Many items have been used to ward off vampires, usually sharp objects such as a knife placed under the pillow, thorns, or sickles, but roses were also used, perhaps because of the thorns. Sewing roses into folk costumes was thus not just for decoration, but also to help ward off evil spirits like the vampire.

Vampires have been the theme of many movies, both serious and humorous. The best known are Bela Lugosi's 1931 film *Dracula* and George Hamilton's 1979 *Love at First Bite*. The actual existence of people who think of themselves as real-life vampires is well documented in Norine Dresser's 1989 book, *American Vampires: Fans, Victims and Practitioners*. The Romanian hero of the 15th century, Count Dracul, actually had no connections with vampires, except for his epithet *dracul*, the Romanian word for devil, and for Bram Stoker's fictional character, who was named Dracula.

See also: REVENANT; WEREWOLF

**3047**

**Vanir** (Vanas, Vanis, Van) (friendly)    In Norse mythology, a race of gods and goddesses who lived in Vanaheim, originally fertility deities. At first the Vanir fought the Aesir, another race of gods, but later they made a truce so that they could fight the giants. Njord and his children, Frey and Freya, went to live with the Aesir gods and goddesses at Asgard in exchange for the

Aesir deities Hoenir and Mimir, who went to live with the Vanir.

See also: AESIR-VANIR WAR; ASGARD; FREY; FREYA; HEIMDALL; HOENIR; MIMIR; NJORD

3048

**Vanishing Hitchhiker**    In American folklore, a classic automobile legend. The story features a revenant, a returning ghost. An automobile motif was added by the early decades of the 20th century. In all variants, some people, usually two young men, were driving along a road when they saw a young woman hitchhiking. They stopped and picked up the girl, and she got into the back seat. She told them that her family lived just a short distance away and said nothing after that. When they came to the house, the driver turned around to tell her that she was home, but when he looked around the young woman was no longer in the back seat. The two occupants of the car were mystified and decided to knock on the front door of the house and tell the people what had happened. They were told by the family that they had indeed had a daughter who fit the description of the girl they had picked up, but she had disappeared, or had been killed in an accident, many years ago. Ever since she had been seen hitchhiking along that very road.

The story is well documented in American legendry and even has variants among the Latter-Day Saints (Mormons) of Utah. There the ghosts are called Nephites, who help stranded motorists on lonely mountainous highways and often foretell the outcome of wars and make predictions about future events or happenings. The vanishing ghost story is not limited to the United States.

There is a Russian variant from around 1890. Along busy Sergievskaya Street in St. Petersburg, a priest carrying the holy sacraments was sent to a certain apartment after mass. When the door was opened, the priest said that he had been sent to administer the sacraments to a dying man. He was told by the person inside that a mistake had been made and that there was no sick

person there. The priest then said that a woman on the street had stopped him, given him this address, and asked that he go there right away to administer the sacraments. The apartment dweller was perplexed. The priest then saw a picture on the wall and told the apartment occupant that it was a picture of the very woman who had approached him on the street. "That is a portrait of my dead mother," said the young man. He was seized with fear and immediately took Communion from the priest. That very evening he was found dead in his apartment.

See also: REVENANT; URBAN LEGEND; VARIANT

3049

**Van-xuong**    In Indo-Chinese mythology, god of literature, who now lives in the Great Bear in heaven. He is portrayed as a man standing, holding a pen in one hand.

See also: CALLISTO

3050

**Var** (truth or promise)    In Norse mythology, a goddess of the vows of love, one of the deities that surround Frigga. In the *Prose Edda* it is said: "She gives a hearing to the oaths of people and the personal agreements that men and women grant one another; thus those agreements are called *varar* [plural]. She takes vengeance on those who violate them."

See also: FRIGGA

3051

**Variant**    In folklore, the term used to designate a variation of a well-known tale type. For most folklorists the terms *variant* and *version* are used as synonyms, but other folklorists make a distinction. A version is a one-time rendering of a specific tale, ballad, or any other traditional oral expressive form. The term variant means a *variation* from what is conceived to be the content of the typical, archetypal, or original tale. Variants have been used in comparative studies of oral expressive forms.

See also: MOTIF; TALE TYPE

*Varuna*

3052

**Varuna** (all-enveloping)   In Hindu mythology, god of the waters who rides on a fantastic animal, the Makara. Varuna is married to the goddess Varuni, who sprang up at the Churning of the Ocean, when the gods and demons sought the Amrita, or water of life. Varuna's son is called Agasti.

See also: AMRITA; CHURNING OF THE OCEAN; MAKARA

3053

**Vasavadatta**   In Buddhist legend, a courtesan who fell in love with Upagupta, one of the Buddha's disciples. Vasavadatta sent a message to Upagupta to come to her, but he replied: "The time has not yet arrived when Upagupta will visit Vasavadatta." Astonished at his reply, she told him she did not want any money, just his love. But again he made the same reply. Later, after Vasavadatta had been punished for the murder of one of her lovers by having her ears, nose, and feet cut off, Upagupta came to see her. "Once this body was fragrant like the lotus, and I offered you my love. In those days I was covered with pearls and fine muslin. Now I am mangled by the executioner and covered with filth and blood." "Sister," Upagupta replied, "it is not for my pleasure that I approach you. It is to restore to you a nobler beauty than the charms which you have lost." He then told her of the teachings of the Buddha and converted her so that she died in peace.

3054

**Vasus**   In Hindu mythology, eight gods originally attendant on Indra, the storm god, who is sometimes called Vasava (of the Vasus); later they attended Vishnu. They are Ap (waters), Dhruva (pole star), Soma (moon), Dhara (earth), Anila (wind), Anala (fire), Prabhasa (dawn), and Pratyusha (light). Sometimes the following are called Vasus: the Aswins, the twin brothers who preceded the dawn; the gods Vishnu, Shiva, and Kubera; and the eight Adityas, children of the goddess Aditi.

See also: ADITI; ASWINS; INDRA; KUBERA; SHIVA; VISHNU

3055

**Vayu** (air, wind)   In Hindu mythology, the wind and the wind god. Vayu rides with Indra, the storm god, in a golden chariot. Vayu married the nymph Ghritachi and had 100 daughters. Vayu wished his daughters to accompany him to the sky, but they all refused. Vayu then cursed them, turning them into deformed creatures. In some texts Vayu is made head of the Gandharvas, the heavenly musicians, and rules over the Anilas, 49 wind gods who are associated with him.

See also: GANDHARVAS: INDRA

**Vedanta** (end of the Veda)  In Hinduism, an interpretation of the Vedas in which everything consists of or is reducible to one substance. This interpretation influenced such Western writers and thinkers as Schopenhauer, Emerson, and Mary Baker Eddy, whose Christian Science is a kind of Western Vedanta.

See also: VEDAS

**Vedas** (the knowledge)  In Hinduism, sacred texts, the foundation of the Hindu religion. They are regarded as divine truth breathed out by the god Brahma. They are the Rig-Veda, Yajur-Veda, Sama-Veda, and Atharva-Veda. The first three are called the triple Veda and are liturgical and public, the last is nonliturgical and private.

See also: BRAHMA; RIG-VEDA

**Vegtala**  In Hindu mythology, demon in human form who haunts graveyards and animates dead bodies. His hands and feet are turned backwards.

See also: PRETA

**Velo Men** (living)  In African mythology (the Malagasy of Madagascar), little clay people. They were created by Earth, the daughter of God, and given life when God breathed into them. They worked for Earth and made her very rich. Since they did not die, it was obvious that Earth would continue to prosper. God, seeing this, demanded half of the wealth they produced, but Earth refused to give up her enormous profits. God then took the breath that he had given to the Velo Men, and since then they grow old and die like ordinary people.

**Vena**  In Hindu mythology, a proud king who was punished by the priests and then saved. When Vena became king he issued a proclamation that said: "Men must not sacrifice or give gifts or present offerings. Who else but myself is the priest of sacrifices? I am forever the lord of offerings." The Brahmans (priests), angry that the king had usurped their power, killed the king. They realized after his death, however, that there was no heir to the throne. The priests then rubbed Vena's thigh or right arm (depending on which text is consulted) and from the corpse came Prithu, "resplendent in body, glowing like the fire god Agni." (Prithu is sometimes called Prithi-vainya, "Prithi, son of Vena.")

With the birth of Prithu, Vena was freed from his sin. In some accounts the king is not killed by the priests but only beaten, so he is then able to retire to a hermitage and do penance. Later the god Vishnu gives Vena the gift of becoming one with himself. Gustav Holst wrote a *Hymn to Vena* for female voices and harp, using his own translation of a Sanskrit text.

See also: AGNI; BRAHMAN; VISHNU

*Venus*

**Venus** (arrival)  In Roman mythology, ancient Italian goddess of love, wife of Vulcan and mistress of Mars; the mother of Cupid; identified with the Greek Aphrodite. Originally, Venus was an Italian goddess who watched over market gardens and was the protector of vegetation. Her name is related to *venire* (come), connected in religion with the arrival of spring. The day on which her temple was founded in Rome was observed as a holiday by the vegetable sellers. Yet it was not as goddess of vegetation that Venus became one of the most important deities in Roman mythology. Instead, she was identified with the Greek goddess Aphrodite. Her role in Roman religion is found in Lucretius's work *On the Nature of Things*, which opens with an invocation to the goddess as the great moving force in life.

At Rome Venus was worshiped as the goddess of erotic love. Vinalia was the festival of Venus and Jupiter. As the mother of Aeneas and the ancestor of the Roman people, she was given special honors. Julius Caesar built a temple to Venus Genetrix, the mother of the Julian family, and established games in her honor. Venus also was the protector of the family as Venus Verticordia. It was this aspect of Venus whose image was bathed and adorned with flowers each spring by women of the upper classes. In the second century C.E. Emperor Hadrian wished to restore the worship of Venus to its rightful place. A poem, the *Pervigilium Veneris* (The Virgil of Venus), believed to be of the same century, deals with Venus's role. It opens: "Let those love now, who never loved before; / And those who always loved, now love the more." The work, in English translation, was set to music by the American composer Virgil Thomson.

Numerous references to Venus are found in literature, since the Roman name for Aphrodite was used more frequently than the Greek. She appears in Ovid's *Metamorphoses*; Chaucer's The Knight's Tale, part of *The Canterbury Tales*; Spenser's "Epithalamium"; and Shakespeare's *The Tempest* and his long narrative poem *Venus and Adonis*, in which she appears as goddess of lust. Milton, less erotic than Shakespeare, writes in *Comus*, "Venus now wakes, and wakens love."

Venus appears in the medieval Christian legend of Tannhäuser. The legend inspired Swinburne's poem *Laus Veneris* and Wagner's opera *Tannhäuser*. She also appears in Dante Gabriel Rossetti's poem *Venus Victrix* as the conquering force of love and in W. H. Auden's poem "Venus Will Now Say a Few Words."

Among the attributes of Venus are a pair of doves or swans, sometimes drawing her chariot; the scallop shell and dolphins, relating to her birth from the sea; her magic girdle or belt, which induced love; a flaming torch that kindled love; and the myrtle, which was evergreen as love. The first day of April was sacred to Venus. She, along with Fortuna Virilis, the goddess of prosperity in the intercourse of men and women, was worshiped by women. With Concordia, Venus was worshiped as Verticordia, the goddess who turns the hearts of women to chastity and modesty. Other holidays in April honored her as the goddess of prostitution.

The Uranian Venus was the title given to Venus for her role as goddess of chastity to distinguish that role from Venus Pandemos, the Venus of erotic love. Tennyson, in his poem *The Princess* (1830), writes:

> The seal was Cupid bent above a scroll,
> And o'er his head Uranian Venus hang
> And raised the blinding bandage from his
>     eyes.

Matthew Arnold's poem "Urania" (1869) is about a cold woman.

In western European art Venus appears in many forms. Sometimes the word *Venus*, with no mythological significance, was used to mean "the female form." The best-known ancient representation of the goddess is the Venus di Milo, a Greek statue now in the Louvre in Paris. It was found on the island of Melos in 1829. (Sometimes it is called Venus of Melos.) A common form of the goddess is the Venus Pudica (Venus of modesty), in which she appears with one arm slightly flexed, one hand covering the pubic area while the other covers the breasts. This form is found in Botticelli's painting *The Birth of Venus*. Other great works portraying the goddess are Veronese's *Venus and Mars*, Titian's *Venus and Adonis*, and Boucher's *Venus and Vulcan*.

Common art motifs portraying the goddess are the Toilet of Venus, in which the goddess is shown reclining, with Cupid holding a mirror. The best-known version of this motif is Velázquez's *Venus at Her Mirror*, painted about 1650.

Another common motif portraying the goddess is that of Sacred and Profane Love. In this, two kinds of love—erotic and Platonic—are portrayed by two Venuses. The Venus Vulgaris is the erotic or common Venus, and the Venus Coelestis is the more spiritual one. The erotic Venus is portrayed in rich garments, and the spiritual Venus is portrayed naked. One example of this type is Titian's *Sacred and Profane Love*.

The Triumph of Venus, another popular motif in art, portrays the goddess enthroned on her triumphal chariot drawn by doves or swans. An unknown American artist of the early 19th century painted *Venus Drawn by Doves* in watercolor. In the work the doves are larger than the goddess, and the landscape is American.

See also: APHRODITE; MARS; OVID; VULCAN

3062
**Venusberg** (mountain of Venus)   In medieval German legend, the mound or hill of Venus, the pagan Roman goddess. Today the Hörselberg, near Eisenach, is still considered to be the Venusberg and is said to be the gathering place for witches and spirits after the Wild Hunt. Here the Christian knight Tannhäuser stayed. Wagner's opera *Tannhäuser* has elaborate music depicting the erotic delights of the mountain.

See also: TANNHÄUSER; VENUS

3063
**Verdandi** (present)   In Norse mythology, one of the three named Norns, personifying the present; the other two are Urd and Skuld.

See also: NORNS; SKULD; URD

3064
**Verethraghna**   In Persian mythology, war god, noted for his 10 incarnations, which are enumerated in the sacred *Avesta*. They are (1) a "strong, beautiful wind"; (2) "a beautiful bull, with yellow ears and golden horns"; (3) "a white, beautiful horse"; (4) "a burden-bearing camel, sharp-toothed, swift"; (5) "a sharp-toothed he-boar"; (6) "a beautiful youth of fifteen, shining, clear-eyed, thin-heeled"; (7) "a raven . . . the swiftest of birds"; (8) "a wild, beautiful ram, with horns bent round"; (9) "a beautiful fighting buck, with sharp horns"; (10) "a man, bright and beautiful," holding "a sword with a golden blade, inlaid with all sorts of ornaments."

Of the 10 incarnations the most popular with the soldiers who worshiped Verethraghna were those of the raven and the boar. The raven was believed to make a man inviolable during battle, and the boar was an ages-old symbol of war gods.

See also: *AVESTA*

3065
**Veritas** (truth)   In Roman mythology, daughter of Saturn and mother of Virtue. She was portrayed as a young virgin dressed in white. Because she was so difficult to find, it was believed that she hid herself at the bottom of a well.

See also: SATURN

3066
**Veronica, St.** (true image)   First century. In Christian legend, patron saint of linen-drapers and washerwomen. Feast, 4 February.

An early Christian legend says that as Christ was bearing his cross to Calvary, a woman, seeing the drops of blood flow from his brow, wiped them off with her veil or handkerchief. When she looked at the cloth, she found the image of Christ impressed on it. The veil was later called the Vera Icon (true image) by Pope Gregory I. According to the same tradition, the name of the woman was Seraphina, but due to a misunderstanding in the transmission of the legend through the ages, the Vera Icon was turned into

*St. Veronica (Dürer)*

a proper name for a woman, and she was called St. Veronica.

That legend is the one generally circulated during the Middle Ages, though there is another account of the origin of the Vera Icon. It tells of a woman's being healed by touching Christ's garment. She then asked St. Luke to paint a picture of Christ on a piece of cloth. When she next saw Christ, she realized that he had changed and that the likeness on the cloth painted by St. Luke was not correct. Then Christ said to her, "Unless I come to your help, all Luke's art is in vain. My face is known only to Him who sent me." He then told her to prepare a meal for him, which she did. After the meal he wiped his face with a cloth, and he left his image on it. "This is like me," he said, "and will do great things."

Various Christian legends credit the Vera Icon with healing. One tells how it healed a Roman emperor (either Vespasian or Tiberius) who was suffering from "worms in the head" or a "wasp's nest in the nose." As a result of seeing the image of Christ, the emperor ransacked Jerusalem and destroyed the Jews, selling them for 30 pieces of silver each. The anti-Semite legend was an attempt to blame the Jews for the death of Christ and to free the Romans from the actual guilt for the deed. (The Romans, not the Jews, killed Jesus.)

St. Brigit, who lived in the sixth century, complained of those who doubted that the face on the Vera Icon was that of Christ. Dante mentions the Vera Icon in *The Divine Comedy*. A statue of St. Veronica, or Seraphina, portraying her holding the Vera Icon, is in St. Peter's Basilica in Rome. Numerous artists have portrayed the subject. In Spanish bull-fighting one movement is called the Veronica. When the cape is swung before the face of the bull, it is said to resemble St. Veronica's wiping of Jesus' face with her scarf.

See also: BRIGIT, ST.; CANDLEMAS; LUKE, ST.

3067
**Vertumnus** (Vortumnus, Virtumnus) (the turner or changer)    In Roman mythology, Italian god of fruits who presided over the changing year. He had the power to assume any shape or

*Vertumnus*

form and used this power when he fell in love with Pomona, the Roman goddess of fruit trees. But the girl refused his advances. None of the various forms assumed by the god pleased Pomona. He appeared as an old woman and pleaded his case. Finally, he transformed himself into his natural shape, a handsome young man. Pomona then accepted him and became his wife. Milton, in *Paradise Lost* (book 9.394–95), describes the innocence of Eve before the Fall, writing: "Likeliest she seemed, Pomona when she fled / Vertumnus. . . ." The tale is told in Ovid's *Metamorphoses* (book 14). A bronze statue of Vertumnus was located in the Tuscan business quarter in Rome, where he was regarded as the protector of business and exchange. His feast was 13 August, at which time sacrifices were made to him in his chapel on the Aventine.

See also: OVID; POMONA

3068

**Vesper** (evening)   In Roman mythology, the planet Venus as the evening star. The Greek form, Hesperus, is often used in English literature. *Vesper* has come to be the name for evening services in the Christian church in western Europe and America.

See also: HESPERUS; VULCAN

3069

**Vesta** (hearth)   In Roman mythology, the goddess of the hearth, equivalent of the Greek Hestia.

Vesta's cult was introduced by Numa Pompilius from Lavinium, where Aeneas, according to Roman myth, had brought the Penates (gods of the store chamber) and the sacred fire from Troy. Roman consuls and dictators, on taking up and laying down their office, sacrificed in the temple of Vesta at Lavinium. It was customary in Italy, as in Greece, for the colonies to kindle the fire of their own Vesta at the hearth of the mother city. The ancient round temple of Vesta, which served as the central point of the city, was built by Numa Pompilius. In its neighborhood

was the Atrium of Vesta, the home of the virgin priestesses of the goddess. Here the goddess was worshiped not in the form of a statue but under the symbol of eternal fire. It was the chief duty of the vestal virgins to keep the flame alive, and every 1 March it was renewed. If it went out, the guilty vestal was scourged by the pontifex. The fire could be rekindled only by a burning glass or by the friction of boring a piece of wood from a fruit tree. A daily sacrifice of food in a clay vessel was made. The daily purifications could be made only with flowing water, which the vestal virgins carried in pitchers on their heads from the fountain of Egeria or from the fountain of the Muses. During the day anyone could enter the temple, except for that part in which the *palladium* and other sacred objects were kept. At night men were not allowed in.

Vesta was the goddess of every sacrificial fire, whether in the home or the temple. She was worshiped along with Janus. His praise opened the service, and Vesta's closed it. Vesta's festival, the Vestalia, was held on 9 June. The matrons of the city walked barefoot in procession to her temple and asked the goddess to protect their households. Millers and bakers also kept the feast. The asses who worked the mills were decked out with garlands, with loaves suspended about their necks. Vesta's worship continued into the Christian era. It was abolished in the fourth century C.E. Although there was no image of the goddess in her temples, statues of Vesta were not uncommon in Rome. She was portrayed clothed and veiled, with chalice, torch, scepter, and palladium. Vergil's *Aeneid* (book 2), Ovid's *Metamorphoses* (book 15) and *Fasti* (book 6), and Macaulay's poem *Battle of Lake Regillus* tell of Vesta.

See also: AENEAS; HESTIA; PALLADIUM; PENATES; TROY

3070

**Vestal Virgins**   In Roman cult, the priestesses of the goddess Vesta. To be called as a vestal virgin, girls had to be not younger than six and not older than 10 years of age. They had to be without personal blemish and of free, respectable families. Their parents had to be living in Italy. The choice was made by casting lots from nominations made by the pontifex. The virgin accepted for the priestly office immediately left her father's authority and entered that of the goddess Vesta. After the rites of entrance the girl was taken into the Atrium of Vesta, her future home; she was ceremonially dressed, and her head was shorn. The time of service was 30 years—10 for learning, 10 for performing the rites, and 10 for teaching the duties. At the end of this time set by law the women were allowed to go and marry. They seldom did.

The vestal virgins were under the complete control of the pontifex. In the name of the goddess he exercised paternal authority over them. He administered corporal punishment if they neglected their duties. If they broke their vow of chastity, they were carried out on a bier to the *campus sceleratus* (the field of transgression) near the Colline Gate, beaten with rods, and buried alive. The guilty man was then scourged to death. No man was allowed to enter their quarters. Their service consisted of maintaining and keeping the eternal flame in the temple of Vesta, watching the sacred shrines, performing sacrifices, and offering prayers for the welfare of the nation. They took part in the feasts of Vesta, Tellus (earth), and Bona Dea (Good Goddess).

The vestal virgins dressed entirely in white, with a coronet-shaped headband ornamented with ribbons suspended from it. When they sacrificed, they covered it with a white veil, a hood made of a piece of white woolen cloth with a purple border, rectangular in shape. It was folded over the head and fastened in front below the throat. The chief part in the sacrifices was taken by the eldest, the *virgo vestalis maxima*.

Various privileges were accorded the vestal virgins. When they went out, they were accompanied by a lictor (guard). At public games they were given the place of honor. When they gave evidence, they did not have to take the oath. They were entrusted with wills and public treaties. If anyone injured a vestal virgin, the penalty was death. If anyone, on the way to punishment, chanced to meet a vestal virgin in the street, the punishment was revoked. They had the honor of being buried in the Forum.

Shakespeare, in *Romeo and Juliet* (3.3.38), speaks of the "pure and vestal modesty" of Juliet's lips, and Alexander Pope in *Eloisa to Abelard* uses the term "the blameless vestal" for a Christian nun. Spontini's opera *La Vestale* (1807) deals with the vestal virgins.

See also: BONA DEA; VESTA

3071
**Vibhishana** (Vibhisana) (terrrifying)    In Hindu mythology, brother of the demon-king Ravana, though in opposition to his brother. He left Lanka (Sri Lanka), Ravana's capital, and sided with the hero Rama in his fight to regain his throne. When Ravana died, Vibhishana was placed on the throne of Lanka.

See also: RAVANA

3072
**Victor de Plancy, St.** (conqueror)    Sixth century. In Christian legend, hermit saint. Feast, 26 February.

According to medieval legend as told by St. Bernard, St. Victor was very good at exorcism. One day St. Victor sent some workers to sow wheat. One of them, however, stole two bushels of seed. Instantly, the thief was possessed by the devil, who made smoke and fire issue from his mouth. St. Victor took pity on the man and made the sign of the cross. The devil fled, and the man confessed his guilt. In another legend St. Victor turned water into wine. One day the king of France, Chilperic, paid a visit to Victor. The saint greeted the king and offered him some water to drink. "O Lord," said Victor, "bless this water and fill the vessel which holds it with heavenly dew." The water was turned into wine.

3073

**Victoria** (victory)   In Roman mythology, goddess of victory, equated with the Greek goddess Nike. In Rome she had a temple, and festivals were held in her honor. Victoria was portrayed with wings, crowned with laurel, and held a branch of palm in her hand. A gold statue of the goddess, weighing some 320 pounds, was given to the Romans by Hiero, king of Syracuse, and placed in the temple of Jupiter on the Capitoline Hill.

See also: JUPITER; NIKE

3074

**Victor of Marseilles, St.** (conqueror)   Fourth century. In Christian legend, Roman soldier martyred under the emperor Diocletian. Patron of millers. Invoked against lightning and on behalf of weak or sick children. Feast, 21 July.

Victor was asked to sacrifice to the Roman god Jupiter. He not only refused, he destroyed the statue of the god. For his crime he was crushed with a millstone and finally beheaded. Three companions who had looked on his suffering became converted to Christianity. At the moment of Victor's death angels were heard singing, "Victory, Victory." St. Victor of Marseilles is portrayed in medieval Christian art with a millstone or dressed in full chain armor with shield and spurs.

See also: JUPITER

3075

**Vidar** (ruler of large territories)   In Norse mythology, son of Odin and the giantess Grid. Known as the silent god, he is the one who will avenge Odin's death by slaying the Fenrir wolf at Ragnarok, the end of the world, and then will rule the new world. The kenning for Vidar is the "silent god."

See also: FENRIR; KENNING; ODIN; RAGNAROK

3076

**Vila**   In south Slavic folklore, a supernatural being, wood nymph, or spirit of forests, mountains, trees, clouds, or lakes, usually seen as a beautiful young woman. In Serbian heroic epic and ballads, the vila competes with mortal men, obstructing human progress, exacting penalties, demanding sacrifices, and determining fate. Although the vila can be a powerful enemy, she also can be a helpmate and strong ally. She appears in several Marko Kraljevich heroic ballads. In an epic on the foundation sacrifice of Scutari (present-day Shkoder, Albania), she thwarts the building of a fortress, demanding the sacrifice of a nursing mother before allowing the walls to be built. In some folk genres, the vila appears with the legs of a horse or donkey. This motif is used in Adolphe Charles Adam's ballet *Giselle, ou les Wilis*. It also supplied the subject for Giacomo Puccini's first opera, *Le Villi*.

See also: KRALJEVICH, MARKO

3077

**Vilacha**   In Inca ritual, a ceremony performed after the sacrifice of a child; it consisted of smearing the sacrificer and other celebrants with the blood of the dead child. The child was laid on an altar, face upward, and strangled, garroted, or cut open with a knife. Another name for the ceremony is Pipano.

See also: VIRACOCHA

3078

**Vili**   In Norse mythology, one of Odin's brothers, along with Ve; sons of Borr and the giantess Bestla.

See also: ASK AND EMBLA; AUDHUMLA; BESTLA; ODIN

3079

**Vimalakirti** (stainless fame)   In Buddhism, a man visited by Manjushri, the personification of wisdom, and thousands of disciples of the Buddha as well as goblins and deities, who all convened in one small square room. A long dialogue ensued, forming a work that has been translated into English as *The Holy Teaching of Vimalakirti*.

See also: MANJUSHRI

**Vimani** In Hindu mythology, the chariot of the storm god, Indra. The charioteer is Matali.

3080

See also: INDRA

**Vincent, St.** (to conquer)    Died 304. In Christian legend, deacon and Christian martyr. Patron of bakers, roofmakers, sailors, schoolgirls, and vine dressers. Patron saint of Lisbon, Valencia, and Saragossa. Feast, 22 January.

3081

Vincent was born in Saragossa, Spain. During the persecution by the emperor Diocletian he was about 20 and a deacon in the church. The proconsul Dacian rounded up all of the Christians of Saragossa, promised them immunity, then ordered them massacred. Vincent was brought before the tribunal along with Bishop Valerius. When they were accused, Valerius answered, but his reply was not heard because he had a speech impediment.

"Can you not speak loudly and defy this pagan dog?" Vincent asked the bishop. "Speak that the world may hear, or allow me, thy servant, to speak in your stead."

Vincent then spoke of the joys of being a Christian. Dacian was unmoved and ordered Vincent tortured. He was torn with iron forks and thrown into a dungeon. Nearly dead, he was miraculously sustained by angels. Dacian then tried to destroy Vincent by other means. He gave the saint every comfort, including a bed of roses. Finally, the saint died. Dacian, however, was still not satisfied. He had the dead body thrown into a garbage ditch. There it was left unburied, to be eaten by wild beasts and birds of prey. However, God sent a raven to watch over the body and to ward off wolves. On being told of this, Dacian had the body wrapped in oxhide, heavily weighted with stones, and cast into the sea. The body was carried out to sea but later appeared on the beach and was buried in the sand. Not long afterward the saint appeared to a widow and told her where he was buried. The widow went to the spot, found the body, and carried it to Valencia.

When the Christians in Valencia were fleeing the Moors in the eighth century, they took the body of the saint with them. Their ship was driven onto a promontory on the coast of Portugal. There they buried the body of the saint, naming the place Cape Saint Vincent, and two ravens guarded the remains. Part of the cape is called El Monte de las Cuervas in memory of the event. In 1147 King Alonzo I removed the saint's remains to Lisbon. This time two crows accompanied the vessel, one at the prow and one at the stern. The crows multiplied at such a rate in Lisbon that taxes were collected to support them.

In medieval Christian art St. Vincent is portrayed as a deacon with a raven nearby. An old missal printed in 1504 contains this proverb for the feast day of the saint:

If on St. Vincent's Day the sky is clear,
More wind than water will crown the year.

See also: RAVEN

**Vincent de Paul, St.** (to conquer)    1576–1660. In Christian legend, founder of Sisters of Charity; also Congregation Missionis, or Priests of the Mission. Patron of all charitable societies, hospitals, lazar-houses (hospices for those afflicted with disease), and prisoners. Invoked to find lost articles and for spiritual help. Feast, 14 July.

3082

Vincent de Paul was born at Puy, in Gascony, France. His father was a farmer, and Vincent tended the flocks. Since his temper was so sweet, his father sent him to a convent school. When his studies were finished, he continued on as a tutor and finally became a priest in 1600. He went to Marseilles on business and when returning was seized by African pirates and sold into slavery in Tunis. He remained there two years, finally converting the wife of his last master, who in turn converted her husband to Christianity. They all eventually escaped. On his return he devoted much of his time to relieving the suffering of galley slaves and founded the hospital of La Madaleine. He also founded the Congregation of the Sisters of Charity.

In L'Abbe Maynard's *St. Vincent de Paul; His Life, His Times, His Works, and His Influence* he writes that Vincent de Paul never uttered a superfluous word and knew how to impose on himself the most rigorous silence, overcoming the malice of others by his silence.

St. Vincent de Paul is usually portrayed in a clerical cassock with a newborn infant in his arms. Sometimes a Sister of Charity is kneeling before him, or he extends his hand to a beggar.

3083

**Vindheim** (home of the winds)  In Norse mythology, the sky.

3084

**Vindsval** (the wind cold)  In Norse mythology, father of winter, sometimes called Vindloni (the wind man). In the *Prose Edda* he is described as having an "icy breath, and is of a grim and gloomy aspect."

See also: *PROSE EDDA*

3085

**Violet**  An herb with a purple flower. In Near Eastern mythology, the violet grew from the blood of the slain Attis, killed by a wild boar. He was consort to the Great Mother goddess Cybele. In Greek mythology, the violet is sacred to Ares and Io, and in Christian symbolism, white violets are associated with the Virgin Mary. In European folklore, the flower also is associated with mourning, suffering, and death and was believed to spring from the graves of virgins. The violet is symbolic of innocence. In *Hamlet*, Ophelia says that the king, the queen, and even

Hamlet, now that he has killed Polonius, are worthy of this symbol.

See also: ARES; ATTIS; IO; VIRGIN MARY

3086

**Viracocha** (Huracocha) (lake of fat, foam of the water)  In Inca mythology, supreme god and creator, lord of the generation of all life.

Viracocha made and molded the sun, endowing it with a portion of his own divinity. He placed the moon to guard and watch over the waters and winds, over the queens of the earth and the parturition of woman. He also created Chasca, the planet Venus. Viracocha was invisible and incorporeal, as were his messengers, called *huaminca* (faithful soldiers) and *hayhuaypanti* (shining ones). These, according to the *Relación anonyma de los costumbres antiquos de los naturales del Piru* (1615), carried Viracocha's message to every part of the world.

The writer says that when the Indians worshiped a river, spring, mountain, or grove, "it was not that they believed that some particular divinity was there, or that it was a living thing, but because they believed that the great god Illa Ticci (another name for Viracocha) had created and placed it there and impressed upon it some mark of distinction, beyond other objects of its class, that it might thus be designated as an appropriate spot whereat to worship the maker of all things; and this is manifest from the prayers they uttered when engaged in adoration, because they are not addressed to that mountain, or river, or cave, but to the great Illa Ticci Viracocha, who, they believed, lived in the heavens, and yet was invisibly present in that sacred object."

Viracocha was invoked in prayers for the dead to protect the body so that it would not undergo corruption or be lost in the earth. He conducted the soul to a haven of contentment.

Part of Viracocha's cult was the sacrifice of children in his temple. The children, brought by their mothers, who considered it a great honor, were either drugged or, if very young, suckled shortly before the sacrifice. The child was laid on an altar, face toward the sun, and was strangled, garroted, or cut open with a knife. With their blood Vilacha, or Pipano, was performed, which consisted of smearing the sacrificer and other celebrants with the blood. Then a prayer was offered: "Oh Lord, we offer thee this child, in order that thou wilt maintain us in comfort, and give us victory in war, and keep to our Lord, the Inca, his greatness and his state, and grant him wisdom that he may govern us righteously."

The *Relación anonyma* says that the great temple at Cuzco, which was afterward the site of a Christian cathedral, was dedicated to Viracocha. It contained only one altar, and on it was a marble statue of the god, which is described as "both as to the hair, complexion, features, raiment and sandals, just as painters represent the Apostle, Saint Bartholomew."

Viracocha was known by several names, among them Usapu (he who accomplishes all that he undertakes or he who is successful in all things); Pachayachachi (teacher of the world); Caylla (the ever-present one); Taripaca (to sit in judgment), used for the god as the final arbiter of the actions and destinies of men; Tukupay (he who finishes); and Zapala (the one or the only one).

See also: BARTHOLOMEW, ST.; CHASCA

3087

**Virgin Mary**    First century. In the Bible, N.T., the mother of Jesus. Her cult during the Middle Ages was the most influential in the development of Christian art and theology.

The Virgin Mary receives small notice in the New Testament. The accounts of Jesus' birth and early years do stress the Virgin, but she is in the background in most of the narratives. She appears at the foot of the cross and receives the Holy Spirit, as do the Apostles. No details are given of her birth or death.

One of the earliest beliefs was that Mary gave birth to Jesus, the Son of God (Luke 1:31–33), without losing her virginity. This doctrine is called the Virgin Birth. By the fourth century she

*Virgin and Child (Dürer)*

was called *Theotokos* (God bearer), and her cult began to spread throughout Christendom. Her cult, however, was based on earlier cults of various pagan goddesses, such as Isis, Diana, Ceres, and Rhea, whose marks of devotion were transferred to the Virgin. Their statues sometimes were used to portray the Virgin and Child. Isis, the great Egyptian goddess, for example, was often portrayed with the infant Horus. The switch from Isis and Horus to the Virgin and Child was therefore easy. Mary inherited not only the statues of pagan goddesses but the cults associated with them. She was called the Queen of Heaven, as were the goddesses, and was often identified with the moon. In France during the Middle Ages the peasants of the Perche district called the moon *Notre Dame* (Our Lady). In Portugal the people called the moon the Mother of God, and in Sicily Christ and the Virgin were identified with the sun and moon. An eclipse was explained as the outcome of a quarrel between mother and son.

Aside from the ancient influences, the medieval cult of the Virgin Mary was in part a reflection of the social background of the Middle Ages themselves. Much that was feudal and chivalrous in concept was applied to her cult. The Court of Heaven was very much like a medieval feudal court. Mary was the queen; the saints were her barons. This belief is expressed in one 14th-century tale written by a Franciscan. "We ought," he wrote, "to imitate the man who has incurred the king's anger. What does he do? He goes secretly to the queen and promises a present, then to the earls and barons and does the same, then to the freemen of the household and lastly to the footmen. So when we have offended Christ we should first go to the Queen of Heaven and offer Mary, instead of a present, prayers, fasting, vigils and alms; then she, like a mother, will come between thee and Christ, the father who wished to beat us, and she will throw the cloak of her mercy between the rod of punishment and us and soften the king's anger against us."

The Virgin Mary not only pleaded for sinners, she could even joust like a knight. Once the knight Walter of Birback was on his way to a tournament. He turned aside to pray to the Virgin Mary in a chapel and became so lost in prayer that he missed all of the jousting. When he finally arrived at the tournament, he was met with shouts of applause from the other knights and learned that he had performed marvelous feats and taken all of the prizes and prisoners. He knew then that it was the Virgin Mary, lance in hand, who had taken his place in the lists.

Mary also appears in a tale associated with St. Thomas à Becket. While a young man in Paris among a company of fellow students, he boasted that he had a mistress "whom I call sweetheart . . . for there is no woman in all France to compare with her in beauty and loving kindness." He was referring to the Virgin Mary, but the students laughed at him because they knew he had no mistress. Thomas left and asked pardon of the Virgin for his deception. Suddenly she appeared to him and gave him a golden casket containing a chasuble (outer vestment) and blade to show to his companions in token of the troth between them.

In her role as mistress the Virgin Mary could be as jealous as any woman. One of many tales is that of a young clerk in minor orders who was deeply devoted to the Virgin Mary, but one day he decided to leave his order and marry. In the midst of the wedding feast the Virgin Mary appeared.

"Tell me," she said, "you that once loved me with all your heart, why now you have cast me aside? Tell me, tell me, where is she who is kindlier and fairer than I? Why this miserable, misled, deceived wretch, which you have chosen instead of me, instead of the Queen of Heaven? What an exchange! You have left me for a strange woman, I that have loved you with true love. Even now in Heaven I have dressed for you a rich bed in my chamber, whereon to rest your soul in great bliss. If you do not quickly change your mind, you bed will be unmade in Heaven and made up in the flames of Hell instead." At midnight the clerk climbed out of his bridal chamber and returned to his hermitage.

Sometimes a person could threaten the Virgin Mary to achieve an end. Once there was a woman who honored the Virgin by placing flowers before her shrine daily. One day the woman's son was taken prisoner. Weeping, the mother went to the shrine of the Virgin and Child and begged the image to return her son: "O Blessed Virgin Mary, often have I asked thee for the deliverance of my son and thou hast not heard me. Therefore, as my son was taken from me, so will I take away thine, and will put him in durance as hostage for mine."

The woman then took the image of the Christ Child from the bosom of the Virgin, went home, wrapped up the image in a clean cloth, and shut it up carefully in a chest. The following night the Virgin appeared to the woman's captive son and said, "Tell your mother to give me my Son." The young boy was then miraculously freed. He came to his mother and told her that the Virgin Mary had freed him from prison. Thankful, the woman took the image of the Christ Child and placed it back in the bosom of the Virgin.

From the many tales that emerged during the Middle Ages regarding the Virgin, a very well defined picture of her character was presented. She loved soldiers, for example, and was often seen on the battlefield defending the Christians. She accompanied the Christian Crusaders when they went to the Holy Land to fight the Muslims. Joinville, the medieval historian, in his *Life of St. Louis*, tells how a man in Syria possessed by the devil was taken to a shrine of the Virgin Mary to be cured. The devil inside the man said when he arrived, "Our Lady is not here; she is in Egypt, helping the king of France and the other Christians who will come to this land this day, they on foot against the pagans all ahorse."

It is interesting to remember that the Virgin Mary also holds an honored place in the religion of Islam. In the Koran, the birth of Mary, her upbringing in the temple, the Annunciation, and the birth of Jesus "under a palm tree" (Suras 3 and 19) are narrated. The incidents do not come from the New Testament, but from the apocryphal writings of the early Christian church. In the Koranic account the angel of the Annunciation, who is understood as the Spirit of God, says to Mary: "God has chosen you over all women" (Sura 3:37). Islam accepts the doctrine that Mary remained a virgin. One saying, attributed to Muhammad, is: "Every child is stung by Satan, except Mary and her Son." Islam, however, stops short of looking upon her as a female substitute for the deity. Sura 5 of the Koran accuses Christians of worshiping Mary as a "third god." Of course, Islam rejects the doctrine that Jesus is God's son by saying, "It is not for Allah to take to Himself any offspring" (Sura 19). Prayer to the Virgin Mary is also forbidden in Sura 39 of the Koran.

The Islamic rejection of the excessive medieval Christian cult of the Virgin Mary was echoed by the Protestant reformers, who also rejected the medieval excess. Eventually, Roman Catholics began to temper the excessive devotion of the Mary cult. Peter Canisius, a Jesuit theologian

in the 16th century, wrote: "We recognize that things have crept into the cult of Mary which disfigures it, and they may do so again. . . . There are some fanatics who have grown crazy enough to practice superstition and idolatry instead of the true cult."

John Donne, the great English poet, wrote in a sermon preached in 1624, "They hurt Religion as much, that ascribe too little to the Blessed Virgin, as they who ascribe too much." Donne thus stated the Anglican middle view of the Virgin's place in Christian theology. In one poem, *A Thanksgiving for the Virgin's Part in the Scheme of Redemption*, he wrote:

For that fair blessed Mother-maid,
Whose flesh redeem'd us;
That she-Cherubin,
Which unlock'd Paradise, and made
One claim for innocence, and disseiz'd sin,
Whose womb was a strange heav'n, for there
God cloath'd Himself, and grew,
Our zealous thanks we pour. All her deeds were
Our helps, so are her prayers; nor can she sue
In vain, who hath such title unto you.

Will Durant in *The Age of Faith*, which is a study of the Middle Ages, wrote concerning the cult of the Virgin: "The worship of Mary transformed Catholicism from a religion of terror—perhaps necessary in the Dark Ages—into a religion of mercy and love."

The six principal feasts of the Virgin Mary observed in the Western Church are those of the Immaculate Conception (8 December), sometimes simply called her Conception to avoid the doctrine of the Immaculate Conception, which is that Mary was born without Original Sin, her Nativity (8 September), the Purification (2 February), the Visitation (2 July), and the Assumption (15 August), sometimes called the Dormation of the Virgin to avoid the Roman Catholic doctrine that the Virgin was taken to heaven body and soul.

See also: DIANA; JESUS; HORUS; ISIS; KORAN, THE; THOMAS À BECKET, ST.

**Virgo** (virgin)    One of the constellations and the sixth sign of the Zodiac. The sun enters it about 23 August. In Greek mythology Erigone, who hanged herself after finding the murdered body of her father, Icarius of Athens, was transformed into the constellation Virgo. Virgo is portrayed as a robed woman holding a sheaf of grain in her left hand.

See also: ERIGONE; ZODIAC

**Viriplaca** (Veraplaca)    In Roman mythology, goddess who presided over the peace of families. If a couple quarreled, they went to the temple of Viriplaca, which was located on the Palatine Hill, and were supposed to be reconciled there.

**Virtus** (manliness, bravery, virtue)    In Roman mythology, the virtues deified. There were two temples to Virtus erected in Rome, one to Virtue and the other to Honor. They were constructed so that to see the temple of Honor it was necessary to pass through the temple of Virtue. The main virtues were Prudence, portrayed as a woman holding a ruler pointing to a globe at her feet; Temperance, with a bridle; Justice, with an equal balance; Fortitude, leaning against her sword; Honesty, dressed in a transparent veil; Modesty, veiled; Clemency, wearing an olive branch; Devotion, throwing incense on an altar; Tranquillity, leaning on a column; Health, portrayed with a serpent; Liberty, with a cap; and Gaiety, with a myrtle.

**Vis and Ramin**    In Persian legend, two lovers who were "joined as bride and groom" after their deaths. The tale of the lovers is told in a narrative poem, *Vis O Ramin*, by the Persian poet Fakhr Ud-Din Gurgani.

**Vishakha**    Fifth century B.C.E. In Buddhist legend, a wealthy woman disciple of the Buddha. She was the first to become the leader of the lay sisters.

*Vishnu*

**Vishnu** (Visnu, Vishnoo) (to pervade, to enter)    In Hinduism, the supreme deity or the second god of the triad made up of Brahma, the creator; Vishnu, the preserver; and Shiva, the destroyer.

Vishnu, along with Shiva and Devi, is among the most popular deities in present-day Hinduism. In the ancient collection of hymns, the Rig-Veda, he is not of the first rank, but in later works, such as *The Mahabharata* and the *Puranas*, he is the embodiment of Sattwa-guna, the quality of mercy and goodness that displays itself as the preserving power, the self-existent, all-pervading spirit. Some worshipers of Vishnu called Varshnavas recognize him as the supreme being from whom all things originate.

Vishnu's preserving and restoring power has been manifested in the world in various avatars (descents), commonly called incarnations, in which a portion or all of his divine nature is wholly or partially in a human or animal form, either constantly or occasionally. All of the avatars were sent to correct some evil in the world. Ten is the number most commonly accepted, though some texts say 22, and others say they are numberless. The most popular are Rama, the seventh, and Krishna, the eighth.

The 10 avatars are as follows:

*Matsya*

*Matsya* (a fish). Vishnu took the form of a fish and saved Manu, one of the progenitors of the human race, from the Great Flood that destroyed the world. Manu found a small fish that asked him for protection. The fish grew rapidly, and Manu recognized it as Vishnu incarnate. When the Great Flood came, Vishnu, as Matsya, led the ark over the waters and saved Manu and the seeds of all living things. There are various accounts of this myth, with Vishnu appearing only in the later ones.

*Kurma* (the tortoise, turtle). The god took the form of Kurma to recover valuable objects lost in the Great Flood. During the Churning of the Ocean, when the gods and demons struggled to obtain the Amrita, the water of life, Vishnu also appeared as Kurma, helping the gods.

*Varaha* (the boar). Vishnu became Varaha to rid the world of the demon giant Hiranyaksha (golden eye). The demon had dragged the earth to the depth of the ocean. Vishnu fought the demon for 1,000 years before he slew him. The epic poem *The Ramayana*, however, says that the god "Brahma became a boar and raised up the earth." The feat was only later ascribed to Vishnu by his worshipers.

*Nara-sinha* (man lion). Vishnu became Nara-sinha to rid the world of the demon Hiranya-kasipu (golden dress), who had control over the three worlds—sky, atmosphere, and earth—for a million years. The demon had obtained the control from either Brahma or Shiva (accounts vary). He had also obtained the boon of being invulnerable to man or beast, by night or day, on sea or land, and to any solid or liquid weapon. (This boon is sometimes ascribed to other deities.) The demon's son, Prahlada, however, worshiped Vishnu, which naturally upset his father. Hiranya-kasipu then tried to kill his son, but the boy was protected by Vishnu. In a scornful tone Hiranya-kasipu asked his son if Vishnu was in a pillar supporting the hall of his palace. The boy said, "Yes." Then the demon said, "I will kill him." He then struck the pillar. Vishnu stepped out of the pillar as Nara-sinha and tore Hiranya-kasipu to shreds.

*Vamana* (the dwarf). Bali (offering), a king, through his devotions and severe austerities, acquired control over the three worlds. He so humbled all of the gods that they asked Vishnu to protect them from Bali's power. Vishnu then took the form of Vamana and came to earth. He asked Bali to be allowed to make three steps (the three strides of Vishnu, mentioned in the Rig-Veda). As much land as Vamana could cover in three steps would then belong to him. Because Vamana was a dwarf, Bali consented. Then Vishnu took two gigantic steps, striding over the heaven and earth, but out of respect for Bali he stopped short of the underworld, leaving that domain for the king. There are numerous variants of the three steps taken by the god. In Hindu texts Bali is sometimes called Maha-bali (great Bali).

*Parashu-rama*

*Parashu-rama* (Rama with the ax). Parashu-rama came to earth to deliver the Brahmans (priests) from the control of the Kshatriyas (the warrior caste). He is said to have cleared the earth of the Kshatriyas 21 times. In his early life Parashu-rama was under the protection of the god Shiva, who taught him the use of arms and gave him the *parashu* (ax), from which he took his name. The first act told of him in the Hindu epic poem *The Mahabharata* relates to his mortal father, Jamadagni (fire-eating). Jamadagni was a king who ordered his sons to kill their mother, Runuka, because she was defiled by unworthy thoughts. Four of Jamadagni's sons would not do so, and as a result the king cursed them, turning them into idiots. The fifth son, Parashu-rama, struck off his mother's head with an ax. Jamadagni then asked Parashu-rama what gift or request he wished. Parashu-rama begged his father to restore his mother to life and his brothers to sanity. The request was granted.

*Rama-chandra* (Rama the charming, beautiful-charming). Rama is regarded by his followers as a full incarnation of Vishnu, whereas the other avatars are only partial ones. Rama's tale is told in many Hindu works, the most famous being the *Ramayana*, which is found in numerous re-tellings.

*Krishna* (the dark one). Vishnu came to save the world from evil spirits who committed great crimes. Among the most famous was the demon-king Kamsa.

*The Buddha* (enlightened). The Buddha rejected the revealed character of the Vedas and the immortality of the deities. His religion became very popular throughout India but largely died out by about 1000 C.E., passing to the rest of Asia, until it was revived in modern times. The Brahmans claimed that the Buddha was an incarnation of Vishnu, who had come either to defeat the *asuras* (who had gained great power by worshiping the Vedas) by telling them the Vedas were not divine, or to draw people away from the worship of the Vedas and thus ensure the decline of the world cycle according to cosmic law.

*Kalki* (impure, sinful). This avatar has not yet occurred. Vishnu is to appear at the end of the world cycle, seated on a white horse, with drawn sword blazing like a comet, for the final destruction of the wicked, the renewal of creation, and the restoration of purity.

Among Vishnu's many titles are Achyuta (unfallen); Ananta (the endless); Ananta-sayana (who sleeps on the waters); Janarddana (whom men worship); Kesava (the hairy, the radiant); Kiritin (wearing a tiara): Lakshmipati (lord of Lakshmi), in reference to his wife, Lakshmi, in his incarnation as Narayana; Madhusudana (destroyer of Madhu); Mukunda (deliverer); Murari (the foe of Mura); Nara (the man); Narayana (who moves in the waters); Panchayudha (armed with five weapons); Padmanabha (lotus navel); Pitam-bara (clothed in yellow garments); Purusha (the man, the spirit); Purushottama (the highest of men, the supreme spirit); Sarngin (carrying the bow Sarnga); Vaikuntha-natha (lord of Vaikuntha), which is his paradise; and Yajneswara (lord of sacrifice).

See also: ASURAS; AVATARS; BRAHMA; BUDDHA; CHURNING OF THE OCEAN; KALKI; KRISHNA; *MAHABHARATA, THE;* MANU; *PURANAS;* RAMA; RIG-VEDA; SHIVA; VEDAS

3094
**Vishvakarman** (all-maker)    In Hindu mythology, a god said to have created man from speech. In the Rig-Veda, the sacred collection of ancient hymns to the gods, Vishvakarman is called the "all-seeing god, who has on every side eyes, faces, arms, and feet, who when producing the heavens and earth, blows them forth with his arms and wings; the father, generator, disposer, who knows all worlds, gives the gods their names, and is beyond the comprehension of mortals." The term was sometimes used for a Prajapati, a progenitor of the human race, and later for Twashtri, the architect and artisan of the gods.

See also: PRAJAPATI; TWASHTRI

3095
**Vishvapani**    In Mahayana Buddhism, one of the five Dhyani-Bodhisattvas, the wielder of the double thunderbolt, which is his symbol.

See also: DHYANI-BODHISATTVAS

3096
**Viswamitra** (friend of all)    In Hindu mythology, a Prajapati, born a member of the warrior class. Through his intense austerities Viswamitra became a Brahman. He appears in both the epics *The Mahabharata* and *The Ramayana*, where he is the adviser of Rama's father and Rama's own guru. Both epics tell of Viswamitra's love for the nymph Menaka. His austerities so alarmed the gods that they sent Menaka to seduce him. She succeeded, and the result was a child, Shakuntala.

See also: *MAHABHARATA, THE;* PRAJAPATI; *RAMAYANA, THE;* RAMA; SHAKUNTALA

3097
**Vitalis, St.** (vital)    First century. In Christian legend, martyr and patron saint of Ravenna, Italy. Feast, 22 September.

St. Vitalis was one of the converts of St. Peter. He was the father of Sts. Gervasius and Protasius. He served in the army of Nero and suffered martyrdom for burying the body of a Christian who had been martyred. After being tortured by a club set with spikes, Vitalis was buried alive.

The church at Ravenna that was dedicated to St. Vitalis during the reign of Emperor Justinian is considered one of the best examples of Byzantine architecture in Italy. The building was erected over the spot where the saint was supposedly buried alive. The Greek mosaics in the vault of the church portray Christ seated on the globe of the universe, and with his right hand St. Vitalis offers Christ his crown of martyrdom.

See also: PETER, ST.

3098
**Vitus, St.**    Died 303. In Christian legend, patron saint of dogs, domestic animals, young people, dancers, coppersmiths, actors, and mummers. Invoked against epilepsy, lightning, St. Vitus' dance, sleeplessness, and snakebite. Patron of Prague, Saxony, and Sicily. Feast, 15 June.

Vitus was the son of noble Sicilian parents who were pagans. The boy, however, was a Christian, having been taught the faith by his nurse Cresentia and his foster father, Modestus. When Vitus' real father heard his son, now 12, was a Christian, he had him locked in a room or dungeon. When he looked through the keyhole to see what was happening, he saw his son dancing with seven angels. The sight so dazzled him that the man went blind. The boy cured his father, but his father still was against him. So Vitus and his nurse Modestus left by boat for Italy. An angel guided the boat safely to Jucania, where they remained for some time preaching to the people and being fed by an eagle sent by God. They then went to Rome, where St. Vitus cured the emperor Diocletian of his evil spirit, but the emperor still wanted Vitus to sacrifice to the pagan gods. Vitus refused and was cast into a caldron filled with molten lead, pitch, and resin. He came out safely. He was then exposed to a lion, but the animal did not touch him. Then, during the Diocletian persecution (303), Modestus, Crescentia, and Vitus were racked on an iron horse until their limbs were dislocated. At this point a great storm arose that destroyed their persecutors as well as their temples. An angel then came down from heaven and set the three free and brought them to Lucania, where they died in peace.

Vitus is often shown with a cock beside him, as in the statue to the saint in the cathedral of Prague. The cock symbol was used for an earlier pagan god and was given to the saint in popular lore. Offering a cock to the saint was practiced in Prague well into the 18th century.

See also: COCK

**3099**
**Vitzilopuchtl** (sorcerer)   In Aztec mythology, a war god who could change himself into any shape. According to various Spanish accounts, Vitzilopuchtl was originally a sorcerer of the black arts who was noted for his strength in battle. When he died, he was deified and slaves were

sacrificed to him. A dragonlike creature was his symbol.

*Viviane (Louis Rhead)*

**3100**
**Viviane** (living, alive?)   In Arthurian legend, the enchantress who was loved by Merlin but later betrayed him. Viviane, called Nimuë in Malory's *Morte d'Arthur*, was a beautiful woman whom Merlin, in his old age, fell madly in love with. Viviane asked Merlin to teach her all of his magic art. After many years, when she had learned all of his magic and had grown tired of him, she asked him to show her how a person could be imprisoned by enchantment without wall, towers, or chains. After Merlin had complied she lulled him into a deep sleep under a whitethorn laded with flowers. While he slept, she made a ring around the bush with her wimple and performed the magic Merlin had taught her. When Merlin awoke he found himself a prisoner. He never freed himself. Tennyson's "Vivien," part of the *Idylls of the King*, and Ernest

Chausson's symphonic poem *Vivian* treat the legend of Merlin and Viviane. Viviane is identified as the Lady of the Lake in many Arthurian legends.

See also: LADY OF THE LAKE; MERLIN

3101
**Vladimir of Kiev, St.**   c. 957–1015. In Christian legend, Apostle of Russia; responsible for that country's conversion to Orthodox Christianity. Feast, 15 July.

Vladimir was the great prince of Kiev, the "God-protected Mother of Russian Cities," during the last quarter of the 10th century. He was brought up a pagan, and, according to the *Chronicle of Nestor*, his "desire for women was too much for him." He had five wives and numerous female slaves. His conversion to Christianity is shrouded in mystery. He was faced with the need to choose a religion for his people and vacilated between Islam, Judaism, the Christianity of the West, and the Christianity of the East, or Byzantium. He sent ambassadors to witness the ceremonies of each religion, and they came back with the report that the Byzantine form of worship was the most beautiful and therefore must be for the true God. St. Vladimir therefore accepted the Byzantine form of Christianity. After his conversion he forced Orthodox Christianity on his subjects, imposing severe penalties on those who refused baptism.

"The Devil was overcome by fools and madmen," says the *Chronicle of Nestor*, stressing the fact that St. Vladimir received grace from God to overcome his evil earlier life. He put away his former wives and mistresses and married Anne, sister of the Greek emperor Basil II, which helped him politically. His bouts with his past life, however, continued. "When he had in a moment of passion fallen into sin he at once sought to make up for it by penitence and almsgiving," the *Chronicle of Nestor* says in support of the saint's varying moods.

3102
**Vlkodlak** (Vukodlak, Vrkolak, Volkun)   In Slavic folklore, a wolfman or werewolf. If a child is born feet first and with teeth, it will become a *vlkodlak*, but one might also be transformed into a *vlkodlak* through witchcraft, in which case only the person who cast the spell could remove it. A *vlkodlak* also can appear as a hen, horse, cow, dog, or cat. The only remedy against the *vlkodlak* is the *kresnik*, a good spirit who will battle it.

3103
**Vodyanik** (water grandfather)   In Slavic folklore, water spirit, the male counterpart of the female water spirit, *rusalka*. Assuming many forms, *vodyanik* can appear as an old man with a fat belly, wearing a cap of reeds and a belt of rushes. When he appears in a village, he assumes he can be spotted by the water oozing from the left side of his coat. Often he stays in the water, where he makes his home, appearing at night to comb his green hair. His nature varies and is either good or bad, depending on his mood at the time. If in a good mood he helps fishermen, but in a bad frame of mind he causes floods, overturns boats, and drowns men. The mood often depends on whether the fishermen return his children to the water after catching them in their nets.

Variants of *vodyanik* in Slavic folklore are Deduska Vodyancy (water grandfather) among the Russians; Vodeni Moz (water man) among the Slovenians; Topielec (drowner) among the Poles; and Vodnik (water goblin) among the Czechs. Dvořák's symphonic poem *Vodník*, often called *The Water Goblin* or *The Water Sprite* in English, is based on a literary folk ballad by Karel Jaromir Erben in his collection *Kytice*.

See also: RUSALKA

3104
**Volkh** (Volga) (sorcerer)   In Russian folklore, Hero of superhuman strength who appears in the *bylini*, the epic songs, as well as in folktales. Volkh is a *bogatyr*, an epic hero, who could turn

himself into a falcon, a gray wolf, a white bull with golden horns, or a small ant. At age one and a half he spoke his first words, telling his mother not to swaddle him but to give him a suit of armor and a helmet of gold. By 15 he had assembled an army of 7,000. He is said to have defeated the infidels as they sought to destroy the churches of Kiev. He then went to India to take control of that country.

See also: BYLINA

3105

**Volos** (Veles, Vyelyes) (ox?)   In Slavic mythology, god of beasts and flocks, worshiped in some sections of Russia into the 19th century. He may have been one aspect of Pyerun.

The demonic aspects of Volos were applied to demons, but his beneficent aspects were attached to St. Blaise (third century), patron saint of physicians, wax chandlers, and wool combers. In Russian Blaise is called Vlas or Vlassy. On his feast day a prayer is addressed to him that resembles an ancient prayer to Volos: "Saint Vlas, give us good luck, so that our heifers shall be sleek and our oxen fat." The rite of "curling Volos's hair" was still practiced in the 19th century, when peasants tied the last sheaf of grain into a knot at harvest time.

The Russian artist Tcheko Potocka portrayed a sacrifice to Volos that shows peasants slaughtering a horse at the feet of a massive statue of the god. In Lithuania, Volos is called Ganyklos.

See also: BLAISE, ST.; PYERUN

3106

*Volsunga Saga*   Scandinavian prose epic, believed to have been written in the 12th century C.E., telling of the hero Sigurd, who appears in Germanic myth as Siegfried.

Volsung, a lineal descendant of the god Odin, built his home around the trunk of the Branstock oak, whose branches overshadowed all that surrounded it. When Signy, Volsung's only daughter, was married against her will to Siggeir, king of the Goths, a one-eyed stranger (Odin in disguise) appeared among the wedding guests. He thrust a sword, Balmung, deep into the oak. Before leaving he said that the weapon should belong to the man who pulled it out. He then promised that Balmung would assure its owner of victory in every fight.

Although conscious that Odin had been among them, Volsung courteously invited the bridegroom, Siggeir, to try his luck first. Siggeir did not succeed, nor did Volsung, nor any of his 10 sons—except for Sigmund, the youngest.

Siggeir offered to purchase the sword, but Sigmund refused. Angry at his refusal, Siggeir left the next day. Although Signy warned her kinsmen that her husband, Siggeir, was plotting revenge, the Volsungs accepted Siggeir's invitation to visit them.

When Volsung and his 10 sons arrived in Gothland, Signy again warned them. The Volsungs were drawn into an ambush and bound fast to a fallen tree in the forest. Each night a wild beast (wolf) devoured one of the boys. Closely watched by her cruel husband, Signy could not aid her family. Only Sigmund, the youngest, was left alive. Signy told a slave to cover Sigmund's face with honey. A wild beast, attracted by the sweet odor, licked Sigmund's face. This enabled Sigmund to catch the animal's tongue between his teeth and struggle free.

When Siggeir went to investigate the next day, his messenger reported that no prisoners were left bound to the tree and that only a heap of bones was visible. Convinced that all of his enemies were dead, Siggeir ceased to watch Signy. She then stole out into the forest to bury the remains of her father and brothers, and there she discovered Sigmund. They both promised to seek revenge. Later Signy sent her two sons to Sigmund to be trained as avengers, but both proved deficient in courage. Signy came to the conclusion that only a pureblood Volsung would prove capable of the task. She disguised herself as a gypsy to visit Sigmund's hut and had a child by him, Sinfiotli. When Sinfiotli grew up, Signy sent him to Sigmund, who did not know it was his sister with whom he had slept.

With Sinfiotli as his helper Sigmund went to the cellar of the palace to capture Siggeir. But warned by two of his young children that murderers were hiding behind the casks, Siggeir had Sigmund and Sinfiotli seized and cast into separate cells. He ordered that they should be starved to death. But before the prison was closed, Signy cast into it a bundle of straw in which she had concealed Balmung, the magic sword.

With the sword the two freed themselves and set Siggeir's palace afire. Siggeir and his men were killed. Sigmund went to save Signy, who merely stepped out of the palace long enough to tell Sigmund that Sinfiotli was his son and then plunged back into the flames.

Sigmund returned home. In his old age he was killed in battle. Before he died, however, he had fathered a son, Sigurd, upon his young wife, Hjordis. In one version the mother died in childbirth, and Sigurd was raised by Mimer, a magician as well as a blacksmith. In a variant version of the saga a Viking discovered the young wife mourning over Sigmund's dead body and carried her off. She consented to become the Viking's wife if he would promise to be a good foster father to Sigmund's child. In his home Sigurd was educated by the wisest of men, Regin, who taught the hero all he needed to know. He advised Sigurd on the choice of a wonderful steed, Grane or Greyfell.

Seeing that the lad was ready for adventure, Regin told him of the gods Odin, Hoenir, and Loki, and how they had killed Otter and had to pay the price for the deed with gold; this gold was now guarded by Fafnir, who had transformed himself into a dragon. Sigurd, with the fragments of his father's sword, forged a new blade and went out to kill Fafnir. A one-eyed ferryman (Odin in disguise) conveyed him to where the dragon was and explained how best to kill the monster.

After Sigurd killed Fafnir, Regin joined him. Regin asked Sigurd to cut out the dragon's heart and roast it for him. Sigurd did as he was told, but while he was cooking the heart, he burned his finger. As he licked the burn, the taste of Faf-

nir's heart blood gave Sigurd the power to understand the language of birds. One bird nearby told him that Regin was coming up behind to kill him with his own sword. Enraged, Sigurd slew Regin. After piling up most of the treasure in a cave, where it continued to be guarded by the dead body of the dragon, Sigurd rode away, taking with him his sword, a magic helmet, and the ring.

Guided by the birds, he came to a place in the forest that was surrounded by flames. He rode through them and came upon Brynhild, asleep. The two fell in love. Brynhild told Sigurd she was a daughter of the god Odin. She had been placed there as punishment for saving a man whom Odin had doomed to death. As a result she was condemned to marry any mortal who could claim her. Sigurd gave Brynhild the ring.

Shortly after, he left and went to Burgundy, the land of the Nibelungs. Their ruler, Giuki, had a beautiful daughter, Gudrun, who fell in love with Sigurd and gave him a love potion, which made him forget Brynhild and fall in love with Gudrun. Sigurd asked for her hand in marriage. The marriage was agreed to if Sigurd would help Gunnar, a brother of Gudrun, to gain Brynhild as his wife.

Taking on Gunnar's form by use of the magic helmet, the Tarnkappe in the *Nibelungenlied*, Sigurd went through the flames again, fought with Brynhild, and took back the ring. Not knowing it was Sigurd, she was forced to marry her "hero" and thus was made Gunnar's bride. When she reached the court, Sigurd did not know her because of the love potion. Brynhild became very bitter.

Brynhild would not have sexual intercourse with her husband, and Gunnar again sought Sigurd for help. The hero, once again using his magic helmet, fought with Brynhild one night and took her girdle and ring, which he carried off and gave to his wife Gudrun. Brynhild believed it was Gunnar who had conquered her.

However, Brynhild's resentment still smoldered. When Gudrun and Brynhild had an argument over who was to be first at bathing in the river, Gudrun showed Brynhild the magic ring and girdle, saying her Sigurd had wooed and won Gunnar's bride. Hogni, a kinsman of the Nibelungs, took Brynhild's side and told her he would help her avenge the insult. In one version Hogni killed Sigurd in bed by discovering his one vulnerable spot. In a variation, Sigurd was killed by Hogni while hunting in the forest.

By order of Gudrun, Sigurd's corpse was placed on a pyre that consumed his weapons and horse. Just as the flames were rising, Brynhild plunged into them and also died. A variant version records that she stabbed herself and asked to be burned beside Sigurd, his naked sword lying between them and the magic ring on her finger.

Atli of the Huns, Brynhild's brother, sought revenge for his sister's death. However, he accepted Gudrun as his wife. Gudrun agreed to the marriage because she was given a magic potion. When it wore off, however, she hated her husband. The end was a battle of Gunnar's and Hogni's men against Atli's forces. When Gunnar and Hogni were caught by Atli, he attempted to force them to tell him the hiding place of the treasure. Gunnar said he would not reveal it as long as Hogni lived because he had given Hogni his word. Atli then had Hogni's heart brought to Gunnar to show him he was dead. Gunnar still refused to tell and was killed. Atli then ordered a festival, but he was killed by Gudrun, who either stabbed him to death with Sigurd's sword or set fire to the palace and perished with the Huns. A third variation recounts that Gudrun was cast adrift and landed in Denmark, where she married the king and bore him three sons. These youths, in an attempt to avenge the death of their stepsister Swanhild, were stoned to death. Gudrun finally committed suicide by casting herself into the flames of a huge funeral pyre.

The *Volsunga Saga* was translated into English in the 19th century by the poet William Morris. He also tells the story in his long narrative poem *Sigurd the Volsung and the Fall of the Niblungs*, an epic in four books.

See also: BALMUNG; BRYNHILD; FAFNIR; GUDRUN; LOKI; *NIBELUNGENLIED*; ODIN; REGIN; SIEGFRIED; SIGMUND; SIGNY; *RING DES NIBELUNGEN, DER*

3107

**Volturnus**   In Roman mythology, a god of the Tiber River. He was identified in later Roman belief with Tiberinus, a legendary king for whom the Tiber was named after he drowned there. His feast was 27 August.

See also: TIBERINUS

3108

**Volva** (carrier of a magic staff)   In Norse mythology, the sibyl who recited the *Voluspa*, the first poem of the *Poetic Edda*, which narrates the creation and destruction of the world.

See also: *POETIC EDDA*; SIBYLS

3109

**Vortigern**   In medieval British mythology, a monk who killed King Constans and usurped his throne. He built a tower, to which he fled when his land was invaded by Ambrosius Aurelius, and he was burned to death.

See also: BRUT; CONSTANS; MERLIN

3110

**Votan** (Voton) (the breast, the heart?)   In Mayan mythology, a culture hero and god. His consort was Ixchel. At some time in the past Votan had come from Valum Votan (the land of Votan) in the far east. He was sent by God to divide out and assign to the different races their portion of the earth and to give each its own language.

His message was brought to the Tzentals (Tzendals), a Mayan tribe living in Mexico. According to Daniel G. Brinton in *American Hero-Myths* (1882), "Previous to his arrival they were ignorant, barbarous, and without fixed habitations. He collected them into villages, taught them how to cultivate the maize and cotton, and invented the hieroglyphic signs, which they learned to carve on the walls of their temples. It was even said that he wrote his own history in them."

Votan also instituted civil laws and reformed religious worship, earning the title "master of the sacred drum" because of its use in ritual dances. He also invented the calendar and founded the cities of Palenque, Nachan, and Huehuetlán. In Heuhuetlán he built an underground temple "by merely blowing with his breath. In this gloomy mansion he deposited his treasures and appointed a priestess to guard it, for whose assistance he created the tapirs."

When it was time for him to depart, after he had civilized the Indians, he "penetrated through a cave into the underground, and found his way to the root of heaven."

See also: IXCHEL

3111
**Vourukasha** In Persian mythology, sea god or the sea. Also the name of the heavenly lake in which grows the tree of life.

3112
**Vretil** In medieval Jewish folklore, angel identified with the "man clothed with linen" carrying "a writer's inkhorn by his side," described by the prophet Ezekiel (9:2). Vretil wears linen since it is ritually clean, whereas wool, coming from an animal, is not. The "man clothed with linen" in Ezekiel (9:4) is to go "through the midst of Jerusalem and set a mark upon the foreheads of the men that sigh and that cry for all the abominations that be done in the midst thereof."

See also: EZEKIEL

3113
**Vritra** (restrainer) In Hindu mythology, the demon of drought, constantly at war with Indra, the storm god. Vritra is sometimes called Vritrasura or Ahi, though in some texts Ahi is a distinct personality.

See also: INDRA

*Vulcan (Hephaestus)*

3114
**Vulcan** (Vulcanus, Volcanus) (volcano) In Roman mythology, the ancient Italian fire god, god of forging and smelting, equivalent of the Greek god Hephaestus.

As smith (or god) of the forge, Vulcan was called Mulciber (the softener or smelter). As a beneficent god of nature who ripens the fruit with his warmth, he was the husband of Maia (or Maiesta), the Italian goddess of spring. Both Vulcan and Hephaestus had sacrifices offered to them by the *flamen Volcanalis* priests after Vulcan became identified with the Greek fire god Hephaestus. When the Roman Venus was identified with the Greek goddess Aphrodite, Vulcan was regarded as her husband. Chaucer, in The Knight's Tale, writes, "Venus . . . spouse to Vulcanus." Vulcan's best-known shrine in Rome was the Volcanal, a level space raised above the surface of the Comitium and serving as the hearth of the spot where the citizens' assemblies were held. Vulcan's chief festival was the Vulcanalia, observed 23 August, when certain fish were thrown into the fire on the hearth and races were held in the Circus Flaminius. Sacrifices were offered to Vulcan as god of metalworking on 23 May, the day appointed for a cleansing of the trumpets used in worship. As lord of fire, Vulcan was also god of conflagrations. His temple in Rome was situated in the Campus Martius. Juturna and Stata Mater, goddesses who caused fires to be quenched, were worshiped along with him at the festival of Vulcanalia.

Shakespeare, in *Hamlet*, has Hamlet speak to Horatio, making reference to Vulcan:

. . . if his occulted guilt
Do not itself unkennel in one speech,
It is a damned ghost that we have seen,
And my imaginations are as foul
As Vulcan's smithy. (3.2.85–89)

The references are to Hamlet's own imagination as well as to his plot to discover the guilt of Claudius.

There is a 17th-century copy of Breughel the Elder's *Venus at the Forge of Vulcan* as well as a brilliant *Forge of Vulcan* by Velázquez, painted in 1630.

In English the word *volcano* comes from Vulcan, as does the verb *vulcanize*, the chemical process for treating crude rubber.

See also: APHRODITE; CHAUCER; HEPHAESTUS; MAIA; VENUS

3115

**Vulture**   A large bird that feeds on dead animals. The ancient Egyptian cult of the vulture dates from predynastic times, when the pharaoh was called Nekhebet (lord of the city of the vulture), referring to the vulture goddess Nekhebet. The bird was also associated with Mut and Neith. Vultures were believed to follow men into battle, hover over those who would die, and later eat their flesh. Thus the bird was sacred to the Greek war god Ares and his Roman counterpart, Mars. All vultures were believed to be female and to be impregnated by turning their backs to the south or southwest wind while flying. They were believed to bring forth their young in three years.

See also: ARES; MARS; MUT; NEITH; NEKHEBET; PHARAOH

**Wabosso** (white hare or maker of white)   In North American mythology (Algonquian), brother of Nanabozho, culture hero and trickster.

See also: TRICKSTER

**Wade**   In northern mythology, giant father of Wayland the Smith, who appears in Anglo-Saxon and Danish tales.

See also: *FRITHJOF'S SAGA*; WAYLAND THE SMITH

**Wahan Tanka** (creator, great spirit)   In North American Indian mythology (Oglala Lakota), Great Spirit, who appears as Wanbli Galeshka, the spotted eagle. The sun, sky, earth, and rock are all Wahan Tanka.

**Waki-Ikazuchi**   In Japanese mythology, one of the Ikazuchi, the eight gods of thunder.

See also: IKAZUCHI

**Wakinyan-Tanka**   In North American Indian mythology (Oglala Lakota), great thunderbird of the west, protector of the sacred pipe.

See also: THUNDERBIRD

**Wakonda**   In North American Indian mythology (Omaha), creator god, in whose mind all things existed until they found a place for bodily existence.

**Walangada** (belonging to the sky)   In Australian mythology, a primal being of unidentified form who ascended to the sky to become the Milky Way.

**Walpurga, St.** (Walpurgis, Walburga, Bugga) Died 779. In Christian legend, abbess of Heidenheim. Invoked against coughs, rabies, frenzy, and plague and for a good harvest. One of her feast days, 1 May, is preceded by the *Walpurgisnacht* in Germany, which, according to folklore and legend, is the night when witches gather together on the Brocken—also called Blocksberg, the highest peak of the Harz Mountains—and revel and carouse with demons.

The name *Walpurgisnacht* derives from the English saint Walpurga, who was the niece of St. Boniface. She spent some 27 years of her life at the monastery in Winburn, in Dorset, England, before she went on a missionary journey with 10 other nuns to Germany. She was made the first abbess of a Benedictine nunnery at Heidenheim, between Munich and Nuremberg. During her lifetime she was noted for her skill in medicine, and her tomb was credited with healing powers. Since the earlier pagan festival marked the beginning of spring, the saint's feast became confused with the pagan one, and the witches' sabbath was named after the nun.

The *Walpurgisnacht* appealed particularly to 19th-century German artists. Goethe twice treated the theme: once in a poem he called a "dramatic-ballad," *Die erste Walpurgisnacht* (The First Walpurgis Night) and in *Faust* (parts 1 and 2). Mendelssohn set Goethe's text for soloists, chorus, and orchestra as *Die erste Walpurgisnacht*, Opus 60, in 1832.

Thomas Mann's novel *The Magic Mountain* has a chapter entitled "Walpurgis-Night," dealing with the Shrovetide festival. Mann, in recalling the name that was used by Goethe, wished to stress the similarity of his theme with that of Goethe's *Faust*.

In art St. Walpurga is usually portrayed as a royal abbess with a small flask of oil on a book. Sometimes she is shown with three ears of corn in her hand (bringing in the symbolism of the pagan festival). Her main festival is now observed on 25 February.

See also: BONIFACE, ST.

3124

**Walwalag Sisters**    In Australian mythology, two sisters who were eaten and regurgitated by the Rainbow Snake. Their story is reenacted in various fertility rites of the tribes.

See also: RAINBOW SNAKE

3125

**Wambeen**    In Australian mythology, an evil being who sends lightning and fire. When he comes down to earth, he kills travelers. He is recognized by an evil odor.

3126

**Wandering Jew**    In medieval anti-Semitic legend, a Jew who was said to have cursed Jesus on his way to be crucified and was punished by having to wait for Christ's Second Coming. The earliest mention of the legend is in the 13th-century chronicles of the Abbey of St. Albans. According to that account, when Jesus was on his way out of Pilate's hall, a porter, called Cartaphilus, "impiously struck him on the back with his hand and said in mockery, 'Go quicker, Jesus, go quicker; why do you loiter?' And Jesus, looking back on him with severe countenance, said to him, 'I am going, and you will wait till I return.'" The chronicle goes on to say that Cartaphilus was 30 at the time. He later became a Christian and, according to the account, is still alive, waiting for the Second Coming of Christ.

Though the name Cartaphilus is given in the earliest account, other names have been given to the Wandering Jew. In Latin versions he is called Johannes Buttadeus (John the God Smiter). He was seen in Antwerp in the 13th century, again in the 15th and a third time in the 16th. His last appearance was in Brussels in 1774. In German versions he is called Ahasuerus, a cobbler, and in other versions he is part of the Wild Hunt. The medieval legend inspired Goethe's *Der ewige Jude*, Edgar Quinet's prose drama *Ahasvérus*, George Groly's *Salathiel*, and Eugene Sue's long novel *The Wandering Jew*.

See also: AHASUERUS

3127

**Wanga**    In Haitian voodoo, an evil spell that causes death in seven days.

**Wang Jung**   305–234 B.C.E. In Chinese legend, one of the seven Chu-lin Ch'i-Hsien (Seven Immortals). He was once a court minister but left his position for a life of pleasure. Once he sold a plum tree cut from his estate only after removing the plums so it could not be grown elsewhere. In Japanese legend he is called Oju.

See also: CHU-LIN CH'I-HSIEN

**Wang Mu** (Mother Wang, Queen Mother)   In Chinese mythology, the spirit of metal, who was born with a tiger's teeth. She is one of the five spirits of natural forces, the Wu Lao.

See also: WU LAO

**Washington, George**   In American history and folklore, first president of the United States, father of his country. The best-known Washington legend was invented by Parson Mason Weems in *The Life of George Washington . . . .* According to Weems, when Washington was about six years old his father gave him a hatchet. "One day, in the garden, he unluckily tried the edge of his hatchet on the body of a beautiful English cherry tree, which he barked terribly." When his father discovered that the tree had been chopped down, he asked who might be responsible. "George," said his father, "do you know who killed that beautiful little cherry tree yonder in the garden?" "I can't tell a lie, Pa; you know I can't. I did cut it with my hatchet." The father then called George into his loving arms. This moral tale, which turns George into an American saint, was painted by Grant Wood.

Nathaniel Hawthorne, the great American novelist, commented that George Washington "had no nakedness but was born with his clothes on and his hair powdered." Though there is no history in the cherry tree tale, there is history in the legend of the crossing of the Delaware in December 1776, as well as in the Valley Forge story. In each case greater drama has been added

by folklore. In Emmanuel Leutze's famous painting of the crossing of the Delaware, for example, the flag portrayed was not in use until 1777. Another example of the sainting of Washington portrays him kneeling in a lonely clearing near Valley Forge. According to legend, a man told his wife, "I am greatly deceived if God do not, through Washington, work out a great salvation for America."

George Washington was far from being a believer in established religion. In fact, he almost had to be dragged to church. The cult of Washington found its greatest growth during the 19th-century. Americans compared him to Moses, Jesus, and various saints. He was often portrayed as a Roman nobleman or a knight. One 19th-century Chinese painting portrays Washington ascending to heaven with an angel.

**Watauineiwa** (the most ancient one)   In the mythology of the Yahgan Indians of Tierra del Fuego, supreme being. He is a beneficent god with no body, and he lives in the heavens. Though not the creator, Watauineiwa sustains life and is believed to be the upholder of moral order.

**Wave Maidens**   In Norse mythology, the nine daughters of the sea god Aegir and his sister-wife Ran, mothers of Heimdall. They are Gialp (yelper), Greip (gripper), Egia (foamer), Augeia (sand strewer), Ulfrun (she-wolf), Aurgiafa (sorrow-whelmer), Sindur (dusk), Atla (fury), Aiarnsaxa (iron sword). They appear in the *Poetic Edda* in the Lay of Hyndla.

See also: AEGIR; HEIMDALL; *POETIC EDDA*; RAN

**Wayland the Smith** (artful smith)   In medieval English legend, the wonder-working smith, sometimes called simply Wayland or Smith and in Norse, Volund the Smith. Wayland was the son of a sailor and a mermaid. He was king of the elves and a maker of magic articles, such as a feather boat, a garment with wings, a solid gold arm ring, and magic swords. Wayland raised the young Siegfried in the forest and made his sword, Balmung, for him. Wayland's brothers married Valkyries. Despite his cleverness, Wayland was made a prisoner by Nidudr, the evil king of Sweden, who had his feet mutilated. Eventually, Wayland killed two sons of Nidudr and raped his daughter Bodhilda. He set the skulls of the slain boys in gold and gave them to Nidudr. He gave their mother jewelry fashioned from their eyes. Their teeth were made into a breast pin for their sister. After he had given his gifts and told Nidudr what they were, he flew away to Valhalla on his magic wings. Sir Walter Scott mentions Wayland in his novel *Kenilworth*, which says that he lived in a cave near Lambourn, Berkshire, since called Wayland Smith's Cave. It was believed that if a traveler tied up his horse there, left sixpence for a fee, and hid from sight, he would find his horse shod when he returned.

See also: BALMUNG; SIEGFRIED; VALHALLA; VALKYRIES

3134

**Weasel**   A small carnivorous mammal with a long slender body. For the ancient Greeks the weasel was a symbol of evil. If one appeared at a meeting, the group would disperse. In Apuleius's *Golden Ass* witches transform themselves into weasels. It was believed by medieval Christians that the weasel conceived through the ear. For the medieval Christian it became a symbol of unfaithfulness, though there was also a medieval belief that the Virgin Mary was impregnated through the ear. The saying was "God spoke through the angel and the Virgin was impregnated through the ear." The *Gesta Romanorum* uses the weasel as a symbol of St. John or Christ himself because the weasel was an enemy of the basilisk, or serpent—the devil. In the 1840s

popular song "Pop Goes the Weasel," the weasel may stand for a whore.

See also: BASILISK; VIRGIN MARY

3135

**Webster, Daniel**   1782–1852. In American history and folklore, lawyer, public official, statesman, and orator. He appears in Stephen Vincent Benét's short story "The Devil and Daniel Webster." In it Jabez Stone, a New Hampshire farmer, sells his soul to Mr. Scratch, the devil. When Mr. Scratch comes to collect, Daniel Webster defends Stone before a jury of depraved characters and wins the case. Benét dramatized the tale, and Douglas Moore wrote the music for the opera *The Devil and Daniel Webster*. A Hollywood film of the tale was made titled *All That Money Can Buy* (1941), starring Walter Huston as Mr. Scratch.

3136

**Wei T'o**   In Chinese Buddhism, a god who protects the Buddhist religion. His image is placed in the first hall of a Buddhist monastery. He is portrayed in complete armor and holding a scepter-shaped weapon of assault.

3137

**Wele** (high one)   In African mythology (Abaluyia of Kenya), creator sky god who built his home, heaven, on pillars and made it always bright. The first human couple also lived in a house that stood up in the air. When they went home, they always pulled up the ladder because there were monsters down below. Wele is said to have sent death as a punishment for man's cruelty. Once Wele observed how a farmer refused food to a hungry chameleon. Angered, the chameleon cursed the farmer, saying the farmer would die. The chameleon left and was later fed by a snake. Wele then decided that humans should die for their evil natures, but the kind snake should be rewarded with renewed life by shedding his skin.

See also: MULUNGU; MWAMBU AND SELA; OLO-RUN; UNKULUNKULU; WERE

**Wenceslaus and Ludmilla, Sts.**  Tenth century. In Christian legend, Wenceslaus is the patron saint of Bohemia. Wenceslaus's feast day is 28 September, and Ludmilla's is 16 September.

Wenceslaus was brought up a Christian by his grandmother, Ludmilla. Drahomia, his mother, and her son Boleslaus were pagans and opposed the conversion of Bohemia to Christianity by Wenceslaus and Ludmilla. Drahomia and Boleslaus had Ludmilla killed by hired assassins who strangled her to death with a veil or a rope. Wenceslaus, however, made peace with his mother and brother. After Wenceslaus married, Boleslaus realized he would not be made king. He therefore arranged for the murder of Wenceslaus. He invited the king to celebrate the feast of Sts. Cosmas and Damien. On his way to mass, Wenceslaus was killed by his brother and some hired henchmen. The people immediately claimed the king as a martyr.

The English carol "Good King Wenceslaus," written in the 19th century by J. M. Neale, is about the sainted king. Antonin Dvořák's oratorio *St. Ludmilla* is based on the medieval legend.

In medieval Christian art St. Wenceslaus is portrayed as a king with an eagle on his banner or shield. St. Ludmilla is shown with a veil or rope, symbols of her martyrdom. Wenceslaus is the English form of the Czech form Vaclav.

See also: COSMAS AND DAMIEN, STS.

**Wen Chang Ti-chun**  Fourth century C.E.? In Chinese Taoist mythology, the deified mortal Chang Ya-Tzu, worshiped as the principal god of literature. In Chinese art he is often portrayed holding a pen and a book on which is written: "Heaven decides literary success." Sometimes he

*Wen Chang Ti-chun*

is portrayed as a handsome young man in a sitting position.

**Wenenut**  In Egyptian mythology, goddess portrayed as a woman with the head of a hare or rabbit. Wenenut usually holds a knife in each

*Wenenut*

hand, identifying her with the destructive goddess Sekhet. But in her more benevolent aspect Wenenut holds a scepter in one hand and the ankh, sign of life, in the other. Her male counterpart was the hare god Wonenu, who was considered a form of Osiris, the god of resurrection.

See also: ANKH; OSIRIS; SEKHET

---

3141

**Were** (father of grace)    In African mythology (Luo of Kenya), creator god, cause of life and death, who punishes evildoers with his thunderbolts. Sacrifices and offerings to Were are made in the morning under large trees.

See also: WELE

---

3142

**Werewolf** (man wolf)    A human being who is transformed into a wolf by any number of methods. The belief in werewolves is international in scope, and in those countries where there are no wolves, the fiercest wild animal of that region replaces the wolf. Information on werewolves can be traced back as far as Herodotus in the fifth century B.C.E. "Scyths and Greeks who live in Scythia tell that every *Neuroi* [Proto-Slav-Eastern Balt] is transformed once a year for some days to wolf, after which he resumes his former shape."

These bloodthirsty animals hunt other animals, occasionally humans, and eat the meat raw. They are nocturnal and must assume their human form before daybreak. Humans can become werewolves by donning a wolf skin or a magic belt. In some countries, particularly in eastern Europe, humans become wolves by passing through a bow formed by poles or stakes driven into the ground or through a natural opening in a live tree. The transformation brings about a radical change in the person's behavior, making him a carnivore. Reversing the process will restore the human form. One legend in the Baltic countries tells of a man who offered a wolf a piece of bread on the point of his knife. The wolf took the bread and the knife and ran into the

woods. Later the man recognized his knife at a merchant's store in Riga, whereupon he was richly rewarded by the merchant. Among some Slavs, werewolves and vampires have merged. Rarely, werewolves also function as protectors of communities. Fear of werewolves may also have contributed to Charles Perrault's rendition of Little Red Riding Hood.

See also: LITTLE RED RIDING HOOD

---

3143

**Wesak** (Vesak)    In Theravada Buddhism, the combined feast of the Buddha's birth, enlightenment, and *parimbbana* (death and Nirvana), observed at the May full moon.

See also: NIRVANA

---

3144

**Whale**    A large air-breathing marine mammal with a fishlike body. In Christian folklore the whale has often been equated with the devil or demonic forces. One medieval Christian belief was that a whale would lure fish by its sweet breath and then eat them, just as the devil would lure a person to sin. One tale found in the Jewish Talmud tells how sailors could mistake a whale for an island and board the monster. After they made a fire, the whale would begin to descend, taking the crew to their watery death. The tale was also told in medieval Europe. Milton's *Paradise Lost* gives a variant of the tale and identifies the whale with Leviathan, the primeval dragon in the Old Testament (Psalm 74:14) that Yahweh, the Hebrew God, subdued. In the biblical Book of Jonah the prophet fled the Lord by boarding a ship so that he would not have to preach. A storm arose; the sailors blamed Jonah and cast him into the sea. "Now the Lord has prepared a great fish to swallow Jonah, and Jonah was in the belly of the fish three days and three nights" (Jonah 1:17). The author of the Gospel According to St. Matthew, not satisfied with "great fish," writes that Jonah "was three days and three nights in the whale's belly" (Matt. 12:40). The symbolism was to suggest that

Christ would be three days and three nights in the tomb before he would arise. The most famous use of the whale in modern literature is Herman Melville's novel *Moby Dick, or The White Whale*, in which scholars see the whale as a symbol of the devil, God, a combination of both,. or man. There are numerous motifs associated with the whale in the *Motif Index of Folk Literature*.

See also: JONAH; KRAKEN; TALMUD; YAHWEH

3145

**Wheat** Cereal grasses cultivated for their grain, often called corn in English literature. Wheat was sacred to the Greek goddess Demeter, who gave it as a gift to humankind. In Roman mythology, wheat was sacred to Ceres, goddess of the harvest. In Christian ritual, wheat, which makes bread, forms part of the Holy Eucharist. In French Christian folklore, the Virgin Mary is sometimes addressed as *Notre-Dame Penetière* (Our Lady the Bread Giver).

See also: CORN; DEMETER

3146

**Whitsunday** In Christian ritual, English name for the Feast of Pentecost, ranking in importance with Christmas and Easter. Whitsunday commemorates the descent of the Holy Spirit on the Apostles and disciples, the founding of the Church, the gifts of the Holy Spirit, and the mission to bring the Christian faith to all peoples throughout the world. The name *Pentecost* comes from the Greek word for 50 and refers to the 50 days after the Jewish Passover, which the ancient Jews celebrated as Shavuoth, a festival of thanksgiving for the year's harvest (Exodus 23:16). The Jewish feast also commemorated the giving of the Law of Moses. The entire time from Passover to Pentecost was also called Pentecost, and thus the disciples were gathered together, as described in Acts 2:1ff, at the end of the 50 days. The early Church adopted the Greek name from the Jewish feast. When the feast is called Whitsunday, as in *The Book of Common Prayer*, it refers to the custom in northern European countries of conferring baptism during the time. The candidates for baptism were dressed in white, thus White-Sunday, or Whitsunday. Since it was too cold in many northern European countries to baptize during the great Easter vigil, many of the customs were transferred to Pentecost.

As part of the great feast the hymn *Veni Sancte Spiritus* (Come Holy Spirit) is sung during the Eucharist. The hymn is attributed to Stephen Langton, archbishop of Canterbury in the early 12th century. In England during the Middle Ages Pentecost was the time when people would contribute to the upkeep of the church building, as well as give money to the cathedral if their house had a chimney. The offering to the cathedral was called Whitsun-darthing or smoke-farthing. Local churches also sold church ale, often called Whitsun ale. Other European Christians would let loose doves from the church rafters or send down hot or lighted coals (or "tongues of fire") to recapture the descent of the Holy Spirit on the Apostles. The doves were released when the priest intoned the *Veni Sancte Spiritus*, and the people made loud noises with drums, whistles, and other noisemakers to symbolize the sound "as of a violent wind blowing," as described in Acts 2:2. In some countries in Europe on the night before Pentecost people still walk barefoot on the grass to obtain its healing power, while others collect the dew of the eve of Pentecost on cakes or bread and serve it to the animals to protect them from illness. The Maypole, so hated by the English Puritans, was also one of the symbols connected with Pentecost. A play on the name referred to it as Wisdom Sunday.

See also: APOSTLE

3147

**Whittington, Dick** d. 1423. In English history and legend, a poor orphaned country boy who becomes the lord mayor of London. Dick heard that London was "paved with gold" and went there to earn a living. At the point of near starvation Dick found work with a kind merchant's family as a cook's helper. The cook, however, mistreated Dick, and the boy ran away. Resting by a roadside, he heard the Cow bells ring, and they seemed to say to him: "Turn again, Whittington, thrice Lord Mayor of London." So Dick returned to his master. In time his master made Dick an offer to go on a ship bound for Morocco. Dick had nothing but a cat, which accompanied him. When he arrived in Morocco, he discovered that the king of Morocco was having trouble with mice, and Whittington's cat eliminated them. This so pleased the king that he bought the cat from Whittington at a fantastic price. Dick invested the money, married his master's daughter, was knighted, and was thrice elected lord mayor of London. An epitaph destroyed in the Great Fire of London said:

Beneath this stone lies Whittington,
Sir Richard rightly named,
Who three times Lord Mayor served in
   London,
In which he ne'er was blamed.
He rose from indigence to wealth
By industry and that,
For lo! he scorned to gain by stealth
What he got by a cat.

3148
**Wi-haru** (the place where the wise words of those who have gone before us are resting)   In North American Indian mythology (Pawnee), an invisible but sacred spot in a traditional Pawnee home, between the buffalo altar at the rear of the lodge and the central fireplace, all of these on a line from the entrance.

3149
**Wihio**   In North American Indian mythology (Cheyenne), the trickster. In one myth Wihio persuades a coyote to dress as a baby, while he dresses as a woman, so that they can get some food from a man who stores tongue. The man

gives the tongue to Wihio, who proceeds to eat it all. "Give me some too; I'm also hungry," the coyote cries out. But Wihio just continues to eat the tongue and dips his fingers in the soup for the coyote to lick. When the coyote threatens to reveal the deception to the man who gave them food, Wihio takes him out and throws him into the lake.

See also: COYOTE; TRICKSTER

3150
**Wild Hunt** (German *wilde Jagd*, French *mesnie Hellequin*)   In German folklore, a series of legends concerning a ghostly hunter often accompanied by dogs or spirits and often engaged in hunting down a woman, a supernatural being. Sometimes the hunter is associated with a historical figure, such as Dietrich of Bern or Satan, but most often with Odin. Legends tell of a woman with huge breasts slung over her shoulder rushing by, then the hunter passes, and finally the hunter returns with the captured woman. There is usually a noise like wind in the trees. In Austria in the 1930s there was an attempt by Otto Höfler and others to suggest a connection with an ecstatic Odin cult, which still survived in the German-speaking lands in many parades and processions, particularly during certain times of the year, Shrovetide for example. Most scholars tend, however, toward an interpretation that sees remnants of an Indo-European warrior cult of young men dressed in animal skins who were being initiated into a warrior band that united them with their fallen companions. The motif of the wild hunt is widely known in folk tales (E501.11ff.).

See also: ASGARDREIA; DIETRICH OF BERN; MOTIF; ODIN; SATAN

3151
**William of Norwich, St.**   Died 1137? In Christian legend, child saint said to have been "ritually murdered" by the Jews. The accusation was quite common during the Middle Ages and was used by secular and religious authorities in

their attempt to destroy the Jews. This is usually referred to as the "blood libel legend." Feast, 9 April.

Thomas de Monmouth in his *History of the Martyrdom of William of Norwich*, a contemporary account, writes that the 12-year-old William, who was apprenticed to a tanner at Norwich, England, was killed on Good Friday, 9 April 1137, by Jews. The lurid account describes how the boy was taken, gagged, and crucified. After he was dead, his body was placed in a sack and carried to the city gates of Thorpe Wood, where it was to be burned. The murderers were surprised and left the body hanging near a tree. A chapel was afterward erected on the spot and dedicated to St. William in the Wood. In 1144 the body was removed to the churchyard of the Cathedral of the Holy Trinity.

Numerous other child saints with similar tales abound in medieval Christian legend. Among them are Hugh of Lincoln, St. Janot of Cologne, St. Richard of Pontoise, St. Michael of Sappendelf, St. Simon of Trent, St. Vernier, and St. Werner or Garnier.

See also: BLOOD LIBEL LEGEND

**William of Orange** (will-helmet)   In the Charlemagne cycle of legends, a hero who appears in numerous French epics. All we know of the historical William is that he was a contemporary of Charlemagne, whom he served as a military leader and administrator. In legend, he is a devoted protector of Louis, Charlemagne's son, as well as a defender of the Christian faith against the Muslims of Spain. Seven French epics describe his life. Dante's *The Divine Comedy* places him in Paradise in the sphere of Crusaders, beside Charlemagne and Godfrey of Boulogne. He also appears in medieval Norse, Italian, and Latin legends. In some accounts he is credited with being a saint because he spent his last years in a monastery.

See also: CHARLEMAGNE

**3152**

**3153**

**William of Palermo**   In medieval legend, a hero, son of King Apulia of Palermo. As heir to the throne, William's life was in danger, so he was carried away by Alphonse, a werewolf prince of Spain who had been transformed by his evil stepmother. Alphonse brought the child to Rome, where William was adopted by a shepherd. When the boy grew up, he became a page to the Roman emperor's daughter, Melior. The two fell in love and after many adventures were married. Alphonse, the werewolf, was finally disenchanted. William appears in the English poem *William of Palerne*, based on a French metrical romance.

See also: WEREWOLF

**3154**

**William of York, St.** (will-helmet)   Died 1154. In Christian legend, William Fitzherbert, archbishop of York. Feast, 8 June.

William's appointment as archbishop was opposed by the Cistercians. St. Bernard, also a Cistercian, described William as a "man rotten from the soles of his feet to the crown of his head." After taking the case to Rome and much arguing back and forth, William finally took his office in 1154. Less than a year later he was dead. He had been seized by violent pains while celebrating mass on Trinity Sunday. Officially, it was said he died a natural death, though he is listed as a martyr in some medieval church calendars. He was canonized in 1220 on account of the many miracles that were reported at his tomb.

In medieval English Christian art William is often portrayed in his episcopal robes. Sometimes he is shown as a tonsured monk praying in the wilderness with a dove nearby. His shield had eight lozenges.

See also: BERNARD, ST.

**3155**

**William the Conqueror**   c. 1027–1087. In English history and legend, king of England and duke of Normandy after the Norman Conquest in 1066. At the Battle of Hastings between the Norman and Saxons, King Harold of the Saxons was killed. William at once marched on to London and was crowned on Christmas Day at Westminster. Many of the people believed that Harold was the rightful king, not William, even though the church supported William's claims. William died after a horseback accident. At his funeral, according to legend, his body burst open, and a foul odor was emitted, forcing the mourners to flee the church. The conquered people said it was God's judgment on the Norman for killing Harold, the last of the Saxon kings. The conflict of William and Harold is the subject of Tennyson's verse play *Harold* and Hope Muntz's novel *The Golden Warrior: The Story of Harold and William*.

3156

**Willow**    A tree; in Near Eastern mythology, sacred to the Great Mother goddess. Called Artemis Lygodesma, she was portrayed as a mother suckling a child decked with branches of the *lygos*, a member of the willow family. In Greek mythology, the willow was sacred to Hera, Circe, Hecate, and Persephone, all forms of the Great Mother goddess and associated with life and death. In Jewish folklore, the willow is associated with mourning, sadness, and death, as reflected in Psalm 137:1. In Christian symbolism, the willow is one of the trees associated with the Virgin Mary, and in Chinese mythology, it is associated with the goddess of mercy, Kuan Yin. Shakespeare combines the image of the willow's sadness with that of death in Desdemona's "Willow Song" before she is murdered on her marriage bed by Othello. In *The Merchant of Venice* (5:1) Lorenzo refers to Dido, queen of Carthage, as holding a "willow in her hand" the night she killed herself for love of Aeneas, who deserted her.

See also: AENEAS; DIDO; HECATE; HERA; PERSEPHONE; VIRGIN MARY

3157

**Windigo** (Windlgo)    In North American Indian mythology (Chippewa/Ojibwa), cannibal ice monster, threat to all who practice evil medicine. During famine, humans can also become Windigo and seek human flesh. Hunters and trappers often reported sightings of Windigos and warned about places to avoid.

3158

**Windingo**    In American folklore, a ghost about 15 feet tall who frightened the citizens of Roseau, Minnesota, for generations. Each time the ghost was seen, a person died. In Indian folklore the Windingo was the terrible cannibal spirit of the cold, and thus the Indians of this region kept their children extra safe during the cold winters.

3159

**Winefred, St.** (Winefride, Wenefrida, Gwenfrewi, Guinevra) (blessed reconciliation)    Died 650. In Christian legend, saint venerated at Holywell, Wales. Feast, 3 November.

According to medieval Christian legend, one day Cradorus (Caradoc), the son of King Alan of North Wales, found Winefred alone in her father's house and tried to rape her. She fled, pursued by Cradorus, who cut off her head. When the head of Winefred hit the ground, a fountain sprang up, later called Winefred's Well or Holywell. Her spiritual teacher, St. Beno (Beuno), came upon her head and set it back on her torso, and the girl returned home in one piece.

In medieval Christian art St. Winefred is portrayed with a sword, a fountain at her feet, and a red ring around her neck to indicate that her head had been cut off. Sometime she is depicted in art like St. Denis, carrying her head in her hands.

See also: DENIS, ST.

**Wisdom to Fools**   Jewish fable found in the Midrash.

One day a woman asked Rabbi Yose bar Halaftah, "Why is it written in the Book of Daniel that God gives wisdom to the wise? Would it not be better if he gave wisdom to fools, who need it?"

The rabbi said he would explain the answer by a parable. "Imagine two people who wish to borrow money from you. One is rich and one is poor. To which of the two would you lend your money?"

"The rich man," replied the woman.

"Why?" the rabbi asked.

"Because if he loses his money, he'll find some means to repay me. But where will a poor man get money to repay me?"

"Well," replied Rabbi Yose, "if God gave wisdom to fools, what would they do with it? They would waste it. That's why he gives wisdom to the wise to use in study."

See also: MIDRASH

---

3161

**Witch of Endor**   In the Bible, O.T., a medium consulted by King Saul on the day of the battle in which the spirit of the dead prophet Samuel was raised. Samuel told Saul that he would be dead the next day and would join him in the land of the dead (1 Sam. 28:7–25). Handel's oratorio *Saul* contains a magnificent scene for the Witch of Endor.

See also: SAMUEL; SAUL

---

3162

**Witch of Wellfleet**   In American folklore of New England, a 17th-century witch, believed to be Goody Hallett, who always wore scarlet shoes. Hallett was 15 years old when she was seduced by a pirate named Samuel "Black" Bellamy. When she was found to be pregnant, she was arrested and whipped by the townspeople. Some said she murdered the child. While she was in prison, the devil, dressed as a handsome French dandy, appeared, and she signed away her soul to get revenge on Bellamy, whose ship was then sunk by the devil. She appeared in many guises over the years, often causing storms to drown seamen. When a storm arose, people said, "Thar be pore Goody, dancin' with the lost souls." Her exact end is not known, although some say she was strangled to death by the devil when she beat him at dice. Others say she married an Indian.

---

3163

**Wiwonderrer**   In Australian mythology, stone animals who kill human beings. They can be destroyed only if speared in the eyes or the mouth.

---

3164

**Woden** (Voden, Votan, Wotan, Wootan)   The Anglo-Saxon name of the Norse god Odin. Wednesday (Woden's day) is derived from his name. He was the god of agriculture, and thus Wednesday was considered to be especially favorable for planting. In Richard Wagner's *Der Ring des Nibelungen* he is called Wotan.

See also: ODIN; *RING DES NIBELUNGEN, DER*

---

3165

**Wolf and the Crane, The**   Aesopic fable found in various collections throughout the world. A wolf, in gorging himself on some poor animal he had killed, got a small bone stuck in his throat. The pain was terrible, and he ran up and down beseeching every animal he met to relieve him. None of the animals, however, felt very sorry for the wolf, for, as one of them put it, "That bone which is stuck in the wolf's throat might just as well be one of mine."

Finally the suffering wolf met the crane. "I'll give you anything," he whined, "if you will help take this bone out of my throat."

The crane, moved by his entreaties and promises of reward, ventured her long neck down the wolf's throat and drew out the bone. She then modestly asked for the promised reward.

"Reward?" barked the wolf, showing his teeth. "Of all the ungrateful creatures! I have permitted you to live to tell your grandchildren that you put your head in a wolf's mouth without having it bitten off, and then you ask for a reward! Get out of here before I change my mind!"

Moral: *Those who live on expectation are sure to be disappointed.*

The fable probably originated in India, where in one account the Buddha tells the story of a lion and a crane to illustrate the ingratitude of the wicked. The fable ends: "The master, having given the lesson, summed up the moral: 'At the time the lion was Devaddatta [the Buddhist Judas] and the crane was myself.'" The Buddhistic form of the fable first became known to Europe in 1691 in De la Loubere's *Description of Siam.* One version, which uses the lion instead of the wolf, was used by Rabbi Jochanan ben Saccai (c. 120 C.E.) to persuade the Jews not to revolt against the Romans. The account is found in *Bereshith Rabba,* a commentary on Genesis. The fable is pictured on the Bayeux tapestry.

See also: AESOPIC FABLES; DEVADDATTA

*The Wolf and the Lamb*

3166

**Wolf and the Lamb, The**   Aesopic fable found in various collections throughout the world.

As a wolf was lapping at the head of a running brook he spied a lamb daintily paddling his feet

some distance down the stream. "There's my supper," thought the wolf. "But I'll have to find some excuse for attacking such a harmless creature." So he shouted down at the lamb: "How dare you foul my stream."

"But you must be mistaken," bleated the lamb. "How can I be spoiling your water, since it runs from you to me and not from me to you?"

"Don't argue," snapped the wolf. "I know you. You are the one who was saying those ugly things about me behind my back a year ago."

"Oh, sir," replied the lamb, trembling, "a year ago I was not even born."

"Well," snarled the wolf, "if it was not you, then it was your father." Without another word he fell on the helpless lamb and tore her to pieces.

Moral: *Any excuse will serve a tyrant.*

The fable appears in Tibet and in Madagascar. In the *Jatakas, or Birth-Stories of the Former Lives of the Buddha,* a panther meets a kid and complains that his tail has been stepped on. The kid gently points out that the panther's face was toward him, so how could he have stepped on his tail?

The panther says: "My tail covers the earth."

The kid replies: "But I came through the air."

The panther says: "I saw you frightening the beasts by coming through the air. You prevented my getting any prey."

See also: AESOPIC FABLES; *JATAKA*

3167

**Wolfgang, St.** (wolf-strife)   Died 994. In Christian legend, bishop who once forced the devil to hold the Gospel book while he read aloud from it. He is the patron saint of carpenters, shepherds, and woodsmen and is invoked against gout, hemorrhage, lameness, stomach troubles, and wolves. Feast, 31 October.

3168

**Wolf in Sheep's Clothing, The**   Aesopic fable, though it does not occur in any early collections attributed to Aesop. It is derived from the

New Testament (Matt. 7:15) by an Italian fabulist, Abstemius, of the 15th century.

A wolf had been lurking near a flock of sheep for several days. But the shepherd had been so vigilant in guarding his animals that the wolf was becoming desperate. Then one day the wolf found a sheepskin that had been thrown away. Quickly, he slipped it on over his own hide and made his way among the flock of grazing sheep. Even the shepherd was deceived by the ruse. When night came the wolf in his disguise was shut up with the sheep in the fold. But that evening the shepherd, wanting something for his supper, went down to the fold and, reaching in, seized the first animal he came to. Mistaking the wolf for a sheep, the shepherd killed him on the spot.

Moral: *Appearances often are deceiving.*

Thackeray makes use of the fable in the Prologue to his novel *The Newcomers.*

See also: AESOPIC FABLES

3169

**Wollonqua**    In Australian mythology, the great snake of the Warramunga, who rose out of the Thapauerlu, a vast water hole in the Murchinson Ranges. Wollonqua is said to be so gigantic that even though he traveled many miles from his water hole, his tail was still in it. Wollonqua's human male companion, Mumumanugara, tried to force the great snake back into his hole, but instead the snake coiled itself around him. In Warramunga ritual the journeys of Wollonqua are acted out by the men. They draw various designs on the ground portraying the adventures of the great snake, who is portrayed covered with red down.

3170

**Wondjina**    In Australian mythology, primal beings who appear in various myths that take place during Ungud (dreamtime). Most Wondjina transform themselves into rock paintings while their spirits inhabit some sacred water hole. The natives frequently retouch these sacred paintings to promote rains or to stimulate fertility. When a person dies his body is painted with red ochre and placed in the cave where his clan's Wondjina resides; the dead man's spirit descends to a nearby pool to await rebirth. Paintings of the Wondjina range from a few feet to 16 feet. Painted against a white ground, the head is outlined in red or yellow. The first nonaborigine to see and comment on them was Sir George Grey in 1838. He interpreted them as priests with halos. The eyes and nose of the Wondjina are linked. No mouth is portrayed because it is believed that would cause it to rain all of the time. The figures are painted with white stripes symbolizing the rain.

See also: DREAMTIME

3171

**Wooden Horse or Trojan Horse**    In Greek and Roman mythology, a large wooden horse in which Greek soldiers hid in order to sack Troy. The horse was designed by Epeius, son of Panopeus. When the horse was taken into Troy, the Greeks came out of hiding at night and destroyed the city.

No mention is made in Homer's *Iliad* of the wooden horse, but in the *Odyssey* (book 11) Odysseus tells the ghost of Achilles in the underworld that his son Neoptolemus had been one of those chosen to go into the device, which was invented by Odysseus. Vergil's *Aeneid* (book 2) gives details of the wooden horse and the fall of Troy.

Sinon, a Greek, pretended that he had been an intended victim of a sacrifice to assure a safe retreat by the Greeks but had escaped as the Greeks sailed away from Troy. He convinced the Trojans that the wooden horse had been built as a tribute to Athena and had been abandoned on the beach when the Greeks decided to retreat. On hearing this, the Trojans decided to bring the horse into the city. Both Cassandra, the king's daughter, and Laocoön, a priest, warned the Trojans not to trust the Greeks. Laocoön hurled his spear into the horse's side and uttered a warning: *Timeo Danaos et dona ferentes* (I fear the Greeks even when they bring gifts). Shortly after that Laocoön was destroyed by a sea monster, and the Trojans took that as a favorable sign for bringing in the wooden horse. During the night, after the horse was safely inside the city walls, the Greeks emerged from it and opened the city gates to their waiting troops. The city fell.

The event was painted by Giovanni Battista Tiepolo in a work titled *The Building of the Trojan Horse* (c. 1760). There is an early Roman wall painting from Pompeii depicting *The Wooden Horse Brought into Troy* (second half of the first century C.E.) and a late 15th-century Franco-Flemish tapestry that shows the Trojan horse within the walls of Troy.

See also: ACHILLES; *AENEID, THE*; CASSANDRA; ILIAD, THE; LAOCOÖN; ODYSSEUS; *ODYSSEY, THE*; TROY

---

3172

**Woodman and the Serpent, The**   Aesopic fable found in various collections throughout the world.

One winter's day as a woodman was homeward bound from market he found a snake lying half dead with cold by the roadside. Taking compassion on the frozen creature, he placed it under his coat to warm it. Then he hastened home and put the serpent down on the hearth where a cheery fire was blazing. The children watched it with great interest and rejoiced to see it slowly come to life again. But as one of them knelt down to stroke the reviving snake, it raised its head and darted out its fangs and would have stung the child to death. Quickly the woodman seized his matlock and with one stroke cut the serpent in two.

Moral: *No gratitude is to be expected from the wicked.*

The fable occurs in the great Indian epic poem *The Mahabharata*. Versions vary as to the threatened victim. In some it is the woodman himself, in others it is one of his children after he arrives home. In one medieval version a woman finds and nourishes the snake.

See also: AESOPIC FABLES

---

3173

**Woodpecker**   Bird with a strong, straight, pointed beak, long tongue with barbs at the tip, and tail feathers that are stiff and pointed at the tip. In Greek mythology the woodpecker was a prophetic bird with great magical power and sacred to Zeus, the sky god, and Ares, the war god. In Roman mythology both Jupiter and Mars, the Latin counterparts of Zeus and Ares, also were associated with the bird. In Hindu mythology the sky god Indra transformed himself into a woodpecker for some of his sexual exploits, as did Zeus in Greek mythology and Mars in Roman mythology. Partly because of the woodpecker's association with Greek and Roman beliefs, the early Christians identified the bird with the devil. In animated cartoons the character of Woody Woodpecker captures the trickster nature ascribed to so many animals in world mythology and folklore.

See also: ARES; INDRA; MARS; TRICKSTER; ZEUS

---

3174

**Work Projects Administration** (WPA)   A government program in the United States during the 1930s and 1940s designed to employ workers who could not find work as a result of the Great Depression. Although the WPA is primarily known for its work on sidewalks, public buildings, and lakes, there was a large division called the Federal Writers Project (FWP), and one portion of FWP was devoted to the collecting of American folklore. Some of the collected materials can still be found in state archives, but some states placed no value on the collections and lost, misplaced, or destroyed them. A small portion of the stories, songs, and other traditional expressive forms found their way into the state guides, published around 1939–1940. Each state published one of these guidebooks that included a chapter devoted to the "Folklore and

Folkways" of that state. The Library of Congress collection includes 2,900 documents representing the work of more than 300 writers from 24 states. These documents are typically 2,000 to 15,000 words in length and consist of drafts and revisions of narratives or even dialogue reports. The oral histories describe the informant's family, education, income, occupation, political views, religion and mores, medical needs, and diet and also include miscellaneous observations. Pseudonyms are common for individuals and sometimes even for places named in the texts.

3175

**Wotan** (Woden, Wuotan, Voden, Votan)   In Germanic mythology, the name given to the Norse god Odin. It is used by Richard Wagner in his *Der Ring des Nibelungen*.

See also: ODIN; *RING DES NIBELUNGEN, DER*

3176

**Wreck of the Hesperus, The**   American literary ballad by Henry W. Longfellow, published in 1841, about the wreck of a schooner named *Hesperus*. Longfellow's ballad was influenced by the old Scottish ballad "Sir Patrick Spens."

3177

**Wu-fu** (the five happinesses)   In Chinese folk belief, the five blessings: long life, riches, tranquillity, a love of virtue, and a good end to one's life. The five characters often appear on chopsticks.

3178

**Wu-kuan wang**   In Chinese mythology, ruler of the fourth hell of Ti Yü, the underworld.

See also: TI YÜ

3179

**Wu Lao** (five odd ones)   In Chinese mythology, spirits of the five natural forces. They are Wang Mu (metal), Mu Kung (wood), Shui

Ching-tzu (water), Ch'ih Ching-tzu (fire), and Huang Lao (earth).

See also: CH'IH CHING-TZU; MU KUNG; SHUI CHING-TZU

3180

**Wulfilaic, St.**   Died 595. In Christian legend, one of the pillar saints of the Western Church. Wulfilaic was a native of Lombardy who spent part of his life in severe austerities on a mountain in the Valley of Chiers in Belgium. St. Gregory of Tours went to see him and wrote down the following account of the saint in his *History of the Franks* (book 8). Wulfilaic tells his own story:

I came to this mountain because here was erected the gigantic statue of Diana, which the inhabitants worshiped as a god. Beside this idol I built a pillar, on the top of which I placed myself barefooted, and my sufferings defy description. In winter the cold froze my feet and all the nails of my toes. . . . The rain which saturated my beard turned to ice, which glistened like candles. . . . My only food was a little bread and a few vegetables and my only drink was water. Though my sufferings were so great, yet I felt satisfaction in my austerities. When I saw the people come to my pillar I preached to them, and told them Diana was no goddess, and the songs which they sang in her honor ought to be addressed to the Creator of heaven and earth. Often did I pray that God would overturn the idol, and snatch the people from the error of their ways. The people listened to my words, the Savior lent an ear to my prayers, and the people were converted. I appealed to some of my converts to assist me in overthrowing the statue of Diana . . . but it resisted all our efforts. I now went to church, prostrated myself on the earth, prayed earnestly, wept, and groaned in spirit, imploring Christ to destroy by His almighty power that which the power of man could not move. My prayer being ended I went to rejoin the workmen. We seized the ropes, and with a vigorous pull succeeded in overthrowing the gigantic image. I broke it to pieces and reduced it to powder with a huge sledge hammer.

That night, the devil covered Wulfilaic "with pustules," but the saint anointed himself "from head to foot with some oil" from St. Martin's tomb and was cured. Later the archbishop of Trier asked that Wulfilaic come down from his pillar and enter a monastery. The saint obeyed.

See also: DIANA; GREGORY OF TOURS, ST.; MARTIN, ST.

3181
**Wulfram, St.**    647–720. In Christian legend, saint venerated at Fontenelle, Frisia, and Sens. Feast, 20 March.

Wulfram succeeded Lambert as archbishop of Sens but left his office to become a missionary among the Frisians, taking with him monks from Fontenelle. Numerous medieval legends are told of the saint. One tells of his ability to make a silver paten float on the sea. As St. Wulfram was sailing from Caudebec to Frisia, mass was being celebrated on board. St. Vando, who was the celebrant, dropped the paten into the sea while wiping it. St. Wulfram told Vando to put his hand into the sea. Immediately, the silver paten was buoyed up into his hand.

Another medieval legend tells how St. Wulfram put an end to human sacrifices. The Frisians used to offer human sacrifices to their pagan gods. These sacrifices were sometimes made by strangulation, the sword, fire, or water. One day the lot fell on two children of one mother, children five and seven years old. St. Wulfram asked King (or Duke) Radbod to prohibit such cruelty, but the king replied he could not violate the laws of his gods. The children were taken to the sacrifice site near where two rivers flowed into the sea. Wulfram prayed to God to save the children, and suddenly the waters of the two rivers stood like a wall around them. Walking on the water, Wulfram took the children and gave them to their mother. The people were amazed, and many became Christians, including King Radbod.

St. Wulfram is often portrayed in medieval Christian art as a bishop baptizing a young king or arriving by ship with monks and then baptizing the king.

3182
**Wu ta chia** (five big families)    In Chinese folklore, the five animals—fox, weasel, hedgehog, snake, and rat—that are feared because they are believed to bewitch people.

See also: FOX; RAT AND MOUSE; SNAKE; WEASEL

3183
**Wu-yuan kuei** (unrelated ghosts)    In Chinese folklore, a ghost who has no descendants to provide him with food offerings.

**Xaman Ek**   In Mayan mythology, god of the North Star, the guide of merchants. Incense was offered to him at roadside altars by his faithful followers. In Mayan art he is portrayed with a snub nose and black markings on his head. Paul Schellhas, classifying the gods in some Mayan codices, gave Xaman Ek the letter *C*, and he is sometimes known as God C.

3184

**Xanthus** (yellow)   In Greek mythology, the name given to the river god of the Scamander River in the Troad. In Homer's *Iliad* (book 20), when Zeus allowed the gods to choose either side in the Trojan War, Xanthus flooded the banks of the Scamander to stop the slaughter of the Trojans by Achilles because their blood was polluting the river. To help Achilles, Hera asked the fire god Hephaestus to set the river aflame. Xanthus surrendered before the holocaust and promised not to reenter the battle. Xanthus is also the name of the immortal horse of Achilles; son of Boreas (or Zephyrus) and Podarge; brother of Balius (piebald). The goddess Hera gave Xanthus the power of speech. He forewarned Achilles of his coming death. Xanthus wept at the death of Patroclus.

See also: ACHILLES; BOREAS; HERA; HEPHAESTUS; *ILIAD, THE*; PATROCLUS; ZEPHYRUS; ZEUS

3185

**Xilonen**   In Aztec mythology, goddess of the growing corn, whose festival, Uei Tecuilhuitl (22 June), was celebrated with corn tortillas wrapped around pieces of spiced vegetables and baked. She was one of the wives of Tezcatlipoca. Some scholars regard Xilonen as an aspect of the great goddess Coatlicue.

See also: COATLICUE; TEZCATLIPOCA

3186

**Xipe Totec** (the flayed one)   In Aztec mythology, god of vegetation, newly planted seeds, penitential torture, and the west. At his festival, captives were flayed alive and then eaten at a ritual meal. After the feast, the skins of the slain could be worn for up to 20 days by anyone who had skin complaints they wished to cure. Because the skins then turned yellow, Xipe Totec became the patron of goldsmiths. Xipe Totec gave himself as food to the world by having himself skinned alive.

3187

**Xiuhtecuhtli** (Xiuhtecutli)   In Aztec mythology, fire god who governed the fifth cardinal point, the center. He was thus worshiped as the center of all things and the spindle of the universe. The god determined the time of death of each individual.

3188

3189

**Xochiquetzal** (lady precious flower, beautiful rose?)   In Aztec mythology, goddess of sexual love and courtesans, patroness of painters, embroiderers, weavers, silversmiths, sculptors, and all whose profession was to imitate nature in crafts and drawings. On the Day of the Dead the goddess was offered marigolds by her faithful followers. She is the female form of the bisexual god Tonacatecutli.

See also: TONACATECUTLI

3190

**Xolas**   In the mythology of the Alacaluf Indians of Tierra del Fuego, supreme being. Xolas puts the soul into each new child. When a man or woman dies, the soul is reabsorbed by Xolas.

3191

**Xolotl Huetzi** (servant?)   In Aztec mythology, lord of the evening star, twin brother of the god Quetzalcoatl. Though credited with animal-like demonic qualities, Xolotl was also responsible for repeopling the earth after it had been depopulated. He went to the underworld and brought back a bone of a previous man. As he was leaving, he was pursued by the god of the underworld (who was not at all pleased with his action), and he fell with the bone. It broke into unequal parts, but Xolotl took what he could of it and sprinkled it with his own blood. After four days a boy was born and after seven days a girl. He then raised the two on the milk of the thistle, and they became the first parents of mankind. Xolotl sometimes appeared as a dwarf or as a dog.

See also: QUETZALCOATL

3192

**Xpiyacoc and Xmucané**   In Mayan mythology, creator deities, the "old man" and "old woman," who were involved with the creation of material objects. The Mayans believed their gods to be sorcerers, and through magic Xpiyacoc and Xmucané aided the creator god Hurakán in forming man through various magic rites.

See also: HURAKÁN

# Y

**Yabons**   In Australian mythology, friendly spirits who aid men, often warning them of danger.

3193

**Yacatecutli** (lord of travelers, he who leads)   In Aztec mythology, god of merchants, whose symbol was a staff, often sprinkled with blood by his worshipers. Slaves also were sacrificed to the god after they had been made sufficiently fat and pleasing because they were to be eaten later at a cannibalistic feast.

3194

**Yaho**   In Australian mythology, a cannibalistic male monster who lives in the mountains. He kills and roasts his victims, who are always women. His evil wife is Kurriwilban. He is also known as Koyorowen.

See also: KURRIWILBAN

3195

**Yahweh** (he causes to be, he brings into existence?)   In the Bible, O.T., the personal name of the god of Israel, preserved only in its four consonants, or the tetragammaton YHWH. By the third century B.C.E. the Jews had either forgotten the correct pronunciation or had omitted

3196

spelling out the entire name out of reverence because in ancient belief to know a god's name was to have power over the god. The Jews substituted the word *Adonai* (Lord or my Lords) for YHWH. The vowels of the word *Adonai* were later added to the consonants YHWH, creating the hybrid form Jehovah, a name never used by the ancient Hebrews. According to one account in the Old Testament, the name Yahweh was revealed to Moses. God spoke to Moses and said, "I am Yahweh. To Abraham and Isaac and Jacob I appeared as El Shaddai; I did not make myself known to them by my name Yahweh" (Exod. 6:2–3, Jerusalem Bible). But the name Yahweh appears in biblical narratives before Moses. In most English Bible translations, including the King James Version, Yahweh is not used; Lord is used in its place. The ancient praise-shout *Hallelujah* (praise the god Yah) contains the name of the god. Yahweh is used in the Jerusalem Bible, but the Revised Standard Version and the New English Bible use Lord.

See also: ABRAHAM; ISAAC; JACOB; MOSES

**Yakushi Nyorai** (master physician Buddha)   In Japanese mythology, god of healing, derived from the *hongji*, the universal Buddhist principle; portrayed holding a small flask that contains

3197

medicine. He is often shown with Gakko (moonlight) and Nikko (sunlight) on either side.

3198

**Yalahau** In Mayan mythology, god of water, darkness, night, and blackness. Yalahau was a fearsome warrior, cruel to his people when he came to earth. In some accounts he is said to be the brother of the culture hero and god Votan, to whom he is an antagonist.

See also: VOTAN

*Yama*

3199

**Yama** (the binder, twin, curb, bridle) In Hindu mythology, the god of death, king of hell.

Variant accounts are given for the origin of Yama. In some texts he is said to have been the son of Surya, the sun, and married to Saranya. Yami, his twin sister, suggested that the two sleep together and people the earth, but Yama refused the offer. In another text Yama was the first mortal to die. He discovered the way to the underworld, earning for himself the title of god of the dead. In the ancient collection of hymns the Rig-Veda, Yama is god of the dead, though he does not punish the wicked, as he does in later

Hindu mythology. One hymn in the Rig-Veda sums up his role:

To the great King Yama homage pay,
Who was the first of men that died,
That crossed the mighty gulf and spied
For mortals out the heavenward way.

Yama has two dogs, each with four eyes and wide nostrils, that guard the road to his kingdom. His scribe is Chitra-gupta, who records the sins and virtues of the dead. The dead are told to hurry past them. The dogs go about as messengers of Yama, calling people to his kingdom. In his kingdom some are allowed sensual pleasures.

In Indian art Yama is portrayed as a green man, dressed in red, crowned with a flower in his hair. He is armed with a club and often rides a buffalo. Among his numerous titles are Antaka (the ender, death), Kritanta (the finisher), Samana (the settler), Dandi or Danda-dhara (the rod bearer), Bhimasasana (of terrible decrees), Pasi (the noose carrier), Pitri-pati (lord of the manes), Preta-raja (king of the ghosts), Sraddha-deva (god of the faithful offerings), and Dharma-raja (just king).

See also: RIG-VEDA; SURYA

3200

**Yama-otoko** (mountain men) In Japanese folklore, wild men who have human-headed she-wolves as companions. They are considered insane and often dangerous.

3201

**Yama-uba** In Japanese folklore, female mountain spirits, sometimes seen as terrifying creatures and at other times as beneficent ones. In the demonic form one often appears as a woman with a mouth on top of her head under her hair, the locks of which transform themselves into serpents, catching small children, on whom she feeds.

**3202**

**Yankee Doodle**  Popular North American ballad, sung during the American Revolution. Believed to have been written in 1775 by Richard Shuckburth, a British army doctor, to ridicule the Continental army, the tune and verse were adopted by the Americans to poke fun at the British. The American version was sung by the Americans when Cornwallis surrendered at Yorktown in 1781. Some scholars believe it is a variant of the nursery rhyme "Lucy Locket." Countless versions and parodies evolved, some of which made fun of officers, including George Washington. There are said to be as many as 190 verses of Yankee Doodle. The Hollywood film *Yankee Doodle Dandy* (1942), starring James Cagney, is about the entertainer George M. Cohan.

*Emperor Yao*

**3203**

**Yao**  2000 B.C.E.? In Chinese legend, culture hero, emperor of the Golden Age, who was born with eyebrows of eight different colors. With the help of Yi, the Divine Archer, he subdued the winds, and with the help of K'un he attempted to quell the floodwaters of the Yellow River. When he wished to pass his throne on to Shun rather than to his own sons, the earth was nearly destroyed by the appearance of 10 suns, which scorched it. Yi stopped the suns by shooting down nine of them.

**3204**

**Yao-Shih Fo**  In Chinese Buddhism, the Healing Buddha, who received his powers from the historical Buddha. He gives spiritual medicine to the sick when they touch part of his image, which is usually made of bronze, though when painted it must be blue. He is known as Yakushi Butsu in Japan, where many early temples are dedicated to him. In Sanskrit he is called Bhaisajyaguru.

**3205**

**Yara**  In the mythology of the Amazonian Indians of Brazil, a siren. The Brazilian journalist and historian Alfonso Arinhos de Melo Franco (1868–1916) tells a tale, *The Yara*, of how a *yara* seduced a youth. Jaguarari is depicted as a handsome hunter loved by all of the villagers. One day he discovered a *yara* at Taruman Point, and from then on he was completely under her spell. He told his mother of the vision, and she warned him never to go back to the enchanted spot. Jaguarari, however, could not resist. He was seen in his canoe "rushing straight toward the sun, as though it would hurl itself into a flaming disk. And beside the young warrior, clasping him like a vine, stood a white figure, of a beautiful form, in a halo of silvery light that contrasted with the ruddy gleam of the setting sun, and crowned the long loose golden tresses."

**3206**

**Yarilo** (Erilo) (ardent, passionate)  In Slavic mythology, god of springtime and fecundity who was worshiped in some Slavic countries as late as the 19th century with various rites to ensure crop fertility.

In legends from White Russia, Yarilo is pictured as young and handsome, riding a white horse and dressed in a white cloak. On his head he wears a crown of wild flowers, and he holds a bunch of wheat ears in his hand. His feet are always bare. In one of his rites, White Russian peasants dressed the most beautiful maiden in Yarilo's costume and put her on a white horse while they sang:

Where he sets his foot,
The corn grows in mountains;
Wherever he glances,
The grain flourishes.

Yarilo's death in the fall after the harvest was celebrated by lamentations and sexual excess. His straw idol was carried in procession, burned, and the ashes scattered on the fields, after which the peasants would again begin feasting and drinking. These rites were condemned by the Russian Orthodox Church.

**Yarrow**   A pungent herb. In Chinese folk belief, yarrow sticks, also called milfoil, are used in the *I Ching* as a form of divination. In European folklore, yarrow is associated with sexual love. Sometimes called the herb of Venus, it was used in the 17th century as a cure for gonorrhea. In English folklore, yarrow was used by lovesick maidens to determine who their future lovers would be. They would pluck the flower from a young man's grave, repeating at the same time:

Yarrow, sweet yarrow, the first that I have
  found,
In the name of Jesus Christ I pluck it from the
  ground
As Jesus loved sweet Mary and took her for
  His dear,
So in a dream this night I hope my true love
  to appear

The chant was supposed to give the yarrow power to bring a vision of the future. But if one dreamed of yarrow, it meant losing the object of one's affection. If one was married and dreamed of the plant, it signified death in the family. Yarrow is often found on gravesites and thus is often associated with death. It also was used against witchcraft during the Christian Middle Ages.

See also: VENUS

**Yashodhara**   Fifth century B.C.E. In Buddhist legend, wife of Gautama, the Buddha, and mother of Rahula. Gautama won the hand of Yashodhara in a contest of arms when he was 16. When he left her and his young son to seek enlightenment, she went into despair. When they met years later she still showed her deep love for her husband. Their son Rahula became a Buddhist monk. Many of the *Jatakas*, or *Folktales of the Former Lives of the Buddha*, are addressed to Rahula. He is said to have died before his father. Some texts give the name Gopa as the wife of the Buddha.

See also: BUDDHA, THE

**Yatawm and Yatai**   In Indo-Chinese mythology, two creator beings, neither spirits nor humans, who were responsible for the creation of animals and people.

Hkun Hsang Long, the creator spirit, or god, looked down from his heavenly home, Mong Hsang, and saw Yatawm and Yatai. He dropped down to them two *hwe-sampi*, or gourds. The two ate the gourds and planted the seeds, which grew to gourds as large as hills, containing animals and people. Yatawm was then called Ta-hsang Kahsi (great all-powerful) and Yatai was called Ya-hsang Ka-hsi (great mother all-powerful).

The myth is not clear as to whether Hkun Hsang Long wanted the two to eat the gourds, because when they ate them, death and sexual passion came into the world. However, the myth may have Christian overtones from missionaries who first recorded it for Western readers.

See also: ADAM AND EVE

**Yayati**    In Hindu mythology, a king who exchanged his old age for the youth of his son Puru.

3210

Yayati, fifth king of the Chandra (lunar) race, was invited by Indra, the storm god, to visit heaven. Matali, the charioteer of Indra, came to fetch Yayati. On their way they held a philosophical discussion that made a deep impression on Yayati. When he returned to earth he administered his kingdom with such virtue that his subjects were exempt from decay and death. Yama, the god of the dead, complained to Indra. Then Indra sent Kama, god of love, and his daughter, Asruvindumati, to arouse passion in Yayati. The king fell in love with Asruvindumati, but he was too old for the young girl. Yayati asked his son Puru, after his other four sons had refused, to exchange his youth for Yayati's old age. Puru agreed. After a while Asruvindumati persuaded Yayati to return to heaven. Before the king left, however, he returned the youth to his son Puru.

In a variant account found in some texts Yayati was given a celestial chariot by Indra. With the chariot Yayati conquered the earth and even subdued the gods. The chariot then passed on to his successors but was finally lost. In the variant legend, Yayati, after restoring his youth to Puru, retired to the forest with his wife and gave himself up to mortification. Abstaining from food, Yayati died and ascended to heaven. He and his five sons are called Rajarshis.

See also: CHANDRA; KAMA; INDRA

**Yazatas**    In Persian mythology, the "adorable" or "worshipful ones," ranking after the good god, Ahura Mazda, and the Amesha Spentas, the seven "immortal bounteous ones." The Yazatas are innumerable and guard the sun, moon, and

3211

stars; they also are personifications of abstract ideas such as blessing, truth, and peace.

See also: AHURA MAZDA; AMESHA SPENTAS

**Yedo Go Nin Otoko** (Edo Go Nin Otoko) In Japanese legend, five men who stole from the rich and gave to the poor. They all dressed alike, and though mischievous, they gained the support of people because of their aid. They usually are portrayed with flutes and big tobacco pouches, either talking to one another or competing in a physical contest.

3212

**Yeh Ching** (karmic mirror)    In Chinese mythology, a magic mirror that shows the dead the form into which they are to be reborn.

3213

**Yen Kung** (Duke Yen)    In Chinese mythology, a deified mortal worshiped as the god of sailors.

3214

**Yen-Mo wang**    In Chinese mythology, ruler of the fifth hell of Ti Yü, the underworld.

3215

See also: TI YÜ

**Yesod** (Yasodiel) (foundation)    In Jewish folklore, angel invoked by Moses to bring death to the firstborn males in Egypt. In the biblical account (Exod. 12:29), however, it says Yahweh "smote all the firstborn in the land of Egypt." In Jewish folklore naming an angel or other spirit as a substitute for Yahweh, God himself, in earthly affairs is quite common; it is done to maintain God's distance from humankind.

3216

See also: YAHWEH

**Yew**    An evergreen tree planted by the Druids near their temples. In European folklore, it was

3217

planted in graveyards to prevent witches from destroying churches and gravestones and sometimes buried with the dead to ward off demons. Because the yew is poisonous, hunting bows made from the tree are said to be doubly fatal, killing both with its poison and as a weapon. Shakespeare's *Hamlet* speaks of the juice of the cursed hebona, believed to be the yew. Christopher Marlowe, in his play *The Jew of Malta*, calls the yew the "juice of hebon."

See also: DRUIDS

3218

**Yggdrasill** (Igdrasil) (Ygg's steed, the horse of the terrible one)   In Norse mythology, the great cosmic ash tree, also known as the world tree. The *Prose Edda* describes Yggdrasill as "the greatest and best of all trees. Its branches spread over the whole world, and even reach above heaven. It has three roots very wide asunder. One of them extends to the Aesir (the gods), another to the Frost-giants in that very place where was formerly Ginnungagap (the primeval abyss), and the third stands over Nifelheim (the land of dark, cold and mist), and under this root, which is constantly gnawed by Nidhogg (the dragon), is Hvergelmir." On top of the Yggdrasill an eagle perches. Between its eyes sits a hawk called Vedurfolnir. The squirrel named Ratatosk runs up and down Yggdrasill, trying to cause strife between the eagle and Nidhogg. Four harts, Dainn, Dvalinn, Duneyr, and Durathor, run across its branches and bite its buds. The Norns sit under the Urdar-fount, which is located at the third root of the tree. Here also the gods sit in judgment. Every day they ride up on horseback over Bifrost. Every day the Norns draw water from the Urdar-fount and sprinkle the ash, so its branches may not rot or wither. This water is so holy that everything placed in the Urdar-fount becomes as white as the film within an eggshell. The dew that falls from it is honey-dew. Two fowls are fed in the Urdar-fount. They are called swans, and from them are descended all of the birds of this species.

Adam of Bremen describes a pagan temple at Uppsala around 1070. There is a large yew tree in front of the temple, and sacrificial victims are hung from its branches. The connection to Yggdrasil seems clear: a large tree at the center of a religious site. The concept of a "world tree" was widespread in Eurasia and was seen as the path into the world of spirits.

See also: AESIR; DVALIN; GINNUNGAGAP; NIDHOGG; NIFELHEIM; NORNS; ODIN; *PROSE EDDA*; RATATOSK; URD

3219

**Yima** (Yam)   In Persian mythology, divine hero, who in some texts is considered the first man, the first king, and the founder of civilization. As the first man he is also the first of the dead, over whom he rules in a region of bliss. Yima becomes the culture hero Jemshid in the Persian epic poem *Shah Namah* by Firdusi.

In the sacred book *Avesta* two myths, somewhat contradictory, are told of Yima. Once Ahura Mazda, the good creator god, asked Yima to receive his law from him and bring it to men as a prophet. "I was not born, I was not taught to be the preacher and the bearer of thy law," Yima told Ahura Mazda.

Then the god said to Yima: "Since thou wantest not to be a preacher and the bearer of my law, then make thou my worlds thrive, make my worlds increase: undertake thou to nourish, to rule, and to watch over my world."

Yima did as Ahura Mazda asked, and the world thrived, "six hundred winters passed away, and the earth was replenished with flocks and herds, with men and dogs and birds and with red blazing fires, and there was no more room for the flocks, herds, and men." Then Yima made the "earth grow larger by two-thirds" to accommodate the new inhabitants.

The second myth narrated in the *Avesta* tells how Ahura Mazda told Yima that a winter was to come that would destroy every living creature. Yima built a *vara*, an underground cavern, and like Noah in the biblical tale, brought "the seed of men and women that are the tallest, best, and the most beautiful" to inhabit his kingdom. "Gather together the seed of all kinds of animals that are the finest on this earth; gather together the seed of all plants and fruits that are the tallest and sweetest. In pairs bring them to your retreat." Again, the people and animals prospered.

The end of Yima is not exactly known. He was condemned by the gods, though the reason is not clear, and killed either by his brother, Spityura, who cut him in two, or by the demon Azhi Dahaka, in the form of a tyrant king, Zahhak, the evil king of Babylon in the Persian epic *Shah Namah* by Firdusi.

See also: AHURA MAZDA; *AVESTA*; AZHI DAHAKA; JEMSHID; NOAH; *SHAH NAMAH*; ZAHHAK

**3220**

**Yin and Yang** (dark side and sunny side of a hill) In Chinese mythology and philosophy, a symbol expressing conflict and resolution. Yin represents the female (negative, dark, the earth) and Yang the male (positive, light, heaven). Heaven, the source of weather, was the realm of Shang-Ti, who was to be offered sacrifices made by the Son of Heaven. This perception of natural forces, weather in particular, may stem from agricultural experiences in the loess country of the Yangtze River. Sudden rains could dramatically alter the landscape. Man had to learn to live with continuing changes. It was viewed as attunement with the pre-established harmony of *li*, the universal pattern.

See also: LI; SHANG-TI

**3221**

**Ymir** (doubled)   In Norse mythology, primeval giant formed from fire and ice, slain by the Aesir gods Odin, Vili, and Ve. From Ymir's body these three gods formed the earth, according to the *Prose Edda*: "From Ymir's blood they made the seas and waters; from his flesh the land; from his bones the mountains; and his teeth and jaws, together with some bits of broken bones, served them to make the stones and pebbles." Ymir's

skull formed the heavens that the gods placed over the earth, with a dwarf at each corner to hold it up. Ymir's brains were tossed in the air to form the clouds.

Ymir is the embodiment of the hermaphroditic procreator. It is interesting to note that to create the universe the gods had to kill a maternal relative. The pagan skalds had many kennings for Ymir; the sky was called "Ymir's skull," and "Ymir's blood" referred to the sea.

See also: AESIR; AUDHUMLA; BESTLA; KENNING; ODIN; *PROSE EDDA*

**3222**

**Yoga** (yoking, harnessing, union)   In Hinduism, various methods of mental and physical self-control or discipline, used for various ends. In the Bhagavad-Gita, part of the Hindu epic poem *The Mahabharata*, the term is widely used to mean a method or discipline leading to salvation.

See also: BHAGAVAD-GITA; *MAHABHARATA, THE*

**3223**

**Yoni** (womb, source)   In Hinduism, the female organ of generation, connected with the great goddess Devi. The *yoni* is worshiped along with the *lingam*, the phallus of the god Shiva, who is the husband of Devi.

See also: DEVI; LINGAM; SHIVA

**3224**

**Yryn-Ajy-Tojon**   In Siberian mythology, white creator god worshiped by the Yakuts, a Turkish people living near the Lena River. He lives in the Tree of Life, in whose roots the mother goddess Ajyset lives.

When Yryn-Ajy-Tojon saw a bladder floating on the waters, he asked what it was. The bladder replied that it was Satan, who lived on the earth under the water. "If there is really earth under the water, then bring me a piece of it," Yryn-Ajy-Tojon said to Satan, who then dived under the water and returned with a piece of earth. It was blessed by Yryn-Ajy-Tojon and placed on the waters, where he sat on it. Angry, Satan tried to drown Yryn-Ajy-Tojon by stretching out the earth, but the more he pulled, the larger it got, until it covered the waters.

In addition to containing elements found in other Siberian myths relating to the origin of the earth and the devil, this myth, by its use of Satan as the name of the devil, suggests that it is a Christian reworking of a pagan myth.

See also: AJYSET; EARTH DIVER; SATAN

*Yü Huang, the Jade Emperor*

**3225**

**Yua**   In Eskimo mythology (Unalit peoples at Bering Strait), spirit of elements, places, and things.

**3226**

**Yuga** (age)   In Hindu mythology, an age of the world, of which there are commonly said to be four:

Krita Yuga, the first age, when men were righteous and in harmony with life. It lasted for a period of 1,728,000 years.

Treta, the second age, when people began to decline in righteousness.

Dvapar, the third age, when more evil came into the world.

Kali, the present age, which began in 3102 B.C.E. and is to last 430,000 years. It will see hunger, fear, and calamities increase.

Each Yuga is shorter than the one before it, and all four make a Maha-Yuga. A thousand Maha-Yugas make a Kalpa, which is a day and night for the Hindu god Brahma, or 4,320,000,000 human years. The term *Mahypralaya* means total destruction of the world and universe, when men and gods are annihilated. Other terms for the age of the world are Jahanaka, Kahita, and Sanhara.

See also: BRAHMA

**3227**

**Yü Huang**   In Chinese Taoist mythology, the Jade Emperor, supreme god; symbol of jade, or absolute purity, who lives in the highest heaven, Ta-lo. He replaced the earlier god, Yüan-Shih T'ien-Tsun, the "heavenly honored one of origin and beginning," who now lives on Yü Shan (the Jade Mountain).

**3228**

**Yuki Onna** (snow woman)   In Japanese folklore, a female ghost who appears in snowstorms, causing travelers to fall asleep and freeze to death.

**3229**

**Yule** (wheel)   A pre-Christian Norse feast held anywhere from mid-November to mid-January, in which sacrifices were made to the Aesir gods. Some Yule customs became absorbed into Christmas customs in the northern countries when the people were converted to Christianity. The most familiar custom was the Yule log burned during the Middle Ages, recalling the pagan custom of lighting a log in honor of Thor with a fragment of the previous year's log. Christians believed that the preservation of the last year's Yule log was effective in preventing fire in the house. Yule is now a term sometimes used for Christmas.

See also: AESIR; THOR; YULE LOG

3230

**Yul-lha** (rural deity)  In Tibetan folklore, lesser gods and demons of the countryside. They are ranked as follows:

Lha. Gods, all male, white in color, and generally genial.

Tsan. Goblins or ghosts, all male, red in color. These are vindictive ghosts of lamas, discontented priests, and haunt temples.

bDub. Devils, all male, black in color. They are the ghosts of the persecutors of Lamaism and cannot be appeased without the sacrifice of a pig.

gZah. Planets, piebald in color.

dMu. Bloated fiends, dark purple in color.

Srin-po. Cannibal fiends, raw-flesh colored and bloodthirsty.

rGyal-po. King fiends, the wealth-masters, white in color, the spirits of apotheosized heroes.

Ma-mo. Mother she-devils, black colored, the disease mistresses. They are sometimes the wives of the demons.

3231

**Yü Shih** (rain master)  In Chinese mythology, the rain god, portrayed in yellow scale armor and wearing a blue hat, standing on a cloud and pouring rain onto the earth from a watering can.

3232

**Yves, St.** (Ives, Ivo, Ybus, Helory) (archer) 1253–1303. In Christian legend, patron of lawyers, judges, and notaries. Feast, 19 May.

Yves was born near Treguier in Brittany and became an ecclesiastical and civil lawyer. As an official of the diocese of Rennes he was noted for his protection of orphans, his defense of the poor, and his impartiality in the administration of justice. In Brittany he is still referred to as "the poor man's advocate." Dom Lobineau, in his *Lives of the Saints of Britain*, recounts the legend of St. Yves, the widow, and two swindlers.

Two swindlers deposited with a widow a valise they said contained 200 gold pistoles. They told her not to give the valise to anyone unless both of them were present. After six days one of the men came for the bag and carried it off. The other swindler then brought the widow before a judge and demanded either the bag or the 200 pistoles. The widow was about to lose the case when St. Yves interfered and said his client could not produce the valise unless *both* of the claimants were present. The plaintiff, therefore, must bring his fellow into court before the valise could be given up. The judge at once saw the justice of this and ordered the plaintiff to produce his companion. He did not and confessed that it was a hoax to get money out of the woman.

Another legend, from the same source, tells how St. Yves multiplied trees. The lord of Rosternen gave St. Yves permission to fell some oak trees in a forest for building the cathedral of Treguier. The steward complained that St. Yves had made "too great havoc with the trees." When the lord was taken to see the "devastation," he found two oaks growing for every one that had been felled.

Still another legend from the same source tells of St. Yves saying mass when a dove, all shining, lighted on his head, then flew to the high altar and almost immediately disappeared. Another day, as the saint was dining with a large number of the poor, a dove entered the room, fluttered around him, then lighted on his head. It did not fly away until St. Yves gave it a blessing.

St. Yves is often shown surrounded by supplicants holding parchment and pointing upward. Sometimes he is shown in a lawyer's gown holding a book.

# Z

**Za'afiel** (wrath of God)    In Jewish and Christian folklore, angel in control of hurricanes and storms. In some accounts he is a good angel, in others, an evil one.

3233

**Zacchaeus** (pure)    First century. In the Bible, N.T., the rich publican at Jericho who was visited by Jesus. According to medieval French legend, he arrived in Gaul to preach the Gospel. His feast in the Coptic Church is 20 April.

3234

**Zacharias** (Yahweh remembers)    In the Bible, name of two characters: one in the New Testament, the father of John the Baptist (Luke 1:15); the other, the Old Testament prophet Zechariah, spelled Zacharias in Greek. In the Koran (sura 6) he is called Zakariya, the father of John the Baptist, and is reckoned, along with John, Jesus, and Elias, among the righteous.

In the New Testament (Luke 1:5–25) Zacharias is a priest married to Elisabeth, who was a kinswoman of the Virgin Mary. While he was performing his priestly duties in the temple, he had a vision in which the archangel Gabriel promised him and his barren wife a son. When old Zacharias doubted the angel's word, he was made speechless. Eight days after the child was born Zacharias went to the temple to have the child circumcised. After making a sign that the boy was to be called John, not Zacharias, his speech was restored. In Islamic legend, after John the Baptist's death Zakariya escapes into a tree that opens for him. The hem of his garment remains outside the tree and is spotted by the demon Iblis, who betrays him. The tree is sawn down and with it Zakariya. Jesus refers to "Zacharias son of Barachias" in Matthew (23:35) as having been slain "between the temple and the altar." Some biblical commentators on the text think Jesus is referring to the father of John the Baptist, but the majority believe Jesus is referring to the Old Testament prophet, Zechariah, though Jewish tradition says the prophet died a natural death. The Jewish, Christian, and Islamic legends evidence influence from one another.

See also: GABRIEL; IBLIA; JOHN THE BAPTIST, ST.; *KORAN, THE*; VIRGIN MARY; ZACHARIAS, ST.

3235

**Zacharias, St.** (Yahweh has remembered) Second century. In Christian legend, second bishop of Vienne, a disciple of St. Peter, according to Christian tradition. A medieval legend says he brought to Vienne the tablecloth on which Jesus instituted the Last Supper. Feast, 26 May.

3236

3237

**Zadkiel** (Zidekiel, Zadakiel, Zedekiel, Tzadkie) (the righteousness of God)   In Jewish and Christian folklore, archangel who held back the knife when Abraham was about to sacrifice his son Isaac (Gen. 22:11–19), though he is not named directly in the biblical text. In another Jewish legend Zadkiel is credited with leading the Israelites out of Egypt. The name Zadkiel was adopted as a pseudonym by the astrologer Richard James Morrison, a naval lieutenant and author of the *Prophetic Almanac*, which was commonly called Zadkiel's Almanac.

See also: ABRAHAM; ISAAC

3238

**Zadok** (just)   In the Bible, O.T., a descendant of Aaron and a high priest of Israel in the time of King David and Solomon. He served as high priest jointly with Abiathar during most of David's reign (1 Chron. 24:3, 2 Sam. 15:24–29; 1 Kings 1:38–39). Handel's choral work *Zadok the Priest*, in praise of the king, is sung at English coronations.

See also: DAVID; SOLOMON

3239

**Zag-Muk** (Zagmuku)   Babylonian New Year festival held in spring in honor of the great hero god Marduk, who on that day decided the fate of men for the coming year. One of the rites associated with the festival was the "visit" paid by the god Nabu, a son of Marduk, to his father. An image of Nabu was carried in a ship to the temple of Marduk and then returned to its own shrine.

See also: MARDUK; NABU

3240

**Zagzagel** (divine splendor)   In Jewish folklore, angel who assisted God, along with Michael and Gabriel, in burying Moses. He is not mentioned in the Old Testament, but arises from folklore.

See also: GABRIEL; MICHAEL; MOSES

3241

**Zahhak** (Zohak, Zuhak, Dahhak)   In the Persian epic poem *Shah Namah*, by Firdusi, an evil king who is defeated by the hero Faridun. King Zahhak had dedicated his life to Iblis, the devil. Out of the king's head came two serpents that had to be fed by human flesh. Human sacrifices of young men and women were made to satisfy the serpents. The hero Faridun challenged the king but was stopped from killing him by a supernatural voice that said:

> Slay him not now—his time is not yet come,
> His punishment must be prolonged awhile;
> And as he cannot now survive the wound,
> Bind him with heavy chains—convey him straight
> Upon the mountain, there within a cave,
> Deep, dark, and horrible—with none to sooth
> His sufferings, let the murderer lingering die
> (James Atkinson translation).

The character of Zahhak is based on the archdemon in Persian mythology, Azhi Dahaka, who was defeated by the hero Traetaona and also imprisoned in a mountain.

See also: AZHI DAHAKA; FARIDUN; *SHAH NANAH*

3242

**Zaka**   In Haitian voodoo, a good loa (deified spirit of the dead), guardian of farmers and the destitute. Offerings of corn, rum, and oil-soaked bread are made to him. He is symbolized by an ear of corn with a hat on it and a pin stuck in it.

See also: LOA

3243

**Zakiqoxol** (Zaquicoxol) (he who strikes from flint)   In the mythology of the Cakchiquels, a branch of the Mayan Indians, demon spirit of fire and the forest. When the heroes Gagavitz and Zactecauh met Zakiqoxol, as told in *The Annals of the Cakchiquels* (16th century), they at first wanted to kill the demon. But instead they gave him a breastplate and sandals, all blood-colored, as a gift, and "he departed and descended to the foot of the mountain." In Cakchiquel folklore, the demon is called "the little man of the woods."

See also: GAGAVITZ

3244

**Zal** In the Persian epic poem *Shah Namah*, by Firdusi, father of the hero Rustum. When Zal was born, he was perfect in all aspects, except one: he had white hair. When Sam, his father, was told that his child possessed this defect, he exposed the babe on a distant mountain. The mysterious and magical bird Simurgh heard the cries of the child and took him to his nest. A voice came from heaven telling Simurgh:

To thee this mortal I resign,
Protected by the power divine.
Let him thy fostering kindness share,
Nourish him with paternal care (James Atkinson translation).

Warned in a dream, Sam repented what he had done to his infant son and went in search of Zal. When he finally found Zal, who had now grown to early manhood, he confessed his crime and asked for forgiveness. Zal then forgave his father.

One of the most interesting episodes in *Shah Namah* relating to Zal is his wooing of Rudabeh (Rudaba, Raduvah), who eventually became his wife and the mother of the great hero of the epic, Rustum.

One day while journeying through his father's domains Zal came to Kabul, where he stayed with Mihrab, who paid Sam an annual tribute to secure the safety of his state. On the arrival of Zal, Mihrab went out of the city to greet him. The young hero entertained Mihrab and soon discovered that Mihrab had a beautiful daughter:

Her name was Rudabeh; screen from public view
Her countenance is brilliant as the sun;
From head to foot her lovely form is fair
As polished ivory . . . (James Atkinson translation).

After some tribulations Rudabeh and Zal were married. The astrologers consulted about the marriage replied that "this virtuous couple will have a son like unto a war-elephant, a stoutly girded son who will submit all man to the might of his sword and raise the king's throne above the clouds. . . ." The name of the son was Rustum, the great hero of the epic poem.

See also: RUSTUM; *SHAH NAMAH*; SIMURGH

3245

**Zamzam** (abundant water) In Islam, sacred well at Mecca, also called Ishmael's Well. According to Islamic tradition the archangel Gabriel opened the well to Hagar when her Ishmael was dying of thirst in the desert. Before leaving Mecca, pilgrims often dip their burial clothes in the well.

See also: GABRIEL; ISHMAEL

3246

**Zao Gongen** In Japanese mythology, patron god of Mount Kimpu in Japan and special guardian of the Buddhist Shugendo sect, a group of wandering mountain ascetics, whose adherents are called *yamabushi* (those who sleep on mountains).

3247

**Zarathustra** (Zardusht, Zartust, Zoroaster) Sixth century B.C.E. Prophet, mystic, and reformer of Persian religion; also known as Zoroaster, the Greek rendering of his name.

Numerous legends surround the life of the historical Zarathustra. According to them, his birth, as with other saviors in world mythology, was foretold. His mother, only 15, bore him after having contact with the sacred Haoma plant. As soon as the child was born, he could converse and spoke with the good god, Ahura Mazda. At the age of 30 Zarathustra had his first vision. After his religious experience he began to teach the Good Religion (one of the names given by his followers to his doctrine). It is also called Mazdaism in some texts. At first no one would accept his teachings. He taught that Ahura Mazda, the good god who had created the world, was in conflict with Ahriman, the evil spirit. In the end, however, the forces of Ahura Mazda would be victorious and evil destroyed. Zarathustra brought his doctrine to the court of King Vishtaspa, who, though impressed by the prophet, still let his own priests jail Zarathustra on charges of being a necromancer.

One day the king's favorite black horse drew up all of its legs into its body so that it could not move. Zarathustra offered to heal the animal if four conditions were granted him: first, that the king should accept his teaching; second, that the great warlike prince, Isfandiyar, fight to spread Zarathustra's doctrine; third, that the queen also accept his doctrine; and fourth, the names of the men who plotted against him should be revealed. As each condition was fulfilled, one of the horse's legs was restored, and it could walk again.

Tradition records that Zarathustra was murdered while he knelt praying. After his death his doctrine was modified by the magi (priests of his religion), who restored some of the earlier beliefs in the old gods and spirits. This form of Zoroastrianism, as it is called, became the faith of Persia and lasted until the Islamic conquest of the country in the seventh century C.E. There are few remaining believers—those called Guebers (Ghebers) by the Islamics, meaning "unbelievers" in the faith of Islam, and some in India called Paris (Parsees) from the ancient name of Persia. The doctrine of Zarathustra, however, had a great impact on Judaism, Mithraism, Gnosticism, Manichaeism, and Christianity.

For the ancient Greeks, Zarathustra was a great magician and philosopher. Plato is said to have wanted to be able to study with the magi.

Socrates is believed to have been taught by one. The magi who visited the infant Christ as the "three wise men" of tradition are perhaps the most celebrated.

The English poet Wordsworth, in the fourth book of his long narrative poem *The Excursion*, wrote on the ancient Persian religion:

. . . the Persian,—zealous to reject
Altar and Image, and the inclusive walls
And roofs of temples built by human
   hands,—
The loftiest heights ascending, from their
   tops,
With myrtle-wreathed Tiara on his brows,
Presented sacrifice to Moon and Stars,
And to the winds and mother Elements,
And the whole circle of the Heavens, for him
A sensitive existence and a God.

Lord Byron, in the third book of his melancholic poem *Childe Harold's Pilgrimage*, wrote also of the Persian belief:

Not vainly did the early Persian make
His altar the high places and the peak
Of earth-o'er-gazing mountains, and thus
   take
A fit and unwalled temple, there to seek
The Spirit, in whose honour shrines are
   weak,
Upreared of human hands. Come and
   compare
Columns and idol-dwellings, Goth or Greek,
With Nature's realms of worship, earth and
   air,
Nor fix on fond abodes to circumscribe thy
   prayer.

A lesser poet than Wordsworth and Byron, the Anglo-Irish Thomas Moore, in his metrical tale *The Fire-Worshippers*, part of his longer *Lalia Rookh*, has a Gueber chief say to an Islamic:

"Yes, I am of that impious race,
Those slaves of Fire, that morn and even
Hail their creator's dwelling place
Among the living lights of heaven;
Yes! I am of that outcast crew
To Iran and to Vengeance true,
Who curse the hour your Arabs came
To desecrate our shrines of flame,
And swear before God's burning eye
To break our country's chains or die."

A brilliant and more interesting description is found in Shelley's poetic drama *Prometheus Unbound*:

. . . Ere Babylon was dust,
The Magus Zoroaster, my dead child,
Met his own image walking in the garden.
That apparition, sole of men, he saw.
For know there are two worlds of life and
    death:
One that which thou beholdest; but the other
Is underneath the grave, where do inhabit
The shadows of all forms that think and live,
Till death unite them and they part no more.

This theme was referred to and expanded by Charles Williams in his novel *Descent into Hell*.

The Frenchman Voltaire, however, was not at all enthusiastic about Zarathustra. He says in his *Ignorant Philosopher* that Zarathustra "established ridiculous superstitions" though the prophet's "morals prove him not corrupt."

In Nietzsche's *Thus Spake Zarathustra* the poet uses Zarathustra for his own mouthpiece. Nietzsche stresses in the complex work that life is the will to power. A man must overcome the beliefs and conventions of common men. He must become an "overman," or as it is usually translated, "superman" (Übermensch). In one section of the work Zarathustra reaches a town where a group of people are watching a tightrope walker. He says to them: "I teach you the overman. Man is something that shall be overcome." He then proceeds to explain that salvation is found in this world and not the next world. His

teachings are rejected. Since he cannot teach the masses, he decides to gather together some few disciples. Nietzsche's work is the basis for the long orchestral work *Also Sprach Zarathustra* by Richard Strauss.

See also: AHRIMAN; AHURA MAZDA; HAOMA; MAGI

3248
**Zaremaya** In Persian mythology, spring that produced oil or butter to feed the souls in paradise.

3249
**Zatik** In Armenian mythology, a vegetation god. The Armenian translation of the Bible calls the Jewish passover "the festival of Zatik," and Armenian Christians call Easter the Festival of Zatik. This has led some scholars to believe that Zatik was a vegetation god, whose resurrection began at the winter solstice and was completed in the spring. Similarly, St. Bede derives the English name for the feast of the resurrection from a pagan spring goddess, Eostre.

See also: BEDE THE VENERABLE, ST.

3250
**Zduh** (Zduhacz) (soul) In Slavic mythology, a term for the soul of either a person or an animal. The *zduh* could leave the body during sleep and engage in a battle with other souls. If it lost the battle, the sleeper would die. Aside from the *zduhs* of people and animals, there were *zduhs* of the land, which caused drought, and a *zduh* of the sea, which caused rain and storms. Another term for the soul in Slavic mythology is *vjedogonja*.

3251
**Zemi** In the mythology of the Indians of the Antilles at the time of Columbus, cult images of animals or humans, worshiped as gods. They were invoked to "send rain or sunshine," according to Peter Martyr d'Anghera in his book *De*

*Orbe Nova* (1516), describing customs and beliefs of the Indians.

3252

**Zeno, St.**   Died 371. In Christian legend, bishop of Verona, invoked for children learning to speak and walk. Feast, 12 April.

The bishop is noted for his kindness to children. *The Life of St. Zeno, Bishop of Verona* by Peter and Jerome Ballerini tells how the daughter of Emperor Gallianus was grievously tormented by the devil and was healed by the saint. One day when she was nearly suffocating she cried out, "I can never be relieved of this torture but by Zeno." The devil added, "And I will never quit my abode here unless compelled to do so by Zeno." The emperor sent for the saint, who arrived quickly and entered the room where the young girl lay. As soon as he entered the devil cried out, "Zeno, you are come to drive me out, for here I cannot abide in the presence of thy holiness." The saint replied, "In the name of the Lord Jesus Christ I command thee to quit the body of this young maiden." The devil came out and said as he left, "Good-bye, Zeno, I am off to Verona, and there you will find me on your return."

St. Gregory the Great, in his *Dialogues*, explains Zeno's connection with the Adige River (Etsch). One day when the clergy and people of Verona were assembled to celebrate the festival of St. Zeno (he was now dead and sainted), the River Adige overflowed its banks, but though the doors of the church "were wide open, the waters were afraid to enter." Instead they formed a wall around the church. Zeno's symbol is usually a fish, stemming from his legend.

See also: GREGORY THE GREAT, ST.

3253

**Zenobio, St.** (force of Zeus)   Fourth century. In Christian legend, bishop of Florence; invoked against headache. Feast, 25 May.

The legendary life of the saint is found in several short biographies, all written after the 11th century and included in the *Acta Sanctorum*, a collection of saints' lives. According to the accounts, Zenobio was born of a noble family. His father, Lucian, and his mother, Sophia, were both pagans. The boy, however, was converted to Christianity and eventually succeeded in converting his parents to the new faith. He lived in Rome as a deacon and was also secretary to Pope Damascus I. He was sent to Florence when two factions, the Catholics and the Arians (a rival Christian group), were fighting to have one of their sect chosen bishop of the city. When Zenobio arrived, both sides agreed that he should be the bishop and elected him to the office. He led a life of poverty and self-denial, keeping the two religious factions at peace.

Many legends center around the saint. Once he made a journey to a city in the Apennines to consecrate a church. On the occasion his friend, St. Ambrose, sent messengers to him with gifts of precious relics. But it happened that the chief of the messengers, in passing through the gorge in the mountains, fell with his mule down a steep precipice and was crushed to death. His companions brought his mutilated body and laid it at the feet of St. Zenobio. The bishop prayed over the corpse, and the man was restored to life.

Another legend says a Frenchwoman, while on a pilgrimage to Rome, stopped off at Florence and left her son in the care of the saint. The boy died the day the woman returned, but when the child was laid at the feet of St. Zenobio, the prayers of the saint restored the child to life. The saint placed him in the arms of his mother.

Still another medieval legend tells how a little child, straying from his mother in the streets of Florence, was run over and trampled by two oxen. Again, the good bishop prayed over the body of the dead child, and the child was restored to life.

Miracles were performed by Zenobio not only while he lived but even after his death. When the remains of St. Zenobio were carried through the city to be deposited under the high altar of the cathedral, the people crowded around to kiss him and touch his garments. In passing through the Piazza del Duomo the body of the saint was thrown against the trunk of a withered elm standing near the spot. Suddenly the tree, which had been dead for years, burst into fresh leaves.

St. Zenobio's life has been a favorite subject for Christian artists. Lorenzo Ghiberti designed a bronze sarcophagus to house the relics of the saint. The bas-reliefs portray the miracle of the restoration of the son of the Frenchwoman, the restoration of the messenger, and the story of the trampled child. Botticelli painted *The Three Miracles of Saint Zenobio*. Masaccio also painted the raising of the dead child. The legendary connection of invoking St. Zenobio against headaches, however, is lost.

See also: AMBROSE, ST.

*Zephyrus*

**Zephyrus**   In Greek mythology, the West Wind, son of Astraeus and Eos; married to Chloris; father of Carpus, god of fruit; also father of Balius and Xanthus, immortal horses of Achilles, by Podarge; called Favionius by the Romans and also known as Caurus. Zephyrus also loved Hyacinthus, a young male, but Hyacinthus loved Apollo. The angry West Wind caused Hyacinthus's death by blowing the quoit of Apollo against Hyacinthus's head. Frequent use is made of Zephyrus in literature. Ovid's *Heroides* (14.39) cites the wind, and Chaucer, in the Prologue to *The Canterbury Tales*, opens with

3254

When Zephirus eek with his swete breeth
Enspired hath in every holt and heeth
The tendre croppes . . .

In *The Bard* Thomas Gray writes:

Fair laughs the Morn and soft the Zephyr
   blows,
While proudly riding o'er the azure realm
In gallant rim the gilded vessel goes;
Youth on the prow, and Pleasure at the helm.

Zephyrus appears in Botticelli's paintings, breathing life into Flora in *Primavera* and wafting Venus to the shore in *The Birth of Venus*. In ancient art Zephyrus is often portrayed as partly unclothed, carrying flowers in the folds of his robe.

See also: ACHILLES; APOLLO; CHAUCER; HYACINTHUS; XANTHUS

3255

**Zetes** (searcher)   In Greek mythology, winged twin of Calais; brother of Chione and Cleopatra; son of Thracian king Boreas and Orithyia. Zetes and his brother Calais took part in the Argonaut expedition and fought the Harpies in Bithynia.

See also: ARGONAUTS; BOREAS; CALAIS; HARPIES

3256

**Zeus** (bright sky)   In Greek mythology, sky god, the chief of the 12 Olympian gods; son of Cronus and Rhea; brother of Hades, Hestia, Demeter, Hera, and Poseidon; married to Hera; called Jupiter or Jove by the Romans.

Cronus had been told by an oracle of Gaea that he would be overthrown by one of his children, even as he had overthrown his father, Uranus. To prevent this, Cronus swallowed his children as soon as they were born. When the time came for Zeus's birth, Rhea was determined to save her child. She went to Mount Lycaeus in Arcadia to a place called Cretea and gave birth to Zeus. When Cronus asked Rhea for the child so that he could swallow him, she gave her husband

*Zeus*

a stone wrapped in swaddling clothes. The god swallowed the stone at once. Rhea then washed the real Zeus in the Neda River and entrusted him to Gaea to be given to the nymphs of Crete to be raised.

Zeus was raised by the nymphs Adrastea and Ida, daughters of Melisseus. The infant god was fed on milk and honey by the goat Amalthea. To drown out the infant's cries and prevent them from reaching the ears of Cronus, the Curetes (people of Crete) crashed their shields.

When Zeus grew up, he went to see Metis, who, some accounts say, was his first wife. Metis was a female Titan who advised Zeus how to force Cronus to disgorge Zeus's brothers and sisters. Metis gave Zeus a potion to give to Cronus. Zeus disguised himself as a cupbearer and gave the drink to his father. Hestia, Demeter, Hera, Hades, Poseidon, and the stone were vomited out. The stone was later set up at Delphi as the Omphalos (navel), or center, of the earth.

Zeus, with his brothers Hades and Poseidon, then made war on his father and the Titans. The war, however, dragged on for 10 years with no end in sight. Then Zeus was told by Gaea that if he released the Cyclopes and the Hecatonchires from their prison in Tartarus, he would defeat Cronus. Zeus descended to Tartarus, killed the woman jailer Campe, and freed the Cyclopes and Hecatonchires. The Cyclopes forged a thunderbolt for Zeus, a magic cap that made Hades invisible, and a trident for Poseidon. The gods, thus armed, defeated Cronus and the Titans. All of the defeated except Atlas were sent to Tartarus to be guarded by the Hecatonchires. Zeus, Hades, and Poseidon then cast lots into a helmet to decide what sections of the universe each god was to rule. Zeus drew the heavens, Hades the underworld, and Poseidon the sea. The earth and Olympus were the common property of all three. Zeus was chosen head.

The marriages of Zeus in Greek mythology are numerous. As the husband of Mnemosyne (memory) he was the father of the Muses; Themis (justice) bore him the Horae, the seasons of the year; and Eurynome (far ruler) was the mother of the Charities or Graces. Zeus is the only Greek god who is the father of other Olympian gods. On Mount Cyllene Zeus was honored as the husband of Maia and the father of Hermes. At Dodona his wife was Dione, but in time his sister Hera was recognized as his legitimate wife and queen. Aside from numerous wives, Zeus also had many love affairs with both women and men. Robert Herrick, the English poet, using the Latin name Jove for Zeus, wrote in *To the Maids to Walk Abroad*:

> But fables we'll relate, how Jove
> Put on all shapes to get a love,
> As now a satyr, then a swan,
> A bull then, and now a man.

Zeus had many roles in Greek mythology, He was the sky god, the god of storms and rain, the mighty thunderer, and master of the lightning. The mountains were his seat. As the god of storms, Zeus was also the god of battles, being the father of Ares and Athena, both war deities. The decision about which side would win in battle was believed to reside with Zeus. The statue of the Olympian Zeus by Phidias carried the Nike (victory) in its right hand. Though the Greeks made the children of Zeus war deities, Zeus was honored as the patron of physical contests. The olive branch of Zeus was awarded to the swift, strong, and skillful at Olympia. In many places in Greece, games were celebrated in honor of Zeus or found expression in the worship of his sons Apollo, Hermes, and Heracles.

As the sky god Zeus revealed his will with signs in the heavens. Prophecy and inspiration belonged to Zeus and his son Apollo. In Aeschylus's *Prometheus Bound*, Prometheus is made to say:

> . . . tokens by the way And flight of taloned birds I clearly marked Those on the right propitious to mankind, And those sinister, and what form of life They each maintain, and what their enmities Each with the other, and their loves and friendships (Translated by Plumptre)

The priest Calchas saw a serpent devouring a sparrow with nine young and knew it was a sign from Zeus that Troy would fall. At Dodona, one of Zeus's great shrines, doves or priestesses made the will of Zeus known. A lofty oak, sacred to Zeus, who sent rain for the farmers, was the home of these doves. The rustling of its leaves revealed the presence of the god. In Athens a spatter of rain or a thunderbolt was a sign that the gods were not looking down with favor, so public assemblies were at once adjourned. Spenser, in the *Faerie Queene* (book 1), using the Latin name Jove for Zeus wrote: "And angry Jove an hideous storme of raine/ Did poure . . ." Pope, in *The Rape of the Lock*, also using Zeus's Latin name Jove, wrote: "Jove's thunder roars, heaven trembles all around."

Aside from his role in the heavens, Zeus was also worshiped as a patron of agriculture. Offerings of fruit were brought to Zeus Polieus, the guardian of the city on the Acropolis. In the variable weather of spring, both public and secret rites were performed to render Zeus propitious. In summer, when heat and drought threatened the crops, the Athenians again joined in the worship of Zeus.

The concept of Zeus changed over the many centuries during which the god was worshiped. In Homer's *Iliad* and *Odyssey* the rule of Zeus over gods and men is set forth. Zeus was always the protector of the state. On the Acropolis at Athens was an altar to Zeus, the protector of the city. The earliest altar of the state was the altar in the king's palace, the altar on which the king sacrificed in behalf of his people. Two kings of Sparta claimed descent from Zeus. At Athens sacrifices were offered to him as the god of phratry, or clan, when children were enrolled in its lists. Though he was not faithful to his wife, he was regarded as the god of the family. He was one of the gods who presided over marriage, along with his wife, Hera.

Zeus was invoked in oaths. The oath breaker feared the vengeance of Zeus. Earlier Zeus had declared that oaths of the gods must be sworn by the waters of the Styx because the Styx and her children had come to his aid in the war against his father and the Titans.

*Cronus and Rhea, father and mother of Zeus*

An elevated concept of Zeus's divine role is found in the *Agamemnon* of Aeschylus. The chorus gives an account of the god's nature:

Zeus—it to The Unknown
That name of many names seem good—
Zeus, upon Thee I call.
thro' the mind's every road
I passed, but vain are all,
Save that which names thee Zeus, the
    Highest One,
Were it but mine to cast away the load,
The weary load, that weighs my spirit down.
He that was Lord of old,
In full-blown pride of place and valor bold,
Hath fallen and is gone, even as an old tale
    told!
And he that next held sway,
By stronger grasp o'erthrown
Hath pass'd away!
And whoso now shall bid the triumph-chant
    arise
To Zeus, and Zeus alone,
He shall be found the truly wise.
'Tis Zeus alone who shows the perfect way
Of knowledge: He hath ruled,
Men shall learn wisdom, by affliction
    schooled (Translation by Morshead).

The eagle and the oak were sacred to Zeus. The eagle, together with the scepter and the lightning, is one of his most frequently encountered attributes. The most famous statue of Zeus in the ancient world was the one Phidias executed for the temple of Olympia. About 40 feet high, it was made of gold and ivory and portrayed the god seated. The bearded head was ornamented with olive leaves, and the upper part of the statue's body was made of ivory; the lower part was wrapped in a golden mantle falling from the hips to the feet, which wore golden sandals and rested on a footstool. Lying beside Zeus were golden lions. Zeus's right hand bore Nike; the left hand bore the scepter surmounted by an eagle.

Zeus had many epithets, among them Cronides (son of Cronus); Coccygius (cuckoo), the bird whose form he assumed when he raped Hera; Aegichus (aegis bearing); Anchesmius (of Anchesmus); Apesantius (of Apesas); Aphesius (releaser); Capotas (reliever); Catharsius (purifier); Chthonius (of the underworld); Clarius (of lots); Ctesius (grain god); Eleutherius (god of freedom); Herceius (of the courtyard); Homagyrius (assembler); Lecheates (in childbed); Leucaeus (of the white poplar); Lycaeus (wolfish); Mechaneus (contriver); Megistus (almighty); Meilichius (gracious); Moeragetes (guide of Fate); Hypaistus (most high); Panhellenius (god of the Greeks); Patrous (paternal); Philius (friendly); Phyxius (god of flight); Semaleus (sign-giving); Soter (savior); Sthenius (strong); Teleius (full grown); and Tropaean (he who turns to flight).

See also: HERA; JOVE; OLYMPIAN GODS

3257

**Ziggurat** (zikkurat, ziqqurat) (pinnacle) Mesopotamian stepped pyramid usually built of brick and forming part of any temple complex. Because Babylonians believed that the gods lived on mountains, they designed the ziggurat in imitation of a natural mountain. The great ziggurat at Babylon was called Etemenaki (the house of the foundation of heaven and earth), and the ziggurat at Nippur was called house of oracle. The Tower of Babel in the Bible (Gen. 11:1–9), as well as Jacob's dream (Gen. 28:11–19), probably stem from the ziggurat; it was the link between heaven and earth, as the tower and Jacob's ladder were in the Hebrew legends.

See also: JACOB; TOWER OF BABEL

3258

**Zin** In African mythology (Songhai of the upper Niger), water spirits. One day a zin, in the form of a snake, sat by its lake sunning itself. When a lovely girl passed by, he immediately fell in love with her. As dowry, her parents asked the zin for possession of the lake. He agreed but on occasion visited his palace at the bottom of the lake. When he grew old and died, his son became the guardian of the lake. It angers the zin when people enter the lake with weapons made of iron.

See also: FARAN; SNAKE

3259

**Zita, St.** (Sitha, Citha) (to seek)    13th century.
In Christian legend, patron saint of domestic
servants; venerated at Lucca, Italy. Feast, 27
April.

Zita became a servant at the age of 12 and
continued to be employed by the same family for
some 48 years. One saying ascribed to the saint is
"A servant is not good if she is not industrious:
Work-shy piety in people of our position is sham
piety." However, the traditional saying seems to
have been invented by her masters.

One legend of the saint in the *Vita Sanctorum*,
a collection of saints' lives, tells how Zita stayed
too long at church and did not have time to make
breakfast for her master. Zita rushed home and
found to her joy that an angel had done the work
for her. The bread was baked and ready to eat.

Another legend tells how Zita, touched with
pity for the half-starved who came to her master's house during a severe famine, gave them the
beans from her master's granary without asking
his permission. Not long afterward the master,
Pagano, was taking stock and went to measure
the beans. Zita was frightened and hid herself behind her mistress. The master found the measure
correct. Zita thanked God for restoring what had
been taken. Zita is portrayed in Christian art as a
serving maid.

3260

**Ziusudra** (Sisouthros, Ziudsuddu)    In Near
Eastern mythology (Sumerian), hero of the flood
myth, which is fragmentary and has in part been
reconstructed. Told of a coming deluge, Ziusudra wrote down the history and traditions of his
people and placed the tablets at Sippar, the city
of the sun god. Then, taking his wife, daughter,
and a pilot, he embarked in an ark, which eventually landed on the top of a mountain as the waters
of the flood receded. When the four disem-
barked from the ark, they offered sacrifices to the
gods. The gods Anu and Enlil gave Ziusudra
"breath eternal like that of a god" as a reward for
his faithfulness. Many of the incidents in the

Sumerian version of the flood myth are also
found in the Hebrew narrative of the flood in the
Old Testament (Gen. 6–9).

See also: ANU; ENLIL; NOAH

3261

**Zoa**    In African mythology (Songhai of the upper Niger), primal ancestor, wise man, and protector.

Word was passed to Zoa that if a pregnant
woman was fed sheep's liver, it was actually the
unborn child who ate it. He opened the stomach
of a pregnant slave and found this to be true. Zoa
performed many other astonishing acts, such as
tending a wounded lioness and then going hunting with her. He predicted that a particular bird
would suddenly die and be cooked on a fire that
would light by itself. All things happened just as
Zoa said they would. His son was greatly sad-
dened when the bird died, and so Zoa commanded the earth to open, predicting that his son
would become the next chief. Zoa told the people what offerings should be brought to him in
times of trouble and which people were unworthy to visit his shrine. Then he entered the
hole in the earth that he had previously ordered
to open, and the ground closed around him.
Four trees grew from that spot. They are taken
to represent the four points of the compass.

3262

**Zodiac** (circle of animals or relating to animals)
Imaginary zone (or belt) in the heavens, extend-
ing about eight degrees to each side of the eclip-
tic, which the sun traverses every year. The signs
of the Zodiac were named after deities and animals whose shape or outline could be seen in the
heavens. The names are derived from Greek and
Roman mythology. The 12 signs of the Zodiac
were often combined in the Middle Ages, in
psalters and books of hours, with the 12 months,
or labors of the month.

The signs with their attributes and the date
when the sun enters their path are

1. Aries, the Ram (Golden Fleece), 21 March.
2. Taurus, the Bull (Europa's mount), 20 April.
3. Gemini, the Twins (Castor and Pollux), 21 May.
4. Cancer, the Crab (Heracles' tormentor), 22 June.
5. Leo, the Lion (Nemean Lion), 23 July.
6. Virgo, the Virgin, 23 August.
7. Libra, the Scales, 23 September.
8. Scorpio, the Scorpion (Orion's torturer), 24 October.
9. Sagittarius, the Archer (Chiron), 22 November.
10. Capricorn, the Goat (Amalthea), 22 December.
11. Aquarius, the Water Bearer (Ganymede), 20 January.
12. Pisces, the Fish (Aphrodite and Eros), 19 February.

Frequent references are made to the Zodiac in European literature throughout the ages. Chaucer wrote a treatise on the *Astrolabe*, which describes the workings of a mechanical device for indicating the movement of the planets. In the prologue to *The Canterbury Tales*, he makes reference to the fact that "the younge sonne / Hath in the Rame his halve cours yronne." In *The Faerie Queene* Spenser gives an elaborate description of the months with figures from the Zodiac. Milton (book 10) also makes use of the Zodiac in *Paradise Lost*.

See also: AQUARIUS; CANCER; CAPRICORN; CHAUCER; VIRGO

3263
*Zohar, The* (splendor)  Medieval Jewish kabalistic work, written partly in Hebrew, partly in Aramaic. It is credited to Moses de León, a 13th-century Castilian cabalist, who died in 1305. It deals with the divine names of God, the soul, the Torah, the Messiah, and other Jewish topics in a mystical way, incorporating many mythical motifs. Its basic belief is that there is a correspondence between the upper world and the lower world—that is, what happens in heaven can affect earth and vice versa.

3264
**Zombie**  In Haitian voodoo, a person who has been "murdered" by poison and brought back to life by a *bocor*, a voodoo witch doctor. It is also used as a generic term for the spirits of the dead.

In Haiti a zombie is one of the most feared of beings, and his or her existence is not doubted. Haiti's criminal code says: "Also shall be qualified as attempted murder the employment . . . against any person of substances, which, without causing actual death, produce a lethargic coma more or less prolonged. If, after the administering of such substances, the person has been buried, the act shall be considered murder no matter what result follows."

An article in *Time* magazine (17 October 1983) quoted Harvard botanist E. Wade Davis, who has made a study of zombies: "Zombism exists and is a societal phenomenon that can be explained logically." The toxin used to poison victims, tetrodotoxin, comes from the puffer fish and is coma-inducing. The effect of the poison depends on the dosage. Too much will actually kill. The zombie must be exhumed about eight hours after burial, or he or she will suffocate. When the victim is awakened, he or she is fed a paste made of sweet potato and datura, a hallucinogenic plant. Often the victim is then used for slave labor.

Zombies are found not only in Haiti but also in movies. Victor Halperin's *White Zombie* was the first sound film on the subject. The term *zombie* was also applied to a strong rum drink said to leave the drinker apparently lifeless with intoxication. In a Ritz Brothers film the three comedians walk up to a bartender and order "Three zombies." "I can see that," the bartender replies, "but what'll you have to drink?"

3265

**Zophiel** (Jophiel, Iophiel, Iofiel, Jofiel) (the beauty of God)   In Jewish and Christian folklore, archangel who drove Adam and Eve from the Garden of Eden. The account in Genesis (3:23–24), however, nowhere mentions an angel but "the Lord God" himself as responsible for casting the two out of the garden. In Genesis cherubim and "a flaming sword which turned every way" guarded the way to the Tree of Life. Cherubim were griffinlike monsters from Near Eastern mythology who were later made into angels in Jewish and Christian mythology. In *Paradise Lost* (book 6:535) Milton calls Zophiel "of cherubim the swiftest wing," and the angel's name forms part of a book-length poem, *Zophiel, or, The Bride of Seven* by the American Maria Gowen Brooks. The poem was quite influential in England, though not as popular in America. Charles Lamb, impressed by the work, could not believe "a woman capable of anything so great!"

See also: ADAM AND EVE; CHERUBIM; GRIFFIN

3266

**Zotz**   In the mythology of the Zotzil Indians who live in the Chiapas, a bat god. One Mayan carving in Copán portrays the hero god Kukulcán battling the Zotz. The term *zotz* also was used by the Mayans for a 20-day period of their calendar.

3267

**Zu**   In Near Eastern mythology (Babylonian), storm god in the form of a massive bird who stole the tablets of fate.

In his greed for power and dominion Zu determined to steal from the great god Bel (variant: Enlil) the tablets of fate, or destiny. The tablets gave their possessor supreme power over men and gods.

"I will possess the tablets," Zu said to himself, "and all things will be under my power and subject to me. The spirits of heaven will bow before me and the oracles of the gods will be under my command. I shall wear the crown, symbol of sovereignty, and the robe, symbol of godhead. I shall rule over men and gods."

Zu entered the great hall of Bel, where he awaited the coming of the day. As Bel was making the day appear, Zu snatched the tablets from Bel's hands and flew off. He then hid himself in his mountain. Zu's act caused consternation among the gods. Anu, the sky god, called an assembly of the gods to find a means of capturing Zu. As he calls on one of the gods to come forth, the text of the myth breaks off. Scholars suggest the gods Shamash, Rimmon, Marduk, or Lugulbanda as possible heroes in the end of the myth.

See also: ANU; BEL; LUGULBANDA; MARDUK; RIMMON; SHAMASH

3268

**Zupay**   In Spanish South American mythology, a forest demon who often seduces women. A *zupay* can take the form of a handsome young man or a satyr. He appears in Ricardo Rojas's short story "The Incubus."

*Zurvan*

3269

**Zurvan** (Akarana, Zarvan, Zervan, Zrvan)   In Persian mythology, god of time-space, father of the good god, Ahura Mazda, and his evil brother, Ahriman. Zurvan appears as the main god in Zurvanism, an offshoot of Zoroastrian belief. One of the main beliefs of Zurvanism was that the universe was not an act of God but an evolutionary development of formless primeval matter, infinite time and space, or Zurvan. This is opposed to Zoroastrian belief in a good creator god, Ahura Mazda, a life after death, and a moral order in which there is reward and punishment.

In one Zoroastrian book, the *Bundahishn*, Zurvan is called Zarman, "the demon who makes decrepit, whom they call old age." Zurvan also appears as a god in Mithraism, where the image of the lion-headed figure with signs of the zodiac on his body is believed to represent the god. Some scholars, however, identify the statue as that of Ahriman.

See also: AHRIMAN; AHURA MAZDA; MITHRAS; ZARATHUSTRA

# ANNOTATED BIBLIOGRAPHY

Any bibliography that attempts to list studies dealing with myth and legend must be viewed as selective. This Annotated Bibliography is no exception. It does, however, list many major translations of original sources available in English as well as scholarly studies of the various mythologies and legends. Since the first publication of the *Facts on File Encyclopedia of World Mythology and Legend* in 1988, numerous new dictionaries, handbooks, and encyclopedias have appeared in print in the United States and abroad. These new works have been added to the bibliography of this revised version. Works in other languages have not been included even though these collections represent major contributions to the study of myth, legend, folktale, and fable. These works, particularly in German, French, and Italian, do, however, frequently appear in the bibliographies of the new works cited here, and the reader is encouraged to consult them for even more sources. Perhaps most useful in the revised Annotated Bibliography are the videos, and Website references, along with maps and illustrations, found in the lists of references of the new items. In addition to these old and new sources, the bibliography also includes the standard and helpful indexes of folktales and motifs, the *Tale Type Index of the Folktale* and the *Motif Index of Folk Literature*. The reader is also encouraged to use the annually published and quarterly updated on-line database of the *Modern Language Association International Bibliography*, which has always listed a broad range of folklore studies, including myth and legend and other narrative forms. In the bibliography below, works are grouped according to category, beginning with general references and proceeding to more specialized groupings according to geographical, cultural, and ethnic divisions. The reader should also consult the "Author's Preface and Users' Guide for further guidance.

## GENERAL REFERENCE WORKS ON MYTHOLOGY, FOLKLORE, AND RELIGION

Aarne, Antti, and Stith Thompson, *The Types of the Folktale: A Classification and Bibliography*; Suomlinen Tiedeakatemia, Helsinki, 1987, second revision. The standard reference work for identifying and classifying of folktales by internationally recognized reference numbers. The individual tales are listed in scholarly texts by AT for Aarne/Thompson and by a number, e.g., 709 for Snow White. Studies of these tales can be searched in the MLA International Bibliography database under AT 709. Unfortunately the scope is primarily Eurocentric.

Aldrich, Keith (ed., trans.), *Apollodorus: The Library of Greek Mythology*; Coronado Press, 1975. A relatively modern translation using a newer text than Frazer (see below), and explanatory notes unencumbered by special theories.

Ann, Martha, and Dorothy Myers Imel, *Goddesses in World Mythology*; ABC-CLIO, Santa Barbara, Denver, and Oxford (England), 1993. A comprehensive guide to the goddesses of the world, covering 30,000 years of goddess worship. Includes a general index.

Ballou, Robert, ed., *The Bible of the World*; The Viking Press, New York, 1939. Excellent anthology, though some of the translations are stilted, of the major religious texts that form so much a part of world mythology. Notes. Index.

Barber, Richard, *A Companion to World Mythology*; Delacorte Press, New York, 1979. An A-to-Z listing, with illustrations by Pauline Baynes on every page. Contains maps, Index of Topics, and Index of Places.

Beard, Mary, John North, and Simon Price, *Religions of Rome* (2 volumes); Cambridge University Press, 1998. A landmark and comprehensive study of Roman religions, with a separate volume of source material.

Bremmer, Jan N., *Greek Religion*; Greece & Rome: New Surveys in the Classics, No. 24. Oxford University Press, 1994. Excellent short introduction to scholarly treatment of Greek religion; includes discussion of the place of mythology within that context.

Brown, Mary Ellen, and Bruce A. Rosenberg, *Encyclopedia of Folklore and Literature*; ABC-CLIO, Santa Barbara, Denver, and Oxford (England), 1998. This work is devoted exclusively to folklore and folklorists and the relationship to primary literary sources. There are helpful cross-references in the text as well as a general index.

Brunvand, Jan Harold, *Encyclopedia of Urban Legends*; ABC-CLIO, Santa Barbara, Denver, and Oxford (England), 2001. An exhaustive compilation of contemporary urban legends from around the world. All entries are cross-referenced and each entry includes a brief source reference. The general bibliography suggests further readings. Illustrations and materials on the Internet are also included.

Bulfinch, Thomas, "Bulfinch's Mythology"; Thomas Y. Crowell, New York, 1970. An edition containing *The Age of Fable* (1855), about Greek and Roman mythology, mainly based on Ovid and Vergil, *The Age of Chivalry* (1858), dealing with medieval legends, and *Legends of Charlemagne* (1863). One of the most popular 19th-century retellings of mythology, leaving out any reference to sexual matters. This particular edition has a helpful dictionary and index. Numerous other editions of "Bulfinch's Mythology" are offered by other publishers.

Burkert, Walter, *Ancient Mystery Cults*; Harvard University Press, 1987. Comprehensive, comparative analysis of mystery religions of Greece and Rome, including Dionysus, Demeter, and Mithras, with emphasis on the original sources.

Campbell, Joseph, *The Hero with a Thousand Faces*; Pantheon Books, New York, [1949] 1968. Now classic study of the subject. Index.

Canney, Maurice A., *An Encyclopedia of Religions*; G. Routledge & Sons, Ltd., London, 1921. Reissued by Gale Research Company, Detroit, 1970. A one-volume work mainly concerned with Christianity, though some of the entries on other religions are of use. No index.

Cavendish, Richard, ed., *Legends of the World*; Orbis Publishing, London, 1982. Dictionary, divided into group sections, such as Hindu, etc., written by various authors. Comparative Survey of World Legends. Bibliography.

———, *Man, Myth, & Magic: An Illustrated Encyclopedia of the Supernatural*; Marshall Cavendish Corp. New York, 1970. A fully illustrated encyclopedia in 24 thin volumes with some excellent articles on mythology. The major problem with the work is its emphasis on occult matters that have little bearing on mythology or folklore. Bibliography. Index.

Cooper, J. C., *An Illustrated Encyclopedia of Traditional Symbols*; Thames and Hudson, London,

1978. A heavily illustrated guide covering a wide spectrum of symbols. Bibliography.

Cotterell, Arthur, *A Dictionary of World Mythology*; Perigee Books, published by G. P. Putnam's Sons, New York, 1979. A short, well-written, illustrated dictionary, done in group sections. Selected Reading list and good index.

Daniel, Howard, *Encyclopedia of Themes and Subjects in Painting*; Harry N. Abrams, Inc., New York, 1971. An A-to-Z listing covering mythological (Greek and Roman), biblical (Christian), historical, allegorical, and topical subjects in Western Art.

Fagles, Robert (trans.), *Homer: The Iliad*; Viking Penguin, 1990. Superb modern translation with a splendid introduction to Homer and the epic by Bernard Knox.

Fagles, Robert (trans.), *Homer: The Odyssey*; Viking Penguin, 1996. Superb modern translation with a splendid introduction to Homer and the epic by Bernard Knox.

Feder, Lillian, *Ancient Myth in Modern Poetry*; Princeton University Press, 1971. Classical myths in the poetry of Pound, Yeats, Eliot, and Auden.

Fontenrose, Joseph, *The Delphic Oracle: Its Responses and Operations with a Catalogue of Responses*; University of California Press, 1978. A thorough catalogue and sober analysis of the evidence surrounding the activity of the oracle at Delphi.

Frazer, James George, *The Golden Bough: A Study in Magic and Religion*; Macmillan & Co. Ltd., London, 1912. A massive, 13-volume work, which is fascinating reading on many levels. Though some of it is dated, it still forms a good basis for the study of mythology and legend. The author published a one-volume abridgment in 1922, also issued by Macmillan. Good index.

Freeman, John, ed., *Brewer's Dictionary of Phrase and Fable*; Harper & Row, Publishers, New York and Evanston, 1963. First published in 1870, eighth revised edition. Very brief entries, but a valuable one volume source.

Gaskell, G. A. *Dictionary of All Scriptures and Myths*; The Julian Press, Inc., New York, 1960. A muddled, misleading dictionary with a very strong occult bias but valuable for its numerous quotations within entries.

Gaster, Theodor H., *The New Golden Bough: A New Abridgment of the Classic Work by Sir James George Frazer*; Criterion Books, New York, 1959. A present-day scholar takes Frazer's work and adds notes to bring it up to date. One of the most valuable editions of Frazer available. Notes. Index.

Georges, Robert A., and Michael Owen Jones. *Folkloristics: An Introduction*; Indiana University Press: Bloomington and Indianapolis. 1995. The most complete and up-to-date study of folklore and folklore methodologies available.

Grant, Michael, *Roman Myths*; Dorset Press, 1984 (1971). The only extensive examination of Roman tales and legends from a serious scholarly point of view as myths within modern critical assumptions. Addresses both "religious" and secular myths and legends.

Green, Thomas A., ed., *Folklore: An Encyclopedia of Beliefs, Customs, Tales, Music, and Art*; ABC-CLIO, Santa Barbara, Denver, and Oxford (England), 1997. A two-volume work and a good source for concepts of folklore, with extensive cross references and a general index. The emphasis is on North American folklore, but some items suggest a more global approach to the topic.

Hall, James, *Dictionary of Subjects & Symbols in Art*; Harper & Row, New York, 1974. Good, well written and researched, with an introduction by Kenneth Clark. Useful for Greek, Roman, and Christian mythology.

Hinnells, John R., ed., *The Facts On File Dictionary of Religions*; Facts On File, New York, 1984. An A-to-Z listing. Good bibliography. Index. Helpful for quick reference.

Ions, Veronica, *The World's Mythology in Colour*; Hamlyn, London, 1974. Richly illustrated in color, with an introduction by Jacquetta

Hawkes, the book makes a quick survey of its subject. Further Reading List. Index.

Kirk, Geoffrey, *Myth: Its Meaning and Functions in Ancient & Other Cultures*; University of California Press, 1970. A comparative treatment of Greek myths and legends within the context of theories of world myths, as well as a kind of historical survey of theory about Greek myths. Careful attention to the impact of scholars such as Max Mueller, B. Malinowski, and C. Lévi-Strauss.

Kirk, Geoffrey, *The Nature of Greek Myths*; Penguin Books, 1974. Intended as a classroom textbook, a level-headed and sound approach to Greek myths, legends, and sagas.

Leach, Maria, ed., *Standard Dictionary of Folklore, Mythology and Legend*; Funk & Wagnalls, New York, 1972. An extensive, one-volume work, written by various hands. Very wide coverage of folklore but lacking in religion and mythology.

Leach, Majorie, *Guide to the Gods*; ABC-CLIO, Santa Barbara, Denver, and Oxford (England), 1992. Michael Owen Jones and Frances Cattermole-Tally, eds. This is an extensive listing of gods from around the world, divided into Cosmological, Celestial, Atmospheric, Terrestrial, Life/Death Cycle deities, sections on Economic Activities, Sociocultural Concepts, and Religion. There is also an extensive index to all of the gods listed in the volume.

Lewis, James R., *UFOs and Popular Culture: An Encyclopedia of Contemporary Mythology*; ABC-CLIO, Santa Barbara, Denver, and Oxford (England), 2000. Includes religious beliefs, legends, movies, TV shows, advertising, celebrities, Internet sites, and photos. General index.

Lewis, James R.. *Satanism Today: An Encyclopedia of Religion, Folklore, and Popular Culture*; ABC-CLIO, Santa Barbara, Denver, and Oxford (England), 2001. This encyclopedia covers popular music and films, contemporary organized Satanic groups, ritual abuse cases, and practices and beliefs. Includes photos and illustrations, a chronology, an index, appendixes, and bibliography.

MacCulloch, John Arnott (general editor), *The Mythology of All Races*; Marshall Jones Co., 1916. Reissued by Cooper Square Publisher, Inc., New York, 1964. A 13-volume work dealing with Greek, Roman (1), Eddic (2), Celtic, Slavic (3), Finno-Ugric, Siberian (4), Semitic (5), Indian, Iranian (6), Armenian, African (7), Chinese, Japanese (8), Oceanic (9), North American (10), American, Latin (11), Egypt, Far East (12), Index (13). Usefulness varies from volume to volume depending on the author. Extensive bibliographies in each volume.

McKinzie, Michael, *Mythologies of the World: The Illustrated Guide to Mythological Beliefs and Customs*; Facts On File, New York, 2001. A good introductory guide book with maps, illustrations, glossary, and tables.

McLeish, Kenneth, *Myth: Myth and Legends of the World Explained and Explored*; Facts On File, New York, 1996. Extensive coverage of myths and legends from around the world. Includes Woodcuts.

Mercatante, Anthony S., *Good and Evil: Mythology and Folklore*; Harper & Row, New York, 1978. A short world study, dealing with the myths, legends, and beliefs surrounding good and evil. Annotated bibliography. Index.

Morford, Mark P. O., and Robert J. Lenardon, *Classical Mythology*, 6th ed.; Addison-Wesley Educational Publishers Inc., 1999. A widely used college-level textbook that includes a thorough survey of the Greek and Roman gods and heroes, with extensive source material translated into English. Some guidance on interpretations of myths, and treatment of the influence of Classical myths on the Middle Ages and Renaissance in art and music.

*New Larousse Encyclopedia of Mythology*; Prometheus Press, London, 1959. Does not list an editor, though the work contains an introduction by Robert Graves and various articles by scholars. Some are excellent. Further reading list. Index.

Oring, Elliott, ed., *Folk Groups and Folklore Genres. An Introduction*; Utah State University Press: Logan, Utah, 1986. A series of excellent and precise essays on the major folklore topics and interpretative techniques.

————, *Folk Groups and Folklore Genres. A Reader*; Utah State University Press: Logan, Utah, 1989. This reader accompanies the essays in the companion volume on the major folklore topics and interpretative techniques.

Parrinder, Geoffrey, *A Dictionary of Non-Christian Religions*; The Westminster Press, Philadelphia, 1971. A good one-volume guide for basic entries on religion, many of which deal with mythology, and sacred books.

————, ed., *Religions of the World: From Primitive Beliefs to Modern Faiths*; Grosset & Dunlap, New York, 1971. Written by a variety of scholars, the book varies in quality but on the whole is worth reading. Heavily illustrated. Bibliography. Good index.

Rosenberg, Donna, *World Mythology: An Anthology of the Great Myths and Epics*; Passport Books, Lincolnwood, Ill., 1986. Retellings of the major myths by often condensing the texts. Selected Bibliography. Index.

Seal, Graham, *Encyclopedia of Folk Heroes*; ABC-CLIO, Santa Barbara, Denver, and Oxford (England), 2001. Mostly short entries, with some longer ones. Includes cross references and suggestions for further reading. Bibliography and general index.

Scullard, H.H., *Festivals and Ceremonies of the Roman Republic*; Cornell University Press, 1981. A complete examination of all known festivals in the pagan Roman calendar.

Thompson, Stith, *Motif-index of Folk-Literature; A Classification of Narrative Elements in Folktales, Ballads, Myths, Fables, Mediaeval Romances, Exempla, Fabliaux, Jest-books, and Local Legends*; Indiana University Press, Bloomington and Indianapolis, 1955–1958. Revised and enlarged edition of the standard motif reference work for folk literature. The six volumes

include individual motifs in an expandable code system. The last volume is the general index to the first five volumes.

Turcan, Robert (Antonia Nevill, trans.), *The Gods of Ancient Rome*; Edinburgh University Press, 2000. An account of what the gods meant to Romans from archaic times to late antiquity; includes a study of the impact of Christianity.

Walker, Barbara G., *The Woman's Encyclopedia of Myths and Secrets*; Harper & Row, San Francisco, 1983. One-volume encyclopedia with some very interesting entries with a very strong bias toward the women's movement. Bibliography.

Whittlesey, E. S., *Symbols and Legends in Western Art*; Charles Scribner's Sons, New York, 1972. An A-to-Z illustrated guide. Helpful for Greek, Roman, and Christian mythology and legend.

## WORLD FOLKTALE COLLECTIONS

Clarkson, Atelia, and Gilbert B. Cross, eds., *World Folktales*; Charles Scribner's Sons, New York, 1980. A selection of folktales with comments. Good introduction. Appendixes covering various aspects of the folktale. Select bibliography.

Cole, Joanna, ed., *Best-Loved Folktales of the World*; Doubleday and Company, Inc., Garden City, N.Y., 1982. A popular collection of tales arranged according to country. Introduction. Index of categories of tales.

Dégh, Linda, ed., *Folktales of Hungary*; translated by Judit Halász; University of Chicago Press, Chicago, 1965. One of the volumes in the series *Folktales of the World* under the editorship of Richard M. Dorson. The present collection contains extensive notes. Index of Motifs and Index of Tale Types. Bibliography. General index.

Foster, James R., ed., *The World's Great Folktales*; Harper & Brothers, New York, 1953. A collection arranged according to types of tales. Introduction. Notes.

Sideman, Belle Becker, ed., *The World's Best Fairy Tales*; The Reader's Digest Association, Pleasantville, N. Y., 1967. A collection of some of the world's best known folktales from a variety of sources.

Thompson, Stith, *The Folktale*; Holt, Rinehart and Winston, New York, 1946. The now classic study of the folktale throughout the world. Introduction. In Appendix B: Principal Collections of Folktales. Index.

Thompson, Stith, *One Hundred Favorite Folktales*; Indiana University Press, Bloomington, 1968. A collection of tales form around the world arranged by cultural area.

## FABLE COLLECTIONS AND REFERENCE WORKS

*Aesop, Fables from*; translated by Ennis Rees; Oxford University Press, New York, 1966. Verse versions of many of the favorite fables derived from a variety of sources. Introduction. Index of titles.

*Aesop, The Fables of*; edited by Joseph Jacobs; Schocken Books, New York, 1966; reissue of 1894 edition. The fables retold by Jacobs. Notes on sources. Index.

*Aesop, Fables of*; translated by S. A. Handford; Penguin Books, New York, 1954. An excellent collection, except the translator insists on using titles not at all familiar to the reader. Introduction. Notes.

Bidpai, *Kalila and Dimna: Selected Fables*; retold by Ramsay Wood; Alfred A. Knopf, New York, 1980. Retelling of classic fables, many of which appear in later Aesopic fables. Based on Sanskrit versions. Introduction by Doris Lessing.

Barius, Valerius, *Aesop's Fables*; translated by Denison B. Hull; The University of Chicago Press, Chicago, 1960. A verse translation of one of the most famous ancient versions of Aesop. Notes. Index.

Jacobs, Joseph, ed., *The Fables of Aesop as First Printed by William Caxton in 1484*; Burt Franklin, New York, 1970; reprint of 1889 edition. A study of the history of the Aesopic

fable. Introduction. Synopsis of Parallels. Index.

Kennerly, Karen, ed., *Hesitant Wolf & Scrupulous Fox: Fables Selected from World Literature*; Random House, New York, 1973. A varied collection of fables from around the world. Biographical notes on the fabulists. Index.

Komroff, Manuel, ed., *The Great Fables*; Tudor Publishing Co., New York, 1928. A massive collection of Aesopic fables ranging the entire world. No index.

La Fontaine, *The Fables*; translated by Elizur Wright; G. Bell and Sons, Ltd., London, 1917; reissue of 1841 edition. A complete edition of all of the fables. Introduction. Brief notes.

———, *The Fables*; translated by Marianne Moore; The Viking Press, New York, 1952. A translation by a major American poet that is often quite good.

———, *Selected Fables*; translated by James Michie; The Viking Press, New York, 1971. A selection of some of the best-known fables in verse. Introduction by Geoffrey Grigson.

*The Panchatantra*; translated by Arthur W. Ryder; The University of Chicago Press, Chicago, 1925. A classic English translation of a classic Sanskrit text of animal fables.

Perry, Ben Edwin, ed. and trans., *Babrius and Phaedrus: Fables*; The Loeb Classical Library, 1965. A collection of fables in Greek by Babrius and in Latin by Phaedrus with English translation. Introduction. Notes.

Shapiro, Norman R., trans., *Fables from Old French: Aesop's Beasts and Bumpkins*; Wesleyan University Press, Middletown, Conn., 1982. A collection of Aesopic fables by Marie de France, Isopet I, Isopet II de Paris, and Isopet de Chartres. Notes. Selected bibliography.

Snodgrass, Mary Ellen, *Encyclopedia of Fable*, ABC-CLIO, Santa Barbara, Denver, and Oxford (England), 1998. Lengthy entries on individual fables, fable writers, and collections of fables from the ancient world down to the present. Sources are listed following each entry, and refer to the extensive bibliography.

Internet sources are also listed, and there is a general index.

## BALLAD COLLECTIONS

Child, Francis James, ed., *The English and Scottish Popular Ballads*; Houghton, Mifflin and Company, New York, 1884–1898. Reissued by Dover Publications, Inc., New York, 1965. The classic five-volume work with the ballads, variants, notes, etc. A standard text.

Friedman, Albert F. *The Viking Book of Folk Ballads of the English-Speaking World*; The Viking Press, New York, 1963. A good one-volume collection of ballads with brief introductions, bibliography, and an Index to Titles and First Lines of the Ballads included.

Kinsley, James, ed., *The Oxford Book of Ballads*; Oxford at the Clarendon Press, Oxford, 1969. A collection with the music. Introduction. Notes.

Leach, MacEdward, ed., *The Ballad Book* Harper & Brothers, New York, 1955. Excellent selection with English, Scottish, and American ballads. Good introduction. Notes. Index.

Lockhart, J. G., ed. and trans., *The Spanish Ballads*; The Century Co., New York, 1907. An edition with notes of one of the most popular 19th-century translations.

Olrik, Axel, ed., *A Book of Danish Ballads*; translated by E. M. Smith-Dampier; Princeton University Press, Princeton, N. J., 1939. A selection of ballads in a wide range. Long, good introduction.

Percy, Thomas, ed., *Reliques of Ancient English Poetry*; edited by J. V. Prichard; Thomas Y. Crowell and Co., New York, 1875. An edition of the classic collection. Introduction. Notes. Glossary.

Wimberly, Lowry C., *Folklore in the English and Scottish Ballads*; Frederick Ungar Publishing Co., New York, 1928. Study of the customs and beliefs in English and Scottish ballads relating to religion and magic. Bibliography. Index.

## FLORA AND FAUNA IN MYTHOLOGY AND FOLKLORE

Davis, Courtney, *Celtic Beasts: Animal Motifs and Zoomorphic Design in Celtic Art*; Blandford, London, 1999. Animals in Celtic art, decoration and ornaments. Bibliography and general index.

Gubernatis, Angelo de, *Zoological Mythology, or The Legends of Animals*; Trubner & Co., London, 1872. Reissued by Singing Tree Press, Detroit, 1968. The work contains a wealth of information as well as summaries of myths, fables, and legends relating to animals. But a major drawback is that the author ascribes nearly every incident in each tale to a natural phenomenon such as dawn, sunset, wind, storm, and others. Index.

Lum, Peter, *Fabulous Beasts*; Pantheon Books, New York, 1951. A popular study of fantastic and mythical animals. Index.

Mercatante, Anthony S., *The Magic Garden: The Myth and Folklore of Flowers, Plants, Trees, and Herbs*; Harper & Row, New York, 1976. A coverage that explores world folklore. Introduction. Illustrations. Annotated bibliography. Index.

———, *Zoo of the Gods: Animals in Myth, Legend, and Fable*; Harper & Row, New York, 1974. A comparative study of world myth and legend relating to various animals. Illustrated. Annotated bibliography. Index.

Porteous, Alexander, *Forest Folklore, Mythology, and Romance*; George Allen & Unwin, Ltd., London, 1928. A general survey of the topic. Index.

Thiselton-Dyer, T. F., *The Folklore of Plants*; Chatto & Windus, London, 1889. Reissued by Singing Tree Press, Detroit, 1968. Basically a coverage of English folklore regarding the plant world. Index.

White, T. H., ed. and trans., *The Bestiary*; Capricorn Books, G. P. Putnam's Sons, New York, 1960. A translation of a medieval bestiary of the 12th century. Wonderful reading. Illustrated. Introduction.

ENGLISH BIBLES, APOCRYPHAL BOOKS,
BIBLICAL LEGENDS, COMMENTARIES,
DICTIONARIES, AND ENCYCLOPEDIAS

*The Apocryphal New Testament*, edited and translated by Montague Rhodes James; Oxford University Press, 1924. An excellent selection but a stiff translation of the various apocryphal gospels, acts, epistles, and apocalypses not included in the New Testament. Index of subjects.

*Apocryphal Gospels, Acts and Revelations*, edited and translated by Alexander Walker; T. & T. Clark, Edinburgh, 1890. An excellent selection of the tales and legends not included in the New Testament. Index.

Ashe, Geoffrey, *The Encyclopedia of Prophecy*; ABC-CLIO, Santa Barbara, Denver, and Oxford (England), 2001. A factual A–Z reference guide, with a global perspective on the role of prophecy in world history, religion, folklore, and literature. Bibliography and general index.

Charlesworth, James H., ed., *The Old Testament Pseudepigrapha*; Doubleday & Company, Inc., Garden City, N. Y., 1985. A massive, two-volume work, containing all of the material not included in the Old Testament but rich in folklore. Notes. Index.

Frazer, James George, *Folklore in the Old Testament*; The Macmillan Company, London, 1918. A three-volume study of the subject. There is also a one-volume abridged edition by Frazer published in 1923.

Gaer, Joseph, *The Lore of the New Testament*; Little, Brown and Co., Boston, 1952. An excellent collection built around the figures of the New Testament. Notes on sources.

———, *The Lore of the Old Testament*; Little, Brown and Co., Boston, 1951. An excellent collection of legends built around Bible stories. Notes on sources.

Gaster, Theodor H., *Myth, Legend, and Custom in the Old Testament: A Comparative Study with Chapters from Sir James G. Frazer's Folklore in the Old Testament*; Harper & Row, New York,

1969. An edition of Frazer updated with much new material. A must for biblical mythology and legend. Introduction. Notes.

Guiley, Rosemary Ellen, *The Encyclopedia of Saints*; Facts On File, New York, 2001. Entries on saints and their journeys. Includes cross-references, appendixes, bibliography, and general index.

Hastings, James, ed., *A Dictionary of the Bible*; Charles Scribner's Sons, New York, 1898. A four-volume work dealing with every aspect of the Bible. An additional volume was included in 1904, bringing it up to that date.

*The Holy Bible: A Translation from the Latin Vulgate in the Light of the Hebrew and Greek Originals*; translated by Ronald Knox; Sheed & Ward, Inc., New York, 1944. An important translation because it is from the Latin Bible, which was the one used during the Middle Ages and had the greatest influence on art.

*The Interpreter's Bible*; Abingdon Press, New York/Nashville, 1952. A 12-volume work with the King James Version and Revised Standard Version as texts. Numerous general articles. Indexes.

*The Interpreter's Dictionary of the Bible: An Illustrated Encyclopedia*; Abingdon Press, Nashville, Tenn., 1964. A four-volume reference work that is a must.

*The Jerome Biblical Commentary*, edited by R. E. Brown, J. A. Fitzmyer, and R. E. Murphy; Prentice-Hall, Inc., Englewood Cliffs, N. J., 1968. A good one-volume Catholic commentary. Index.

Sanmel, Samuel, gen. ed., *The New English Bible with the Apocrypha*; Oxford Study Edition. Contemporary British translation of the Bible. Introductions. Annotations. Cross-references. Indexes.

*The New Jerusalem Bible*; Doubleday & Company, Inc., Garden City, N. Y., 1985. A revision of the earlier 1966 version, which is very popular. Must be used with caution. Numerous misprints. Very Roman catholic notes.

*The Oxford Annotated Bible with the Apocrypha; Revised Standard Version*, edited by H. G. May and B. M. Metzger, Oxford University Press, New York, 1965. A handy one-volume annotated RSV Bible. Charts. Tables. Indexes.

*Peake's Commentary on the Bible*, edited by M. Black and H. H. Rowley; Thomas Nelson and Sons, Ltd., London, 1962. A good one-volume commentary on the Bible. Index.

*Tanakh: A New Translation of The Holy Scriptures According to the Traditional Hebrew Text*; The Jewish Publication Society, Philadelphia, 1985. A new English translation of the Hebrew Scriptures. Reading it against standard Christian translations of the Old Testament is very enlightening. Notes.

## ANCIENT AND MODERN NEAR EAST MYTHOLOGY

*Gilgamesh, The Epic of*; Penguin Book, Baltimore, 1960. A prose version of the epic by N. K. Sandars, pulling together various ancient versions. Contains a long introduction giving background. Glossary.

Gray, John, *Near Eastern Mythology: Mesopotamia, Syria, Palestine*; Hamlyn Publishing Group, Ltd., London, 1969. A very useful, short, illustrated study of a very complex subject. Reading list. Index.

Heidel, Alexander, *The Gilgamesh Epic and Old Testament Parallels*; The University of Chicago Press, Chicago, 1946. A translation and interpretation of the ancient epic poem, with other myths and legends relating to it. No index.

Jastrow, Morris, *The Religion of Babylonia and Assyria*; Ginn & Company, Boston, 1898. Classic, 19th-century study by a well-known scholar. Bibliography. Index.

Pritchard, James B., ed., *The Ancient Near East: An Anthology of Texts and Pictures*; Princeton University Press, Princeton, N. J., 1958. A collection of important Near Eastern texts, many relating to mythology, such as Gilgamesh. Illustrations. Notes. Glossary. Index.

Pritchard, James B., *Ancient Near Eastern Texts Relating to the Old Testament*; Princeton University Press, Princeton, N. J., 1955. An important collection of texts, many of which are original sources for myths and legends relating to the Near East. The work is fully annotated. Some of the translations, however, are very stiff and awkward. Index of biblical names.

Sandars, N. K., ed., *Poems of Heaven and Hell from Ancient Mesopotamia*; Penguin Books, Baltimore. An excellent collection of texts. Notes. Glossary.

Spence, Lewis, *Myths & Legends of Babylonia and Assyria*; Harrap & Co., London, 1916. Reissued by Gale Research Company, Detroit, 1975. A popular study of these fascinating myths but often confusing. Glossary. Index.

## EGYPTIAN MYTHOLOGY

Aldred, Cyril, *Akhenaten: Pharaoh of Egypt—A New Study*; McGraw-Hill, New York, 1968. Deromanticizes Akhenaten as a religious revolutionary. One of the few books to mention Akhenaten's homosexuality. Chronology. Notes. Select Bibliography. Index.

*The Book of the Dead: The Hieroglyphic Transcript of the Papyrus of Ani*; translated by E. A. Wallis Budge; Medici Society Edition, 1913. Reissued by University Books, New Hyde Park, N. Y., 1960. Based on various editions published by Budge, 1890, 1894, and 1913. A major source book but very difficult to read. It contains rubrics and rituals and alludes to mythology. It is similar to trying to reconstruct Christian mythology from a hymnal.

Budge, E. A. Wallis, *Egyptian Religion: Egyptian Ideas of the Future Life*; reissued by Bell Publishing Company, New York, 1969. Original edition, London, 1900. A short study of the cult of Osiris, the major god of death and resurrection in ancient Egypt. No index.

———, *The Gods of the Egyptians, or Studies in Egyptian Mythology*; The Open Court Publishing Company, Chicago, 1904. Reissued by Dover Publications, New York, 1969. Classic study with quotes from many ancient Egyptian texts, but it is poorly arranged and often contradicts itself from one section to another. Illustrations. Index.

Erman, Aldolf, *The Ancient Egyptians: A Sourcebook of Their Writings*; translated by Aylward M. Blackman; Harper Torchbooks, New York, 1966. An interesting anthology, though many of the translations are very stiff and awkward. The Harper Torchbook edition is a republication of *The Literature of the Ancient Egyptians* (1927 English translation).

Frankfort, Henri, *Ancient Egyptian Religion*; Columbia University Press, New York, 1948. Reissued by Harper Torchbooks, New York, 1961. A short survey of Egyptian gods and goddesses, way of life, art, and literature. Index.

Ions, Veronica, *Egyptian Mythology*; Hamlyn, London, 1965. A fully illustrated study of the gods and goddesses of ancient Egypt. Index.

James, T. G. H., *Myths and Legends of Ancient Egypt*; Grosset & Dunlap, New York, 1971. Popular retellings of various Egyptian myths with contemporary illustrations. Index.

Maspero, Gaston C. C., *Popular Stories of Ancient Egypt*; translated by A. S. Johns; reissued by University Books, New Hyde Park, N. Y., 1969. Original edition in English, 1915. Contains 17 complete Egyptian stories and six fragments. Many of the tales are classics in world folklore.

Mercatante, Anthony S., *Who's Who in Egyptian Mythology*; Clarkson N. Potter, Inc., New York, 1978. An A-to-Z dictionary of Egyptian mythology, illustrated by the author. Numerous cross-references. Introduction by Dr. Robert S. Bianchi of the Department of Egyptian and Classical Art, The Brooklyn Museum. Bibliography.

Pinch, Geraldine, *Handbook of Egyptian Mythology*; ABC-CLIO, Santa Barbara, Denver, and Oxford (England), 2002. The work covers Egyptian culture from c. 3200 B.C.E. Introduction provides background information. Cross-references, glossary, and listing of non-print resources including videos, Websites, and CD-Roms.

Quirke, Stephen, *Ancient Egyptian Religion*; Cornell University Press, Ithica, New York, 2001. A publication for the Trustees of the British Museum. A good summary of the religion(s) of Egypt. Index.

Simpson, William Kelly, *The Literature of Ancient Egypt: An Anthology of Stories, Instructions and Poetry*; Yale University Press, New Haven, Conn., and London, 1972. An excellent anthology. Translations vary in merit. Introduction.

Zecchi, Marco, *A Study of the Egyptian God Osiris Hemag*; Editrice La Mandragora, Imola, Italy, 1996. A detailed study of a single Egyptian god, Osiris. Bibliography, Index.

## PERSIAN MYTHOLOGY AND FOLKLORE

Christensen, Arthur, ed., *Persian Folktales*; translated by Alfred Kurti; G. Bell & Sons Ltd., London, 1971. Good selection of folktales. Notes and Sources.

Curtis, Vesta Sarkhosh, *Persian Myths*; University of Texas Press, Austin, 1993. Published in cooperation with British Museum Press. Good illustrations. Includes bibliography and a general index.

Fardusi, *The Shah-Namah*; translated by Alexander Rogers; reissued by Heritage Publishers, Delhi, India, 1973. Original edition, 1907. An abridged translation of the massive epic poem in both prose and verse.

Hinnells, John R., *Persian Mythology*; Hamlyn Publishing Group, Ltd., London, 1973. Excellent, illustrated short study. Bibliography. Index.

## HEBREW AND JEWISH MYTHOLOGY AND FOLKLORE

Ausubel, Nathan, *A Treasury of Jewish Folklore*; Crown Publishers, New York, 1948. An excellent anthology, covering stories, traditions, legends, humor, wisdom, and folk song. Glossary. Index.

Bin Gorion, Micha Joseph bin, collector, *Mimekor Yisrael: Classical Jewish Folktales*; translated by Dan Ben-Amos; Indiana University Press, Bloomington, Ind., and London, 1976. A three-volume collection made up of religious tales, national tales, folktales, and oriental tales. Sources and references.

Gaster, Theodor H., *Customs and Folkways of Jewish Life*; William Sloane Associates Publishers, New York, 1955. A reissue of *The Holy and the Profane*, covering various aspects of Jewish beliefs and rituals in relation to world folklore. Bibliography. Index.

————, *Festivals of the Jewish Year*; William Sloane Associates, New York, 1952. Excellent study with rich folklore background. Notes. No index.

Ginzberg, Louis, *The Legends of the Jews*; translated by Henrietta Szold; The Jewish Publication Society of America, Philadelphia, 1900. A seven-volume collection of Jewish legends built around biblical themes. Sources. Index.

Noy, Dov, ed., *Folktales of Israel*; translated by Gene Baharav, University of Chicago Press, Chicago, 1963. One of the volumes in the series *Folktales of the World* under the editorship of Richard M. Dorson. The present collection contains extensive notes. Index of Motifs and Index of Tale Types. Bibliography. General index.

*Talmud, The, Selections*; translated by H. Polano; Frederick Warne & Co., Ltd., London, reprinted 1965. Good selection of various biblical themes and stories built around them. No index.

## CHRISTIAN MYTHOLOGY, LEGEND, AND FOLKLORE

Ballou, Robert O., *The Other Jesus*; Doubleday & Co., Garden City, N. Y., 1972. A narrative based on the apocryphal stories of Jesus not included in the canon of the New Testament but very much a part of Christian legend. Sources.

Brewer, E. Cobham, *A Dictionary of Miracles*; J. B. Lippincott Co., Philadelphia, 1884. Reissued by Gale Research Co., Detroit, 1966. Absolutely fascinating reading about the saints and miracles.

Butler, Alban, *The Lives of the Saints*; edited by Herbert Thurston and Donald Attwater; P. J. Kennedy & Sons, New York, 1965. A four-volume set, based on Butler but drastically rewritten. Florid prose. Major source book for lives of the saints. Arranged according to the Christian calendar.

Cross, F. L., ed., *The Oxford Dictionary of the Christian Church*; Oxford University Press, London, 1957. The best one-volume guide to the Christian Church, its saints, and customs.

Jameson, Mrs. *The History of Our Lord*; Longmans, Green, and Co., London, 1872. The classic two-volume study of the life of Jesus as portrayed in works of art. Gives numerous legends. Index.

———— *Legends of the Madonna*; Longmans, Green, and Co., London, 1879. The classic study of the Virgin Mary in works of art. Gives numerous legends. Index.

————, *Legends of the Monastic Orders*; Longmans, Green, and Co., London, 1880. A study of saints connected with monastic orders and their portrayal in art. Numerous legends. Index.

————, *Sacred and legendary Art*; Longmans, Green, and Co., London, 1879. Longmans, Green, and Co., London, 1879. A two-volume set covering angels, archangels, evangelists, apostles, doctors of the church, and Mary Magdalene, as portrayed in art. Numerous legends. Index.

Metford, J. C. J., *Dictionary of Christian Lore and Legend*; Thames and Hudson, Ltd., London, 1983. Excellent one-volume, illustrated guide to Christian lore and legend.

Voragine, Jacobus, *The Golden Legend*; translated and adapted by Granger Ryan and Helmut Ripperger, Longmans, Green and Co., New York, 1941. A shortened version that often omits the best parts of the legends because they might seem outlandish to present-day Roman Catholics. Index.

———, *The Golden Legend or Lives of the Saints*; translated by William Caxton; J. M. Dent and Co., London, 1900. An edition of Caxton's English version, with modern spelling, in seven volumes.

## ARMENIAN MYTHOLOGY AND FOLKLORE

Ananikian, Mardiros H., *Armenian Mythology*; Marshall Jones Company, Boston, 1925. Volume 7, *The Mythology of All Races*; reissued by Cooper Square Publishers, Inc., New York, 1964. Notes. Bibliography. No index, except in final volume of full set.

Arnot, Robert, ed., *Armenian Literature*; The Colonial Press, New York, 1901. An anthology containing poetry, drama, and folklore.

## ISLAMIC MYTHOLOGY, LEGEND, AND FOLKLORE

*Arabian Nights' Entertainments, or The Thousand and One Nights*; translated by Edward William Lane; Tudor Publishing Co., New York, 1946. A contemporary edition of the famous Lane translation, published in 1838 and 1840. Extensive notes.

*The Book of the Thousand Nights and One Night*; rendered into English from the literal and complete French translation of Dr. J. C. Mardrus by Powys Mathers; St. Martin's Press, New York, 1972. A four-volume edition of the classic work in a very readable English form.

Gibb, H. A. R., and Kramers, J. H., eds., *Shorter Encyclopedia of Islam*; E. J. Brill, Leiden, 1961. A very scholarly one-volume edition on Islam. Helpful for background. Various entries on legendary persons, heaven and hell. Register of subjects.

Hughes, Thomas Patrick, *Dictionary of Islam*; Cosmo Publications, New Delhi, India, 1977. Reprint of 1885 edition. A one-volume dic-tionary with some entries on mythology and folklore in Islam. Index.

Jeffery, Arthur, ed., *Islam: Muhammad and His Religion*; The Liberal Arts Press, New York, 1958. Anthology covering varying aspects of Islam, some of which deals with folklore. Glossary.

Leick, Gwendolyn, *A Dictionary of Ancient Near Eastern Mythology*; Routledge, London and New York, 1991. Short and lengthy entries, with a chronological chart, a glossary, bibliography, and a general index. There are also 44 black-and-white photographs and illustrations.

*The Koran*; translated by J. M. Rodwell; J. M. Dent & Sons, Ltd., London, 1909. An edition of the classic English translation. Notes.

*The Qur'an*; translated by Richard Bell; T. & T. Clark, Edinburgh, 1937. A two-volume edition of the Qur'an (The Koran) with a rearrangement of the suras. Notes.

*The Quran: The Eternal Revelation Vouchsafed to Muhammad, The Seal of the Prophets*; translated by Muhammad Zafrulla Khan; Curzon Press, 1971. An English translation with Arabic text facing; it presents the book in English by a believer. Index.

## GREEK AND ROMAN MYTHOLOGY AND LEGEND (CLASSICAL)

Apollodorus, *The Library*; translated by James George Frazer; Loeb Classical Library, New York, 1921. A two-volume edition of one of the basic sources for Greek mythology. Introduction. Notes. Appendix comparing Greek myth with world myth. Index.

Dixon-Kennedy, Mike, *Encyclopedia of Greco-Roman Mythology*; ABC-CLIO, Santa Barbara, Denver, and Oxford (England), 1998. Good entries on both Greece and Rome, most are short but substantial, with cross-references following the entry. In addition to the bibliography there are also chronologies for ancient Greece and Rome and a list of Roman emperors. General index.

Gilbert, John, *Myths and Legends of Ancient Rome*; Hamlyn, London, 1970. A short collection of myths and legends.

Godolphin, F. R. B., ed., *Great Classical Myths*; The Modern Library, New York, 1964. A collection of myths from a variety of sources in a variety of translations. Introduction. Glossary. Index.

Grant, Michael, *Myths of the Greeks and Romans*; World Publishing Company, Cleveland, Ohio, 1962. A study with numerous references to art, music, and literature. Bibliography. Index.

Graves, Robert, *The Greek Myths*; George Braziller, Inc., New York, 1955. Excellent retellings of the myths based on the ancient sources. Complete notes. One may disagree with Graves's interpretations, but the stories are very well told. Index.

Greene, David, and Richmond Lattimore, eds., *The Complete Greek Tragedies*; The University of Chicago Press, Chicago, 1959. A four-volume set of the complete works of the Greek dramatists in contemporary English poetic translations. Introductions.

Hendricks, Rhoda A., ed. and trans., *Classical Gods and Heroes; Myths as Told by Ancient Authors*; Frederick Ungar Publishing Co., New York, 1972. Modern translations of original sources for many myths. Introduction. Glossary.

Hesiod, *Theogony, Works and Days*; translated by Dorothea Wender; Penguin Books, Baltimore, 1973. A prose translation of the important texts. Introduction. Notes.

———, *Works and Days*; translated by Hugh G. Evelyn-White; Loeb Classical Library, 1914. A Greek text with English prose translation. Book also includes the Homeric Hymns and other Homerica. Introduction. Index.

———, *The Works and Days, Theogony, The Shield of Herakles*; translated by Richmond Lattimore; The University of Michigan Press, Ann Arbor, Mich., 1959. A poetic translation of some basic texts on Greek mythology. Introduction.

Homer, *The Iliad*; translated by Richmond Lattimore; The University of Chicago Press, Chicago, 1951. A modern verse translation of the epic. Introduction. Glossary.

———, *The Iliad*; translated by Alexander Pope; edited by Reuben A. Brower and W. H. Bond; The Macmillan Co., New York, 1965. The most famous translation into English. Introduction. Textual notes.

———, *The Iliad, The Odyssey and The Lesser Homerica*; edited by Allardyce Nicoll; Princeton University Press, Princeton, N. J., 1967. An edition in two volumes of the classic Chapman's translations. Introduction. Notes. Commentary.

———, *The Odyssey*; translated by E. V. Rieu; Penguin Books, Baltimore, 1946. A simple prose version of the epic poem. Introduction.

Kravitz, David, *Who's Who in Greek and Roman Mythology*; Clarkson N. Potter, Inc., New York, 1975. An A-to-Z listing, important in that it gives all of the relationships—mother, father, husband, wife, offspring, etc.

*Lempriere's Classical Dictionary of Proper names Mentioned in Ancient Authors*; edited by F. A. Wright; E. P. Dutton & Co., Inc., New York, 1955. An edition of a classic dictionary, used by Keats and other Romantic poets. The names, however, are listed under their Roman forms.

Mayerson, Philip, *Classical Mythology in Literature, Art and Music*; Xerox College Publishing, Lexington, Mass., 1971. Excellent illustrated coverage of Greek and Roman mythology in relation to the arts. Introduction. Index.

Melas, Evi, *Temples and Sanctuaries of Ancient Greece*; translated by F. Maxwell Brownjohn; Thames and Hudson, London, 1970. A rich study of Greek temples and the cults surrounding them. Illustrated. Index.

Norton, Dan S., and Peters Rushton, *Classical Myths in English Literature*; Rinehard & Company, Inc., 1952. A very thorough coverage of the myths and how they are used in English literature, arranged A to Z.

Ovid, *Heroides and Amores*; translated by Grant Showerman; Loeb Classical Library, New York, 1921. Latin with English prose translation on facing page.

———, *The Metamorphoses*; translated by Horace Gregory; The Viking Press, New York, 1958. A major poetic translation of the poem. Introduction. Glossary.

———, *The Metamorphoses*; translated by Rolfe Humphries; Indiana University Press, Bloomington, Ind., 1964. A spirited blank-verse translation of one of the major sources of Greek and Roman mythology. Glossary. Index.

———, *The Metamorphoses*; translated by Mary M. Innes; Penguin Books, Baltimore, 1955. A modern, somewhat stiff prose translation of the brilliant poem. Introduction.

———, *The Metamorphoses*; translated by Frank Justus Miller; Loeb Classical Library, New York, 1916. A two-volume prose translation with Latin on facing pages.

*Ovid's Metamorphoses: The Arthur Golding Translation (1567)*; edited by John Frederick Nims; The Macmillan Co., New York, 1965. A modern edition of the classic English translation read by Shakespeare. Notes. Glossary.

*Ovid's Works*; translated into English prose by Henry T. Riley; G. Bell & Sons, Ltd., London, 1912. A three-volume set containing all of the works, translated into a very dull English but useful because of its completeness.

Perowne, Stewart, *Roman Mythology*; Paul Hamlyn, London, 1969. Excellent, fully illustrated study. Introduction. Further reading list. Index.

Rose, H. J., *A Handbook of Greek Mythology*; Methuen & Co., Ltd., London, 1928. Interesting study. Notes. Bibliography. Indexes.

Scherer, Margaret R., *The Legends of Troy in Art and Literature*; Phaidon Press, New York and London, 1963. A study, with illustrations, of the rich art works and books produced from the Troy legend. Contains a list of works of literature and music dealing with the Trojan War. Index.

Seyefert, Oskar S., *A Dictionary of Classical Antiquities, Mythology, Religion, Literature and Art*; William Glaisher, Ltd., London, 1891. An excellent dictionary compiled in the 19th century.

Tripp, Edward, *Crowell's Handbook of Classical Mythology*; Thomas Y. Crowell Company, New York, 1970. Dictionary-length entries and a pronunciation index.

Vergil, *The Aeneid*; translated by Patrick Dickinson; The New American Library, New York, 1961. A poetic translation of the classic.

———, *The Aeneid*; translated by John Dryden; edited by Robert Fitzgerald; The Macmillan Co., New York, 1965. The most famous English translation in heroic couplets. Introduction. Notes.

———, *The Aeneid*; translated by Robert Fitzgerald; Random House, New York, 1981. A new poetic translation by an important poet.

———, *The Aeneid*; translated by William Morris; Longmans, Green, and Co., London, 1900. A very interesting translation by the 19th-century English designer and poet.

Zimmerman, J. E., *Dictionary of Classical Mythology*; Harper & Row, New York, 1964. A concise dictionary with references to literature. Introduction.

## MEDIEVAL LEGENDS (GENERAL)

*Gesta Romanorum*; translated by Charles Swan; Bohn Library Edition, 1876. Reissued by Dover Publications, New York, 1959. The classic medieval collection of tales from a variety of sources.

Guerber, H. A., *Legends of the Middle Ages*; American Book Co., New York, 1896. A popular retelling of many medieval legends, connecting them to literature. Glossary. Index.

Guido dele Colonne, *Historia Destructionis Troiae*; translated by Mary Elizabeth Meek; Indiana University Press, Bloomington, Ind., 1974. The medieval version of the destruction of Troy, which had a great influence on the legends in Europe. Introduction. Notes.

Jones, Charles W., ed., *Medieval Literature in Translation*; Longmans, Green and Co., New York, 1950. An excellent anthology with a variety of literature, including much legendary material. Introduction. Bibliography.

Lindahl, Carl, John McNamara, and John Lindow, eds., *Medieval Folklore: An Encyclopedia of Myths, Legends, Tales, Beliefs, and Customs*; ABC-CLIO, Santa Barbara, Denver, and Oxford (England), 2000. A two-volume set written by contributors from around the world, even though the entries are primarily on European topics. Cross-references, sources, and references for further reading follow each entry. Indexes of tale types and motifs, and general index.

*Medieval Epics*; The Modern Library, New York, 1963. An anthology, no listing of an editor, of *Beowulf*, translated by William Alfred (1963), *The Song of Roland*, translated by W. S. Merwin (1959), *The Nibelungenlied*, translated by Helen M. Mustard (1963), and *The Poem of the Cid*, translated by W. S. Merwin, 1959.

Schlauch, Margaret, trans., *Medieval Narrative: A Book of Translations*; Gordian Press, New York, 1928. A varied collection, including Icelandic sagas, chansons de geste, the Tristan legend, the legend of the Holy Grail, the Nibelung cycle, the tale of Troy, the legend of Alexander the Great, saints' lives, and *fabliaux*.

Spence, Lewis, *A Dictionary of Medieval Romance and Romance Writers*; Routledge & Kegan Paul Ltd., London, 1913. Reissued by Humanities Press, Inc., New York, 1962. A dictionary of much medieval legend but somewhat difficult to follow.

## ARTHURIAN LEGENDS

*The High History of the Holy Graal*; translated by Sebastian Evans; J. M. Dent & Sons, Ltd., London, 1898. A classic translation of the legend surrounding the Holy Grail.

Jenkins, Elizabeth, *The Mystery of King Arthur*; Coward, McCann & Geohegan, Inc., New York, 1975. A study of the legends, with numerous illustrations.

Kennedy, Edward Donald, ed. and introduction, *King Arthur: A Casebook*; Garland, New York, 1996. A collection of studies by authors from around the world on King Arthur. Illustrations and bibliography.

Malory, Sir Thomas, *Le Morte D'Arthur*; edited by A. W. Pollard; University Books, New Hyde Park, N. Y., 1961. An edition of the classic Arthurian account in English. Glossary.

———, *Le Morte D'Arthur*; edited by Edward Stachey; Macmillan and Co., Ltd., London, 1868. An edition of Caxton's text. Introduction. Notes. Glossary.

Steinbeck, John, *The Acts of King Arthur and His Noble Knights*; edited by Chase Horton; Farrar, Straus and Giroux, New York, 1976. An edition of Malory from the Winchester manuscript. A reworking of the Arthurian legends by a modern novelist.

## BRITISH AND WELSH MYTHOLOGY AND LEGEND

*Beowulf*; translated by Burton Raffel; The New American Library, New York, 1963. A poetic translation. Afterword by Robert P. Creed. Glossary of names.

*Beowulf*; translated by Chauncey Brewster Tinker; Newson & Company, New York, 1902. A prose translation of the great epic. Notes. Index of proper names.

Briggs, Katharine, and Ruth M. Tongue, eds., *Folktales of England*; University of Chicago Press, Chicago, 1965. One of the volumes in the series *Folktales of the World* under the editorship of Richard M. Dorson. The present collection contains extensive notes. Index of Motifs and Index of Tale Types. Bibliography. General index.

Briggs, Katharine M., ed., *A Dictionary of British Folk-Tales*; Indiana University Press, Bloomington, Ind., 1971. The most complete collection to date. Introduction. Notes.

Ebbutt, M. I., *The British: Myths and Legends Series*; George G. Harrap & Co., London, 1910. Reissued by Avenel Books, New York, 1986. Popular retellings of the major myths and legends from Beowulf to Robin Hood. Glossary and Index.

Geoffrey of Monmouth, *Histories of the Kings of Britain*; translated by Sebastian Evans; J. M. Dent and Co., London. A translation of one of the major sources of British mythology.

————, *The History of the Kings of Britain*; translated by Lewis Thorpe; Penguin Books Ltd., 1966. A modern translation. Excellent introduction.

*The Mabinogion*; translated by Charlotte Guest; Bernard Quaritch, London, 1877. Reissued by Academy Press Ltd., Chicago, 1978. A classic translation of the tales that made them popular with English-speaking peoples. Introduction Notes.

*The Mabinogion*; translated by Gwyn Jones and Thomas Jones; Everyman's Library, New York, 1949. A more exact translation of the text than that of Guest. Introduction. Notes.

Spaeth, J. Duncan, trans., *Old English Poetry*; Gordian Press, New York, 1967; reprint of 1921 edition. A collection, translated into verse, ranging from Beowulf to legends of the saints. Introduction. Notes.

Weston, Jessie L., ed. and trans., *The Chief Middle English Poets: Selected Poems*; Phaeton Press, New York, 1968. Reprint of 1914 edition. A collection in verse ranging from Layamon to romances, such as Havelok the Dane. Bibliography. Index.

## CELTIC MYTHOLOGY AND FOLKLORE

Colum, Padraic, ed., *A Treasury of Irish Folklore*; Crown Publishers, Inc., New York, 1954. A collection of stories, traditions, legends, humor, wisdom, ballads, and songs. Index.

Cross, Tom Pette, and Chark Harris Slover, eds., *Ancient Irish Tales*; Barnes & Noble, Inc., New York, 1936. Very good collection of myths. Introduction. Bibliography. Glossary.

Curtin, Jeremiah, *Myths and Folk-Lore of Ireland*; Little, Brown and Co., Boston, 1890. Reissued by Singing Tree Press, Detroit, 1968. Selection of folktales. Glossary.

Graves, Alfred Perceval, *The Irish Fairy Book*; Crescent Books, New York, 1987. A reissued volume of a collection made by the father of the poet Robert Graves.

Jacobs, Joseph, ed., *Celtic Fairy Tales*; World Publishing Co., New York, 1971. A volume that combines Jacobs' *Celtic Fairy Tales* (1891) and *More Celtic Fairy Tales* (1894), both published by David Nutt, London. Notes and References.

Joyce, P. W., *Old Celtic Romances: Tales from Irish Mythology*; David Nutt, London, 1879. Reissued by Devin-Adair Co., New York, 1962. Well-known 19th-century collection of tales. Introduction. Notes. List of proper names.

Lover, Samuel, and Thomas Crofton Crokes, *Legends and Tales of Ireland*; Crescent Books, New York, 1987. A volume that reprints in one volume Samuel Lover's *Legends and Tales of Ireland* and Thomas Crofton Croker's *Fairy Legends of the South of Ireland*, both works written in the last century.

MacCana, Proinsias, *Celtic Mythology*; Hamlyn, London, 1970. An excellent study of a very involved and complex subject. Illustrated. Bibliography. Index.

MacKillop, James, *Dictionary of Celtic Mythology*; Oxford University Press, Oxford and New York, 1998. Entries are dictionary length, but substantial. There is a pronunciation guide for the Celtic words, a good bibliography divided into sections such as Irish, Welsh, and Manx, and a general index.

McGarry, Mary, ed., *Great Folktales of Old Ireland*; Bell Publishing Company, New York, 1972. A collection of 17 stories, myths, legends from a variety of sources.

O'Sullivan, Sean, ed. and trans., *Folktales of Ireland*; University of Chicago Press, Chicago, 1966. One of the volumes in the series *Folk-*

*tales of the World* under the editorship of Richard M. Dorson. The present collection contains extensive notes. Index of Motifs and Index of Tale Types. Bibliography. General index.

Squire, Charles, *Celtic Myth and Legend*; Newcastle Publishing Co., Inc., Hollywood, Calif., 1975. Originally published as *The Mythology of the British Isles* (1905) in London. Index.

## ITALIAN MYTHOLOGY

Ariosto, Ludovico, *Orlando Furioso*; translated by Guido Walkman; Oxford University Press, London, 1974. A prose translation of the entire work, which is based on medieval legend and lore. Introduction.

———, *Orlando Furioso*; translated by Sir John Harington; edited by R. Gottfried; Indiana University Press, Bloomington, Ind., and London, 1963. The classic Elizabethan translation of one of the most popular European works based on medieval legend.

Boccaccio, *The Decameron*; anonymous translation, published in 1620; The Heritage Press, New York, 1940. The great collection of tales, many of which are part of European folklore.

Calvino, Italo, *Italian Folktales*; translated by George Martin; Pantheon Books, New York, 1956. A wonderful collection, but in many cases there is more Calvino than Italian folklore in the tales.

Crane, Thomas Frederick, *Italian Popular Tales*; Houghton, Mifflin, Boston, 1885. Reissued by Singing Tree Press, Detroit, 1968. Good selection with many variants of the tales. Notes. Sources.

Dante Alighieri, *The Comedy of Dante Alighieri*; translated by Dorothy L. Sayers; Basic Books, Inc., New York, 1963. A three-volume poetic translation with copious notes. Long introduction. Excellent version.

———, *The Divine Comedy*; translated by John Ciardi, The Franklin Library, Franklin Center, Pennsylvania, 1977. A poetic translation

with notes. One of the best contemporary versions available.

———, *The Divine Comedy*; translated by Charles S. Singleton; Princeton University Press, Princeton, N. J., 1970. A six-volume set with original text, prose translation. Introduction. Notes.

Tasso, Torquato, *Jerusalem Delivered*; translated by Joseph Tusiani; Fairleigh Dickinson Press, Rutherford, N. J., 1970. A contemporary poetic translation of the Renaissance epic based on medieval legends. Introduction.

Toynbee, Paget, *Concise Dictionary of Proper Names and Notable Matters in the Works of Dante*; Phaeton Press, New York, 1968. Reprint of the 1914 edition. Extremely helpful in locating legendary and mythological references, but you must know the spelling in Dante's Italian text.

## SPANISH MYTHOLOGY

Don Juan Manuel, *Count Lucanor; or the Fifty Pleasant Stories of Patronio*; translated by James York; Gibbings & Company, Ltd., London, 1899. An edition of the work originally published in 1868. Preface. Notes.

*The Lay of the Cid*; translated by Leonard Bacon and Selden Rose; University of California Press, Berkeley, Calif., 1919. A poetic translation of the Spanish epic poem.

Ruiz, Juan, *The Book of True Love*; translated by Saralyn R. Daly; The Pennsylvania State University Press, University Park, Pa., and London, 1978. A bilingual edition of the text with an English verse translation. Introduction. Notes. Reader's Guide.

Spence, Lewis, *Spain: Myths and Legends*; George C. Harrap & Co., London, 1920. Reissued by Avenel Books, New York, 1986. A popular retelling of Spanish myths and legends, including those of the Cid and Amadis de Gaul, and the ballads.

## FRENCH MYTHOLOGY

Delarue, Paul, ed., *The Borzoi Book of French Folk Tales*; translated by Austin E. Fife; Alfred A. Knopf, New York, 1956. An excellent collection of French tales. Sources and Commentary.

*Marie de France, Lays of*; translated by Eugene Mason; J. M. Dent & Sons, Ltd., London, 1911. The book not only includes tales ascribed to Marie de France but other French legends.

Massignon, Genevieve, ed., *Folktales of France*; translated by Jacqueline Hyland. University of Chicago Press, Chicago, 1968. One of the volumes in the series *Folktales of the World* under the editorship of Richard M. Dorson. The present collection contains extensive notes. Index of Motifs and Index of Tale Types. Bibliography. General index.

Morris, William, trans., *Old French Romances*; Charles Scribner's Sons, New York, 1896. A classic translation of the French medieval tales and legends.

Perrault, Charles, *Fairy Tales*; translated by A. E. Johnson and others; Dodd, Mead & Co., New York, 1961. All of the classic tales are included in this edition, such as "Blue Beard" and "Cinderella."

*The Song of Roland*; translated by Charles Scott Moncrieff; The Heritage Press, New York, 1938. An English poetic version that tries to capture the beauty of the original.

## NORSE, AND GERMANIC MYTHOLOGY, LEGEND, AND FOLKLORE

Christiansen, Reidar Thorwald, ed., *Folktales of Norway*, translated by Pat Shaw Iversen; University of Chicago Press, Chicago, 1964. One of the volumes in the series *Folktales of the World* under the editorship of Richard M. Dorson. The present collection contains extensive notes. Index of Motifs and Index of Tale Types. Bibliography. General index.

Craigie, William A., ed. and trans., *Scandinavian Folk-Lore*; Alexander Gardner, London, 1896. Reissued by Singing Tree Press, Detroit, 1970. A collection of documents relating to Scandinavian folk beliefs. Notes. Index.

Dasent, George Webbe, compiler, *Popular Tales from the Norse*; David Douglas, Edinburgh, 1888. Reissued by Grand River Books, Detroit, 1971. A translation of 59 Norwegian folktales from the *Norske Folke-eventyr* published by Peter Christen Asbjornsen and Jorgen Moe in 1843 and 1844 and expanded in 1852. The collection was also republished by Dover Publications in 1970 as *East o' the Sun and West o' the Moon*.

Davidson, H. R. Ellis, *Gods and Myths of Northern Europe*; Penguin Books, Baltimore, 1964. One of the best current studies on the subject. Index.

———, *Scandinavian Mythology*; Paul Hamlyn, London, 1969. A well-written, concise, illustrated study. Bibliography. Index.

*The Elder Edda: A Selection*, translated by W. H. Auden and Paul B. Taylor; Random House, New York, 1967. A poetic translation by one of the great poets of the century. Introduction. Notes. Glossary.

*The Elder Edda and the Younger Edda*, translated by Benjamin Thorpe and L. A. Blackwell; Norroena Society, London, 1907. *The Elder (or Poetic) Edda*, translated into stiff prose by Thorpe, and *The Younger (or Prose) Edda*, translated by Blackwell. Glossary.

Grimm, Brothers, *The Complete Fairy Tales of the Brothers Grimm*; Bantam Books, Toronto, New York, London, Sydney, Auckland, 1988. The best new translation of the Grimm tales, by Jack Zipes, including the 32 tales included in various publications by the Grimms but not included in the final canon of 210 tales. Original German titles and informant sources are included.

———, *The German Legends of the Brothers Grimm*, edited and translated by Donald Ward; Institute for the Study of Human Issues, Philadelphia, 1981. Two volumes of the legend collection by the Grimms, including extensive notes on each tale, a bibliography and a general index.

———, *Grimm's Household Tales*, translated by Margaret Hunt; George Bell and Sons, London, 1884. Reissued by Singing Tree Press, Detroit, 1968. A two-volume edition of the famous folktales. Good introduction by Andrew Lang. Notes.

Grimm, Jacob, *Teutonic Mythology*; George Bell and Sons, London, 1883. Reissued by Dover Publications, New York, 1966. A four-volume complex study of Germanic mythology. Not at all as interesting as the folktale collection but filled with information. Index.

Guerber, H. A., *Myths of Northern Lands*; American Book Co., New York, 1895. A popular retelling of various myths and legends associated with the North countries. Constant references to art. Glossary. Index.

Jones, Gwynn, *Scandinavian Legends and Folk-Tales*; Oxford University Press, London, 1956. Popular retellings of various myths and legends from a variety of sources.

Lindow, John, *Handbook of Norse Mythology*; ABC-CLIO, Santa Barbara, Denver, and Oxford (England), 2001. This is the best new source for Nordic mythology, and includes not only the individual entries, but also a lengthy section on the "Print and Nonprint Resources." This latter section is in place of a listing of bibliographical sources. There is also a general index.

Mackenzie, Donald A., *Teutonic Myth and Legend*; The Gresham Publishing Co., London, n. d. A popular retelling of various Norse and Germanic myths. Numerous editions available. Index.

Munch, Peter Andreas, *Norse Mythology: Legends of Gods and Heroes*, translated by Sigurd Bernhard Hustvedt; The American-Scandinavian Foundation, New York, 1927. Classic 19th-century study. Notes. Index.

Palmer, Philip Mason, and Robert Pattison More, *The Sources of the Faust Tradition*; Oxford University Press, Ltd., London, 1936. Reissued by Octagon Books, New York, 1969.

A collection of documents on the Faust legend serving as background for Goethe's *Faust*. Good source book. Index.

*The Poetic Edda*, translated by Henry Adams Bellows; American-Scandinavian Foundation, New York, 1923. Reissued by Biblo and Tannen, New York, 1969. A complete translation. Introduction. Notes. Index.

*The Prose Edda: Tales from Norse Mythology*; translated by Jean I. Young; University of California Press, Berkeley, Los Angeles, and London, 1954. A very good and readable translation. Includes a general index of names and places.

Ranke, Kurt, ed., *Folktales of Germany*, translated by Lotte Baumann; The University of Chicago Press, Chicago, 1966. Good selection. Part of the series *Folktales of the World*, under the editorship of Richard M. Dorson. Notes. Sources. Index.

Sturluson, Snorri, *The Prose Edda: Tales from Norse Mythology*, translated by Jean I. Young; University of California, Berkeley, Calif., 1964. A contemporary translation. Introduction. Notes. Index.

### FINNISH MYTHOLOGY AND FOLKLORE

*The Kalevala, or Poems of the Kaleva District*, compiled by Elias Lönnrot, translated by Francis Peabody Magoun, Jr.; Harvard University Press, Cambridge, Mass., 1963. A prose translation. The was the best edition of the work available in English until the 1988 edition by Eino Friberg. Introduction. Glossary.

"The Old Kalevala and Certain Antecedents", compiled by Elias Lönnrot, translated by Francis Peabody Magoun, Jr.; Harvard University Press, Cambridge, Mass., 1969. An earlier edition of *The Kalevala* compiled in 1835, translated into prose. A perfect companion to Magoun's translations of the 1849 *Kalevala*. Introduction. Glossary.

*The Kalevala, Epic of the Finnish People*, translated by Eino Friberg, introduction by George C. Schoolfield, illustrated by Björn Landström;

Otava Publishing Company, Helsinki, 1988. A one-volume edition of the epic done in the original meter. The best edition of the work available in English.

## SLAVIC MYTHOLOGY AND FOLKLORE

Afanasiev, compiler, *Russian Fairy Tales*, translated by Norbert Guterman; Pantheon Books, Inc., New York, 1945. The best one-volume edition of Russian folktales in English. Index.

Azadovskii, Mark Konstantinovich, *A Siberian Tale Teller*, translated by James R. Dow, introduction by Robert A. Georges; Center for Intercultural Studies in Folklore and Ethnomusicology, Austin, 1974. The first translation into English of the German publication *Eine sibirische Märchenerzählerin* (1926). Azadovskii's new theories of the "narrator complex" are exemplified through the tales of his Siberian informant, N.O. Vinokurova.

Curcija-Prodanovic, Nada, *Heroes of Serbia*; Oxford University Press, London, 1963. Folk ballads retold by the author in prose.

Curtin, Jeremiah, ed., *Myths and Folktales of the Russians, Western Slavs and Magyars*; Little, Brown and Co., Boston, 1890. Interesting collection of folktales. Notes. Good introduction.

Dixon-Kennedy, Mike, *Encyclopedia of Russian and Slavic Myth and Legend*; ABC-CLIO, Santa Barbara, Denver, and Oxford (England), 1998. Good entries on all Slavic cultures, as well as some related but not Slavic: Balto-Slavic, Hungarian, Armenian, etc. The culture area is identified for each entry, e.g., Russia, Ukraine, and there are cross-references in the text. Several appendixes: glossary of terms, Cyrillic to Latin transliterations, the rulers of Russia, and a topic finder as well as a general index.

Guerney, Bernard Guilbert, ed., *A Treasury of Russian Literature*; Vanguard Press, New York, 1943. Excellent anthology, containing a complete version of the epic *The Lay of Igor's Army* as well as excerpts from the Ilya Muromets legends.

Krylov, Ivan, *Fables*, translated by Bernard Pares; Harcourt, Brace and Co., New York, n. d. A complete edition of one of the best writers of Aesopic fables. Introduction. No index.

Machal, Jan, *Slavic Mythology*; Vol. 3 in *The Mythology of All Races*; The Marshall Jones Co., Boston, 1918. Reissued by Cooper Square Publishers, Inc., New York, 1964. Useful for much information. Bibliography. No index, except in last volume of complete set.

Mijatovies, Csedomille, ed., and trans., *Serbian Folklore*; Benjamin Bloom, Inc., New York, 1968; reissue of 1874 edition. A collection of folktales.

Obolensky, Dimitri, ed., *The Penguin Book of Russian Verse*; Penguin Books, England, 1962. Russian texts and prose translations at the bottom of the page. Contains *The Lay of Igor's Army*, some *Byliny*, and a selection of Ivan Krylov's fables.

Petrovitch, Woislav M., *Hero Tales and Legends of the Serbians*; George G. Harrap & Co., Ltd., London, 1914. A collection of tales, prose ballads, and folklore. Glossary. Index.

Ransome, Arthur, ed., *Old Peter's Russian Tales*; T. C. and E. C. Jack, Ltd., London, 1916. Reissued by Dover Publications, Inc., New York, 1969. Many of the tales are from Afanasiev's collections, but the editor has often softened them or changed the endings.

Simonov, Pyotr, *Essential Russian Mythology: Stories that Change the World*; Thorsons, London, 1997. Retelling of Slavic myths, and suggestions for further reading.

Zenkovsky, Serge A., ed., *Medieval Russia's Epics, Chronicles and Tales*; A Dutton Paperback, E. P. Dutton, Inc., New York, 1974. A massive collection of hard-to-find material in English translation. Includes a generous selection from *The Tale of Bygone Years* and a complete version of *The Lay of Igor's Army*. Good introduction. Notes.

## HINDU MYTHOLOGY AND FOLKLORE

*Atharva-Veda, Hymns of the*, translated by Maurice Bloomfield; Volume 42 of the *Sacred Books of the East*; Oxford University Press, 1897. Reprinted by Motilal Banarsidass, India, 1964. The hymns, plus extracts from the ritual books and commentaries. The translation is somewhat awkward. Introduction. Notes.

Beck, Brenda E.F., et al., eds., *Folktales of India*; University of Chicago Press, Chicago, 1987. One of the volumes in the series *Folktales of the World*. The present collection contains extensive notes. Index of Motifs and Index of Tale Types. Bibliography. General index.

*Bhagavadgita, The Sanatsugatiya and the Anugita*, translated by Kashinath Trimbak Telang; Volume 8 of the *Sacred Books of the East*; Oxford University Press, 1882. Reprinted by Motilal Banarsidass, India. 1965. Three important texts; the most important being the *Bhagavadgita*.

*Bhagavad-Gita: The Song Celestial*, translated by Edwin Arnold from the Sanskrit text into English verse; The Heritage Press, New York, 1965. A modern edition of the classic 19th-century translation in blank verse. Introduction by Shri Sri Prakasa.

*Dandin's Dasha-Kumara-Charita: The Ten Princes*, translated by Arthur W. Ryder from the Sanskrit; The University of Chicago Press, Chicago, 1927. A modern translation of a classic Indian collection of tales.

Das, Tulasi, *The Holy Lake of the Acts of Rama*, translated by W. Douglas; Oxford University Press, London, 1952. A classic Hindu retelling of the epic of Rama. Appendix listing the main characters in the epic.

Dimmitt, Cornelia, and J. A. B. van Buitenen, *Classical Hindu Mythology: A Reader in the Sanskrit Puranas*; Temple University Press, Philadelphia, 1978. Excellent collection of myths. Glossary. Notes on Sources. Bibliography of Sanskrit Puranas. Index.

Dowson, John, *A Classical Dictionary of Hindu Mythology and Religion, Geography, History and Literature*; Turbner's Oriental Series, Routledge & Kegan, London, 1878. Reissued. Excellent A-to-Z guide to Hindu mythology and legend.

Gaer, Joseph, *The Fables of India*; Little, Brown and Co., Boston, 1955. An excellent collection of tales from *The Panchatantra*, *The Hitopadesa*, *The Jatakas*. Good introduction. Annotated bibliography.

*Hindu Scriptures*, translated by R. C. Zaehner; Everyman's Library, London, 1966. A selection of hymns from the *Rig-Veda*, the *Atharva-Veda*, the *Upanishads*, and the complete *Bhagavad-Gita*. Difficult reading, and a rather heavy translation of the texts. Zaehner's edition replaces the earlier Hindu Scriptures edited by Nicol Macnicol (1938), which had a different emphasis.

*Institutes of Vishnu*, translated by Julius Jolly; Volume 7 of the *Sacred Books of the East*; Oxford University Press, 1880. Reprinted by Motilal Banarsidass, India, 1965. The *Vishnu-smriti*, or *Vaishnava Dharmasastra*, is a collection of ancient aphorisms on the sacred laws of India. Part 1 contains a discussion between the god Vishnu and the earth goddess. Difficult reading.

Ions, Veronica, *Indian Mythology*; Paul Hamlyn, London, 1967. A concise, well-illustrated book on Hindu mythology. In addition to Hindu mythology, there is a section on Buddhist mythology and Jain mythology.

Jacobs, Joseph, ed., *Indian Fairy Tales*; David Nutt, London, 1892. Reissued by Dover Publications, Inc., New York, 1969. Popular collection of folktales. Notes and references at back of volume to show relationship to similar folk tales throughout the world.

*The Laws of Manu*, translated by G. Bühler; Volume 25 of the *Sacred Books of the East*; Oxford University Press, 1886. Reprinted by Motilal Banarsidass, India, 1964. An important book of Hindu thought with a long introduction. Aside from the *Manu* text, it contains extracts from seven commentaries.

*The Mahabharata*, edited by Chakravarthi V. Narasimhan; Columbia University Press, New York, 1965. An English-language version based on selected verses. Introduction. Genealogical tables. Glossary. Index of verses on which the English prose version is based.

*The Mahabharata of Krishna-Dwaipayana Vyasa*, translated by Pratap Chandra Roy; reissued by Munshiram Manoharlal Publishers, India, 1974. Complete translation in 12 volumes done in the last century.

O'Flaherty, Wendy Doniger, ed., and trans., *Hindu Myths: A Sourcebook Translated from the Sanskrit*; Penguin Books, Baltimore, 1975. Excellent collection of Hindu myths with a very good introduction. Selected bibliography. Notes. Glossary. Index of Proper Names.

*The Ramayan of Valmiki*, translated into English verse by Ralph T. H. Griffith; The Chowkhamba Sanskrit Series Office, India, 1963. A reprint of the complete translation published between 1870 and 1875. The poetics of the translation often have leave much to be desired. Introduction. Notes.

*The Ramayana of Valmiki*, edited and translated by Hari Prasad Shastri; Shantisadan, London, 1962. Complete prose translation of the epic in three volumes. The best English edition available. Appendixes and glossaries.

*Rigveda, The Hymns of the*, edited and translated by Ralph T. H. Griffith; 1896. Reissued by Motilal Banarsidass, Delhi, India, 1973. A reissue, edited by J. L. Shastri, of a complete translation (with notes) of the hymns of the *Rig-Veda*. Appendixes. Index of hymns according to deities and subjects. Index.

Stutley, James, and Margaret Stutley, *A Dictionary of Hinduism: Its Mythology, Folklore and Development 1500 B.C.–A.D. 1500*; Routledge & Kegan Paul, London and Henley, 1977. Dictionary-length entries and cross-references following the entry. Bibliography and a special section on English Subjects and Their Sanskrit Equivalents.

Thompson, Stith, and Jonas Balys, *The Oral Tales of India*; Indiana University Press, Bloomington, 1958. A good collection of tales from India. Index of Motifs and Index of Tale Types.

*The Upanishads*, translated by F. Max Müller; Volumes 1 and 15 of the *Sacred Books of the East*; Oxford University Press, 1879 and 1884. Reprinted by Motilal Banarsidass, India, 1965. A long introduction and 12 Upanishads in a stiff, awkward translation.

*Vedanta-Sutras*, translated by George Thibaut; Volumes 34, 38, and 48 in the *Sacred Books of the East*; Oxford University Press, 1904. Reprinted by Motilal Banarsidass, India, 1962. The *Vedanta-Sutras* with commentary by Sankaracarya and a book-length introduction in volumes 34 and 38. Volume 48 contains the *Vedanta-Sutras* with the commentary by Ramanuja. Myth and legend scattered throughout but very difficult reading.

*Vedic Hymns*, translated by Max Müller and Hermann Oldenberg, Volumes 32 and 46 in the *Sacred Books of the East*; Oxford University Press, 1891. Reprinted by Motilal Banarsidass, India, 1964. Volume 32, with a long introduction and copious notes by Max Müller, contains hymns to the Maruts, Rudra, Vayu, and Vata. Volume 46 contains hymns to Agni. The translations in both cases are stiff and awkward.

Weber, Max, *The Religion of India*; The Free Press, New York, 1958. A study of the sociology of Hinduism and Buddhism. Notes. Index.

Wilkins, W. J., *Hindu Mythology: Vedic and Puranic*; Curzon Press, London, and Rowman & Littlefield, Totowa, N. J., 1973. Reissue of 1892 edition. Popular retelling of Hindu mythology and legend. Illustrated. Index.

Wilson, Epiphanius, ed., *Hindu Literature*; The Colonial Press, New York, 1900. An anthology containing *The Book of Good Counsels*, the 'Nala and Damayanti" episode from the epic *Mahabharata*, the drama *Sakoontala*, and a shortened version of the epic poem, *The Ramayana*.

## BUDDHIST MYTHOLOGY AND FOLKLORE

Burtt, E. A., ed., *The Teachings of the Compassionate Buddha*; New American Library, Mentor Books, New York, 1966. Excellent collection of original texts in English translation with a commentary. Introduction.

Carus, Paul, *The Gospel of Buddha; Compiled from Ancient Records*; The Open Court Publishing Co., LaSalle, Ill., 1894 (numerous reprints). A classic retelling of the life and teaching of the Buddha, strung together, and written in a pseudo-biblical style. Contains many of the important legends associated with Buddha's life. Glossary of Names and Terms.

Conze, Edward, ed. and trans., *Buddhist Scriptures*; Penguin Books, Baltimore, 1959. An excellent collection and translation of important Buddhist texts. Introduction. Sources. Glossary.

————, *Buddhist Texts Through the Ages*; Bruno Cassier, Oxford, 1954; reissued by Harper Torchbooks, New York, 1964. A collection of various Buddhist texts from a variety of sources. Introduction. Bibliography. Glossary.

Coomaraswamy, Ananada, *Buddha and the Gospel of Buddhism*; University Books, New Hyde Park, N. Y., 1964; reissue of 1916 volume. A popular, classic study of the entire realm of Buddhism. Bibliography. Glossary. Index.

Cowell, E. B., ed. and trans., *Buddhist Mahayana Texts*; Volume 49 of the *Sacred Books of the East*; Oxford University Press, 1894. Reissued by Motilal Banarsidass, India, 1965. A collection of various original texts in English translation. Notes. Introduction.

*The Dhammapada*; translated by P. Lal; Farrar, Straus & Giroux, New York, 1967. A translation from the Pali text. Excellent introduction. Select bibliography.

Getty, Alice, *The Gods of Northern Buddhism*; Oxford University Press, 1928; reissued by Charles E. Tuttle Co., Rutland, Vt., 1962. A fully illustrated study of the history, iconography, and development of various Buddhist deities, with explanations of various Sanskrit words used in the text. Index.

Humphreys, Christmas, *Buddhism*; Penguin Books, Middlesex, England, 1951. A short, popular study of the vast subject with illustrations. Bibliography. Glossary. Index.

*The Jataka, or Stories of the Buddha's Former Births*; edited by E. B. Cowell; reissued by Cosmo Publications, India, 1973 of 1895 edition. A six-volume set, translated by different hands, of all of the fables relating to the Buddha's former lives. A must for the folklore of Buddhism. Index in volume 6 of the entire set.

Ling, Trevor, *The Buddha: Buddhist Civilization in India and Ceylon*; Charles Scribner's Sons, New York, 1973. A modern life of the Buddha that attempts, not too successfully, to interpret the social and religious background of the time. Notes. Index.

Rhys, T. W., ed. and trans., *Buddhist Suttas*; Volume 11 of the *Sacred Books of the East*; Oxford University Press, 1881. Reissued by Motilal Banarsidass, India, 1965. A collection of short texts, originally in Pali. Introduction. Notes. Index.

Roveda, Vittorio, *Khmer Mythology: Secrets of Angkor*; Weatherhill, New York, 1998. An illustrated presentation of relief sculptures of the Khmer in Cambodia. Maps.

*The Tibetan Book of the Dead*; edited by W. Y. Evans-Wentz; Oxford University Press, London, 1960. Popular edition of one of the standard texts on dying and Buddhism.

Waddell, L. Austin, *The Buddhism of Tibet, or Lamaism*; W. H. Allen & Co., London, 1895. Reissued by Dover Books, New York, 1971, under the title *Tibetan Buddhism*. An illustrated, turn-of-the-century study of the "mystic cults, symbolism and mythology" of Tibetan Buddhism. Index.

Warren, Henry Clarke, ed. and trans., *Buddhism in Translations*; Harvard University Press, Cambridge, Mass., 1896. Reissued by Atheneum, New York, 1972. An excellent translation of original sources in Pali. No index.

### CHINESE MYTHOLOGY AND FOLKLORE

Birrell, Anne, *Chinese Mythology: An Introduction*; Johns Hopkins University Press, Baltimore, 1993. Includes bibliographical references and a general index.

———, *Chinese Myths*; University of Texas Press, Austin, 2000. Published in cooperation with British Museum Press, includes illustrations, bibliographical references, and a general index.

Chai, Ch'u, and Winbert Chi, eds. and trans., *The Sacred Books of Confucius and Other Confucian Classics*; Bantam Books, Inc., New York, 1965. Contemporary and useful translation of some of the major texts. A help in understanding the background of much Chinese belief.

Christie, Anthony, *Chinese Mythology*; Paul Hamlyn, London, 1968. Excellent study with numerous illustrations. Bibliography. Index.

Dennys, N. B., *The Folk-Lore of China and its Affinities with That of the Aryan and Semitic Races*; Trubner and Co., London, 1876. Reissued by Tower Books, Detroit, 1971. An interesting work dealing with such subjects as birth, marriage, and death as well as superstitions, ghosts, witchcraft, and demonology. Index.

Eberhard, Wolfram, ed., *Folktales of China*; translated by Desmond Parsons; University of Chicago Press, Chicago, 1965. One of the volumes in the series *Folktales of the World* under the editorship of Richard M. Dorson. Many of the tales in this collection originally appeared in *Chinese Fairy and Folk Tales*. The present collection contains extensive notes. Index of Motifs. Bibliography. General index.

Ferguson, John C., *Chinese Mythology*; Volume 8 in the *Mythology of All Races*; Marshall Jones Co., Boston, 1928. Reissued by Cooper Square Publishers, New York, 1964. A short study, with numerous illustrations, giving a general view of Chinese mythology. Bibliography. Index only in last volume of the complete set.

Legge, James, ed., and trans., *The Sacred Books of China*; Clarendon Press, Oxford, 1891. Reissued by Motilal Banarsidass, Delhi, India, 1966. These six volumes contain translations of the texts of Confucianism and Taoism. The Confucian texts are the *Shu King* the *Religious Portions of the Shi King*, the *Hsiao King*, the *Yi King*, and the *Ki Ki*. The Taoist texts are the *Tao Teh king*, the writings of *Kwang-Tze* (Chuang-Tsu), and *Thai-Shang Tractate of Actions and Their Retributions*. Extensive notes. Introduction. Various indexes.

Palmer, Martin, and Zhao Ziaomin, with Joanne O'Brien and James Palmer; *Essential Chinese Mythology*; Thorsons, London and San Francisco, 1997. General overview of the subject. General index.

Roberts, Moss, ed. and trans., *Chinese Fairy Tales and Fantasies*; Pantheon Books, New York, 1979. A popular collection of various types of tales found in China. Introduction. Sources.

Smith, D. Howard, *Chinese Religions from 1000 B.C. to the Present*; Holt, Rinehart and Winston, New York, 1968. General overview of a complex subject. Glossary. Index.

Weber, Max, *The Religion of China*; The Free Press, New York, 1951. A sociological study of Confucianism and Taoism. Notes. Index.

Werner, E. T. C., *A Dictionary of Chinese Mythology*; Kelley and Walsh, Ltd., Shanghai, 1932. Reissued by The Julian Press, New York, 1961. A standard work in the field, but one that must be used with extreme caution because it contains numerous mistakes. Bibliography.

———, *Myths and Legends of China*; Arno Press, A New York Times Company, 1976 reissue of the 1922 edition. Chinese myths and legends in a popular style for the general reader. Introduction. Index.

Williams, C. A. S., *Outlines of Chinese Symbolism and Art Motives*; Kelly and Walsh, Ltd., Shanghai, 1941. Reissued by Charles E. Tuttle Co., Rutland, Vt./Tokyo, Japan, 1974. This popular study, illustrated with line drawings from various sources, is an alphabetical listing of various legends, gods, customs, etc. Index.

Wilhelm, Richard, ed., *Chinese Folktales*; translated by Ewald Osers; G. Bell & Sons, London, 1971. Good selection of tales. Notes.

Wilson, Epiphanius, ed., *Chinese Literature*; The Colonial Press, New York, 1900. An anthology containing *The Analects of Confucius, The Sayings of Mencius, The Shi-King, The Travels of Fa-Hien* in 19th-century translations.

Wu Ch'eng-en, *Monkey*; translated by Arthur Waley; The John Day Co., New York, 1943. The classic English translation, shortened from the original, of the classic Chinese novel that contains so much folklore and mythology.

## JAPANESE MYTHOLOGY AND FOLKLORE

Anesaki, Masaharu, *History of Japanese Religion*; Kegan Paul, Trench, Trübner & Co., London, 1930. Reissued by Charles E. Tuttle Co., Vermont/Tokyo, 1963. A classic study of Japanese religious beliefs with emphasis on Shinto practices.

Czaja, Michael, *Gods of Myth and Stone: Phallicism in Japanese Folk Religion*; Weatherhill, Tokyo/New York, 1974. A very thorough study of various Shinto deities worshiped in Japan. Illustrations. Notes. Bibliography.

Hearn, Lafcadio, *Kwaidan: Stories and Studies of Strange Things*; The Shimbi Shoin, Ltd., Tokyo, 1932 (for the Limited Editions Club). Reissued by Dover Publications, New York, 1968. A classic collection of Japanese ghost tales with an introduction by Oscar Lewis and illustrations by Yasumasa Fujita.

Joly, Henri L., *Legend in Japanese Art*; John Lane The Bodley Head, London, 1908. Reissued by Charles E. Tuttle Co., Vermont/Tokyo, 1967. An A-to-Z listing of over a 1,000 figures, etc., from myth, legend, and folklore in Japan, with 700 illustrations. Generally an invaluable guide, though weak in entries on mythology.

Kiej'e, Nikolas, compiler, *Japanese Grotesqueries*; Charles E. Tuttle Co., Rutland, Vt./Tokyo, Japan, 1973. A collection of Japanese prints of various demons and spirits, with short comments. Helpful introduction by Terence Barrow.

*Kojiki*; edited and translated by Donald L. Philippi; Princeton University Press, University of Tokyo Press, 1969. A modern, up-to-date translation of a classic text on Japanese mythology. Long introduction. Glossary of over 200 pages. A must for any study of Japanese mythology.

*Ko-Ji-Ki: Records of Ancient Matters*, edited and translated by Basil H. Chamberlain; Lane, Crawford & Co., Kelly & Co., Yokohama, 1883. One of the main original sources for Japanese mythology in a rather stiff translation that avoids the 'obscene" passages of the work.

McAlpine, Helen and Wiliam, *Japanese Tales and Legends*; Oxford University Press, Oxford, 1958. A collection of epic and legends retold, including *Tales of the Heike*. Glossary.

*Nibongi: Chronicles of Japan from the Earliest Times to AD 697*, edited and translated by W. G. Aston; Kegan Paul, Trench, Trübner & Co., London, 1896. Reissued by Allen and Unwin, London, 1956. An original source book of Japanese mythology, forming with the *Kojiki* the main source for the study of Japanese mythology.

Ozaki, Yei Theodora, compiler, *The Japanese Fairy Book*; Archibald Constable & Co., Ltd., 1903. Reissued by Dover Publications, New York, 1967. An excellent collection of Japanese folktales compiled at the suggestion of the folklorist Andrew Lang, the great compiler of folktales in 19th-century England.

Piggott, Juliet, *Japanese Mythology*; Paul Hamlyn, London, 1969. A fully illustrated study of Japanese mythology and legend. Bibliography. Index.

Redesdale, Lord, ed., *Tales of Old Japan*; Macmillan and Co., Ltd., London, 1908 edition. A popular collection of Japanese tales from various sources.

Seki, Keigo, ed., *Folktales of Japan*, translated by Robert J. Adams; University of Chicago Press, Chicago, 1965. One of the volumes in the series *Folktales of the World* under the editorship of Richard M. Dorson. The present collection contains extensive notes. Index of Motifs and Index of Tale Types. Bibliography. General index.

Ury, Marian, trans., *Tales of Times Now Past: Sixty-Two Stories from a Medieval Japanese Collection*; University of California Press, Berkeley, Calif., 1979. An interesting collection of tales, chosen from over 1,000 in the collection. Good introduction.

## AMERICAN INDIAN MYTHOLOGIES

Alvarado, de Pedro, *An Account of the Conquest of Guatemala in 1524*, translated by Sedley J. Mackie; The Cortes Society, New York, 1924. A classic Spanish study of the encounter of Christianity with native American beliefs. Notes. Bibliography.

Burland, C. A., *The Gods of Mexico*; Eyre & Spottiswoode, London, 1967. A concise and informative treatment of a very complex subject. Short annotated bibliography. Index.

Burland, Cottie, *North American Indian Mythology*; Hamlyn Publishing Corp., London, 1965. An excellent short, illustrated volume on the subject. Bibliography. Index.

Burland, Cottie, and Werner Forman, *Feathered Serpent and Smoking Mirror*; Orbis Publishing, London, 1975. An beautifully illustrated volume on the Mesoamerican gods and myths. Glossary, chronology, bibliography, and index.

Burr, Hartley, *North American Indian Mythology*; Volume 10 of *The Mythology of All Races*; Marshall Jones Company, Boston, 1916. Reissued by Cooper Square Publishers, New York, 1964. A discussion of North American Indian mythology by area, such as the Far North, etc. Introduction. Notes. Bibliography.

Clark, Cora, and Texa Bowen Williams, eds., *Pomo Indian Myths and Some of Their Sacred Meanings*; Vantage Press, Inc., New York, 1954. A diverse collection of myths and legends as well as some native Indian explanations of their meanings.

Curtin, Jeremiah, ed., *Myths of the Modocs: Indian Legends of the Northwest*; Benjamin Blom, Inc., New York, 1971; reissue of 1912 edition. An early collection of tales by a famous collector. Notes.

Curtin, Jeremiah, *Creation Myths of Primitive America*; edited with an Introduction by Karl Kroeber, ABC-CLIO, Santa Barbara, Denver, and Oxford (England), 2002. Translations of Native American myths recorded in the 19th century. Cross References and a general index.

Dixon-Kennedy, Mike, *Native American Myth and Legend: An A-Z of People and Places*; Blandford, London, 1996. Dictionary length entries, maps and a brief bibliography.

Durán, Fray Diego, *Book of the Gods and Rites* and *The Ancient Calendar*; translated by Fernando Horcasitas and Doris Heyden; University of Oklahoma Press, Norman, 1971. A must. A Christian view of the ancient rites, but filled with rich information. Glossary. Bibliography. Index.

————, *The History of the Indies of New Spain*; translated by Doris Heyden and Fernando Horcasitas; Orion Press, New York, 1964. Eyewitness account by a Spanish priest who attempts to understand native American religious beliefs and rites. Bibliography. Index.

Gill, Sam D., and Irene F. Sullivan, *Dictionary of Native American Mythology*; ABC-CLIO, Santa Barbara, Denver, and Oxford (England), 1992. Dictionary-length entries, black-

and-white pictures and illustrations, maps, bibliography, and a very useful index by tribe.

Hausman, Gerald, *Turtle Island Alphabet: A Lexicon of Native American Symbols and Culture*; St. Martin's Press, New York, 1992. Illustrations and bibliography.

Hirschfelder, Arlene, and Paulette Molin, *Encyclopedia of Native American Religions*; Facts On File, Inc., New York, 2000. This is an updated edition of a 1992 publication, and includes dictionary-length entries. There are also suggestions for further reading, a subject index, and a general index.

Leland, Charles G., ed., *The Algonquin Legends of New England, or Myths and Folk Lore of the Micmac, Passamaquoddy, and Penobscot Tribes*; Houghton, Mifflin and Co., Boston, 1884. Reissued by Singing Tree Press, Detroit, 1968. Classic retellings done in the 19th century in a stilted and unnatural English.

Lyon, William S., *Encyclopedia of Native American Shamanism: Sacred Ceremonies of North America*; ABC-CLIO, Santa Barbara, Denver, and Oxford (England), 1998. A continuation of ABC-CLIO's *Encyclopedia of Native American Healing* (1996), by the same author. This volume includes maps locating the various tribes of North America, an extensive bibliography with a separate section on ethnobotany, and a general index.

Macfarlan, Allan A., ed., *American Indian Legends*; The Heritage Press, New York, 1968. A varied collection, mainly from literary sources but valuable. Introduction. Sources.

Marriott, Alice, and Carol K. Rachlin, eds., *American Indian Mythology*; Thomas Y. Crowell Co., New York, 1968. An excellent collection, mainly derived from oral sources. Introduction. Bibliography.

*Popul Vuh: The Sacred Book of the Ancient Quiché Maya*, edited and translated by Delia Goetz and Sylvanus G. Morley; University of Oklahoma Press, 1950. An English version by the editors based on the Spanish translation of Andrián Recinos. The book is one of the most important documents for the mythology of the Maya. This edition contains a long introduction. Notes. Index.

Radin, Paul, *The Trickster: A Study in American Indian Mythology*; Philosophical Library, New York, 1956. A very useful study of the role of the Trickster in North American Indian as well as other cultures. Commentaries by Karl Kerényi and C. G. Jung included.

Read, Kay Almere, and Jason J. González, *Handbook of Mesoamerican Mythology*; ABC-CLIO, Santa Barbara, Denver, and Oxford (England), 2000. Useful list of Annotated Print and Nonprint Resources, which includes books and articles, videos, Websites, a reference list, a glossary, and a general index.

Schoolcraft, Henry R., ed., *The Myth of Hiawatha and Other Oral Legends, Mythologic and Allegoric of the North American Indian*; J. B. Lippincott & Co., Philadelphia, 1856. Reissued by Kraus Reprint Co., New York, 1971. One of the first collections in English of North American Indian myths and legends. However, Schoolcraft made the mistake of identifying Hiawatha, the historical personage, with the god Manabozho, calling them both Hiawatha.

Taube, Karl A., *Aztec and Maya Myths*; University of Texas Press, Austin, 1993. Published in cooperation with British Museum Press. Includes illustrations, an extensive bibliography, and a general index.

Thompson, Stith, ed., *Tales of the North American Indians*; Indiana University Press, Bloomington, Ind., 1929. A collection of tales including mythological stories, mythical incidents, trickster tales, hero tales, journeys to the other world, animal wives and husbands, miscellaneous tales, tales borrowed from Europeans, and tales based on Bible stories. One of the best collections. Introduction. Notes. Bibliography.

Toor, Frances, *Mexican Folkways*; Crown Publishers, New York, 1947. Excellent collection of customs, myths, folklore, traditions, etc. Introduction. Glossary. Index.

Turner, Frederick W., ed., *The Portable North American Reader*; The Viking Press, New York, 1973. An excellent anthology with more than 200 pages devoted to North American Indian myths and legends. Introduction.

Wherry, Joseph H., *Indian Masks and Myths of the West*; Funk & Wagnalls, New York, 1969. An interesting, helpful, and understanding account. Illustrations. Bibliography. Index of mythical beings. Index.

## NORTH AMERICAN FOLKLORE AND LEGEND

Axelrod, Alan, and Harry Oster, *The Penguin Dictionary of American Folklore: Arts and Crafts, Ballads and Beliefs, Real and Imaginary Heroes*; Penguin Reference Books, New York, 2000. A very rich collection of short and long entries, from definitions and descriptions of terms and objects. Over 750 entries and 228 photographs and line drawings.

Botkin, B. A., ed., *A Treasury of American Folklore*; Crown Publishers, New York, 1944. An anthology from a variety of sources, most of which were written, not oral, causing Richard Dorson to coin the term *fakelore* for the Botkin collections. Index. Botkin also produced other "Treasurie" of folklore, including collections on Southern Folklore (1949), Western Folklore (1951), the Civil War (1960), and the Mississippi River (1978).

Brewer, J. Mason, ed., *American Negro Folklore*; Quadrangle/The New york Times Book Co., New York, 1968. A collection of tales, songs, superstitions, etc. Index.

Brunvand, Jan Harold, *The Baby Train and Other Lusty Urban Legends*; Norton, New York and London, 1993. This only one of many collections of urban legend published by Jan Brunvand, but it is of particular importance for the Type-Index of Urban Legends included as an appendix. Legends are divided into 10 categories. Includes legends about automobiles, animals, horrors, accidents, sex and scandals, business, government, celebrities, and academics.

Brunvand, Jan Harold, ed., *American Folklore: An Encyclopedia*; Garland, New York and London, 1996. One of the new generation of reference books, with entries written by well-known folklore scholars. There are good cross-references, limited references, and an extensive general index.

Clough, Ben C., ed., *The American Imagination at Work: Tall Tales and Folk Tales*; Alfred A. Knopf, New York, 1947. Rich, excellent collection from a variety of sources. Introduction. Bibliography.

Coffin, Tristram Potter, and Hennig Cohen, eds., *The Parade of Heroes: Legendary Figures in American Lore*; Anchor Press, Doubleday, Garden City, N. Y., 1978. A selection from the journals and archives of American folklore and culture. Notes. Index.

Dresser, Norine, *American Vampires: Fans, Victims and Practitioners*; Norton, New York, 1989. A well-documented study of vampire culture in United States, based on personal interviews with practitioners and with medical doctors who explain the need for consuming blood on the part of some individuals.

Dundes, Alan, ed., *Mother Wit from the Laughing Barrel: Readings in the Interpretation of Afro-American Folklore*; Jackson and London, University Press of Mississippi, [1973] 1990. An extensive collection of essays about African-American folklore covering a wide spectrum of traditions, folk speech, verbal art, belief, music, narrative, and humor.

Flanagan, John T., and Arthur Palmer Hudson, eds., *The American Folklore Reader: Folklore in American Literature*; A. S. Barnes & Co., New York, 1958. A collection of works by American writers on folklore themes, ranging from the American Indian to devil tales, witchcraft, literary ballads, heroes, Yankees, Negro tales, and folk songs and ballads. Bibliographical notes. Bibliography. Index of authors and titles.

Fritze, Ronald H., *Travel Legend and Lore: An Encyclopedia*; ABC-CLIO, Santa Barbara, Denver, and Oxford (England), 1998. Legends of fabulous places, from Atlantis to Vinland. Includes cross-references, illustrations, and a general index.

Lamar, Howard R., ed., *The Reader's Encyclopedia of the American West*; Thomas Y. Crowell Co., New York, 1977. An excellent, one-volume encyclopedia, filled with fascinating information, much regarding American legend.

Editors of *Life*, *The Life Treasury of American Folklore*; Time, Inc., New York, 1961. A heavily illustrated, popular guide to the subject. Index.

Reader's Digest, *American Folklore and Legend*; The Reader's Digest Association, Inc., Pleasantville, N.Y., 1978. A popular, illustrated collection from a variety of sources. Index.

Slatta, Richard W., *The Mythical West: An Encyclopedia of Legend, Lore, and Popular Culture*; ABC-CLIO, Santa Barbara, Denver, and Oxford (England), 2001. Western figures, events, and places that appear in folk legends, art, literature, and popular culture. Includes numerous illustrations, a bibliography, and a general index.

## VOODOO

Deren, Maya, *Divine Horsemen: Voodoo Gods of Haiti*; Chelsea House Publishers, New York, 1970. Often interesting, though one may disagree with many of its theories.

Pelton, Robert W., *Voodoo Secrets from A to Z*; A. S. Barnes and Co., South Brunswick, N. J., 1973. A short A-to-Z listing of Voodoo terms. Helpful for quick reference.

Rigaud, Milo, *Secrets of Voodoo*; translated by Robert B. Cross; Arco, New York, 1969. A sympathetic study of the subject. Book lacks an index, making it difficult for reference.

## OCEANIC MYTHOLOGY AND LEGEND

Alpers, Anthony, *Legends of the South Seas: The World of the Polynesians Seen through Their Myths and Legends, Poetry and Art*; Thomas Y. Crowell Co., New York, 1970. Excellent col-

lection of myths, relating to creation, heroes, etc. References. Glossary. Index.

Dixon, R. B., *Oceanic*; Vol. 9, *The Mythology of All Races*; Marshall Jones Publishing Corp., Boston, 1916. Reissued by Cooper Square Publishing, Inc., New York, 1964. A study, rather stiff, of a very rich subject. Bibliography.

Grey, George, *Polynesian Mythology*; edited by W. W. Bird; Taplinger Publishing Co., New York, n. d. A slightly reedited version of Grey's 1855 book. Index.

Massola, Aldo, *Bunjil's Cave: Myths, Legends and Superstitions of the Aborigines of Southeast Australia*. Lansdowne Press, Melbourne, 1968. Myths, legends, and folk beliefs. Introduction. Glossary.

Parker, K. Langloah, collector, *Australian Legendary Tales*; Bodley Head Ltd., London, 1978. A volume that combines two collections made by Parker, one in 1896 and the other in 1898, published by David Nutt in London.

Poignant, Roslyn, *Myths and Legends of the South Seas*; Hamlyn, London, 1970. An excellent little book covering Melanesia, Micronesia, Polynesia. Index.

———, *Oceanic Mythology*; Paul Hamlyn, London, 1967. A fully illustrated volume covering Polynesia, Micronesia, Melanesia, and Australia. Reading list. Index.

Reed, A. W., *Myths and Legends of Australia*; Taplinger Publishing Co., New York, 1965. A selection of myths and legends, creation myths, myths of the sun, moon, stars, animals, etc. Introduction. Glossary.

Schmitz, Carl August, *Oceanic Art, Myth, Man and Images of the South Seas*, translated from the German by Norbert Guterman; H.N. Abrams, New York, 1971. More than 300 illustrations, 50 in color. Bibliography.

## AFRICAN MYTHOLOGIES AND FOLKLORES

Carey, Margaret, *Myths and Legends of Africa*; Paul Hamlyn, London, 1970. An excellent retelling of some African folktales. Good introduction.

Courlander, Harold, *Tales of Yoruba Gods and Heroes*; Fawcett Publications, Inc., New York, 1974. Intelligent collection of Yoruba folklore and customs.

————, *A Treasure of African Folklore*; Crown Publishers, Inc., New York, 1975. A collection of the oral traditions, myths, legends, epics, tales, recollections, wisdom, sayings, and humor of Africa. Brief bibliography and index included.

Dorson, Richard, ed., *African Folklore*; Doubleday, Garden City, N. Y., 1972. Scholarly treatment of folklore concepts applied to oral traditions of Africa. Introduction.

Herskovits, Melville J. and Frances, *Dahomean Narrative: A Cross-Cultural Analysis*; Northwestern University Press, Evanston, 1958. A collection of folktales with a very long introduction of over 100 pages.

Feya, Abayomi, *Fourteen Hundred Cowries and Other African Tales*; Washington Square Press, New York, 1971. Detailed retellings of the Yoruba people's West African tales.

Parrinder, Geoffrey, *African Mythology*; Paul Hamlyn Group, Ltd., London, 1967. Valuable book for those not familiar with the vast scope of African mythology. Bibliography. Index.

Scheub, Harold, *A Dictionary of African Mythology: The Mythmaker as Storyteller*; Oxford University Press, Oxford and New York, 2000. Very useful listing of myths in three appendixes: by country, by language and culture, and by topics such as Beginnings, Separation, Struggles between God and Man, Mythic Heroes, and Endings. Includes a general index.

# Cultural and Ethnic Index

## A

Abipone Indians of South
America
Aharaigichi 0108
Aesopic
Aesopic fables 0085
Ant and the Grasshopper,
0266
Ass in the Lion's Skin, The
0365
Ass's Brains 0366
Avaricious and Envious,
The 0419
Belly and Its Members, The
0533
Cat Maiden, The 0746
Cock and the Pearl, The
0845
Dog and His Shadow, The
1000
Eagle and the Arrow, The
1049
Fox and the Crow, The
1205
Fox and the Grapes, The
1206
Fox and the Mosquitoes,
The 1207
Frog and the Ox, The 1225
Goose That Laid the Golden
Eggs, The
1305
Hawk and the Nightingale,
The 1403
Jay and the Peacock, The
1615

Juno and the Peacock 1673
Lion and the Mouse, The
1893
Lion in Love, The 1894
Lion's Share, The 1895
Mice in Council, or Belling
the Cat, The
2071
Milkmaid and Her Pail,
The 2082
Mountain in Labor, The
2122
Old Man and Death, The
2280
Piper, The 2428
Serpent and the File, The
2679
Sick Lion, The 2713
Tortoise and the Birds, The
2936
Town Mouse and the
Country Mouse, The
2938
Tree and the Reed, The
2939
Two Pots, The 2977
Wolf and the Crane, The
3165
Wolf and the Lamb, The
3166
Wolf in Sheep's Clothing,
The 3168
Woodman and the Serpent,
The 3172
African
Abuk and Garang 0024
Adu Ogyinae 0062

Aiwel 0127
Ala 0138
Anansi 0233
Atai 0378
Bomazi 0605
Bumba 0658
Cagn 0686
Da 0889
Deng 0949
Efé 1060
Eka Abassi 1067
Eshu 1123
Fa 1153
Faran 1161
Gikuyu (Kikuyu), Masai, and
Kamba 1273
Golden Stool, The 1296
Gu 1330
Haitsi-aibed 1362
Iku 1544
Ilé-Ifé (house wide) 1546
Imana 1549
Imilozi 1551
Iruwa 1574
Jok 1646
Juok 1674
Kalumba 1696
Kholumolumo 1734
Khonvum 1737
Kibuka 1738
Kintu and Nambi 1745
Kitamba 1749
Lebe 1855
Le-eyo 1858
Legba 1859
Leve 1878
Leza 1879

# General Index

## A

Aa 0001
Aarne, Antti 2816
Aaron 0002, 2321
Aaron's rod 0183
Aaron's rod blossomed 0183
Aba 0003
Abaris 0004
Abassi 0378
Abbas Stultorum 1913
Abbate, Niccolo
dell'(1512–1571); Aristaeus
0330
Abbot of Misrule 1913
Abbot of Unreason 1913
Abdallah and Amina 2128
Abd Al Muttalib 2128
Abdera 0005
Abderus 0005
Abdhi-nagari 1783
Abdiel 0006
Abdu'llah (The Servant of
Allah) 1621
Abednego 0922
Abel 0007, 0689
*Abe Lincoln in Illinois* 1889
Abenalmao, Moorish Infante
0008
*Abenamar and King Don Juan*
0008
Abe no Seimei 0009, 0010

Abe no Yasuna 0010
Abere 0011
Abezi-thibod 0012
Abgar 0013
*Abhaya mudra* 2127
*Abhidhamma Pitaka* 2909
Abhinandana 2912
Abhinna 0014
Abhra-pisacha 2504
Abiathar 3238
Abigail 0015
Abiram 0002
Ab Kin Xoc 0016
Abominable Snowman 0570
Abomination of desolation
0017
Abore 0018
Abracadabra 0019, 0021
Abraham 0020, 1681
*Abraham Being Blessed by
Melchizedek* 0020
*Abraham Lincoln* 1889
Abraxas 0021
Absalom 0022
*Absalom, Absalom!* 0022
*Absalom and Achitopel* 0022
Absyrtus 0023, 2046
Abu-Bakr 0424
Abuk and Garang 0024

abundance; Chinese symbol
of 1319; Near Eastern
gods of 0504
Abu Talib 2128
Abyrga 1915
Acacallis 0291
Acamas 0025, 1425, 1837,
2417
Acantha 0026
acanthus 0027
Acarnan and Amphoterus
0028
Acarnania 0028
Acastus 0029
Acca Larentia 0030
accidend; Islamic demon of
1528
accidents 1123
Accolon of Gaul 0031
*Account of the Antiquities of
Peru* 1493
Acesis 0345
Acestes 0032
Acetes 0983
*Achaeans* 0319, 0915
Achaius 0241
Achates 0033
Achatius 1203
Acheflour 0034
Achelous 0035, 0198
Achemorus 2363

the Baptist 1643; St. Matthew 2034; St. Peter 2401; St. Sebastian 2662
carbuncles 0645
Cardea 0722
Cardiff Giant 0723
Carlisle, Helen 2765
Carloman 0782
Carlos, Don 0724
Carlyle, Thomas; Koran 1769
Carme 0725
Carmelites 2864
*Carmen Deo Nostro* 2022
*Carmen Nuptialis* 2257
Carmenta 0726
Carmentalia 0726
*Carmina* 0401
*Carmina burana* 1201
Carna 0727
Carnarvon, Lord 2970
carnation 0728
carnivore 3142
Carolsfeld, Julius Schnoor von; St. Roch 2565
Caron, Antoine; St. Thomas More 2889
Caros 0721
carpenters 1655, 2401, 2886, 3167; Chinese god of 1937; Melanesian god of 2568
carpet snake 0571, 1303
Carpo 0729
Carrez, Florence 1634
Cartaphilus 3126
Carter, Howard 2970
Carthage 0975
Carthismandu 0720
Carus, Paul 1109
Carya 0731
caryatids 0732
Caryatis 0340, 0732
Casey at the Bat 0733
Casey Jones 0734
Casilda, St. 0735

Casimir of Poland, St. 0736
Caspar 1956
Cassandra 0091, 0128, 0737, 3171; warns against wooden horse 0076
Cassiopea 0738
Cassiopea's Chair 0738
Cassiopeia 0245
Cassius 0960
Castalia 0739
Castel Sant' Angelo 2072
Castillo, Bernal Díaz del 1503
Castor 0699, 1422, 1856, 1876, 2802
Castor and Polydeuces 0740, 0984
*Castor et Pollux* 0740
castration 0401, 0766, 0829, 1440, 1516; pine tree as symbol of 2426
Castro, Guillén de (1569–1631); El Cid 0828
Caswallawn 0741
cat 0742, 3023
Catacombs of Alexandria 2685
*Catalogue of Famous Women* 1440
Catamitus 1248
Catequil 0743
caterpillar 0669, 0686
Catharsius 3256
Catherine of Alexandria, St. 0744, 1203
Catherine of Siena, St. 0100, 0745
Cather, Willa (1876–1947); Kit Carson 1750
Cathman, St. 0884
Catholic universities 2888
*Cat Maiden, The* 0746
*Cato* 0747
Cato the Younger, Marcus Porcius 0747
Catreus 0748
cattle 0404, 1868

Cattle of the Sun 0749
cattle pest 2662
Catullus, Gaius Valerius (c 84–c. 54 B.C.E.); Ariadne 0324; Attis 0401; Berenice 0544; nut 2257; Peleus 2388
Caucasus 0750
Cauchon, Bishop 1634
Caunus and Biblis 0751
Caurus 3254
Cavall 0752
Cave-in-Rock gang 0576
Caxton, William 1295
cayman 0409, 1949
Cecilia, St. 0753
Cecropia 0754
Cecrops 0303, 0754
Cedalion 0755
cedar 0756, 0874
Cedar Tree 1275, 1504
Ceiuci 0757
Celaeno 0076, 0758
Celeus, King 0946
Cellini, Benvenuto (1500–1571); Perseus 2400
cemeteries 0491
Cenn Cruaich 0759
centaurs 0760, 1140, 2205; Chiron 0345, 1612; Rhoecus 2549; Ripheus 2558
Centeotl 0842
Central Plains 2767
*Centuries* 2246
centurion 1910
Cepheus 0245
Cerberus 1433
Cercym 2880
Ceres 0946, 3145
Ceridwen 0761
Cernunnos 0762
Cervantes, Miguel de (1547–1616); Melisenda 2050; Rodomont 2567
Cerynean hind 1433
Cessair 0763